YOUTH AT RISK

A Prevention Resource for Counselors, Teachers, and Parents

Third Edition

Edited by

David Capuzzi
and
Douglas R. Gross

AMERICAN
COUNSELING
ASSOCIATION

YOUTH AT RISK
Third Edition

10 9 8 7 6 5 4 3 2

American Counseling Association
5999 Stevenson Avenue
Alexandria, VA 22304

Director of Publications
Carolyn C. Baker

Copyeditor
Lucy Blanton

Cover design by Brian Gallagher

Library of Congress Cataloging-in-Publication Data

Youth at risk : a prevention resource for counselors, teachers, and parents /
    David Capuzzi, Douglas R. Gross, [editors] — 3rd ed.
        p.   cm.
    Includes bibliographical references and index.
    ISBN 1-55620-219-9 (alk. paper)
    1. Socially handicapped youth—United States.   2. Youth—
Counseling of—United States.   3. Deviant behavior.   4. Adolescent
psychopathology—United States.   5. Adolescent psychotherapy—United
States.   6. Dropout behavior, Prediction of.   I. Capuzzi, Dave.
II. Gross, Douglas R.
HV1431.Y68   2000   99-41560
362.74—dc21   CIP

DEDICATION

To: *Kevin and Keith Capuzzi*

Your supportiveness and quick wit made this book possible. You are wonderful role models, each in your own way, for other young people.

To: *Lola Gross*

With love all is possible.

CONTENTS WITHDRAWN

PREFACE

Youth At Risk: A Prevention Resource for Counselors, Teachers, and Parents is a revision of the 1996 second edition. In this third edition, major emphasis has again been placed on prevention efforts with at-risk populations as well as practical guidelines for successful intervention with behaviors most often identified as placing youth at risk. Selected chapters include case studies that explore prevention efforts from individual, family, school, and community perspectives. Every effort has been made to address the complexities of working with vulnerable youth in a way that provides professionals, as well as parents, with an information base and guidelines for working within the parameters of the prevention-intervention paradigm. This text differs from similar texts because of the attention placed on counseling and systems applications with youth at risk.

The text is developmental in orientation. Part One presents information dealing with population identification, definition, and behaviors descriptive of youth at risk. Information is also included that serves as a foundation for understanding the prevention-intervention paradigm. A new and exciting feature of the third edition is a chapter in Part One that addresses prevention from the point of view of identification and promotion of resiliency in our youth.

Part Two of the text deals with parameters that often serve as causal factors for the development of at-risk behaviors. Included in this section are chapters dealing with the effects of a dysfunctional family, low self-esteem, depression, and stress and trauma. Each chapter in this section not only identifies various aspects of the causal factors but also presents information related to prevention strategies designed to deal with these factors.

Part Three of the text deals with behaviors most often identified as placing youth at risk. These behaviors include those that lead to eating disorders, pregnancy, AIDS, suicide, gang membership, violence on school campuses, substance abuse, homelessness and school dropout. Each chapter in Part Three provides definitive information related to the specific behavior, includes a case study to illustrate the information presented, and provides approaches to prevention and intervention from individual, family, school, and community perspectives. Adaptations for diversity are also addressed because prevention and intervention efforts usually need to be modified to meet the needs of minority and disenfranchised youth served by school, community, and mental health practitioners.

Every effort has been made by the editors and contributors to provide the reader with current and relevant information in each of the 16 areas of focus. We hope that this new edition of *Youth At Risk: A Prevention Resource for Counselors, Teachers, and Parents* will prove to be an invaluable resource for individuals committed to assisting young people in the often difficult transition between adolescence and adulthood.

ACKNOWLEDGMENTS

We would like to thank the 23 authors who contributed their expertise, knowledge, and experience in the development of this text. We would also like to thank our families who provided the freedom and encouragement to make this endeavor possible. Our thanks are also directed to ACA staff for their encouragement and assistance with copy-editing and ultimately the production of the book. Thanks also to Patty Muller, graduate assistant for this project and a student in the community counseling specialization of the Counselor Education Program at Portland State University, who eased the burden of this task.

Special acknowledgment must be given to Dr. Cheryl Livneh and Dr. Joel Arick of the Graduate School of Education at Portland State University. Their support for the funding of the graduate assistantship made it possible to employ Patty Muller, an excellent scholar, research assistant, and manuscript reviewer.

ABOUT THE AUTHORS

David Capuzzi, PhD, NCC, LPC, is a past president of the American Counseling Association (formerly the American Association for Counseling and Development) and is professor of counselor education in the Graduate School of Education at Portland State University in Portland, Oregon.

From 1980 to 1984, Dr. Capuzzi was editor of *The School Counselor*. He has authored a number of textbook chapters and monographs on the topic of preventing adolescent suicide and is coeditor and author, with Dr. Larry Golden, of *Helping Families Help Children: Family Interventions With School-Related Problems* (1986) and *Preventing Adolescent Suicide* (1988). In 1989 and 1996 he coauthored and edited *Youth at Risk: A Prevention Resource for Counselors, Teachers, and Parents*; in 1991 and 1997, *Introduction to the Counseling Profession*; in 1992 and 1998, *Introduction to Group Counseling*; and in 1995 and 1999, *Counseling and Psychotherapy: Theories and Interventions* with Douglas R. Gross. He has authored or coauthored articles in a number of ACA-related journals.

A frequent speaker and keynoter at professional conferences and institutes, Dr. Capuzzi has also consulted with a variety of school districts and community agencies interested in initiating prevention and intervention strategies for adolescents at risk for suicide. He has facilitated the development of suicide prevention, crisis management, and postvention programs in communities throughout the United States; provides training on the topics *youth at risk* and *grief and loss*; and serves as an invited adjunct faculty member at other universities as time permits. He is the first recipient of ACA's Kitty Cole Human Rights Award.

Douglas R. Gross, PhD, NCC, is a professor emeritus at Arizona State University, Tempe, where he served as a faculty member in the counseling program for 29 years. His professional work history includes public school teaching, counseling, and administration. He is currently retired and living in Three Rivers, Michigan. He has been president of the Arizona Counselors Association, president of the Western Association for

Counselor Education and Supervision, chairperson of the Western Regional Branch Assembly of the American Counseling Association, president of the Association for Humanistic Education and Development, and treasurer and parliamentarian of the ACA.

Dr. Gross has contributed chapters to seven texts: *Counseling and Psychotherapy: Theories and Interventions* (1995, 1999); *Youth at Risk: A Resource for Counselors, Teachers, and Parents* (1989, 1996); *Foundations of Mental Health Counseling* (1986, 1996); *Counseling: Theory, Process, and Practice* (1977); *The Counselor's Handbook* (1974); *Introduction to the Counseling Profession* (1991, 1997); and *Introduction to Group Counseling* (1992, 1998). His research has appeared in the *Journal of Counseling Psychology; Journal of Counseling and Development; Association for Counselor Education and Supervision Journal; Journal of Educational Research, Counseling, and Human Development; Arizona Counselors Journal; Texas Counseling Journal;* and *American Mental Health Counselor Association Journal.*

Dr. Gross serves as a consultant to Carondolet Management Institute and provides national training for certification in the areas of bereavement, grief, and loss.

Valerie E. Appleton, EdD, MFCC, ATR, NCC, is associate professor and the director of counselor education at Eastern Washington University. She teaches full-time in the two CACREP-accredited programs: mental health and school counseling. A licensed marriage, family, and child therapist, Dr. Appleton worked for 10 years as the art therapist to the intensive care burn unit at Saint Francis Memorial Hospital in San Francisco. There she developed a unique program to provide art and play therapy to trauma patients and their families. In Washington State, she was the principal investigator for a federal grant (DOE) serving at-risk secondary students. Under this grant, Dr. Appleton implemented Project Success, a program of creative arts and skills-based learning in seven rural county school districts and Indian reservations.

Mit Arnold, EdD, is associate professor of special education at the University of Mississippi. She teaches classes and has published articles related to adolescents and young adults with disabilities. Her work with at-risk youth has been supported by state and federal grants for demonstration programs, and serves to increase the independence and productivity of the nation's most vulnerable youths.

Michael T. Barta, PhD, has just completed his doctorate in counselor education at the University of Northern Colorado. He has worked with children and adolescents for the past 10 years as both a teacher in public education and a counselor in mental health centers. Dr. Barta is interested in educational reform and in making our schools safer and more secure for all children.

Sonja Burnham, EdD, is currently an assistant professor of educational psychology at the University of Mississippi. She received her BA in education at Michigan State University and her MEd and EdD at Mississippi State University. She has coordinated federal transition school-to-work demonstration grants and taught in counselor education programs at Delta State University in Cleveland, Mississippi, and at Augusta State University in Augusta, Georgia. Her research interests include issues facing school counselors, career issues for individuals from kindergarten through retirement, and clinical supervision of counselors. She is active in her state counseling association and her state and regional counselor educators associations.

Donna A. Champeau, PhD, CHES, is currently an assistant professor in the Department of Public Health at Oregon State University. She received her master's degree from the University of Wisconsin, LaCrosse, in school health, and her PhD in public health from Oregon State University. Her research interests include adolescent sexuality issues, women's health issues, and end-of-life decision making.

Cass Dykeman, PhD, is an associate professor of counselor education at Oregon State University. He is a National Certified Counselor, Master Addictions Counselor, and National Certified School Counselor. Dr. Dykeman received a master's in counseling from the University of Washington and a doctorate in counselor education from the University of Virginia. He served as principal investigator for a $1.5 million federal school-to-work research project. In addition, he is the author of numerous books, book chapters, and scholarly journal articles. Dr. Dykeman is past president of both the Washington State Association for Counselor Education and Supervision and the Western Association for Counselor Education and Supervision. He is also past chair of the School Counseling Interest Network of the Association for Counselor Education and Supervision. His current research interests include school violence, addiction counseling, and brief counseling techniques.

Irit Gat, MA, received her master's degree in clinical psychology from the University of Colorado, Colorado Springs, and her bachelor's degree from Emory University. She is currently a doctoral candidate in the counseling psychology program at the University of Nebraska-Lincoln. Her doctoral dissertation is focused on incarcerated mothers, recidivism, moral development, empathy, and state hope. Ms. Gat has been published in the *Personality and Social Psychology Bulletin* and *Journal of Sport Behavior.*

Alberta M. Gloria, PhD is an assistant professor in the Department of Counseling Psychology at the University of Wisconsin-Madison. She has published and presented in areas related to educational issues for racial and ethnic minority students in higher education, in particular for

Latino/a students, and professional practice issues for counselors in training. She is an active member of the American Psychological Association (APA) and the National Association for Chicana and Chicano Studies, and is an editorial board member for the *Journal of Multicultural Counseling and Development* and the *Journal of Counseling and Development*. She is also the secretary for APA's Division 17 (Counseling Psychology) Section on Ethnic and Racial Diversity. Some of her recent journal articles are published in *The Counseling Psychologist*, *Education and Urban Society*, *Professional Psychology*, *Journal of Substance Abuse Treatment*, and *Hispanic Journal of Behavioral Sciences*.

Lizbeth A. Gray, MSW, PhD, has been a counselor educator at Oregon State University for over 15 years. She is a sexual therapist who lectures internationally on HIV/AIDS, particularly in developing countries. Dr. Gray's research and publications focus on sexuality, HIV/AIDS, and social advocacy.

Rebecca S. Hart, MA, received her master's degree in counseling psychology from Northwestern University in 1996. She is currently a third-year doctoral student in the counseling psychology program at the University of Oregon. Ms. Hart is interested in the prevention of child abuse and intervening with abusive families to promote positive outcomes.

Paula Heariold-Kinney, MA, has a bachelor's degree in English and a master's degree in psychology. She was the director of alternative education programs for Portland Public Schools, Portland, Oregon, from 1983 to 1988. She developed and maintained programs for students who were at risk of not succeeding in school. Ms. Heariold-Kinney currently is arts administrator in the Portland School District. Her responsibilities include the evaluation and supervision of visual and performing arts staff. She is a strong advocate for arts education and how it has prevented many students from dropping out of school.

Reese M. House, EdD, program specialist, is a nationally recognized counselor educator. He is professor emeritus at Oregon State University where he focused on preparing school counselors to be proactive change agents and advocates for social, economic, and political justice. He has experience as a school counselor, community activist, and HIV/AIDS educator. He currently works at the Education Trust in Washington, D.C., on the DeWitt Wallace-Reader's Digest Fund's Transforming School Counseling Initiative.

Sharon E. Robinson Kurpius, PhD, received her doctorate from Indiana University in 1978 and has been a member of the counseling faculty at Arizona State University since that time. She holds fellow status in the Counseling Psychology and the Consulting Psychology divisions of APA.

She has been active at both state and national levels of ACA and most recently was the associate editor for the *Journal for Counseling and Development*. Professional areas of interest include at-risk youth, ethics, consultation, and health counseling. She recently co-authored (with Neil Weiner) the book *Shattered Innocence: A Practical Guide for Counseling Women Survivors of Childhood Sexual Abuse*.

James W. Kushman, PhD, works with schools and school districts on school improvement, action research, and strategic planning. He also conducts research and evaluation studies on school-community partnerships, school reform models, and programs for youth at-risk.

Rolla E. Lewis, EdD, is an assistant professor in counselor education in the Graduate School of Education at Portland State University, where he serves as coordinator of the school counseling specialization for the master's program in counselor education. Dr. Lewis has taught, led groups, and counseled students in alternative and public school settings for more that 15 years. He is a past president of the Oregon Association for Counselor Education and Supervision, and has authored a number of book chapters and journal articles.

Benedict T. McWhirter, PhD, received his doctorate in counseling psychology from Arizona State University in 1992 and is currently director of training of the Counseling Psychology Program at the University of Oregon. He is a licensed psychologist and spent 5 years as an assistant professor at the University of Nebraska-Lincoln. He has had extensive experience living and working in Latin America. He has taught in Peru and is currently a regular consultant for two school guidance/prevention programs in Santiago, Chile. Dr. McWhirter's teaching focuses on counseling practica, supervision, counselor skills training, and on community and prevention interventions. His two programmatic areas of research include college student development, with a particular focus on loneliness, and at-risk children and adolescents, with a particular focus on examining the effectiveness of school-based small-group interventions for high-risk adolescents. Dr. McWhirter has published more than 35 articles and book chapters and has presented more than 30 papers at professional conferences in these and other areas. He has recently completed, with members of his family, the second edition of the book *At-Risk Youth: A Comprehensive Response*.

J. Jefferies McWhirter, PhD, ABPP, a professor at Arizona State University and a diplomate in counseling psychology, has had nearly 40 years experience as a teacher, counselor, psychologist, and university professor. For over 25 years he has served as a consultant to school personnel and mental health clinic personnel on a variety of topics, including substance abuse, group work, peer intervention strategies, and high-risk young people. He is the senior author of a major text, *At-Risk Youth: A Comprehensive Response* (2nd ed, 1998), that focuses on prevention and early intervention strategies for high-risk school children and adolescents. He has developed the group training course sequence for the Division of Psychology in Education at Arizona State University, and over half of his over 130 publications (books, book chapters, and journal articles) deal with issues related to the chapter in this book on preventing and treating depression in youth.

Sandra S. Meggert, PhD, NCC, president of Unfinished Business Business, is deeply involved in the areas of humor and career development. She has facilitated over 500 Creative Humor at Work seminars throughout the country and in Europe for counselors, educators, businesses, and various civic groups. She received her PhD in counselor education/counseling psychology from Arizona State University and has taught in counselor education programs, counseled, and consulted for several years. Dr. Meggert has written articles on career guidance and humor, and she has developed career guidance materials and the original chapter on self-esteem in this publication.

Russell D. Miars, PhD, is an associate professor in the counselor education program at Portland State University. Previously, Dr. Miars was director of the Counseling and Student Development Center and adjunct associate professor in clinical psychology at Indiana University of Pennsylvania. His research and scholarly interests include counselor supervision, legal and ethical issues, life-span human development, career development, and assessment in counseling. An emphasis in all his work is translating theory and research into effective clinical practice.

Ardis Sherwood-Hawes, MS, is both a mental health counselor in private practice and an employee of a mental health agency. Her training includes a BS in psychology and an MS in counselor education at Portland State University in Portland, Oregon. She has worked extensively with women who experience economic, academic, and/or social barriers at the community college level. She has published articles covering a wide range of topics, including counseling and therapy for children and adolescents, teenage pregnancy, and issues related to adolescent suicide.

Conrad Sieber, PhD, completed a postdoctoral fellowship in the counselor education program at Portland State University, where he taught courses on program evaluation in educational and social service agencies and supervised counseling practicum students and interns. He also pursued interests in treating posttraumatic stress disorder, in person-centered psychology, and in developing educational/counseling programs for disadvantaged youth. Dr. Sieber received his doctoral degree from Colorado State University and completed his internship at the Ohio State University.

He has 5 years of professional experience in university counseling centers, where he coordinated and developed group therapy programs, evaluated clinical services, and was actively involved in training graduate students. Currently, he maintains a private practice in Portland, Oregon, evaluates educational and counseling programs, and consults with public schools and institutions of higher education. Dr. Sieber has authored counseling book chapters and articles for professional publication.

Melissa Stormont, PhD, is currently an assistant professor of special education at the University of Missouri-Columbia. In addition to her interest in at-risk youth, her other expertise area is attention deficit/ hyperactivity disorder (ADHD). Dr. Stormont has published numerous articles for practitioners that review research literature and give feasible intervention options for the purpose of meeting the needs of children in the classroom.

Kimberely Wright, PhD, is a licensed psychologist and has worked with eating disordered clients at several universities. She earned her bachelor's and master's degrees from California State University, Long Beach, and her doctorate in counseling psychology from Indiana State University. She is currently eating disorders coordinator at Arizona State University, working in conjunction with counseling and consultation and student health services. In addition, she serves as adjunct faculty for the Arizona State University Counselor Education Department.

PART ONE | INTRODUCING THE PROBLEM

All persons who either work with or live with youth have become increasingly aware of the potential that exists for the development of at-risk behaviors. This awareness is enhanced by media coverage, educational reform, mental health programming, governmental mandates, and law enforcement reporting. This ongoing bombardment of the vulnerability of youth provides a call to action for all persons involved with this population. Prior to taking such action, however, it is important to understand not only the demographics of this population but also current definitions, at-risk behaviors, generic causal factors, and preventive and interventive approaches to dealing with youth at risk. Part One of this text provides the reader with this foundational information. Chapter 1, Defining Youth At Risk, introduces the topic of *at-riskness* by providing the reader with foundational information related to definitions, at-risk behaviors, and causal factors that enhance the development of at-risk behaviors. The chapter concludes with an introduction to the two approaches that are used to work with this population, namely prevention and intervention.

Building on this foundation, chapter 2, Approaches to Prevention, lays the groundwork for understanding the various strategies incorporated in the term *prevention*. In meeting this goal, information presented includes goals and purposes of prevention; primary, secondary, and tertiary concepts related to prevention; and program examples to illustrate prevention's place in the broad spectrum of helping. Some discussion of the schools' efforts to develop tragedy response plans is included. The chapter concludes with an explanation of how to plan prevention and intervention strategies.

Chapter 3, Resiliency: Pathway to Protective Factors and Possibilities for Self-Righting Narratives, adds a new dimension to the prevention par-

1

adigm by offering professionals an alternative view that sees youth at promise rather than at risk. This new chapter for the third edition provides ideas for practices promoting resiliency that can guide counselors, teachers, and parents in their efforts to ensure possibilities for success for all youth.

These first three chapters provide a necessary foundation for all persons wishing to reduce the vulnerability of youth for the future development of at-risk behaviors.

1 | Defining Youth at Risk

Douglas R. Gross and David Capuzzi

As John Patron sat down at the large table in the conference room, he hoped that something positive could come from this meeting, that perhaps something finally could be done to help some of the students in his classroom. He knew that he had been instrumental in forcing Ms. Callis, his principal, to call this meeting. He hoped that all of his colleagues attending shared his view on the urgency for taking some positive action.

This was John's third year of teaching, and each day he was confronted with problems in his classroom. The problems were not those of math, his subject area, but problems that he observed and that were reported to him by many of his students. The problems covered a wide range of areas including pregnancy, gangs, drugs and alcohol, violence, eating disorders, and dropping out of school. Certainly, he was not the first to notice these problems, or the only teacher in whom students confided. If these problems were so obvious to him, why hadn't something been done to deal with them? Most of his students were now juniors in high school, and he was sure that the problems did not have their origins in attaining junior status.

He did the best he could, but he was not trained to handle these issues. In seeking direction, he talked with the school counselor, the school psychologist, and Ms. Callis. Although all of the persons contacted wanted to help, they were also overwhelmed by the demands upon their time. His questions for the most part went unanswered. If he was correct that these problems did not begin during the junior year in high school, why hadn't something been done earlier? Hadn't former school personnel recognized the difficulties these students were having? Hadn't parents asked for help with their children? Why hadn't something been done to prevent these problems from developing? John hoped that maybe answers would be forthcoming at the meeting.

John sat in his classroom after the meeting and reflected on what had happened. He was very pleased that he was not alone in his concern about students and that his colleagues had raised many of the same questions that plagued him. He was also pleased that many of his colleagues saw a need for adding trained personnel to work with teachers, students, and parents in developing strategies to intervene in the disrupted lives of many of the students before it was too late. John felt that several helpful outcomes resulted from the meeting. The first of these was that of exploring the development of prevention strategies aimed at early identification of problem behaviors and establishing programs directed at impeding their development. This outcome generated much discussion centering around such questions as "What constitutes prevention?" "How does prevention differ from intervention?" "What have other schools tried and what has worked?" "Do we need to go beyond the school to build a prevention program?" and "What part will the community and parents play in the prevention program?" The second outcome dealt with the identification of other at-risk issues such as suicide, increased sexual activity and the danger of sexually transmitted diseases including AIDS, and the impact of homelessness on a small percentage of the students. This outcome led to a discussion of the questions "Are there community resources we can use to aid us in better dealing with these identified problems?" and "Where in the community can we find suicide prevention/intervention programs, AIDS education, and services to aid the homeless?"

A third outcome dealt with the concept of *resiliency* and the related questions "What makes some young people resilient to high-risk environments while other succumb to these same environments?" and "What are the characteristics of both the individual and his or her environment that make him or her resistant to these high risks?" John had not thought much about resilience and was excited over finding answers to these questions. He sensed that the questions came more easily than would the answers.

The major directives that came from the meeting were the establishment of a committee to investigate what is currently being done by other schools to develop an approach to prevention, to develop a list of community mental health services that could be utilized by the school to supplement the work currently being done by the school staff, and to gather data relative to the concept of resiliency and how these data would impact the development of a prevention program. John had volunteered to serve as chairperson of the committee investigating current programs and to assist in gaining more information about the issue of resiliency. He looked forward to the next meeting that was scheduled in 2 weeks.

This hypothetical situation has been repeated over and over in school districts across the country as teachers, administrators, community leaders, and parents attempt to better understand what needs to be done to provide effective programs to help with the growing numbers of young people who are labeled *at risk* due to their involvement in certain destructive behaviors as well as to help prevent the development of these destructive behavioral patterns. The question these concerned citizens are striving to answer is "Do we continue to deal from a crisis management perspective with the problem behaviors of youth, or do we take a preventive approach to attempt to stop these problem behaviors from developing?"

The answer to both parts of this complex question is "yes." With the growing numbers of young people entering our educational systems identified as at risk, it is not possible to say "no" to continuing our crisis management strategies. Due to these increasing numbers, however, most educational systems are not equipped to address this problem from a purely crisis management perspective. Therefore, steps must be taken to attempt to stop its development. Such steps are usually described in terms of prevention modalities aimed at providing programs that will identify young people with the highest potential for developing at-risk behaviors, stop these destructive behaviors from developing, and work to identify individual and environmental characteristics that enhance the resiliency of the individual and his or her environment. Thus we must continue to intervene at the points of crisis and at the same time set into place prevention programs that will eventually reduce the need for crisis intervention.

This chapter first provides a foundational perspective on at-risk youth by presenting the definition, identifying the population, and describing the population's behavioral and causal characteristics. The chapter then introduces the concept of resiliency and concludes with a discussion of a prevention and crisis management paradigm.

A FOUNDATIONAL PERSPECTIVE

Many problems are encountered in attempting to understand the concepts and issues that surround the term *at-risk youth*. Such problems center upon definition, cause and effect, calculating and determining the population, and the development and implementation of both prevention and crisis management programs that impact the various destructive behaviors that place youth at risk. According to Conrath (1988), "principals and teachers have known at-risk youth for a long time. They have recently been discovered by policy makers and budget sculptors" (p. 36). Simple answers and agreed-upon definitions do not currently exist. The best we have at this time are experimental programs, a host of opinions, definitions, and population descriptors, and a high motivation to find workable solutions. The concepts that surround the students at risk and the most effective ways to deal with this at-riskness are complex, filled with frustration for those who attempt to understand them, filled with despair for those who attempt to affect them, and often filled with tragedy for the individuals so labeled.

Overwhelming statistics place the concepts and issues surrounding at-risk youth high on the priority lists of educators, mental health workers, counselors, social workers, psychologists, parents, and community leaders. According to researchers Donmoyer and Kos (1993), Dryfoos (1990), Kronick (1997), Kushman and Heariold-Kinney (1996), McWhirter, McWhirter, McWhirter, and McWhirter (1998), and the National Center for Education Statistics (NCES) (1997), approximately

- 700,000 students drop out of high school each year;
- 500,000 teenagers give birth each year;
- 24,000,000 children live in poverty;
- 14,000,000 children are being raised by a single parent;
- 2,000,000 children suffer from some form of abuse each year;
- 3,000,000 students and teachers are victims of crime each year;
- 500,000 robberies, burglaries, assaults, and rapes are committed in schools each year; and
- 7,000 teenagers commit suicide each year.

It is important to keep in mind that each day steps are being taken to reduce these staggering numbers. Educational, psychological, sociological, governmental, and community-based entities are developing and applying prevention and crisis management strategies directed toward a society at risk. This book has as its major purpose providing these entities with information and direction in meeting their difficult tasks.

The Definition

Tracing the exact origins of the term *at risk* as it applies to education and youth is impossible, but during the past 25 years, the term has appeared frequently in educational literature, federal reports, and legislative mandates from the individual states. In 1988, *Education Week* reported that three out of four states have either adopted or are preparing a definition of their populations determined to be at risk (Minga, 1988); and although current data are not available, it is assumed that all states have by now established legislative parameters for their at-risk populations. A review of the known definitions reveals not only that there is a lack of clarity and consensus but also that the term is explained most often from an educational perspective and indicates individuals at risk of dropping out of the educational system. The characteristics of at-risk youth presented in these definitions include the well-known risk factors of tardiness, poor grades, low math and reading scores, and failing one or more grades (Kushman & Heariold-Kinney, 1996; Wehlage, 1991).

A more interesting listing of characteristics was adopted by the Montana State Board of Education in April 1988. This definition (reported by Minga, 1988) is as follows:

> . . . at-risk youths are children who are not likely to finish high school or who are apt to graduate considerably below potential. At-risk factors include chemical dependence, teenage pregnancy, poverty, disaffection with school and society, high-mobility families, emotional and physical abuse, physical and emotional disabilities, and learning disabilities that do not qualify students for special education but nevertheless impede their progress. (p. 14)

This definition speaks directly to the confusion that surrounds the issue of being at risk and somewhat indirectly addresses concerns regarding cause versus effect. From this definition, it could be concluded that behaviors such as tardiness, truancy, and low grades are the effects of identified causal factors, for example, chemical dependency, teenage pregnancy, and poverty (Aruffo, Gottlieb, Webb, & Neville, 1994; Donmoyer & Kos, 1993; Homebase, 1993).

If programs dealing with at-risk youth first attempt to deal with factors such as tardiness, truancy, and low grades, they may be placing the proverbial cart before the horse. If the desired effects are to reduce tardiness and truancy and to improve grades, with the ultimate aim of reducing the dropout rate, perhaps more attention needs to be directed toward such identified causal issues as are listed by the Montana State Board of Education. Underlying much of the confusion surrounding at-risk youth is the amount of emphasis placed on either cause or effect (behavior) or both. Whichever position is selected often determines both definition and strategies to operate within that definition. For example, if we approach this area from an effect (behavior) point of view, then what we need to do is identify the behaviors that place the individual at risk and develop strategies to change these behaviors. Or if we approach this area from a causal perspective, then we must try to determine what caused the development of the effect (behavior) and attempt to develop strategies that eliminate the causal factors, thereby stopping the development of the effect (behavior). But if we approach from both cause and effect perspectives, then we must develop strategies both to identify and eliminate the causal factors, and at the same time put into motion programs to change the behavior.

This latter approach—from both cause and effect perspectives—forms the basis for our definition of *at risk*. In this book, the term *at risk* encompasses a set of causal/effect (behavioral) dynamics that have the potential to place the individual in danger of a negative future event. This definition not only considers the effect (behavior) that may lead to a negative future event but also attempts to trace the causal factors that led to the development of the effect (behavior). For example, with school-age persons, one of these negative future events may be that of dropping out of school. The causal/behavioral approach identifies not only the behaviors that lead to this event but also the myriad causal factors that aided in the development of this behavior. This definition speaks directly to the need for programs to change existing negative behaviors and for prevention programs to tackle the precipitating events that serve as causal factors in the development of the negative behavior. When viewed from the causal/effect (behavioral) perspective, the concept of being at risk broadens, and dropping out is only one of many possible outcomes. Other risks include, but are not limited to, graduating without an education, without goals and objectives, without direction for what comes next, without an understanding of potentials and possibilities, without appreciation for self, or without a knowledge of one's place in the larger society.

When viewed from this causal/effect (behavioral) perspective, the concept of being at risk takes on new dimensions and places the emphasis on individual and systemic dynamics that may or may not lead to a wide range of destructive outcomes. Such a viewpoint emphasizes the vulnerability of all youth to be at risk and provides a strong rationale for the development of prevention programs directed toward stemming the negative impact of certain individual and systemic dynamics. This viewpoint directs attention to a set of causal issues and resultant behaviors that often have proven to be significantly related to the development of many personal and educational dilemmas faced by today's youth. Any one of these dilemmas could result in personal and educational impairment. In combination, the results could be both personally and educationally fatal. This book uses the causal/effect (behavioral) definition of being at risk and presents both information and strategies to deal with at-riskness from a preventive perspective.

The Population

One of the basic issues confronting those wishing to work in the area of at-risk youth centers on the identification of the population. Who are these persons identified as being at risk? Is it possible to identify young people who, by behavior or circumstance, are more at risk than others? Are not all young people, based upon behaviors, environments, and developmental patterns, at risk? Specific answers to these questions are not readily available. The research literature in this area is as yet replete with more opinion and supposition than fact. Interest in this population is recent. Population identification may be possible only after the fact, as exemplified by the studies that deal with placing the label of at-risk youth on those who drop out of school, abuse alcohol and/or drugs, become involved in gangs, and attempt and/or complete suicide. In such studies, the population is identified by the specific behaviors manifested. Such an approach to identification, although interesting, limits the identification process of at-riskness to those who currently manifest the specified behaviors.

Another factor that may hinder gaining a comprehensive perspective on the population of at-risk youth is the fact that the terms *at-risk youth* and *adolescence* are used somewhat interchangeably. It seems that to be at risk is to be between the ages of 13 and 18. Such parameters are understandable when we realize that most of the behaviors that are used to describe at-risk youth are those that coincide with the turbulent and exploratory developmental period called adolescence. Factors such as sexual experimentation, first-time drug and alcohol utilization, ego and self-concept development, and peer inclusion and/or exclusion are descriptive of both adolescence and of the population labeled at-risk youth. Such age-specific parameters, however, are limiting and often rule out a large segment of youth, namely those younger than 13, who also need to be a focus in any discussion of at-risk youth. If we limit our identification process of at-risk youth to adolescence, we may also limit issues of cause and effect. From this perspective, both causal and behavioral dynamics are correlated with entrance into and exit from the developmental stage termed adolescence. Based upon the definition of at-risk youth stated earlier and knowledge of human development, we take a somewhat different viewpoint in identifying this population and view adolescence as simply the emerging period for behaviors that have been developing over a much longer period of time.

In keeping with this definition and viewpoint, the population identified as at risk includes all youth regardless of age. All young people have the potential for the development of at-risk behaviors. The key words in this statement are *potential for*. All young people may move in and out of at-riskness depending on personal, social, educational, and family dynamics. No one can be excluded.

By expanding the at-risk population to include all youth, the doors are open to begin work with this population at a much earlier age, to identify causal factors in the individual's environment that may either encourage or impede the later development of at-risk behaviors, and to develop prevention programs for all youth regardless of age or circumstance. If all youth have the potential for the development of at-risk behaviors, preventive steps can be taken to see that the young person does not reach his or her at-risk potential. If this population also includes those who have achieved their at-risk potential, then crisis management steps can be taken to reduce the level of at-riskness and return them to a level more descriptive of *potential for*.

Behaviors and Causal Factors

Based on the assumption that all youth have the potential for at-riskness, how then are we able to identify both behaviors and causal factors that make these behaviors reality? Is it possible to spell out a direct cause-effect relationship, or is this relationship much more indirect and circular in nature? The answers to these questions are at best speculative and perhaps best understood by looking at the developmental period that describes this population and then by identifying the behaviors and causal factors related to this population from school, mental health, and home perspectives.

The developmental period from childhood through adolescence is characterized by rapid physical change, striving for independence, exploration and implementation of new behaviors, strengthening peer relationships, sexual awakening and experimentation, and seeking clarity relating to self and one's place in the larger society. Pressures exerted by family, school, peers, and society to conform or not conform to established standards contribute to the highly charged environment in which this developmental process takes place and the degree of vulnerability that exists within it for the individual. Ingersoll and Orr (1988), in an article about adolescents at risk, discussed G. Stanley Hall's 1904 view of adolescence as a phase of "storm and stress" and painted a graphic picture of this developmental process in which adolescence is simply the emerging period for behaviors that have been developing over a much longer period of time:

> Still, for those who deal with adolescents in a therapeutic context, there remains a subgroup that does experience storm and stress, whose transition to adulthood is marked by turmoil and trial. Further, only a recluse could be unaware of the statistics that show an upsurge in adolescent suicide, pregnancy, and venereal disease, as well as continued patterns of drug and alcohol use and abuse, school dropouts, and delinquency. For some young people, adolescence is an extended period of struggle; for others the transition is marked by alternating periods of struggle and quiescence. During periods of stress and turmoil, the latter group's ability to draw on effective adaptive coping behaviors is taxed. The resulting maladaptive behavior risks compromising physical, psychological, and social health. These young people are at risk. (p. l)

Terms such as *turmoil, trial, struggle, compromise,* and *stress* lend credence to the difficulty that surrounds this developmental period of youth. Research dealing with this developmental period includes but is not limited to such impacting factors as eating disorders (Brownell & Rodin, 1994; Wright, 1996), homelessness (Rafferty & Schinn, 1991; Stormont-Spurgin & De Reus, 1996), sexual behaviors (Katz, Mills, Singh, & Best, 1995; Melchert & Burnett, 1990), abuse (Goldman & Galgino, 1990; Rencken, 1996), affective disorders (Pinto, Grapentine, Francis, & Picariello, 1996; Meggert, 1996), substance use and abuse (Gloria, Trainer, Beasley, & Robinson Kurpius, 1996), pregnancy (Alan Guttmacher Institute, 1994; Sherwood-Hawes & Thompson, 1996), suicide and suicide ideation (Capuzzi & Gross, 1996; Durlak & Wells, 1997), and violence (Burden, Miller, & Boozer, 1996; Wilson, 1997). Each of these factors is descriptive of either behaviors or causal factors that can be identified from the perspective of the school, the mental health community, and the home. The behaviors and causal factors are separated for purposes of discussion only. Many items could appear in each perspective's listing.

From a School Perspective.

At-risk behaviors.   From an educational perspective, there seems to be a good deal of consistency regarding the behaviors of youth who fall within the parameters of the at-risk population. According to Aksamit (1990), Cohen and de Bettencourt (1991), Kushman and Heariold-Kinney (1996), and McMillen, Kaufman, Hausken, and Bradby (1993), the following behaviors are red flags for those at risk:

- tardiness;
- absenteeism;
- poor grades;
- truancy;
- low math and reading scores;
- failing one or more grades;
- rebellious attitudes toward school authority;
- verbal and language deficiency;
- inability to tolerate structured activities;
- dropping out of school; and
- aggressive behaviors.

Causal factors.   Behaviors such as those just listed, viewed either individually or in combination, aid in the identification process. However, this type of identification focuses on existing behaviors that need crisis management strategies to attempt to change them. A different approach, and one we support, identifies the causal factors that lead to these behaviors and suggests prevention programs that may keep these behaviors from developing.

Ekstrom, Goertz, Pollack, and Rock (1986) attempted to address these causal issues in their analysis of data from the U.S. Department of Education's High School and Beyond national sample of 30,000 high school sophomores and seniors. The researchers looked at sophomores in 1980 and 1982 and concentrated on the differences between graduates and nongraduates. Their findings indicated that behavior problems and low grades were major determinants of dropping out. Other determinants included family circumstances with few educational supports and parents uninvolved in the ongoing process of their child's education. Further, dropouts tended to have close friends whose attitudes and behaviors also indicated alienation from school.

In a study of a comprehensive high school in upper Manhattan, Fine (1986) concluded that the structural characteristics that may lead to dropping out include a school that has a disproportionate share of low-achieving students and insufficient resources to provide for this population; overcrowded classrooms; teachers who are predominantly White, leading to poor communication with minority students and a lack of understanding; and teaching styles based more on control than conversation, authority than autonomy, and competition than collaboration.

Barber and McClellan (1987) and Paulu (1987) addressed the dropout problem from the students' perspective and reported that the reasons students gave for leaving school included personal reasons such as family problems, pregnancy, and academic problems. Other reasons that spoke directly to problems inherent in the educational structure included the absence of individual help, more challenging classes, smaller classes, more consistent discipline and more understanding, support, and help by teachers as well as the presence of boredom and communication problems with teachers, counselors, and administrators.

From a Mental Health Perspective.
At-risk behaviors. Today more and more young people are seen by mental health agencies either in terms of clients who present for treatment or through the mental health agency's consulting relationships with schools. Regardless of the nature of the involvement, the following behaviors are most often presented:

- drug and alcohol use and abuse;
- eating disorders;
- gang membership;
- pregnancy;
- suicide or suicide ideation;
- depression;
- sexual acting out;
- aggression;
- withdrawal and isolation;
- low self-esteem; and
- school-related problems.

Causal factors. Based upon the behaviors identified, it is easy to realize that no single causal factor provides the answer as to why such behaviors develop, that it may be better to answer in terms of combinations of causal factors leading to somewhat predictable behaviors. Often listed as causal factors for many of the behaviors just identified are dysfunctional family dynamics, peer group pressure for inclusion/exclusion, lack of positive adult models, an uninspired educational system, learning difficulties that go untreated, increased violence within the community and the school, homelessness and economic hardship, single-parent households, living in a highly stressed society, and physical, sexual, or psychological abuse (Cashwell, Bloss, & McFarland, 1995; Dryfoos, 1990; McCarthy, Brack, Lambert, Brack, & Orr, 1996; McWhirter et al., 1998; Zanarini et al., 1997).

From the Perspective of the Home.

At-risk behaviors. Parenting in today's society presents many challenges, not the least of which is attempting to understand children and the various factors that have an impact on them. Parents do not have the objective, somewhat clinical, viewpoint of at-risk behaviors as do either school personnel or members of the mental health profession. Because of their close relationship with their children, the following is descriptive of what they might list if asked to identify behaviors that place their children at risk:

- failing to obey rules or directives;
- avoiding taking part in family activities;
- spending a great deal of time alone in their room;
- being secretive about friends and activities;
- not communicating with parents or siblings;
- displaying values and attitudes different from family;
- resisting going to school or discussing school activities;
- arguing about everything; and
- staying away from home as much as possible.

Causal factors. As the family and its dynamics are generally viewed as one of the major contributors (causal factors) to at-risk behaviors, what does the family identify as causal factors and where do they look for explanations? Families must look inside the family structure as well as to entities outside the family to arrive at causal factors. These include the educational system, the peer group, the media, the economic conditions that necessitate both parents working, the lack of time for family interaction, the violence so common in both the community and the society at large, the absence of extended family, the availability of drugs and alcohol, and the lack of funds or governmental support for child care (Baumrind, 1990; Capuzzi & Gross, 1996; McWhirter, McWhirter, & Gat, 1996; Nock & Kingston, 1991).

Origins of Causal Factors

The three perspectives illustrate not only the differing behaviors identified but also the differing opinions as to the origins of the causal factors that aid in the development of these behaviors. Is one more accurate than the other two? Does one provide a better answer than the other two? Are all three perspectives accurate? The answer to all three of these questions could be "yes" depending on the setting, the perspective of the person in the setting, and the individual under evaluation. No one single factor can explain the development of at-riskness; only in combination are we able to understand the impact these factors have on the developmental process. For example, the young person growing up in a dysfunctional family often internalizes aspects of this dysfunction. Such internalization may stem from physical, sexual, or psychological abuse and result in low self-esteem, poor school performance, drug and alcohol use, or gang membership. The causal factors stem both from the degree of dysfunctionality within the family and how the young person reacts to that dysfunctionality. We know that not all young people who live in a dysfunctional family environment achieve at-risk status. We do know, however, that the potential for at-risk-ness in this type of environment is high.

This same situation exists when we move from the family environment to the school environment. The child who enters school for the first time may find this environment both frightening and difficult. So much depends upon what is done to recognize these reactions in the child and to develop programs to aid the child in making the transition from home to school. First impressions can have a far-reaching impact on this person's movement though the educational system—an impact that has the potential for such future behaviors as poor grades, lack of interest in learning, disruptive behaviors, and eventually dropping out of the educational system.

Aligned closely with the school environment is the developing pressured environment of the peer group. Part of the developmental process from childhood through adolescence is the growing importance of the peer group and the need to conform or to belong. The peer group impacts youth in areas such as self-identification, self-esteem and self-worth, interactive styles, attitudes, values, and beliefs. As youth develop, the peer group is like a magnet that continually pulls them away from family and often encourages behaviors that are decidedly different from those espoused by the family. Young people attempting to find their place in the world are faced with making choices, choices that for the most part place them at odds with one of two pulling forces: the family or the peer group. The ensuing stress demands the use of coping strategies and decision-making skills, both of which are often not part of the young person's behavioral repertoire. Unless something is done to relieve this pressure, the young person may develop a wide range of emotional reactions or behavioral dynamics in an attempt to relieve the stress, including depression, aggressiveness, use of alcohol and drugs, eating disorders, and suicide or suicide ideation. Any one of these classifies the young person as being at risk.

Society provides a further environment that has the potential for causing at-riskness in young people. One influencing element within today's society is conflicting standards for youth. On one hand, through legislative actions persons under the age of 18 have few rights. Decisions regarding many aspects of their life are made by parents or other adults. The message is clear: You are too young to make these important decisions. On the other hand, the media, which permeate so much of society, provide and promote all types of models that encourage youth to be more adult in terms of behaviors, clothes, physical appearance, and relationships. The pull that the media hold for youth is like that of the peer group. The only difference is that the pull may be even stronger and again may encourage youth to move away from the demands of the family, culture, racial and/or ethnic orientations, and religious teachings.

A second influencing element on youth in today's society is best summed up in the term *violence*. It is difficult to read a paper or view a newscast without being confronted with stories detailing robbery, rape, assault, murder, drive-by shootings, and gang-related retaliations. In 1998 and 1999, schools in Pearl, Mississippi; Paducah, Kentucky; Jonesboro, Alabama; Edinboro, Pennsylvania; Springfield, Oregon; Green River, Wyoming; and Littleton, Colorado made national headlines as armed students killed and/or wounded both peers and school personnel. All of these involved young people and took place in environments generally thought of as safe, that is, elementary and high school playgrounds and campuses. Faced with vivid examples of such violent responses together with the death of friends, peers, and teachers, youth experience a great deal of uncertainty about their future. Such uncertainty creates stress, frustration, and often an attitude of hopelessness and helplessness. Any one of these enhances the at-riskness potential of youth; in combination, they almost assure it (NCES, 1997; Wilson, 1997). Due to the growing significance of violence in schools, we have devoted an entire chapter (chapter 13) to a discussion of the issues surrounding violence in schools together with prevention information from individual, family, school, and community perspectives.

Within these four environments—the family, the school, the peer group, and society—are found most of the causal factors that lead to at-riskness in youth. However, the internal environment (what the individual brings to and takes from these environments) of the individual needs also to be considered in terms of its place in this causal paradigm. What part does the individual play in response to these various environments? Are youth simply the victims without recourse, or do they play an active role in determining their own at-riskness? Answers to these questions may be found in the growing body of research surrounding the concept of resiliency.

Resiliency

The term *resiliency*, when applied to at-risk youth, describes certain skills, abilities, and personal qualities or attributes that enable certain youth, exposed to significant stress and adversity, to cope with and even thrive in spite of the stress and adversity. These youth, unlike many of their peer counterparts, do not succumb to the stresses and adversities present in their environment and, in fact, may develop strength and positive coping strategies from the exposure (Bernard, 1991; Garmezy, 1993; Rak & Patterson, 1996).

The research on resiliency (Canino & Spurlock, 1994; Sayger, 1996; Werner, 1992; Werner & Smith, 1992; Wolin & Wolin, 1993) identifies various sets of characteristics that when present in youth provide a screening device that allows them to adjust to and cope with the negative conditions within their environments. Such listings often include but are not limited to:

- approaching life's problems in an active way;
- constructively perceiving pain, frustration, and negative experiences;
- gaining positive attention from others;
- having a view of life as both positive and meaningful;
- possessing positive self-esteem;
- comprehending, appreciating, and producing humor;
- being willing to risk and accept responsibility;
- being proactive;
- being adaptable; and
- being competent in the school, social, and cognitive dimensions.

There are no data to indicate what percentage of youth fits this profile. Based upon the staggering figures presented earlier, it seems that the percentage is perhaps small. The research on resiliency, however, does provide direction for those working with at-risk youth (Bradley, Parr, & Gould, 1995; Parr, Montgomery, & Debell, 1998; Sayger, 1996). Based upon our view of its growing importance in prevention programming, we have devoted an entire chapter (chapter 3) to a discussion of resiliency and its application to prevention programs for at-risk youth.

PREVENTION AND CRISIS
MANAGEMENT PARADIGM

The description of at-risk youth in terms of causal factors, behaviors, and factors of resiliency provides a logical entry into a discussion of the prevention and crisis management paradigm as this relates to developing programs that will assist in either preventing the development of the problem behaviors, treating the problem behaviors that have developed, or enhancing resiliency factors.

Prevention

Two basic criteria underly the development of effective prevention programs for at-risk youth: the causal factors that lead to at-riskness can be enumerated, and the population of young people who are impacted by these factors can be identified. Causal factors are enumerated for a variety of identified problems in this chapter and the chapters that follow, and there seems to be a good deal of similarity across these factors. The population of young people impacted by these factors is also identified in this chapter: all young people have the potential for at-riskness. With these two basic criteria established, prevention programs can be developed to keep the identified population from achieving its at-risk potential.

Prevention programs can be and have been developed for a wide range of potential at-risk behaviors. The theory behind prevention is simply "stop certain behaviors from developing." Prevention programming for at-risk youth applies this theory but in a somewhat more comprehensive manner. Effective prevention programs directed at at-risk youth are generally viewed as multidisciplinary and are developed based upon the knowledge and expertise of several publics. For example, a prevention program directed at alcohol and drug abuse might involve not only school personnel (teachers, counselors, administrators) but also parents, students, community leaders, religious leaders, police, and representatives from various human service organizations. A multidisciplinary approach assures the widest range of expertise, involvement of those most likely to be affected by the program, and a commitment from the community in making the program work. It enhances the physical and financial resources of the proposed program and alerts young people to the fact that this is not just a school-based program but one that has the backing of both their parents and the community. Because the program has prevention as its purpose, as opposed to crisis management, information can be provided regarding alcohol and drug use, redesigning environments to remove the availability of alcohol and drugs, changing existing policies and procedures within the educational system to enhance the prevention of alcohol and drug use, changing parenting styles and rules and regulations within the home to better accommodate the needs of the young person, designing alternative activities for young people that do not include alcohol and drug use, and providing peer mentoring systems to allow young people to learn from each other. These are just examples. One of the key factors in prevention program development is individualizing the programs to better meet the unique needs of the targeted population, the school, and the community.

According to Coyne (1994), many of the identified problems of at-risk youth are preventable. What is needed are well-designed programs that take into consideration such factors as knowledge and understanding of the concepts that define prevention, local assessments to define target populations, information regarding existing programs both locally and nationally, and the selection of multiple strategies for implementation of the program. This is best done through a team composed of many individuals representing a broad spectrum of the community. This broadened base not only expands the knowledge and skill base of the program but also assures financial and personal commitment from the many publics impacted by the program, including students, parents, school personnel, and members of the community (Keys, Bemak, Carpenter, King-Sears, 1998; Keys, Bemak, & Lockhart, 1998). Once the program is designed, it can be piloted and then restructured as needed. When the team is satisfied that the program is ready, formal implementation can take place. Evaluation is continual and the program is revised as necessary. A more in-depth discussion of prevention is found in chapter 2, and each of the 14 chapters that follow present prevention programming with a problem-specific focus.

Crisis Management

Although crisis management is not the main thrust of this book, it is important to understand the basic differences between prevention and crisis management. Whereas prevention programs have as one of their basic goals reducing the at-risk potential for youth, crisis management programs have as one of their basic goals eliminating at-risk behaviors and providing new behaviors, coping skills, and knowledge that will keep the at-risk behaviors from reoccurring. In the first, we attempt to stop something before it begins (primary prevention), and in the second, we attempt to stop something from continuing (secondary and tertiary prevention). Underlying the development of either secondary or tertiary prevention programs are the facts that many of the behaviors discussed in this chapter are currently present in a large percentage of youth and that steps need to be taken to change or remediate these behaviors. It is too late to prevent these behaviors from developing; they are present. Therefore, programs are designed to eliminate or reduce the behaviors that have placed the individual at risk. In so doing, programs, which may be aimed at either individuals or groups of individuals, identify the problematic behavior(s), identify the individual(s) operating within this behavioral pattern, design programs based upon current knowledge or select existing programs that have proven effective, implement strategies, and then evaluate the results of the implementation. Similarities between programmatic aspects of primary prevention and secondary and tertiary prevention are obvious. Differences also exist. Secondary and tertiary prevention often occur in a structured setting such as a treatment center, mental health clinic, or school counseling office. In these settings, counseling/therapy is provided to address specific problem behaviors and varies according to identified problem behaviors, theoretical orientation of the counselor/therapist, institutional/organization policies, parameters of insurance reimbursement, and the willingness of the individual to take part in the process. Secondary and tertiary prevention are often of a more immediate nature than primary prevention due to the severity of the presenting at-risk behavior. Programs aimed at preventing youth from developing suicidal behaviors do not have the same immediacy as programs developed to deal with youth who have attempted suicide. Primary prevention programs tend to deal with healthy individuals or those with the potential for at-risk behaviors, whereas secondary and tertiary prevention programs tend to deal with individuals who have moved from healthy lifestyles to unhealthy lifestyles. A final difference is that primary prevention programs tend to be group or population based, and secondary and tertiary prevention programs focus more on the individual and his or her place in the larger group. Similarities and differences among these differing levels of prevention will become clearer in the chapters that follow.

SUMMARY

This chapter provides a working definition of at-risk youth, information pertaining to the causal factors and behaviors that are descriptive of this population, a list of the factors of resiliency, and general information related to the similarities and differences between prevention and crisis management. Such information could have helped our hypothetical teacher, John Patron. It could have provided some foundational material to aid him in better understanding the various parameters that surround the students in his classroom. It could have provided him with directives as he began to seek out information regarding what is currently being done to develop approaches to prevention, community resources that could be utilized by the school, and insight into factors of resiliency. If John had had the opportunity to read the following 15 chapters, he could be in a much better place in terms of answering the many questions raised at the meeting. For those who share some of John's concerns, have questions similar to John's, and feel the need to know more about the areas of at-risk youth and prevention, this book can be of great assistance. The true benefit of the knowledge gained will be not only better service for those youth who have a potential for developing at-risk behavior but also better preparation for dealing with those youth whose behaviors currently place them at risk.

REFERENCES

Aksamit, F. L., Jr. (1990). Mildly handicapped and at-risk students: The graying of the line. *Academic Therapy, 25,* 277–289.

Alan Guttmacher Institute. (1994). *Sex and America's teenagers.* New York: Author.

Aruffo, J., Gottlieb, A., Webb, R., & Neville, B. (1994). Adolescent psychiatric inpatients: Alcohol use and HIV risk-taking behavior. *Psychosocial Rehabilitation Journal, 17*(4), 150–156.

Barber, L. W., & McClellan, M. C. (1987). Looking at America's dropouts. *Phi Delta Kappan, 69,* 264–267.

Baumrind, D. (1990). Rearing competent children. In W. Damon (Ed.), *New directions for child development: Child development today and tomorrow.* San Francisco: Jossey-Bass.

Benard, B. (1991). *Fostering resiliency in kids: Protective factors in the family, school, and community.* Portland, OR: Western Center for Drug-Free Schools and Communities.

Bradley, L., Parr, G., & Gould, L. J. (1995). Counseling and psychotherapy: An integrative perspective. In D. Capuzzi & D. Gross (Eds.), *Counseling and psychotherapy: Theories and interventions* (pp. 589–614). Englewood Cliffs, NJ: Merrill.

Brownell, K. D., & Rodin, J. (1994). The dieting maelstrom: Is it possible and advisable to lose weight? *American Psychologist, 49,* 781–791.

Burden, C.A., Miller, K.E., & Boozer, A.E. (1996). Tough enough: Gang membership. In D. Capuzzi & D. Gross (Eds.), *Youth at risk: A prevention resource for counselors, teachers, and parents* (2nd ed., pp. 283–306). Alexandria, VA: American Counseling Association.

Capuzzi, D., & Gross, D. (1996). *Youth at risk: A prevention resource for counselors, teachers, and parents* (2nd ed.). Alexandria, VA: American Counseling Association.

Canino, I. A., & Spurlock, J. (1994). *Culturally diverse children and adolescents: Assessment, diagnosis, and treatment.* New York: Guilford Press.

Cashwell, C. S., Bloss, K. K., & McFarland, J.E. (1995). From victim to client: The cycle of sexual reactivity. *The School Counselor, 42,* 233–238.

Cohen, S. B., & de Bettencourt, L. V. (1991). Dropout: Intervening with the reluctant learner. *Intervention in School and Clinic, 26,* 263–271.

Conrath, J. (1988). A new deal for at-risk students. *NAASP Bulletin, 14,* 36–39.

Coyne, R. K. (1994). Preventive counseling. *Counseling and Human Development, 27*(1), 21–28.

Donmoyer, R., & Kos, R. (1993). *At-risk students: Portraits, policies, programs, and practices.* Albany: State University of New York Press.

Dryfoos, I. C. (1990). *Adolescents at risk: Prevalence and prevention.* New York: Oxford University Press.

Durlak, J. A., & Wells, A. M. (1997). Primary prevention mental health programs for children and adolescents: A meta-analytic review. *American Journal of Community Psychology, 25*(2), 115–152.

Ekstrom, R. R., Goertz, M. E., Pollack, J. M., & Rock, D. A. (1986). Who drops out of school and why: Findings from a national study. *Teachers College Record, 87,* 356–373.

Fine, M. (1986). Why urban adolescents drop into and out of public high school. *Teachers College Record, 87,* 393–409.

Garmezy, N. (1993). Children in poverty: Resilience despite the risk. *Psychiatry, 56,* 127–136.

Gloria, A. M., Trainer, C. M., Beasley, J. F., & Robinson Kurpius, S. E. (1996). Adolescent substance abuse: Past, present, and future. In D. Capuzzi & D. Gross (Eds.), *Youth at risk: A prevention resource for counselors, teachers, and parents* (2nd ed., pp. 307–333). Alexandria, VA: American Counseling Association.

Goldman, R., & Galgino, R. (1990). *Children at risk: An interdisciplinary approach to child abuse and neglect.* Austin, TX: Pro.ed.

Homebase. (1993). *Reaching and teaching children without housing: Improving educational opportunities for homeless children and youth.* San Francisco: Author.

Ingersoll, G., & Orr, D. (1988). Adolescents at risk. *Counseling and Human Development, 20,* 1–8.

Katz, R., Mills, K., Singh, N., & Best, A. (1995). Knowledge and attitudes about AIDS: A comparison of public high school students, incarcerated delinquents, and emotionally disturbed adolescents. *Journal of Youth and Adolescence, 24*(1), 117–130.

Keys, S. G., Bemak, F., Carpenter, S. L., & King-Sears, M. E. (1998). Collaborative consultant: A new role for counselors serving at-risk youths. *Journal of Counseling and Development, 76*(2), 123–133.

Keys, S. G., Bemak, F., & Lockhart, E. J. (1998). Transforming school counseling to serve the mental health needs of at-risk youth. *Journal of Counseling and Development 76*(4), 381–388.

Kronick, R. F. (1997). *At-risk youth: Theory, practice, reform.* New York: Garland.

Kushman, J. W., & Heariold-Kinney, P. (1996). Understanding and preventing school dropout. In D. Capuzzi & D. Gross (Eds.), *Youth at risk: A prevention resource guide for counselors, teachers, and parents* (2nd ed., pp. 353–381). Alexandria, VA: American Counseling Association.

McCarthy, C., Brack, C., Lambert, R., Brack, G., & Orr, D. (1996). Predicting emotional and behavioral risk factors in adolescents. *The School Counselor, 43,* 277–286.

McMillen, M. M., Kaufman, P., Hausken, E. G., & Bradby, D. (1993). *Dropout rates in the United States: 1992.* Washington, DC: National Center for Education Statistics.

McWhirter, B. T., McWhirter, J. J., & Gat, I. (1996). Depression in childhood and adolescence: Working to prevent despair. In D. Capuzzi & D. Gross (Eds.), *Youth at risk: A prevention resource for counselors, teachers, and parents* (2nd ed., pp. 105–128). Alexandria, VA: American Counseling Association.

McWhirter, J. J., McWhirter, B. T., McWhirter, A. M., & McWhirter, E. H. (1998). *At-risk youth: A comprehensive response* (2nd ed.). Pacific Grove, CA: Brooks/Cole.

Meggert, S. S. (1996). Who cares what I think: Problems of low self-esteem. In D. Capuzzi & D. Gross (Eds.), *Youth at risk: A prevention resource for counselors, teachers, and parents* (2nd ed., pp. 81–104). Alexandria, VA: American Counseling Association.

Melchert, T., & Burnett, K. (1990). Attitudes, knowledge, and sexual behaviors of high-risk adolescents: Implications for counseling and sexuality education. *Journal of Counseling and Development, 68*(3), 293–298.

Minga, T. (1988). States and the "at-risk" issues: Said aware but still "failing." *Education Week, 8*(3), 1–16.

National Center for Education Statistics, Fast Response Survey System. (1997). *Principal/school disciplinarian survey on school violence* (FRSS 63) [On-line]. Available: NCESwebmaster@ed.gov

Nock, S. L., & Kingston, P. W. (1991). Time with children: The impact of couples' work/time commitments. *Social Forces, 67*, 59–85.

Parr, G. D., Montgomery, M., & DeBell, C. (1998). Flow theory as a model for enhancing student resilience. *Professional School Counseling, 1*(5), 26-31.

Paulu, N. (1987). *Dealing with dropouts: The urban superintendents' call to action.* Washington, DC: Office of Educational Research and Improvement, U.S. Department of Education.

Pinto, A., Grapentine, W. L., Francis, G., & Picariello, C. M. (1996). Borderline personality disorder in adolescents: Affective and cognitive features. *Journal of the American Academy of Child and Adolescent Psychiatry, 34*, 1338–1343.

Rafferty, Y., & Schinn, M. (1991). The impact of homelessness on children. *American Psychologist, 46*(11), 1170–1179.

Rak, C. F., & Patterson, I.E. (1996). Promoting resilience in at-risk children. *Journal of Counseling and Development, 74*(4), 368–373.

Rencken, R. H. (1996). Body violation: Physical and sexual abuse. In D. Capuzzi & D. Gross (Eds.), *Youth at risk: A prevention resource for counselors, teachers, and parents* (2nd ed., pp. 59–80). Alexandria, VA: American Counseling Association.

Sayger, T. V. (1996). Creating resilient children and empowering families using a multifamily group process. *Journal for Specialists in Group Work, 21*(2), 81–89.

Sherwood-Hawes, A., & Thompson, R. A. (1996). Adolescent pregnancy and childbearing: A focus on prevention. In D. Capuzzi & D. Gross (Eds.), *Youth at risk: A prevention resource for counselors, teachers, and parents* (2nd ed., pp. 183–216). Alexandria, VA: American Counseling Association.

Stormont-Spurgin, M., & De Reus, L. A. (1996). No where to turn: Homeless youth. In D. Capuzzi & D. Gross (Eds.), *Youth at risk: A prevention resource for counselors, teachers, and parents* (2nd ed., pp. 335–352). Alexandria, VA: American Counseling Association.

Wehlage, C. C. (1991). School reform for at-risk students. *Equity and Excellence, 23*(1), 15–24.

Werner, E. E. (1992). The children of Kauai: Resiliency and recovery in adolescence and adulthood. *Journal of Adolescent Health, 13*, 262–268.

Werner, E. E., & Smith, R. S. (1992). *Overcoming the odds: High risk children from birth to adulthood.* Ithaca, NY: Cornell University Press.

Wilson, K. J. (1997). *When violence begins at home.* Alameda, CA: Hunter House.

Wolin, S. J., & Wolin, S. (1993). *The resilient self: How survivors of troubled families overcome adversity.* New York: Villard Books.

Wright, K. S. (1996). The secret and all-consuming obsessions: Anorexia and bulimia. In D. Capuzzi & D. Gross (Eds.), *Youth at risk: A prevention resource for counselors, teachers, and parents* (2nd ed., pp. 153–182). Alexandria, VA: American Counseling Association.

Zanarini, M. C., Williams, A. A., Lewis, R. E., Reich, R. B., Vera, S. C., Marino, M. F., Levin, A., Yong, L., & Frankenburg, F. R. (1997). Reported pathological childhood experiences associated with the development of borderline personality disorder. *American Journal of Psychiatry, 154*, 1101–1106.

2 | Approaches to Prevention

David Capuzzi and Douglas R. Gross

The number of children and adolescents who engage in behaviors (e.g., unprotected sex, substance use and abuse, abnormal eating patterns, suicide attempts) and are exposed to environmental factors (e.g., abuse, violence, homelessness) that place them at risk for adverse mental and physical health consequences is increasing at alarming rates (Kazdin, 1993; Popenhagen & Qualley, 1998). In addition, many children and adolescents are experiencing serious psychological and emotional impairment. Because the impairments that youth experience can persist and increase in severity across the life span, the importance of early prevention and intervention efforts has increased in significance.

Robert Conyne (1994) emphasized the significance and importance of early prevention efforts by offering examples of some of the problems that characterize contemporary residents of the United States:

- There are 20 million illiterate adults. This amounts to 13% of the U.S. population.
- Nineteen percent of the population (or 43 million adults) have been identified as experiencing some type of mental disturbance.
- The number of youth dropping out of school each year has reached 1 million or 25% of those enrolled in K–12 settings.
- AIDS has become one of the leading causes of death among the 15- to 24-year-old age group.
- Nearly 5,000 infants are born each year with fetal alcohol syndrome.
- Adolescent suicide ranks second or third in most reports of the leading causes of death in the 11- to 24-year-old age group.
- First marriages end in divorce 50% of the time, and 50 to 75% of child mental health referrals are for children impacted by divorce.
- Almost 18.5 million Americans abuse alcohol, and over 100,000 alcohol-related deaths occur annually.
- Increasing numbers of women—3 to 4 million annually—are physically assaulted by intimate male partners.

More recently, Joy Dryfoos (1997) summarized data supplied by the U.S. Bureau of the Census, the Centers for Disease Control, the U.S. Department of Justice, and the National Center for Education Statistics with respect to the prevalence of at-risk behaviors of the 14- to 17-year-old population. The data indicated that 25% of all the young people in this age range are behind in grade and that 5% have already dropped out. Between 18 and 48% are involved in some form of substance abuse, and 53% are sexually active. More than 9% have been adjudicated as delinquents, 22% carry some form of weapon, and 21% have frequently been truant. About one fourth of this population report that they have been preoccupied with suicidal thoughts, and 9% report that they have made suicidal attempts.

The cost associated with these examples in terms of economics is staggering: approximately $273 billion was spent in 1990 in treatment and social services associated with alcohol, drug abuse, and mental illness (Horner & McElhaney, 1993). These costs do not include those associated with teenage pregnancy, AIDS, eating disorders, suicide, homelessness, and school dropout. When these additional areas are taken into consideration, the estimated figure increases to incomprehensible levels. As significant as these dollar amounts are, however, they do not include the immeasurable costs associated with human loss and suffering and the concomitant issues related to grief and loss.

In the wake of the need for counseling and therapy created by conditions in the North American culture, the availability of counselors, social workers, psychiatric nurses, psychologists, and psychiatrists pales by contrast (Conyne, 1994). Mandates connected with managed care and the understaffing of social service agencies further compounds the difficulties experienced by children, adolescents, and adults in need of assistance from the professionally prepared, licensed helper.

Prevention is based upon a different approach to help giving than that associated with prevalent diagnostic/prescriptive approaches. Prevention is not focused on dysfunction and associated remediation; it is focused on a proactive approach designed to empower the individual, change systemic variables, and forestall the development of dysfunction. Prevention is also based on awareness of the risk factors that researchers have identified as the most common antecedents of at-risk behaviors (Dryfoos, 1997):

1. Parents' ability to provide nurturing and support are closely connected to a child's ability to mature and develop. Parents who are unable to parent in ways that convey a sense of nurturing and support provide barriers to optimal development.
2. The schooling experience is also a significant precursor to maturation and development. Poor grades, deficits in basic skills, low aca-

demic expectations, and repeated school discipline problems are predictors of involvement in at-risk behavior.

3. Peer influences are strong determinants of youth behavior during the middle school years and sometimes earlier. Youth who engage in high-risk behaviors lack ability to resist joining their friends in experimenting with drugs, sex, and other delinquent behavior.

4. Young people who are depressed or conduct disordered (engaging in multiple problem behaviors such as truancy, stealing, cheating, running away, arson, cruelty to animals, unusually early sexual intercourse, theft, and excessive fighting prior to age 15) are extremely vulnerable to making choices that are far from responsible and productive.

5. Life in a low-income family and an impoverished neighborhood also increases the probability of at-risk behavior because economically disadvantaged youth often lack access to quality education and safe environments.

6. Race and ethnicity are also factors effecting youth's vulnerability, not because of race and ethnicity alone but because African American, Hispanic, and Native American youth may be at a disadvantage economically, and live in poorer, less safe neighborhoods.

QUALITIES OF PREVENTION

As noted by Conyne (1994), Dryfoos (1997), Gilliland and James (1993), and Janosik (1984), prevention efforts focus on averting human dysfunction and promoting healthy functioning. The emphasis in prevention is on enhancing optimal functioning or well-being in psychological and social domains and on the development of competencies. This emphasis is in contrast to an emphasis on the identification and diagnosis of various disorders or maladaptive behavioral patterns in individuals and the provision of treatment to lessen impairment (Kazdin, 1993). Prevention efforts are characterized by a number of defining qualities:

1. *Prevention efforts are proactive.* Prevention initiatives address individual and systemic strengths and further develop those strengths so that dysfunction either does not develop or does not manifest itself to the point that impairment occurs. This contrasts with reactive approaches that are designed to intervene after problems have developed.

2. *Prevention efforts focus on functional people and those who are at risk.* As noted by Conyne (1994), prevention services (e.g., classroom guidance, individual or small group counseling) focus on those who are healthy and coping well so that strengths may be identified and

enhanced and additional skills can be learned. Prevention efforts are also directed to those known to be at risk, such as children of divorce, children of alcoholics, or the homeless. The purpose is to provide proactive intervention so that future difficulties are avoided.

3. *Prevention efforts are cumulative and transferable.* When professionals help others through prevention, every effort is made to point out relationships and to assist clients to master a hierarchy of skills. For example, elementary aged children who have participated in groups designed to enhance self-esteem may, at a later date, feel good enough about themselves to participate in assertiveness training. Ability to use assertiveness skills may be useful in the context of refusing drugs; these same skills may prevent a youth from being victimized in some other situation.

4. *Prevention efforts are used to reduce incidence* (Conyne, 1994). Prevention activities are used before the fact so that problems do not develop. They might also be used to reduce the incidence of a new dysfunction.

5. *Prevention efforts promote peer helping.* When elementary, middle school, and high school youth learn to enhance communication, assertiveness, problem solving, and other related abilities, they are better able to help peers, encourage friends to seek professional assistance, and participate in supervised peer-helper programs. In many instances, the power of a member of the peer group outdistances that of a concerned adult in terms of providing encouragement, support, and straightforward feedback (Dryfoos, 1997).

6. *Prevention efforts can be group based, population based, or individual based.* Many are focused upon at-risk populations (e.g., information and discussion about the HIV virus or hepatitis B may be shared with sexually active adolescents, or victims of abuse may be assisted so that they do not develop lifelong dysfunctional patterns). Prevention may also be focused entirely on an individual so that suicidal preoccupation can be eliminated or depression can be overcome. When larger populations are reached through prevention programming, it is possible to impact the life space of large numbers of people (Conyne, 1994).

7. *Prevention efforts can be used early in the life span.* We know that children who are homeless or who have been physically or sexually abused may develop traits and self-concepts that put them at risk during adolescence and adulthood. Early prevention efforts can effect changes in self-esteem, behavior, feelings, and thinking so that these children are not at risk of substance abuse, prostitution, depression, and suicide at a later time (Dryfoos, 1997).

8. *Prevention efforts target more than a single system.* Because each person must simultaneously interact in a variety of environments, practitioners do not emphasize one system to the exclusion of others. Healthy individuals must learn to cope with the demands of several systems on a daily basis (Dryfoos, 1997).

9. *Prevention efforts are sensitive to the needs of diverse populations.* No constellation of services or approach to prevention can make equal impact on all groups. Diverse populations present unique challenges; what one population finds acceptable may be totally incompatible with the needs of another. Practitioners must be sensitive to the traditions, needs, and differences presented by subcultures in North America (Conyne, 1994; Dryfoos, 1997).

10. *Prevention efforts are collaborative.* As noted by Conyne (1994), prevention efforts can be complex and must be conducted in concert with professionals from a number of disciplines. For example, a counselor working with a depressed adolescent may need the assistance of a psychiatrist or nurse practitioner if medication is needed along with counseling to control a body-chemistry-related bipolar pattern of depression. Often the expertise needed to assist an individual, a family, or a larger population may require input and teaming among professionals from several disciplines.

11. *Prevention efforts are applicable in more than one context.* Faculty and staff in a school setting, for example, may seek the assistance of someone who can provide staff development, train a crisis team, and provide input relative to a written crisis management plan. Such efforts may be focused, initially, on substance abuse prevention or suicide prevention. After the adults connected with a particular school or school district have been prepared with respect to one particular at-risk population, they can usually apply the same principles and process to providing prevention services to another at-risk group.

12. *Prevention efforts are empowering* (Conyne, 1994). Empowerment should be the primary goal of all prevention efforts. This empowerment should apply not only to the recipients of prevention efforts but also to the providers of prevention services. When those receiving assistance build on strengths and learn new coping skills, they feel better about themselves and their ability to make responsible, healthy decisions. As professionals increase their ability to enrich the lives of others, they, too, feel productive, competent, and capable of impacting change.

13. *Prevention efforts involve parents.* Inviting parents to be responsible participants in their children's schools, such as in roles as paid or volunteer classroom aides or voting members of school reorgani-

zation initiatives, results in more positive outcomes for children and adolescents. Establishment of parent centers in schools for parents and youth for whom English is a second language or for whom assistance with health and social services, transportation, child care, or meals is needed has been found to be effective (Dryfoos, 1997).

14. *Prevention efforts make connections to the world of work.* Many at-risk youth have little exposure to the world of work and may not have adult role models who are consistently employed. When these youth are exposed to curricula that provide career information, skills training, and opportunities for volunteer or paid work experience, their involvement in at-risk behaviors decreases (Dryfoos, 1997).

15. *Prevention efforts include social and life skills training.* Improving social, decision-making, and assertiveness skills lead to more positive outcomes. Research also demonstrates that consistency of participant involvement and opportunities for booster sessions are required to maintain long-term effects (Dryfoos, 1997).

16. *Prevention efforts include in-service training for both faculty and staff.* Prevention efforts rarely succeed unless time and money are committed to the in-service training necessary to provide the adults in the school with the insight, skills, and motivation needed to implement initiatives aimed at aspects of systemic reform successfully.

17. *Prevention efforts include the presence of dedicated adults.* Successful prevention programs are usually the result of the efforts of adult role models who have a great deal of empathy and provide high levels of support for young people who have risk factors in their lives that predispose them to engaging in at-risk behaviors. It is very difficult to implement new programs and policies in a school in which the faculty and staff are not receptive to new ways of enhancing the school climate or to the needs of youth who may be quite different than themselves.

APPROACHES TO PREVENTION

A number of experts in contemporary prevention strategies (Hadge, 1992; Janosik, 1984; McWhirter, McWhirter, McWhirter, & McWhirter, 1998; Roberts, 1991) identify prevention as either primary, secondary, or tertiary. As practitioners consider prevention strategies for possible implementation with an individual, a family, a school, or a community, it is important to be able to assess needs and identify strategies relative to whether these strategies can be categorized as primary, secondary, or tertiary.

Primary Prevention

Primary prevention involves proactive planning of strategies and activities to keep specific problems or crises from developing in the first place (Gilliland & James, 1993). In primary prevention, the purpose is to reduce the incidence of future problems by reinforcing internal coping ability, modifying external variables, or both. Primary prevention provides assistance prior to the development of problems through counseling, teaching, or other services that emphasize anticipatory planning. Through anticipatory planning, individuals of all ages are given the opportunity to select and practice behaviors that are helpful in both present and future circumstances.

Examples of primary prevention include parent education programs to prevent child neglect and abuse, and educational programs on university campuses to prevent sexual harassment, date rape, or violation of affirmative action guidelines. School programs for teenage men and women regarding the consequences of teenage pregnancies, the impact of school dropout, or the importance of effective communication skills are additional examples of primary prevention. Entire communities might also benefit from primary prevention efforts. For example, a series of mental health education seminars might be offered, free of charge, to residents of a community and might be collaboratively planned by representatives from the local schools, mental health services, and business sectors. Television and radio journalists might provide coverage of the services offered by women and children's shelters or local crisis hot lines. Whatever the emphasis, the focus is always upon preventing future and, more often than not, long-term pain or impairment.

Chapter 3 of this edition of our text presents valuable, additional information on primary prevention from a resiliency point of view. This provides an additional perspective that may prove helpful to those whose practice focus is working with children and adolescents.

Secondary Prevention

Secondary prevention consists of early intervention with people in crisis for the purpose of restoring equilibrium as soon as possible and reducing the impact of the distress. During periods of crisis, people are aware that the situation is out of control; they may feel helpless. Unless secondary prevention is made available, a crisis may escalate to the point at which it may be difficult to contain or consequences may be irreversible. For example, a suicidal adolescent who does not obtain assistance may attempt suicide, survive, and be left with lifelong physical impairment and emotional turmoil that overlay the traits and characteristics that precipitated the suicidal crisis in the first place. When individuals, families, schools, or communities recognize the parameters connected with a crisis situation, they may be quite motivated and extremely receptive to secondary prevention efforts.

Examples of secondary prevention include support groups for students who are experiencing the grief and loss associated with the unexpected death of a peer, school and community collaborative efforts to provide child care and alternative education opportunities for teenage parents, residential or outpatient treatment for teenagers who abuse alcohol, or counseling services established to stop battering or other violent behavior. During the secondary prevention process, emphasis should be placed on individual, family, school, and community resources and abilities. Preoccupation with defeat and negative consequences seldom results in the management of a particular crisis situation and the reestablishment of equilibrium.

It is important to note that more and more school districts are writing *tragedy response plans* for the purpose of planning and coordinating efforts of school personnel who are suddenly presented with a sudden crisis situation. The plans are developed so as to prevent the systemic chaos and resultant negative impact on individuals and groups on a school campus when an unanticipated crisis occurs. These tragedy response plans usually delineate not only the roles of members of the crisis team and the roles of all other school personnel but also the roles of individuals or groups in the community that the school may need to call upon in the midst of a crisis. Among the advantages of developing plans in advance is the opportunity to have such plans evaluated in advance by experts in crisis management and by the school or district's legal team so that modifications and additions can be made.

Tragedy response plans usually outline crisis responses to natural disasters (e.g., earthquakes, tornados, release of airborne toxins), fire, death, accidents, child abduction, violence, and other events that need to be addressed immediately and may not have been anticipated. These plans are usually comprehensive and may include guidelines for possible evacuation and transportation of students as well as for contacting parents, responding to the inquiries of journalists, and working with police and disaster relief workers from the community. Many school districts are beginning to publish their plans on the World Wide Web, and we encourage school/community groups planning to commence work on tragedy response plans to read what other school/ community groups have developed and to contact representatives from schools that have experience in this realm. Making such contacts can provide opportunities for collaborative sharing and evaluation and can eliminate the necessity of starting from scratch.

Tertiary Prevention

Tertiary crisis prevention attempts to reduce the amount of residual impairment that follows the resolution of some crisis. Adolescents who complete residential or outpatient programs for substance abuse may benefit through participation in weekly support groups, facilitated by a professional, for the purpose of providing the reinforcement and support needed to prevent relapse. These same adolescents may need to participate, concurrently, in individual counseling or therapy to address the unmet needs that led to the abuse of a substance in the first place because emotional development and coping skills are usually arrested about the time substance use begins. Victims of sexual abuse may participate in either group or individual (or both) counseling or therapy long after the abuse has ceased for the purpose of repairing damaged self-esteem and rebuilding the capacity to trust and share intimacy with significant others.

As emphasized by Janosik (1984), crisis in contemporary society is so prevalent that it is not possible for all those experiencing crisis to access the help of professionals. It is possible, however, to identify factors that place individuals, families, schools, and communities at risk; thus it is of paramount importance to reduce emotional pain, residual impairment, and cost to the society as a whole through judicious use of prevention, whether primary, secondary, or tertiary in nature.

TYPES OF PRIMARY PREVENTION

The youth of today are faced with coping amidst a society that is more populated, more connected by advanced communication technology, and more complex with respect to a variety of psychosocial stressors. This edition of *Youth At Risk* places yet more emphasis on prevention with respect to causative factors (such as low self-esteem, stress, depression) and a number of at-risk behaviors (such as drug abuse, unprotected sex, eating disorders, suicidal preoccupation, gang membership). The chapters that follow highlight secondary and tertiary prevention efforts. This chapter provides information on primary prevention efforts based on the types described by McWhirter et al. (1998): developing life skills, enhancing interpersonal communication, learning strategies for cognitive change, achieving self-management and self-control, and coping with stress.

Developing Life Skills

Life skills can be defined as the ability to make use of personal resources for the purpose of expressing needs and positively influencing the environment. Such skills influence the formation of relationships and friendships, nonviolent methods of conflict resolution, and communicating with adults (McWhirter et al., 1998). Developing life skills can be accomplished through education and training in life skills, school peer mediation, peer tutoring, and peer facilitation.

Education and training in life skills involve developing and incorporating instructional modules into the curriculum at elementary, middle, and high school levels. Also involved is the collaborative input of a variety of professionals (counselors, nurses, physicians, social workers, psychologists, physical educators, classroom teachers) for the purpose of teaching skills needed by most individuals on a day-to-day basis. The format for teaching any targeted skill should, ideally, contain the following components: teach, model, role-play, provide feedback, and assign homework. Almost any skill can be taught within this paradigm, and the fact that implementation is most often effected in the classroom means that entire populations can be accessed so that more and more young people can master skills that can help them avoid future problems.

School peer mediation, peer tutoring, and peer facilitation all involve training and supervising students to perform interpersonal helping tasks. School peer mediation requires trained peer mediators who work in partnerships with other students for the purpose of facilitating problem solving between disputing students. As noted by McWhirter et al. (1998), peer mediation ensures that both peer mediators and peer disputants increase experience with critical thinking, problem solving, and self-discipline.

Peer tutors are students who teach other students in both formal and informal learning situations. Peer tutoring can provide a cost-effective means of meeting individual needs, developing better ownership of the value of the educational experience, and enhancing self-esteem and motivation.

Peer facilitation, sometimes called peer helping, is a process in which students are trained to listen, paraphrase, support, and provide feedback to other students in the school. Peer facilitation is an effective way to empower children and adolescents and to provide adjunct support to the professional counselor or other human service specialist.

Enhancing Interpersonal Communication

Interpersonal communication skills are primary factors in the development of mutually beneficial relationships. Most programs designed to enhance interpersonal communication skills offer training in verbal and nonverbal communication, creation of constructive friendships, avoidance of misunderstanding, and the development of long-term relationships with significant others (McWhirter et al., 1998). Lack of ability to communicate well with others can lead to lowered self-esteem, isolation, and the development of future at-risk behaviors. Assertiveness training as well as resistance and refusal training are often important components of training in interpersonal communication.

Assertiveness training is most often accomplished in the context of small groups. It can include providing assistance with expressing positive and negative feelings; the ability to initiate, maintain, and end conversations; and practice on setting limits. Nonverbal communication is an important component of assertiveness training because the manner in which something is communicated—body language, eye contact, personal distancing, voice tone—can influence the message as much as the context of the message itself.

Resistance and refusal training is provided to help children and adolescents resist peer pressure or other negative social influence. Students are taught to label and recognize various forms of pressure and develop behavior to resist such pressure and influence. Both assertiveness training and resistance and refusal training provide numerous modeling, role-play, feedback, and reinforcement opportunities during the process of acquiring such interpersonal communication skills so that new behaviors are more likely to be used in day-to-day interactions with peers.

Learning Strategies for Cognitive Change

Because cognition mediates both behavior and affect, cognitive restructuring can be an effective primary prevention strategy. Techniques used in problem solving and decision making, self-management and self-control, and cognitive restructuring are among the primary prevention strategies that can be taught to children and adolescents.

All young people have the potential to problem solve and make decisions. At times, however, the emotional components connected with a particular problem, the egocentric focus commonly associated with the early years of human growth and development, and the lack of experience with systematically approaching problem-solving situations provide barriers to effective problem solving and decision making (McWhirter et al., 1998). Instruction can be provided, however, in each step of the problem-solving and decision-making process. Teaching children and adolescents how to resolve problematic situations can help them enhance self-esteem, overcome feelings of being helpless, and promote a generalized sense of empowerment. McWhirter et al. (1998) suggested that the following steps/components be taught:

1. *Define the problem.* The problem is defined as clearly as possible and is stated as a goal to be achieved. This goal is assessed: Does it meet the underlying needs? If it is attained, does it help the individual achieve satisfaction?
2. *Examine variables.* The specifics of the total situation are examined. Background issues and environmental factors are considered, so it may be necessary to gather and appraise additional information. It is particularly important to identify the feelings and thoughts of the youngster at this step. Often earlier maladaptive responses must be

modified. In both this step and step 1, questions and suggestions from other students in the classroom or the group are useful.

3. *Consider alternatives.* Various means of solving the problem are considered. The strengths and weaknesses of each possibility are evaluated. Again, the teacher or counselor may call for brainstorming to generate ideas from other students about alternatives and strategies.

4. *Isolate a plan.* The alternatives are gradually narrowed down until what seems like the best response or solution remains. A plan for carrying out this alternative is prepared, and the potential consequences are considered in more detail.

5. *Do action steps.* After a plan is decided upon, action must be taken to implement it. Thus youngsters are systematically encouraged to follow through on the necessary steps to carry out their plan. They perform the behaviors that make up the solution plan.

6. *Evaluate effects.* Finally, youngsters need to evaluate the effectiveness of the solution. Teaching them to look for effects in their thoughts and feelings is important. They analyze and evaluate the outcome, review the decision, and, if necessary, develop another plan to achieve their goal. (pp. 276–277)

McWhirter et al. called their model the DECIDE model and reported that it is an effective strategy for teaching problem solving and decision making.

Achieving Self-Management and Self-Control

Self-management means that self-control has been achieved. It implies that individuals can develop the ability to control, to a great extent, thoughts, feelings, and behaviors. Teaching children and adolescents the techniques of self-management and self-control can result in outcomes similar to those connected with teaching problem solving and decision making, enhanced self-esteem, overcoming feelings of being helpless, and a sense of empowerment. Teaching self-management and self-control involves teaching children and adolescents self-assessment, self-monitoring, and self-reinforcement (McWhirter et al., 1998). Self-assessment means that the individual learns to evaluate his or her own behaviors against a standard that has personal meaning in order to determine whether the behavior is adequate. Self-monitoring requires that the individual observes his or her own behavior and records it. Record keeping may involve notation of contingencies in the environment prior to and immediately following the behavior. Self-reinforcement involves supplying one's own consequences for a given behavior (e.g., self-praise, buying something of personal significance). Generally, children and adolescents who master the techniques of self-management and self-control feel energized, motivated, and positive about themselves.

Coping With Stress

The term *coping with stress* is particularly significant in contemporary society. There are so many potential stressors encountered by each of us on a day-to-day basis that it behooves the adults in our society to teach children and adolescents as much as possible about stress and stress management. It is an important primary prevention strategy. Chapter 7, Stress and Trauma: Coping in Today's Society, addresses this topic fully through discussion and analysis of perspectives on the stress concept, including stimulus-oriented views, response-oriented views, stress as a transaction between person and environment, trauma and posttraumatic stress, life event stressors, daily stress, traumatic stress, home and family stress, school stress, and developmental stress.

PLANNING PREVENTION PROGRAMS

Laudatory prevention efforts of schools and communities have failed because planning efforts have not included important steps or because a group of concerned adults has moved to the implementation stage and short-changed the entire planning process. The following steps, based on our experience in a variety of school and community settings, will help assure success.

1. *Read the research on prevention programs.* There are excellent reviews and monographs on approaches to prevention (Dryfoos, 1997; Gager & Elias, 1997; Goldston, Yager, Heinicke, & Pynoos, 1990; Romano, 1997; Weisberg, Caplan, & Harwood, 1991). Often practitioners who are anxious to implement programs and services do not take the time to learn about and build upon the successes and failures of others. Based on numerous outcome studies, a number of generalizations can be made:

    • Prevention programs directed to the early years (e.g., pre- and postnatal parents and children during preschool years) can reduce factors that increase risk for maladaptive behaviors. Most of these efforts are focused on primary prevention and reduce the incidence of dysfunction in childhood and adolescence (Lally, Mangione, & Honig, 1988).
    • Prevention programs that involve parents, connect to the real world of work, incorporate social and life skills training, incor-

porate staff development, and involve dedicated, role model adults seem to have the most lasting and positive impact (Dryfoos, 1997).

- School-based programs targeting adolescents have improved prosocial competence and decreased at-risk behaviors (such as the behaviors discussed in Part Three) (Schinke, Botvin, & Orlandi, 1991; Schneider, Attili, Nadel, & Weisberg, 1989).
- Broad-based programs aimed at several causative factors or at-risk behaviors seem to be the most successful because youth at risk usually present with a number of conditions (Caplan & Weissberg, 1989).
- Occasionally programs have not been effective or have made problems escalate (Bangert-Drowns, 1988). Finding out why could be extremely important to practitioners prior to implementing any prevention effort.

2. *Assess needs.* Sometimes the professional helper fails to target the right population, the best combination of causative factors, or the at-risk behaviors of most concern to children, adolescents, and their families. It is important to touch base with the population being served prior to doing much planning. Children and adolescents, families, school faculty and staff, and components of the community (e.g., hospitals, businesses, churches, social service agencies) should be asked about their views of factors creating risk, problematic behaviors, and skill deficits. Prevention programming should always be designed to address needs and concerns identified by recipients of future services.

3. *Meet with administrators, elected officials, and business owners.* Prevention efforts take time, commitment, and money to implement. Numerous prevention programs have met with failure because planners failed to obtain the input and support of those in positions to reinforce efforts and keep programs and services funded and in place on a long-term basis. This is a critical step in planning for program support.

4. *Establish a broad-based planning group.* Educators, parents, youth, administrators, mental health professionals, physicians, nurses, and police should all be included in planning efforts for prevention programming. The more interdisciplinary and representative the group, the richer the input. The best prevention efforts have been based on the collaborative teaming of members of the community to be served.

5. *Target the population, the causative factors, or the at-risk behaviors.* Often planning groups are too ambitious with respect to goals and expectations. There is always more to be accomplished than can be

realized with respect to a given prevention program. It is important to use the results of a needs assessment to target initial efforts so that initiatives are well planned and supported by adequate resources. Once a focus has been established, findings of research conducted relative to similar populations, risk factors, or at-risk groups should be utilized so that problems can be circumvented and past successful practices can be employed.

6. *Identify existing prevention programs and resources.* Sometimes planning groups recreate programs, services, or resources that already exist and could be built upon or used as adjuncts to newly created programs. It is important to identify existing prevention programs and assess them in terms of whether they offer primary, secondary, or tertiary prevention. Planning groups can then determine how to focus new initiatives (i.e., primary, secondary, or tertiary) and do a better job of effectively utilizing newly committed funding and resources.

7. *Carefully describe policies and procedures.* Before implementing a new program, it is extremely important to draft a description of all policies and procedures to be followed. This insures that everyone involved in the program can be clear about roles and responsibilities. A written description also provides opportunity for input, revision, and refinement. Program descriptions can (and should) be checked in advance of implementation for legal and ethical implications.

8. *Plan variations for diversity.* For many young people, minority status is associated with low socioeconomic status, poor living conditions, fragmented families, and a variety of critical cultural, ethnic, and racial differences. All human service specialists must be flexible about making adaptations in prevention programming in a way that shows sensitivity and respect for diversity. Variations for diversity are addressed throughout this edition of *Youth At Risk.*

9. *Plan staff development.* Whether prevention programming is centered in school or community settings, all staff need to be educated, supervised, and prepared in advance of program implementation. Adults working on behalf of children and adolescents need to be carefully prepared and provided with opportunities to have their questions answered and their concerns addressed.

10. *Make sure adjunct services and referral options have been identified.* Those working on behalf of children and adolescents often need the assistance of other medical and social service professionals. Identifying adjunct services and referral options and acting as a liaison with employees in those settings, in advance, should never be overlooked.

11. *Plan evaluation procedures prior to program implementation.* Practitioners often neglect the evaluative component of prevention programming efforts. Evaluation procedures should be preplanned, and data collection should be an integral part of efforts on behalf of youth. Data can be used to modify and improve the services offered and can provide justification for continued funding and commitment of other needed resources.

SUMMARY

Our overview of prevention has provided introductory material highlighting the problems that underscore the need for escalation of prevention efforts; defined the qualities of prevention programming; described the differences among primary, secondary, and tertiary prevention, and noted the need for additional primary prevention programs; and suggested guidelines and steps for prevention programming. We hope that this information provides an enriched perspective with which to approach the material in the chapters that follow. The context of this chapter is reflective of our belief that more emphasis needs to be placed on proactive prevention efforts so that, as time passes, individuals, families, schools, and communities can lessen the amount of time and energy directed toward remediation and containment of impairment and dysfunction.

REFERENCES

Bangert-Drowns, R. L. (1988). The effects of school-based substance abuse education: A meta-analysis. *Journal of Drug Education, 18,* 243–264.

Caplan, M. Z., & Weisberg, R. P. (1989). Promoting social competence in early adolescence: Developmental considerations. In B. H. Schneider, G. Attili, J. Nadel, & R. P. Weisberg (Eds.). *Social competence in developmental perspective* (pp. 371–385). Norwell, MA: Kluwer Academic.

Conyne, R. K. (1994). Preventative counseling. *Counseling and Human Development, 27*(1), 1–10.

Dryfoos, J. D. (1997). Adolescents at risk: Shaping programs to fit the need. *Journal of Negro Education, 65*(1), 5–18.

Gager, P. J., & Elias, M. J. (1997). Implementing prevention programs in high-risk environments: Application of the resiliency paradigm. *American Journal of Orthopsychiatry, 67*(3), 363–373.

Gilliland, B. E., & James, R. K. (1993). *Crisis intervention strategies.* Pacific Grove, CA: Brooks/Cole.

Goldston, S. E., Yager, J., Heinicke, C. M., & Pynoos, R. S. (Eds.). (1990). *Preventing mental health disturbances in childhood.* Washington, DC: American Psychiatric Association.

Hadge, C. (1992). *School-based prevention and intervention program: Clearinghouse fact sheet* (Report No. CG 025 63 1). Piscataway, NJ: Center of Alcohol Studies, Rutgers University. (ERIC Document Reproduction Service No. ED 372 329)

Horner, J., & McElhaney, S. (1993). Building fences. *American Counselor, 2,* 17–21, 30.

Janosik, E. H. (1984). *Crisis counseling: A contemporary approach.* Monterey, CA: Wadsworth Health Sciences.

Kazdin, A. E. (1993). Adolescent mental health: Prevention and treatment programs. *American Psychologist, 48,* 127–141.

Lally, R., Mangione, P. L., & Honig, A. S. (1988). The Syracuse University Family Development Research Program: Long-range impact on an early intervention with low-income children and their families. In D. Powell (Ed.), *Parent education as early childhood intervention: Emerging directions in theory, research, and practice* (pp. 79–104). Norwood, NJ: Ablex.

McWhirter, J. J., McWhirter, B. T., McWhirter, A. M., & McWhirter, E. H. (1998). *At-risk youth: A comprehensive response* (2nd ed.). Pacific Grove, CA: Brooks/Cole.

Popenhagen, M. P., & Qualley, R. M. (1998). Adolescent suicide: Detection, intervention, and prevention. *Professional School Counseling, 1*(4), 30–36.

Roberts, A. R. (Ed.). (1991). *Contemporary perspectives on crisis intervention and prevention.* Englewood Cliffs, NJ: Rutgers University Center of Alcohol Studies.

Romano, J. L. (1997). School personnel training for the prevention of tobacco, alcohol, and other drug use: Issues and outcomes. *Journal of Drug Education, 27*(3), 245–258.

Schinke, S. P., Botvin, G. J., & Orlandi, M. A. (1991). *Substance abuse in children and adolescents: Evaluation and intervention.* Newbury Park, CA: Sage.

Schneider, B. H., Attili, G., Nadel, J., & Weisberg, R. P. (Eds.). (1989). *Social competence in developmental perspective.* Norwell, MA: Kluwer Academic.

Weissberg, R. P., Caplan, M., & Harwood, L. (1991). Promoting competent young people in competence-enhancing environments: A systems-based perspective on primary prevention. *Journal of Consulting and Clinical Psychology, 55,* 542–549.

3 | Resiliency: Pathway to Protective Factors and Possibilities for Self-Righting Narratives

*Rolla E. Lewis**

The resiliency paradigm offers education, prevention, and a counseling pathway that emphasizes optimism and mental health and can expand our perception of how counselors view and work with youth. The resiliency paradigm also provides an alternative view that sees youth at promise rather than at risk and that shows a different and viable professional perspective for prevention work with youth. The resiliency paradigm is not a singular point of view, however. Thus this chapter looks at resilience research and practice not to synthesize but rather to call attention to the evolving resiliency paradigm's capacity to expand opportunities for the counseling and teaching professions to provide hopeful and rewarding service to youth, and to highlight how the resiliency paradigm can inform and guide counselors, teachers, and parents.

The resiliency paradigm (for the purposes of this chapter) is an empowerment paradigm that has evolved from multidisciplinary research and practices emerging from the prevention, counseling, education, social work, and youth development fields (Benard, 1991, 1996, 1997). The paradigm moves primary prevention perspective and practices away from short-term, individual interventions toward long-term, comprehensive interventions designed to foster positive youth development in and beyond the school into the community (Benard, 1996, 1997; Benard & Marshall, 1997; Henderson & Milstein, 1996; Linquanti, 1992). In many

*The author wishes to thank Kathy Marshall for her review of an early draft and clarification regarding tapping resilience: a framework for practice. The author would also like to thank Jeanne Slingluff for sharing her expertise and information about her work in the schools.

ways, the resiliency paradigm offers school counselors a pathway back to and forward from the counseling profession's roots in human development and education, back to and forward from the assumption that growth and development are human imperatives. In following this pathway, the chapter is guided by key research, effective practices, and professional possibilities.

1. *Key research.* Key resiliency research and prevention efforts acknowledge the inborn, self-righting capacity of people (Benard, 1991, 1993, 1996, 1997; Werner, 1989, 1996, 1998; Werner & Smith, 1982, 1992). A notable body of resiliency research and practice has at its heart the radical notion that "resilience is innate in all of us— our innate wisdom, mental health, common sense, etc." (Personal communication, Bonnie Benard, October 23, 1998). Such a view shifts professional perspective to seeing that youth have what they need to navigate through life. Counselors, teachers, and parents are in a position to help youth realize this, but counselors and teachers must perceive their own self-righting capacities if they are going to help youth understand their own health. In other words, in order to promote the health of youth at risk, helpers are advised to begin recognizing their own resiliency and health.

   In an effort to expand the possibilities for counseling theory and practice guiding work with youth, this chapter shares practices that begin with the assumptions that resiliency is a self-righting quality fostered transactionally in the presence of certain environmental variables, and that risk should be considered in a broader context of poverty, racism, and injustice. Metaphorically, youth stand as diverse seeds with great potential, like acorns with the capacity to become oak trees but dependent upon adequate soil, water, and sun from the environment. The resiliency paradigm can guide school counselors, teachers, and parents to appreciate the true meaning of education (*e-ducare* means to lead out rather than put in), and school counselors and teachers are in a position to lead students to realize their own self-righting capacities.

2. *Effective practices.* Narratives and narrative counseling practices can be used to foster resiliency. The narrative perspective has the power to transform counselors and those they work with because narrative counselors assume counseling is a coexploration in search of hidden talents, understandings, and abilities (Monk, Winslade, Crocket, & Epston, 1997). Narrative fosters resiliency by enabling people, both helpers and helpees, to speak about the world from different, more empowering perspectives (Bruner, 1986, 1990; Monk et al., 1997; Parry & Doan, 1994; Robinson, 1999; Saleebey, 1997; Sarbin, 1986; White & Epston, 1990; Winslade &

Monk, 1999). Central to the narrative perspective is the assumption that "We live our lives according to the stories we tell ourselves and the stories that others tell about us" (Winslade & Monk, 1999, p. 2). Helping others revise their stories calls for a different kind of listening. By listening deeply to clients' stories for the hidden meanings, gaps, spaces, and evidence that suggest possibilities for challenging taken-for-granted assumptions, counselors help clients to realize their capacity to spring back despite adversity and to seek relationships that support their sense of social, academic, and vocation competence. Listening for possibilities enables counselors to collaborate with clients to discover and detail stories that identify their resiliency.

3. *Professional possibilities.* Practices promoting resiliency can guide school counselors and teachers in their efforts to ensure possibilities for success for all students. Because success in schools depends upon students' personal/social, academic, and career development, this chapter shares how the resiliency paradigm offers keys to how positive personal/social, learning, and career development can be fostered in youth. As Masten (1994) pointed out, "Fostering resilience is an attempt to deflect a developmental pathway in a more positive direction" (p. 21). Schools and communities have numerous possibilities for helping youth recognize their self-righting capacities and their hope that they can shift their life trajectory in a positive direction. Such hope and recognition of self-righting capabilities are fundamental. As Werner & Smith (1992) concluded in their longitudinal study,

> The central component in the lives of the resilient individuals in this study which contributed to their effective coping in adulthood appeared to be a confidence that the odds can be surmounted. Some of the luckier ones developed such hopefulness early in their lives, in contact with caring adults. (p. 207)

By beginning with youth as resources and listening deeply, school reform efforts may open possibilities for students to perceive their own ability to spring back from adversity, to realize their own self-righting capacities, to understand their own ability to learn, and to fulfill their own power to engage passionately in meaningful activities. Part of social-emotional development has to do with individuals' ability to get up after they have been knocked down, to have heart, gumption, determination, and compassion. Moreover, social-emotional maturity has to do with grasping the role of thought in interpreting experience in life (Mills, 1995; Pransky, 1998). Learning development is related to individuals' ability to learn from difficulties and failures, to struggle with uncertainty and let solutions and the deeper wisdom emerge (Bruner, 1986, 1990; Claxton, 1997; Clinchy, 1996; Langer, 1997). Career development is connected to individuals' ability to adjust to the ongoing and continual changes in their livelihoods as students and adults. More importantly, career development concerns the capacity to be passionate about the work we choose to do and doing things we find meaningful (Quattrociocchi & Peterson, 1997). The resiliency paradigm begins by seeing youth as resources and offers primary prevention direction in helping youth develop pathways to learn to live, learn to learn, and learn to work.

To further describe this pathway offered to counselors by the resiliency paradigm, the chapter now defines resiliency, explicates resiliency's causal factors, and discusses risks and strengths. It then presents four approaches to prevention and interventions exemplifying resiliency (structured narrative, framework for tapping resilience, health realization, structure-relationship model) and a discussion of additional interventions for youth with disabilities. The chapter concludes with a brief but emphatic emphasis on adaptations for diversity.

RESILIENCY DEFINED

Given the diversity within the resiliency paradigm, the definition for resiliency used in this chapter expands upon Benard (1993): "resiliency is the process of healthy human development that is based on and grows out of nurturing, participatory relationships grounded in trust and respect" (p. 27). Resiliency is the process of healthy human development based on and growing out of nurturing relationships that support social, academic, and vocational competence and the capacity to spring back despite exposure to adversity and other environmental stressors. When counselors, teachers, parents, and others realize the self-righting capacity for healthy human development in themselves, they are more capable in facilitating resiliency in others. The power inherent in the realization is pointed out by Benard and Marshall (1997): "Resilience is an inside-out process that begins with one person's belief and emanates outward to transform whole families, classrooms, schools, and communities. . . . it means we shift from a focus on fixing individuals to creating healthy systems" (p. 1). Individuals who foster resiliency promote prevention.

Because diverse professional fields contribute to the evolving resiliency paradigm, there are a variety of perspectives about the resiliency paradigm and resiliency that lead to misunderstandings. On one hand, as Matsen (1994) pointed out,

Studies of resilience suggest that nature has provided powerful protective mechanisms for human development. . . . When adversity is relieved and basic human needs are restored, then resilience has a chance to emerge. Rekindling hope may be an important spark for resilience processes to begin their restorative work. (p. 20–21)

On the other hand, one of McWhirter, McWhirter, McWhirter, and McWhirter's (1998) concerns about resiliency was that

the justice system has used the term *resiliency* to help punish offenders— contending that a violent and abrasive upbringing provides no explanation for violent behavior because some youth who grow up in the same type of environment do not engage in violence. (p. 80)

Such practices by those in the justice system totally misunderstand the research and practices emerging from the resiliency paradigm. As made clear by Werner (1998),

As long as the balance between stressful events and protective factors is favorable, successful adaptation is possible even for youngsters who live in "high risk" conditions. However, when stressful life events outweigh the protective factors in a child's life, even the most resilient individual can develop problems. (p. 8)

As diverse as it is, the resiliency paradigm does not support institutionalizing ways to blame individuals in need of help. Such practices are contrary to the assumptions guiding prevention practices cited in this chapter; the imperative for growth and development unfolds naturally when certain environmental attributes are present.

"Resilience is not the cheerful disregard of one's difficult and traumatic life experiences; neither is it the naive discounting of life's pains. It is rather the ability to bear up in spite of these ordeals" (Saleebey, 1997, p. 9). Blum (1998) offered this perspective regarding what should be done in response to the positive findings in the resiliency research:

Rather than viewing the findings from resiliency research as a rationale for inaction, we should redouble our efforts. The good news is that for those reared in adversity, the outcomes are not necessarily bleak . . . It is likewise clear that, as the African proverb states, "it takes a community to rear a child." (p. 374)

To embody this proverb, individuals can learn to draw upon their own resiliency, foster resiliency in others, and work within their schools and communities to encourage collaborative and systemic approaches that foster resiliency in youth.

RESILIENCY CAUSAL FACTORS

Multiple factors influence the developmental trajectories of youth, and there are many explanations for the difficulties they face (Durlak, 1998). Identifying risks and causal factors does not always work; Benard's (1991) resiliency research synthesis showed that identifying risks does not translate into strategies for reducing those risks. This section explores how prevention efforts viewed in the broader social context (and not in individuals, families, and communities) shift the reasons why some children are not damaged or spring back from deprivation and adversity (Benard, 1994). This section does not attempt to capture the scope of the theory, research, and prevention efforts informing the evolving resiliency paradigm, but rather focuses upon longitudinal resiliency research that points toward the self-righting capacity in people. Research spanning over 30 years conducted by Werner and her colleagues (Werner, 1989, 1996, 1998; Werner & Smith, 1982, 1992) that describes protective factors within youth, within the family, and within the community is highlighted; Benard's (1991, 1993, 1994, 1996, 1997) research synthesis that profiles qualities of resilient youth and three protective factors that enhance student resiliency in the schools are presented.

Werner: The Mother of Resiliency

The life-span, crosscultural studies, such as those exemplified in the longitudinal studies of Werner and her colleagues, have concluded resiliency is the natural human capacity for self-righting (Werner, 1996; Werner & Smith, 1982, 1992). That the human organism has an imperative for growth and development is supported by their theory and research. Werner and Smith (1992) were guided by a transactional-ecological model of human development that posits people are active, self-righting organisms continuously adapting to their environment.

Their influential resiliency research used a prospective—developmental and longitudinal—design to assess how youth, at various stages of development and growing into high-risk conditions, respond to risk factors (Werner, 1989, 1996, 1998; Werner & Smith, 1982, 1992). According to Werner and Smith, "prospective longitudinal studies have fairly consistently shown that even among children exposed to potent risk factors it is unusual for more than half to develop serious disabilities or persistent problems" (1992, p. 4). Thus the longitudinal perspective essentially has resulted in the finding that most delinquent youth do not develop into career criminals (Werner, 1996, 1998; Werner & Smith, 1992). This prospective research design, which is different from the retrospective design, changed how the individuals being studied were discerned and what researchers found. Researchers using prospective designs study groups of youth over time, whereas researchers using retrospective designs are more likely to investigate risk factors linked to the history of a person with identified difficulties. Prospective design offers researchers different possibilities in describing youth who grow up in high-risk environments, whereas retrospective designs focus on events that lead to or interventions that are devised to diminish pathology. Longitudinal research offers an alternative way of understanding and learning about human self-righting capacities.

This hopeful and optimistic view needs to be explained in the context of research, commentary, and life stories supporting inborn, self-righting capacities. Werner and her colleagues' study (Werner, 1989; Werner, Bierman, & French, 1971; Werner & Smith, 1977, 1982, 1992) has extended 40 years and has found there are protective factors within youth, the family, and the community. Beginning with the entire population of 698 youth born in 1955, the study has followed 505 individuals on Kauai, Hawaii, from the prenatal stage to the adult stage of development. Data have been collected from cohort members in the prenatal period, at birth, and at ages 1, 2, 10, 18, 32, and 40. By birth, one third of the group was considered at risk due to four or more factors, including significant poverty, being reared by parents with little formal education, moderate to severe perinatal stress, family discord, divorce, alcoholism, or mental retardation. One third of these high-risk youth did not develop difficulties as a result of the exposure to risk, and another one third rebounded as they reached adulthood to become competent adults (Werner, 1998; Werner & Smith, 1992).

Research data have been presented in

- *Children of Kauai* (Werner, Bierman, & French, 1971), which documented the development from birth to age 10 and the cumulative effects of poverty, perinatal stress, and disorganized caretaking;
- *Kauai's Children Come of Age* (Werner & Smith, 1977), which analyzed the likelihood of persistent problems into childhood by examining learning disorders, mental health problems, and antisocial behavior of high-risk youth in their teens;
- *Vulnerable but Invincible* (Werner and Smith, 1982), which documented vulnerable and stress-resistant youth up to the transitional phase when they were about to leave high school; and
- *Overcoming the Odds* (Werner & Smith, 1992), which traced the long-term effects of childhood adversity and examined the protective factors that led most of the youth to adapt successfully as adults.

Werner and Smith (1992) found that resiliency is not something that is fixed and concrete, but a quality that is enhanced by protective buffers that appear to transcend ethnic, social class, and geographical boundaries. Individual variability had to be taken into account, but the majority of resilient youth in the Kauai study had a variety of internal or external protective factors (Werner, 1996). Those youth who overcame the odds were described as resilient, and as Werner and Smith (1992) pointed out, "they began to perceive themselves as movers of their destiny rather than as pawns in a power game played by outsiders" (p. 21).

The vast majority of delinquent youth in the study did not become adult career criminals. The majority of chronic criminals from the study cohort consisted of a small group of individuals who had averaged four or more arrests before becoming 18 years old. Those who did become persistent offenders needed remedial educational help (usually reading) prior to age 10, were considered troublemakers by their fifth-grade teachers and parents, and had grown up in homes where significant caregivers were absent for extended periods of time during adolescence (Werner & Smith, 1992). Youth

> exposed to adversities in early childhood are not predestined to grow into adults with failed marriages, criminal records, or psychiatric disorders. At each developmental stage, there is an opportunity for protective factors (personal competencies and sources of support) to counterbalance the negative weight exerted by adverse experiences. (Werner & Smith, 1992, p. 171)

Second chance opportunities are usually found at major life transitions. Such opportunities enable high-risk individuals to rebound and are frequently found in adult education programs, military service, active participation in a church community, or a supportive friend or spouse.

Werner and Smith (1992) asserted that the protective factors within the individual, family, and community have a more profound impact on the lives of youth than risk factors. Key protective factors within the individual, the family, and the community that were pointed out by Werner and Smith (1992) and expanded by Werner (1998) are worthy of note for professionals working with youth.

Within the Individual. Resilient individuals can be characterized by their caregivers as

- being active, affectionate, cuddly, good-natured, and easy to deal with in infancy;
- having effective reading skills by age 10 or grade 4;
- having communication and reasoning skills;
- being responsible and achievement oriented, and having competence and self-efficacy as general hallmarks;
- being more nurturant, compassionate, and socially perceptive;
- being more socially mature and possessing an internalized set of values;

- having a special interest or hobby;
- being liked by peers and adults;
- being reflective rather than having an impulsive dominant cognitive style;
- having an internal focus of control—believing that they can influence the environment around them;
- being flexible in coping strategies when dealing with adversity; and
- being resilient as adults if they set career and/job success as a high priority.

Within the Family. Resiliency is enhanced when

- child-rearing practices for boys and girls are different. Households with male role models and those providing structure and rules fostered resiliency in males. Male role models who encouraged the expression of emotion fostered resiliency.
- there is an emphasis on risk taking and independence for young women, a tendency not to overprotect, and reliable emotional support from another woman, such as a mother, grandmother, older sister, or aunt.
- there are affectional ties with alternate caregivers. Caring, nonjudgmental, adults, not necessarily family members, are critical in fostering resiliency.
- youth from chaotic families have an association with friends from stable households.
- there is an emphasis on youth being more helpful. Chores and domestic responsibilities prove to be sources of strength and competence.
- faith provides a sense of coherence, and rootedness gives youth a sense of meaning and compassion. Such faith helps men and women overcome great odds.

Within the Community. Resilience is enhanced when

- youth are able to make and keep friends. Resilient youth keep friends into adulthood and look to them for emotional support.
- there is a favorable attitude toward school.
- there is structure and clear limits for boys, nuturance and assumption of responsibility for girls.
- there is positive mentoring from school personnel. Those remembering one or more teachers are more resilient (most frequently identified role models are favorite teachers). The impact of positive mentoring may last a lifetime.

Werner and Smith (1992) concluded that the protective factors

> appear to transcend ethnic, social class, geographical, and historical bound-
> aries. Most of all, they offer a more optimistic outlook than the perspective
> that can be gleaned from the literature on the negative consequences of peri-
> natal trauma, caregiving deficits, and chronic poverty. They provide us with
> a corrective lens—an awareness of the self-righting tendencies that move
> children toward normal adult development under all but the most persis-
> tent adverse circumstances. (p. 202)

Counselors, teachers, parents, and others can foster the protective
buffers that support positive life trajectories for youth in which competence, confidence, and ability to care for others will flourish, but those
helping youth must believe in youth if this is going to happen.

> The life stories of the resilient youngsters now grown into adulthood teach
> us that competence, confidence, and caring can flourish, even under adverse
> circumstances, if children encounter persons who provide them with the
> secure basis for the development of trust, autonomy, and initiative. (Werner
> & Smith, 1992, p. 209)

Kitashima (1997), a youth from the Kauai study, embodied this point
in sharing what made a difference in her life growing up in a high-risk
household. Kitashima found caring and supportive people in school significant contributors to her success. At the same time, she found that
some professionals in the school made her a target of racism and put-
downs. She described a time when her fifth-grade math teacher told her,
"You are a good-for-nothing Hawaiian and will never amount to anything," whereas her school principal told her, "You are Hawaiian, and
you can be anything you choose to be" (p. 34). At age 16, when she got
pregnant and had a child, another school principal supported her desire
to stay in school. As for many youth from the Kauai study, the protective
factors counterbalanced the risks, and Kitashima went on to become a
successful adult.

One factor having a profound impact upon her resiliency was her
faith in something greater than herself. Thus faith led Kitashima to conclude, "Treasures exist in each one of our children—be they our own or
somebody else's—and we need to be patient until they realize their
promise. . . . Never give up on kids" (1997, p. 36). Her guiding beliefs
and comments opened a larger question that Werner and her colleagues
did not have to concern themselves with: the growing discussion about
spirituality in public education.

Palmer (1998/1999) has illustrated this point by saying that

> I advocate any way we can find to explore the spiritual dimension of teach-
> ing, learning, and living. By *spiritual* I do not mean the creedal formulation

of any faith tradition. . . . I mean the ancient and abiding human quest for connectedness with something larger and more trustworthy than our egos—with our own souls, with one another, with the worlds of history and nature, with the invisible winds of the spirit, with the mystery of being alive. (p. 6)

Such discussion and position should cause counselors and teachers to pause because they place professionals in a position where they must wrestle with complex issues regarding "the spirit of education" where educators can "neither ignore religion nor proselytize a particular belief" (Scherer, 1998, 1999, p. 5). Ultimately, as Kitashima's experience and beliefs showed, the act of believing in youth "becomes a concern of the spirit" (Wesley, 1998/1999, p. 42). Counselors and teachers thinking deeply about spiritual issues are forced to recognize and appreciate the issues raised and how beliefs foster resiliency.

Benard: On Changing Perspective and Practices

Benard's (1991) review of the resiliency research described personal and environmental sources of healthy development that shift prevention away from a problem-focused approach to human development and toward health promotion. Her review and subsequent work stand as a synthesis of the resiliency research that identifies major factors contributing to the enhancement of youth resiliency; her synthesis and practice continue to inform prevention efforts with youth and adults (Benard, 1991, 1993, 1994, 1996, 1997; Benard & Marshall, 1997).

Benard (1991, 1993, 1994, 1996, 1997) identified and referred to the self-righting characteristics of individuals as resilience traits and the characteristics found in facilitative environments as protective factors. Drawing on the transactional-ecological model of human development, Benard stated,

> personality and individual outcomes are the result of a transactional process between self, agency, and environmental influences. To be successful, prevention interventions must focus on enhancing and creating positive environmental contexts—families, schools, and communities that, in turn, reinforce positive behaviors. (1997, p. 169)

The individual traits include social competence, problem-solving skills, autonomy, and a sense of purpose and belief in a bright future. These resilience traits and protective factors support the self-righting tendencies within the person. Youth with a positive sense of well-being demonstrate

- *social competence:* responsiveness, flexibility, empathy and caring, communication skills, and a sense of humor;

- *problem-solving skills:* thinking abstractly and reflectively, planning skills, and flexibility;
- *autonomy:* internal locus of control, sense of power, self-discipline, and adaptive distancing; and
- *sense of purpose and future:* healthy expectations, goal-directedness, success orientation, educational aspirations, persistence, hopefulness, hardiness, belief in a bright or compelling future, and a sense of coherence or meaning (Bernard, 1991).

Protective factors are also needed. Environmental characteristics or protective factors that support positive youth development include

- *caring relationships:* The single most important factor in fostering resiliency in youth is having a connection with at least one caring person. Relationships noted for stable care, affection, attention, intergenerational social networks, and a basic sense of trust foster a climate of caring and support.
- *high expectations:* This implies that adults see potential for maturity, responsibility, self-discipline, and common sense in youth. The focus is on strengths and assets and not on problems and deficits. Having structure, order, clear expectations, and cultural traditions; being valued; and promoting social and academic success fosters high expectations.
- *opportunities for participation:* These are a natural outcome of "high expectations for youth, for viewing youth as resources and not problems" (Benard, 1991, p. 17). Participation connects youth to other people, to interests, and to valuing life itself. Being valued participants, having socially and economically useful tasks, and having responsibilities for decision making, planning, and helping others provide opportunities for participation.

According to Benard (1994), human development is a fluid process, and prevention efforts must focus on processes that foster both resilience traits and protective factors.

> Resiliency research . . . promises to move the prevention, education, and youth development fields beyond their focus on program and *what* we do, to emphasis on process and *how* we do what we do; to move beyond our fixation with content to a focus on *context.* (Benard, 1996, pp. 9–10)

This shift requires invitations for youth to connect with adults who offer all youth hope by providing care and support, high expectations, and opportunities for participation.

Benard (1993) summed up the hope for all youth inherent in the resiliency paradigm: "Solutions do not come from looking at what is missing; solutions will come by building on strengths" (p. 28). Like solution-focused and narrative counseling, the strengths perspective inherent in the resiliency paradigm places professionals as partners in helping people draw upon their own power to help themselves (Benard, 1991, 1993, 1994, 1996; De Jong & Berg, 1998; Monk et al., 1997; Parry & Doan, 1994; Saleebey, 1997; White & Epston, 1990; Winslade & Monk, 1999). Seeing people as inherently possessing power shifts the professional role away from authority, expert, and director to that of collaborator working with others who have resources, expertise in their own lives, and the capacity to recognize their own well-being. In narrative counseling, problems are defined as external to the person, and both Benard (1991, 1993) and narrative counselors (White & Epston, 1990) have stated that the person is not the problem; the problem is the problem. The next section explores professional and personal discourse around risks and strengths and how both the resiliency paradigm and narrative counseling address problems as problems.

RISKS AND STRENGTHS DISCOURSE

The strengths perspective inherent in the resiliency paradigm, in solution-focused counseling, and in narrative counseling does not overly remediate and target client weakness. Rather the strengths perspective guides efforts to create healthy systems that support human development in which counselors and teachers find themselves in collaborative dialogue with people regarding their beliefs and assumptions about the world and actions they take in the world (Saleebey, 1997). Collaborative dialogues create contexts in which professionals are challenged to look deeply at themselves and their own resiliency in a context that assumes people are experts on their own experiences and capable of drawing on their resiliency (Saleebey, 1997).

Professionally reflecting on and looking deeply at the individual and environmental attributes fostering personal and professional development set up a number of demands. A special issue of the *Journal of Counseling and Development* on racism (Robinson & Ginter, 1999) captured how our lives are woven into stories that illustrate racism's toxic effects in counselors' personal and professional lives. As Kitashima's (1997) account demonstrated, racism infects both individual and environmental attributes fostering resiliency; and most counselors and teachers recognize that not every youth has Kitashima's individual and environmental attributes when faced with racism at school.

Counselors, teachers, parents, and others are challenged to understand how dominant discourses affect how their clients' stories are heard, understood, and responded to. For instance, "Counselors must avoid attributing certain occupations, attitudes, and experiences to their clients due to the visibility of their race, gender, and other identities. Making judgments about people's humanity and its quality due to established criteria is to rely on tried but extremely powerful discourse steeped in oppression" (Robinson, 1999, p. 78). In other words, counselors have to know themselves, their privilege, and the cultural context in which they meet others, and be able to listen deeply to the stories of others without judgment if they are to engage in profoundly human conversations. Robinson argued that if counselors' practice takes a constructionist perspective, they do not assume a preferred position in any dialogue; and that such a perspective allows for a plurality of ways for viewing the world, and shows how power, privilege, and disadvantage do not have to be deemed as absolute and fixed.

The resiliency paradigm focuses on learning about and from individual stories and truths, and how the individual variation within groups having risk status might inform youth to see possibilities and hope in the world (Benard, 1994). The risks and strengths discourse, the role story, connectedness, and developmental processes play important roles in understanding resiliency. To look from one perspective, our society is at risk. Among industrialized nations, the United States ranks first in military technology, military exports, gross domestic product, number of millionaires and billionaires, health technology, and defense expenditures. However, the United States ranks 18th in the gap between rich and poor, 16th in the living standards among the poorest one fifth of children, and last in protecting children against gun violence (Children's Defense Fund, 1997). Risk is frequently located in individual youth, giving professionals a sense of being overwhelmed by the difficulties confronting youth and society and reducing complex social problems to trying to fix youth who are the causalities of social policies (Saleebey, 1997). Further,

> our culture is obsessed with, and fascinated by, psychopathology, victimization, abnormality, and moral and interpersonal aberrations. A swelling conglomerate of businesses and professions, institutions and agencies, from medicine to pharmaceuticals, from the insurance industry to the mass media turn handsome profits by assuring us that we are in the clutch (or soon will be) of any number of emotional, physical, or behavioral maladies. (Saleebey, 1997, p. 4)

There is a generalized discourse that troubled families, schools, and communities perpetrate harm on youth. The problems are bound in the individuals composing those families, schools, and communities. By fixing those people, youth living in high-risk contexts might avoid becoming adults with serious problems.

> Labeling youths, their families, and their communities as at risk means we are acting on stereotypes, on unquestioned assumptions about who people really are. . . . In contrast, resilience research focuses on learning . . . individual stories and truths, on studying the individual variation within groups having risk status. (Benard, 1994, p. 4)

Swadener and Lubeck (1995) stated that describing youth as at risk creates an

> ideology of risk, which has embedded in it interpretations of children's deficiencies or likelihood of failure due to environmental, as well as individual variables. The problem of locating pathology in the victim is the most objectionable tenet of much of the dominant rhetoric of risk. (p. 18)

In other words, describing youth as at risk creates political consequences that result in the victims of social injustice being blamed for the results of that injustice. For Swadener and Lubeck, the need to confront structural injustices is lost when professional conversations and actions focus on fixing youth at risk. For Fine (1995),

> youth at risk is an ideological and historical construction. While numbers and their skewed class and racial distributions are intolerable, and the academic and economic consequences are severe, we must remember that today more students graduate from high school than was true 15 years ago. . . . Fundamentally, the notion of risk keeps us from being broadly, radically, and structurally creative about transforming schools and social conditions for all of today and tomorrow's youth. (p. 90)

Although Swadener and Lubeck (1995) and Fine (1995) did not locate themselves in the counseling profession, resiliency paradigm, or even in prevention work, such perspectives should prompt counselors, teachers, parents, and others to pause and think. By taking advantage of the deconstruction of the at-risk construct, counselors and teachers can critically reflect upon their own practice and open up possibilities for different kinds of professional practice. As Rak and Patterson pointed out, "The guidance and counseling professions have long emphasized a model based more on health than illness" (1996, p. 368). Counselors focusing on resiliency and health build on strengths and communicate hope to youth.

Health-promoting stories may guide individuals, families, groups, and even professional practice (Saleebey, 1997). A brief review of solution-focused counseling, narrative counseling, and resiliency practice shows health-promoting practices that draw upon individual, family, and community strengths. Solution-focused approaches promote resiliency because they are committed to health (Rak & Patterson, 1996). By committing to client strengths, solution-focused counseling empowers clients to draw upon multiple possibilities for defining solutions that will help individuals and families develop more productive and satisfying lives (De Jong & Berg, 1998). Solution-focused counseling shifts away from emphasizing client problems and expert solutions and toward helping clients discover the considerable power and possibilities they have in themselves (De Jong & Berg, 1998; Saleebey, 1997).

Narrative counseling draws upon people's strengths by placing the counseling conversation and all conversations in a social context (Monk et al., 1997; Saleebey, 1997; White & Epston, 1990; Winslade & Monk, 1999). When conversations are placed in a social context, the political nature (power) of those conversations has to be considered. When counselors enter conversations about taken-for-granted assumptions, talk leads to certain discourses about thought and action. Inherent in those taken-for-granted assumptions, "people are often unaware of how discourses restrict their knowledge and volition about how to think and act" (Winslade & Monk, 1999, p. 26). Narrative counselors argue this lack of awareness limits individuals' appreciation of their own knowledge and ability to respond to oppressive circumstances. In practice, narrative counselors

> view the young person as someone who has knowledge, but may never have had encouragement to access his or her own ability to make sense of the problem. Giving a person this kind of respect [possessing valid personal knowledge] calls forth hidden resourcefulness and promotes a respect-full relationship. (p. 27)

Such a position forces counselors to wrestle with the political dimensions of the narratives they use to describe the world.

Given the storied nature of our lives, both the resiliency paradigm and narrative counseling signify the dynamic quality descriptions and thought have in guiding and defining our lives (Lifton, 1993; Monk et al., 1997; Sarbin, 1986; White & Epston, 1990; Winslade & Monk, 1999). Like the resiliency paradigm, narrative counseling begins with certain assumptions that are derived from different professional fields, such as anthropology, psychology, history, biology, and systems theory. Like resiliency practice, narrative is not a set of fancy tricks and techniques but a way of being with people. Unlike resiliency, narrative counseling is led by a different set of assumptions. Writing about narrative counseling, Winslade and Monk (1999) offered nine assumptions that can inform how counselors and teachers can foster resiliency:

1. People live their lives according to stories. Such stories shape an individual's social reality.
2. The stories people live are not produced in a vacuum. Stories emerge from conversations and are found in social contexts.
3. Discourses are embedded within stories. Discourses are "what gets exchanged in conversation" and are the taken-for-granted assumptions that exist just beneath the surface of many conversations.
4. "The modern world is characterized by societal norms that are kept in place by surveillance and scrutiny" (p. 24). The notion of *the gaze*, derived from Michel Foucault, a postmodern French historian, refers to the scrutiny individuals subject themselves to by comparing and evaluating themselves to others or to cultural expectations. Anorexia, bulimia, and steroid abuse are examples of what occurs to individuals who respond to cultural expectations for perfection.
5. Contradictory or alternative discourses are always available.
6. Severe limits are placed on people seeking to create change in their lives by the dominant cultural stories. For example, though currently fading as a dominant cultural story, a young woman might be influenced by traditional female discourses in her family to seek a safe career, do what men say, catch the right man.
7. New possibilities for living may occur when dominant discourses are deconstructed. *Deconstruction* is a narrative counseling process where individuals take apart, unpack, or develop an understanding of the discourses embedded in their lives.
8. "There is always lived experience that does not get encapsulated in stories" (p. 27). Every lived story has parts that are not stated, such as details and gaps. There are parts of the story that may be more satisfying and offer a different perspective than the parts of the story being lived.
9. Counselors can help individuals construct a more satisfying and appealing story. Narrative counselors help discover counterplots and different ways of seeing and understanding problem-saturated stories in order to begin revising more appealing stories.

The nine narrative counseling assumptions open space for seeing how dominant and alternative discourses might guide stories and narrative interventions used to foster resiliency. White and Epston (1990) showed counselors the importance of externalizing the problem by personifying the constraint that is hampering the youth. Counselors begin to talk about the influence of trouble and the way trouble tricks or pushes around youth. Externalizing places the problem outside of the youth in discourse and frees the youth to develop an alternative story for guiding life.

Using the narrative approach, counselors, teachers, and parents can engage youth in conversations that offer alternative discourses and stories. Discourses are embedded in our cultural assumptions, in things taken for granted. For example, many White individuals do not see or understand the notion of White privilege, whereas African Americans and other traditionally disenfranchised groups cannot escape the impact of White privilege. For another example, Macfarlane (1998) developed an approach for Maori special education students in New Zealand that utilized culturally appropriate discourse. "In New Zealand it is the dominant culture that provides the guidelines for conventional and special education, as well as the majority of professionals determining 'who is the problem'" (p. 2). Like minority youth in the United States, Maori youth frequently find themselves alienated from school. Macfarlane's bicultural approach begins with a meeting, or what the Maori refer to as *hui*, where school officials and Maori youth could "speak with each other about difficult things in a way that avoids sliding back into the dynamics that gave rise to the problems in the first place" (p. 3). By moving away from punitive and judgmental discourse, the *hui* promotes culturally appropriate alternatives to suspension based on community partnerships with the school. The conference is embedded in a culturally appropriate discourse that draws on Maori culture and values, such as the four principles of consensus, reconciliation, examination, and harmony. The conference starts by saying in Maori and English, "I am who I am. You are who you are. Let us move together in tandem" (p. 11). That being said, the youth are introduced to a new school discourse that places their values and culture central to finding solutions to the problems being faced at school. The youth experience discourse in school that embeds Maori students' success and well-being.

According to Rockwell (1998), youth are capable of remarkable growth and achievement when adults do not fall prey to four fundamental myths: the myth of irreparable damage, the myth of predetermination, the myth of identity, or the myth that, ultimately, "it doesn't matter." Rockwell countered the four myths with anecdotal stories. The myth of irreparable harm is countered by Lauren Slater, "a Harvard graduate with awards for her writing and administrative duties as the director of a mental health facility . . . [who] was hospitalized repeatedly for suicide attempts as a teenager" (p. 16). The myth of predetermination is countered by a youth who made a decision to change his aggressive behavior because he did not want to go to prison like his father. The myth of identity is countered by seeing that abuse is what happens to youth, and that abuse does not define who children are. By helping youth reframe self-descriptions around abuse, they can become heroes in their own struggles to self-right themselves rather than become "abused or damaged youth." The myth that, ultimately, it doesn't matter is countered by alternative explanations when helpers recognize that kindness, compassion, and grace are the qualities that matter most for youth living in a difficult world.

The importance of developing what narrative therapists call counterplot is a significant dimension in understanding human resiliency. There are numerous possibilities for developing counterplot. Counselors might offer youth counterplots by helping them discover strengths and resources needed to confront risks via specific prevention interventions, like those described in the next section. Counselors could also bring in adults who are capable of connecting with youth in roles such as big brothers and big sisters, or they could work with teachers and other school staff in a context where stories are shared, and positive, compassionate, and mentoring relationships are developed.

Additionally, it is important for counselors to help youth recognize the counterplots existing in their own families or in the lives of others. For example, in a bestselling memoir, Goodwin (1997) described how her father's counterplot developed when he was 18 years old.

> In little more than a decade, my father had lost his two brothers, his mother, his father, and, finally, his sister. . . . My father somehow emerged from this haunted childhood without a trace of self-pity or rancor; on the contrary, he seemed to possess an absolute self-confidence and a remarkable ability to transmit his ebullience and optimism to others. (p. 31)

Such stories are preventative and hopeful, and the value of sharing them is well-known (Brooks, 1997; Fredericks, 1997; Gladding, 1997, 1998). We are surrounded by stories both as actors and audience. Listening to the stories of others deepens a sense of community and fosters the view that people are resilient. The next section focuses on approaches that help youth take actions to guide their own life stories and counselors and teachers to advise their professional lives.

APPROACHES TO PREVENTION

Four approaches—structured narrative, a framework for tapping resilience, health realization, and a structure-relationship model—exemplify practices and connections within the resiliency paradigm. Other approaches are also grounded in resiliency, but the approaches presented here best illustrate how resiliency interventions begin with believing in individuals, families, schools, and communities, and like Rutter (1987), see human thinking as a protective mechanism. Each approach shows how the resiliency perspective is a collaborative process, respectful of multicultural perspectives, and hopeful about engaging youth as resources.

Structured Narrative

Schools are one of the places where youth have opportunities to create stories of success or stories of woe regarding their abilities to learn to live, learn, and work. The structured narrative is a written counseling intervention was developed in an effort to address the cold efficiencies necessitated by high school counselor-to-student ratios.

The structured narrative writing intervention is designed to help students cultivate positive stories about their possibilities for renewal and redirection, and to provide normally anonymous students with voices during the critical transition into high school (Berliner, 1993). Students have space to tell their stories and know someone will take time to "listen" to every story by reading them. In this written approach, structured prompts help students clarify or redefine personal narratives and see possibilities for living with greater hope and power.

The structured narrative as an intervention grows out of a tradition that uses narrative and writing in counseling (Bruner, 1986, 1990; Desetta & Wolin, 1998; L'Abate, 1992, 1994; Pennebaker, 1997; Riordan, 1996; Sarbin, 1986; White & Epston, 1990). The nature of narrative is nonnormative and can be optimistic because every person has numerous possibilities for describing experience. Structured narrative lessons may be used in a number of ways, from lessons designed to enhance transition into high school to lessons created to enhance the mindful practice required by graduate students in the teaching and counseling professions. Such lessons orient individuals to requirements defined by organizations, such as schools, or prompt individuals to explore the narrative possibilities that entering the teaching and counseling profession provide. The lessons may also be used to assess individuals who might need additional help in developing their writing skills, making connections with caring adults, or reaching personal and professional goals.

An example of a structured narrative intervention is A Write Way, which consists of six structured narrative lessons that can be used to help youth during their transition into high school (Lewis, 1996, 1999). The prompts are formatted on a page to limit the length of responses, to make responding more attractive to reluctant writers, and to focus respondents on time-limited tasks. (The second of the six lessons is included in the appendix to this chapter.) The prompts, which must be adapted to local needs, range from closed-ended questions to short essays that open opportunities for creative responses. For instance, in a study focusing on youth transitioning into high school, youth were asked the closed-ended question, "Do you plan to graduate from high school? Yes or No." They were also given the prompt, "Describe a time when you were a positive leader or participant at home, school, or elsewhere" (Lewis, 1995). The study concluded that creating structures helps students understand high expectations, but that caring and supportive face-to-face relationships are equally important (Lewis, 1995, 1999).

One purpose of the A Write Way lessons is to help youth see possibilities for viewing or rewriting their school story in a positive way by assisting them to become oriented to the organizational demands of the school, document their own perspective about learning, and open them up to seeing more possibilities for living and learning in themselves. Prompts are designed to help youth explore developmental possibilities and not leap to conclusions about themselves as learners or as people because drawing conclusions too quickly might close off possibilities for discovering the world and themselves anew (Claxton, 1997).

Structured narratives assist individuals in seeing that their life trajectories are not set by the stars or fates. People can change their life stories, and the vast majority of youth do become successful adults. Structured narratives attempt to give youth greater agency in describing their lives and are especially useful when youth see their life stories in the context of other life stories. Stories supporting positive relationships or overcoming the odds not only are critical to children but also encourage students to take action in their own stories. Resiliency is fostered by taking action in developing one's own ever-changing story and by listening to the success stories of others. At the same time,

> no one ever fully becomes the author of her/his own story; any such assumption can only lead back to the illusions of control, individual autonomy, isolated selfhood, and single truth. The person goes forth instead to join with others in the universal human action of multiple authorship. (Parry & Doan, 1994, p. 43)

The structured narrative and other active approaches thus facilitate youth in becoming agents in their own life narratives, and reflective approaches like bibliotherapy facilitate youth in valuing the stories of others. These approaches focus on individual youth in organizational contexts. However, what is frequently called for is to change the beliefs guiding the organization.

A Framework for Tapping Resilience

Tapping resilience is an "inside-out process," according to Benard and Marshall (1997). Individual change can thus be encouraged and more successfully tapped with systems change and education rather than with risk-focused therapeutic interventions. Benard, associate for program development of the University of Minnesota National Resilience Resource Center, and Marshall, executive director of the center, have developed a tool for guiding school community systems change initiatives designed to foster resilience in children, youth, adults, and organizations. Also according to Benard and Marshall, successful systemic interventions are not quick fixes but require 3 to 5 years to implement. The framework is only one part of their comprehensive approach to establishing a resilience operating philosophy in major systems such as school districts. Ultimately the purpose is to help adults foster the resilience of individuals by first learning to discover and tap their own resilience.

The planning framework encourages planners to focus on four arenas:

1. beliefs planners hold about the natural resilience and promise of human beings;
2. conditions for empowerment revealed in research and best practice;
3. program strategies to create these conditions and tap resilience; and
4. individual and societal outcomes to be evaluated as part of the process.

This framework cuts new ground. It directs planners to explore their fundamental beliefs about human functioning and how it is fully realized. Traditional prevention planning guides, for example, have primarily focused on needs assessment and on community assets and deficits as precursors to poor youth outcomes. Staff development and technical assistance services offered by the National Resilience Resource Center use the framework for tapping resilience to shift the local focus from *at risk* to *at promise*. Benard and Marshall have suggested that our beliefs about the capacity of youth determine the degree to which youth are ultimately able to realize their own potential.

Belief is the foundation of the planning framework. Adults must "see how conditioned thoughts prevent us from recognizing students' natural strengths" (Benard & Marshall, 1997, p. 2). Understanding the power of conditioned, limiting beliefs and learning how to tap one's own resilience—the health of the helper—are of paramount importance. The key questions in the early planning phase are What do we believe about the capacity for resilience in all people? Is it natural and inborn in all human beings even though it is not always realized or manifested in behaviors, skills, and characteristics? If we look through behaviors can we discern health? Is it there waiting to be tapped?

With the framework, planners also study resilience research and best practices. What creates the conditions of empowerment? What taps resilience? What evidence supports our beliefs about human resilience? This phase of program development unites common sense, research, and program evaluation. What do we know works? Where is more study needed? In simplest terms (and as already noted), Benard has categorized the conditions of empowerment as three major protective factors: caring and support, high encouraging expectations, and meaningful opportunities for participation (Benard, 1991). The challenge is how to prepare adults to provide these critical protective factors, that is, to be caring, to believe youth can succeed, and to invite genuine participation, even when behavior is highly problematic, past performance meager, and social behavior completely obnoxious or even personally threatening.

Based on an understanding of both beliefs and evidence, planners are guided to develop or select strategies that will tap resilience. After an exhaustive search for effective prevention and youth development strategies, Benard and Marshall (1997) settled on health realization as one of the most efficient and effective ways school and community representatives could be taught to foster resilience. (The experiences of a district student assistance director trained by the National Resilience Resource Center using this systems change approach in fostering resilience are described in the next section.)

The framework also pushes planners to think about evaluation from the very beginning. Key questions to address include

- What will it look like if a young person realizes his or her resilience?
- How will it look in adults?
- How does resilience look in a school, family, neighborhood, community?
- Do we know what we are looking for and trying to make happen?
- Will we know healthy human functioning when we see it?

Resilience is not about labels:

To label a child, family, community, or culture resilient—or not resilient—misses the mark. Labeling one child resilient implies another is not and contradicts the resilience paradigm in which resilience is part of the human condition and the birthright of all human beings. (Benard & Marshall, 1997, p. 4)

The systems change Benard and Marshall have called for shakes traditional prevention, special education, and mental health services at the very core. Are human beings capable by nature? As professionals can we teach healthy functioning and in an organized fashion tap resilience? Can school counselors be most effective if they point students to their health rather than cementing student, parent, and professional thoughts about diagnosis, labels, problems, risks, and looming danger and failure? The framework for tapping resilience can assist counselors, teachers, and parents in encouraging school leaders to begin a systematic paradigm shift to health rather than dysfunction.

Health Realization: The Psychology of Resiliency

Health realization's psychology of resiliency begins with the assumption that every person has the innate capacity for mental health, for common sense, and for living in a mature and responsible manner regardless of his or her past and current circumstances (Mills, 1995). As a prevention and education approach, health realization focuses upon inside-out change and innate resiliency (Mills, 1995; Pransky, 1998). This subsection presents the principles of the health realization approach as well as its impact on a high-risk public housing site in Miami and concludes with stories from a district student assistance director from St. Cloud, Minnesota, who used health realization to guide her work with youth.

Health realization's three guiding principles—mind, thought, consciousness—are described as providing a basis for the renaissance of psychology (Pransky, 1998), as the source of human experience and psychological functioning (Mills, 1995; Pransky, 1998).

- *Mind* is defined as the source of thought and consciousness (Pransky, 1998). As in physicists' use of the term *energy* or in terms like *life force*, mind is the power that makes thought and consciousness possible.
- "*Thought* as a function originates beyond our individual psychological personage just as the life force originates beyond our individual physical personage" (p. 38). The brain processes thoughts moment to moment, giving each person a different experience of reality. "The function of thinking, the ability to think is universal, but the content of that thinking is determined by each person" (p. 38).
- *Consciousness* is the process of experiencing our thinking through our senses. "If you mistakenly thought you were in extreme danger, you would have a sensory experience of being in danger" (p. 39).

Mills (1995) and Pransky (1998) saw individual problems as emerging from the way people think about themselves, and well-meaning efforts that focus on symptom reduction usually fail to point people toward the principle of thought. Because individuals construct their personal realities, health realization focuses on those qualities of thought that elicit a sense of well-being in the moment and do not explore the psychic damage resulting from past trauma. Mills found that "people's ability to change their outlook, and the quality of their lives, varied directly in relation to their understanding of thought" (1995, p. 61). The therapeutic process is approached as educational (Mills, 1995, 1996; Pransky, 1998). "We concluded that we could help people much more by teaching them to elicit their own intrinsic health, rather than encouraging them to explore their dysfunctions" (Mills, 1995, p. 53). As products of thought, psychological difficulties were approached as thoughts rather than as existing independently and having a life of their own. The intervention shifted to eliciting and teaching people to understand the source of their mental health. Individuals were helped to understand the moment-to-moment thinking and two modes of thought: the processing mode and the free-flowing mode. Modes of thinking are ways of going about something (Mills, 1995; Pransky, 1998).

- The *processing mode* draws upon memory and frees individuals from having to learn things like tying shoes and driving a car over and over; it is also the mode that keeps people stuck trying to do the same thing over and over.
- The *free-flowing mode* is more relaxed and has greater vitality; it is the source of objectivity, common sense, good judgment, and wisdom.

The crisp and clear way of thinking found in the process mode of thinking can be contrasted to the relaxed free-flow mode of thinking (Mills, 1995; Pransky, 1998). By helping people understand how they experience the two modes of thought and not focusing upon the content of the thought, health realization assists individuals to access their free-flowing mode much more and bypass getting stuck in the processing mode where they might repeat the same thoughts over and over.

People who understand what mental health is and live effortlessly in mental well-being are able to live with their mind free in receiver [free-flowing] mode because they avoid thought processes like worry and overanalysis that relegate the thinker to computer [processing] mode. (Pransky, Mills, Sedgeman, & Blevens, 1997, p. 412)

The innate resiliency is accessed when individuals recognize that reality is formed from moment-to-moment thought, and that the trajectory of a life story can be changed by recognizing the role of thought in creating that story (Mills & Spittle, 1998). Individuals and groups are taught to recognize that the processing mode has a positive function that enables people to store and retrieve information as well as a negative function that may lead to insecure habits of thinking. They are also taught to recognize that free-flowing thought enables people to draw upon an open, receptive source of common sense, wisdom, and good judgment from which they are not compelled to force answers.

Teaching individuals about the two modes of thought, coupled with community building activities, has resulted in impressive preliminary results. For example, the health realization model was used as a community intervention at the Modello-Homestead Gardens Project in Metro-Dade County, Florida. Staff were initially trained in health realization prior to conducting outreach activities for project residents. These outreach activities included initiating PTA meetings, parenting classes, and individual and family counseling sessions. Residents were taught about how their thinking formed their outlook and behavior, and how to recognize the difference between their learned, conditioned, or processing thinking from the past and their more free-flowing, here-and-now, common-sense thinking. All staff contact with the residents was respectful, and residents were viewed as being resilient and healthy.

After 3 years, the program had served 142 families and 600 youth. Resident surveys after 3 years found that

- 87% of parents reported that their children were more cooperative and that they experienced significantly less frustration with or hostility toward their children;
- over 60% of residents involved in programs became employed, from a baseline of 85% on public assistance;
- school discipline referrals and suspensions decreased by 75% from baseline at the middle school level;
- attendance improved and school truancy rates improved around 80%;
- parent involvement in schools improved by 500%;
- school failure dropped from 50% to 10%;
- middle school teen pregnancy dropped 80%; and
- the Homestead police reported that they had not had any calls for drug trafficking or criminal activities such as stolen cars or burglaries for almost a year. (Mills, 1997, p. 2)

In addition, parents stopped hitting their children and got more involved with schools, and children improved their school performance. The community became a better place to live for both adults and youth. With communities typically defined as at-risk, the health realization approach has been helpful in promoting positive individual and community outcomes. Other communities and programs reporting successes using health realization range from the South Bronx in New York City to the Avalon Gardens in South Central Los Angeles (Mills, 1995). The work is not merely directed toward high-risk communities.

Jeanne Slingluff, the district student assistance director in St. Cloud, Minnesota, was trained in health realization by the National Resilience Resource Center to improve the performance of student assistance teams, which are committees of teachers, principals, social workers, counselors, and others who focus on improving the performance of at-risk youth. Slingluff initially found that some teams met on a regular basis, and others did not, and that their success could be improved. Two pilot schools with staffs of 15 to 20 were selected for health realization training.

Staff were taught to talk about innate resilience and to teach youth the source of thought. One teacher used peanut M&Ms to move youth along; there were many different colors but a common interior. Youth were taught about the "busy mind" during a group exercise designed to help them "get quiet" and "clear their minds" on their own. The exercise used the following steps:

- Students were told they had been given a call slip to the office to talk to the principal and to write down their thoughts on a half sheet of paper.
- After writing, the students broke into groups and summarized their thoughts on post-its.
- Then, individually and in small groups, they were asked to put their post-its on their teacher's glasses as she sat in front of the class. It was only moments before the teacher's glasses were covered with post-its, and soon her nose and other parts of her face were covered as well. The teacher said, "When you have a busy mind, you can't see." A busy mind can lead to problems.
- The teacher then posed some questions: "What would happen if this student had to go to a test after meeting with the principal? How would the student perform?"
- The teacher then asked, "What can you do to clear your thoughts?" The students offered suggestions and strategies for getting quiet. Some suggestions were as simple as close your eyes or picture something relaxing.

Once the students have the concept, they know how to quiet their minds. Slingluff said that when the class starts to get overly busy, the teacher can simply tell the class, in a respectful way, "Put your heads down just for a minute to clear your heads." The students stop and clear their minds.

Slingluff was clear that this occurs because teachers, counselors, and administrators believe in students' innate capacities. To illustrate her point, she shared the story of a young man who was sent to her after he expanded a one-paragraph assignment about conflict into a five-page catharsis that described his experience of being sexually abused and having substance abusing parents. The teacher was concerned that the student was suicidal; Slingluff said that she normally would think in terms of getting an ambulance, but that this time she decided to clear her own mind before meeting the young man, to listen deeply to him without letting her mind get busy. He brought in a friend when they met. She listened to the child as he told his story. The three of them talked about strengths that could be found in the story he told. From there he generated options and a plan for taking care of himself.

The data and the stories point to a variety of possibilities for the health realization model. As more schools experiment with the approach and more research studies are conducted, there will be more opportunities to assess the impact the approach has on individuals and organizations.

Structure-Relationship Model for Fostering Resiliency: Balancing School Reform

The structure-relationship model for fostering resiliency integrates Benard's (1991) three protective factors with L'Abate's (1994) notion of structure and relationship to guide pedagogical and counseling practices that foster resiliency (Lewis, 1996, 1999; Lewis & Siefer, 1997). In the broad sense, the model attempts to address the loss of faith in and need to explore alternatives to the modernist attempts to plan an ideal social order rationally and define a standardized knowledge (Hayes & Oppenheim, 1997). Clearly, there is a need to balance school reform efforts (Hayes, 1993; Hayes, Glickman, & Lunsford, 1996). In a more practical sense, the model offers counselors, teachers, and parents a model for entering conversations regarding restructuring efforts and school reform. The model also offers a frame for guiding counselor conversations that might suggest different ways for administrators to look at systems (Fullan, 1993) or for teachers to look at new ways of teaching (Gibbs, 1994).

The model integrates both relationship and structure into contexts that provide opportunities for meaningful participation. Relationships between youth and adults in schools are enhanced by caring and support, accepting where youth are developmentally, and appreciating each as unique individuals. Relationship focuses upon youths' *becoming*. Benard pointed out that "Resilience research shows the field that the blueprint for building this sense of home and place in the cosmos lies in relationships. . . . effective interventions must reinforce, within every arena, the natural social bonds between young and old, between siblings, between friends" (1994, p. 8). Significant relationships develop over time and include just hanging around, listening to another person's story, struggling with difficult tasks, and being alive in the moment with another person. Youth perceiving one caring adult in their lives have one more protective factor than other youth who are isolated; the single consistent known protective factor found across the resiliency research is a caring adult (Benard, 1991, 1993, 1996; Gregg, 1996; Resnick et al., 1998; Reynolds, 1998; Werner, 1996; Werner & Smith, 1982, 1992).

Relationships with little or no structure can make school and life chaotic. Structure in schools requires clearly communicating high expectations for youth to achieve. Structure focuses upon youths' *doing*. Many of the current school reform efforts seem to value maximizing the structure inherent in defining high expectations at the expense of creating relationships, which are viewed as costing too much money and time, or as not having as much importance as delivering content to youth. Significantly, those elements of school reform emphasizing high expectations at the expense of building relationships should be considered thoughtfully; high structure with little or no relationship makes school drudgery. Ultimately, the overemphasis on structure can diminish schools' social capital and lead to social Darwinism; schools and organizations high in structure can become highly productive at best, or oppressive and dehumanizing at worst. Schools that define goals in terms of easily measured structures, like normative tests, at the expense of other more meaningful activities and human relationships must be considered in terms of the civic education and the resiliency of youth.

The natural tension between relationship and structure is balanced by providing youth with opportunities for meaningful participation; in such balanced contexts, meeting scholastic and social challenges can be more positive when youth are provided with meaningful opportunities that put them in touch with caring adults who have high expectations of what youth can do. Meaningful participation integrates *becoming-doing* into actions that have value to youth, the school, and community; meaningful participation is the praxis that integrates reflection and action (Claxton, 1997; Freire, 1970).

School counselors are not viewed as critical players in school reform (Paisley & Borders, 1995). The structure-relationship model offers a guide for empowering school counselors to foster relationships in schools that provide care and support for all youth, facilitate youth opportunities for meaningful participation, and encourage all youth to meet high scholastic expectations. Expanding caseloads, quasiadministrative tasks, and other demands challenge school counselors to respond creatively, and this model guides conversations in a manner easily understood by youth, teachers, and administrators.

Resiliency and Youth With Disabilities

Youth with disabilities may require specific interventions in addition to enhancing schoolwide protective factors, such as designing multidisciplinary and multimodal teams to address the needs of the whole person. Counselors may be designated on those teams as strengths advocates and define an important role for looking for strengths. In fact, individualized educational programs (IEPs) can identify and maximize strengths without eliminating the need to detect and accommodate weaknesses that add to risk, and remediation efforts can be directed toward building up youth competence (Gregg, 1996).

For example, "Children with ADHD exhibit many characteristics attributed to creativity and giftedness" (Gregg, 1996, p. 6). They need help with their social skills, but more importantly, they need the unconditional support of at least one "prosocial adult who believes in the child." To help foster the resiliency of disabled youth, conditions must be present that

- give opportunity for bonding to take place;
- increase academic, social skills, and self-esteem to assist youth in successful bonding; and
- recognize and reinforce accomplishments in a consistent and systematic manner (Gregg, 1996).

One responsible and caring adult—teacher, counselor, administrator, relative—can help youth with disabilities become more prosocial. Providing youth with disabilities with coaches or mentors is one way to initiate the bonding relationship. Supporting all facets of a youth's education from art to athletics to reading helps youth with disabilities to find and express possible talents and encourages them to work effectively with others. Developing creative "alternatives to suspension and expulsion— like community service—for all but the most serious offences, to keep from further isolating and alienating" youth with disabilities enables them to remain attached to the school culture (Gregg, 1996, p. 9). Helping these youth find something meaningful to do at school is critical to their future success. Besides encouraging youth with disabilities to acquire the critical skill of reading (there is a high correlation between reading and income), these youth must be encouraged to develop a passion for what they do.

Similarly, it is vital to identify and reinforce each youth's strengths because "every person possesses at least one small 'island of competence,' one that is, or has the potential to be, a source of pride and accomplishment" (Brooks, 1997, p. 391). Teachers who are taught to show personal interest in youth by spending a few extra moments or writing words of encouragement on papers or in notes foster resilience in youth. According to Brooks (1997), "Adults must constantly walk a tightrope when discipline is concerned, maintaining a delicate balance between rigidity and permissiveness, striving to blend warmth, nurturance, acceptance, and humor with realistic expectations, clearcut regulations, and logical and natural consequences" (p. 393). In order to foster resiliency, schools must be made places where youth with and without disabilities experience a growing sense of competence and resulting self-esteem (Brooks, 1994).

ADAPTATIONS FOR DIVERSITY

Diversity is integral to the resiliency paradigm because listening deeply to the experience of others opens up possibilities for understanding and compassion. Each section in this chapter has raised concerns that call upon counselors, teachers, parents, and others to become aware of their personal and professional discourse, to wrestle with the scourge of racism, to listen deeply to the stories of their clients, and, most of all, to see the strengths in their clients, to see the self-righting capacities in all people, and to understand that resiliency approaches are ultimately about empowerment.

SUMMARY

The resiliency paradigm and practice offer counselors, teachers, parents, and others a path back to their roots in education and development. Resiliency research supports an optimistic, longitudinal view of the person and offers a proactive approach for enhancing human development. Benard (1996) has stated emphatically that "The astounding finding from these long-term studies was that at least 50%—and often closer to 70%—of youth growing up in these high-risk conditions did develop social competence despite exposure to severe stress and did overcome the odds to lead successful lives" (p. 7). The paradigm offers counselors, teachers, parents, and others an optimistic and hopeful developmental perspective; a viewpoint that sees people as having innate self-righting capacities for changing their life trajectories; a landscape that defines risks in social contexts rather than in people; and an outlook that asks people to slow down enough to listen deeply to the stories embedded in everyday lives. As Benard (1996) has asserted, the shift to resiliency has the power to "recreate a social covenant grounded in social and economic justice" (p. 11). Resiliency interventions are primarily systemic; link individual, family, school, and community; and require counselors, teachers, parents, and others to consider the ground they stand upon.

At the very least, fostering resiliency in the schools is vital to the well-being of youth (Henderson & Milstein, 1996). Counselors, teachers, parents, and others can look to prevention and practices designed to foster resiliency to help youth learn to live, learn to learn, and learn to work. Helping youth to develop more empowering learning stories is one tool. Benard and Marshall (1997), Mills (1995), and Pransky (1998) have offered powerful approaches for teaching students to recognize their healthy thinking. Lewis (1996; Lewis & Siefer, 1997) has enabled teachers and counselors to initiate conversations that call for high expectations in contexts that provide care and support and opportunities for meaningful participation. Gregg (1996) and Brooks (1997) have reminded counselors, teachers, parents, and others that every youth has a gift or an island of competence that can be tapped if we look. Indeed, the resiliency pathway to protective factors and self-righting narratives calls upon counselors, teachers, parents, and others to see that all people have the innate capacity for common sense and well-being.

REFERENCES

Benard, B. (1991). *Fostering resiliency in kids: Protective factors in the family, school, and community.* Portland, OR: Northwest Regional Educational Laboratory.

Benard, B. (1993). *Turning the corner: From risk to resiliency.* Portland, OR: Northwest Regional Educational Laboratory.

Benard, B. (1994, December). *Applications of resilience: Possibilities and promise.* Paper presented at the Conference of the Role of Resilience in Drug Abuse, Alcohol Abuse, and Mental Illness, Washington, DC.

Benard, B. (1996). From research to practice: The foundations of the resiliency paradigm. *Resiliency in Action, 1*(1), 7–11.

Benard, B. (1997). Changing the condition, place, and view of young people in society: An interview with youth development pioneer Bill Lofquist. *Resiliency in Action, 2*(1), 7–18.

Benard, B., & Marshall, K. (1997). *A framework for practice: Tapping innate resiliency* [On-line]. Center for Applied Research and Educational Improvement (CAREI), College of Education and Human Development, University of Minnesota. Available: http://carei.coled.umn.edu/ResearchPractice/v5n1/benard.htm

Berliner, B. A. (1993). *Adolescence, school transitions, and prevention: A research-based primer.* San Francisco: Far West Regional Educational Laboratory.

Blum, R. W. (1998). Healthy youth development as a model for youth health promotion. *Journal of Adolescent Health, 22,* 368–375.

Brooks, R. B. (1994). Children at risk: Fostering resilience and hope. *American Journal of Orthopsychiatry, 64 ,* 545–553.

Brooks, R. B. (1997). A personal journey: From pessimism and accusation to hope and resilience. *Journal of Child Neurology, 12,* 387–396.

Bruner, J. (1986). *Actual minds, possible worlds.* Cambridge, MA: Harvard University Press.

Bruner, J. (1990). *Acts of meaning.* Cambridge, MA: Harvard University Press.

Children's Defense Fund. (1997). *The state of America's children: Yearbook 1997.* Washington, DC: Author.

Claxton, G. (1997). *Hare brain, tortoise mind: Why intelligence increases when you think less.* London: Fourth Estate.

Clinchy, B. M. (1996). Connected and separate knowing. In N. R. Goldberger, J. M. Tarule, B. M. Clinchy, & M. F. Belenky (Eds.), *Knowledge, difference, and power: Essays inspired by women's ways of knowing.* New York: BasicBooks.

De Jong, P., & Berg, I. K. (1998). *Interviewing for solutions.* Pacific Grove, CA: Brooks/Cole.

Desetta, A., & Wolin, S. (1998). Youth communication: A model program for fostering resilience through the art of writing. *Resiliency in Action 3*(1), 19–23.

Durlak, J. A. (1998). Common risk and protective factors in successful prevention programs. *American Journal of Orthopsychiatry, 68,* 512–521.

Fine, M. (1995). The politics of who's "at risk." In B. B. Swadener & S. Lubeck (Eds.), *Children and families "at promise": Deconstructing the discourse of risk.* Albany: State University of New York Press.

Fredericks, L. (1997). Why children need stories: Storytelling and resiliency. *Resiliency in Action, 2*(3), 26-29.

Freire, P. (1970). *Pedagogy of the oppressed.* New York: Continuum.

Fullan, M. (1993). *Change forces: Probing the depths of educational reform.* Bristol, PA: Falmer Press.

Gibbs, J. (1994). *Tribes: A new way of learning.* Santa Rosa, CA: Center Source.

Gladding, S. T. (1997). Stories and the art of counseling. *Journal of Humanistic Education and Development, 36,* 68–73.

Gladding, S. T. (1998). *Counseling as an art: The creative arts in counseling* (2nd ed.). Alexandria, VA: American Counseling Association.

Goodwin, D. K. (1997). *Wait until next year: A memoir.* New York: Touchstone.

Gregg, S. (1996). Preventing antisocial behavior in disabled and at-risk students. *Policy Briefs.* Charleston, WV: Appalachia Educational Laboratory.

Hayes, R. L. (1993). A facilitative role for counselors in restructuring schools. *Journal of Humanistic Education and Development, 31,* 156–162.

Hayes, R. L., Glickman, C. D., & Lunsford, B. (1996). *Restructuring schools through teacher empowerment.* Unpublished manuscript, University of Georgia, Athens.

Hayes, R. L., & Oppenheim, R. (1997). Constructivism: Reality is what you make it. In T. L. Sexton & B. L Griffin (Eds.), *Constructivist thinking in counseling practice, research, and training* (pp. 19–40). New York: Teachers College Press.

Henderson, N., & Milstein, M. M. (1996). *Resiliency in schools: Making it happen for students and educators.* Thousand Oaks, CA: Corwin Press.

Kitashima, M. (1997). Lessons from my life: No more "children at risk" . . . all children are "at promise." *Resiliency in Action, 2*(3), 30–36.

L'Abate, L. (1992). *Programmed writing: A paratherapeutic approach for intervention with individuals, couples, and families.* Pacific Grove, CA: Brooks/Cole.

L'Abate, L. (1994). *A theory of personality development.* New York: Wiley.

Langer, E. J. (1997). *The power of mindful learning.* Reading, MA: Addison-Wesley.

Lewis, R. (1995). *A Write Way: Programmed writing effects on high school math students' attendance, homework, grades, and attributions.* Unpublished doctoral dissertation, University of San Francisco, California.

Lewis, R. E. (1996). Writing changes lives: Counselors and English teachers working together. *Oregon English Journal, 18,* 8–12.

Lewis, R. E. (1999). A Write Way: Fostering resiliency during transitions. *Journal of Humanistic Education and Development, 37,* 200–211.

Lewis, R. E., & Siefer, R. L. (1997). Teacher education: A course shifts to resiliency. *Resiliency in Action, 2*(4), 29–31.

Lifton, R. J. (1993). *The protean self: Human resilience in an age of fragmentation.* New York: Basic Books.

Linquanti, R. (1992). *Using community-wide collaboration to foster resiliency in kids: A conceptual framework.* Portland, OR: Northwest Regional Educational Laboratory.

Macfarlane, A. H. (1998, November). Hui: *A process for conferencing in schools.* Paper presented at the Western Association for Counselor Education and Supervision Conference, Seattle, WA.

Masten, A. S. (1994). Resilience in individual development: Successful adaptation despite risk and adversity. In M. C. Wang & E. W. Gordon (Eds.), *Educational resilience in inner-city America: Challenges and prospects* (pp. 3–25). Hillsdale, NJ: Erlbaum.

McWhirter, J. J., McWhirter, B. T., McWhirter, A. M., McWhirter, E. H. (1998). *At-risk youth: A comprehensive response* (2nd ed.). Pacific Grove, CA: Brooks/Cole.

Mills, R. C. (1995). *Realizing mental health: Toward a new psychology of resiliency*. New York: Sulzburger and Graham.

Mills, R. C. (1996, August). *Empowering individuals and communities through health realization: Psychology of mind in prevention and community revitalization*. Paper presented at the meeting of the American Psychological Association, Toronto, Canada.

Mills, R. C. (1997). *Comprehensive health realization community empowerment projects: List of completed and current projects*. Long Beach, CA: R.C. Mills & Associates.

Mills, R. C., & Spittle, E. B. (1998). *A community empowerment primer*. Long Beach, CA: R.C. Mills & Associates.

Monk, G., Winslade, J., Crocket, K., Epston, D. (Eds.). (1997). *Narrative therapy in practice: The archaeology of hope*. San Francisco: Jossey-Bass.

Paisley, P. O., & Borders, L. D. (1995). School counseling: An evolving speciality. *Journal of Counseling and Development, 74*, 150–153.

Palmer, P. J. (1998/1999, December/January). Evoking the spirit in public education. *Educational Leadership, 56*, 6–11.

Parry, A., & Doan, R. E. (1994). *Story re-visions: Narrative therapy in the postmodern world*. New York: Guilford Press.

Pennebaker, J. W. (1997). *Opening up: The healing power of confiding in others*. New York: Guilford Press.

Pransky, G. S. (1998). *The renaissance of psychology*. New York: Sulzburger and Graham.

Pransky, G. S., Mills, R. C., Sedgeman, J. A., & Bleven, J. K. (1997). An emerging paradigm for brief treatment. In L. Vandecreek, S. Knapp, T. L. Jackson (Eds.), *Innovations in clinical practice: A source book* (Vol. 15, pp. 401–420). Sarasota, FL: Professional Resource Press.

Quattrociocchi, S. M., & Peterson, B. (1997). *Giving children hope and skills for the 21st century*. Olympia, WA: WOIS/Career Information System.

Rak, C. F., & Patterson, L. E. (1996). Promoting resilience in at-risk children. *Journal of Counseling and Development, 74*, 368–373.

Resnick, M.D., Bearman, P.S., Blum, R. W., Bauman, K. E., Harris, K. M., Jones, J., Tabor, J., Beuhring, T., Sieving, R. E., Shew, M., Ireland, M., Bearinger, L. H., & Udry, J. R. (1998). Protecting adolescents from harm: Findings from the national longitudinal study on adolescent health. *Journal of the American Medical Association, 278*, 823–832.

Reynolds, A. J. (1998). Resilience among Black urban youth: Prevalence, intervention effects, and mechanisms of influence. *American Journal of Orthopsychiatry, 68*, 84–100.

Riordan, R. J. (1996). Scriptotherapy: Therapeutic writing as a counseling adjunct. *Journal of Counseling and Development, 74*, 263–269.

Robinson, T. L. (1999). The intersections of dominant discourses across, race, gender, and other identities. *Journal of Counseling and Development, 77*, 73–79.

Robinson, T. L., & Ginter, E. J. (1999). Introduction to the special issue on racism. *Journal of Counseling and Development, 77*, 3.

Rockwell, S. (1998). Overcoming four myths that prevent fostering resilience. *Reaching Today's Youth, 2*(3), 14–17.

Rutter, M. (1987). Prosocial resilience and protective mechanisms. *American Journal of Orthopsychiatry, 57*, 316–331.

Saleebey, D. (Ed.). (1997). *The strengths perspective in social work practice* (2nd ed.). White Plains, NY: Longman.

Sarbin , T. R. (Ed.). (1986). *Narrative psychology: The storied nature of human conduct.* New York: Praeger.

Scherer, M. (1998/1999, December/January). Linking education with the spiritual. *Educational Leadership, 56*, 5.

Swadener, B. B., & Lubeck, S. (Eds.). (1995). *Children and families "at promise": Deconstructing the discourse of risk.* Albany: State University of New York Press.

Werner, E. E. (1989). Children of the garden island. *Scientific American, 260*(4), 106–111.

Werner, E. E. (1996). How children become resilient. Observations and cautions. *Resiliency in Action, 1*(1), 18–28.

Werner, E. E. (1998). Resilience and the life-span perspective: What we have learned—so far. *Resiliency in Action, 3*(4), 1, 3, 7–9.

Werner, E. E., Bierman, J. M., & French, F. E. (1971). *The children of Kauai.* Honolulu: University of Hawaii Press.

Werner, E. E., & Smith, R. S. (1977). *Kauai's children come of age.* Honolulu: University of Hawaii Press.

Werner, E. E., & Smith, R. S. (1982). *Vulnerable but invincible: A longitudinal study of resilient children and youth.* New York: McGraw Hill.

Werner, E. E., & Smith, R. S. (1992). *Overcoming the odds: High-risk children from birth to adulthood.* Ithaca, NY: Cornell University Press.

Wesley, D. C. (1998/1999, December/January). Believing in our students. *Educational Leadership, 56*, 42–45.

White, M., & Epston, D. (1990). *Narrative means to therapeutic ends.* New York: Norton.

Winslade, J., & Monk, G. (1999). *Narrative counseling in schools: Powerful and brief.* Thousand Oaks, CA: Corwin Press.

APPENDIX 3–1

Name _____ Date _____

LESSON: THE STORY OF SCHOOL

We all have stories about school. Some of them are good, some of them are not. In fact, some stories about school can be painful, even when we say they were not. This lesson's goal is to help you look at your own school story and to take steps toward strengthening it.

This lesson will ask a series of questions related to your school story.

TIME

Stories exist in time and space. Let's begin first by looking at your past, then by looking at your future.

Four years ago, you were probably in the fifth grade. Now you are in the ninth. By meeting the requirements, you will graduate in 4 years.

1. Who were important people to you back in grade school? _____

2. What did you like about school? _____

3. What did you not like about school? _____

4. Where did you go when you needed help with school or problems?

   _____

5. Who helped you the most? _____

6. Think back 4 years, describe two important things you learned or experienced since the fifth grade.

   1. _____

   2. _____

7. Describe your best or most powerful moment in the last 4 years.

   _____

Look forward 4 years: What you will be able to say about what you have learned or experienced at Resiliency High? Write a few lines for Resiliency's school newspaper about what a great student you have been at Resiliency. Remember, this is a story. Make it up.

_____

SUBJECTS

We are better in some classes than others.

Which subject has been your favorite? Why?

_____

Which subject have you not liked or avoided? Why? _____

_____

TEACHERS

Who is the best teacher you ever had? (Maybe that teacher is really your mother, father, uncle, aunt, friend, etc.)

    Name _____

What did this person do to help you learn?

_____

Who is the worst teacher you ever had? What did this other teacher do to make you feel bad about yourself as a learner?

_____

Write a make-believe letter to this person about the following:

1. How you view what happened.
2. Why it was a problem for you.
3. How it hurt or got you angry.
4. How you are going to get the most from your education.

Note: You can use any language or words you want to.

Dear _____:

_____

_____

_____

MATH, TEACHERS, AND PRACTICING APPROACH

Many people avoid math because it is difficult. For many people, it is easier to avoid some things than face them. Math is frequently one of those things that students avoid. At Resiliency High, given the two required math proficiency exams and the 30-credit requirement, it is impossible to avoid math if you want to graduate.

What do you like most or least about math? _____

Running away from any problem does not always help, and it does take some courage to approach problems.

Describe two problems that you face everyday (for instance, getting to class on time, finishing homework, helping the family, or even math).

_____

Give an example of a time you tackled a problem _____

Would things have been better or worse if you avoided the problem?

_____

Finish this sentence: The problem with math is _____

Let's look at approaching math. During the time between this lesson and the next one, practice asking your math teacher at least one question per day. If too many other students in math ask, practice asking one of your other teachers questions.

Here's the trick. Start with what you know, then ask about what you do not know. For instance, I know $2 + 2 = 4$ but I do not know what $2 + -2$ equals.

Here are three basic question stems to use with your teacher:

Could you tell me how to _____

Could you show me how to _____

What have I done right?

Now, could you tell me how Lesson Two helps? _____

_____

_____

Thank you for your efforts.

PART	EXAMINING
TWO	THE CAUSES

Building on the foundational information in Part One, the four chapters that compose Part Two provide the reader with current and comprehensive information regarding the factors generally considered to be causal to the development of at-risk behaviors. It is important to keep in mind that it is impossible to draw a direct cause-effect relationship between any one of the four major factors identified—dysfunctional family, low self-esteem, depression, and stress and trauma—and any of the nine specific behaviors identified in the nine chapters of Part Three of this text. Authors in Part Two understand this and caution their readers to view these causal factors as both cumulative and cyclical. This perspective enhances the awareness that taken separately any one of these causal dimensions enhances the likelihood of at-riskness in youth. When viewed from a cumulative and cyclical perspective, the development of at-risk behaviors is almost inevitable.

Chapter 4, The Harmful Effects of Dysfunctional Family Dynamics, spells out the various gradations of family dysfunctionality and couples this with case examples to enhance the readers' understanding. The authors elaborate on five causal factors within the family dynamic that enhance the possibility of at-riskness in youth: at-risk adults parenting, parental conflict, family denial, parentification of children, and serious illness and disability within the family. Again, case examples highlight these explanations. After presenting some invaluable information on the incidence and impact of abuse and neglect, the chapter ends with a discussion of prevention approaches aimed at ameliorating the identified causal factors.

Chapter 5, Who Cares What I Think: Problems of Low Self-Esteem, touches upon a causal factor that permeates any discussion of at-risk behaviors. The information in this chapter includes not only definitions and indicators of low self-esteem but also causal factors from parental, social, psychological, physical, environmental, and cultural perspectives. Prevention approaches are presented from individual, family, school, community, and global perspectives. The case study provides a realistic application of the approaches described.

Chapter 6, Preventing and Treating Depression in Children and Adolescents, approaches the topic by illuminating the complex issues of both definition and diagnosis. The case study of Esteban provides a central theme around which the authors present information dealing with causal factors from biological, psychodynamic, behavioral, cognitive, and family perspectives. Individual, family, school, and community based prevention and treatment programs are described. The chapter ends with the presentation of the authors' approach to comprehensive intervention and adaptions for multicultural sensitivity.

Chapter 7, Stress and Trauma: Coping in Today's Society, begins by presenting the confusion surrounding the definition of stress and delineates four perspectives on stress and traumatic stress: stimulus-oriented views, response-oriented views, stress as a transaction between the person and the environment, and trauma and posttraumatic stress. From this foundation, the author presents six factors that may have a causal relationship to the development of at-risk behaviors. Approaches to prevention from individual, family, school, and community perspectives, followed by a discussion of coping from an ethnocultural perspective, conclude the chapter.

4 | The Impact of Dysfunctional Family Dynamics on Children and Adolescents

Cass Dykeman and Valerie E. Appleton

In their influential work on high-risk youth in schools, Pianta and Walsh (1996) defined the term *at-risk status* in reference to youth. They described at-risk status as the likelihood that a given youth will attain a specific outcome, given certain conditions. The specific outcomes of concern for this book were presented in chapter 1. This chapter explores dysfunctional family dynamics as the certain condition. In addition, this chapter provides readers with some practical ways to prevent at-risk status in youth.

The level of dysfunction in families can vary widely. Moreover, severity of at-risk status runs parallels to severity of family dysfunction. Thus this chapter first defines the multileveled nature of family dysfunction and then examines causal factors, that is, the specific family situations that both precede and fuel at-risk behaviors. The final section considers prevention at the individual, family, school, and community levels.

DEFINITIONS OF FAMILY DYSFUNCTION LEVELS

When examining the level of dysfunction in family dynamics, it is possible to classify families at either the moderate dysfunction level or severe dysfunction level. This classifying is important because severity level suggests the appropriate interventions to be used. This section defines the distinctions between the moderate and severe levels of dysfunction so as to enable the reader to be better able to consider family dynamics when planning work with youth and/or parents.

Moderate Dysfunction

In families at the moderate dysfunction level, each parent presents an appropriate image to the outside world. Hence, it is difficult to believe that there may be severe problems with one of the children. However, below the surface and hidden from the community view are problems that the family is not willing to reveal. The at-risk youth becomes the not-so-popular messenger, letting the community know that the family has secrets and is not perfect. The advantage of working with families at the moderate dysfunctional level is that the adults are competent in dealing with the basic aspects of life (e.g., work, providing food). The following case study fleshes out how a family at this level of dysfunction may present itself:

> *Case study.*   Derek Jones was a high school junior who was failing several classes. In addition, he appeared quite depressed at times. Mr. and Mrs. Jones were college-educated professionals who were well known in the local community. In terms of family dynamics, Mr. Jones had a very bad temper and engaged in frequent arguments with Derek. When these arguments happened, Mrs. Jones always sided with Derek against his father. Mrs. Jones' consistent siding with Derek caused significant problems between Mr. Jones and Mrs. Jones. The tension in the Jones family all came to a head when Derek's failing quarter grades were posted. After these grades were posted, Derek's counselor Mr. Dykeman called together Derek, his parents, and his teachers for a before-school conference.
>
> At the start of the conference, Mr. and Mrs. Jones voiced their concern and willingness to do what was necessary to have Derek be more successful and happy. However, as the conference proceeded, the dysfunctional patterns of communication just noted appeared. In the middle of the conference a heated argument on TV privileges broke out between Mr. Jones and Derek. After a few minutes of arguing, Derek broke down in tears. Derek's teariness led Mrs. Jones to put her arm around him and cry as well. At this point, the school bell rang signaling 5 minutes until the start of first period for Derek and his teachers. The teachers immediately got up and headed for their classes. After his tears had stopped, Derek was given a hall pass and also left for first period.
>
> With Derek gone, Mr. Jones expressed his remorse for fighting with Derek and his frustration that Mrs. Jones did not enforce the TV rules when he was gone. Mr. Dykeman first empathized with Mr. Jones' remorse and frustration as well as Mrs. Jones' sadness. Then he noted that the Joneses had problems that were common to parents of teenagers, and that were fixable. Mr. Dykeman referred the Joneses to Ms. Appleton, a local family therapist known for brief and effective treatment of families with communication problems. Because Mr. Dykeman couched his description of the Joneses' difficulties as both normative and fixable, the Joneses were able to consider his advice without further loss to their self-esteem or self-efficacy. Indeed, the Joneses appeared grateful for Mr. Dykeman's suggestions as well as his confidence in their ability to heal their family.

In family therapy, Mr. and Mrs. Jones began to understand the need for cooperation between themselves if there was to be any change in Derek. After a few weeks, Mr. Jones began simply to talk with Derek rather than yell. Mrs. Jones no longer took Derek's side during arguments and did not undercut Mr. Jones' attempts to enforce appropriate rules. Derek eventually quit using one parent against the other to get his way. Moreover, Derek and his father were able to establish a satisfying relationship with each other.

Severe Dysfunction

In the family at the severe dysfunction level, one or more adults may exhibit many at-risk behaviors such as substance abuse. In working with severely dysfunctional families, a professional encounters adults functioning at an even lower level than their children! This collapse of adult child differentiation in functioning limits the extent to which professionals can effectively intervene in the life of an at-risk child. The following case study illuminates this difficulty:

Case study. Susan Smith was a high school junior with a long history of school attendance problems. She lived with her mother, Ms. Baker, and her mother's new live-in boy friend, Mr. Green. Susan has never met her biological father. Ms. Baker and Mr. Green both currently abuse alcohol and marijuana. On more than one occasion, Susan and her mother smoked marijuana together. Ms. Baker and Mr. Green are both currently unemployed and live on public assistance. The relationship between Ms. Baker and Mr. Green has been conflictual since he moved in 6 months ago. The two have frequent battles over money, friends, and drugs.

In the summer between her sophomore and junior year, Susan lived with her Aunt Joan and her older cousin Katie in a town on the other side of the state. Susan was impressed by how Katie seemed to have her life all together. When Susan moved back home at the end of the summer, she vowed to "get her act together." In contrast to previous years, Susan's attendance during the first quarter of her junior year was excellent. She was well liked by both teachers and peers and maintained a B average. Susan dreamed of going to the local community college to study fashion merchandising like her older cousin Katie. However, as winter quarter began, the fighting at home between Ms. Baker and Mr. Green worsened exponentially. As Susan sought to escape this fighting by smoking marijuana, her attendance began to slide.

Concerned about the slip in attendance of a talented fashion design student, Susan's consumer and family life teacher asked if the school counselor, Mr. Dykeman, would talk to Susan. Mr. Dykeman called Susan into his office and expressed the concern everyone at school had about Susan's sliding attendance. Susan claimed that she had been feeling ill lately and that other than that, everything was fine. She rebuffed all of Mr. Dykeman's gentle invites to talk about the issues that concerned her. After the conference with Susan, Mr. Dykeman attempted to call Ms. Baker. However, Ms. Baker's phone had been disconnected. Mr. Dykeman sent a letter to Ms.

Baker asking her to contact him. However, she never responded to that letter. By the middle of winter quarter, Susan had stopped coming to school
completely.

CAUSAL FACTORS

Before working with at-risk youth, it is important to understand how dysfunctional family dynamics can lead to specific destructive behavioral
patterns in youth. Dysfunctional family dynamics create an invidious
emotional atmosphere for at-risk youth. Such an atmosphere produces
severe personal stress and emotional upheaval. Moreover, this highly
charged emotional atmosphere causes the at-risk youth to accommodate
his or her behavior in such a way as to reduce the internal stress and
upheaval. Accommodating the stress and upheaval creates problem
behaviors such as poor school performance, depression, anorexia, loss of
control, and a myriad other at-risk behaviors. This section first examines
specific family factors that lead to these problem behaviors and then the
incidence and impact of abuse and neglect.

Specific Family Factors

At-risk adults parenting, parental conflict, family denial, parentification
of children, and serious illness and disability are among the specific family factors that contribute to youth at-riskness.

At-Risk Adults Parenting.   We can gain critical insight on the direction
and depth of the problems exhibited by an at-risk youth through cultivat-
ing an awareness of the problems of the youth's parents. The problematic
behaviors of the at-risk youth and his or her at-risk parents may differ, but
the end goals of these separate behaviors are typically parallel. The following case study illustrates this point:

> *Case study.*   Bob Adams was a 45-year-old father of two who had been
> married for 24 years to Terri. Both were professional people with highly
> responsible jobs. Bob had a severe drinking problem that had affected the
> family for years. Also, Bob had been consistently impervious to suggestions
> that he address his problem. Bob and Terri's two daughters, aged 17 and 19,
> were both high achievers in high school. Despite Bob's problems the
> Adamses appeared as a picture-perfect family to other members of the com-
> munity. However, when the oldest daughter Mary left for college this
> appearance began to give way, and the family's underlying dysfunction
> emerged.
> Although initially excited to go off to college, Mary soon found herself
> consumed with worries about her family; she had always been the one to

smooth over conflicts between mom and dad. She found that these worries left her little time for peers or academics. She returned home after only passing one course during the fall quarter. After being home for the entire year, she applied to another college and went off to school once again. Needless to say, she could not stay at the new college either, returning home after only a few weeks. At about this time, Bob had a severe alcoholic episode and had to be brought home in a taxi one evening because of his drunkenness. He fought with his wife and destroyed the house before being hospitalized for several days. He checked out of the hospital before treatment was completed and against medical advice.

Mary's reaction to all of the confusion in her life was to take a bottle of pills. Her attempt at suicide was a cry for help—one that almost cost Mary her life. In trying to fix her parents and their marriage, she became unable to manage her own life.

This case demonstrates several important points. First, the father's severe drinking problem both produced and directed his daughter's at-risk behavior. Second, by never getting her life together, Mary avoided leaving home and abandoning her parents for whom and to whom she feels responsible. As many family therapists would conclude, Mary rescued the marriage and family by putting herself at risk. Thus if a counselor attempted to work with Mary's suicidal feelings independent of her family role as the rescuer, the counseling would be doomed to fail.

One final note of importance needs to be mentioned. The transmission of at-risk tendencies from parent to child is much easier to see in families at the severe dysfunction level. Families at the moderate level generally possess the skills to hide problems. The at-risk behaviors in youth from families at this level can appear to exist without cause. However, rarely does an at-risk youth emerge sui generis (i.e., self-generated). While keeping mindful that exceptions do exist, we should always seek to understand the underlying family aspects of a youth's at-risk behavior. Otherwise, work with at-risk youth may never amount to more than the bandaging of symptoms.

Parental Conflict. If parents are having difficulty processing conflict between themselves, the situation is likely to deteriorate into communication problems between the parents. This problem also extends to communication problems between parents and children. Secrets begin to exist between the parents. In the conflict between parents, children often become the emotional pawns in the intensified atmosphere of the home. For instance, Shaw, Keenan, Vondra, Delliquandri, and Givannelli (1997) found parent conflict to be a direct correlate of at-risk behaviors in children.

Conflict between parents also leads to power struggles in parenting children. Each parent attempts to structure his or her relationship with the child as an individual instead of as a member of the marital unit. Loyalty issues are pressed onto the child. For example, a teenager comes home after curfew and is grounded for a week by the father. However, after 2 days mother allows the teenager to visit friends but says, "Don't tell Dad!" This pattern of deceit between parents empowers the at-risk youth in two ways. First, the youth learns not to follow rules, and second, the youth learns to be deceitful. As family functioning begins to deteriorate, the youth will begin to demonstrate increasingly maladaptive behavior (Cumsille & Epstein, 1994). The following case study concretizes this process:

> *Case study.* James Cooper was a 10-year-old fourth grader who was in frequent difficulties at school and in the community. His teacher reported him to be an aggressive, high-energy boy with a low attention span. However, his level of inappropriate conduct was never very severe until the day he assaulted another student on the playground during recess. The student he assaulted had to go to the emergency room for four stitches. At that time, James' parents were forced to enter counseling in order to assist him with his anger management program. Completion of this anger management program was the main prerequisite for the school district's lifting of James' suspension. In the family counseling part of the anger management program, it was immediately evident that Mr. and Mrs. Cooper had a very long history of marital and parental discord. Mr. Cooper was upset with Mrs. Cooper over numerous issues. These included an affair, overspending, poor discipline of the children, and meddling in-laws. Both Mr. and Mrs. Cooper reported that their fighting had escalated recently. Given the Coopers' marital trauma, the assault can be viewed as the inevitable act of a high-energy, aggressive boy who needed to create a major problem in order to bring his parents back together.

This brief example demonstrates several important points about the struggles faced by at-risk youth. First, it is difficult to discipline a youth having severe difficulties without complete cooperation between the parents. One parent undercutting the effectiveness of the other makes it impossible to bring about change in the family, and creates a situation in which the youth can become at risk. Second, loyalty issues between family members can create severe problems if the loyalty lines are inappropriately drawn (Visher & Visher, 1996). A youth who is dependent upon one parent can become angry at the other parent and attempt various at-risk behaviors. In other words, Parent A will fight Parent B through the at-risk behavior of their children.

Third, a youth's temperament will shape the at-risk behaviors the youth uses to heal family trauma. For example, an aggressive youth may choose fighting, whereas a depressed youth may choose a self-destructive act such as a suicide attempt. Finally, parental conflict can lead to divorce. To oversimplify a difficult and complex problem, a divorce happens when two people fail to communicate and resolve conflicts. Following divorce, if a youth exhibits at-risk behaviors, it usually takes a significant problem to force the parents to face the gravity of the issues. Kitzman and Emery (1994) reported that parental conflict after divorce is a significant problem for children—a problem because youth give voice to their concerns over parental conflict through at-risk behaviors.

Family Denial. Denial is the defense mechanism in which problems and/or their intensity are ignored or redirected. Denial is acted out in two ways within families. The first way is by burying one's head in the sand, that is, by ignoring the reality of the situation. The second way is by finger pointing, that is, by blaming other persons or events for the problems. Both methods of enacting denial lead to youth becoming at risk. The following case study illustrates the effect of denial on the development of at-risk youth:

> *Case study.* Kathy was a 17-year-old senior who had become increasingly defiant with her parents. The parents attributed the defiance to Kathy's boyfriend of the past 8 months. She began to stay out beyond her assigned curfew, her grades at school declined, and her attitude at home became progressively negative. At various times over the end of her junior year and the beginning of her senior year, Kathy became ill and was unable to work or attend school. Her parents suspected that she was pregnant, but Kathy denied that she was. Throughout this period of time, the parents were concerned about Kathy's relationship with her 20-year-old boyfriend. They had frequent violent arguments with Kathy about her need to see him less or break off the relationship.
>
> During the second month of her senior year, Kathy had a baby. The parents never knew she was pregnant until the night Kathy's water broke at home. After being rushed to the hospital, Kathy gave birth to a baby with numerous disabilities who lived only several months. During this time, the parents and Kathy continued to battle over the relationship with the baby's father.

This tragic case study presents the ultimate example of denial of a major problem while focusing on a serious, but tangential problem. Kathy's parents ignored the issue of the pregnancy, even though they strongly suspected something was physically wrong with their daughter. Rather than having their daughter examined by a physician, the parents went along with Kathy's denial. Instead of directly confronting issues with children, parents tend to allow them to have the power over major decisions in their lives. The parents wanted to believe that Kathy was fine, but knew in their own minds she was not. Therefore, not wanting to risk a battle with Kathy, they denied that anything was wrong and placed their daughter in the at-risk category.

If Kathy's parents had become involved earlier in the process, a tragedy could have been avoided. Because the parents could only focus on Kathy's relationship, they could not see the larger picture. Kathy's relationship with her boyfriend was symbolic of the gap in the relationship between herself and her parents. Specifically, Kathy's parents had lost control of their relationship with Kathy, and they could not face their responsibility in having let this loss occur. Kathy's parents used denial to avoid examining the problems they had, and affixed all the blame to the boyfriend. Because of their strong denial, they placed their child in an at-risk situation.

Parentification of Children. One dysfunctional pattern of family dynamics that begins in the early years of childhood is parentification of children. This pattern occurs when parents give responsibilities and privileges to younger children that would be more appropriate for older children or adults. Young children, by their actions and requests, maintain the control of the household and frequently dictate the mood of the entire family. Parents, fearful of disrupting the family calm, refrain from effective discipline techniques. Thus the children gain control of the family.

Parentified children are placed in situations in which they are given the power to make decisions that belong with the parents. The parents, by giving the power to the child, abdicate their responsibility for protecting the child from potentially dangerous situations. A brief case study helps to demonstrate this parentification process:

Case study. Ray, a 10th grader, was referred by a student to Mrs. Wall, an English teacher and the Natural Helpers adviser. Ray was referred by the student because he was overheard saying that he wanted to die. After talking with Ray, his school counselor assessed that Ray was at moderate risk for suicide and thus immediately contacted Ray's parents. The school counselor referred Ray's parents to three private practice counselors known for their strong skills with adolescents. Ray objected to the counseling and said he would not go to see anyone. The parents contacted one of the referred counselors and asked for a suggestion as to how they could get him into counseling. The counselor told them to tell Ray that he had no choice in the matter and that he had to go to counseling. This approach worked, and Ray and his family appeared at the counselor's office for help.

Ray was seen for three sessions alone and one family session. After these sessions, the counselor provided the family with his feedback, suggesting that Ray remain in counseling to deal with his depression, mood swings, and suicidal tendencies. The parents were told that some family counseling would help them to deal more effectively with Ray. After the feedback session, the mother and father said they would let Ray decide because the counseling was for him! Even though they were told about Ray's depression and suicidal ideation, they felt Ray had to make the decision because they did not want to have to "fight" with him to get him to attend counseling sessions.

In this instance, the well-being of the child was left with the child because the parents did not take control of the situation. By permitting a child to make such decisions, the at-risk status increases significantly. The parentification process not only impacts dramatic issues such as suicide but also accelerates the at-risk status of youth confronting common teenage problems such as academic failure or alcohol use.

This parentification is a common byproduct of divorce. As the conflict between divorcing parents escalates, more and more self-care is left to the child. Very young children are sometimes even expected to carry the burden for maintaining the well-being of the parents during the separation and divorce process. As long as the child is behaving, giving attention to the parents, and causing no apparent difficulty, life is fine. The burden can become intense as the child grows and matures. It is very tiring to always be happy, provide love for a parent, care for other children, and be adult-like. In these cases, the parents report that the child has never been a difficulty, but rather the ideal child who always took care of everything.

Children and youth want to be in control of the decisions that affect their lives and will take every opportunity to gather more power. Parents must be encouraged to involve their children in the decision-making process, but they should be reminded that involvement is different from making a final decision. Final decisions belong to the parents, not the children. When the child makes the choices alone, at-risk status is inevitable.

Serious Illness and Disability Within the Family. Serious illness and disability can catapult a family into a trauma response and affect their ability to maintain healthy coping. Consider an example in which the father has a newly diagnosed heart condition but denies his symptoms to his family. He might fear his role as the provider will be questioned. If the parents are unable to discuss the issue with each other, or with the children, the family members are left more vulnerable to fears and fantasies about how bad the situation is. As secrecy or even dishonesty or deceit increase, these families become more at risk and sensitive at home, work, or school.

Kazak , Christakis, Alderfer, and Coiro (1994) discussed the impact of illness in families. They suggested that (a) family members tend to overreact to simple problems, (b) parents are protective of the children, and (c) in general, the entire family is acutely sensitive. In an attempt to cope with this sensitivity, the family may focus on less serious problems and concerns. Thus denial becomes a major risk aspect. This denial can be considered dysfunctional. However, it can also be understood as an expected part of the reaction to trauma (Aguilera & Messick, 1986).

Typically, families go through a series of stages in coping with the shock of diagnosis of an illness, disability, hospitalizations, and treatment. There is a movement from defensive coping strategies such as denial or anger toward more functional ways of coping. The families at greatest risk are those unable to move toward the last stage. They remain mired in defensive coping patterns that affect all members in negative ways. The following case study illustrates the high at-risk status of families in which there is an inability to address a child's suffering:

Case study. Jeff Stone was a 7-year-old brought to the Riverbend Pediatric Hospital for rehabilitation surgery. The surgery was for a hand, deformed at birth, that was shrunken and twisted. All Stone family members referred to this appendage as "the paw." When Jeff experienced anxiety about reconstructive surgery, the Stones were unable to discuss the hand with him because this issue had been avoided from the time of Jeff's birth. Mr. and Mrs. Stone felt tremendous guilt over their boy's disability. The consulting counselor to the surgery unit, Mrs. Macintosh, suggested the boy draw a person as part of his initial assessment. The boy drew an image of a teddy bear with a deformed paw. Mrs. Macintosh also observed the defensive nature of the family coping.

After the initial assessment, Mrs. Macintosh worked to increase family communications and to address denial. She invented a game called Secrets. In it, the family members examined the names they gave things that bothered them at home, school, or work. While playing the game, Mrs. Stone was able to disclose that the paw was her way to avoid discussing the boy's disability, or embarrassing him or the other family members. Mrs. Stone hoped that the reference to a paw was easier on Jeff and family. When this issue arose, the father and siblings spoke of the the paw despairingly. With Mrs. Macintosh's assistance, the boy was able to share his feelings of inferiority in the family and of feeling like a nonperson (or stuffed bear). Through these disclosures it was clear no one in the family was comfortable with the term *the paw*.

In follow-up counseling, medical staff were accessed to discuss the diagnosis and plans for rehabilitation of the boy's weak hand. Mrs. Macintosh explored ways for the family to discuss the disability openly. In this way both medical information and counseling encouraged exploration of more open communication during and after the surgery process. The Stones had begun to learn a new way to cope with difficult issues by discussing them together.

As the case example demonstrates, the family faced with an illness or disability must handle many emotionally charged issues. Because there is relatively little support in the medical setting for such issues, appropriate referral is critical. In most instances, problematic family issues that existed before the medical crisis are exaggerated during the trauma of illness, loss of function, surgery, and other medical interventions. Fortunately, diagnosis and medical intervention also provide an opportunity for change. In states of crisis and trauma, otherwise rigid or resistant families may be responsive to psychosocial resources. In this way, the danger of the illness can provide new opportunities for change in the communication and coping systems within the family.

The Incidence and Impact of Abuse and Neglect

Atrocities of violence against children are among the most difficult to discuss. However, abuse is a historical problem that does not go away. In fact, as professionals are trained to understand and report abuse, the number of reported cases has risen dramatically. A consideration of the incidence and impact of abuse and neglect will help us recognize those children who are at the highest risk for maltreatment.

In 1973, the Child Abuse Prevention and Treatment Act (Public Law 93-247) defined the legal responsibilities of health care providers encountering child abuse or neglect. Intervention is defined as social, legal, medical, or any combination of the aforementioned. Congress declared that child abuse and neglect means the physical and mental injury, sexual abuse, negligent treatment or maltreatment, of the child under age 18 by a person who is responsible for the child's welfare under circumstances that indicate the child's health or welfare is thereby harmed or threatened. Every state now has within its statutes a legal definition of abuse.

Incidence. The United States Congress mandated reports documenting the incidence of child abuse and neglect in this country. For each National Incidence Study of Child Abuse and Neglect (NIS), professionals across a spectrum of schools and agencies act as sentinels and gather data about abuse incidences. In this way, the NIS estimates provide a more complete measure of the scope of child abuse and neglect than is known to community professionals but that may not be included in official statistics. The most recent NIS study is NIS-3 (Sedlak & Broadhurst, 1996).

NIS-3, which covered a 7-year period, reported an alarming increase in the incidence of child abuse and neglect. This report revealed that the number of abused and neglected children had nearly doubled between 1986 and 1993, and that an estimated 1,553,800 children in this country were abused or neglected. Physical abuse had almost doubled; sexual abuse had more than doubled. The number of children seriously injured and endangered had quadrupled.

The NIS-3 study also found specific characteristics of the abused and neglected children and the families in which abuse and neglect occurred most often. The factors that contributed to the highest incidence of abuse include the child's gender and age, the family's income, and the family's size. Race was not a significant factor in the incidence of maltreatment or injury.

Child's age. There is little reporting of sexual abuse in children from ages 1 to 3, but the number of children vulnerable to sexual abuse is consistent from age 3 forward, with reports of sexual abuse distributed evenly across these children. This flattening of the age differences is provocative and suggests a broad range of vulnerability for sexual abuse starting in preschool. In terms of neglect, there is a near linear comparison between the child's age and risk for maltreatment. However, the lower incidence of reported abuse in young children might reflect under-coverage of these children. As children mature, they are involved with an increasing number of community professionals who can observe them and make appropriate investigations. They may also be better able to escape, retaliate, or ask for help.

Child's gender. Girls are most vulnerable to sexual abuse, at a rate three times higher than boys. Because serious injury can accompany sexual abuse, girls have higher incidence rates for injury. Boys are at greater risk for other forms of maltreatment, and they are 24% more likely than girls to be emotionally neglected and to suffer serious injury resulting in death.

Child's family. The demographics of the family are also linked to incidences of child maltreatment (Sedlak & Broadhurst, 1996). Children of single parents have a 77% greater risk of being harmed by physical abuse, and an 87% higher risk of physical neglect, than children living with both parents. Children in the largest families are physically neglected at about three times the rate of those who are single children. Children in poverty that is, in families with an annual income of less than $15,000, are 25 times more likely to suffer some form of maltreatment than children in families with an annual income of more than $30,000 per year. Moreover, poverty is directly linked with the incidence of sexual abuse and serious harm. Children in the lowest income families are more likely to be sexually abused and to suffer serious injury from maltreatment.

Impact. Abuse is an issue of control and power, whether it is perpetrated within or outside the family. The impact of physical and sexual abuse is directly related to intensity, the amount of coercion, and level of conflict involved. Terr (1988) distinguished between two kinds of trauma. A single traumatic event in an otherwise normal life is called Type I trauma, and the effects of prolonged and repeated trauma are called Type II trauma. Within families, children are more likely to suffer Type II trauma and endure repeated and anticipated pain, violence, and chaos.

The Type II syndrome, according to Terr, includes coping mechanisms of denial, psychological numbing, self-hypnosis, dissociation, and extreme shifts between rage and passivity.

When observing children suspected of being maltreated, it is helpful to understand the form their trauma and symptoms take. According to Gil (1991), children exhibit the impact of abuse and neglect through either internalized or externalized behaviors. Children who cope through internalized behavior negotiate the pain by themselves. They are likely to avoid interaction and appear depressed, joyless, phobic, hypervigilant, and regressed. Given the stress of coping without help, these children manifest physical symptoms including sleep disorders and somatic problems (e.g., headaches and stomachaches). Additionally, they withdraw emotionally and may appear overcompliant. In more severe cases they disassociate, self-mutilate, and may become suicidal. They are also likely to use drugs to numb both the physical and emotional pain of abuse.

Conversely, children who cope through externalized behavior direct their pain outwardly and toward others. They express emotions that are often hostile, provocative, and violent. They may kill or torture animals, destroy property through fire settings, and exhibit sexualized behaviors, and they may become youthful offenders.

The impact and effects of physical and sexual abuse differ markedly from those of neglect, and they may be affected by stress resistance. However, the effects are not, for most, multigenerational.

Physical abuse effects.   Physically abused children have deficits in gross motor development, speech, and language. The impact of physical abuse includes psychic trauma, chaos, rejection, deprivation, distorted parental perceptions, and unrealistic expectations. Further disruptions of family life occur with hospitalizations, separation, foster placement, and frequent home changes.

At a minimum, children hurt by others suffer an impaired capacity to enjoy life. When the abuse is more extreme, psychiatric symptoms appear (e.g., enuresis, hyperactivity, and bizarre behavior). In school, abused children who exhibit more internalized behaviors present learning problems, compulsiveness, hypervigilance, and suicidal tendencies. Children who cope with abuse through more externalized behaviors are oppositional. Typically, these children have problems managing aggressive behavior and cannot establish relationships with other children (Kent, 1980).

Sexual abuse effects.   The impact of child sexual abuse can be measured along a continuum from neutral to very negative (Friedrich, 1990). At its extreme, the effects of sexual abuse manifest in dissociation. The term *dissociation* refers to a disturbance in the normal functions of identity, memory, and consciousness (American Psychiatric Association, 1994).

Dissociation occurs when the child is exposed to overwhelming events that result in extreme feelings of helplessness. In the traumatic situation, the child attempts to cope by dissociating the self from the act being perpetrated. This dissociation becomes part of the child's development and results in long-term difficulties. In this way, internalized behaviors such as eating disturbances, substance abuse, and depression can be understood as behavioral readouts of dissociation. Externalized behaviors accompanying sexual abuse include school difficulties, anger, running away, delinquency, and sexualized behaviors.

Sexualized behavior is an externalized behavior that is shaped by sexual experiences, feelings, and attitudes that occur in the abuse process (Finkelhor, 1984). Early and manipulated exposure to sex may result in a child's excessive or preoccupying interest in it. There is a difference between normal sexual curiosity and sexualization. Unlike other children, the sexualized child (a) completes intercourse without coercion, (b) is not inhibited about masturbating, and (c) exhibits focused sexual behavior in front of others. This lack of inhibition can extend to play, art, or conversation that is imitative of adult sexual relationships.

The sexualized child is clearly at risk for developmentally inappropriate sexual behavior as well as pregnancy, sexually transmitted diseases, and prostitution. Thus it is critical for the professional to understand and differentiate what is normal sexual development in children from behaviors that indicate trauma.

Neglect effects. The dynamics of neglect differ markedly from those of physical or sexual abuse. The main difference is the attention received by the parents. The attention associated with abuse is inappropriate, excessive, harsh, and damaging, but the parent is still involved with the child. Neglecting parents do the opposite. For example, they fail to stimulate or interact on an emotional or a physical level. In extreme cases, it is as though the parent does not know the child exists.

The effects of child neglect and deprivation occur across all levels of development, including social, affective, physical, emotional, behavioral, and cognitive. We can expect to see internalized behaviors including a lack of affect (feelings), social detachment, impaired empathy, and externalized behaviors including violence, and delinquency. Neglected youth can be identified by behaviors that convey low self-esteem, a negative worldview, and internalized or externalized anxieties or aggressions. Because of the lack of nurturance, poor intellectual development, developmental disabilities, and developmental delays are typical. Neglected children are also seriously bereft of personal or family resources for care.

Stress resistance. Interestingly, some abused and neglected children appear relatively less traumatized than others. Garbarino, Guttman, and

Seeley (1986) proposed the concept of *stress-resistant children* who become prosocial and competent despite harsh or even hostile upbringing. It is speculated that these children receive compensatory psychological nurturance and sustenance. This nurturance may come from school professionals, neighbors, or family friends. Perhaps the experience of even minimal care enables the child to cope better and to develop social competence. With a basis of social competence, the child's view of the world, and his or her role within it, remain more positive. In a time when counseling is reduced to a bare minimum of contact with at-risk youth, school professionals might examine what the good-enough intervention is that can promote the natural adaptability of young people.

Continuing effects/youthful offenders. It is important to recognize that the majority of abuse victims do not become perpetrators. Further, the great majority of abuse survivors protect their children from enduring the fate they lived (Kaufman & Zigler, 1987). In this way, the concept of multigenerational abuse cycles is confounded.

According to Herman (1992), the small minority of survivors who take on the role of the perpetrator, and become youthful offenders, may be literally reenacting their childhood experiences. In the literature on this issue, youthful offenders are described as those who rape, initiate intrafamilial sexual contact between an adolescent and a prepubertal child, or exploit young children through sex or coercion (Okami, 1992). They may engage also in pseudosexual behaviors such as genital touching, exhibitionism, and voyeurism with a younger child who knows them (Higgs, Canavan, & Meyer, 1992).

Despite the aggressiveness of the young offenders' behavior, they are observed to be more asocial than antisocial. These adolescents suffer isolation, alienation, and lack of intimacy. In addition, the young offender may be rather compliant, withdrawn, and isolated from peers. This inability to form successful relationships with peers is marked by feelings of low self-esteem and inadequacy. There may also be a generalized preference for nonsexual contact with younger children. School adjustment difficulties are to be expected.

PREVENTION

The preceding section has reviewed a number of dysfunctional family situations and some of the youth at-risk behaviors that could flow from such family situations. The impact of physical and sexual abuse on youth was also explored. However, when faced with at-risk youth, professionals need more than knowledge; they need to be armed with practical ways to help these youth. Such arming is the goal of this section.

Forms of Prevention

Pianta and Walsh (1996) posited that three forms of prevention operate in work with at-risk youth. These forms are primary prevention, secondary prevention, and tertiary prevention. We have placed the focus and timing aspects of all three forms in a table for review (see Table 4–1).

An example of primary prevention is Washington State's Elementary School HIV/AIDS Education Law. This law mandates that all students in grades K-6 receive HIV/AIDS prevention education each year. The law represents primary prevention because it is directed to all students before the period when at-risk behaviors (e.g., IV drug use) begin. A transition-to-middle-school support group for students with low grades is an example of secondary prevention because it is directed at a specific population before it obtains at-risk status (e.g., school dropout). An example of tertiary prevention is a school-based aftercare group for students who have recently returned from a stay at a drug rehabilitation center. The goal of tertiary prevention is to remediate students who have already obtained an at-risk status.

With the forms of prevention defined, attention now turns to the levels of prevention: individual, family, school, and community.

Table 4–1 | Form, Focus, and Timing of Prevention Activities

Focus and Timing	Form		
	Primary	Secondary	Tertiary
All students	•		
Potential at-risk students		•	
At-risk students			•
Before at-risk status is obtained	•	•	
After at-risk status is obtained			•

Prevention at the Individual Level

Counseling. Individual counseling can be a secondary or tertiary prevention activity. Counselors who work with at-risk youth must exemplify the importance of well-defined rules and responsibilities. In working with the at-risk youth, the counselor must be sure to follow the rules of the counseling process. Just as the at-risk youth attempts to alter the rules in other settings for personal gain, the youth will attempt to have the professional alter, change, and ignore the rules of the counseling process.

For example, the youth may have a simple request, such as asking the counselor to write an excuse that will allow him or her to miss a class at school or be permitted to miss detention. Other, more critical violations of the rules may be requests for emergency appointments late at night or over the weekend. One counselor from a rural district spent 6 hours with a youth along a country road following a phone call requesting her help. It was considerate of the counselor but also very risky and ethically questionable. The youth did not follow the rules of counseling—attending the counseling session—in the appropriate location. One way to decrease the at-risk behavior is to define up front the role of the counselor and the rules of the counseling process.

Another aspect of prevention within the individual counseling process is the determination of the severity of the at-risk youth's actions and interactions. Whether the youth is abusing alcohol, is pregnant, or is a runaway, the counselor needs to determine the extent of danger to the well-being of the youth. The prudent counselor takes few chances with at-risk youth. Risk taking on the part of the counselor is ill-advised because these youth tend to be impulsive in their actions and prone to hurting themselves physically.

In determining severity, the counselor needs to be highly aware of the concept of duty to warn. This is prevention of the highest order. At the initiation of counseling, the at-risk youth and the family are both informed that any suspicious or questionable behaviors will be reported. Confidentiality and at-risk status are both clearly defined early in the process, reinforcing the professional's responsibility to follow the rules.

If there are questions about the level of severity of the behavior the youth exhibits, professionals need to follow a very cautious route and involve the parents. Following the rules may mean having a crisis team available to give the youth the appropriate treatment including the possibility of hospitalization. If the youth is suicidal, a coordinated professional effort may need to be utilized to resolve the problem. The sooner the at-risk youth is involved in treatment, the greater the opportunity for successful resolution and prevention of problems.

In principle, the counselor should always involve a family in at-risk prevention planning. However, there are situations where individual counseling with an at-risk student should be emphasized over family counseling. These situations include those in which (a) the relationship between the parents is questionable, (b) parenting skills are almost nonexistent, (c) one parent is an alcoholic, and (d) the parents are frequently absent from the home.

An emphasis on individual counseling places even more responsibility on the counselor to follow the rules. In order to treat effectively the myriad difficulties of at-risk youth, the professional must maintain a high level of confidence. Treating the at-risk youth can be a substantial test of a counselor's self-confidence. Thus appropriate attention to the counselor's own self-care against stress and anxiety is warranted. This self-care is the best antidote to counselor burnout.

Abuse Prevention.
Providing care. It is critical that professionals who work with the difficult issues of child abuse and neglect are trained in the specifics of these issues. Hurt children evoke complex responses in caregivers. At some point, the most skilled practitioner wants to rescue the child from trauma. Therefore, a support system and professional contact base are essential in this work. Also, specific resources for reporting, legal issues, safe housing, and community support services are necessary for effective interventions to occur.

Clarification of roles, empowerment, and the stages of intervention. Given the issues of control and coercion in child abuse, it is particularly important for the counselor to define his or her role with the young person. For example, Herman (1992) suggested that at the outset of working together, the counselor and client must be able to name the problem. To debate the story or the existence of an abuse report undermines the potential for recovery. By acknowledging the story, the professional begins to form an alliance. This alliance is critical because abused and neglected children have poor and often brutalized experiences with trust and intimacy. When hearing the story, the young person must understand that he or she is the survivor, not merely a victim. Further, the young person needs to know that he or she carries no responsibility for the abuse.

At the first stages of intervention, the counselor can work to develop small steps of self-care, plans for safety, and other support resources. The young person must be told at the outset that the counselor must report the threat of harm to self or others. Depending on the severity of the abuse or neglect, the later stages of counseling will help the young person toward self-care and independence. In this way, the counselor can help the young person toward the future. This process cannot be rushed and will depend on the young person's internal, familial, and other support resources. As gains are made in a transfer of learning to the world outside counseling, prevention and education become important. When intention is delayed, group counseling is a valuable approach. Mutual support is critical and can reinforce affective awareness and empowerment.

Empowerment also occurs through mastery. As seen in other developmental sequences, children develop a sense of mastery by practicing. Nonverbal processes give an outlet for raw emotion and a place to practice or work through the trauma impact. The following case study of a child's abuse reflects the complexity of issues surrounding at-risk families:

> *Case study.* Janet Firwood, aged 13, was brought to the intensive care burn unit of a local pediatric hospital for reconstructive surgery. This

surgery was for burns sustained when she was age 3. She had been burned when her nightgown ignited while jumping over a candlestick. Janet lived with her mother. Her father was the mother's boyfriend. This man had an intact family with a wife and several children and lived separately from Janet and her mother. Her mother was molested by this man when she was babysitting for him at age 17, and their relationship had continued since then.

The hospital's counselor began the assessment by talking with the medical staff and school personnel. A nurse reported seeing Janet holding hands with a 22-year-old patient during movie night. The hospital's schoolteacher also reported provocative behavior in class. In fact, Janet had shown other children her burn scars, including removing her underpants, if they gave her money. This pattern of premature sexual behavior such as flirting with an older man and exhibitionism are indicators of sexual abuse.

The counseling intervention started at the first step by naming the problem. Janet did not see herself as having a problem. However, she was happy to have attention from the counselor. Eventually, through artwork, Janet portrayed her feelings of powerlessness and of being divided by her loyalties to her mother and father who fought with one another. Before discharge, she revealed that her father sexually abused her. The referral to the local child abuse agency resulted in investigation and incarceration of the father. Unfortunately, Janet's case is one where serious identity and role confusion for the survivor resulted. This confusion was the product of delayed identification of abuse and the lack of social services. Besides identity and role confusion, Janet also exhibited characteristics of the youthful offender discussed earlier in this chapter. These characteristics include exhibitionism and peer coercion. Intensive counseling and support services were necessary to help Janet and her mother begin to resolve the chaos of their lives.

Prevention at the Family Level

The Family Role of the At-Risk Youth.　When an at-risk youth is identified, attention is often given directly to the youth without commensurate attention to the entire family. This inattention is unfortunate because at-risk behavior is simply a behavioral readout of family dysfunction. In other words, the youth's at-risk behavior is not sui generis, but rather the acting out of a script provided by the family system.

One common role in such a script is that of the identified problem. The family of the at-risk youth asserts that all in the family is well except for the at-risk youth. In truth, the at-risk youth's behaviors are merely the symptoms of family dysfunction. The greater the difficulties demonstrated by the youth, the larger the number of issues that need attention within the family. It is inappropriate to assume that the identified problem child is the only family member with mental health needs or the only family member who may be at risk. The case of Justin llustrates the identified-problem role.

Case study. Justin, a 14-year-old high school freshman, was referred for counseling by his school counselor following the interception of a suicide note. Two of Justin's friends found a letter describing how he planned to shoot himself. Justin, along with his mother and father, came to counseling. It was apparent in the initial session that Justin did not want to be there. He was rude, obnoxious, and embarrassing to his parents. Mother was tearful; father remained stoic. Both parents were obviously shaken by Justin's recent behaviors. The counselor attempted to understand the relationship between the issues Justin expressed and the problems that the family faced but no clear correlation emerged. Justin's behaviors were so disruptive that it was difficult to have his parents in the counseling session. Although several more counseling appointments were set up, the mother called the next day and canceled them. Two weeks later the counselor received a call from the mother asking for help. Her husband had been placed in the psychiatric unit of the local hospital. She explained that her husband had been laid off from work for the last 6 months and was becoming more and more withdrawn. He seemed devastated by the problems with Justin. In despair, he pulled out his shotgun and threatened to kill himself. Justin's mother called the police, and eventually her husband was placed in inpatient psychiatric care.

Impact of Malevolent Family Dynamics.   Once a youth demonstrates at-risk behaviors, family dynamics play a significant role in whether or not the at-risk behaviors will escalate or decline. If the dysfunctional aspects of the family dynamics are not identified, discussed, and changed, the behaviors of the at-risk youth will continue to escalate. Moreover, parental conflict has a compounding effect for the at-risk youth (Wasserman, Miller, Pinner, & Jaramillo, 1996). Thus involvement of the family is vital to preventing at-risk behaviors from escalating.

Families and Change of At-Risk Behavior.   The involvement of the family of the at-risk youth in assessment, diagnosis, and treatment planning is essential. The counselor provides a model of behavior to the parents, and the parents provide a wealth of information, spoken or unspoken, to the counselor. Many counselors wonder which family members should be involved in the counseling process. It is important to consider all members of the household as potential participants in the work with at-risk youth.

Frequently, one of the most effective treatment modalities to bring about change in youth is counseling the parents. If the parents can commit to working on their relationship, and be willing to learn different parenting approaches with their children, the chances of successfully assisting an at-risk youth increase significantly. However, as demonstrated throughout the case studies, there frequently is much disarray in the relationship between the parents. Such disarray makes it easy to understand why the youth may be having emotional difficulty. Further, parents provide an inappropriate model for the developing youth when they work too much, drink too much, or allow their lives to be out of control (Fincham, 1994). Once parents can be taught to reorient and redirect some of their energies, the positive changes in youth are absolutely astounding. Therefore, parent counseling along with family counseling can produce remarkable changes in dysfunctional family structures.

Thus family counseling must be part of the intervention and prevention plan for at-risk youth. In working with the family, the counselor must maintain a neutral position and avoid a position of being on someone's side. The youth and the parents will both attempt to enlist the counselor's support in their attempts to maintain the dysfunctional family system. Situations that represent some of the influence peddling family members try include phone calls by the youth or a parent, damaging evidence brought to the session to demonstrate someone's problems, or requests for additional sessions. It is important to remember that the goal is not to fix the at-risk youth but rather to support the development of a new and functional family interaction system.

Postabuse Family Intervention. The critical issue for children not removed from their families is monitoring the risk factors for the child and his or her parents. Any postabuse plan must assess and insure a safe environment by evaluating parental abuse proneness, the vulnerability of the child, and environmental stresses that trigger abuse (Green, 1988). The counselor also needs to assess the family's level of coping and complexity. At-risk families are typically ones with multiple problems, poor ability to cope with stress, and few resources for help internally or in the community. Therefore, it is important for the counselor to devise realistic goals. Postabuse counseling is a process of mediating the need for the family members to express their feelings and safety from punishment or retaliation for this behavior at home. Self-help groups such as Daughters & Sons United, Parents Anonymous, and Parents United may be helpful to families as well.

Prevention at the School Level

Preservice/In-Service Needs. School counselors and teachers are the frontline soldiers in the war against at-risk behaviors. To be capable soldiers, school counselors and teachers need to possess adequate knowledge in the following areas: parent consultation, referral and networking, and professional comportment.

Parent consultation. All school professionals need to be comfortable with the principle of parent consultation. If a school professional does not contact parents regarding at-risk behaviors, the professional is maintaining too much responsibility for the at-risk youth. Parents need to be encouraged to take responsibility for their at-risk children and to become actively involved in the prevention process as soon as possible.

Providing an effective consultation with the parents assists the family in understanding the necessary steps of the helping process. It is very important for the school professional making the initial contact with the family to understand the critical nature of his or her role. It is essential to provide the family with a clear understanding of the helping process. The initial consultation should be used to encourage and assist the family in receiving the most effective services possible. If the initial consultation is a positive experience, the family will more than likely be ready to pursue the necessary steps of the treatment process.

Referral and networking. Another necessary knowledge area for school counselors and teachers is referral and networking. If school professionals cannot provide the at-risk youth with appropriate services, they must refer the at-risk youth and the family to an appropriate agency, institution, or private practitioner. Frequently, the at-risk youth is identified by school professionals, but the services required for treatment are offered elsewhere. Thus schools must link their efforts for at-risk youth with the efforts of local agencies, practitioners, and hospitals.

Maintaining a comprehensive referral network of helping professionals is probably one of the most important aspects of prevention as well as a major responsibility for school professionals treating at-risk youth. The network should include both medical and nonmedical mental health service providers. Specifically, referral sources need to include psychiatrists, drug and alcohol counselors, mental health counselors, clinical psychologists, marriage and family specialists, and clergy. School professionals treating at-risk youth must have a thorough knowledge of the variability and comprehensiveness of various services in the community.

Professional comportment. Critical to proper professional comportment is knowledge of how to act in an ethical and legal manner when working with at-risk youth. One key ethical and legal concern in work with at-risk youth is the issue of confidentiality. Too often school professionals maintain confidentiality without considering the ramifications to the youth as well as to themselves. Being direct and up-front with the youth about the types of information and behavior that are treated in a confidential manner versus those to be reported to the parents helps avoid potential problems later.

School counselors and teachers often serve as the primary connection between at-risk youth and their families. Thus it is essential for school professionals to possess knowledge of parental consultation, referral and networking, and proper professional comportment. Using professional colleagues for support and consultation, making effective and necessary referrals of particularly difficult cases, and seeking personal counseling when the stress becomes too great are some ways a school counselor or teacher can maintain a high level of self-confidence and effectiveness.

Curriculum-Based Interventions. When people think of school counselors working with at-risk youth, they usually think of school counselors performing secondary and tertiary prevention activities, such as facilitating support groups or conducting individual counseling. However, school counselors have an important role to play with the primary prevention of at-risk status in youth.

In 1997, the American School Counselor Association published national standards for school counseling programs. The model program contained K-12 guidance curriculum goals in three areas: personal/social development, career development, and academic development. Lapan, Gysbers, and Sun (1997) have found that full implementation of a guidance program serves as a powerful antidote to at-risk status. Students in schools with a more fully implemented guidance program reported that (a) they earned higher grades, (b) their education was better preparing them for the future, (c) their school made more career information available to them, and (d) their school had a more positive climate. School guidance programs are not the sole domain of school counselors. In fact, because of their small numbers, the main role of the school counselor in the guidance program is that of facilitator. The key deliverer of the curricular parts of the guidance program is the teacher. Thus the student outcomes just noted are only possible if school counselors and teachers work in concert.

School counselors are not the only education professionals with a curriculum that serves as an at-risk primary prevention activity. Family and consumer sciences teachers have also published a national curriculum. This curriculum aims to help young people develop the social skills and decision-making skills that can serve as a protection against at-risk behaviors. In addition, this curriculum contains standards on parent training for youth. There is no better example of a primary prevention activity than giving people parenting skills before they become parents! Thus national curricula exist in this country that directly address the skill deficits that can lead to an at-risk status for youth. Such curricula have been shown scientifically to be efficacious. Unfortunately, none of these curricula are universal in America's schools.

Mentoring Programs. To prevent the development of at-risk behaviors may mean that the child needs to find other role models and mentors in his or her own day-to-day experiences. At-risk youth sometimes find their own ability to develop appropriate roles and responsibilities from interactions with peers, school teachers, neighbors, and other community leaders. For at-risk youth to change their pattern of behavior means that they need to see an alternative way to life.

Physical and Sexual Abuse Education for Children. The NIS-3 report (Sedlak & Broadhurst, 1996) stressed that schools play a central role in identifying and helping abused and neglected young people. School professionals are the frontline observers who form relationships of care with young people. Rencken (1989) has advocated three axes of prevention for abuse that are useful at the school and community levels. These axes are empowerment, sex education, and gender equity. The first axis includes teaching assertiveness and the ability to say "no" from a foundation of self-esteem, responsibility, and age-appropriate control. The second axis is sex education to remediate ignorance for young people and their families. The third axis is a discussion of gender role differences between males and females in our society and the development of equitable power arrangements.

It is clear that physically abused and neglected children are not always helped even with reporting. Child protection agencies and the court system are already seriously overworked. Often they are unable to follow up on cases except where there is threat of fatality. To address this problem, grassroots support systems are being developed. Schools and mental health agencies are teaming together to develop individualized and tailored care that uses the natural support systems in communities to help protect children. These support systems include safe places for children to go after school, neighborhood police stations, child mentorship, and after-school activities such as tutoring and gym nights. Schools can become a place to provide support to at-risk youth and their families. Grants and donations of time and money are typically used by school and agencies to development these support resources.

Prevention at the Community Level

Parent Education. A powerful prevention activity is parent education. Both schools and community agencies can sponsor such an activity for minimal cost. If only one activity could be selected to prevent at-risk status in youth, the thing to select is parent education. Nothing provides more bang for the buck.

Two parent education activities that have solid research support are STEP and parent monitoring. It is important to note that these activities can be easily sponsored and led not only by school personnel but also by local community agencies or churches. Neither is the kind of fancy, complex activity that garners media attention. Rather, they are doable, proven at-risk prevention activities that can make a difference in the lives of youth and their parents. As such, they merit the consideration of anyone looking for ways to address the at-risk youth problems they encounter in their workplace or in their community.

STEP. Systematic Training for Effective Parenting is a widely used parent education program. The STEP program curriculum presents practical ideas for parents based upon Adlerian psychology. There are a wide variety of STEP modules including those for parents of young children, parents of teens, Christian parents, and Latino parents. Although designed for the average parent, there is even evidence of STEP's effectiveness with parents who have previously abused their children (Fennell & Fishel, 1998).

The STEP program is well laid out with clear lesson plans and appropriate participant activities. A training facilitator's handbook provides support (Dinkmeyer, 1997). A person who has had some previous training in developmental psychology and in communication skills could do an excellent job of facilitating STEP training.

Parent monitoring. Although it may sound like an incredibly simplistic solution, extensive research supports the idea that at-risk behaviors can be substantially decreased by increasing parental monitoring of youth. Murray, Kelder, Parcel, and Orpinas (1998) developed a parent education program that taught parents practical skills for monitoring middle school students. They identified four skills that are essential in building competent monitoring in parents:

1. Parents will ask their child where he or she is going.
2. Parents will obtain a list of telephone numbers of their child's friends.
3. Parents will call parents of their child's friends.
4. Parents will visit their child's school.

Learning objectives are identified for each skill. For example, one of the learning objectives for the second skill is "Parents will be able to recognize most of their child's friends on the street and know their names" (p. 50).

Community Capacity Building. At-risk behaviors of youth do not wreak havoc in just families and schools. The social and economic costs of such behaviors impact every community. As such, building the capacity of communities to prevent at-risk behaviors benefits all citizens. Given the central role of schools in most communities, school personnel can be key instigators of a community's focusing on at-risk prevention. In terms of community-wide prevention efforts, school personnel should work toward two goals: education on family dynamics, and community-wide networking.

Education on family dynamics. One key community prevention goal is educating the general public about variation in family structures and individual differences. It is still difficult for many local institutions such as churches, hospitals, and other community organizations to make allowances for the various family structures such as blended families, single-parent families, interracial families, and dual-career families. Moreover, if at-risk youth are to find surrogate role models in the community, it is important for the potential role models to understand the dysfunctional and non-traditional aspects of family life in the current culture.

Community-wide networking. Another key community prevention goal is the successful networking of school personnel with other professionals in the community that serve at-risk youth. These professionals include private practice counselors, community agency counselors, probation officers, law enforcement officers, and pediatricians. This networking is a must given the multifaceted nature of youth at-risk status. For example, substance abuse may lead to both academic and health problems. Given this multifacetedness, school professionals must have an effective network of other professionals in order to offer the youth and the family the best services possible. The network should include knowledge of runaway shelters, crisis intervention teams, support groups, hospitals, and outpatient services.

SUMMARY

This chapter provides an overview of how dysfunctional family dynamics both precede and fuel at-risk behavior. In addition, the chapter presents some ideas about how best to provide a program of prevention to assist at-risk youth and their families. Several points needs to be emphasized for those charged with working with at-risk youth.

First, there is no more difficult population to serve than at-risk youth. They tend to be more professionally demanding, emotionally draining, and behaviorally unpredictable than youth as a whole. Professionals assigned to work with this population must learn to be direct and honest with the youth as well as his or her family. As mentioned in the discussion of prevention, these same professionals must learn to follow the rules in serving these youth.

Second, the at-risk family is a special entity that needs tremendous amounts of attention to keep it functioning without tragedy. When a professional works with an at-risk individual, he or she has always to be aware of the remaining family members to make sure that another member does not manifest a severe behavioral difficulty. Consultation with other important adults surrounding the family members is a must for effective work with the at-risk family.

Finally, treating at-risk youth mandates that professionals be involved with families and community agencies. There is no place in work with at-risk youth for the professional Lone Ranger. The biggest mistake made by caring professionals is to assume too much individual responsibility for the at-risk youth and his or her family. Find a support system to assist in the treatment process and be sure to have a support system available for yourself. Maintaining physical energy and emotional balance is as important as any decision the professional can make.

REFERENCES

Aguilera, D. C., & Messick, J. M. (1986). *Crisis intervention: Theory and methodology.* St. Louis, MO: Mosby.

American Psychiatric Association. (1994). *Diagnostic and statistical manual of mental disorders* (4th ed.). Washington, DC: Author.

Cumsille, P. E., & Epstein, N. (1994). Family cohesion, family adaptability, social support, and adolescent depressive symptoms in outpatient clinic families. *Journal of Family Psychology, 8,* 202–214.

Dinkmeyer, D. (1997). *Systematic training for effective parenting: Leaders resource binder.* Circle Pines, MN: American Guidance Service.

Fennell, D. C., & Fishel, A. H. (1998). Parent education: An evaluation of STEP on abusive parents' perceptions and potential abuse. *Journal of Child and Adolescent Psychiatric Nursing, 11,* 107-121.

Fincham, F. D. (1994). Understanding the association between marital conflict and child adjustment: Overview. *Journal of Family Psychology, 8,* 123–127.

Finkelhor, D. (1984). *Child sexual abuse.* New York: Free Press.

Friedrich, W. N. (1990). *Psychotherapy of abused children and their families.* New York: Norton.

Garbarino, J., Guttman, E., & Seeley, J. W. (1986). *The psychologically battered child.* San Francisco: Jossey-Bass.

Gil, E. (1991). *The healing power of play: Working with abused children.* New York: Guilford Press.

Green, A. H. (1988). The abused child and adolescent. In C. J. Kestenbaum & D. J. Williams (Eds.), *Handbook of clinical assessment of children and adolescents* (Vol. 2, pp. 841–863). New York: University Press.

Herman, J. L. (1992). *Trauma and recovery: The aftermath of violence from domestic abuse to political terror.* New York: Basic Books.

Higgs, D. C., Canavan, M. M., & Meyer, W. J. (1992). Moving from defense to offense: The development of an adolescent female sex offender. *Journal of Sex Research, 29,* 131-139.

Kaufman J., & Zigler, E. (1987). Do abused children become abusive parents? *American Journal of Orthopsychiatry, 57,* 186–192.

Kazak, A. E., Christakis, D., Alderfer, M., & Coiro, M. J. (1994). Young adolescent cancer survivors and their parents: Adjustment, learning problems, gender. *Journal of Family Psychology, 8,* 74–84.

Kent, J. T. (1980). A follow-up study of abused children. In G. J. Williams & J. Mahoney (Eds.), *Traumatic abuse and neglect of young children at home* (pp. 221–233). Baltimore, MD: Johns Hopkins University Press.

Kitzman, K. M., & Emery, R. E. (1994). Coping 1 year after mediated and litigated custody disputes. *Journal of Family Psychology, 8,* 150–159.

Lapan, R., Gysbers, N. C., & Sun, Y. (1997). The impact of more fully implemented guidance programs on the school experiences of high school students: A statewide evaluation study. *Journal of Counseling and Development, 75,* 292–302.

Murray, N., Kelder, S., Parcel, G., & Orpinas, P. (1998). Development of an intervention map for a parent education intervention to prevent violence among Hispanic middle school parents. *Journal of School Health, 68,* 46–53.

Okami, P. (1992). Child perpetrators of sexual abuse: The emergence of a problematic deviant category. *Journal of Sex Research, 29,* 109–130.

Pianta, R. C., & Walsh, D. J. (1996). *High-risk children in schools.* New York: Routledge.

Rencken, R. H. (1989). *Intervention strategies for sexual abuse.* Alexandria, VA: American Counseling Association.

Shaw, D. S., Keenan, K., Vondra, J. I., Delliquandri, E., & Givannelli, J. (1997). Antecedents of preschool children's internalizing problems: A longitudinal study of low-income families. *Journal of the American Academy of Child and Adolescent Psychology, 36,* 1760–1768.

Sedlak A., & Broadhurst, D. (1996). *Third national incidence study of child abuse and neglect: Final report.* Washington, DC: U. S. Department of Health and Human Services, Administration of Children and Family.

Terr, L. (1988). What happens to the memories of early childhood trauma? *Journal of the Academy of Child and Adolescent Psychiatry, 27,* 96–104.

Visher, E. B., & Visher, J. S. (1996). *Therapy with stepfamilies.* New York: Brunner/Mazel.

Wasserman, G. A., Miller, L. S., Pinner, E., & Jaramillo, B. (1996). Parenting predictors of early conduct problems in urban, high-risk boys. *Journal of the American Academy of Child and Adolescent Psychology, 35,* 1227–1237.

5 | Who Cares What I Think: Problems of Low Self-Esteem

Sandra S. Meggert

We observe many adolescents in pain. We see many with negative attitudes or low self-esteem and suspect there are many more. Many researchers believe that one of the major causes of deviant or potentially destructive behavior is low self-esteem (Kaplan, 1975; Leung & Drasgow, 1986; Maternal and Child Health Branch, Hawaii State Department of Health, 1991; Yanish & Battle, 1985). A review of the literature supports the belief that negative self-esteem affects behavior in negative or destructive ways (Aronson & Mettee, 1968; Graf, 1971; Kaplan, 1975; Kaplan, Martin, & Johnson 1986; Lorr & Wunderlich, 1986; Yanish & Battle, 1985). Kaplan (1976) stated that poor self-esteem or "negative self-attitudes increase the probability of later adoption of each of a range of different types of deviant responses" (p. 788). Low self-esteem is a critical factor in at-risk behavior. Eskilson, Wiley, Meuhlbauer, and Dodder (1986) reported that adolescents who feel excessive demands to succeed academically are apt to disclose involvement in deviant activities, to have low self-esteem, and to feel inadequate and unable to fulfill their families' aspirations for them. Aronson and Mettee (1968) used college students as subjects in a study of dishonesty. They hypothesized that students with "low self-esteem are more likely to engage in immoral behavior" (p. 74). Results showed that 87% of the subjects with induced low self-esteem cheated on a test as compared to 60% of the neutral group and 40% of the induced high self-esteem group. In a similar study, Graf (1971) reported that 40% of those with induced low self-esteem, 17% of the neutral group, and 14% of the group with induced high self-esteem engaged in dishonest behavior.

Kaplan's (1976) theory suggests that low self-esteem influences a person to adopt delinquent or other behaviors that are deviant from the norm. The theory identifies two routes that negative self-attitudes may take to influence deviant behavior. One is that these attitudes make conformity to membership group patterns painful or distressing; the other is "by influencing the person's need to seek alternatives to the disvalued normative patterns in order to satisfy the self-esteem motive" (p. 788). More recently, the Maternal and Child Health Branch of the Hawaii State Department of Health (1991) collected data on adolescent health in Hawaii and found adolescents with low self-esteem were more likely to exhibit high-risk behaviors than their peers with high self-esteem.

The results of a study of adolescents at risk for compulsive overeating (Marston, Jacobs, Singer, Widaman, & Little, 1988) showed that students designated *at risk* perceived their life quality as poor, and the authors hypothesized that this meant they are getting along poorly with the person to whom they feel closest. Because esteem is closely tied to perceived evaluations from significant others, the quality of significant relationships is a crucial ingredient of self-esteem. The research findings of Yanish and Battle (1985) supported the importance of significant others to the adolescent. They found depression in adolescents to be more strongly affected by the relationship with parents than with peers. A longitudinal study by Cohen, Burt, and Bjorck (1987) indicated that low self-esteem and depression, which is an indicator of low self-esteem, are positive predictors of controllable negative events, such as expulsion from school.

Simmons, Burgeson, Carlton-Ford, and Blyth (1987) stated that young people who encounter several important life events at the same time they are adjusting to the changes of adolescence are expected to be at greater risk than those who have longer periods of time to adjust to adolescence. Findings in this study showed that girls suffer loss of self-esteem, and both boys and girls show declines in grade point averages (GPA) and participation in extracurricular activities. For girls, each subsequent life change brings more difficulty with coping. The authors suggested that, in terms of self-esteem, this group of young adolescents does better if one aspect of their life is comfortable. If this is accomplished, then the timing and pacing of major changes are of primary importance.

As discussed in the many preceding examples, adolescents who exhibit signs of low self-esteem may be considered at risk or as adopting or experimenting with deviant or potentially destructive behaviors. These young people may or may not be responding to life situations with deviant behaviors currently. However, when the signs indicate low self-esteem, interventions designed to improve self-esteem are important to help them avoid at-risk behaviors.

This chapter examines low self-esteem as one of the primary causes of the at-risk behaviors just described and delineates strategies and programs to prevent low levels of self-esteem. Self-esteem is defined in relation to at-risk youth, and behavioral descriptions or indicators frequently linked to low self-esteem are discussed. Causal factors that influence the development of self-esteem as well as prevention strategies that can be used by the individual, parents, schools, and communities to make young people feel valued and significant participants in making their environment a satisfying, safe, and rewarding place are presented. A case study describes a successful experimental program with at-risk students that has brought about changes that reflect improved levels of self-esteem.

DEFINITIONS OF SELF-ESTEEM

Self-esteem refers to subjective evaluations of worth. These value judgments develop through personal success or failure experiences, interactions with others, maturation, heredity, and social learning, and are formulated from an individual's perspective. Kaplan (1975) discussed the self-esteem motive as being an individual's need to optimize positive feelings about self while reducing negative feelings. It is the process of increasing feelings of self-respect, approval, worth, and esteem. When the balance is on the negative side, a person is said to feel self-rejection, self-derogation, and, in many cases, self-hate.

Self-esteem is also a function of perceived evaluation by significant others. Mack and Ablon (1983) believed that no human is ever totally independent of the evaluation of others, and everyone retains "to some degree, a dependence upon connectedness with others for validation of . . . worth" (p. 10). A person's self-evaluation is referred to as self-esteem (Robison-Awana, Kehle, & Jenson, 1986). It is influenced by the individual's feelings of competence and efficacy. Two other terms are sometimes used interchangeably with self-esteem: *self-concept* and *self-acceptance*.

Self-concept refers to the perception individuals have about their personal attributes and the roles they fulfill. Some of these perceptions are accurate, and some are not. We receive feedback about the roles we play and internalize information about the character and quality of our role performance (Beane & Lipka, 1980). "Self-concept refers to the valuative assessment of those descriptions" (p. 3). For example, individuals have an academic self-concept, a social self-concept, or a physical appearance self-concept. Elliott (1988) maintained that anyone with low self-esteem has an unstable self-concept. The term *self-acceptance* pertains to the degree to which people are comfortable with their self-concept (Frey & Carlock, 1984).

For purposes of this discussion, *self-esteem* is defined as the pattern of beliefs an individual has about self-worth. It is the subjective part of self-concept, the evaluation of self and behaviors based on an individual's perceptions of personal experiences and feedback from significant others. It is expressed in feelings of power or helplessness, called efficacy, or in beliefs about personal control.

INDICATORS OF LOW SELF-ESTEEM

Beliefs about self develop as a result of perceptions and evaluations of success and failure experiences. In this process, an individual forms some beliefs about personal control (internal vs. external) and personal effectiveness (self-efficacy).

Locus of control refers to a person's belief about outcomes. Locus of control is the conviction that success or failure at a task is internally determined by one's own actions or ability, or that the outcome is due to external influences such as luck, fate, or chance. According to Johnson (1981), "internal attributions for success are associated with higher levels of self-esteem," and low self-concept "was predicted independently and significantly by internal attribution for failure and external attribution for success" (p. 174). Abramson, Seligman, and Teasdale (1978) suggested that low-achieving students ascribe any failures to internal causes and all successes to external causes.

Personal effectiveness, or self-efficacy, as defined by Benoit and Mitchell (1987), has four essential elements: awareness of required behavior to bring about success, expectation that this behavior will be successful, belief that there is a relationship between behavior and outcome and that this behavior will have an impact, and belief that the outcome will provide something valued.

Evidence supports the fact that an individual with low self-esteem does most likely believe in luck (external control) rather than ability (internal control) to achieve success. However, failure is attributed to personal shortcomings (internal control). Because self-esteem judges whether such an individual can, in fact, succeed at a given task, the lack of belief in self makes it likely that someone with low self-esteem will also exhibit feelings of helplessness or powerlessness, in other words, low levels of self-efficacy. In this case, a possible defense might be to deny that the outcome of the behavior has any value, and to withdraw or drop out.

Individuals with low self-esteem often find it necessary to develop defenses. People who have low self-esteem hurt. To avoid this hurt there is a tendency either to shun experiences such people believe will bring additional pain or to change these experiences in some way. They erect barriers or defenses. At times the individual might be hostile, critical, or suspicious of others, or lack identification with others. Sometimes retreating defenses are exhibited when a person avoids coming to grips with problems or denies reality (Kaplan, 1975). A person might retreat into an "I don't care" stance or simply resist trying. It is too much of a risk for someone with feelings of poor self-worth to be exposed to additional hurt or situations in which failure is expected.

Persons with low self-esteem may be distractible, timid, shy, withdrawn, inhibited, anxious, and less academically able (Domino & Blumberg, 1987), and have a narrow range of interests. They are more likely to daydream and to want to find jobs where they have little or no supervision and where there are minimal amounts of competition. From their perspectives, an ideal situation is one in which they have no supervision because then no one can confirm their failure. Generally, they express the idea that they do not really want to get ahead in life. This could be because they will not place themselves in a position where they expect to fail. This too is a defense.

Individuals with low self-esteem have few coping strategies. They often feel a lack of control over life events. They do not feel connected and have few, if any, expectations of future success. They lack a sense of belonging. Possibly, dropping out is a defensive way of demonstrating some power, self-defeating though it may be.

Low self-esteem can cause emotional distress as well. Many individuals who question their worth are sad, lethargic, tense, anxious, and angry. Some of these feelings stem from concurrent feelings of helplessness and powerlessness. Physically they may exhibit sleeplessness, headaches, or nightmares.

Those who have low self-esteem are generally dissatisfied with themselves and their lives, contemptuous of self, and have low levels of self-respect. Typically, they are fearful of new experiences and have a poor physical appearance and a low energy level. Apologizing, criticizing others, showing an interest in material things, and bragging are all indicators of low self-esteem.

CAUSAL FACTORS

Parental, social, psychological, physical, environmental, and cultural influences affect self-esteem. They all contribute to the development of self-esteem to the extent that each or all of these are valued or devalued by significant others who provide feedback. This feedback is both verbal and nonverbal, overt and covert, and dramatically affects how adolescents see themselves.

Parental Influences on Self-Esteem

Frey and Carlock (1984) identified a representative list of "psychological pathogens" to self-esteem (pp. 25–31). Many of these are associated with parental influences. These pathogens may persist throughout life and, if so, may consistently keep self-esteem low unless someone or something intervenes. Among the pathogens they identify, and the problems that might arise when these are present during childhood, are the following:

- *Expecting perfection.* Nobody has achieved this state yet, but many people try! Carrying a burden of always trying to be perfect out of childhood guarantees failure. Those who have learned to set idealistic or unrealistic goals for themselves are constantly frustrated, critical, and impatient with themselves and others, always trying harder and never quite feeling successful. Negative self-evaluations, which are formulated by the individual from perceptions of adult reactions, deeply affect his or her feelings about self. Unless a person learns to set realistic goals and acknowledge small steps on the way, self-esteem remains low because the person never feels adequate.

- *Inconsistency and failure to set limits.* Though some people believe consistency is a myth, children often search for consistency and limits, apparently seeking the security that structure and predictability provide. When that is missing, the result is anger, insecurity, and hostility.
- *Failure to give positive feedback.* Many parents and significant others assume that children know positive behavior is appreciated and only respond to negative or improper behavior. Being constantly reminded or punished when behavior is inappropriate, and seldom being appreciated when behavior is appropriate, create feelings of inadequacy and inferiority.
- *Failure to listen.* Failing to listen to a child indicates a lack of respect and communicates that the child or what the child is trying to communicate is not important. When this feeling is carried through childhood, it fosters additional feelings of inferiority and inadequacy that are sometimes expressed in anger or hostility.
- *Rejection.* Consistent rejection critically impacts an individual's self-esteem. The rejected child's basic needs are not being met, in some cases deliberately. Death, divorce, severe illness, or ignoring the child can all be viewed as rejection by a child with the ensuing feelings of inadequacy, guilt, self-hate, or self-rejection.
- *Being a maladjusted role model.* Children who model their behavior after an adult who is maladjusted often end up disliking themselves because of those behaviors. Their self-esteem is greatly diminished in such cases.
- *Failure to help children adapt.* Societal and cultural values are being questioned more now than ever before. It is difficult for children to feel adequate in a society where values are shifting or unclear. It becomes even more difficult when children try to adapt to a different culture and values conflict.
- *Forcing children into a pattern.* Sometimes parents try to fit children into certain behaviors or patterns that may restrict their unique development or be beyond their capacity. This is sometimes called *living vicariously* and creates frustration, feelings of worthlessness, and inadequacy in both parent and child.
- *Allowing and supporting procrastination.* Believing that one does not have the self-discipline necessary to complete a task contributes to poor self-esteem. The longer the child procrastinates, the more the

feelings of inadequacy and worthlessness multiply. Concurrently, there is a loss of self-respect.

Frey and Carlock (1984) listed several additional pathogens and observed that "one can be the recipient of several of these dynamics" (p. 31). Each of these, or a combination of several, is detrimental to a child's self-esteem.

Parents have significant impacts on the self-esteem of their children. Parental attitudes and behaviors have been shown to affect children (Buri & Kircher, 1993; Lord, Eccles, & McCarthy, 1994; Ohannesian, Lerner, Lerner, & Von Eye, 1994). The number of divorces and remarriages and the child's subsequent adjustment were the focus of a study that found some evidence of a "negative linear relationship" between these variables (Lord et al., 1994, p. 28). Buri and Dickinson (1994) reported that although parental authority was predictive of self-esteem, these behaviors were less important than overgeneralization, particularly in females. The authors described overgeneralization as the inclination for a person to view a failure as an indication of his or her general inadequacy.

A consequence of the dynamics just described is that young people today feel unimportant or even irrelevant in their families (Glenn & Nelson, 1989). Many believe that they are important only when they are doing what someone else wants them to do. The authors speculated that this is one impetus for early sexual involvement. Sex becomes a strategy to make the individuals involved believe themselves to be significant in the eyes of someone else. The irony is that if the female has a child she is automatically treated as an adult when, in fact, there are now two children.

The need to feel significant is also a powerful motivator to become a gang member. News stories report daily regarding the initiation rites to join a gang. Some young people want so badly to belong that they lose their lives during the entry process.

Note that many of the pathogens identified are behaviors found in extremely inexperienced parents who may use the child to satisfy personal needs not previously filled. The child will not feel valued, may be confused, and, most likely, will develop low self-esteem. The cycle will remain unbroken unless there is some type of intervention.

Social Influences on Self-Esteem

A basic assumption in social psychology is that self-concepts are heavily influenced by social contexts (Bachman & O'Malley, 1986). Each of us has a long history of dependency during infancy and childhood during which we need to receive positive responses from adults. We are motivated to behave in ways that increase the likelihood of receiving these positive responses. As children we internalize adult standards in this manner, and we attempt to regulate our own behavior and react with positive or negative self-feelings at the perceived evaluations/reactions of significant adults (Kaplan, 1976).

Kaplan (1976) further noted that low self-esteem is thought to be caused by self-perceptions that either our behavior or our characteristics do not meet personal standards valued by the social system; by self-perceptions that significant others do not value us positively or perhaps even negatively; or that a person might not have developed "normatively acceptable coping mechanisms" that could protect one from the effect of "self-perceptions of failure or rejection by others" (p. 790). Someone with a history of being devalued is most likely to have low self-esteem. This can be said to evolve from two sources: an individual's history of negative self-evaluation and perception, and perceptions of highly valued others in the environment responding to the individual with less than positive attitudes (Kaplan, 1975). An individual is more likely to value the attitudes of those persons "who were associated with need gratification or deprivation" (p. 37).

Society imposes strong gender-based role behaviors that continue their impact on self-esteem long after adolescence. A recent study has demonstrated that masculine bias is still strong in America (Burnett, Anderson, & Heppner, 1995). Masculinity, defined as having high levels of traditional masculine behaviors (such as competitiveness, decisiveness, and independence) as opposed to feminine characteristics (such as focus on relationships and nurturing), has been shown to be "significantly correlated with self-esteem for both men and women, but individual femininity was not significantly related to self-esteem in either sex" (p. 325).

Even though masculine behaviors are clearly valued in America, they are not generally characteristic of at-risk youth. If they are evident in some, they are not generally evident in socially acceptable ways. For example, aggressiveness and rebelliousness might substitute for independence and competitiveness. Enns (1992) stated that "there is some evidence that the socialization process is even more stringent for men than it is for women, and that boys and men experience higher costs for straying from traditional gender roles than do girls and women" (p. 11). There is the possibility that absence of masculine skills in boys, and to some extent girls, has the potential of contributing to low self-esteem. Bower (1993) reported that development of self-esteem in males and females is different due to societal pressures that dictate male and female role behaviors. Some research has also indicated that teenage girls have lower self-esteem than teenage boys (Dwyer, 1993). A recent *U.S. News & World Report* article (Saltzman, 1994) surveyed research regarding self-esteem of adolescent girls. After examining several research studies, the author concluded that social science has no conclusive answers and that parents have to assess and address the needs of their daughters individually.

Many of the social changes are high-risk changes. As young people are alienated from society and practice more violent methods to feel significant and powerful, many die or become incapacitated. Wars are fought on TV and children feel threatened. Technology has changed the world of work, and many parents or parental figures are unemployed. Divorce is common; homes are broken. Values are lost. Young people hear of people their own age dying from the variety of perils to which they are exposed. Many of them believe that they will live short lives. No one has prepared them for the choices they have to make.

Psychological Influences on Self-Esteem

It is "questionable, indeed, whether human beings can deeply experience positive self-worth except as the result of a relationship" (Mack & Ablon, 1983, p. 9). Everyone knows two basic truths about the self. One is that the self is alone and private, and the other is "that one is a real self only to the extent that caring and reaching beyond the self continue" (Yankelovich, 1981, p. 240). Therefore, an important psychological determinant of self-esteem is the individual's feelings about the level of success within relationships.

The whole notion of connectedness or belonging to someone is central to the development of self-esteem. Belonging to a family, a culture, a community, or a school provides a connection to aid in sustaining a sense of worth. Lacking such a feeling, a person is likely to feel not valued, or not of value, and retreat into a defensive posture to protect the self from the pain of feeling isolated, hopeless, worthless, and unconnected. "Virtually all maladaptive defensive patterns in childhood, adolescence, and adult life have as at least one major purpose, protection of the pain associated with lowered self-esteem" (Mack & Alblon, 1983, p. 38).

Television has become a psychological determinant of self-esteem (Glenn & Nelson, 1989). Young people receive messages about the society in which they live in a passive manner. They do not have to participate to learn. In the past, people learned about functioning in society while they were actively involved in living and working. The learning might be trial and error, role modeling, or direct teaching, but individuals were active. The authors referred to this as on-the-job training or OJT. Today, with the use of television, children's reality becomes distorted. Within a short time, they see problems solved through miracles, violence, various medications, sex, and drinking. According to Glenn and Nelson, they learn the following:

1. In productive and desirable social interactions, drinking or substance abuse is necessary.
2. Pain, fatigue, listlessness, and boredom are all dispelled through self-medication.
3. Indiscriminate or uninvolved sexual encounters are appropriate ways to communicate.
4. Problems can be resolved instantly through manipulation, violence, and breaking the law.
5. Deferred gratification, hard work, and personal initiative are unacceptable, and drinking and self-medication can help a person avoid these stresses. Any stressful situation can be alleviated by using specific products and/or services. (1989, pp. 42–43)

These "truisms" are further complicated by parents who foster the belief that most material possessions can be obtained in ways other than hard work. So because things come easily, there is no respect for possessions and there are no positive messages about the purpose of life. It is easy to speculate that if no active role modeling or teaching of healthier, more productive attitudes dispute these claims, young people may feel alienated, angry, and confused. When they use these same behaviors that work on television to solve their problems, they get into trouble. The nonacceptance of their behaviors confirms their sense of worthlessness and insignificance. The only way they can feel any sense of worth is when they are with others who feel and think as they do.

Physical Influences on Self-Esteem

Inherited physical characteristics, such as physique, appearance, and handicaps also may influence self-esteem. The physical attributes that an individual has inherited can affect others' perceptions and behavior. Others may respond negatively to an individual's handicapping condition or physical appearance, thus affecting that individual's self-esteem, even though the individual's initial self-perception may not have been negative.

Others' reactions are also influenced by maturational rates. Adults treat children differently at differing maturation levels. Early maturing children are quite often treated as adults and develop positive self-esteem. But those who mature later and continue to be treated as children tend to develop low self-esteem. Even when this latter group matures, they often maintain old self-perceptions and the corresponding low self-esteem. Maturation also affects mastery of developmental tasks. Social disapproval, maladjustment, and increased difficulty in mastering higher level developmental tasks are all possible results of delayed maturation (Frey & Carlock, 1984).

Environmental Influences on Self-Esteem

It is difficult to define the effect environment plays in the development of low self-esteem. A person learns values and has needs satisfied within the environment through social interaction with significant others, and if needs are not met and the expression of beliefs and values meet with disapproval within the environment, self-esteem is likely to be damaged.

An additional aspect of environment has to do with the groups within the environment with which the person identifies. Each member of a group is evaluated by every other member. If the group is significant to an individual, these evaluations affect self-esteem. For example, if a person's perception is one of not being valued by the group, low self-esteem is probable. Esteem is related to one's rank in a group rather than rank of the group when compared to other groups (Rosenberg, 1965).

As the population has moved from country to city areas, the environment in which children had built-in networks and role models has diminished and, in many cases, been lost. In the past, grandparents, aunts, uncles, cousins, neighbors, and friends were available to help educate and advise young people, and that was a given. In the absence of such an array of support, young people have turned to their peers for guidance and approval. In doing so, they use peer norms, created out of lack of experience, for evaluating behavior rather than the collective experience and wisdom of a network of adult role models (Glenn & Nelson, 1989).

Parents have also suffered a loss of support. In most cases, the parents have no network of relatives nearby to assist in parenting, and they have to depend on themselves to make the right choices. And they have no experience being parents. Because both parents usually work, they parent part time. In single-parent families, even part-time parenting is shared with other stresses involved in survival. So now we have time factors as well as inexperienced parents as well as the challenges presented to children in today's world. It becomes easier to see why parents use the same stress reducers as their children.

Cultural Influences on Self-Esteem

Self-esteem develops within the cultural environment in which an individual lives (Hales, 1990). Culture defines how roles will be played by members. An individual's success or failure in fulfilling cultural role expectations influences self-esteem. Success brings with it a feeling of belonging to a group, of being an important contributing member of that culture, of feeling good about self. Failure, of course, brings the opposite.

A problem occurs when at-risk youth belong to a nondominant culture and are faced with living in another culture, one with new or different expectations. Conflict is inevitable. A person who is respected for specific behaviors in one culture, and chastised or punished for the same behavior in another, could easily develop lowered self-esteem. We see evidence of this in at-risk youth today. Brendtro (1990) suggested that a feeling of competence is one aspect essential to the development of self-esteem, and in the scenario just described an individual may not feel competent.

Phinney (1992) suggested that continuing to identify with one's own culture as well as with the main culture is an important component of high self-esteem. Problems arise if the cultural or national group is not viewed as esteemed by other cultures/nations. Those identifying with the original culture/group may suffer low self-esteem. It becomes difficult when minorities identify with their own culture, are accepted and develop positive feelings of worth and belonging within that culture, and do not receive the same positive responses in the new culture. Ishiyama (1995) referred to this phenomenon as *cultural dislocation*. This is particularly painful when the culture of origin does not appear to be valued in the new culture, and the beliefs and values of the two cultures are divergent. We see this occurring with minorities when they experience difficulty assimilating another culture's values.

Another issue was highlighted in a recent discussion with immigrants to the State of Washington. Conflicts have emerged between those children who were born and lived in another country and culture before emigrating with their parents, and those who were born in the United States after the move. Members of the same family are conflicted, some wanting to retain what is known and familiar, and some wanting to fit in and not be associated with the old culture. Whatever the resolution of the conflict, it is a direct threat to self-esteem.

Sheets (1995) and Washington (1989) discussed the impact of school culture on self-esteem. Describing different ethnic cultures, they both agreed that teaching and programs that are culturally appropriate can help minorities maintain a positive level of self-esteem and self-validation.

To add to any existing conflicts between dual cultures' norms and values, Kumamoto (1997) explained that people's views of self and culture are changing because of the massive changes in the world today. The changing (or perhaps conflicting) guidelines for roles for everyone, regardless of culture, impact members of both the dominant and the minority cultures. With the resulting confusion, the success or failure in adapting to new ways of acting and interacting creates an additional assault on self-esteem.

In previous generations young people had roles to play that confirmed their value as important contributors to the welfare of the family and community. This gave them a meaningful role in their community and ensured the transfer of cultural beliefs and values (Glenn & Nelson, 1989). In contemporary society, with single-parent families and population mobility, that is less likely to occur. Changes in society have provided more passive ways for values to be transmitted to the young; the roles that are depicted in the media often do not reflect appropriate cultural beliefs and values. Further, many young people do not have multiple adult role models that can correct inappropriate perceptions of behaviors and beliefs illustrated in the media.

APPROACHES TO PREVENTION

The pervasive distress and too frequent demise of our young people seems to be out of control. Jason et al. (1993) reported that in Chicago schools, "more than 40% of children do not graduate [from] high school" (p. 69). These researchers believed that the problems leading to dropout often begin in the elementary schools. It is clear that some interventions, some low self esteem prevention strategies, must be integrated into every level of the community. In this section specific approaches for parents, individuals, schools, and communities are discussed. No one segment of the population is solely responsible for providing prevention. All groups should overlap, and building and maintaining high levels of self-esteem should become an integral part of the total community structure. Though parents are charged with the initial environment for the child, they too are part of a community and have need of resources from the community. A global approach that could be utilized by the entire community is described at the end of this section

Family

The environment in which a child is raised has a significant impact on the individual's self-esteem (Barber, Chadwick, & Orter, 1992; Blake & Slate, 1993; Cerezo & Frias, 1994; Harvey & Byrd, 1998; Shek, 1997). Historically, children were born into an intact family, and that was the primary environment in which the child learned about being an adult. Today, families vary in structure. Households where both parents work outside the home are common. Single parenting, stepparenting, joint parenting, parenting by someone other than the biological parent, and homelessness have altered family structures and added to the pressures young people face as they grow into adulthood. Many who find themselves in parenting roles have no idea how to accomplish this and fall back on personal experience. They feel the loss of assistance and experience that an extended family provides, so they parent as they were parented, as best as they can remember. They may have low self-esteem as a result of their own childhood experiences and perpetuate their own feelings of worth in their children. Their own parental role models may not have had the wisdom of the extended family experience either, and lack of parenting skills continues from one generation to the next.

In terms of prevention, steps must be taken to teach parents how to parent. Recognizing and admitting the need to learn parenting is a primary step in the process of building self-esteem. Today's parents have access to parenting classes and special support groups to help them learn to work with their children. These groups are sponsored by school specialists as well as churches and agencies in the community. Joining a class or support group serves a dual purpose. The parents learn skills at the same time that they are increasing their network of support. Getting to know neighbors is another excellent way to extend their support network and can serve as a means to check perceptions of neighborhood situations.

Parents must understand their own needs for success, status, and control as these needs relate to their childrearing practices. They must be able to put these needs aside and respond to each child as a unique person and to recognize and accept the contributions their children make in the family. There may have to be conscious efforts made to include each child and to discover ways in which each child can successfully contribute to the well-being of the family. Taking out the garbage can become significant if a child understands that his or her contribution is important to the family. When a parent asks a child for assistance with a task or project, one that cannot be done alone, the child learns that his or her contribution is an integral part in the task completion. In this case, it is essential that the child understands his or her help is not gratuitous but essential. For example, if the family pet has a thorn in a paw, it is difficult for one person to hold the animal, examine or probe the paw, and extract the thorn. It is much easier if someone else holds the animal. Asking for the child's assistance, and pointing out that this task is difficult or impossible for one person to do alone, validates the value of the individual's contribution.

Another way to prevent low self-esteem is to allow children to do what they can do and not do it for them. Often adults, who can do it faster or better, become impatient and complete tasks for the children. This indicates a lack of respect for the child and gives negative messages about the child's abilities and worthwhileness. These negative messages are both overt and covert and have a powerful effect on self-esteem. Though it may be difficult, allowing a child to complete a task more slowly and in a different manner or to make a mistake brings greater opportunities for learning. Using the mistake as a teachable moment is of greater value than scolding, punishing, or doing it for them.

Spending time with the child, talking or playing, gives positive messages about the child's importance. Letting children know that they are valued is critical in building self-esteem. Ironically this is often the most difficult prevention technique; it takes time and is the first date to be canceled when schedules get tight. During regularly scheduled time together, bonds are cemented, relationships are nurtured, and both parent and child feel important. In using this strategy, parents must listen carefully, suspend judgment, and be accepting of the child's point of view. Children will discuss serious topics if they believe what they say will be heard and valued. They also learn from the role modeling.

Many families hold regularly scheduled meetings to discuss family matters. These meetings are used to resolve conflicts, plan outings, make decisions about the household, test out new ideas, and involve the whole family in a variety of discussions. Again, these should not be canceled except with solid reasons. If meetings are canceled too often, their usefulness diminishes. The interesting effect of using preventative measures is that the parents' or parental figures' self-esteem grows as well. When parent-child interactions are positive and productive, both participants feel valued.

Individual

Self-esteem develops as a result of interaction with and feedback from others. It is doubtful whether an individual can build self esteem in a vacuum. If the feedback is negative, either verbal or nonverbal, the individual internalizes negative feelings about self and has poor feelings of worth. If feedback is positive and the individual feels successful, self-esteem is enhanced. An individual who feels valued and worthwhile has high self-esteem and responds to others in a manner that communicates this level of self-esteem.

It is difficult, perhaps impossible, for someone suffering from low self-esteem to undertake a prevention program alone. Most of the feedback that builds or destroys self-esteem comes either directly or indirectly from others. An individual is influenced by role models and can be encouraged to learn skills and attitudes that will lead to success experiences. As self-esteem is raised, a person may seek out avenues that will bring more success.

Volunteering, learning to be assertive, learning to cope with anger and conflict constructively, attending workshops and special classes to learn life skills, and entering programs that are specifically designed for young people are all ways an individual can build self-esteem. In each of these possibilities, external guidance is often necessary for a person with low self-esteem.

School

Because every child has the opportunity to attend school, this is an ideal place to continue the low self-esteem prevention programs. Hamachek (1995) noted that school performance and "self-attitudes" (i.e., self-esteem) are interactive. Johnson, Johnson, and Taylor (1993) reported higher levels of self-esteem achievement and cohesion in fifth graders who participated in cooperative learning environments. Strategies for improving school performance cannot be developed without attending to methods to "help students feel better about themselves" (p. 422). Educators have long been aware of the need for students to feel good about themselves and what they can do. Many schools have peer-tutoring or lower-grade-tutoring programs, peer helpers, and student aides. In such tutoring programs students are paired with students for teaching or coaching. The tutored students are either peers or, in many cases, younger students in elementary schools. Peer helper programs train selected young people in listening skills and have them talk with and listen to their peers. Student aides assist teachers and office staff. Some of these programs tend to exclude the high-risk populations.

Reasoner (1994) described several programs that have been successful in improving self-esteem and reducing crime and violence. A Florida high school program focused on positive adviser/advisee relationships and reported that within 3 weeks grade point averages and attendance, both indicators of levels of self-esteem, improved (Testerman, 1996). Still another study (McCormick & Wold, 1993) found positive changes in self-concept of gifted and talented females who had exhibited underachievement in science and math after exposure to a program describing nontraditional career choices.

Hains (1994) reported on the effectiveness of a cognitive stress management program that helped high school participants make significant improvements in developing self-esteem and in reducing anxiety, depression, and anger. In another cognitive restructuring program, subjects either were exposed to a computer-based program that targeted irrational beliefs or to a relaxation training program. Those participating in the computer-based program improved self-esteem (Horan, 1996).

A mediation intervention program was piloted at a middle school in Georgia in which results indicated a decrease in suspensions, a school morale improvement, and an increase both in requests for peer mediation and the belief that it works (Thompson, 1996). Edmondson and White (1998) found significant improvement in the self-esteem of students who participated in both a tutorial and a counseling program. Conclusions drawn from a 3-year longitudinal study of urban children in Georgia stressed the importance of both early and developmentally specific interventions (Spencer, 1991). Kraizer (1990) discussed skills children need to master the stresses of development. She identified a list of life skills essential to successful passage into adolescence, then advocated early and continuing intervention to prevent development of inappropriate behaviors.

Because schools are community institutions and have the most contact with children, and because many services were available to families, but delivery was fragmented and/or crisis oriented, the West Virginia Education Association and Appalachia Educational Laboratory (1993) surveyed the existing school/community partnerships in that state. In this survey process, the researchers gathered information about problems inherent in school-linked services and about additional school-linked service possibilities. With these data, the research team developed profiles for each of these social service programs and made recommendations for changes at the school, district, and policy-making levels.

School and district level recommendations
- The responsibilities of schools should include serving as a focal point to connect families with health and social service providers.
- The mission of the school should include health and social services provision.
- Educational focus should be on prevention and early intervention.
- Schools should provide training to staff to teach them to work effectively with health and social service problems of students.
- Research and evaluation should be undertaken regularly to assess program success and recommend any needed improvements.
- Districts should establish foundations whose funds would be used to develop programs to benefit children and families. Independent sources would donate these funds. (p. 36)

Policy recommendations
- Funding for programs for at-risk populations should be provided for in the budget, which would serve to standardize school-linked programs. These programs should be protected from budget cuts.
- Early intervention and prevention programs should be given priority.
- Operational procedures of schools and service providers should be examined and changed if these procedures interfere with effective delivery of services. (p. 37)

The recommendations reflect the belief that no one group or institution is totally responsible for bringing health and social services to those community members who need them. The philosophy is that the entire community must work as a team, with the school being the common link between service providers and families.

Jones and Watson (1990) studied high-risk students in higher education. Several of their findings can be considered for earlier educational experiences as well. Recommended prevention programs and strategies are to

- market benefits of persistent, positive student behaviors;
- provide career information beginning at an early age, and encourage goal identification;
- use low-achieving college students to tutor students K–12—which raises self-esteem of each participant;

- encourage and market counseling services as part of the curriculum, and involve teachers in the referral process;
- provide in-class programs designed to teach positive attitudes and skills that include acceptance of others, such as high-risk students;
- use peer advisers;
- enlist school organizations to develop programs to assist fellow students;
- provide educational programs to teach teachers how to teach, and provide opportunities for teachers to learn alternative teaching techniques and ways to empower students;
- evaluate testing materials to see that needs of high-risk students are being assessed effectively;
- develop orientation programs addressing the needs of high-risk populations;
- acknowledge school personnel who work with high-risk students by reducing class loads; develop methods to assure high-risk students an in-school support system; use local businesses to provide opportunities for high-risk students to do visits, internships, or part-time work in the community; consider inviting business people into the classroom to work with students as many schools do; and
- provide programs for teachers and school personnel to examine their attitudes toward minorities, women, and other high-risk populations. (pp. 85–88)

Community

If we accept the philosophy that at-risk students and families and the school are all part of the total community, any of the just listed strategies can be offered throughout the community and sponsored by any business or agency. Specific programs located in a major metropolitan area that may be similar to programs available in other areas are as follows:

YMCA Teen Services (1994)

- *County Youth Initiative* provides opportunities for leadership training, public speaking, project planning and delivery of community services, and employment.
- *Earth Service Corps* provides opportunities for environmental education and action, leadership development, and project planning and implementation.
- *The Manifesto Newspaper* provides an opportunity, through a youth-produced countywide newspaper, for teenagers to share their ideas and creativity with members of the community.
- *Y-Zone* provides a safe, alternative environment for youth to participate in activities and special events on a weekend night. This has

expanded in adjacent communities to being available both weekend nights.
- *Youth Employment* sponsors a youth-run espresso cart at a local YMCA. The youth are hired and trained before they begin working this cart.

Central Area Youth Association (CAYA) (1992)
- *TeenPATH (Teen Parent Assistance and Transitional Housing Program)* provides assistance to homeless or near-homeless teen parents under the age of 18. The program's goal is to provide assistance to teen parents in breaking out of the poverty cycle. Through Teen-PATH, stable, safe housing is found. In return, the teen parent(s) are required to complete high school, get work training and/or employment, and be responsible parents.
- *Mentorship* assigns role models who offer companionship, guidance, and support and help empower participants to be free of gang and drug involvement.
- *STARS (Special Tutor for At-Risk Students)* provides one-on-one tutorial services to at-risk students in grades K-8. Tutors are available both in school and after school in churches, libraries, and community centers.
- *Sports Program* provides adult role models who focus on team work, mental health, physical health, and individual and group responsibilities.
- *4-H Challenge* teaches participants, particularly minority males, coping skills, communication skills, problem-solving skills, and decision-making skills.
- *Introduction to Challenge* places youth in support groups and introduces rules, concepts, and benefits of the Challenge program.
- *Boot Camp/National Guard* introduces youth to orderly, disciplined environments and provides opportunities for building self-esteem.
- *Job Power* allows youth to explore assets and liabilities in regard to employment.
- *Ropes Course* provides outdoor activities to help adult and youth participants learn and develop problem-solving, goal-setting, and communication skills while experiencing total commitment.
- *I'll Take Charge* provides opportunities for youth to take responsibility for their choices.
- *Self-Determined Projects* allow members to determine, with guidance, their own projects that might not be available otherwise.
- *Multimedia* teaches students techniques and technology involved in video production while exposing them to drama, music, and arts.
- *Job Readiness* helps youth create contacts without turndowns, teaches them job interviewing skills, and brings the community together to help youth become productive, responsible members of society.

- *Elite Boxing* provides a meaningful outlet for physically aggressive youth in a positive, acceptable manner.
- *BALANCE (Beautiful, Ambitious Ladies Able to Negotiate with Commitment to Self-Esteem and Excellence)* provides weekly support groups for young women, through which substance abuse education and services are provided.

STARS I and II

- Two community-based programs for African American youth, STARS I and II, target at-risk youth aged 6 to 10 years and 11 to 17 years and their parents or guardians. In STARS I "sessions focused on cultural legacy family communication, the role of the extended family, and decision making" (Dabrowski, Avety, Gyger, & Emshoff, 1993, p. 4). The program for the older children focused on drug education, assertiveness, resisting peer pressure, raising self-esteem, and family communication. Program outcomes showed improvement in all areas for both adults and the children.

Other programs and types of programs that may be available include adventure-based counseling as an intervention to foster self-esteem (Nassar-McMillan & Cashwell, 1997) and a similar wilderness program for youth with attention deficit hyperactive disorder (ADHD) in which activities are built to address the characteristic behaviors of this population (Kennison, 1996). Camp Elsewhere has provided a program for adolescent females with eating disorders and has reported a positive impact (Tonkin, 1997). A university-sponsored 2-week residential leadership education program for adolescent girls has also reported a positive impact on participants' self-confidence (Taylor & Rosselli, 1997).

The HAWK federation, which focuses on issues unique to Black adolescent males and is rooted in African traditions, is another type of program that may be available. Initial reports have indicated that those who are involved improve their academic achievement (Nobles, 1989). Delgado 1997) has described a substance abuse program for Puerto Rican teenagers. Another program with a cultural focus is MAAT Center for Human and Organizational Enhancement, Inc., a rites-of-passage program for Egyptian adolescents (Harvey & Coleman, 1997). (*Maat* is an Egyptian word meaning virtuous or moral life.)

Additional community programs to consider include volunteer chore services; training to become volunteers; volunteer opportunities in social service agencies, churches, and community agencies; and community projects sponsored by individual clubs and organizations, for example, Junior Chamber of Commerce and Boys and Girls Clubs. Many of these offer training and provide built-in support and networking sources.

A Global Approach to Prevention

Seven tools that are critical to the parenting process and building of self-esteem have been identified by Glenn and Nelson (1989). These tools can also be used in schools, in the community, and by individuals. The authors noted that they discovered these tools, which are basic to survival in times of change, while they were studying failure, not success (p. 48).

The Significant Seven
1. Perceptions of personal capabilities
2. Perceptions of personal significance
3. Perceptions of personal power or influence over life
4. Intrapersonal skills
5. Interpersonal skills
6. Systemic skills
7. Judgmental skills. (pp. 48–49)

Perception, as described by the authors, is "the conclusion we reach after we have had time to reflect on that experience" (p. 51). Perception guides our attitudes and behaviors, and as we mature, we become more and more creatures of perception. Perceptions include four components: "the experience, what we interpret as significant about the experience, why it is important, and how we generalize the experience" (p. 55). Because perceptions change as we mature and because they are unique to each individual, it is important that the four components reflect the perceiver's point of view. Even if an experience is shared, perceptions of the experience differ for each participant. It is significant to each person in different ways and important to each person for different reasons, and the experience is generalized individually. In terms of building self-esteem, the learner must see the personal importance and value of an experience for himself or herself. As teachers or role models, we have to suspend our own perceptions, judgments, and beliefs, and genuinely and respectfully listen to the learner's perspective.

In teaching the first tool and helping young people develop a strong idea about their personal capabilities, there are some critical behaviors we have to give up (Glenn & Nelson, 1989). We must give up assuming that we know how someone else will react in situations and acting as if that were true. We no longer need to rescue or explain, expect attainment of perfection, or dominate and control. Instead, we must learn to listen and hear individual perceptions; check out assumptions; be open to, accepting, and respectful of a young person's thoughts and feelings; and be encouraging and celebrate successes. These changes in adult behaviors will help young people begin to feel valued and respected in the community.

As noted earlier, years ago each family member used to feel that his or her contributions were essential to the family's maintenance and survival.

For the most part, this reality has been lost. What has not been lost is the need to be needed. The individual's perception of personal significance is of primary importance. To develop this second tool, we must find ways to acknowledge each individual's personal worth, to help them see that the family is richer because this person is contributing his or her uniqueness. This can be done by listening, understanding, and accepting another's perspective, by soliciting ideas and perceptions from young people, by having frequent personal contact, and by providing a loving, warm family climate.

The third tool, the individual's belief in his or her ability to influence life, refers to the earlier discussion of internal versus external locus of control. Adults can help children build this internal power by establishing firm boundaries for behavior. One of the purposes for maladaptive behavior is to see if limits are real. If an adult cares enough to set limits and adhere to them, the child learns that he or she is valued and loved and knows the parameters within which to make decisions about behavior. At the same time, he or she also learns about the natural or logical consequences of stepping outside of these parameters. Children will learn from their mistakes if allowed to do so. They will build a belief system that says they have influence over their world. As already noted, adults have to be good listeners so there can be continued discussions with the child as he or she matures and encounters new decision-making opportunities.

Intrapersonal skills, the fourth tool, refer to an individual being able to understand and express feelings, to exercise self-control and self-discipline (Glenn & Nelson, 1989). As a child learns to make decisions within established boundaries, in new situations he or she can consider available responses and choose appropriately. The parent who does not allow the child to make a decision, and does it for him or her, is a primary interference here. A better intervention is to provide a list of alternatives, discuss with the child the consequences of each action (from the child's perspective), and allow the child to decide.

Interpersonal skills, the fifth tool, refer to those skills that allow people to communicate with each other. The extent to which a young person learns these skills is closely related to how well he or she gets along with others. Adults can teach these skills through modeling and talking with children.

The systemic and judgmental skills, identified by Glenn and Nelson (1989) as the sixth and seventh tools, are not always specifically taught. They are based on, composed of, and the result of earlier lessons learned. Understanding how the system in which we live works is to become aware of the connection between what we do and the result of our actions. By becoming aware of cause and effect, we learn to predict outcomes and are able to set attainable, realistic goals. We learn to be flexible and to take responsibility for our actions because we know the possible outcomes or consequences. In order for children to learn and increase these skills, adults must provide information about behavior in a caring, respectful climate. Helping an individual to develop good judgment skills requires adults to allow the person most affected by the decision to make it, to provide opportunities for young people to make decisions and experience the consequences, and to collaborate with them during the process. As part of the learning process, we also need to help them evaluate their decisions.

CASE STUDY: PROJECT REACH

Project Reach is an alternative program for at-risk students in the Socorro School District in Texas (Heger, 1992). Students in this program are in serious trouble in school and have reached the stage where the next step is expulsion. Health education, drama, group therapy, and computer-assisted instruction are blended in a program designed to prevent dropouts or expulsions and to assist in the reintegration of these at-risk students into the mainstream.

The curriculum is a traditional curriculum delivered in a nontraditional way, through computers. In the remaining time during the school day, students participate in health and drug education, drama, and personal log writing. The psychological part of the program is described as similar to Tough Love and Boot Camp, which are highly structured programs that leave no doubt as to limits and consequences of misbehavior.

The school day starts at 11 a.m. and continues into early evening, and admission is for an undetermined length of time. Students have levels of tasks to complete, and when these stages are accomplished, they are readmitted into the mainstream. The pace of progress is individualized.

Evaluators have found dramatic results. Attrition rates went from 84% in 1990-91 to 2.9% in 1992-93. At the same time, 76% of the students reported better grades. Students were surveyed periodically, and 86% believed the program was helpful to them. The longer they were in the program, the more helpful they reported it to be.

The success of this program is attributed to the design, the staff, and the execution. Staff members are from nontraditional backgrounds, and many have turned to teaching after trying other occupations. Some are not fully certified, but all have prior experience in helping people in nontraditional curricula.

SUMMARY

In our society, young people daily exhibit deviant behaviors. There is evidence every day that there are many more adolescents demonstrating characteristics that are understood to be at risk. These young people are considered at risk because unless they are helped to succeed, they will become part of the deviant subculture. Research has shown that there is a connection between how a person feels about himself or herself and how that person acts (Kaplan, 1975; Kaplan, Martin, & Johnson, 1986; Marston et al., 1988). Self-esteem is an issue that must be confronted as a cause of at-risk behaviors.

This chapter identifies specific symptoms of low self-esteem and factors that influence self-esteem as well as specific prevention programs and strategies for parents, individuals, schools, and communities. The activities and programs designed to be used with at-risk youth are not extensive. We must look within our own communities to discover available and successful youth programs. Additional information and resources may also be found in popular magazines (Corbett in *Essence*, 1995; Cordes in *Parenting*, 1994; Herman in *Utne Reader*, 1992; McMahon in *Cosmopolitan*, 1994; McMillan, Singh, & Simonetta in *Education Digest*, 1995; Tafel in *McCalls*, 1992). The goal is to reach all adolescents, particularly those at risk, and give them a chance to succeed and feel worthwhile.

REFERENCES

Abramson, L Y., Seligman, M.E.P., & Teasdale, J. D. (1978). Learned helplessness in humans. Critique and reformulation. *Journal of Abnormal Psychology, 87*, 49–74.

Aronson, M., & Mettee, S. (1968). Dishonest behavior as a function of differential levels of induced self-esteem. *Journal of Personality and Social Psychology, 9*, 121–127.

Bachman, J. G., & O'Malley, P. M. (1986). The frog's pond revisited (again). *Journal of Personality and Social Psychology, 50*(1), 35–46.

Barber, B. K., Chadwick, B. A., & Orter, R. (1992). Parental behaviors and adolescent self-esteem in the United States and Germany. *Journal of Marriage and Family Therapy, 54*(1), 128–141.

Beane, J. A., & Lipka, R. P. (1980). Self-concept and self-esteem. A construct differentiation. *Child Study Journal, 10*, 1–6.

Benoit, R. B., & Mitchell, L. K. (1987). Self-efficacy: Its nature and promise as an approach to dealing with high school dropout among minorities. *CACD Journal, 8*, 31–38.

Blake, P. C., & Slate, J. R. (1993). A preliminary investigation into the relationship between adolescent self-esteem and parental verbal interaction. *The School Counselor, 41*(2), 81–85.

Bower, B. (1993). Gender paths wind toward self-esteem. Gender differences in self-esteem development. *Science News, 143*(20), 308.

Brendtro, L.K. (1990). *Reclaiming youth at-risk: Our hope for the future*. Bloomington, IN: National Education Service.

Buri, J. R., & Dickinson, K. A. (1994, May). *Comparison of familial and cognitive factors associated with male and female self-esteem*. Paper presented at the annual meeting of the Midwestern Psychological Association.

Buri, J. R., & Kircher, A. (1993, April). *Parental hostility, adolescent high standards, and self-esteem*. Paper presented at the 65th Annual Meeting of the Midwestern Psychological Association, Chicago.

Burnett, J. W., Anderson, W. P., & Heppner, P. P. (1995). Gender roles and self-esteem: A consideration of environmental factors. *Journal of Counseling and Development, 73,* 323–326.

Central Area Youth Association (CAYA). (1992). *A history and overview* (paper and brochures). (Available from CAYA, 119 23rd Ave., Seattle, WA 98122)

Cerezo, M., & Frias, D. (1994, November). Emotional and cognitive adjustment in abused children. *Child Abuse and Neglect: The International Journal, 18,* 23–32.

Cohen, L. H., Burt, C. E., & Bjorck, J. P. (1987). Life stress and adjustment: Effect on life events experienced by young adolescents and their parents. *Developmental Psychology, 23*(4), 583–592.

Corbett, C. (1995). The winner within: A hands-on guide to healthy self-esteem. *Essence, 26*(2), 56–70.

Cordes, H. (1994). Resources: Groups, books, magazines, and other tools for building girls' self-esteem. *Parenting, 8*(3), 96.

Dabrowski, R. M., Avetry, M. E., Gyger, R. L., & Emshoff, J. G. (1993). *Community-based, family-focused prevention of youth substance use*. Paper presented at the Southeastern Psycholocical Association, Atlanta, GA.

Delgado, M. (1997). Strengths-based practice with Puerto Rican adolescents: Lessons from a substance abuse prevention project. *Social Work in Education, 19*(2), 101–112.

Domino, G., & Blumberg, E. (1987). An application of Gough's conceptual model to a measure of adolescent self-esteem. *Journal of Youth and Adolescence, 16*(2), 87–90.

Dwyer, V. (1993). Eye of the beholder: Young women have self-image problems. *Maclean's, 106*(8), 46–47.

Edmondson, J. H., & White, J. (1998). A tutorial and counseling program: Helping students at risk of dropping out of school. *Professional School Counseling, 1*(4), 43-47.

Elliott, G. C. (1988). Gender differences in self-consistency: Evidence from an investigation of self-concept structure. *Journal of Youth and Adolescence, 17*(1), 41–57.

Enns, C. Z. (1992). Self-esteem groups: A synthesis of consciousness-raising and assertiveness training. *Journal of Counseling and Development, 71,* 7–13.

Eskilson, A., Wiley, G., Meuhlbauer, G., & Dodder, L. (1986). Parental pressure, self-esteem, and adolescent reported deviance: Bending the twig too far. *Adolescence, 21*(83), 501–515.

Frey, D., & Carlock, C. J. (1984). *Enhancing self-esteem*. Muncie, IN: Accelerated Development.

Glenn, H. S., & Nelson, J. (1989). *Raising self-reliant children in a self-indulgent world*. Rocklin, CA: Prima.

Graf, R. C. (1971). Induced self-esteem as a determinant of behavior. *Journal of Social Psychology, 85,* 213–217.

Hains, A. A. (1994). The effectiveness of a school-based, cognitive-behavioral stress management program with adolescents reporting high and low levels of emotional arousal. *The School Counselor, 42*(2), 114–25.

Hales, S. (1990, Winter). Valuing the self: Understanding the nature of self-esteem. *The Saybrook Perspective*, pp. 3–17.

Hamachek, D. (1995). Self-concept and school achievement: Interaction dynamics and a tool for assessing the self-concept component. *Journal of Counseling and Development, 73*, 419–423.

Harvey, A. R., & Coleman, A. A. (1997). An Afrocentric program for African American males in the juvenile justice system. *Child Welfare, 76*(1), 197–211.

Harvey, M., & Byrd, M. (1998). The relationship between perceptions of self-esteem, patterns of familial attachment, and family environment during early and late phases of adolescence. *International Journal of Adolescence and Youth, 7*(2), 93–111.

Heger, H. K. (1992, October). *Retaining Hispanic youth in school: An evaluation of a counseling-based alternative school program*. Paper presented at the annual conference of the Rocky Mountain Educational Research Association, Stillwater, OK.

Herman, E. (1992). Are politics and therapy compatible? A lesson from the self-esteem movement. *Utne Reader*, pp. 97–100.

Horan, J. J. (1996). Effects of computer-based cognitive restructuring on rationally mediated self-esteem. *Journal of Counseling Psychology, 43*(4), 371–75.

Ishiyama, F. I. (1995). Culturally dislocated clients: Self-validation and cultural conflict issues and counseling implications. *Canadian Journal of Counseling, 29*(3), 262–273.

Jason, L. A., Weine, A. M., Johnson, J. H., Danner, K. E., Kurasaki, K. S., & Warren-Sohlberg, L. (1993). The school transition project: A comprehensive preventative intervention. *Journal of Emotional and Behavioral Disorders, 1*, 65–70.

Johnson, D. S. (1981). Naturally acquired learned helplessness: The relationship of school failure to achievement behavior, attributions, and self-concept. *Journal of Educational Psychology, 73*(2), 174–180.

Johnson, D. W., Johnson, R. T., & Taylor, B. (1993). Impact of cooperative and individualistic learning on high-ability students' achievement, self-esteem, and social acceptance. *Journal of Social Psychology, 133*(6), 839–844.

Jones, D. J., & Watson, B. C. (1990). *High-risk students and higher education*. Washington DC: Clearinghouse on Higher Education, George Washington University.

Kaplan, H. B. (1975). *Self-attitudes and deviant behavior*. Pacific Palisades, CA: Goodyear.

Kaplan, H. B. (1976). Self-attitude and deviant response. *Social Forces, 54*, 788–801.

Kaplan, H. B., Martin, S. S., & Johnson, R. J. (1986). Self-rejection and the explanation of deviance: Specification of the structure among latent constructs. *American Journal of Sociology, 92*(2), 384–411.

Kennison, J. A. (1996). Therapy in the mountains. *Proceedings of the 1995 International Conference on Outdoor Recreation and Education*.

Kraizer, S. (1990). Skills for living: The requirement of the 90s. In *Critical issues in prevention of child abuse and neglect—Adolescent parenting life skills for children* (pp. 131–139). Children's Trust Fund of Texas.

Kumamoto, C. C. (1997, March). *Unison in variety, congeniality in difference: Sifting beyond the multicultural sieve*. Paper presented at the 48th annual meeting of the Conference on College Composition and Communication, Phoenix, AZ.

Leung, K., & Drasgow, F. (1986). Relation between self-esteem and delinquent behavior in three ethnic groups. *Journal of Cross-Cultural Psychology, 17*(2), 151–167.

Lord, S., Eccles, J. S., & McCarthy, K. A. (1994). Surviving the junior high school transition: Family processes and self-perceptions as protective and risk factors. *Journal of Early Adolescence, 14*(2), 162–199.

Lorr, M., & Wunderlich, R. A. (1986). Two objective measures of self-esteem. *Journal of Personality Assessment, 50*(1), 18–23.

Mack, J. E., & Ablon, S. L. (Eds.). (1983). *The development and sustenance of self-esteem in childhood.* New York: International Universities Press.

Marston, A. R., Jacobs, D. F., Singer, R. D., Widaman, K. F., & Little, T. D. (1988). Characteristics of adolescents at risk for compulsive overeating on a brief screening test. *Adolescence, 23*(89), 59–72.

Maternal and Child Health Branch, Hawaii State Department of Health. (1991). *Adolescent health in Hawaii: The adolescent health network's teen health adviser report.* Rockville, MD: Health Resources and Services Administration.

McCormick, M. E., & Wold, J. S. (1993). Programs for gifted girls. *Roeper Review, 16*(2), 85–88.

McMahon, S. (1994). Let us now praise me. *Cosmopolitan, 217*(2), 68–70.

McMillan, J. H., Singh, J., & Simonetta, L. G. (1995). Self-oriented self-esteem self-destructs. *Education Digest, 60*(7), 9–12.

Nassar-McMillan, S. C., & Cashwell, C. S. (1997) Building self-esteem of children and adolescents through adventure-based counseling. *Journal of Humanistic Education and Development, 36*(2), 59–67.

Nobles, W. W. (1989, July 25). *The HAWK Federation and the development of Black adolescent males: Toward a solution to the crises of America's young Black men.* Testimony before the Select Committee on Children, Youth, and Families in the Congressional Hearings on America's Young Black Men: Isolated and in Trouble, Washington, DC.

Ohannesian, C., Lerner, R., Lerner, J- V., & Von Eye, A. (1994). A longitudinal study of perceived family adjustment and emotional adjustment in early adolescents. *Journal of Early Adolescence, 14*(3), 370–390.

Phinney, J. S. (1992). Acculturation attitudes and self-esteem among high school and college students. *Youth and Society, 23*(3), 299–312.

Reasoner, R. W. (1994). *Self-esteem as an antidote to crime and violence.* Unpublished manuscript.

Robison-Awana, P., Kehle, T. J., & Jenson, W. R. (1986). But what about smart girls? Adolescent self-esteem and sex-role perceptions as a function of academic achievement. *Journal of Educational Psychology, 78*(3), 179–183.

Rosenberg, M. (1965). *Society and the adolescent self-image.* Princeton, NJ: Princeton University Press.

Saltzman, A. (1994). Schooled in failure? Fact or myth—teachers favor boys; girls respond by withdrawing. *U.S. News & World Report, 117*(18), 88–93.

Sheets, R. H. (1995). From remedial to gifted: Effects of culturally centered pedagogy. *Theory Into Practice, 34*(3), 186–193.

Shek, D.T.L. (1997). Family environment and adolescent psychological well-being, school adjustment, and problem behavior: A pioneer study in a Chinese context. *Journal of Genetic Psychology, 153*(1), 113–128.

Simmons, R. C., Burgeson, R., Carlton-Ford, S., & Blyth, D. A. (1987). Impact of cumulative change in early adolescence. *Child Development, 58,* 1220–1234.

Spencer, M. B. (1991). *Adolescent African American male self-esteem: Suggestions for mentoring program content.* Mentoring program structures for young minority males, conference paper series. (Available from the Publications Office, Urban Institute, P.O. Box 7273, Department C, Washington, DC 20044)

Tafel, R. (1992). How your self-esteem affects your child's. *McCalls, 119*(6), 40–42.

Taylor, E. L., & Rosselli, H. (1997). *The effect of a single gender leadership program on young women.* Paper presented at the annual meeting of the American Educational Research Association, Chicago, IL.

Testerman, J. (1996). Holding at-risk students. *Phi Delta Kappan, 77*(5), 364–65.

Thompson, S. M. (1996). Peer mediation: A peaceful solution. *The School Counselor, 44*(2), 151–154.

Tonkin, R. S. (1997). Evaluation of a summer camp for adolescents with eating disorders. *Journal of Adolescent Health, 20*(6), 412–413.

Washington, E. D. (1989). A componential theory of culture and its implications for African American identify. *Equity and Excellence, 24*(2), 24–30.

West Virginia Education Association and Appalachia Educational Laboratory. (1993). *Schools as community social-service centers: West Virginia programs and possibilities.* (Available from Appalachia Educational Laboratory, P.O. Box 1348, Charleston, WV 25325)

Yanish, D. L., & Battle, J. (1985). Relationship between self-esteem, depression, and alcohol consumption among adolescents. *Psychological Reports, 57,* 331–334.

Yankelovich, Y. D. (1981). *New rules: Search for self-fulfillment in a world turned upside down.* New York: Random House.

YMCA. (1994). *YMCA teen services* [Flyer]. Seattle, WA: Seattle YMCA.

6 | Preventing and Treating Depression in Children and Adolescents

Benedict T. McWhirter, J. Jeffries McWhirter, Rebecca S. Hart, and Irit Gat

The incidence, nature, and treatment of depression during childhood and adolescence has been a topic of extensive research in recent years (Birmaher, Ryan, Williamson, Brent, & Kaufman, 1996; Brent et al., 1996; Kovacs & Devlin, 1998; Lewinsohn, Clarke, Rohde, Hops, & Seeley, 1996; Milling & Martin, 1992; Mufson, Moreau, & Weissman, 1996; Sheras, 1992). Currently, depression in youth is viewed as a significant problem that affects approximately 30% of the adolescent population (Lewinsohn, Hops, Roberts, Seeley, & Andrew, 1993) and between 2% and 5% of younger children (Milling & Martin, 1992). In fact, one in five youth report a minimum of one episode of major depression by the age of 18 (Lewinsohn et al., 1993). Furthermore, the prevention of depression in childhood and adolescence is critical to reducing the high cost of treating this disorder among adults (King, 1991). Therefore, child and adolescent depression is a major phenomenon and deserves the full attention of mental health and educational professionals.

This chapter focuses on the problem of child and adolescent depression. First presented are some of the definitional and diagnostic issues in child and adolescent depression. Next, the story of Esteban, a Latino adolescent who is struggling with depression, illustrates some of its causes and related intervention strategies. Some of the causal factors associated with this disorder are discussed, as are the prevention and treatment strategies that have been found to be effective for children and adolescents suffering from depression. The strategies discussed include interventions at the individual, family, school, and community levels. The chapter concludes with an exploration of how the various prevention and treatment strategies discussed can be combined to form a responsible and comprehensive response to young people experiencing depression.

PROBLEM DEFINITION AND
DIAGNOSTIC ISSUES

Until recently, depression in childhood and adolescence was not well addressed in the psychological literature. Early concepts, such as *adolescent turmoil* and the *masked depression* model either led practitioners to discount depression or hindered their understanding of depression in childhood and adolescence. For instance, adolescent turmoil suggests that all adolescents go through a period of turmoil that may appear to be pathological (Garrison, Shoenbach, & Kaplan, 1985). But the symptoms of inner unrest and deviant behavior that characterize adolescent turmoil were thought to be a normal part of adolescence and, therefore, clinically unimportant (Garrison et al., 1985). The notion of masked depression also confused, rather than clarified, this clinical problem. This model suggested that although depression is experienced in childhood and adolescence, it is not manifested as such. Instead, it is masked by other behaviors associated with depression. These include anxiety, aggressiveness, delinquency, somatic complaints, substance abuse, poor peer relationships, negative body image, poor school performance, school phobia, loss of initiative, social withdrawal, and sleep difficulties (Aseltine, Gore, & Colten, 1998; Lewinsohn et al., 1996; Miller-Johnson, Lochman, Coie, Terry, & Hyman, 1998; Windle & Windle, 1997).

Current research, however, has refuted those ideas, and experts agree that depression in childhood and adolescence is a valid psychological disorder. In fact, adolescents seen in mental health centers are most frequently diagnosed with an affective disorder (Marcotte, 1997). Extensive research efforts to understand the course of depression in children and adolescents, and to find efficacious treatment, have been undertaken. It is now known that youth who have had depression are likely to have another episode within a few years (Birmaher, Ryan, Williamson, Brent, Kaufman, et al., 1996; Kovacs & Devlin, 1998; Lewinsohn et al., 1996). The importance of addressing depression among children and adolescents is apparent; therefore, it is appropriate to describe the procedures for the diagnosis of depression among youth.

For the last four decades, the most widely used diagnosis and classification system has been the *Diagnostic and Statistical Manual of Mental Disorders* (*DSM*; American Psychiatric Association). The revised, third edition, *DSM-III-R* (1987), began the clarification and classification of depression in children and adolescents by providing symptom descriptions. The most recent version, *DSM-IV* (1994), added precision to the diagnosis of depression in childhood and adolescence. The *DSM-IV* has addressed differential aspects of adolescent depressive symptomatology as opposed to common symptoms experienced by adults. It appears that in childhood the rates are relatively equal between boys and girls, but during adolescence females have increased rates of depression closely paralleling the gender differences found in adulthood (Birmaher, Ryan, Williamson, Brent, Kaufman, et al., 1996; Kazdin, 1994). There is further symptom delineation between prepubescent children and adolescents. For example, children commonly display irritable mood rather than depressed mood, somatic complaints, and social withdrawal, whereas depressed adolescents typically display psychomotor retardation and hypersomnia. Furthermore, depression is comorbid in childhood and adolescence more often than in adulthood (Rohde, Lewinsohn, & Seeley, 1991). Prepubertal children typically display major depressive episodes in conjunction with disruptive behavior disorders, attention-deficit disorders, and anxiety disorders (American Psychiatric Association, 1994; Kovacs & Devlin, 1998). Adolescent depression is more commonly associated with anxiety, disruptive behavior disorders, attention-deficit disorders, substance-related disorders, and eating disorders (American Psychiatric Association, 1994; Birmaher, Ryan, Williamson, Brent, Kaufman, et al., 1996; Lewinsohn et al., 1996). In addition, the depressed adolescent is likely to have a depressotypic cognitive style, negative body image, less social support (peer and familial), and more conflictual family interactions than nondepressed peers.

In the *DSM-IV* mood disorders are divided into three major categories: depressive disorders, bipolar disorders, and mood disorders due to a general medical condition. The depressive disorders include major depressive disorder, characterized by one or more depressive episodes without history of mania, and dysthymic disorder, characterized by conditions indicating mood disturbance that has been chronic or intermittent for at least 2 years but without the degree of severity to warrant a diagnosis of major depressive disorder. Bipolar disorders include bipolar I disorder, bipolar II disorder, and cyclothymic disorder. The bipolar disorders are distinguished by the presence of a manic episode. Cyclothymia, of course, is a milder form of bipolar disorder. The final category includes mood disturbances judged to be of medical etiology. This condition is found with increasing frequency among younger populations. The *DSM-IV* also includes specifiers such as seasonal pattern indicators (such as seasonal affective disorder) in which people become more depressed during certain times of the year. Practitioners should also pay attention to adjustment disorders that may be accompanied by depressed mood as another important diagnostic category. In summary, the *DSM-IV* can be a useful tool for the clarification and diagnosis of childhood and adolescent depression. It certainly can be helpful for assisting the young man in the following story.

CASE STUDY: THE STORY OF ESTEBAN

Esteban was a 15-year-old Mexican American high school sophomore who was referred to counseling at a community mental health center by his mother after he threatened to kill her with a kitchen knife. He had straight black hair—long on top and shaved from 1 inch above his ears on down. He had an earring in his left ear, crooked teeth, jeans that were fashionably oversized, and an untucked flannel shirt. Esteban attended a school where the majority of students were European American from middle-class backgrounds. In our first session, Esteban sat silently and played with his hands while his mother provided information about the family and described her concerns.

Esteban had two sisters, Reynalda (Reina), age 16, and Catalina, 13. His mother, Irma, and his father, Reynaldo, were married when they were 18 and 20, respectively. According to Irma, Reynaldo began a series of extra-marital affairs shortly after Esteban was born. He had always been a heavy drinker and lost his job with the mining company after "too many Monday flus." The family environment described by Irma included harsh and inconsistent discipline by Reynaldo and guilt-induced permissiveness by Irma, in a context of poverty, frequent moves, and anxiety regarding Reynaldo's next binge. On several occasions, Reynaldo hit Irma in front of the children and was frequently verbally abusive toward her. Irma had finally divorced Reynaldo 3 years ago, and within 2 months he was remarried to an 18-year-old. Currently, Irma was working the 3 to 11 p.m. shift at a factory. Reynaldo has had intermittent contact with his children since the divorce. Reina and Esteban "hated" his new wife, Tina, and Reynaldo refused to spend time with them apart from Tina.

Irma described Esteban as a sweet little boy who had grown into a monster like his father. When he entered high school last year, his average grades began slipping, he started to smoke, and he skipped classes. Whenever Irma confronted him, she reported that Esteban would use the same verbally abusive language that his father used, such as "It's none of your business, you dirty whore." He refused to help out around the house and spent most of his time locked in his room listening to Savage Garden CDs with "a girl who dresses like a boy." When asked whether she had concerns about sexual activity between Esteban and this young woman, Irma said scornfully, "Even if she did want it—and that girl don't want it—he wouldn't know what to do." Esteban visibly flinched as she said this—his first overt reaction since arriving in the office.

Irma made the appointment for Esteban after an argument in which he shouted "If you don't leave me alone I'm going to come after you with that big ol' knife! Everybody hates you, and if I killed you they would laugh." Irma said that although she didn't think Esteban would kill her or even attempt to hurt her, she was frightened by the hatred in his voice.

When asked what she hoped counseling would accomplish, she said "Find my sweet little boy and bring him back to me."

The remainder of that first session was spent alone with Esteban. As soon as his mother left he asked if he could smoke. That was his only question and his only spontaneous communication. It quickly became obvious that he was painfully shy, embarrassed, and very nervous. His brief answers to my questions did not seem to convey hostility or resentment but a profound sense of frustration and inadequacy. Additional information slowly emerged in the one-on-one meeting. His mother had a string of boyfriends, none of whom he liked; he communicated very little with his siblings and knew nothing of how they felt; he had only one friend—the aforementioned "girl who don't want it"—who did, in fact, want it but so far had only permitted him to lie in bed naked with her. This they did regularly while listening to Savage Garden CDs and smoking cigarettes. When asked how he felt toward others—his mother, teachers, people at school—he stated, unconvincingly, that he hated them. He frequently stated, more convincingly, that he didn't care or didn't know about much of what was going on around him most of the time.

In subsequent sessions, Esteban began to communicate more openly, using longer sentences and asking more questions. It was clear that Esteban lacked many basic social skills. He spent much of his time at home while his mother worked. Often, her current boyfriend would hang out there while she worked. He didn't like this, but it was the only time that he would talk with his sisters—they would hang out in his room to avoid their mother's boyfriends. There were no indications of any attempted sexual contact between any of the boyfriends and the three children. Esteban indicated that he was embarrassed to ask his teachers for help and so he never tried to talk to them. He also reported that he felt responsible for his father's behavior—that if he wasn't the way that he was, his father would not have been a drunk and been so violent.

Esteban seemed to hate himself as much, if not more, than others around him. He was clearly experiencing a great deal of pain, frustration, guilt, and depression. Although he did not want to feel so isolated from others, he felt "stuck" and had never been taught the skills to move forward.

CAUSAL FACTORS

Esteban's depression could have been caused by any number of factors. In this section, some of the more central causal and conceptual models of depression—biological, psychodynamic, behavioral, cognitive, and family systems—and how each of these models might apply to Esteban are described. In the next section, how these causal models flow into effective prevention and treatment is discussed.

Biological Models of Depression

Biological models of depression can be divided into two main categories: those that focus on the role of genetic factors and those that emphasize biochemical aspects of depression. There is a strong genetic component in the risk of depression (Kovacs & Devlin, 1998). Based on adult twin and adoption research, genetic factors account for approximately 50% of the variance in the transmission of mood disorders (Birmaher, Ryan, Williamson, Brent, Kaufman, et al., 1996). They also report that children of depressed parents are three times more likely to have a major depressive episode at some point during their lives; this likelihood increases when the parent has had multiple depressive episodes (Garber & Robinson, 1997). Moreover, in studies of depressed children, 25% to 54% percent of first-degree relatives, and approximately 15% of second-degree relatives have major depression (Kovacs & Devlin, 1998). The specific nature of genetic transmission has not been determined, and further studies using children and adolescents may help to clarify the genetic contributions to the onset and maintenance of depression.

Another biological model of depression focuses on biochemical processes such as growth hormones, seritonergic systems, hypothalmus-pituitary-adrenal axis, and so forth (Birmaher, Ryan, Williamson, Brent, Kaufman, et al., 1996). Neurotransmitter actions and their interactions with antidepressant medications have been the focus of much biochemical research on depression. Whether a primary cause of depression or a secondary component, some evidence suggests that abnormalities in the metabolism of neurotransmitters are present in people who are depressed and can be counteracted with antidepressant drugs. Research has indicated more success in treating depressed adults with antidepressant medication, but studies with children and adolescents have continued to focus on pharmacological interventions with youth (Birmaher, Ryan, Williamson, Brent, & Kaufman, 1996; Kye et al., 1996; Sommers-Flanagan & Sommers-Flanagan, 1996).

Although psychopharmacological interventions are commonly and successfully used with adults, the results with youth have not been as promising (Birmaher, Ryan, Williamson, Brent, & Kaufman, 1996; Kye et al., 1996; Sommers-Flanagan & Sommers-Flanagan, 1996). Most medication trials using antidepressants and youth have failed to demonstrate significant differences between the active medications and the placebos (Brent et al., 1996). Controlled trials of tricyclic antidepressants (TCA) (e.g., amitriptyline, imipramine) have not been demonstrated to be effective with improving adolescent depression (Kye et al., 1996). Sommers-Flanagan and Sommers-Flanagan (1996) reviewed five studies using tricyclic antidepressants and two studies and one chart review using selective serotonin reuptake inhibitors (SSRI) and depressed youth. They found TCA to have serious side effects and low efficacy on the depression (Boulos et al., 1991; Geller, Cooper, Graham, Marsteller, & Bryant, 1990; Geller, Cooper, McCombs, Graham, & Wells, 1989; Kutcher et al., 1994; Puig-Antich et al., 1987). Results with the SSRIs were inconclusive, but more promising than those using the TCAs (Boulos, Kutcher, Gardner, & Young, 1992; Jain, Birmaher, Garcia, Al-Shabbout, & Ryan, 1992; Simeon, Dinicola, Ferguson, & Copping, 1990). The lack of significant results must be interpreted with caution. Many of the trials had small or heterogeneous sample sizes, used the medications for a short duration, or did not obtain self-report information on the participants perceived mood in addition to the doctors' reports. It is clear that biological and chemical functioning of the developing child or adolescent reacts differently to traditional antidepressants that have been efficacious with adults; further investigation is warranted to determine appropriate use of antidepressants with children and adolescents (Birmaher, Ryan, Williamson, Brent, & Kaufman, 1996).

In Esteban's case, evidence suggests that both of his parents may have experienced depression. His mother's patterns of developing relationships and his father's alcoholism and abusiveness both support the notion that they suffered from a lack of coping skills and poor self-esteem—which is almost always a concomitant of depression. The weakness of this model in explaining Esteban's depression is that it does not attend to the profound impact of Esteban's environment in forming his behavior and feelings about himself and others.

Psychodynamic Models of Depression

Psychodynamic models of depression focus on the loss of meaning or satisfaction in one's life and its affect on self-esteem regulation (Bemporad, 1988; Wolf, 1988). Depression is generally expressed in one of two ways: anger turned inward or feelings of emptiness and loss. Heightened self-blame and rejection, often linked with the failure to live up to an idealized view of oneself, are viewed as reflections of the anger turned inward (Wolf, 1988). Low self-esteem develops because it is impossible to meet the standards of this idealized view of self. In contrast, the latter expression of depression relates to the loss of something important in one's life (e.g., relationship, job, academic achievement) without which one feels worthless or empty (Bemporad, 1988). This type of depression is viewed as a result of never being valued or accepted when young, so one's positive self-esteem does not develop. In this person, self-esteem is dependent on external sources rather than on an internal sense of worth so when the external source is lost the person is unable to maintain his or her self-worth. The reliance of these theories on untestable, intrapsychic constructs has prevented their validation, but these perspectives provide important conceptualizations of depression that can be useful for practitioners.

In Esteban's case, for example, it is likely that he did not feel valued while younger, so he did not learn to value himself. After the loss of his father he may feel no one will ever love him because he is unworthy of being loved. He may also believe that if only he was perfect, his father would not have left. His realization that he will never be perfect then becomes anger that is directed inward because he is unable to achieve perfection. Over time, these feelings have severely damaged Esteban's self-esteem. In order for Esteban to resolve his depression he must learn to value himself and accept realistic expectations for himself instead of trying to live up to an unachievable ideal.

Behavioral Models of Depression

Behaviorists view depression as a result of significant loss (Kovacs & Beck, 1977; Schwartz & Johnson, 1985) and the consequence of inadequate or insufficient reinforcement (Ferster, 1973, 1974). Lewinsohn's social learning theory provides a concise behavioral model of depression. This theory suggests that depressive behaviors are determined by the presence or absence of reinforcers and maintained through the reduction of response-contingent reinforcing events (Lewinsohn & Hoberman, 1985). Depression may be the result of limited positive reinforcement for the individual, which is determined by the number of potentially reinforcing events, the number of these events available in the environment, and the individual's social skills to elicit accessible reinforcers (Levitt, Lubin, & Brooks, 1983). Depression may also result from an excess in punishment, especially when it occurs at high rates, when the individual is highly sensitive to punishment, and when necessary coping skills to terminate punishment are limited (Lewinsohn & Hoberman, 1985). Unfortunately, the depressive behaviors stimulated by inadequate reinforcement are further reinforced by the concern or sympathy expressed by significant others. Eventually though, others avoid the depressed person because of the nature of his or her depressive behaviors, which minimizes positive reinforcement and further exacerbates the depression (Lewinsohn & Hoberman, 1985).

To illustrate this model, Esteban receives almost no positive reinforcement, except perhaps from his female friend. Further, his lack of social skills does nothing to elicit positive reactions from others. On the contrary, his surly manner elicits negative reactions from others so that he never receives the social reinforcement that he so desperately needs to help lift his feelings of depression. He feels more and more isolated, less liked by others, and subsequently more depressed.

Cognitive Models of Depression

Research has also supported the role of cognition in depression (Beck, 1967; Rehm, 1977; Seligman, 1974, 1975). The following cognitive models of depression are helpful in understanding this perspective.

- The first model, proposed by Beck (1967), suggests that cognition and affect are interactive, and that the prior occurrence of cognition determines a person's affective response to an event. If cognitions are distorted or inaccurate, the individual's emotional response is inappropriate. Dysphoria may be the affective response of one's tendency to interpret experiences and events as negative or self-devaluative, indicating a cognitive role in the experience of depression.

    Beck, Rush, Shaw, and Emery (1979) pointed to three cognitive components central to depression: the cognitive triad, schemas, and cognitive errors. The cognitive triad includes three negative thought patterns: a negative view of self, of the world, and of the future. Schemas, like personality traits, represent a stable cognitive pattern that individuals create in order to organize and evaluate information and events. People who experience depression develop schemas that distort environmental stimuli to coincide with a derogatory self-image. These dysfunctional or negative schemas are often created and exacerbated by faulty information processing, or consistent errors in logic, called cognitive errors. The person suffering from depression uses these automatic cognitive errors to evaluate events, often leading to negativistic, categorical, absolute, and judgmental thinking (Levitt et al., 1983; Lewinsohn & Hoberman, 1985).

- The second model of depression, Seligman's (1974, 1975) learned helplessness model, contends that depression exists in people who perceive that they have no control over their environment. They develop self-defeating attributions. They make internal (feeling responsible for an event), stable (the causes of an event remain constant), and global (event outcomes impact all areas of life) attributions for failure. In contrast, they attribute successful outcomes to external (caused by others), unstable (causes of events are transitory), and specific (situation specific) causes (Kaslow & Rehm, 1983). According to this model, this self-defeating attributional style results in the lowered motivation and reduced self-esteem common in depressed clients (Kaslow & Rehm, 1983). Self-defeating attributional style has been correlated with depression (Garber & Robinson, 1997; Lewinsohn & Hoberman, 1985). Cole, Martin, and Powers (1997) proposed a similar, competency-based model of depression. Their model links a child's perceived helplessness, pessimism, and depression to a negative self-construct based on a lack of competence across five important domains within his or her life (school, attractiveness, social, conduct, and athleticism). Thus if the child is unable to master tasks in one or more of these domains, he or she forms negative self-constructs leading to depression and helplessness.

- Rehm's (1977) self-control theory represents the third cognitive model of depression. Problems of self-control are manifested through deficits in three cognitive processes: self-monitoring, self-reinforcement, and self-evaluation. Depressed clients fail to view situations with an orientation to the future, and tend to concentrate on immediate consequences of events (Gilbert, 1984). They selectively attend to negative outcomes and focus on immediate reinforcements, a negative view of the self, the environment, and future results. Similarly, depressed individuals tend to have negative attribution styles in which events are seen as being due to either external causes beyond their control or to internal, unchangeable skill deficits. They tend to set high standards for positive self-evaluation and at the same time have low standards for negative self-evaluation (Lewinsohn, et al., 1996; Stark, Swearer, Kurowski, Sommer, & Bowen, 1996). They are likely to take credit for failures but not successes.

In accord with these models, cognitions play a key role in Esteban's depression. For example, Esteban maintains the faulty belief that he is responsible for his father's behavior and for the demise of his family. Likewise, he attributes negative outcomes to deficiencies in himself (a negative internal attribution) instead of to the dysfunctional family and unstable economic environment around him.

Family Models of Depression

A family systems approach to understanding the development of childhood and adolescent depression attends to family dynamics and the family environment. These dynamics are of considerable importance. Proponents of this perspective suggest that young people who experience depression are symptoms of family malfunction. The homeostasis of a maladaptive family system is maintained when a child or adolescent performs the role of the sick family member. This person is often referred to as the identified patient. In accord with this model, other family members often resist any positive change in the adolescent because it risks upsetting the homeostasis of the family. This reality necessitates the involvement of the entire family system in treatment interventions (Guttman, 1983; Nichols & Schwartz, 1995).

This approach requires Esteban's entire family to be involved in the treatment process. Although Esteban's concerns may be more acute right now, his sisters are both at risk for a variety of behavioral problems as well. Family intervention may help not only to resolve his issues but also to prevent future problems from being expressed by his siblings. Furthermore, the behaviors and messages of Esteban's mother and father must be explored in order for each family member to recognize the resulting consequences. Clearly, the ideal is for Esteban's mother and father to be involved in treatment and to make changes. But if his father is no longer involved with the core family, then at least Esteban's mother needs to understand and modify her patterns of communication and behavior. It is also important that the entire family receives support and validation in treatment, especially given the economic marginalization and racial victimization they experience. According to this model, if family members are unwilling to be involved in treatment, any individual intervention focused solely on Esteban is likely to be ineffective.

The next section discusses how these causal models of depression flow into effective prevention and treatment. We begin by presenting a conceptual framework for discussing intervention As before, we follow Esteban's treatment as a way of highlighting the practical aspects of the prevention and treatment strategies presented.

APPROACHES TO PREVENTION
AND TREATMENT

A conceptual model for understanding and intervening with at-risk youth has been proposed by McWhirter, McWhirter, McWhirter, and McWhirter (1998). This model is based on two key assumptions: (a) being at-risk for problematic behavior reflects not only a current condition but also an element of prediction for future problems, and (b) at-riskness must be viewed not so much as discrete and unitary but rather as a series of steps along a continuum. This continuum begins with youth who are at *minimal risk* for problematic behavior, proceeds through *remote risk, high risk,* and *imminent risk,* and ends with those already engaged in *category activity.* Category activity refers to participation in one or more destructive behaviors such as drug use, delinquent activity, and sexual promiscuity. A child or adolescent's placement along the at-risk continuum is mediated by demographics, family and school environments, psychosocial stressors, and personal characteristics of the youth (e.g., critical school competencies, concept of self, communication skills, coping ability, and control—McWhirter, McWhirter, McWhirter, & McWhirter, 1994). This model also proposes that prevention, early intervention, and treatment must involve the family, school, and community. In short, interventions must attend to current problems, to the potential for future difficulty, and to multiple aspects of a young person's life.

Using the McWhirter et al. (1998) model, for example, Esteban would be considered at imminent risk. He has a very negative family environment, comes from a poor socioeconomic background, experiences a great many psychosocial stressors including subtle and direct racial discrimination, and does not have effective coping skills or clear goals for his future. Further, he has already developed gateway behaviors, such as smoking, being sexually explorative, and having violent outbursts, that highly predict category behavior.

In accord with this model, practitioners should (a) use generic skills training prevention programs for children in early elementary grades, (b) move into more focused and topic-specific prevention/intervention efforts for youth around middle-school age or earlier if risk factors demand it, and (c) use more topic-specific treatments and second-chance programs for older youth or those already engaged in category activity. At the prevention end of the continuum, efforts are focused on the building of general skills, such as assertiveness, communication, recognizing feelings, and resolving conflict. At the treatment end of the continuum, interventions are focused on resolving specific problems that have already developed, such as depression, drug use, or delinquency, as well as on techniques that enhance a broad range of skills in order to prevent more serious problems from emerging as adolescents become young adults. For instance, Esteban needs treatment focused specifically on his depression and on its root causes as well as treatment focused on helping him develop skills for dealing with future problems across a wide range of areas. He could be helped by interventions for the entire family, by cognitive and behavioral strategies focused on him individually, by school intervention programs, and by community-based treatment approaches. Bronfenbrenner's (1979) ecological model is one way to conceptualize treatments across a variety of domains. He described four systems within a person's life: the micro-, meso-, exo-, and macrosystems. Each system represents a level of interaction of the person within his or her multiple contexts—from the immediate family to the political structures that organize society. We refer to this model when discussing subsequent interventions.

This section now discusses how the core components of prevention as well more specific treatment strategies might be applied to youth at-risk for depression. We describe these prevention and treatment strategies with a focus on the individual, family, school, and community, and we conclude by discussing a comprehensive intervention that reaches across domains.

Individual Approaches to Prevention and Treatment

Individual approaches vary, and practitioners should follow their own orientation in attending to child and adolescent depression. Frequently, individual approaches involve both individual and family sessions with the focus remaining on the depressed child or adolescent. Approaches include individual cognitive-behavioral interventions and interpersonal psychotherapy as well as pharmacological treatment.

Cognitive-Behavioral Interventions.   The focus here is on cognitive-behavioral approaches that can be used to prevent and treat depression because they have demonstrated proven effectiveness. For instance, Reinecke, Ryan, and DuBois (1998) conducted a meta-analysis of cognitive-behavioral therapy for depression and dysphoria. All of the 24 studies they included demonstrated positive results in the treatment and alleviation of depression in adolescents due to the cognitive-behavioral interventions employed. Similarly, Rosselló and Bernal (1996) modified a cognitive-behavioral treatment for depressed Puerto Rican adolescents, and their preliminary findings showed positive results for its use with this population. One caution is that in young children a cognitive focus may not be as effective because higher order thinking may not have developed yet.

Cognitive-behavioral treatments for depression flow directly from the cognitive and behavioral models described earlier. For example, Beck et al. (1979) developed a therapy with both behavioral and cognitive components designed to reduce automatic negative cognition with the goal of challenging the assumptions that maintain these faulty cognitions. Because clients often have difficulty utilizing cognitive tasks, behavioral strategies should be used first in the therapeutic process. These strategies include scheduling pleasant activities, relaxation training, graduated task assignments, social skills training, role-plays, and behavioral rehearsal (Lewinsohn et al., 1996; Reinecke et al., 1998). Behavioral strategies increase an individual's activity level and, therefore, the frequency of potentially rewarding activities, which may also increase the level of response-contingent reinforcement. During depression, there is a tendency to withdraw from activities and interactions with others. Behavioral strategies directly address withdrawal behaviors and encourage children and adolescents to be active, which in turn lessens the attention to and perseverance of depressogenic cognitions. Behavioral interventions appear appropriate for Esteban. Unless he becomes more involved in more positive peer interactions and in pleasant activities, he may have great difficulty in improving his depressed mood and in learning more positive cognitions about himself and his environment.

After these strategies are successfully utilized, emphasis is moved to cognitive interventions that emphasize identifying, testing, and modifying cognitive distortions. Strategies that have been successfully used include

- recognizing the connection between cognition, affect, and behavior;
- monitoring negative automatic thoughts;

- examining evidence related to distorted automatic cognition;
- substituting more realistic interpretations for distorted cognitions;
- learning to identify and modify irrational beliefs;
- altering biased attentional processes;
- affect regulation; and
- impulse control (Brent et al., 1996; Ellis, 1962; Ellis & Bernard, 1983; Marcotte, 1997; Reinecke et al., 1998).

Such strategies could be implemented with Esteban as part of individual treatment in order to address his distorted cognitions and their relation to his mood and behavior. Of course, these strategies could be used as part of a prevention program in the school setting as well, which we discuss later.

Another cognitive-behavioral approach for depression is based on Rehm's self-control model. This intervention has been described as a primary prevention method, useful in teaching the skills necessary to avoid depression (Kaslow & Rehm, 1983). Kolko (1987) recommended that treatment in self-control involve specific training in monitoring positive events and self-statements, engaging in positive behaviors and cognitions, emphasizing long-term positive consequences, developing more realistic and achievable goals, making more legitimate attributions, and creating more frequent self-reinforcements.

Consistent with these models, we have found two cognitive-behavioral techniques to be particularly helpful. First, ask the child or adolescent to repeat a standard, positive phrase, such as "I am a good person" every time they take out a pen from their backpack. Second, ask the child or adolescent to write down on three-by-five cards a positive, affirming self-statement (e.g.,"I am an honest and decent person," "I am attractive and caring."). When three or four cards are completed, add one blank card and place them inside the child or adolescent's class notebook. Each time the notebook is used, the child or adolescent silently reads one of the cards. When the blank card turns up, the client must spontaneously make up a new, positive sentence. These types of interventions may prove helpful to Esteban who clearly needs to augment his positive self-statements.

Interpersonal Psychotherapy. Another individual approach that has received significant research attention and demonstrated positive results in alleviating depression in children and adolescents is interpersonal psychotherapy. Preliminary results indicate that, after appropriate cultural modifications, interpersonal psychotherapy had moderate success in treating depressed Puerto Rican adolescents (Rosselló & Bernal, 1996). Interpersonal psychotherapy conceptualizes depression as conflict taking place in the context of interpersonal relationships (Mufson et al., 1996). There are five areas that form the problem areas and treatment goals in interpersonal psychotherapy:

1. grief;
2. interpersonal role disputes;
3. role transitions;
4. interpersonal deficits; and
5. single-parent families (this is a modification for use with adolescents).

Goals in interpersonal psychotherapy are to reduce depression and address the underlying conflict that was associated with the depression. Examples of techniques used in this approach include exploratory questioning, linking affect and events, clarifying conflicts and communication patterns, and behavior modification strategies. This approach has received promising empirical support (Mufson & Fairbanks, 1996; Rosselló & Bernal, 1996). In the case of Esteban, interpersonal psychotherapy could focus on his grief over his parents' divorce as well as on interpersonal deficits (poor social skills) and coping in a single-parent family. Role transitions around adolescence and increasing independence may also be an area on which to focus.

Pharmacological Treatment. Pharmacological interventions are, in some cases, required with depressed clients. Medication usage for depressed youth has followed the trend of adult research. Since the 1960s tricyclic antidepressants have been prescribed for young patients (Hodgman, 1985). Although frequently used in the clinical setting, the effectiveness of antidepressants for children and adolescents has not yet been established through controlled research (Brent et al., 1996). Nevertheless, case studies and informal clinical lore consider pharmacological interventions as useful in the treatment of depression, especially severe and chronic depression.

In the case of bipolar disorders, medication is probably essential. The effectiveness of lithium carbonate with this type of depressive disorder has been well established. Of course, during a severe manic episode the behavior often causes problems that result in hospitalization. With adolescents, counselors and other practitioners need to be attentive to less severe mood swings or problems with a view to referral. Although the existence of a bipolar disorder does not seem probable in Esteban's situation, a medical referral for his depression may still be important.

Family Approaches to Prevention and Treatment

The role of the family in the successful treatment of the depressed child or adolescent is crucial. Family counseling has been shown to be even more important in the effective treatment of childhood disorders, in part due to the extensive influence families have over young children compared with adolescents (Nichols & Schwartz, 1995). Counselors using only an individually based intervention strategy may, in fact, be doomed to failure because from this perspective the entire family system needs to change. Clinicians must be prepared to work with all family members, especially parents who may also suffer from an affective disorder or have marital conflict, in order to be successful. Therefore, in Esteban's family, if his mother and sisters are not engaged in treatment, he is likely to continue to suffer from the same environment that contributed to his depression in the first place.

In many circumstances parent training and education can benefit the family and help prevent depression and other problems. Workshops for parents can be particularly useful and cost effective, especially those that focus on developing communication skills, enhancing family interactions, and sharing information about issues (such as birth control and signs of drug use). Workshops also offer parents a forum for discussing fears, concerns, and frustrations with other parents and with a professional facilitator, which can increase parental confidence and comfort with discussing issues with their children. In families with greater dysfunction, therapeutic programs attending to child abuse and neglect, parental dysfunction, and family violence may be extremely beneficial.

Parent training may also be utilized as prevention as well as treatment for many problems, including childhood and adolescent depression. Parent training includes parent effectiveness training (PET), family effectiveness training (FET), and systemic-behavioral family therapy (SBFT).

- *Parent effectiveness training* (Gordon, 1975, 1977) combines lectures, role-playing, and homework exercises to train parents in healthy confrontation, conflict resolution, and active listening skills.
- *Family effectiveness training* (Szapocznik, Santisteban, Rio, Perez-Vidal, & Kurtines, 1986a, 1989) is a preventative training model for Latino families of preadolescents at risk for future drug abuse. FET is designed to address three problems that often serve as antecedents to adolescent behavior problems: maladaptive family interactions, intergenerational conflict, and intercultural conflict. It is one of few empirically tested programs that directly address cultural differences. The model has three components.

  The first component, family development, helps the family to negotiate the childhood-to-adolescence transition. All family members learn constructive communication skills and take increased responsibility for their own behaviors. Parents become educated about drugs so that they can teach their children; they also learn the skills to become democratic rather than authoritarian leaders.

  The second component, bicultural effectiveness training (BET; Szapocznik, Santisteban, Kurtines, Perez-Vidal, & Harris, 1984; Szapocznik et al., 1986b), is designed to bring about family change by (a) temporarily placing the blame for the family's problems on the cultural conflict within the family and (b) establishing alliances between family members through the development of bicultural skills and mutual appreciation of the values of both cultures. The family learns to handle cultural conflicts more effectively and reduces the likelihood that such conflicts will occur. BET represents an excellent parent training program in and of itself. This program will be particularly helpful for Esteban's family who contends with acculturation issues as well as overt and covert racism on a daily basis.

The third component of FET is the implementation of brief strategic family therapy. Based on the work of Minuchin (1974), this component involves a series of family therapy sessions and is the most experiential aspect of this didactic/experiential model. The entire training consists of 13 sessions that last from 1 1/2 to 2 hours; the entire family is present for each session. In addition, FET can be modified to deal specifically with other child and adolescent behavior problems.

- *Systemic-behavioral family therapy* (Brent et al., 1996) is a combination of functional family therapy (FFT; Alexander & Parsons, 1973, cited in Brent et al., 1996) and a behavior component developed by Robin and Foster (1989, cited in Brent et al., 1996). In this approach the counselor joins with each family member and obtains commitment and engaged participation from each person. Then the problem is clarified and goals are set. Deficient communication and problem-solving skills, as well as structural difficulties (parent-child alliances), are conceptualized as the focus of the difficulty. Interventions include family tasks, self-monitoring, and positive practice. Although the study by Brent and colleagues is still in progress, early results indicated that this treatment remitted depression in approximately two thirds of the adolescent participants.

These programs represent some of the effective parent training programs that are useful for preventing depression. Others include some of the extensive, empirically based, parent training models developed by Carolyn Webster-Stratton and her colleagues and others (e.g., Dinkmeyer & McKay, 1989; Webster-Stratton, Kolpacoff, & Hollingsworth, 1989). Additional parent training is often available at local community counseling centers on a variety of topics including behavior management and discipline, nutrition, family budgeting, and preventing chemical dependency.

Parent training programs could help Esteban, but because he already shows clear signs of depression, direct therapeutic intervention with the whole family is indicated. Helping Irma and her children communicate more effectively with each other, and clarifying roles and boundaries, have the potential of creating a great deal of change in the family. In addition, helping each of the children to see their value and importance in the family is important. The family can become a primary source of support and encouragement if family members can share their needs, wants, and feelings more effectively.

School-Based Approaches to Prevention and Treatment

The occurrence of depression among children and adolescents has increased in recent years and may be due, in part, to environmental stressors (Birmaher, Ryan, Williamson, Brent, Kaufman, et al., 1996). This finding supports the need for early prevention and intervention in the school setting. One goal school personnel can achieve is the early identification of depressed children and adolescents who sometimes are overlooked for depression due to acting-out behaviors (Hart, 1991). The discussion here on school prevention is quite extensive because schools are an ideal setting for prevention: most children and adolescents can be reached, and most can be taught critical life skills as an integral part of school-based curriculum. Training in life skills can reduce existing problems as well as prevent more serious ones from occurring. As such, school-based programs can prevent child and adolescent depression as well as many other problems.

In responding to depression, school-based prevention programs engage multiple strategies. School counselors should use instruments to assess depression. To be effective, assessment should consider the youngster's cognitive and affective characteristics, environment, life stressors, and relationships with others (Hart, 1991; Vernon, 1993). School prevention and treatment should include a mixture of affective, cognitive, and behavioral strategies; self-acceptance; problem solving and decision making; and social skills or interpersonal relationships (Vernon, 1989a, 1989b). Further, group interventions are central to many school-based prevention programs because of their ability to reach a large number of children and their adaptability to the classroom format.

Early prevention in the schools can take the form of educational programs focused on forming friendships (social skills), nonviolent conflict resolution, assertiveness training, relating to adults, dealing with peer pressure, and improving critical school competencies such as basic academic skills and academic survival skills (McWhirter et al., 1994). Broad-based skills training programs such as these not only prevent depression but also help to prevent other critical problems, such as teenage pregnancy and drug use. Schools are important focal points in building these prevention programs because they provide access to both families and communities. In Esteban's case, such programs might have provided the social skills training that he did not receive at home as well as assistance in mastering academic survival skills that he may have missed due to his frequent moves.

The core components of good life skills prevention programs include (a) interpersonal communication, (b) strategies for cognitive change, (c) coping with stress, and (d) managing health (McWhirter et al., 1998). Life skills are those that involve behaviors and attitudes necessary for coping with academic challenges, communicating with others, forming healthy, stable relationships, and making good decisions. Life skills training programs emphasize the acquisition of generic social and cognitive skills. The theoretical foundation of life skills training includes Bandura's (1977) social learning theory and Jessor and Jessor's (1977) problem behavior theory. In accord with these perspectives, children and adolescents are not blamed for causing their problems, but are viewed as capable of learning new ways to behave that reduce the likelihood of future problems.

Counselors and other mental health professionals can all be involved in teaching life skills. Procedures for teaching life skills resemble those used in the teaching of any other skill. Overall tasks are broken down into smaller stages or component parts and taught systematically, moving from simple to more complex skills. Each life skills session follows a five-step model: (a) instruction (teach); (b) modeling (show); (c) role-play (practice); (d) feedback (reinforce); and (e) homework (apply). Within this general framework, steps may be modified in accord with the needs of the classroom or group. Three broad skill categories are usually included in basic life skills programs:

- *interpersonal communication skills*, including assertiveness and refusal skills;
- *cognitive change strategies*, including problem solving, decision making, self-control and self-management skills, and cognitive-behavioral restructuring approaches; and
- *anxiety coping approaches*, including relaxation, imagery training, and exercise.

Learning effective social skills is core to life skills training because it improves and increases the positive feedback and reinforcement that is received from others (Lewinsohn, Biglan, & Zeiss, 1976). Treatment here focuses on the improvement of interpersonal style and on the development of skills, such as peer etiquette and group entry (Frankel, Cantwell, & Myatt, 1996). Modeling, feedback, role-playing, instruction, situation logs, and homework practice are all utilized to help augment social skills and minimize the depression caused by an inability to elicit positive consequences. The prevalence of social skills deficits and the results of social skills training among children and adolescents have received limited attention; generalizability from group to external environments has had mixed results (Frankel et al., 1996). Nevertheless, such approaches seem especially appropriate for Esteban. Given the fact that he has had relatively little peer group interaction, and prefers to be by himself, it appears that he has not developed effective social skills with his peer group. Indeed, he seems unable to cope with the responses of his classmates and family. Thus social skills training appear to be a very useful strategy to help lift his depression.

Life skills training can also be achieved through leadership training programs. For example, students provided with leadership opportunities exercise decision-making skills and learn the importance of self-control (What Schools Can . . . , 1987). Some researchers have found very positive effects from improving adolescent students' problem-solving and decision-making skills (Beyth-Marom, Fischhoff, Jacobs, & Furby, 1989). Specifically, schools have reported marked reduction in disruptive behaviors after teaching students to mediate disputes on their own (Lane & McWhirter, 1992). The ability of students to solve their own problems and peacefully settle disputes directly and positively impacts student climate and reduces the likelihood of violence. The development of school mediation programs as models of student-centered conflict resolution have been especially helpful in this regard (Lane & McWhirter, 1992; Schrumpf, Crawford, & Usadel, 1992).

Exercise, nutrition, and additional self-care habits are often ignored in prevention efforts, but are also very helpful. In a study by Brown, Welsh, Labbe, Vitulli, and Kulkarni (1992), a group of psychiatrically institutionalized adolescent boys and girls were assigned to a 9-week aerobic exercise program. The treated girls showed lower incidence of depression, anxiety, hostility, confused thinking, and fatigue, and both the adolescent males and females in the aerobics program showed improved vigor and self-efficacy. The added benefits of employing exercise and nutritional strategies with youth are multifold because forming healthy habits early in life is easier than changing habits later in life. Similarly, utilizing stress reduction techniques in school, such as relaxation training, biofeedback, autogenic training, meditation, affirmations, and guided visual imagery, may also be helpful in preventing or reducing depression among children and adolescents.

School-based small group intervention programs for depression and other psychosocial problems have not often been rigorously evaluated, but existing outcome studies indicate some positive results. For example, Vernon (1989a, 1989b) developed an effective emotional education curriculum based on rational emotive therapy by Albert Ellis. This program targets thoughts, affect, and behavior and has specific grade level interventions targeted to the young person's developmental level. Topics such as self-acceptance, feelings, behaviors, problem solving, decision making, and interpersonal relationships are addressed. In addition, groups that help adolescents cope with parental divorce have also proven to be effective in ameliorating loneliness (Lesowitz, Kalter, Pickar, & Chethik, 1987) and have helped raise self-esteem and increased a sense of control in life (Omizo & Omizo, 1987). Groups for violent youth have also shown several positive effects in reducing school behavior problems (Roth, 1991). However, although results are promising, more research on school-based depression interventions is needed.

Community Approaches to Prevention and Treatment

Thus far we have reviewed individual, family, and school approaches for the prevention and treatment of childhood and adolescent depression. Many of the interventions discussed in this chapter could easily be employed by counselors, psychologists, social workers, and other mental health professionals who work in community agencies. But approaches that specifically involve the larger community acknowledge the role of the larger context in which depression and other problems of childhood and adolescence emerge. Thus we focus now on a larger community program. Given the high correlation between delinquency and depression (McWhirter et al., 1998), the community program described here can be seen as a treatment as well as a prevention measure for depression and other concerns.

Teencourt (McWhirter, 1994; McWhirter et al., 1998), a community program that is used in Gila County, Arizona, is for first-time juvenile offenders between the ages of 8 and 17 who have committed a misdemeanor offense, status offense, or minor traffic violation. The Teencourt program incorporates leadership skills, critical thinking, career exploration, taking responsibility, and influencing peer norms. Youth referred to Teencourt have a choice of (a) pleading guilty, participating in the program, and keeping their record clean; or (b) going through the traditional juvenile court system. Teencourt sentencing is designed to fit the offense and usually includes community service, tutoring, attending workshops, and/or traffic survival school.

Each session of Teencourt lasts 4 months and involves six attorneys, 20 jurists, one court clerk, and three bailiffs, all of whom are trained high school students. Thus offenders passing through Teencourt are tried by their peers; the judge is the only adult representative of the legal system. All defendants are required to serve a term of jury duty after their own sentencing. This is consistent with the goals of Teencourt, which include preventing repeat offenses among those who are tried; preventing first-time offenses among the many students who voluntarily participate as attorneys, bailiffs, jurists, and clerks; educating adolescents about the legal system; and utilizing peer pressure to evoke conformity to positive behaviors. The recidivism rate for Teencourt participants is well below both state and national averages (McWhirter, 1994). This program models an empowerment philosophy as defined by McWhirter (1994) because it not only prevents future problems but also helps young people develop skills for helping others and for changing their communities.

Thus far, Esteban has not been accused of any legal violation, although he does smoke prior to the legal age. However, his involvement in some offense could not be surprising given his current alienation, anger, and apathy. Participation in a program such as Teencourt as an offender and then a jury member could have a considerable positive effect on Esteban. Teencourt's philosophy of empowerment is manifested in a variety of ways: by increasing adolescents' awareness of the legal system, providing specific skills training as well as the broader experience of leadership and citizenship, utilizing peers (of equal power status) rather than adults, involving adolescents with community organizations, tailoring sentences to individual offenses, and emphasizing responsibility for behavior (McWhirter, 1994). In the context of Seligman's model of learned helplessness, the Teencourt program addresses many of the deficiencies and apathetic responses from which Esteban suffers.

Adaptations for Diversity

We have discussed the issues of individual, family, school, and community interventions, but we are still confronted with a very depressed 15-year-old who needs support. The comprehensive model we propose here is built on the foundation of a solid interpersonal relationship between the depressed child or adolescent and the helpers in his or her environment: counselors, teachers, and parents. This relationship, although necessary and yet not sufficient for fully treating depression, must incorporate the basic conditions of empathy, genuineness, warmth, and respect for differences. It must also incorporate multicultural awareness and sensitivity. In this case, multicultural sensitivity involves more than knowledge of Mexican American cultural norms; it must include awareness of the effects of societal influences such as racism, oppression, and economic marginalization on people of color and their communities.

Bronfenbrenner's (1979) ecological model describes the dynamic interaction of four basic systems within an individual's life and provides a framework for a comprehensive intervention. At the most basic level of the ecological model is the *microsystem* that is composed of the individual and his or her interactions within small contexts such as the family, classroom, and friends. Esteban's microsystems include his sibling relationships, relationship with his mother, family interactions, his classes, and his peers. Next is the *mesosystem*, in which interactions become more complex. This system involves the interactions of the individual and significant others across microsystems, such as a conference with Esteban,

Irma, and one of his teachers. The *exosystem* is the even larger systems that indirectly influence the child. It does not include the direct interaction of the youth. This could refer to a school in-service that the individual's teacher attends that may indirectly affect the child. Finally, the *macrosystem* represents the larger societal influences that distantly relate to the individual. Government educational policies, race relations, and economic barriers within a person's community are all examples. Using this model helps counselors and others to examine the direct and indirect influences on a youth's depression and can illuminate possible ways to prevent or intervene.

Given the complexity of Esteban's present problems and the threat of future overtly violent behaviors, we recommend employing a comprehensive treatment strategy that addresses Esteban's different contexts (micro- and mesosystems) and his cognitions, behaviors, and affect as well as attends to larger environmental issues (exo- and macrosystems). The nature and severity of his depression should be assessed thoroughly, via a family intake with measures of anxiety, depression, anger, and self-esteem. Vernon (1993) suggested that counselors and other helping professionals use the HELPING model developed by Keat (1979, cited in Vernon, 1993) who adapted it from multimodal therapy (Lazarus, 1976, cited in Vernon, 1993) as a comprehensive assessment strategy. Each letter stands for a domain within the child's life: health, emotions, learning, personal relationships, imagery, need to know, guidance of actions, behaviors, and consequences. In sum, in order to be accurate and clinically useful, Esteban's comprehensive assessment needs to include individual factors as well as contextual and interpersonal factors such as family dynamics, poor school performance, fear of interaction with others, peer rejection, and the overt and covert racism that he experiences regularly.

After the assessment, an intervention should be collaboratively developed with Esteban and his family. This plan should be responsive to Esteban's degree of risk along the continuum presented earlier. He is currently depressed, but a skill-building intervention—the core of any prevention program—can prevent future depressive episodes and other problems. Effective intervention for Esteban should include

- behavioral interventions of life skills training and increasing age-appropriate pleasurable activities;
- cognitive interventions designed to identify, test, and modify his dysfunctional beliefs about himself, his family, his future;
- family interventions designed to improve the communication within the family and to improve his mother's parenting consistency; and
- school interventions designed to attend to his poor performance and relationships with peers.

In future work, Esteban may choose to become active in Mexican American groups at school or within the community. In addition, some understanding and potential use of biological and pharmacological interventions may be necessary if his depression does not remit.

SUMMARY

Depression is a significant and complicated mental health problem among children and adolescents. Its manifestation in childhood varies, but in adolescence is more similar to that found in adulthood. It has been linked to other at-risk factors such as suicide, school attrition, substance abuse, and behavior problems, further augmenting the difficulty in making appropriate diagnosis and establishing effective treatment interventions. Current research supports several treatment approaches as being equally successful in remitting depression. Future research should continue to examine the active ingredients in depression prevention and intervention in order to improve efficacy as well as to further our understanding of depression among children and adolescents. In light of effective medications for treating adult depression, but less effective results with youth, pharmacological research for depression in youth is especially recommended.

What is very clear is that depression can have a catastrophic effect on youngsters and on those around them. This is true for young Esteban. The interventions described that involve the individual, family, school, and community could all be employed in a comprehensive way to help tackle the depression that Esteban, and many young people, experience. Parents, counselors, teachers, and other school personnel who play primary roles in the lives of children and adolescents must be especially aware of and responsive to the symptoms, causes, and problems associated with depression. Recognizing and responding quickly to depression and to its root causes are especially important in avoiding the potentially devastating effects of this disorder on the young people with whom we live and work.

REFERENCES

American Psychiatric Association. (1987). *Diagnostic and statistical manual of mental disorders* (3rd ed., rev.). Washington, DC: Author.

American Psychiatric Association. (1994). *Diagnostic and statistical manual of mental disorders* (4th ed.). Washington, DC: Author.

Aseltine, R. H., Jr., Gore, S., & Colten, M. E. (1998). The co-occurrence of depression and substance abuse in late adolescence. *Development and Psychopathology, 10,* 549–570.

Bandura, A. (1977). Self-efficacy: Toward a unifying theory of behavioral change. *Psychological Review, 84,* 191–215.

Beck, A. T. (1967). *Depression: Causes and treatment.* Philadelphia: University of Pennsylvania Press.

Beck, A. T., Rush, A. G., Shaw, B. F., & Emery, G. (1979). *Cognitive therapy of depression.* New York: Guilford Press.

Bemporad, J. R. (1988). Psychodynamic treatment of depressed adolescents. *Journal of Clinical Psychiatry, 49*(9, Suppl.), 26–31.

Beyth-Marom, R., Fischhoff, B., Jacobs, M., & Furby, L. (1989). *Teaching decision making to adolescents: A critical review.* Washington, DC: Carnegie Council on Adolescent Development.

Birmaher, B., Ryan, N. D., Williamson, D. E., Brent, D. A., & Kaufman, J. (1996). Childhood and adolescent depression: A review of the past 10 years. Part II. *Journal of the American Academy of Child and Adolescent Psychiatry, 35*(12), 1575–1583.

Birmaher, B., Ryan, N. D., Williamson, D. E., Brent, D. A., Kaufman, J., Dahl, R. E., Perel, J., & Nelson, B. (1996). Childhood and adolescent depression: A review of the past 10 years. Part I. *Journal of the American Academy of Child and Adolescent Psychiatry, 35*(11), 1427–1439.

Boulos, C., Kutcher, S., Gardner, D., & Young, E. (1992). An open naturalistic trial of fluoxetine in adolescents and young adults with treatment-resistant major depression. *Journal of Child and Adolescent Psychopharmacology, 2,* 103–111.

Boulos, C., Kutcher, S., Marton, P., Simeon, J., Ferguson, B., & Roberts, N. (1991). Response to desipramine treatment in adolescent major depression. *Psychopharmacology Bulletin, 27,* 59–65.

Brent, D. A., Roth, C. M., Holder, D. P., Kolko, D. J., Birmaher, B., Johnson, B. A., & Schweers, J. A. (1996). Psychosocial interventions for treating adolescent suicidal depression: A comparison of three psychosocial interventions. In E. D. Hibbs & P. S. Jensen (Eds.), *Psychosocial treatments for child and adolescent disorders: Empirically based strategies for clinical practice* (pp. 187-206). Washington, DC: American Psychological Association.

Bronfenbrenner, U. (1979). The ecology of human development: Experiments by nature and design. Cambridge, MA: Harvard University Press.

Brown, S. W., Welsh, M. C., Labbe, E. E., Vitulli, W. F., & Kulkarni, P. (1992). Aerobic exercise in the psychological treatment of adolescents. *Perceptual and Motor Skills, 74,* 555–560.

Cole, D. A., Martin, J. M., & Powers, B. (1997). A competency-based model of child depression: A longitudinal study of peer, parent, teacher, and self-evaluations. *Journal of Child Psychology and Psychiatry, 38,* 505–514.

Dinkmeyer, D., & McKay, G. D. (1989). *Systematic training for effective parenting* (3rd ed.). Circle Pines, MN: American Guidance Service.

Ellis, A. (1962). *Reason and emotion in psychotherapy.* New York: Stuart.

Ellis, A., & Bernard, M. E. (Eds.). (1983). *Rational-emotive approaches to the problems of childhood.* New York: Plenum Press.

Ferster, C. B. (1973). A functional analysis of depression. *American Psychologist, 28,* 857–870.

Ferster, C. B. (1974). Behavioral approaches to depression. In R. J. Friedman & M. M. Katz (Eds.), *The psychology of depression: Contemporary theory and research* (pp. 29-53). New York: Winston-Wiley.

Frankel, F., Cantwell, D. P., & Myatt, R. (1996). Helping ostracized children: Social skills training and parent support for socially rejected children. In E. D. Hibbs

& P. S. Jensen (Eds.), *Psychosocial treatments for child and adolescent disorders: Empirically based strategies for clinical practice* (pp. 595–618). Washington, DC: American Psychological Association.

Garber, J., & Robinson, N. S. (1997). Cognitive vulnerability in children at risk for depression. *Cognition and Emotion, 11,* 619–635.

Garrison, C. Z., Shoenbach, V. J., & Kaplan, B. H. (1985). Depressive symptoms in early adolescence. In A. Dean (Ed.), *Depression in multidisciplinary perspective* (pp. 60-82). New York: Brunner/Mazel.

Geller, B., Cooper, T. B., Graham, D. L., Marsteller, F. A., & Bryant, M. (1990). Double-blind placebo-controlled study of nortriptyline in depressed adolescents using a "fixed plasma level" design. *Psychopharmacology Bulletin, 26,* 85–90.

Geller, B., Cooper, T. B., McCombs, H. G., Graham, D., & Wells, J. (1989). Double-blind placebo-controlled study of nortriptyline in depressed children using a "fixed plasma level" design. *Psychopharmacology Bulletin, 25,* 101–108.

Gilbert, P. (1984). *Depression: From psychology to brain state.* London: Erlbaum.

Gordon, T. (1975). *PET: Parent effectiveness training.* New York: American Library.

Gordon, T. (1977). Parent effectiveness training: A preventive program and its delivery system. In G. W. Albee & J. M. Joffe (Eds.), *Primary prevention of psychopathology* (pp. 175–186). Hanover, NH: University Press of New England.

Guttman, H. A. (1983). Family therapy in the treatment of mood disturbance in adolescence. In H. Golombek & B. Garfinkel (Eds.), *The adolescent and mood disturbance* (pp. 263–272). New York: International Universities Press.

Hart, S. L. (1991). Childhood depression: Implications and options for school counselors. *Elementary School Guidance and Counseling, 25*(4), 277–289.

Hodgman, C. H. (1985). Recent findings in adolescent depression and suicide. *Developmental and Behavioral Pediatrics, 6,* 162–170.

Jain, U., Birmaher, B., Garcia, M., Al-Shabbout, M., & Ryan, N. (1992). Fluoxetine in children and adolescents with mood disorder: A chart review of efficacy and adverse effects. *Journal of Child and Adolescent Psychopharmacology, 2,* 259–265.

Jessor, L. C., & Jessor, S. L. (1977). *Problem behavior and psychosocial development: A longitudinal study of youth.* New York: Academic Press.

Kaslow, N. J., & Rehm, L. P. (1983). Child depression. In R. J. Morris & T. R. Kratochwill (Eds.), *The practice of child therapy* (pp. 27–51). New York: Pergamon Press.

Kazdin, A. E. (1994). Psychotherapy for children and adolescents. In A. E. Bergin & S. L. Garfield (Eds.), *Handbook of psychotherapy and behavior change* (4th ed., pp. 543–594). New York: Wiley.

King, S. R. (1991). Recognizing and responding to adolescent depression. *Journal of Health Care for the Poor and Underserved, 2,* 122–129.

Kolko, D. J. (1987). Depression. In M. Herson & V. Van Hassalt (Eds.), *Behavior therapy with children and adolescents: A clinical approach* (pp. 137-183). New York: Wiley.

Kovacs, M., & Beck, A. T. (1977). An empirical-clinical approach toward a definition of childhood depression. In J. G. Schulterbrandt & A. Raskin (Eds.), *Depression in childhood: Diagnosis, treatment, and conceptual models* (pp. 1–25). New York: Raven Press.

Kovacs, M., & Devlin, B. (1998). Internalizing disorders in childhood. *Journal of Child Psychology and Psychiatry, 39*(1), 47–63.

Kutcher, S., Boulos, C., Ward, B., Marton, P., Simeon, J., Ferguson, H. B., Szalai, J., Katic, M., Roberts, N., Dubois, C., & Reed, K. (1994). Response to desipramine treatment in adolescent depression: A fixed-dose, placebo-controlled trial. *Journal of the American Academy of Child and Adolescent Psychiatry, 33*, 686–694.

Kye, C. H., Waterman, G. S., Ryan, N. D., Birmaher, B., Williamson, D. E., Iyengar, S., & Dachille, S. (1996). A randomized, controlled trial of amitriptyline in the acute treatment of adolescent major depression. *Journal of the American Academy of Child and Adolescent Psychiatry, 35*, 1139–1144.

Lane, P. S., & McWhirter, J. J. (1992). A peer mediation model: Conflict resolution for elementary and middle school children. *Elementary School Guidance and Counseling, 27*, 15–23.

Lesowitz, M., Kalter, N., Pickar, J., & Chethik, M. (1987). School-based developmental facilitation groups for children of divorce: Issues of group process. *Psychotherapy, 24*(1), 90–95.

Levitt, E. E., Lubin, B., & Brooks, J. M. (1983). *Depression: Concepts, controversies, and some new facts.* Hillsdale, NJ: Erlbaum.

Lewinsohn, P. M., & Hoberman, H. M. (1985). Depression. In A. S. Bellack, M. Herson, & A. E. Kazdin (Eds.), *International handbook of behavior modification and therapy* (student ed., pp. 173–207). New York: Plenum Press.

Lewinsohn, P. M., Biglan, A., & Zeiss, A. M. (1976). Behavioral treatment of depression. In P. O. Davidson (Ed.), *The behavioral management of anxiety, depression, and pain* (pp. 91–146). New York: Brunner/Mazel.

Lewinsohn, P. M., Clarke, G. N., Rohde, P., Hops, H., & Seeley, J. R. (1996). In E. D. Hibbs & P. S. Jensen (Eds.), *Psychosocial treatments for child and adolescent disorders: Empirically based strategies for clinical practice* (pp. 109-136). Washington, DC: American Psychological Association.

Lewinsohn, P. M., Hops, H., Roberts, R., Seeley, J. R., & Andrew, J. (1993). Adolescent psychopathology: I. Prevalence and incidence of depression and other *DSM-III-R* disorders in high school students. *Journal of Abnormal Psychology, 102*, 183–204.

Marcotte, D. (1997). Treating depression in adolescence: A review of the effectiveness of cognitive-behavioral treatments. *Journal of Youth and Adolescence, 26*, 273–283.

McWhirter, E. H. (1994). *Counseling for empowerment.* Alexandria, VA: American Counseling Association.

McWhirter, J. J., McWhirter, B. T., McWhirter, A. M., & McWhirter, E. H. (1994). High- and low-risk characteristics of youth: The five Cs of competency. *Elementary School Guidance and Counseling, 28*, 188–196.

McWhirter, J. J., McWhirter, B. T., McWhirter, A. M., & McWhirter, E. H. (1998). *At-risk youth: A comprehensive response* (2nd ed.). Pacific Grove, CA: Brooks/Cole.

Miller-Johnson, S., Lochman, J. E., Coie, J. D., Terry, R., & Hyman, C. (1998). Comorbidity of conduct and depressive problems at sixth grade: Substance use outcomes across adolescence. *Journal of Abnormal Child Psychology, 26*, 221–232.

Milling, L., & Martin, B. (1992). Depression and suicidal behavior in preadolescent children. In C. E. Walker & M. C. Roberts (Eds.), *Handbook of clinical child psychology* (2nd ed., pp. 319–339). New York: Wiley.

Minuchin, S. (1974). *Families and family therapy.* Cambridge, MA: Harvard University Press.

Mufson, L., & Fairbanks, J. (1996). Interpersonal psychotherapy for depressed adolescents: A 1-year naturalistic follow-up study. *Journal of the American Academy of Child and Adolescent Psychiatry, 35,* 1145–1155.

Mufson, L., Moreau, D., & Weissman, M. M. (1996). Focus on relationships: Interpersonal psychotherapy for adolescent depression. In E. D. Hibbs & P. S. Jensen (Eds.), *Psychosocial treatments for child and adolescent disorders: Empirically based strategies for clinical practice* (pp. 137–156). Washington, DC: American Psychological Association.

Nichols, M. P., & Schwartz, R. C. (1995). *Family therapy: Concepts and methods* (3rd ed.). Boston: Allyn & Bacon.

Omizo, M. M., & Omizo, S. A. (1987). Group counseling with children of divorce: New findings. *Elementary School Guidance and Counseling, 22,* 46–52.

Puig-Antich, J., Perel, J., Lupatkin, W., Chambers, W. J., Tabrizi, M. A., King, J., Goetz, R., Davies, M., & Stiller, R. L. (1987). Imipramine in prepubertal major depressive disorders. *Archives of General Psychiatry, 44,* 81–89.

Rehm, L. P. (1977). A self-control model of depression. *Behavior Therapy, 8,* 787–804.

Reinecke, M. A., Ryan, N. E., & DuBois, D. L. (1998). Cognitive-behavioral therapy of depression and depressive symptoms during adolescence: A review and meta-analysis. *Journal of the American Academy of Child and Adolescent Psychiatry, 37*(1), 26–34.

Rohde, P., Lewinsohn, P. M., & Seeley, J. R. (1991). Comorbidity with unipolar depression II: Comorbidity with other mental disorders in adolescents and adults. *Journal of Abnormal Psychology, 100,* 214–222.

Rosselló, J., & Bernal, G. (1996). Adapting cognitive-behavioral and interpersonal treatments for depressed Puerto Rican adolescents. In E. D. Hibbs & P. S. Jensen (Eds.), *Psychosocial treatments for child and adolescent disorders: Empirically based strategies for clinical practice* (pp. 157–186). Washington, DC: American Psychological Association.

Roth, H. J. (1991). School counseling groups for violent and assaultive youth. *Journal of Offender Rehabilitation, 16,* 113–131.

Schrumpf, F., Crawford, D. K., & Usadel, H. C. (1992). *Peer mediation: Conflict resolution in schools.* Champaign, IL: Research Press.

Schwartz, S., & Johnson, J. H. (1985). *Psychopathology of childhood* (2nd ed.). New York: Pergamon Press.

Seligman, M. E. (1974). Depression and learned helplessness. In R. J. Friedman & M. M. Katz (Eds.), *The psychology of depression: Contemporary theory and research* (pp. 83–125). New York: Wiley.

Seligman, M. E. (1975). *Helplessness: On depression, development, and death.* San Francisco: Freedman.

Sheras, P. L. (1992). Depression and suicide in adolescence. In C. E. Walker & M. C. Roberts (Eds.), *Handbook of clinical child psychology* (2nd ed., pp. 587-606). New York: Wiley.

Simeon, J. G., Dinicola, V. F., Ferguson, B. H., & Copping, W. (1990). Adolescent depression: A placebo-controlled fluoxetine study and follow-up. *Progress in Neuro-Psychopharmacology and Biological Psychiatry, 14,* 791–795.

Sommers-Flanagan, J., & Sommers-Flanagan, R. (1996). Efficacy of antidepressant medication with depressed youth: What psychologists should know. *Professional Psychology: Research and Practice, 27,* 145-153.

Stark, K. D., Swearer, S., Kurowski, C., Sommer, D., & Bowen, B. (1996). Targeting the child and family: A holistic approach to treating child and adolescent depressive disorders. In E. D. Hibbs & P. S. Jensen (Eds.), *Psychosocial treatments for child and adolescent disorders: Empirically based strategies for clinical practice* (pp. 207-238). Washington, DC: American Psychological Association.

Szapocznik, J., Santisteban, D., Kurtines, W. M., Perez-Vidal, A., & Hervis, O. (1984). Bicultural effectiveness training: A treatment intervention for enhancing intercultural adjustment in Cuban-American families. *Hispanic Journal of Behavioral Sciences, 6*, 317–344.

Szapocznik, J., Santisteban, D., Rio, A., Perez-Vidal, A., & Kurtines, W. M. (1986a). Family effectiveness training (FET) for Hispanic families. In H. P. Lefley & P. B. Pedersen (Eds.), *Cross-cultural training for mental health professionals* (pp. 245–261). Springfield, IL: Charles C Thomas.

Szapocznik, J., Santisteban, D., Rio, A., Perez-Vidal, A., & Kurtines, W. M. (1986b). Bicultural effectiveness training (BET): An experimental test of an intervention modality for families experiencing intergenerational/intercultural conflict. *Hispanic Journal of Behavioral Sciences, 8*, 303–330.

Szapocznik, J., Santisteban, D., Rio, A., Perez-Vidal, A., & Kurtines, W. M. (1989). Family effectiveness training: An intervention to prevent drug abuse and problem behaviors in Hispanic adolescents. *Hispanic Journal of Behavioral Sciences, 11*, 4–27.

Vernon, A. (1989a). *Thinking, feeling, behaving: An emotional education curriculum for adolescents: Grades 7–12.* Champaign, IL: Research Press.

Vernon, A. (1989b). *Thinking, feeling, behaving: An emotional education curriculum for children: Grades 1–6.* Champaign, IL: Research Press.

Vernon, A. (1993). *Developmental assessment and intervention with children and adolescents.* Alexandria, VA: American Counseling Association.

Webster-Stratton, C., Kolpacoff, M., & Hollingsworth, T. (1989). The long-term effectiveness and clinical significance of three cost-effective training programs for families with conduct problem children. *Journal of Consulting and Clinical Psychology, 57*, 550–553.

What schools can do to help disadvantaged children. (1987). *Education Digest, 53*, 14–18.

Windle, R. C., & Windle, M. (1997). An investigation of adolescents' substance use behaviors, depressed affect, and suicidal behaviors. *Journal of Child Psychology and Psychiatry, 38*, 921–929.

Wolf, E. S. (1988). *Treating the self: Elements of clinical self-psychology.* New York: Guilford Press.

7 | Stress and Trauma: Coping in Today's Society

Russell D. Miars

Multiple, conflicting time demands; social, economic, and political competition; and the complex and ever-changing nature of technology and the world of work characterize the society in which we live. As popularized in numerous self-help guides (Davis, Eshelman, & McKay, 1988; Girdano, Everly, & Dusek, 1990), coping with stress has become synonymous with modern adult life. Interestingly, however, the image of a carefree childhood void of stress and trauma has dominated our cultural view of youth for most of this century. Since the mid-1980s, however, there has been an increasing awareness that not only do children and adolescents experience stress and trauma (Dinicola, 1996; Humphrey, 1988; Youngs, 1985), but that also, in complex fashions yet to be understood, the numerous stresses and trauma youth actually do experience are linked to the alarming rise in their at-risk behavioral difficulties (Gottlieb, 1991). In addition, there is increasing interest in the role trauma (extreme stress) and posttraumatic stress play in at-risk behaviors and mental health problems of youth (Kilpatrick & Williams, 1998; Parson, 1995).

Paradoxically, although youth and adults alike seem to know what it means to be stressed (being under pressure; being tense or anxious about problems at work, school, or in the family), there has yet to emerge a uniformly agreed-upon definition of the stress concept by researchers. This problem of definition in the literature complicates any discussion of stress and coping in youth. Until recently, an additional complication in understanding stress in youth has been that most stress research has been conducted exclusively with adults (Johnson, 1986; Lazarus, 1991). This results in a temptation to extrapolate and apply our understanding of stress and coping in adults to youth (Ryan-Wenger, 1992). It is doubtful, however, that stress and coping in adults is the same, or directly similar, to stress and coping in youth (Johnson, 1986). In fact, several authors (Dise-Lewis, 1988; Humphrey, 1988; Sandler, Wolchik, MacKinnon, Ayers, & Roosa, 1997; Youngs, 1985) are quite clear that stress in youth must be regarded as distinct. Yet the research evidence to support this claim is preliminary and only now beginning to appear in the literature (Aneshensel & Gore, 1991; Colten & Gore, 1991; Ryan-Wenger, 1992; Wertlieb, 1991; Wolchik & Sandler, 1997).

This chapter examines what is currently known about human stress, trauma, and coping processes in general, giving special attention to causes and prevention of stress in youth. The chapter first reviews the predominant ways stress and trauma have been conceptualized over the past three decades and then concentrates on causal factors, that is, on the sources of stress and trauma in children and adolescents, with consideration of how developmental stages interact with the experience of stress as well as of the coping strategies used by youth when faced with stress and trauma. The chapter next addresses approaches to prevention of stress and trauma from family, individual, school, and community perspectives. It concludes with a brief consideration of stress and trauma from a cultural perspective.

In this chapter the term *children* refers to ages preschool to 10, and the term *adolescents* refers to ages 11 to 19. This is a useful convention (cf. Peterson, Kennedy, & Sullivan, 1991) because of the key developmental transition from childhood to adolescence broadly represented by the start of the second decade of life at age 10, with individual variation in the starting of adolescence occurring with the timing of puberty. As used here, the term *youth* is inclusive of ages preschool to 19.

PERSPECTIVES ON STRESS AND TRAUMATIC STRESS

As just noted, researchers and theorists have had difficulty agreeing upon a consistent definition of stress (Johnson, 1986). *Trauma* is more consistently defined in the literature as a form of stress that is extreme and overwhelming, and that is subjectively experienced as uncontrollable or unpredictable (Allen, 1995). Stress research historically has focused more on the consequences of stress for organismic functioning (Selye, 1993) than on how stress is aroused (Pearlin, 1993) and subsequently coped with at the emotional and behavioral levels (Moos & Schaefer, 1993; Sandler et al., 1997).

Although acknowledging that a complete and uniform definition of stress has yet to emerge in the literature, Johnson (1986) asserted that the stress concept has been conceptualized from only three major perspectives: stimulus-oriented views, response-oriented views, and stress as a transaction between person and environment. These three perspectives, however, do not include the special attention that is given in the research literature to trauma and posttraumatic stress as forms of debilitating stress (van der Kolk, McFarlane, & Weisaeth, 1996). For this reason, trauma and posttraumatic stress are included in this section as a fourth perspective on the stress concept.

Stimulus-Oriented Views

From this perspective, the focus is on stress as a specific stimulus: ". . . stress is seen as resulting from experiencing any of a number of situations that are noxious or threatening or that place excessive demands on the individual" (Johnson, 1986, p. 16). Research that has defined stress from a life events perspective (divorce, death in the family) falls under this view. Although useful, particularly when relating stress to the onset of physical disease (Creed, 1993; Holmes & Rahe, 1967), this perspective alone is significantly limiting in that it cannot account for why some individuals experience potential stressors negatively while others experience the same stressor as a positive challenge (Johnson, 1986).

Response-Oriented Views

Up until the 1960s stress was almost exclusively defined from a stimulus perspective, meaning the effects of destructive environmental demands (Lazarus, 1993a). Embedded in this framework was an engineering analogy of stress in which an external force created a strain on the object and deformed it in proportion to the pressure of the stressor (Lazarus, 1993a, p. 22). After several decades of work around the stress concept, Hans Selye (1974) asserted that stress is the organism's physiological response to external stressors. His work popularized a physiological version of the engineering analogy by conceiving of stress as having three distinct phases: alarm, resistance, and exhaustion. This sequence was termed the *general adaptation syndrome* (GAS) and refers to the "manifestations of stress in the whole body" (Selye, 1974, p. 139).

In the *alarm reaction* phase, considered to be the most important element of the GAS, the organism responds with a series of complex biochemical alterations. Numerous bodily systems speed up (breathing, blood sugar release) through the discharge of hormones preparing the body for fight or flight (Selye, 1993).

Because a state of alarm cannot be maintained continuously, a second phase, the *stage of resistance*, ensues. If the stressor continues to impinge on the organism, its limited adaptational energy is focused more singularly on resisting further the threat presented by the stressor. Unfortunately, when the organism's adaptational energy is focused on selected stressors in an ongoing fashion, it leaves itself vulnerable to other ensuing stressors (Ivancevich & Matteson, 1980). This "biological stress syndrome" (Selye, 1974) is how numerous stress studies have successfully linked various stressors with the onset of psychiatric (Rabkin, 1993) and somatic disease processes (Creed, 1993; Holmes & Rahe, 1967; Selye, 1993).

The final and third phase of the GAS is the *stage of exhaustion*. Selye (1993) emphasized that the body is limited in adaptability, or the amount of adaptational energy available to withstand stress. Once the adaptational energy has been expended, significant efforts at restoration must follow, and even then there is some wear and tear on the body's total reserve of adaptational energy. If the body cannot engage in replenishment and restore itself to the level of resistance, a phase of burnout (Pines, 1993) may ensue. Most adults have had some experience with burnout in terms of their involvement with work, career, or other prolonged life stress events. We tend to forget, however, that because of the incredible energy that youngsters expend in multiple spheres of activity, they too, by their very developmental nature, are equally vulnerable to burnout (Youngs, 1985).

Two limitations of the response-oriented perspective are that some individuals do not show the stressful response even in the face of a presumably stressful stimulus, and that a stressful stimulus cannot be specified independently of a person's stressful response to it (Johnson, 1986).

Stress as a Transaction Between Person and Environment

Because of the limitations of the stimulus-oriented and response-oriented views, an additional model has emerged in the literature that not only incorporates many aspects of the stimulus and response perspectives but also takes into account the interaction between the person and the environment in accounting for stress and coping. This view has been most fully developed by Lazarus (Lazarus & Folkman, 1984). Of critical significance from this perspective is how the person views (appraises) the stressfulness of the environmental event, whether the event is seen as threatening or nonthreatening, desirable or undesirable, controllable or uncontrollable, and if the person believes coping resources are readily available for dealing with the events. Out of this perspective Lazarus and Folkman (1984, p. 19) offer their definition of stress: "Psychological stress is a particular relationship between the person and the environment that is appraised by the person as taxing or exceeding his or her resources and endangering his or her well-being." The emphasis in this definition is on the psychological processes (cognitive and mediational variables) in the person's experience of stress. As Lazarus has developed his theory from the mid-1960s to the present, he has argued that stress should be seen as a subset of emotion (Lazarus, 1993a). This view is adopted for two reasons. First, knowing that a person is experiencing "emotions resulting from harms, losses, and threats" (anger, anxiety, fear) or from "emotions resulting from benefits" (joy, pride) in response to stress is very useful and says a lot more about how a troubled "person-environment" relationship is being coped with than when the subjective experience of emotion is omitted (p. 24). As Houston (1987) has noted, "an event cannot be regarded as a stressor without reference to the affective response it elicits" (p. 379). Second, the more striking issue in understanding stress is the person's various coping responses to stressors, not just the body's physiological response and adaptation to stress.

Although it is beyond the scope of this chapter to present a full discussion of Lazarus's theoretical model (Lazarus, 1991, 1993b; Lazarus & Folkman, 1984), it is useful to highlight here that a significant portion of stress research has shifted from an emphasis on the physiological response aspects of stress (although that is an inseparable aspect of stress—Arnold, 1990b) to an examination of the psychological experience of stress and the ways in which the organism copes with or buffers (is resilient to) stress (Houston, 1987; Lazarus, 1993b). This is particularly true of research on stress and coping in youth.

Trauma and Posttraumatic Stress

Trauma is the extreme stress reaction that results from the experience of a threatening and overwhelming (traumatic) life event (Allen, 1995). The American Psychiatric Association (1994) has defined traumatic stress events "to include both the witnessing and/or involvement in a threatening (to self or others) situation (including death or serious injury), and the person's psychological response of intense fear, helplessness, or horror" (pp. 427–428). Posttraumatic stress includes the "generalized reaction pattern to traumatic events, which is predetermined by the limited response range of affective, cognitive, and behavioral responses that humans have to overwhelming stress" (McFarlane & Girolamo, 1996, pp. 129-130). Only since the 1980s has it been acknowledged that exposure to trauma, over and beyond stress in general, is a widespread human experience, being reported as high as 40% in the population of young adults in one study (Breslau, Davis, & Andreski, 1991). Like adults, youth are exposed to traumas of various types and are vulnerable to posttraumatic stress reactions including the most severe form, posttraumatic stress disorder (PTSD). PTSD is a syndrome that includes three clusters of symptoms: hyperarousal, reexperiencing the trauma, and avoidance or numbing (Allen, 1995). Although PTSD can be construed (paradoxically) as a form of adaptation to trauma (Allen, 1995), its dysfunctional and self-damaging nature causes maladaptive functioning in the person's present life experience (including coping with common life stressors). PTSD symptoms may be acute (less than 3 months' duration) or chronic (more than 3 months), and for some traumas (war-related, rape) the disorder can occur and/or recur weeks, months, or even years after exposure to the traumatic event (Freedy & Donkervoet, 1995). Children and youth frequently show posttraumatic stress symptoms and PTSD from such traumas as child sexual/physical abuse, domestic violence, criminal violence, and any number of natural or human-made (caused) disasters.

The traumatic stress field has become a major subspecialty within the larger stress and coping field. The area of traumatic stress research includes youth, and adults as youth, who have experienced trauma and show posttraumatic effects including PTSD (Freedy & Donkervoet, 1995), and those who do not show such symptomatic responses, and who are somehow resilient to the effects of the traumatic event(s) and show no or minimal posttraumatic reaction. Preventive factors that appear to buffer the effects of trauma in some youth as well as preventive factors that facilitate faster recovery from posttraumatic stress will be noted in the Approaches to Prevention section. Because the research literature on traumatic stress has burgeoned over the past two decades, it is not possible to provide a complete review of the many important aspects of traumatic stress and PTSD. For more comprehensive presentations consult Allen (1995), Freedy and Hobfoll (1995), Marsella, Friedman, Gerrity, and Scurfield (1996), or van der Kolk, McFarlane, and Weisaeth (1996).

CAUSAL FACTORS

Exact causal factors relating stress to certain emotional or behavioral outcomes are exceedingly difficult to show in the stress field, and researchers may never be able to make many exact causal inferences from the available data (Johnson, 1986). Part of the difficulty is that it is now known that the experience of stress and traumatic stress are multiply determined by personality characteristics and contextual factors (Allen, 1995; Peterson et al., 1991) compounded even further by a large range of individual response variation around any one given source of stress (Lazarus, 1991, 1993a). This is particularly true for children and adolescents as developmental age changes interact with stressors to produce varied outcomes in coping responses (Compas & Phares, 1991). Thus the identified sources of stress highlighted in this section do not prove a causal relationship between the identified source and a stress outcome, especially when applied to an individual case.

Because whole volumes have been compiled on current research and theory on stress and coping in youth and the effects of traumatic stress, what follows are selected highlights of what is currently known about the sources of stress and traumatic stress in childhood and adolescence. For more complete presentations on these topics numerous excellent sources are available including Allen (1995), Arnold (1990a), Colten and Gore

(1991), Goldberger and Breznitz (1993), Humphrey (1988), Marsella et al. (1996), van der Kolk et al. (1996), and Wolchik and Sandler (1997).

Life Event Stressors

Life event scales have been developed for children (Coddington, 1972) similar to those originally developed for adults (Holmes & Rahe, 1967). The key feature of these scales is that they index *the source* and the *amount of change* demanded by the occurrence of specific events that are common across the developmental age range of youth. For example, the death of a parent is regarded uniformly as a very stressful major life change across preschool, elementary, junior, and senior high, whereas change to a different school is regarded as a minor change for preschoolers and progresses to a moderately challenging change for high school students (Johnson, 1986). Each stress event has its own rated level of life change units that varies across the preschool to senior high age range. There are 41 life events listed in Coddington's (1972) scale, including such events as divorce or remarriage of parents, increase in arguments between parents, arguments with parents, and death of brother or sister (see Johnson, 1986, p. 34, for the complete life events checklist).

Two problems arise with the life events approach to the causes of stress in children and adolescents. One is that the external view of raters such as parents, teachers, and other adults is questionable in terms of whether the ratings actually correspond well with children's self-ratings of the same events (Johnson, 1986). The other is that life events are regarded as stressful (i.e., negative) without consideration of their desirability (e.g., getting married). An alternative approach to address these issues, and one that may be more useful in practice settings, is to ask the child to indicate events as either *good* or *bad* and then provide self-ratings of the extent of impact of the event (e.g., *none* to *great*) in the child's life (see the life events checklist in Johnson, 1986). The child or adolescent's evaluation and subjective perspective is thus preserved and may be a more valid indicator of childhood stress. Johnson (1986) summarized a number of studies that show that child/adolescent adjustment and life stress scores using either measurement approach have shown a significant relationship between increased levels of life stress and difficulties with self-esteem, delinquent behavior, poor school performance, and overall level of psychiatric symptomatology. This includes such specific psychological problems as suicidal tendencies and anorexia nervosa. The implication of these studies was that the accumulation of unchecked stressful life events may set the stage for vulnerability to, and possible development of, at-risk emotional (e.g., depression) and behavioral (e.g., conduct disorder) problems in youth. Further, when the coping resources of youth are strained or depleted, they are particularly vulnerable to traumatic stress reactions when faced with trauma (Hobfoll, Dunahoo, & Monnier, 1995).

Daily Stress

A source of stress that has been identified over and beyond the occurrence of specific life events is the stress-inducing potential of mundane, chronic daily events or what has been called *daily hassles* (Vingerhoets & Marcelissen, 1988). In adults, DeLongis, Coyne, Dakoff, Folkman, and Lazarus (1982) have shown that not only do daily hassles have the potential to induce stress but also may play an even stronger role in a person's physical health status than traditional life event stressors.

With respect to children, Youngs (1985) has suggested that the abundance of choices in modern society, especially in urban environments, and the increased cultural emphasis placed on self-fulfillment create a chronic underlying current of stress in children. In the adolescent years a similar stress may exist stemming from so many choices around forming interpersonal relationships (Compas & Wagner, 1991) and pursuing career/vocational options (Youngs, 1985). In both these arenas, however, choice also means the stress of relinquishment: not all desired peer relationships are possible, and career/vocational aspirations may be frustrated by today's economic environment of low growth and diminishing expectations in the rapidly changing world of work (Zunker, 1994).

Traumatic Stress

The most extreme and disruptive stressors youth face are traumatic events that result from some human action, such as violence, or a natural disaster, such as an earthquake. The defining characteristics of trauma are that the event is perceived as a potential threat to survival, and that on a subjective level the event is experienced as uncontrollable or unpredictable (Friedman & Marcella, 1996). Many traumas are possible from human-made and natural sources, but those affecting youth the most are likely to be violence or violent crimes, domestic violence, physical abuse, sexual abuse (incest or rape), life-threatening illness or severe accidental injury, or one of numerous natural disasters. Traumatic stress from any of these sources differs from challenging or painful stress in that an acute or chronic posttraumatic stress condition results because normal coping resources are ineffective or depleted (Hobfoll, Dunahoo, & Monnier, 1995).

The key to whether a traumatic event leads to a posttraumatic stress condition is based on a complex matrix of preexisting genetic factors (proneness to anxiety), developmental factors (disruption of attachment), and coping style (resilience) that interact with length of exposure to the traumatic experience, the subjective intensity of the traumatic experience, and posttrauma factors such as quickness of treatment intervention, strength of the person's social support (especially family), and overall coping resources. When extreme or negative levels of these factors converge in one person's experience and coping fails, the clinical syndrome of posttraumatic stress disorder is the likely outcome. PTSD can be acute or chronic, and as a diagnosable psychiatric condition includes symptoms of intrusive recollection (flashbacks), emotional numbing to avoid the trauma-based memories, and hyperarousal (generalized anxiety, insomnia, irritability) (American Psychiatric Association, 1994). PTSD requires clinical diagnosis and intervention at the individual and family levels as the condition rarely resolves on its own (Allen, 1995) and may actually induce secondary traumatic stress in spouses, children, and other family members (Steinberg, 1998).

Home and Family Stress

Home and family are important contexts for understanding stress in children and adolescents and represent a large portion of the types of stressors youth experience (Humphrey, 1988). Numerous studies have identified significant relationships between the extent of parental stress and levels of child distress (Compas & Phares, 1991; Steinberg, 1998). Most, but not all, of these studies show that as one or both parents' stress and maladjustment increases so does the level of stress and maladjustment in the child or adolescent. Discussions of child abuse, divorce and marital dissolution, family economic problems, and adolescent-parent conflict are considered to illustrate how home and family stress can be strong sources of stress for many youth.

Child Abuse. Physical, sexual, emotional, and negligent abuse of children is an enormous concern in our society, and in spite of the increased effort to combat child abuse over the past half century, the true incidence and damaging consequences of abuse, including later posttraumatic reactions in adults, are still not fully known or understood (Johnson & Cohn, 1990). Relevant to a discussion of abuse and family stress is that parental stress is considered to be the major cause of child abuse (Straus, 1980), with child abuse being a major family stressor in the lives of those youth who are abused. Typically, the stress the child or adolescent experiences from the abuse is not expressed as such, but rather is expressed through a wide range of posttraumatic-linked emotional and behavior difficulties such as anger, apathy, delinquency (Widom, 1991), school problems, shame, and eating disorders. Johnson and Cohn (1990) have provided a comprehensive list of reported effects. Interestingly, the typical runaway is likely to have come from an abusive family and may regard life on the street as less stressful than the home environment (Farber, Kinast, McCoard, & Falkner, 1984). This is just one example of how the ongoing effects of the stress of child abuse can be displaced in the form of other at-risk coping strategies in youth.

Divorce and Marital Dissolution. From a life events perspective, parental divorce is ranked second only to death of a parent as the most stressful life event a child or adolescent might experience (Coddington, 1972). Current statistics indicate that as many as 60% of youth will spend a portion of childhood or adolescence in a single-parent situation (Norton & Glick, 1986). Researchers have expanded their concern about the effects of divorce from a more singular life event readjustment to the chronic effects of divorce on children's mental, emotional, social, and academic development (Kalter, 1987; Wertlieb, 1991). The antecedents (emotional conflict and diminished support) and aftermath (divorce wars) of divorce are now considered as more inclusive aspects of the actual stress youth experience from marital dissolution (Arnold & Carnahan, 1990). These researchers have also summarized a number of studies that showed an interaction between sex, age, time of divorce in the youth's life, and the stress of readjustment. In general boys appear to experience the stress of divorce more intensely at the elementary level while girls at this age fare about as well as those in intact families. Later, however, adolescent girls of divorcing parents show significantly increasing problems with self-esteem and, later still, in heterosexual relationships. Overall, one of the better ways to understand divorce as a source of stress for youth is to recognize the significant loss/change in access to parents the experience usually represents. Diminished access to parents can significantly reduce the felt social support youth receive from parents at times when they may critically need it (e.g., around the stress of school). As noted further in the section on prevention approaches, for a variety of life event and chronic stressors, social support plays a critical role in buffering the negative effects of stress (Gottlieb & Wagner, 1991).

Economic Stress. No discussion of home and family stress is complete without mentioning the chronic and often devastating effects of economic stress in the family (Committee for Economic Development, 1991). Poverty creates an overall psychological environment in the family that is stressful for parents and youth alike, and is linked to the incidence of numerous mental health adjustment issues of children, such as child abuse and its associated stresses. But economic stress is not limited to those families struggling to make ends meet. Occupational stress in adults has been associated with a number of health and psychological adjustment variables (Holt, 1993), contributing to the overall level of stress in the family. The dual roles of career and parent, especially for women but increasingly for men as well (Zunker, 1994), create stress in the form of daily hassles, such as child-care arrangements, and strain in the parenting role. Further, job loss, career change, and being a displaced worker are all stresses deriving from economic change/uncertainty and the stress inherent in the rapid change to a technology- and service-based economy. Whether directly through financial strain or indirectly through parent job/career stress, economic stressors are a significant source of stress for today's youth.

School Stress

All aspects of the school experience challenge youth to adapt to the stresses of the educative process. Sears and Milburn (1990) listed 25 common school-age stressors. These include "anxiety about going to school, changing schools, competitiveness (including fear of failure and fear of success), conflict with teacher, failing an exam, worrying about taking tests, and peer teasing" (p. 225).

Paradoxically, although for some youth school is a major source of stress, for others school can be a source of motivational challenge and stress relief (Elias, 1989). Thus when assessing the stress experienced by a child or adolescent, the nature and impact of the stress can only be ascertained in the context of the child's whole life space—background, home life, school life, age, and gender (Humphrey, 1988).

For many youth, and possibly increasing numbers of youth, the school experience is not the benign academic learning experience it was once regarded to be (Elias, 1989; Skinner & Wellborn, 1997). School reform pressures, which overemphasize academic success at the expense of psychosocial learning/development, may be contributing to "debilitating student stress" in up to 30% of the student population (Elias, 1989, p. 394). Rather than providing a balance between academics and preparation of students for adult citizenship, social competence, and the world of work, schools are under tremendous pressure from parents who are "looking to the schools to guarantee their children's future success" (Elias, 1989, p. 395). As this singular pressure for academic success and test score performance has increased, so has the stress level of students, to the point that for some the stress is debilitating. Students display the effects of this debilitating stress through physical symptoms of fatigue, headaches, and nausea; a sense of alienation from satisfaction gained through effectiveness and success; and delinquent and antisocial behavior, such as substance abuse or gang involvement, as a means of coping with the stress of thwarted expectations for a positive future (Elias, 1989). Elias' recommendations for addressing the pervasive and debilitating effects of school stress are included in the section on approaches to prevention.

Developmental Stress

The biological, cognitive, and emotional changes in youth from childhood to adolescence are complex and numerous. They also interact with the perception of and response to other life stress (Peterson et al., 1991; Trad

& Greenblatt, 1990). Some of these additional as well as interactive sources of stress in youth—biological, cognitive-emotional, gender, and interpersonal—are briefly discussed here. For a more comprehensive review of the literature on these complex interactions, see Arnold (1990a, 1990b) and Colten and Gore (1991).

Biological Changes.   Puberty is the most dramatic of all the developmental transitions in the human life span (Peterson et al., 1991). Biological changes in early adolescence leading to adult appearance and size, reproductive capacity, and internal endocrine changes produce challenges and stresses in the intrapersonal and social adaptation spheres of adolescent functioning. Issues of sexuality and sexual behavior emerge as a result of these biological changes and are often very stressful for early adolescents and their parents. Further, sex has become an issue for more young people at an earlier age than in previous generations (Youngs, 1985). This observation supports the belief that there is a downward age trend for today's youth in the timing of the stress of emerging sexuality.

Cognitive-Emotional Changes.   The increase in cognitive and emotional complexity required for expanding from a concrete and certain experience of the world to a capacity for abstract and relativistic thinking and emotion (Piaget & Inhelder, 1969) is a developmental stressor of enormous implications in the transition from childhood to adolescence. Larson and Asmussen (1991) reported data that show there is an increase in the experience of negative emotion (anger, worry, hurt) from preadolescence to adolescence. In a certain sense, maturing cognitive and emotional capacities set the stage for adolescence to be the first major confrontation with the existential issues of choice, responsibility, and freedom in the life span (Bugental, 1981). As is commonly recognized, the inherent stress of this developmental transition can be overwhelming for many youth. What is less commonly recognized is the adolescent's critical need for parent and peer support (Peterson & Ebata, 1987) as a means of navigating through this challenging transitional period of life.

Gender Differences.   Gender socialization has emerged as a significant moderator variable in the experience of stress in youth (Gore & Colten, 1991). Some of the conclusions emerging from the literature in this area are extremely relevant to our understanding of the sources of stress in youth, particularly in older adolescents. For example, Peterson et al. (1991) concluded from a number of studies that although in early adolescence there is only one gender divergence (for body image, with girls showing a decline), by late adolescence there is marked gender divergence across all measures of self and negative affect, with girls becoming markedly more depressed as adolescence proceeds. The available evidence suggests that girls "amplify" negative moods as a form of coping with developmental stressors while boys are "more likely to distract themselves from a depressed mood" (p. 105). Thus girls' coping response to stress changes along gender lines during adolescence, suggesting they become more vulnerable to various stressors, but boys' coping responses appear to remain the same. Paradoxically, girls' coping response to developmental stress in adolescence may set a lifelong pattern of coping with stress with depressive affect. Similarly, the pattern of boys' coping may be protective for gender-based functioning in instrumental and achievement spheres, but it may also be quite maladaptive for future interpersonal relationships requiring emotional intimacy (Peterson et al., 1991).

Interpersonal Stress. Interpersonal relationships increasingly become a source of stress for youth as they progress from childhood to early adolescence and through late adolescence. This appears to be true for both girls and boys, but adolescent girls report greater interpersonal stress than boys (Compas & Wagner, 1991). Further, they noted that when stressful life events occur in an adolescent's life they are likely to be "*directly related to others in their social networks, especially their parents*" (p. 75). In a study that directly examined adolescent-parent conflict, Smetana, Yau, Restrepo, and Braeges (1991) found that conflict, although stressful, provides a context for debates over the extent of adolescents' developing autonomy, and thus serves an adaptive function. However, when the interaction style between parent and adolescent is negative (i.e., constraining, devaluing, or judging) adolescent development is inhibited, causing further intrapersonal stress and interpersonal conflict. Interestingly, another significant finding was that adolescent-parent conflict is greater in married than divorced families, and that children and adolescents who have had to deal with the stress of parental divorce may actually increase their coping competence and resilience to future life stress (Smetana et al., 1991). In addition, Compas and Wagner (1991) have noted that interpersonal stress shows a reliable developmental variation: in junior high negative family interaction is the predominant source of interpersonal stress, but by senior high conformity and concerns about acceptance by the peer group are the dominant interpersonal stressors. Stress arising from dependency on the peer group subsides by later adolescence, and with entry into college, academic events become the predominant source of stress.

APPROACHES TO PREVENTION

Primary and secondary prevention strategies are both important in reducing stress in youth. *Primary prevention* consists of attempts to minimize youths' vulnerability to stress or actually prevent its occurrence, and *secondary prevention* consists of teaching vulnerable youth therapeutically the coping skills they need to know (Lazarus, 1991). *Tertiary prevention* consists of clinical treatment of stress and posttraumatic stress after the damage has occurred, and although not preventive in an absolute sense, such intervention can prevent the exacerbation of traumatic stress as well as lessen the secondary traumatic stress of family members of the traumatized individual (Steinberg, 1998).

Because so many stressors of youth, especially in children, are outside of their control and related to situations with parents, other family members, teachers, or socioeconomic conditions (Ryan-Wenger, 1992), it is particularly relevant to approach the prevention of stress in youth from a systemic perspective. At the same time, many life and traumatic stressors are unavoidable for youth, or stem from normal developmental challenges. Given this, an additional prevention strategy becomes maximizing the coping resources of youth so that the negative effects of stress are buffered to the greatest extent possible (Gottlieb, 1991; Sandler et al., 1997). This latter strategy reflects the current research emphasis on understanding individual coping processes (Lazarus, 1991, 1993a, 1993b) and psychosocial protective factors (Kimchi & Schaffner, 1990; Roosa, Wolchik, & Sandler, 1997) when the person is under stress. In this overview of approaches to prevention in the family, individual, school, and community, consideration is given to possible systemic prevention of stress as well as various coping and protective factors that appear to buffer the effects of stress and trauma in youth.

Family

From a larger systems perspective, those services that reduce stress in family life can directly prevent the stress in children that can interfere with normal development (Wagner, 1994) or cause secondary traumatic stress reactions in children (Steinberg, 1998). Peterson et al. (1991) observed that when such a strategy can be implemented from childhood to early adolescence, and through adolescence, a positive trajectory of coping with the stress of developmental transitions is set in motion. The earlier and the more consistent the support is from parents in this process, the more positive is the overall mental health trajectory of the child. Further, Peterson et al. (1991) noted that positive mental health in children and adolescents is related to greater internal coping resources when youth are faced with unexpected life event stressors. Given this overall picture, school-based health clinics (Sleek, 1994) that can provide family support (Gottlieb, 1991) in the form of integrated social, health, and mental health services may be one of the most effective means of ameliorating family stress and, by extension, preventing stress in youth. In addition, the school context can be a good intervention and referral point for youth needing therapeutic services for posttraumatic stress reactions or PTSD.

A more direct way in which the family plays a role in the prevention of stress in youth is through the family's function as an informal social support network (Sandler et al., 1997; Willis, 1987). Willis (1987) believed the extent to which the family functions as an "informal help-seeking" support system is the extent to which such "informal support may serve to reduce the stressful impact of adverse events" (p. 34). This idea has also been advanced for posttraumatic stress reactions (Dinicola, 1996), although the caregivers of traumatized youth may also be at risk for developing secondary traumatic stress reactions (Steinberg, 1998). Dimensions of parent/family support that appear to make a real difference in buffering the negative effects of stress are esteem support, informational support, motivational support, and instrumental support. In contrast, one of the reasons child abuse is so likely to have posttraumatic stress features is that the various forms of family support are so lacking in the abusive family. Other family factors that appear to be protective of stress in youth are noted by Kimchi and Schaffner (1990) and include such dimensions as adequate rule setting and structure, family cohesion, lower parental conflicts, open communication, warmth toward the child, and being patient in parenting style. As noted earlier, the family can be a powerful source of stress in youth; likewise, it can be a powerful buffer to stress when functioning effectively.

Individual

As already noted, secondary prevention of stress consists of teaching therapeutic stress and coping skills to the individual in hopes that the negative effects of stress will not escalate. This may be done in a remedial fashion once stress reduction has been identified as needed, or more broadly and in advance through coping skills training (Elias, 1989; Sandler et al., 1997). Because children, and to a certain extent adolescents, are less able to identify the sources of stress or know how to cope with a variety of stressors (Ryan-Wenger, 1992), adults in the lives of youth must facilitate the referral of youth for remedial stress reduction and/or anticipate the need for and benefits of coping training (Folkman, Chesney, McKusick, Ironson, & Coates, 1991). Stress reduction strategies and techniques that rely on progressive muscle relaxation, visual imagery, and biofeedback have been shown to be effective for both adults (Girdano et al., 1990) and children (Humphrey, 1988; Humphrey & Humphrey, 1981; Romano, 1997; Youngs, 1985). Stress reduction in children might best focus on the aspects of body relaxation, nutrition, and exercise to counter the effects of stress (Humphrey, 1988), while as cognitive development increases, cognitive, emotional, and social support coping skills training are additional forms of preventive intervention for adolescents (Folkman et al., 1991). Interestingly, however, Romano (1997) found that cognitive coping strategies were being used in the school environment by children as early as the fourth and fifth grades.

With respect to coping, researchers have identified three conceptual frameworks that relate to the present discussion of coping effectiveness in the individual as a preventive measure against stress (Ebata & Moos, 1991). The first is identified as the approach/avoidance coping model (Lazarus & Folkman, 1984) and distinguishes between active approach-oriented coping (toward threat) versus passive or avoidance-oriented (away from threat) coping. Approach coping includes efforts to change ways of thinking about a problem (stressor) as well as behavioral attempts to resolve or address the problem. Avoidant coping includes cognitive attempts to deny or minimize threat and behavioral attempts to avoid or get away from the problem. Research has shown that adolescents who use more approach coping than avoidance coping are better adjusted and less distressed (Ebata & Moos, 1991). Further, they concluded that adolescents who show a pattern of avoidance coping may be at greater risk for poorer adjustment to subsequent life stressors and crises. Through coping skills training, adolescents can be shown the positive value of approach-coping and encouraged to engage in approach coping behavior when faced with life event and developmental stressors.

A second framework for thinking about stress prevention for the individual from a coping perspective is highlighted by the problem-focused/emotion-focused distinction (Lazarus, 1993b). In this framework, coping efforts can be focused on modifying the stressor itself (problem-focused coping) or on attempts to regulate the emotional responses that accompany the stressor (emotion-focused coping). Ebata and Moos (1991) reported research that suggests that adolescents who used more problem-focused coping with interpersonal stressors (i.e., talking with the other person) reported fewer stressful emotional and behavioral reactions than those who used emotion-focused strategies, such as ignoring the situation or yelling at the other person. It should be noted, however, that although problem-focused coping is a more effective coping strategy in general, emotion-focused coping may be more effective for certain types of stressors over which the person can exercise no useful action (Lazarus, 1993a).

The third framework for understanding and facilitating positive coping in the individual is related to the role of seeking social support as a coping response. Ebata and Moos (1991) summarized several studies that examined the relationship among family and peer support, active coping strategies, and substance use in adolescents. In general, adolescents who used active behavioral and cognitive coping as well as the seeking of adult support showed less substance use while those adolescents who relied more on peers and acting out to cope showed more substance use (Ebata & Moos, 1991). Other authors (Gottlieb, 1991; Hendron, 1990) have also noted that attachment, support, and guidance from at least one adult figure in an adolescent's life can buffer the effects of stress and facilitate approach and problem-focused coping.

The prevention of traumatic stress can take two additional forms. First, preliminary research has shown that when trauma occurs immediate crisis intervention and critical incident stress debriefing can minimize the risk of posttraumatic stress reactions in many individuals (Saylor, Belter, & Stokes, 1997). This type of prevention applies more to singular events (natural disasters, catastrophic accidents, violent crime) than it does to repeated or more hidden traumas (child sexual abuse, domestic violence). In the latter case posttraumatic symptoms or PTSD often show a delayed onset in the individual and require corrective therapy in the form of psychological and/or pharmacological therapies (Allen, 1995). In all cases of traumatic stress in the individual, crisis intervention is preventive of an intensification of posttraumatic stress reactions. Thus community efforts to have services in place in advance of trauma, whether in disaster agencies, hospitals, schools, or clinics, are the best prevention when traumatic events inevitably occur in the lives of youth (Saylor, Belter, & Stokes, 1997).

School

Elias (1989) has outlined a number of recommendations that reflect both primary (systemic) and secondary (coping skills) stress prevention strategies in the schools. Basing his perspective on the assumption that school stress does interfere with both academic and social growth in youth, which in turn diminish the coping resources available to youth, he asserted that "It is . . . logical and necessary to rethink our view of 'academic time' and incorporate the teaching of coping and learning-to-learn skills into the mainstream of educational programming" (p. 400). More recently Skinner & Wellborn (1997) corroborated this idea and suggested that interventions promoting academic coping are both preventive and developmental in nature. Using this general perspective, Elias (1989) made the following recommendations to reduce school stress:

- *promote accomplishment* by expanding opportunities for children to feel connected to schools as well as feel efficacious in all learning contexts of the school;
- *teach coping skills and learning-to-learn skills* as part of the mainstream educational programming;
- *adjust the culture of classrooms and schools* to reflect an integrated approach to social and coping skills development rather than the isolated clinical approach to intervention that is common;

- *ensure that schools are physically safe* because safety is paramount to managing stress;
- *increase the value placed on long-term educational planning* to address complex issues rather than favor a tendency to seek short-term "a program in place" solutions, which eventually fade;
- *use action research* as "a procedure in which new programs are tried, monitored, evaluated, refined, and tried again" (p. 402); and
- *shift the emphasis of current training programs* for teachers so that debilitating stress in schools is recognized and addressed through social development education of the child and changes in the learning environment.

As another means of countering the stress adolescents experience in school, Gottlieb (1991) emphasized the benefits of social support interventions. Because inclusion, acceptance, and approval from one's peer group are so important in adolescence, peer counseling programs in schools can materially increase the social support adolescents feel. With such added peer/social support, the stressful aspects of school and the challenges of developmental changes can be minimized.

Further, Humphrey (1988) has suggested that stress from academic competition needs to be offset by an increased emphasis on cooperative learning experiences. For example, the stress of math anxiety is centrally based on the way in which math is often taught—in a context of time pressure to finish first, humiliation when being called upon to perform in front of the class, and an emphasis on one right answer. All three of these elements are negative and stressful for many youth and reveal a child's weakness rather than his or her competence (Humphrey, 1988). By altering this approach to learning math, teachers can significantly reduce stress in the classroom and produce more confident and capable students.

Community

Wagner (1994) observed that the povertization of childhood is the single largest threat to the welfare of children today. Clearly poverty is stressful for parents and families and plays a large role in the chronic stress that many youth experience in the family, school, and community. In addition, poverty may also be associated with more frequent witnessing of violent crime by many youth, serving as a source of traumatic stress and its associated risks (Parson, 1995). There are no simple or direct ways to prevent poverty, but communities can advocate for changes in public policy that empower children, protect their rights, and facilitate access to social and mental health services to reduce stress (Stern & Newland, 1994). Such efforts when successful can go a long way in preventing stress in youth while benefiting all children as a social group.

The stress associated with violence in the schools can be another important target of community prevention. The threat of violence in schools affects nearly all students, and the fear that results can inhibit a sense of industry, achievement, and self-confidence (Christie & Toomey, 1990). Further, posttraumatic reactions and PTSD are likely for those in immediate proximity to a violent crime at school or a school shooting. Given that schools are embedded in the larger community, the stress of violence must be prevented by community-based programs. Because it is commonly believed that much of the violence in schools is related to the problems of gangs and drugs in and around schools, school-community prevention strategies that address these issues (see chapters 12, 13 and 14) reduce an aspect of chronic stress in youth.

In addition, the community can play a preventive role in reducing stress in youth by publicly supporting the continuing efforts of schools to integrate psychosocial education and other intervention at-risk programs into the schools (Elias, 1989). McWhirter, McWhirter, McWhirter, and McWhirter (1994) have identified five C's of competency that distinguish high- and low-risk youth: critical school (academic) competencies; concept of self and self-esteem; communication with others; coping ability; and control—over decision making, delay of gratification, purpose in life. Parents, teachers, clergy, and all adults in the community can help prevent stress in youth by teaching and valuing these coping competencies that are so necessary to deal with a rapidly changing world.

Stress and Trauma: A Cultural Perspective

Considering stress, traumatic stress, and coping from an ethnocultural perspective is the most recent development in the stress field (de Vries, 1996; Marsella et al., 1996). Cross-cultural applicability is an important question and begins with whether the stress concept (including posttraumatic stress) validly applies to children, adolescents, and adults from other cultures (de Vries, 1996). Based on the available research, Marsella et al. (1996) concluded that PTSD is a valid and clinically meaningful diagnosis in non-Western cultures. These authors cautioned, however, that in most cases there are culture-specific responses to trauma not captured in the universal aspects of the diagnosis. Similarly, de Vries (1996) supported the concept that traumatic stress is valid cross-culturally, but added that a person's unique culture or ethnic subculture may offer protective responses to stress that are integrated into the culture's existing framework for holding problems and illnesses, including stress/traumatic stress. For example, fatalistic cultures may assign external (unalterable) causation to stress and trauma and, therefore, have cultural rituals in place to accept and support traumatized individuals, but other cultures may medicalize trauma and expect curative solutions from expert treatment providers. Clearly, subtle cultural factors do exist beyond the apparent universality of the trauma construct, and therefore, sensitivity to and inclusion of unique ethnocultural definitions and experiences of stress and trauma are required in treatment and prevention efforts (Dinicola, 1996; Dragnus, 1996).

From the same perspective, Gonzales and Kim (1997) indicated that the available literature on stress, coping, and overall mental health of youth also requires specific consideration of cultural factors. In addition to all the life stress and coping adaptation concepts outlined in the literature, working with ethnic minority youth requires consideration of their "cultural ecology," which includes the stress-related variables of socioeconomic status, neighborhood context, migration/acculturation, and ethnic/racial discrimination. Although beyond the scope of the present discussion, Gonzales and Kim's (1997) cultural ecological process model for ethnic minority children provides a comprehensive picture of how ethnicity and cultural protective factors interact to produce varied stress and coping outcomes.

SUMMARY

In this chapter stress is discussed from three perspectives: stimulus-oriented view, response-oriented view, and person-environment transaction view. In addition, trauma and posttraumatic stress are considered as extreme stress and significant challenges to coping. Recent research and theory emphasize the person-environment transactional model in which both the perception of stress and coping responses to stress play an active role in the stress phenomenon (including traumatic stress). Only since the mid-1980s has research focused specifically on stress and coping in youth, and only in the past decade has a fuller appreciation of trauma and posttraumatic stress in youth, especially ethnocultural considerations, emerged in the literature. Causal factors for stress and trauma in youth are multiple and varied, and are complexly interwoven with the developmental challenges of childhood and adolescence. Life events, daily hassles, traumatic stress, family stress, child abuse, divorce, economic factors, school stress, and developmental challenges are highlighted as causal factors for stress in youth. Approaches to prevention are considered across family, individual, school, and community from a larger systems perspective as well as from individual coping skills and social support factors that are preventive of stress in youth. Important ethnocultural factors are also highlighted as they relate to the cross-cultural validity of posttraumatic stress and stress and coping in ethnic minority youth.

REFERENCES

Allen, J. G. (1995). *Coping with trauma: A guide to self-understanding*. Washington, DC: American Psychiatric Press.

American Psychiatric Association. (1994). *Diagnostic and statistical manual of mental disorders* (4th ed.). Washington, DC: Author.

Aneshensel, C. S., & Gore, S. (1991). Development, stress, and role structuring: Social transitions of adolescence. In J. Eckenrode (Ed.), *The social context of coping* (pp. 55–77). New York: Plenum Press.

Arnold, L. E. (Ed.). (1990a). *Childhood stress*. New York: Wiley.

Arnold, L. E. (1990b). Stress in children and adolescents: Introduction and summary. In L. E. Arnold (Ed.), *Childhood stress* (pp. 1–19). New York: Wiley.

Arnold, L. E., & Carnahan, J. A. (1990). Child divorce stress. In L. E. Arnold (Ed.), *Childhood stress* (pp. 373–403). New York: Wiley.

Breslau, N. D., Davis, G. C., & Andreski, P. (1991). Traumatic events and posttraumatic stress disorder in an urban population of young adults. *Archives of General Psychiatry, 48,* 216–222.

Bugental, J. F. T. (1981). *The search for authenticity* (Rev. ed.). New York: Irvington.

Christie, D. J., & Toomey, B. G. (1990). The stress of violence: School, community, and world. In L. E. Arnold (Ed.), *Childhood stress* (pp. 297–323). New York: Wiley.

Coddington, R. D. (1972). The significance of life events as etiological factors in the diseases of children: A study of a normal population. *Journal of Psychosomatic Research, 16,* 205–213.

Colten, M. E., & Gore, S. (Eds.). (1991). *Adolescent stress: Causes and consequences*. New York: Aldine de Gruyter.

Committee for Economic Development. (1991). *The unfinished agenda: A new vision for child development and education*. New York: Author.

Compas, B. E., & Phares, V. (1991). Stress during childhood and adolescence: Sources of risk and vulnerability. In E. M. Cummings, A. L. Greene, & K. H. Karraker (Eds.), *Life-span developmental psychology: Perspectives on stress and coping* (pp. 111–129). Hillsdale, NJ: Erlbaum.

Compas, B. E., & Wagner, B. M. (1991). Psychosocial stress during adolescence: Intrapersonal and interpersonal processes. In M. E. Colten & S. Gore (Eds.), *Adolescent stress: Causes and consequences* (pp. 67-85). New York: Aldine de Gruyter.

Creed, F. (1993). Stress and psychosomatic disorders. In L. Goldberger & S. Breznitz (Eds.), *Handbook of stress: Theoretical and clinical aspects* (pp. 496–510). New York: Free Press.

Davis, D., Eshelman, E. R., & McKay, M. (1988). *The relaxation and stress reduction workbook* (3rd ed.). Oakland, CA: New Harbinger.

Delongis, A., Coyne, J. C., Dakoff, G., Folkman, S., & Lazarus, R. A. (1982). Relationship of daily hassles, uplifts, and major life events to health status. *Health Psychology, 1,* 119–136.

de Vries, M. W. (1996). Trauma in cultural perspective. In B. A. van der Kolk, A. C. McFarlane, & L. Weissaeth (Eds.), *Traumatic stress: The effects of overwhelming experience on mind, body, and society* (pp. 398–413). New York: Guilford Press.

Dinicola, V. F. (1996). Ethnocultural aspects of PTSD and related disorders among children and adolescents. In A. J. Marsella, M. J. Friedman, E. T. Gerrity, & R. M. Scurfield (Eds.), *Ethnocultural aspects of posttraumatic stress disorder: Issues, research, and clinical applications* (pp. 389–414). Washington, DC: American Psychological Association.

Dise-Lewis, J. E. (1988). The life events coping inventory: An assessment of stress in children. *Psychosomatic Medicine, 50,* 484–489.

Dragnus, J. G. (1996). Ethnocultural considerations in the treatment of PTSD: Therapy service considerations. In A. J. Marsella, M. J. Friedman, E. T. Gerrity, & R. M. Scurfield (Eds.), *Ethnocultural aspects of posttraumatic stress disorder: Issues, research, and clinical applications* (pp. 459–482). Washington, DC: American Psychological Association.

Ebata, A. T., & Moos, R. H. (1991). Coping and adjustment in distressed and healthy adolescents. *Journal of Applied Developmental Psychology, 12,* 33–54.

Elias, M. J. (1989). Schools as a source of stress to children: An analysis of causal and ameliorative influences. *Journal of School Psychology, 27,* 393–407.

Farber, E. D., Kinast, C., McCoard, W. D., & Falkner, D. (1984). Violence in families of adolescent runaways. *Child Abuse and Neglect, 18,* 295–299.

Folkman, S., Chesney, M., McKusick, L., Ironson, D. S., & Coates, T. J. (1991). Translating coping theory into an intervention. In J. Eckenrode (Ed.), *The social context of coping* (pp. 239–260). New York: Plenum Press.

Freedy, J. R., & Donkervoet, J. C. (1995). Traumatic stress: An overview of the field. In J. R. Freedy & S. E. Hobfoll (Eds.), *Traumatic stress: From theory to practice* (pp. 3–28). New York: Plenum Press.

Freedy, J. R., & Hobfoll, S. E. (Eds.). (1995). *Traumatic stress: From theory to practice.* New York: Plenum Press.

Friedman, M. J., & Marsella, A. J. (1996). Posttraumatic stress disorder: An overview of the concept. In A. J. Marsella, M. J. Friedman, E. T. Gerrity, & R. M. Scurfield (Eds.), *Ethnocultural aspects of posttraumatic stress disorder: Issues, research, and clinical applications* (pp. 11–32). Washington, DC: American Psychological Association.

Girdano, D., Everly, G., & Dusek, D. (1990). *Controlling stress and tension: A holistic approach* (3rd ed.). Englewood Cliffs, NJ: Prentice-Hall.

Goldberger, L., & Breznitz, S. (1993). *Handbook of stress: Theoretical and clinical aspects.* New York: Free Press.

Gonzales, N.A., & Kim, L.S. (1997). Stress and coping in an ethnic minority context: Children's cultural ecologies. In S. A. Wolchik & I. N. Sandler (Eds.), *Handbook of children's coping: Linking theory and intervention* (pp. 481–511). New York: Plenum Press.

Gore, S., & Colten, M. E. (1991). Adolescent stress, social relationships, and mental health. In M. E. Colten & S. Gore (Eds.), *Adolescent stress: Causes and consequences* (pp. 1–14). New York: Aldine de Gruyter.

Gottlieb, B. H. (1991). Social support in adolescence. In M. E. Colten & S. Gore (Eds.), *Adolescent stress: Causes and consequences* (pp. 281–306). New York: Aldine de Gruyter.

Gottlieb, B. H., & Wagner, F. (1991). Stress and support processes in close relationships. In J. Eckenrode (Ed.), *The social context of coping* (pp. 165–188). New York: Plenum Press.

Hendron, R. L. (1990). Stress in adolescence. In L. E. Arnold (Ed.), *Childhood stress* (pp. 247–264). New York: Wiley.

Hobfoll, S. E., Dunahoo, C. A., & Monnier, J. (1995). Conservation of resources and traumatic stress. In J. R. Freedy & S. E. Hobfoll (Eds.), *Traumatic stress: From theory to practice* (pp. 49–72). New York: Plenum Press.

Holmes, T. H., & Rahe, R. H. (1967). The social readjustment rating scale. *Journal of Psychosomatic Research, 11,* 213–218.

Holt, R. R. (1993). Occupational stress. In L. Goldberger & S. Breznitz (Eds.), *Handbook of stress: Theoretical and clinical aspects* (pp. 342–367). New York: Free Press.

Houston, K. B. (1987). Stress and coping. In C. R. Snyder & C. E. Ford (Eds.), *Coping with negative life events* (pp. 373–399). New York: Plenum Press.

Humphrey, J. H. (1988). *Children and stress.* New York: AMS Press.

Humphrey, J. H., & Humphrey, J. N. (1981). *Reducing stress in children through creative relaxation.* Springfield, IL: Charles C Thomas.

Ivancevich, J. M., & Matteson, M. T. (1980). *Stress and work: A managerial perspective.* Glenview, IL: Scott, Foresman.

Johnson, C. F., & Cohn, D. S. (1990). The stress of child abuse and other family violence. In L. E. Arnold (Ed.), *Childhood stress* (pp. 267–295). New York: Wiley.

Johnson, J. H. (1986). *Life events as stressors in childhood and adolescence.* Beverly Hills, CA: Sage.

Kalter, N. (1987). Long-term effects of divorce on children: A developmental vulnerability model. *American Journal of Orthopsychiatry, 57,* 587–599.

Kilpatrick, K. L., & Williams, L. M. (1998). Potential mediators of posttraumatic stress disorder in child witnesses to domestic violence. *Child Abuse and Neglect, 22,* 319–330.

Kimchi, J., & Schaffner, B. (1990). Childhood protective factors and stress risk. In L. E. Arnold (Ed.), *Childhood stress* (pp. 475–500). New York: Wiley.

Larson, R., & Asmussen, L. (1991). Anger, worry, and hurt in early adolescence: An enlarging world of negative emotions. In M. E. Colten & S. Gore (Eds.), *Adolescent stress: Causes and consequences* (pp. 21–41). New York: Aldine de Gruyter.

Lazarus, R. S. (1991). *Emotion and adaptation.* New York: Oxford University Press.

Lazarus, R. S. (1993a). Why we should think of stress as a subset of emotion. In L. Goldberger & S. Breznitz (Eds.), *Handbook of stress: Theoretical and clinical aspects* (pp. 21–39). New York: Free Press.

Lazarus, R. S. (1993b). Coping theory and research: Past, present, and future. *Psychosomatic Medicine, 55,* 234–247.

Lazarus, R. S., & Folkman, S. (1984). *Stress, appraisal, and coping.* New York: Springer.

Marsella, A. S., Friedman, M. J., Gerrity, E. T., & Scurfield, R. M. (1996). Ethnocultural aspects of PTSD: Some closing thoughts. In A. J. Marsella, M. J. Friedman, E. T. Gerrity, & R. M. Scurfield (Eds.), *Ethnocultural aspects of posttraumatic stress disorder: Issues, research, and clinical applications* (pp. 529–538). Washington, DC: American Psychological Association.

McFarlane, A. C., & de Girolamo, G. (1996). The nature of traumatic stressors and the epidemiology of posttraumatic reactions. In B. A. van der Kolk, A. C. McFarlane, & L. Weissaeth (Eds.), *Traumatic stress: The effects of overwhelming experience on mind, body, and society* (pp. 129–154). New York: Guilford Press.

McWhirter, J. J., McWhirter, B. T., McWhirter, A. M., & McWhirter, E. H. (1994). High- and low-risk characteristics of youth: The five Cs of competency. *Elementary School Guidance and Counseling, 28,* 188–196.

Moos, R. H., & Schaefer, J. A. (1993). Coping resources and processes: Current concepts and measures. In L. Goldberger & S. Breznitz (Eds.), *Handbook of stress: Theoretical and clinical aspects* (pp. 234–257). New York: Free Press.

Norton, A., & Glick, P. (1986). One-parent families: A social and economic profile. *Family Relations, 35,* 9–17.

Parson, E. R. (1995). Posttraumatic stress and coping in an inner-city child: Traumatic witnessing of interparental violence and murder. *Psychoanalytic Study of the Child, 50,* 135–147.

Pearlin, L. I. (1993). The social context of stress. In L. Goldberger & S. Breznitz (Eds.), *Handbook of stress: Theoretical and clinical aspects* (pp. 303–315). New York: Free Press.

Peterson, A. C., & Ebata, A. T. (1987). Developmental transitions and adolescent problem behavior: Implications for prevention and intervention. In K. Hurrelmann, F. X. Kaufmann, & F. Losel (Eds.), *Social intervention: Potential and constraints* (pp. 167–184). New York: Aldine de Gruyter.

Peterson, C. A., Kennedy, R. E., & Sullivan, P. (1991). Coping with adolescence. In M. E. Colten & S. Gore (Eds.), *Adolescent stress: Causes and consequences* (pp. 93–110). New York: Aldine de Gruyter.

Piaget, J., & Inhelder, B. (1969). *The psychology of the child.* New York: Basic Books.

Pines, A. M. (1993). Burnout. In L. Goldberger & S. Breznitz (Eds.), *Handbook of stress: Theoretical and clinical aspects* (pp. 386–402). New York: Free Press.

Rabkin, J. G. (1993). Stress and psychiatric disorders. In L. Goldberger & S. Breznitz (Eds.), *Handbook of stress: Theoretical and clinical aspects* (pp. 477–495). New York: Free Press.

Romano, J. L. (1997). Stress and coping: A qualitative study of fourth and fifth graders. *Elementary School Guidance and Counseling, 31,* 273–282.

Roosa, M. W., Wolchik, S. A., & Sandler, I. N. (1997). Preventing the negative effects of common stressors: Current status and future directions. In S. A. Wolchik & I. N. Sandler (Eds.), *Handbook of children's coping: Linking theory and intervention* (pp. 515–533). New York: Plenum Press.

Ryan-Wenger, N. M. (1992). A taxonomy of children's coping strategies: A step toward theory development. *American Journal of Orthopsychiatry, 62,* 256–263.

Sandler, I .N., Wolchik, S. A., MacKinnon, D., Ayers, T. S., & Roosa, M. W. (1997). Developing linkages between theory and intervention in stress and coping processes. In S. A. Wolchik & I. N. Sandler (Eds.), *Handbook of children's coping: Linking theory and intervention* (pp. 3–40). New York: Plenum Press.

Saylor, C. F., Belter, R., & Stokes, S. J. (1997). In S. A. Wolchik & I. N. Sandler (Eds.), *Handbook of children's coping: Linking theory and intervention* (pp. 361–383). New York: Plenum Press.

Sears, S. J., & Milburn, J. (1990). School age stress. In L. E. Arnold (Ed.), *Childhood stress* (pp. 223–246). New York: Wiley.

Selye, H. (1974). *Stress without distress.* New York: Lippincott.

Selye, H. (1993). History of the stress concept. In L. Goldberger & S. Breznitz (Eds.), *Handbook of stress: Theoretical and clinical aspects* (pp. 7–17). New York: Free Press.

Skinner, E. A., & Wellborn, J. G. (1997). Children's coping in the academic domain. In S. A. Wolchik & I. N. Sandler (Eds.), *Handbook of children's coping: Linking theory and intervention* (pp. 387–422). New York: Plenum Press.

Sleek, S. (1994, September). Psychology is finding a home in school-based health clinics. *APA Monitor*, pp. 1, 34.

Smetana, J. G., Yau, J., Restrepo, A., & Braeges, J. L. (1991). Conflict and adaptation in adolescence: Adolescent-parent conflict. In M. E. Colten & S. Gore (Eds.), *Adolescent stress: Causes and consequences* (pp. 43–65). New York: Aldine de Gruyter.

Steinberg, A. (1998). Understanding the secondary traumatic stress of children. In C. R. Figley (Ed.), *Burnout in families: The systemic costs of caring* (pp. 29–46). New York: CRC Press.

Stern, M., & Newland, L. M. (1994). Working with children. *The Counseling Psychologist, 22,* 402–425.

Straus, M. A. (1980). Stress and physical child abuse. *Child Abuse and Neglect, 4,* 75–88.

Trad, P. V., & Greenblatt, E. (1990). Psychological aspects of child stress: Development and the spectrum of coping responses. In L. E. Arnold (Ed.), *Childhood stress* (pp. 23–49). New York: Wiley.

van der Kolk, B. A., Mcfarlane, A. C., & Weisaeth, L. (Eds.). (1996). *Traumatic stress: The effects of overwhelming experiences on mind, body, and society.* New York: Guilford Press.

Vingerhoets, A. J., & Marcelissen, F. H. (1988). Stress research: Its present status and issues for future developments. *Social Sciences in Medicine, 26,* 279–291.

Wagner, W. G. (1994). Counseling with children. *The Counseling Psychologist, 22,* 381–401.

Wertlieb, D. (1991). Children and divorce: Stress and coping in developmental perspective. In J. Eckenrode (Ed.), *The social context of coping* (pp. 31–54). New York: Plenum Press.

Widom, C. S. (1991). Childhood victimization: Risk factors for delinquency. In M. E. Colten & S. Gore (Eds.), *Adolescent stress: Causes and consequences* (pp. 201–221). New York: Aldine de Gruyter.

Willis, T. A. (1987). Help-seeking as a coping mechanism. In C. R. Snyder & C. E. Ford (Eds.), *Coping with negative life events* (pp. 19–50). New York: Plenum Press.

Wolchik, S. A., & Sandler, I. N. (Eds.). (1997). *Handbook of children's coping: Linking theory and intervention.* New York: Plenum Press.

Youngs, B. (1985). *Stress in children.* New York: Arbor House.

Zunker, V. G. (1994). *Career counseling: Applied concepts of life planning.* Pacific Grove, CA: Brooks/Cole.

PART THREE

WORKING WITH YOUTH AT RISK: PREVENTION AND INTERVENTION

In Parts One and Two, the topic of youth at risk was introduced and the causes were examined. In Part Three, Working With Youth At Risk: Prevention and Intervention, the text addresses behaviors most often identified as placing youth at risk. Each of the chapters in this part contains an introduction, problem identification, a case study, approaches to prevention, intervention strategies, adaptations for diversity, and a summary. Authors discuss both prevention and intervention from individual, family, school, and community perspectives. In this way the reader is able to obtain a comprehensive and comparative overview of the material in each chapter.

Chapter 8, The Secret and All-Consuming Obsessions: Eating Disorders, provides excellent introductory material with respect to the impact of the media, gender socialization, and body image on youth at risk for eating disorders. Risk factors such as gender, age, socioeconomic status, family characteristics, and identification with socialized norms are also discussed. Such background information, along with a thorough discussion of definitions, symptoms, and etiology, create the context for the case study and subsequent presentation of approaches to prevention and intervention. The chapter includes an extremely current and well-done section on diversity issues including those faced by men, gay and lesbian individuals, and athletes.

It is estimated that over 1 million adolescent women become pregnant each year. Thousands of these infants are raised by children under the age of 14; likewise, thousands will be the second child born to a 16-year-old mother. Chapter 9, Children Having Children: Teenage Pregnancy and Parenthood, is based on the assumption that universal remedies are necessary for the successful reduction of adolescent pregnancy and childbearing. Traditional sex education, life management skills training, the impact of the Adolescent Family Life Act, school-based clinics, community family planning services, residential programs, and life options' programs are just a few of the possibilities discussed in this comprehensive treatment of the topic.

Chapter 10, A Future in Jeopardy: Adolescents and AIDS, provides an indispensable resource for those working with this at-risk population. As noted by the writers of this chapter, researchers are currently struggling to acquire the information and medical technology needed to develop a cure for HIV/AIDS. The outlook for a cure, however, is not optimistic; some say we must learn to live with some form of HIV as long as there are human beings on this planet. Others say that even with a cure, elements such as poverty, racism, sexism, and homophobia will continue to contribute to the far-reaching consequences of HIV/AIDS. In addition to the introduction, case study, prevention approaches, and intervention strategies in this chapter, an appendix of national AIDS resources is also provided.

The adolescent at risk for suicide has become an increasing concern for schools and communities throughout the United States. Between 1960 and 1988 the adolescent suicide rate rose by 200% compared to an increase in the general population of approximately 17%. According to some experts, one teenager attempts suicide every 90 seconds, and one completes the act of suicide every 90 minutes. Chapter 11, I Don't Want to Live: The Adolescent At Risk for Suicidal Behavior, discusses information all professionals and all parents should know if prevention and/or intervention efforts are to succeed. Discussions of ethnic and gender differences, methods, risk factors, precipitants, myths, and profiles provide the groundwork for the subsequent case study, prevention approaches, intervention strategies, and adaptations for diversity. An adolescent who is suicidal is communicating the fact that he or she is experiencing difficulty with problem-solving, self-esteem, managing stress, expressing feelings. It is important for all of us to respond in constructive, safe, informed ways when working with this very vulnerable adolescent population.

Chapter 12, I Am Somebody: Gang Membership, examines the youth gang phenomenon. Robin Hood and his Merry Men are perhaps the most celebrated gang in literature. Not unlike some gangs operating today, Robin Hood's gang was believed to be helpful by some people in the communities in which it operated. Often modern street gangs first present themselves as protectors of the community. Yet Robin Hood's Merry Men carried weapons, and their behavior, even though they robbed from the rich to give to the poor, was illegal under the criminal codes of the era.

Setting the modern youth gang within the context of history and literature, the discussion in chapter 12 includes an examination of views as to why gangs form, risk factors for gang involvement, and statistics that set the stage for understanding gangs and their impact upon society. A case study profiles a young man involved in gangs as a way of understanding the reality of those factors shaping the choices and lives of our youth. From the information about gang organization, risks, and statistics, the focus shifts to an understanding of diversity and gang involvement, prevention approaches, and strategies for intervention.

Death in the Classroom: Violence in Schools is a new chapter (13), and it addresses the recent escalation of violence in schools. This is a particularly timely chapter given the fact that the Littleton, Colorado, incident occurred just about the time this third edition was scheduled to go into production. We think readers will find this chapter to be an important and helpful addition to the text and will find merit in the application of William Glasser's ideas to creating safe school environments.

Research has shown that use of alcohol is associated with 60% of all murders, 40% of all assaults, and 33% of all rapes and child molestation. In spite of our technologically advanced modern society, America is fighting an age-old problem: drug and alcohol abuse. This is not a problem limited to adults. Significant percentages of youth and adolescents are experimenting with and becoming regular users of chemical substances, particularly tobacco, alcohol, marijuana, inhalants, and cocaine. Chapter 14, I Can't Live Without It: Adolescent Substance Abuse From a Cultural and Contextual Framework, focuses on why teens turn to drugs, the physiological mechanisms of drug use, and the roles that individuals, families, schools, and the community have in both prevention and intervention.

Nowhere to Turn: Homeless Youth is the topic of chapter 15. At least half a million youth in the United States are homeless, with incidence increasing at a rate of 25% a year. From the most recent statistics available, it is clear that the faces of the homeless have changed drastically since the days of the White, male, alcoholic, skid-row bum. Forty percent of the homeless are families, and 25% are children. Homeless children's differences in appearance, behavior, and ability demand tolerance and flexibility from teachers and school administrators. The purpose of this chapter is to describe homelessness both demographically and more descriptively using a case example. The chapter discusses preventive measures society must take to avoid the problem of homelessness and offers several interventions to help the increasing numbers of homeless youth in the classroom and address their educational needs.

The text concludes with chapter 16, This Isn't the Place for Me: School Dropout. The placement of this chapter at the end of the book is fitting because the problem of the school dropout involves many of the personal, family, and social issues discussed in previous chapters. Demographic correlates, early warning signs, underlying causes, two case studies, clinical and systemic approaches to prevention and intervention, and adaptations for diversity form the basis for this informative and cutting-edge chapter.

8 | The Secret and All-Consuming Obsessions: Eating Disorders

Kimberly Wright

The standard for body size and weight is socially determined. It is a cultural phenomenon that demands that the current ideal physique is slim. Countries that commonly experience the threat of famine have virtually no cases of anorexia or bulimia, and obesity is considered desirable (Bruch, 1973). In previous eras in the United States, larger bodies were associated with prosperity, in contrast with current mores that associate thinness with affluence. Obesity is now considered a correlate of the lower class. Continuous images indoctrinate the public with the message that to be considered successful, masterful, and acceptable, one must display a thin physique (Vandereycken, 1993). This image is one that emphasizes self-control and discipline over self-indulgence. For women, this message is especially strong. Since Twiggy reigned as a premier fashion model in the late 1960s, America has promoted a thinner and thinner standard for the female ideal (Garner, Garfinkel, Schwartz, & Thompson, 1980). It is within this context that the current escalation of eating disorders in the United States is occurring.

Among the most powerful transmitters of social standards are the media. According to Garner et al. (1980), "the potential impact of the media in establishing identificatory role models cannot be overemphasized" (p. 652). Newspapers, television, movies, magazines, and billboards bombard the public with images and messages about appropriate behavior, dress, food, entertainment, appearance, and beliefs. Avoiding the overt and covert messages of society portrayed through the media is virtually impossible. For men, the standards portrayed include fitness, power, and independence. For women, the standards portrayed include thinness, femininity, and beauty.

The female ideal as defined by the culture fluctuates. The power of these fluctuations is revealed by a study (Garner et al., 1980) comparing the weights and measurements of *Playboy* centerfolds and Miss America

Pageant contestants from 1959 to 1978. There was a significant decrease in body weight and body measurements for both groups, despite an increase in height. Additionally, the Miss America Pageant winners were significantly slimmer than the average contestant in the same pageant. This trend also occurred at the same time period that the average woman under age 30 was becoming heavier.

The trend toward a slim female ideal is also illustrated by the recent changes in diet advertisements. Between 1973 and 1991, the United States witnessed a consistent increase in television commercials featuring diet products (Wiseman, Gunning, & Gray, 1993). Another study of media messages compared food and diet advertisements from 48 women's magazines and 48 men's magazines (Silverstein, Perdue, Peterson, & Kelly, 1986). Interestingly, 1,179 different food and diet advertisements appeared in the women's magazines, compared to 10 in the men's magazines. Anderson and DiDomenico (1992) also found that women's magazines contain over 10 times the number of diet advertisements and articles as do men's magazines. The inherent double message is that women need to indulge in various foods and that they need to diet in order to avoid weight gain.

Few argue that men and women are socialized in different ways. The female and male socialization experiences can be viewed as representative of different cultures. Women are socialized to draw their self-esteem from their physical appearance rather than from what they do (Beattie, 1988). For men, self-esteem tends to be more frequently related to success. This discrepancy, combined with the ideal standards for female appearance, increases a woman's vulnerability to eating disorders but does not rule out the vulnerability among men.

Body image is the perception of one's own shape and size. Those who compare themselves to models or other ideals often distort their own body image negatively (Kalodner, 1997). The body is perceived to be inadequate if it fails to meet ideal criteria. It is not unusual to hear women, or even young girls, say "I feel so fat" even when their weight is normal. Among women, it is now the norm to diet. Although it may not be healthy, Polivy and Herman (1987) found that the majority of women are dissatisfied with their bodies and have dieted.

Body image distortions are more prevalent among women than among men. In a study of college males, 65% of a sample of 340 reported that they weighed within 5 percentage points of their ideal weight (Franco, Tamburrino, Carroll, & Bernal, 1988) in contrast to the typical body dissatisfaction of their female peers. Women tend to exhibit greater body dissatisfaction and body image distortion than do men (Connor-Greene, 1988). Even among men with bulimia, the desired ideal weight has been found to be more realistic than the desired ideal weight of women with bulimia (Schneider & Agras, 1987).

This chapter first defines the problem of eating disorders by looking at risk factors and at the symptoms and etiologies of anorexia nervosa, bulimia nervosa, and binge-eating disorder. The chapter then presents a case study, considers approaches to prevention, and discusses intervention strategies from individual, family, school, and community perspectives. The chapter concludes with an exploration of adaptations for diversity in relation to ethnicity, gender, affectional orientation, and athletes.

PROBLEM DEFINITION

The prevalence of eating disorders has consistently increased in the United States across the last 30 years. Increasing emphasis on thinness and physical fitness has altered the standard for appearance for women and men. The term *fitness movement* is misleading. Many individuals flock to gyms and aerobics classes under the guise of cardiovascular health and physical fitness, but with the goal of achieving their physical ideal of attractiveness. The current trends are not in danger of reversing, which leaves the social climate primed for a continuing increase in eating pathology.

Risk Factors

Gender. Anorexia, bulimia, and, to a lesser extent, binge eating disorder are typically characterized as female afflictions, but they also cross gender lines. Although these disturbances do appear more frequently among females, males can develop these disorders. It is likely that many cases of anorexia or bulimia among males go unreported for several reasons: (1) the reluctance of men to admit symptoms of a female disorder, (2) eating large quantities of food is not considered abnormal by adolescent boys and young men, and (3) clinicians are less likely to explore eating disorder symptoms among males. Even considering the potential underreporting among males, women are at higher risk for developing anorexia or bulimia due to the value placed on their appearance. (The gender differences are reflected by the primary use of the female pronoun throughout, unless specifically referring to males.) Binge eating, typically associated with obesity, is less gender specific but also occurs more frequently in women than in men (Bruce & Agras, 1992). It is important to note, however, that *binge eating* and *obesity* are not comparable terms. Binge eating refers to a behavior; obesity refers specifically to having excess body fat. Obesity may be a likely consequence of binge eating behavior, but because weight is regulated by a variety of biological and behavioral factors, obese persons are not necessarily binge eaters.

Age. Adolescence is a high-risk period for the development of eating disorders. The most frequent period for the emergence of anorexia and bulimia is between the ages 14 and 18; however, atypical onset patterns exist. Late adolescence is also the most likely period for the development of binge eating disorder, with 18 being the modal age of onset (Streigel-Moore, 1993). The developmental tasks of adolescence interact with the physical and social demands of maturation to create a vulnerability to developing eating disorders during adolescence or early adulthood. Binge eating disorder may also develop in adulthood, and it is not unusual for the disorder to be diagnosed once bulimia is in remission.

Race. Anorexia and bulimia have historically been more frequently associated with upper middle-class White populations, and the greatest risk for these disorders continues to be in this group. However, there is recent evidence suggesting that the risk and prevalence are increasing for minority groups (Sanders & Heiss, 1998). In addition, binge eating and obesity are more common among some minority populations such as African American and some Native American groups (Klesges, DeBon, & Meyers, 1996).

Socioeconomic Level. Women with anorexia and bulimia have most frequently come from the middle to upper-middle socioeconomic classes (Anderson & Hay, 1985), and obesity (and by extension, binge eating) tend to be associated with lower socioeconomic status. This pattern is not consistent, however, especially among youth with upwardly mobile aspirations, such as first generation college students.

Family Characteristics. The families of those with bulimia are described as chaotic and conflicted (Schwartz, Barrett, & Saba, 1985), and the families of those with anorexia as overcontrolling and rigid (Sargent, Liebman, & Silver, 1985). Those with binge eating disorder report being neglected or overlooked as children, as well as experiencing overinvolvement or lack of structure around meals (Pike & Wilfley, 1996). Although these are simplified, stereotypical portrayals, family problems are common among the eating disordered population. It is also common for another family member to have struggled with weight problems or an eating disorder. Eating disturbances among women have been found to be related to weight concerns expressed by parents (Keel, Heatherton, Harnden, & Hornig, 1997). Previous research and a review of the literature has indicated convergent evidence that the families of eating disordered individuals have a higher rate of affective disorders, alcoholism, and conflictual and controlling family relationships (Kog & Vandereycken, 1985; Pike & Wilfley, 1996).

Identification With Socialized Norms. Among a sample of 682 college students, Mintz & Betz (1988) reported that disordered eating similar to that found in anorexia and bulimia was strongly related to the endorsement of sociocultural norms that regard female thinness and attractiveness as an indication of worth. Those women who hold beliefs similar to the traditional gender expectations are at greater risk for these eating disorders. Persistent weight and shape concerns are also reported to pose a risk for the development of eating pathology among high school females (Killen et al., 1996).

Although many of the risk factors prominent in eating disorders are featured in other disturbances of youth, such as alcohol and drug abuse or depression, the sociocultural and gender pressures are the distinguishing features of anorexia nervosa and bulimia. Risk factors for binge eating disorder are less clearly identified.

Anorexia Nervosa: Symptoms and Etiology

The prevalence of anorexia nervosa (typically referred to as anorexia) among the general population is reported to be between 0.5% to 1.0% (American Psychiatric Association, 1994), but the prevalence is believed to be higher among high school and college populations (Mintz & Betz, 1988). Approximately 90% of the cases of anorexia nervosa are female. Cases with eating disturbances that do not meet all of the criteria for anorexia nervosa are more common. The onset is most likely to occur in adolescence and early adulthood, but cases of earlier and later onset have been reported, with a later onset more common among ethnic minorities (Anderson & Hay, 1985).

Anorexia nervosa is a constellation of symptoms in which an extreme drive for thinness, fear of becoming fat, and a restriction of food intake are central. Anorexia nervosa is actually a misnomer. Literally translated, anorexia nervosa means "nervous lack of appetite." Although there is a denial of hunger, actual hunger loss does not occur until the very advanced stages of the disorder.

The most recent diagnostic criteria presented in the *DSM-IV* (American Psychiatric Association, 1994) allow for specificity in diagnosis and highlight the similarity of some symptoms common to both anorexia nervosa and bulimia nervosa. (See Tables 8–1, 8–2, and 8–3.)

The critical elements of anorexia include

- refusal to maintain body weight at or above a minimally normal weight for age and height (e.g., weight loss leading to maintenance of body weight less that 85% of that expected; or failure to make expected weight gain during periods of growth, leading to body weight less than 85% of that expected);

- intense fear of gaining weight or becoming fat, even though underweight;
- disturbance in the way in which one's body weight or shape is experienced, undue influence of body weight or shape on self-evaluation, or denial of the seriousness of the current low body weight; and
- in postmenarcheal females, amenorrhea, i.e., the absence of at least three consecutive menstrual cycles. (A woman is considered to have amenorrhea if her periods occur only following hormone, e.g., estrogen administration.)

Further, the *DSM-IV* specifies two types of anorexia:

- *restricting type.* During the current episode of anorexia nervosa, the person has not regularly engaged in binge eating or purging behavior (i.e., self-induced vomiting or the misuse of laxatives, diuretics, or enemas).
- *binge eating/purging type.* During the current episode of anorexia nervosa, the person has regularly engaged in binge eating or purging behavior (i.e., self-induced vomiting or the misuse of laxatives diuretics, or enemas).

Among the first noticeable symptoms of anorexia are a preoccupation with food, particularly a focus on the fat and calorie content of food. The woman with anorexia may begin by restricting herself to a "healthy" diet or may begin exercising more than usual. She may slowly add to her list of forbidden foods until the list of foods she allows herself to consume becomes scant. The most striking feature is the determination she evidences. As the disorder progresses she may begin removing herself from social dining situations. She may claim to be too busy to eat lunch with friends or excuse herself from an invitation by claiming to have already eaten. As her weight begins to drop she may conceal herself with loose-fitting clothes or wear warmer clothing than necessary. She may become compulsive with list making, being sure that no free time exists in her schedule. As her work or activities begin to consume all of her day, she may stay up late at night in an effort to burn more calories. As others begin to notice the change in her appearance or behavior, she is likely to become defensive and isolate herself further. She takes any comment regarding her weight loss as a compliment and a sign of success. As the disorder progresses, her cognitive functions become less sharp, decisions are more difficult, and her obsession with food becomes unrelenting.

Throughout the process, she becomes more and more entrenched in her behavior. She appears rigid, reacts with denial if confronted, and becomes more secretive in her eating rituals. Thoughts of food, calories, and weight consume her daily. She becomes more depressed and anxious, and mood swings are frequent. She may develop comorbid obsessive-compulsive symptoms unrelated to her weight and food obsessions, such as ensuring her room is orderly, frequent checking behavior, or repetitive counting. Her sense of self-worth becomes intimately linked with her control of food, largely as a mask for her pervasive feeling of ineffectiveness and inadequacy. She strives for extreme achievement and perfection in her endeavors. Her emotional development and social interactions are less mature than that of her peers. (See Table 8–1.)

A single etiology of anorexia has yet to be determined. It is currently accepted that the disorder is of a multidimensional nature. Although the anorexic female appears to the world to be a perfect child who is a high achiever, is compassionate toward others, and is respectful toward authority, it is believed that personality deficits precede the onset of the illness (Steiger & Houle, 1991). The extreme control exhibited in the young woman with anorexia becomes a compensation for poor coping skills and feelings of instability (Bruch, 1973).

Table 8–1 | Symptoms of Anorexia Nervosa

Psychological

Perfectionism	Denial of problem
Depression	Anxiety
Distorted body image	Thoughts of suicide
Intense fear of food and weight gain	High need for control
	Mood lability
Inflexibility in thought and behavior	Poor self-esteem
	Compliance
Feelings of guilt about eating	

Behavioral

Extreme food restriction	Preoccupation with food and eating
Isolation from friends and family	
Fatigue and irritability	Compulsive exercise
Extreme physical activity	Vomiting meals
Eating alone	Abuse of laxatives, diet pills, or diuretics
Adoption of loose clothing	
High caffeine intake	

Physical

Noticeable weight loss—15% or more of total body weight	Lanugo—growth of fine facial and body hair
Absent or erratic menses	Exhaustion
Cognitive disturbances	Cardiac disturbances
Electrolyte imbalance	Malnutrition
Distortion of hunger and satiety	Tooth decay/gum disease
	Lowered metabolism
Hypersensitivity to cold	

Psychoanalytic theory postulates that anorexia serves as a defense against maturation. Fears about becoming a woman and developing sexually inspire attempts to control the body. The maintenance of a child-like physique is seen as an unconscious strategy to forestall adult relationships and sexuality. Developmentalists view anorexia as an adaptive tool used to combat great anxiety about developmental crises, such as increased expectations and responsibilities associated with maturation. Sociocultural theorists claim that it is the striving for perfection in appearance as a visible hallmark of success that motivates the woman with anorexia. Learning theory is related to this sociocultural explanation in that initial weight loss is met with praise and positive reinforcement. As she becomes emaciated, the attention received from others turns to concern that may be positively reinforcing as well. Internal reinforcement operates simultaneously as the anorexic prides herself on her self-control. The control issue escalates as she resists others' attempts to feed her and refuses external intervention. Negative reinforcement maintains the pattern as the fears of food and fat provide the incentive for the avoidance of food. Family theorists hypothesize that the behavior is a means of gaining control and independence from a critical and overcontrolling parent. Food and the body become the areas in which the anorexic can exert control. It is most reasonable to propose a multietiological perspective that incorporates several theoretical considerations while recognizing that no single etiological course can apply to each case.

Bulimia Nervosa: Symptoms and Etiology

Prevalence estimates for bulimia nervosa vary from 1% to 3% for women and 0.3% for men (American Psychiatric Association, 1994) to 11% to 13% in college populations (Coric & Murstein, 1993; Gray & Ford, 1985). Despite these considerable statistics, a great number of people exhibit bulimic symptoms without meeting the complete diagnostic criteria. As with anorexia, the typical onset of bulimia nervosa is during adolescence and early adulthood.

Bulimia nervosa is commonly known as bulimia. Roughly translated from the ancient Greek, bulimia means "ravenous or ox-like hunger" (Stunkard, 1993) and is a disorder characterized by cyclical periods of binge eating, typically followed by purging behavior (vomiting, laxative use, diuretic use, or excessive exercising). Many individuals engage in purging behavior without a binge precursor. This behavior would be classified as eating disorder not otherwise specified (ED NOS) and often takes the form of purging small or normal meals or purging a forbidden food eaten in a small quantity. The latest diagnostic criteria in the *DSM-IV* have specified two types of bulimia, although in practice the occasional overlap of symptoms with those of anorexia make the distinctions less clear. The diagnostic criteria for bulimia nervosa are

- recurrent episodes of binge eating in which an episode of binge eating is characterized by both of the following:
  —eating, in a discrete period of time (e.g., within any 2-hour period), an amount of food that is definitely larger than most people would eat during a similar period of time and under similar circumstances; and
  —a sense of lack of control over eating during the episode (e.g., a feeling that one cannot stop eating or control how much one is eating).
- recurrent inappropriate compensatory behavior in order to prevent weight gain, such as self-induced vomiting; misuse of laxatives, diuretics, enemas, or other medications; fasting; or excessive exercise;
- the binge eating and inappropriate compensatory behavior both occur, on average, at least twice a week for 3 months;
- self-evaluation is unduly influenced by body shape and weight; and
- the disturbance does not occur exclusively during episodes of anorexia nervosa.

Further, the *DSM-IV* specifies two types of bulimia nervosa:

- *purging type*. During the current episode of bulimia nervosa, the person has regularly engaged in self-induced vomiting or the misuse of laxatives, diuretics, or enemas.
- *nonpurging type*. During the current episode of bulimia nervosa, the person has used other inappropriate compensatory behaviors, such as fasting or excessive exercise, but has not regularly engaged in self-induced vomiting or the misuse of laxatives, diuretics, or enemas.

Perhaps the first identifiable symptom of bulimia is an occasional binge eating episode. The episode may be in response to feeling a need to nurture oneself with food, or to indulge oneself following a period of dieting or restricted food intake. The reinforcement of the binge (feeling soothed, reducing anxiety) leads to repeated binges. The fear of weight gain is often the impetus for later purging behavior, but the relief the purge provides can also be an accidental discovery (as when spontaneous vomiting following a large meal affords physical relief). As with addictive behaviors, the cycle escalates from an occasional episode to a daily habit.

Binges most commonly occur in the late afternoon or late evening, often after a day of food restriction, but may begin in the early morning. It is not unusual for bingeing to occur on a daily basis, and for normal meals during the day to be vomited as well. Binges are frequently planned, and time alone must be negotiated. Social activities become limited as activities are scheduled with bingeing and purging episodes in mind. The woman with bulimia may withdraw most noticeably from meals where she will be observed, and will become very anxious if prevented from purging (either by interruption or situational factors). Mood swings are common. As the disorder progresses, the bulimic's body image becomes more distorted, and her sense of being out of control is less tolerable. As she puts more effort into controlling her food intake, she increases her sense of deprivation and sets the scenario for future binges. Increasingly, the binge/purge cycle becomes a means of managing all painful emotions, and her awareness of her feelings becomes muted. Although her weight is likely to remain stable, fluctuating within 5 pounds, she begins to look less physically well. Her face and neck may appear swollen and she may develop a burst blood vessel in the eye from the force of vomiting.

The woman with bulimia is susceptible to depression, and typically has low self-esteem and poor impulse control. She may abuse drugs or alcohol in the way that she abuses food. Her body image is invariably distorted, and she is highly self-critical. She may define herself as a people pleaser and be fearful of confrontation, conflict, or anger. Frequently she identifies feeling lonely, despite the fact that her isolation is often self-imposed. (See Table 8–2.)

The etiology of bulimia is not agreed upon, and it appears that there may be many avenues to onset. Some women develop bulimic symptoms following a diet. A developmental transition or move may trigger bulimic behavior or intensify existing symptoms (as in the transition to high school or a move away to college) (Smolak & Levine, 1996). Losses (such as deaths, parental separations) are particularly painful and difficult for the bulimic to manage (Armstrong & Roth, 1989).

Increasingly, the etiology of bulimia nervosa is being viewed as multidimensional. A risk factor model has been proposed that posits an interaction between biological, family, developmental, personality, and sociocultural factors (Johnson, Tobin, & Steinberg, 1989). The biological factor most implicated is the correlation between bulimia and affective disorders, particularly depression. The affective instability typically appears prior to the onset of bulimia and suggests a biological vulnerability to bulimic symptoms. Although the disorder may begin with restrictive dieting, the biological urge for food preempts a binge episode. This cycle is maintained by the physical need for food and the soothing emotional benefits of the binge (Lacey, Coker, & Birtchnell, 1986).

Research has supported the position of family theorists that eating disorders are a response or adaptation to coping with a dysfunctional family (Lundholm & Waters, 1991). The family factors that tend to be related to bulimia include a family environment that is chaotic, conflicted, and neglectful, resulting in children who feel insecure, anxious, and disorganized. The inability of the bulimic to identify internal states is seen as a developmental deficit resulting from the parent's inablility to respond to

Table 8–2 | Symptoms of Bulimia Nervosa

Psychological

Low self-esteem
Depression
Anxiety
Feelings of
  worthlessness
Over concern with weight and
  body image

Feeling out of
  control
Suicidal
  thoughts/feelings
High need for
  approval

Behavioral

Cyclical bingeing and purging
Bingeing on high calorie foods
  (carbohydrates/fats)
Increasing time
  spent on bingeing/purging
Abuse of laxatives, diet
  pills, diuretics, or exercise
Abusing alcohol or drugs
Restroom visits after
  meals

Preoccupation with
  food and body image
Eating in secret
Hoarding food
Isolating from friends
  and family
Poor impulse control

Physical

Normal weight
Dehydration
Irritability and fatigue
Tooth decay/gum disease
Chronic illness
Swollen neck glands
Cardiac irregularities
Electrolyte imbalance

Occasional burst blood vessel in
  the eye
Chronic sore throat
Esophageal erosion
Gastrointestinal problems

Table 8–3 | Distinguishing Features Between Anorexia Nervosa and Bulimia Nervosa

Anorexia	Bulimia
Great weight loss	Minor weight fluctuations
More introverted	More extroverted
Pride in weight and food control	Shame in bulimic behavior
Less sexually active	More sexually active
Feels in control with food	Feels out of control with food

the child in a manner that allowed the child to internalize her own awareness. Contributing personality factors are low self-esteem, feelings of ineffectiveness, sensitivity to rejection, and compliance with others. They have persistent shame and guilt about not meeting their idealized goals. Sociocultural factors include the changing gender roles in the dominant culture, the increased pressure for thinness, and the use of the pursuit of thinness as a means of adaptation and social acceptability.

Binge Eating Disorder: Symptoms and Etiology

Binge eating disorder is a more recently recognized eating disorder that afflicts approximately 5% to 10% of the general population (Yanovski, Nelson, Dubbert, & Spitzer, 1993). Currently, binge eating disorder falls under the diagnostic criteria of eating disorder not otherwise specified (ED NOS) but has been proposed as a disorder of its own in the *DSM-IV*. Binge eating disorder is characterized by binge eating (eating a large amount of food in a short period of time and feeling out of control during the binge episode). The disorder may develop in the absence of a history with anorexia or bulimia, or may result when the purging aspects of bulimia have been discontinued. The disorder is somewhat more common among women (ratio of 3:2) and is equally common among White and African American women. The modal age of onset is 18, but many experience some episodes of overeating behavior at earlier ages.

The diagnostic category of ED NOS includes other types of eating pathology that do not meet criteria for anorexia and bulimia. Examples of ED NOS are

- for females, meeting all of the criteria for anorexia nervosa except that the individual has regular menses;
- meeting all of the criteria for anorexia nervosa except that, despite significant weight loss, the individual's current weight is in the normal range;
- meeting all of the criteria for bulimia nervosa except that the binge eating and inappropriate compensatory mechanisms occur at a frequency of less than twice a week or for a duration of less than 3 months;
- regular use of inappropriate compensatory behavior by an individual of normal body weight after eating small amounts of food (e.g., self-induced vomiting after the consumption of two cookies);
- repeatedly chewing and spitting out, but not swallowing, large amounts of food;
- binge eating disorder, that is, recurrent episodes of binge eating in the absence of the regular use of inappropriate compensatory behaviors characteristic of bulimia nervosa.

The *DSM-IV*'s proposed criteria for binge eating disorder include

- recurrent episodes of binge eating in which an episode of binge eating is characterized by both of the following:
  —eating, in a discrete period of time (e.g., within any 2-hour period), an amount of food that is definitely larger than most people would eat in a similar period of time under similar circumstances; and

   —a sense of lack of control over eating during the episode (e.g., a feeling that one cannot stop eating or control what or how much one is eating);
- binge eating episodes are associated with three (or more) of the following:
   —eating much more rapidly than usual;
   —eating until feeling uncomfortably full;
   —eating large amounts of food when not feeling physically hungry;
   —eating alone because of being embarrassed by how much one is eating; and
   —feeling disgusted with oneself, depressed, or very guilty after overeating;
- marked distress regarding binge eating is present;
- the binge eating occurs, on average, at least 2 days a week for 6 months; and
- the binge eating is not associated with the regular use of inappropriate compensatory behaviors (e.g., purging, fasting, excessive exercise) and does not occur exclusively during the course of anorexia nervosa or bulimia nervosa.

Although there are many consistencies among those with binge eating disorder, a typical progression is more difficult to describe because binge eating disorder develops in more varied ways. It is common, but not invariable, for the seeds of binge eating to begin in childhood and for the symptoms to develop slowly throughout adolescence and adulthood. Binge eaters may begin as larger children who develop an overreliance on food for comfort to assuage hurt feelings or to disconnect from painful events of childhood. They may experience a period of chubbiness during which they are teased or are made to feel self-conscious about weight. Parental concern may take the form of restricting snacks allowed for other children in the family, criticizing or mocking size or weight, or encouraging them to become more physically active in order to slim down. During this time they may begin to hoard food without the family's awareness and hide it for later consumption in private. They may be sent to special summer camp programs for overweight children and later refer to it as "fat camp." They may seem undisturbed by the remarks about their weight or robust appetite, and may even develop a self-deprecating sense of humor. They may begin to isolate self to spare self from critical remarks or, later, the harsh judgments of peers. As they enter adolescence they may become less socially engaged and find solace in food rather than take the risks required for adolescent socialization. As they become more lonely, their use of food for managing distressing feelings increases their overconsumption of food, and bingeing becomes more frequent. This begins a cycle of bingeing in response to negative affective states, which leads to increased weight, which leads to further guilt and isolation and increasingly recurrent binges. Feelings of depression may also escalate simultaneously. Their sense of shame (about their inability to control eating and increasing weight) is pervasive and hinders the development of interpersonal relationships. Once their binge eating produces considerable weight gain, medical complications, such as hypertension and diabetes, may arise. (See Table 8–4.)

As with anorexia and bulimia there is disagreement about the etiology of binge eating disorder. There is some similarity in the etiologies of binge eating disorder and bulimia. Developmentalists note that the passage through adolescence into adulthood stresses coping skills beyond their capacity. This is the time when female sex-role socialization promotes an excessive emphasis on appearance and the value of thinness (Striegel-Moore, 1993). The mechanisms operating for men during this time have been less defined, but it is reasonable to assume that the sex-role expectations of boys during adolescence are also challenging. A restraint model posits that binge eating develops in response to a period of dieting, but there is sufficient evidence that this is not always the case. A significant number (approximately half) of binge eaters develop the disorder without a history of intake restriction or body dissatisfaction (Wilson, Nonas, & Rosenblum, 1993). A *conditioning model*, based on learning theory, suggests that the comfort derived from food gradually reinforces a pattern of self-soothing that relies on food. An *addictions model* contends that the processes for binge eating are similar to those of an alcohol or drug addiction, and some treatment programs and self-help groups (Overeaters Anonymous) have been based on the 12-step model of recovery (Westphal & Smith, 1996).

The high rate of comorbidity of binge eating disorder with depression has led to the proposition that binge eating is a variant of affective disorders and that the binge eating serves to regulate negative emotional states. Some contend, however, that the most promising model of binge eating disorders is a *biopsychosocial model* that takes into account biological vulnerability as well as the cognitive, behavioral, and social determinants of binge eating (Polivy & Herman, 1996). The difficulty with this type of model is that it does not account for the various factors operating at different stages of the disorder. Polivy and Herman (1996) have suggested that identifying the phases of the disorder would provide valuable information to the research and treatment of binge eating disorder.

CASE STUDY

Carrie is a 19-year-old female of White/Latina heritage. She is in the second semester of her freshman year at a large university. She originally

Table 8–4 | Symptoms of Binge Eating Disorder

Psychological

Low self-esteem	Feeling out of control
Depression	Preoccupation with food
Anxiety	
Shame about bingeing and weight	

Behavioral

Frequent, recurrent bingeing	Avoidance of emotional or sexual
Eating alone in private	intimacy
Hoarding food	
Social isolation	

Physical

Higher than normal weight or obesity	Sexual impairment
High blood pressure	Fatigue
Risk of diabetes	Difficulty with physical activity
Joint strain	Lack of hunger or satiety awareness
Edema of the lower extremities	Renal disease
Coronary disease	Osteoarthritis

sought counseling to deal with her increasing sense of depression. During her first session with the psychologist, she presented as bright and cheerful, in contrast to her reported feelings of sadness and hopelessness. She was immaculately groomed, of normal weight, and casually dressed.

As Carrie described her current situation, her pain was evident even as she smiled through the tears she fought to keep from falling. She just didn't understand why she couldn't control herself. She had been bingeing and purging (via vomiting) since her junior year of high school and was feeling increasing shame and powerlessness. Although there had been periods when she binged and purged less often (such as during the football season when she was busy with cheerleading and had less time alone), the transition to college escalated the pattern from occasionally to daily. She was also now taking laxatives several times a week, and often went for an entire day without eating in order to pay for having binged the day before. This would eventually led to another late night binge, which she vomited, and the cycle began again. However, even these efforts in conjunction with 2 hours of daily aerobic exercise did little to conquer her intense fear that she would gain an enormous amount of weight.

She had begun by self-inducing vomiting when she had overeaten or had been drinking alcohol. She had been an unpopular child, and once she had made the cheerleading squad in high school she feared that she would gain weight and lose her newfound social status. She lived in terror that she would be discovered to be as inadequate as she felt.

She described her parents as "perfect" and her younger sister as the "baby" of the family. Mom was a perfectionist who was hardworking and demanded the same from her oldest daughter. Dad worked long hours and was not as involved with the family. Carrie did not mention until a later session that her mother was generally quite critical, especially of Carrie's appearance, and had very high expectations, or that her dad drank frequently on the occasions when he was home with the family.

During the first session Carrie described the painful pattern of her daily life:

Carrie: I just can't seem to control anything. It feels like this is never going to end.

Dr. W: That sounds pretty hopeless.

Carrie: It is hopeless. I've been depressed since I first got here. At first I thought it was just homesickness, but everything seems to be falling apart. I can barely get out bed, except to eat, and I can't have another semester with the grades as bad as last semester. Everything seems dark, like there's no escape.

Dr. W: Can you tell me what feels so overwhelming?

Carrie: Every day feels overwhelming. It starts out with my planning not to eat at all. As long as I don't eat, I feel okay and pretty happy. But once I start eating I know it's all over.

Dr. W: All over?

Carrie: Yeah, I'll start to eat and I won't be able to stop. When I finally realize how much I've eaten it's too late and my stomach is huge and I have to get rid of it.

Dr. W: It sounds like you aren't aware of your behavior when you're in the middle of a binge.

Carrie: I'm not. It's like I just go numb. Then I feel horrible at what I've done and I get sick.

Dr. W: Does that mean that you intentionally vomit?

Carrie: I don't call it that, but that's the only way I truly feel better. If I can get rid of it, then maybe I'm not so bad and maybe I don't have to feel too guilty.

Dr. W: It doesn't feel like you deserve to eat?

Carrie: Not when I can't control myself. And I usually end up eating bad food anyway.

Dr. W: Bad food?

Carrie: You know, crackers and cookies and ice cream and bread and pizza.

Dr. W: And how are those bad?

Carrie: Do you know the calorie and fat content of that stuff? I don't allow myself to eat that kind of food. If I can just make it through the day without eating, everything will be okay. But even when I make it through the day, I can never seem to have the willpower at night. That's the most dangerous time.

Dr. W: So the food you don't feel you deserve is the food you end up craving. Can you tell me what happens right before you binge?

Carrie: Nothing happens. I just start eating and don't stop.

Dr. W: Are you aware of the circumstances or what you are feeling?

Carrie: I've never thought about it, but I guess I'm scared and lonely, which I feel all the time, but mostly at night.

Dr. W: And what makes you frightened?

Carrie: I'm afraid I'll get fat.

Dr. W: What else?

Carrie: I'm afraid that I won't make it at college, that I'll never be good enough.

Dr. W: How about when you get angry?

Carrie: I never get angry, but I cry a lot.

Dr. W: Could it be that you know when you're scared or sad or hurt but not when you're angry?

Carrie: No, I just don't get angry. Except at myself when I eat a bunch of bad stuff. I get mad when I don't do what I should.

Dr. W: When would that be?

Carrie: Like when I don't study enough, or call my mom enough, or work out enough, or when I eat too much.

Dr. W: Sounds like you're pretty hard on yourself, and your expectations are pretty high. I wonder if anyone could expect to live up those expectations? It doesn't seem like you give yourself much room to make mistakes or to be human.

Carrie: I'm supposed to be better than that—I shouldn't have to make mistakes.

APPROACHES TO PREVENTION

Prevention in the area of eating disorders has recently come under greater scrutiny. Primary prevention has been aimed at preventing the development of eating disorders in unafflicted individuals. The goal of secondary prevention has been to detect early warning signs of eating disorders and encourage treatment for those in the early stages of the disorders. The effectiveness of prevention efforts are currently being called into question, however. Although many school and college programs are designed and administered in an attempt to prevent disturbed eating and the associated psychological problems, there is some evidence that such programs are ineffective (Carter, Stewart, Dunn, & Fairburn, 1997; Mann et al., 1997). Research has suggested that psychoeducational interventions intended to reduce the risk and incidence of eating pathology may, in fact, increase the likelihood that a participant will develop disturbed eating symptomology (Carter et al., 1997). It has been further considered that using the same psychoeducational strategy to accomplish both primary and secondary prevention goals may be ill-advised. Mann et al. (1997) contended that primary prevention efforts that stress the severity of the disorders and secondary prevention programs that tend to normalize the disorders in order to encourage those in need to seek help have conflicted goals. Their study of the effects of prevention programs on female college freshmen revealed that the participants had more symptoms of eating disorders at follow-up than did the control group. Prevention interventions may have an unintentional effect of reducing the stigma and normalizing eating disorders, thereby increasing the likelihood that individuals will engage in such behaviors. The authors emphasized that prevention programs may be more effective if they do not attempt to address both primary and secondary prevention goals simultaneously. The conclusions drawn by these studies has been challenged (Cohn & Maine, 1998), however, and it has been suggested that the methodology of these studies in assessing the effectiveness of prevention programs was faulty and that prevention must be viewed as a developmental process rather than a single effort.

Although abandoning prevention programs based on limited data is not prudent, more investigation of the impact of prevention programs is necessary. One prevention study with 11- and 12-year-old girls concluded that prevention programs are most effective with high-risk groups rather than the general population (Killen, 1996). A study of self-selected college women reported positive outcomes from an 8-week prevention program (Franko, 1998), and although eating patterns were not altered as a result, body image concerns and the importance of appearance were reduced. Some authors have recommended ongoing prevention programs that emphasize health promotion along with opportunities for girls and women to develop attributes beyond attractiveness (Huon, 1996) and the introduction of feminist processes to validate fully the female experience (Piran, 1996). Others have suggested that teaching girls and women to be media literate and educated consumers of the media images that permeate our culture will allow them to evaluate the media more critically (Berel & Irving, 1998). This may be especially important for those with some eating disorder symptomology, given the finding that those with eating disorders are more significantly influenced by the body ideals presented in the media (Murray, Touyz, & Beumont, 1996). Most experts have agreed, however, that given the health risk of eating disorders and their complex etiology, prevention alone can not extinguish eating disorders (Levine, Smolak, & Striegel-Moore, 1996).

Individual

Approaches to prevention at the individual level are typically identified as educational programming, especially among groups of high-risk individuals, and early detection of symptoms. In the case of Carrie, high-risk factors were prominent. Her low self-esteem was not ameliorated by her acceptance to a popular peer group and her cheerleading status (a high-risk group in itself). In addition, her family situation compounded her low self-esteem and depression. Never feeling adequate for her mother's standards, and feeling alienated from her father, left her feeling no sense of safety or acceptance, making her acceptance within her peer group that much more significant.

Programs aimed at high-risk groups might have helped Carrie to identify her problems earlier. A more important task may be to assist young, developing women in maintaining self-esteem through adolescence when their sense of self-esteem is most tenuous. One program aimed at junior high school girls (Friedman, 1998) reported some success in helping girls to cope with the demands of adolescence and maturation, including respecting their bodies' development and challenging the societal pressure for women's appearance. As has been noted by Huon (1996), girls need opportunities to develop and demonstrate their own sense of power and competence. In addition to programming, secondary prevention efforts at the individual level also require that friends and family members take an active role in identifying the warning signs and confronting the behavior of the person.

Family

The role of the family in the prevention of eating disorders is rarely discussed. Although the stereotypical dysfunctional characteristics of the family with an eating disordered member have been identified, intervention at the family level is more common than prevention. The family can, however, be significant in deterring the development of these disorders.

Avoiding the dysfunctional dynamics that contribute to eating pathology is prudent for family members. Family environments that foster an eating disorder tend to be overcontrolling, neglectful, and conflictual, but members do not express their feelings. Families should be encouraged to keep communication open, including discussing unpleasant feelings like anger and disappointment. Further, parents should be taught to nurture developmental maturation and separation, as is appropriate throughout the adolescent years. With each year, the child is learning to take on new levels of independence and responsibility. This task is impeded when the parents are critical or doubtful, or refuse to allow the child the freedom to grow.

The family can also model an acceptance of making mistakes. This includes a tolerance of human mistakes made by themselves and their children. Tolerance is also warranted with regard to appearance. Families who place a strong emphasis on appearance (how each member looks) and on appearances (what others think) tend to imbue this value in their children. It is the lack of tolerance with imperfection that characterizes the unrealistically high self-standards and shame of the eating disordered adolescent. Removing the value of appearance from the family environment also requires a reduced emphasis on food and weight. Even learning to manage such concerns by family activity or exercise is an improvement over the diet-obsessed family.

Some authors have suggested that parents can play a key role in the prevention of eating disorders (Graber & Brooks-Gunn, 1996). They have recommended that parents be educated about the normal progression of puberty, the importance of staying involved in the meal practices of adolescents, and the negative impact of parental comments about appearance. They also have emphasized the need to address the changing relationship between parent and child throughout adolescence.

Secondary prevention can take the form of early symptom identification. Because pathological eating is so common (Betz & Fitzgerald, 1993; Polivy & Herman, 1987) and eating disorders are difficult to understand, many families do not acknowledge the problem until the illness is in the advanced stages. In their study of 14 European exchange students diagnosed with eating disorders while in the United States, Van den Broucke and Vandereycken (1986) noted that most of the students had evidence of disturbed eating or weight preoccupation prior to their departure from home. These disturbances were ignored by the parents and were not identified in the medical examination required before leaving home. These authors recommended becoming aware of the more obvious risk factors and early detection of preliminary symptoms by family members and professionals (doctors, school nurses, and teachers).

Carrie's family could have been most helpful had they identified the dysfunctional family patterns that allowed Carrie's disorder to escalate without acknowledgment. Addressing the family conflicts, critical style, and withdrawal via alcohol could likely have prevented an extended course of her bulimia.

School

High school and junior high personnel are in an important position to assist with the prevention and early detection of eating disorders among adolescents, but it should also be noted that children, particularly girls, are showing evidence of weight preoccupation and disturbed body image at younger ages. It is not unusual to find girls in elementary school demonstrating concern about their weight and dieting. Some prevention programs have been targeted at this younger audience with minimal results (Levine, Smolak, & Schermer, 1996). Omizo and Omizo (1992) suggested that a school counselor should be aware of the risk factors and be watchful of those in high-risk groups such as cheerleaders, drill team members, wrestlers, track team members, gymnasts, and those in the performing arts. In addition to the emphasis on weight and appearance, these are highly competitive environments made more stressful by perfectionistic tendencies and the potential for failure.

The first responsibility of the school counselor is recognition of the symptoms of anorexia, bulimia, and compulsive overeating. The counselor should be aware that some students will not admit eating problems or acknowledge their behavior as a problem. Without the student's willingness to participate, treatment is likely to be ineffective.

Although some school counselors may be trained to work with eating disordered clients, a decision to undertake treatment in a high school setting should be made with caution. Despite the ethical consideration of counseling minors, especially those with serious disorders, the treatment is likely to be more involved than an overextended school counselor could manage.

Due to the setting and frequent contact with groups at high risk for eating disorders, school counselors might most profitably aim their energies toward education and prevention programs. Some programs that have incorporated eating disorder education and evaluation into the school curriculum have been successful in prevention and early detection efforts (Moriarty, Shore, & Maxim, 1990). Given the recent research challenging prevention programming (Carter et al., 1997; Mann et al., 1997), however, the impact of such programs may be most significant among at-risk groups (Killen, 1996; Killen et al., 1993) because most adolescents will not develop an eating disorder.

Recent research has also indicated that eating disorder behaviors may be a response to a crisis (Troop & Treasure, 1997). In this research, anorexic symptoms seemed to be related to cognitive avoidance in response to a crisis, whereas bulimic symptoms seemed to be related to cognitive rumination about the event or situation. In both groups, women who felt helpless were more likely to develop an eating disorder. The authors recommended that primary and relapse prevention of eating disorders should focus on facilitating the development of coping skills. Such programs might have helped Carrie more quickly identify her dilemma, improve her coping strategies, and recognize that help was available.

Community

At present, community prevention has occurred primarily through the media by publicizing famous cases of anorexia. Perhaps because anorexia is considered more glamorous than bulimia or binge eating, less public attention has been given to the latter. Primarily female actors, fashion models, and athletes who have struggled with anorexia have been highlighted through news programs and magazine articles. Talk shows have aired episodes that interview eating disordered individuals with less fame. Television movies have portrayed the consequences of the progression of eating disorders. We have yet to see public service announcements that warn of the dangers of extreme dieting, however. Given the heavy investment in thinness as the social norm and the enormous profits generated by the diet industry, warnings against dieting are not likely to emerge soon.

The most important community intervention might be to address the larger societal issues. The strong influence of the media on the development and maintenance of eating disorders has led most authors to suggest that a change in the societal norms is necessary (Cohn & Maine, 1998; Jasper, 1993; Levine, Smolak, & Striegel-Moore, 1996; Polivy & Herman, 1987; Ussery & Prentice-Dunn, 1992). Without a reduced emphasis on the value of thinness within the society, prevention efforts will remain primarily early detection devices. The task of shifting societal standards, although seemingly monumental, is central to the prevention effort at the community level. One organization in particular, Eating Disorders Awareness and Prevention (EDAP), has as its central mission to educate the public about the dangers of dieting, about eating disorders, and about the need for media literacy in relation to media's inpact on body image and self-esteem. It is less likely that Carrie would have developed an eating disorder as a means of managing her distress had the emphasis on women's appearance not been so prominent in our culture.

INTERVENTION STRATEGIES

Given the enormity of the challenge in preventing eating disorders, the majority of theorizing and research has been in the area of intervention and treatment of eating disorders.

Individual

Individual interventions vary depending upon the theoretical approach used in conceptualization. Psychoanalytic, cognitive-behavioral, developmental, and feminist counselors may approach the treatment of eating disorders in different ways; however, there are some central unifying principles. Regardless of counseling orientation, a first consideration is the medical stability of the client. Consultation with a physician is essential during the assessment phase. The medical complications arising from anorexia, bulimia, and binge eating are dangerous, and the need to monitor the client's physical condition is imperative.

A medical evaluation of blood pressure, heart rate, and body temperature helps to determine the extent of the client's physical danger. Further laboratory tests—electrolyte levels, estrogen and cholesterol levels, liver and thyroid functioning, and cardiac functioning—are necessary to evaluate vulnerable physical conditions. Continued monitoring by a physician is appropriate when the medical condition of the client warrants close observation, but a medical evaluation should be a component of treatment with all eating disordered clients as a precaution.

A second consideration is the need for nutritional restabilization. Without adequate nutrition, counseling is less effective due to the cognitive and affective disturbances that result from starvation and/or bingeing. For bulimics as well as anorexics, the quality of the nutritional state is highly compromised as a result of the eating pathology (Story, 1986). For the anorexic, the nutritional goal is a restoration of body weight. For the bulimic, the goal is a restabilization of the nutritional process. For the binge eater, the goal is regulation of the caloric intake. Consultation with a nutritionist skilled at nutritional restoration among an eating disordered population is a useful adjunct to treatment.

A third consideration is type of intervention. Intervention strategies for individuals include individual counseling, family counseling, group counseling, pharmacological treatment, inpatient treatment, and bibliotherapy.

Once a therapeutic relationship is built through support and trust, individual counseling will proceed based on the counselor's therapeutic orientation. Cognitive-behavioral treatment protocols and interpersonal therapy have been the most frequently identified effective treatments of eating disorders (Garner, Vitousek, & Pike, 1997; Marcus, 1997; Wilson, Fairburn, & Agras, 1997). Unfortunately, some therapeutic approaches are less amenable to research and have not been experimentally tested. An eclectic approach may be most suited to the multidimensional nature of eating disorders. Treatment should address the behavioral, cognitive, affective, and interpersonal disturbances as they apply to each client. Initial steps in counseling may include helping the client manage affect in more appropriate ways. Learning alternate means of expressing emotions and self-soothing can interrupt the dysfunctional behavioral patterns. By increasing the client's awareness of the distinction between physiological and emotional states, the client becomes more adept at managing denied feelings. Expressing affect, becoming more self-directed and autonomous, and tolerating ambiguity are reasonable goals for counseling. Cognitive interventions are intended to challenge the distorted thought processes that have served to maintain and support the disordered eating. Challenging the irrational beliefs inherent in eating disorder pathology can address issues of body image and self-esteem. Progress in these areas may lead to the exploration of interpersonal and intrapersonal conflicts that plague eating disordered clients. A necessary treatment goal is "helping individuals develop a more internalized sense of self-worth independent of the eating disorder" (Pike & Wilfley, 1996, p. 381).

When feasible, family counseling can be a powerful component of treatment for the adolescent or young adult eating disordered client with anorexia or bulimia (Pelch, 1999; Sargent et al., 1985; Schwartz et al., 1985). In addition to addressing the distress created in the family by the eating disorder, family counseling can intervene in any dysfunctional interpersonal relationships. Common issues in these families are enmeshment, overprotection, hostility, and rigidity (Kog & Vandereycken, 1985). The goals of family counseling might include expression of feelings, resolution of conflict, and fostering autonomy. Families should be discouraged from monitoring the client's weight or food intake, however. Further, families tend to be less involved if the client is an independent adult (Pike & Wilfley, 1996).

Family therapy has not been frequently described in the treatment of binge eating disorder, perhaps because binge eating disorder is more frequently treated in adulthood. It is more likely that family counseling will address issues in the client's current relationships, such as marital or parenting issues, in addition to attempting to resolve those in the family of origin (Pike & Wilfley, 1996).

Group counseling has also been used successfully with eating disordered clients, although it has been less frequently recommended for anorexics (Lee & Rush, 1986; Polivy & Federoff, 1997). The use of group counseling in conjunction with individual counseling or for individuals at a more advanced stage of recovery allows clients to reduce the isolation and shame of their disorders. Groups can be effective venues for developing interpersonal skills and challenging dysfunctional thoughts and behaviors. Anorexic clients should be carefully screened for level of rigidity and weight competitiveness prior to admission in a counseling group (Hall, 1985).

Pharmacological treatment, especially for bulimia, has gained favor in recent years (Garfinkel & Walsh, 1997; Mitchell, 1988). The use of antidepressant medication may have some merit in treating the related depression and in reducing the compulsion to binge. A review of the literature has suggested that antidepressant medication is the most effective when combined with cognitive-behavioral counseling for bulimia (Garfinkel & Walsh, 1997). In the treatment of anorexia, the issue is more complicated. Although medications may assist the client with co-occurring depression and obsessional thinking, many of these symptoms remit without medication once weight stabilization has occurred. Antidepressant medication may also be helpful in the treatment of binge eating disorder, in treating co-occurring depression, and in helping to break the cycle between negative mood and bingeing (Marcus, 1997). Although controversial, treatments employing a pharmacological component may be a reflection of the current trend toward a biological-based etiology.

Inpatient treatment is warranted in severe cases. Especially for anorexic clients who have lost 25% of their expected body weight, inpatient treatment is considered necessary. Some bulimic clients, especially those who refuse or are unable to sustain any meals or who have severe depression associated with their disorder are recommended for inpatient treatment. Inpatient treatment is less often discussed for binge eating disorder, but should follow a protocol similar to that for bulimia. Individuals with eating disorders may also be referred for inpatient treatment if they have not responded to outpatient treatment. Clients may be admitted by the family if they are under legal age, but it is most therapeutically useful if the client voluntarily agrees to inpatient care. A program specifically designed for eating disorder treatment is more effective than a general psychiatric inpatient center.

The structured environment of an inpatient setting often helps to reduce the anxiety of the eating disordered client. The treatment protocol differs, however, depending on the disorder. The focus for anorexic clients is often weight restoration. For bulimic clients, the focus is on a normalization of the eating process. Both of these strategies are used in combination with individual, group, and family therapy during the inpatient stay. Inpatient programs vary in length depending on the individual needs of the client and can range from 1 week to several months. Close follow-up and extensive outpatient treatment are necessary for these clients due to the high rate of relapse.

Bibliotherapy or self-help books are becoming increasingly common and have carved a niche in this field. This medium can provide a useful adjunct to counseling or may be an introduction to the treatment process. Many individuals strive to avoid the stigma of psychological disorders and are reluctant to present for treatment. The shame that arises from eating disorders makes this population particularly likely candidates for self-help literature. Books are available on a variety of topics, including anorexia, bulimia, binge eating, self-esteem, and body image. Many of these books contain testimonials that sufferers find helpful in alleviating their sense of isolation and fears that they are alone in their distress. Many communities also offer self-help groups. A self-help approach may be less appropriate for more severe cases, however (Fairburn & Carter, 1997).

Prognosis of eating disorders has been related to type of disorder and body weight. Bulimia has a more positive prognosis than anorexia, and anorexic clients with lower body weights have the poorest prognosis (Herzog et al., 1993). Clinical observation as well indicates that anorexia is the more untractable disorder and requires longer term counseling. Research on binge eating disorder treatment has indicated that the relapse rate is high, but that approximately one third of those in short-term treatment remain abstinent at follow-up (Agras, 1996).

Family

Family therapy is considered by some to be among the most effective treatments for eating disorders, especially with adolescents, and at the very least, it should be considered as an adjunct to other treatment modalities (Pelch, 1999; Schwartz et al., 1985). The families of anorexic clients have been described as overcontrolling and rigid (Sargent, Liebman, & Silver, 1985), and the families of bulimic clients have been described as conflicted and chaotic (Schwartz et al., 1985). Despite these differences, some universal principles in family counseling for eating disordered clients have been prescribed.

Common issues to be addressed in family counseling often include strengthening boundaries between parents and children, dealing with family and parental conflict in more healthy ways, and openly dealing with other disorders such as depression or alcoholism of another family member (Schwartz et al., 1985). Reducing the family's focus on food, weight, and appearance is often an immediate goal of the process. The family members need to learn healthy expression of emotions in order to move beyond the past issues (Pelch, 1999). Teaching the family to allow appropriate development of adolescents (which includes allowing less reliance on the parents) is also necessary. Particularly for younger clients, family counseling is considered an important piece of the treatment process.

School

Although few school counselors are trained in the treatment of eating disorders, it may be the school personnel who first identify disturbed eating patterns. School personnel should be aware of the eating disorder symptomology and be prepared to encourage youths suspected of such disturbances to seek counseling. Resources and referrals that are available to the students seeking treatment should be current.

Some school settings offer support groups for eating disorders, and this is reasonable if the counselor is skilled in group counseling with eating disordered clients and treatment consent can be obtained from parents. An assessment of the extent of the student's disorder is prudent prior to beginning any type of intervention at the school level.

Athletic coaches should be especially vigilant in identifying disturbed eating patterns. Thompson (1998) has warned that given the central role that coaches play in the lives of athletes, coaches must avoid encouraging, even tacitly, unhealthy eating practices. Thompson admonished those coaches who are aware of and allow dangerous weight-cutting practices by competitive wrestlers. This emphasis was provided by the deaths of three competitive wrestlers as a direct result of the common practice of trying to "make weight," which entails efforts to drop weight rapidly in order to compete in a lighter weight class.

Community

Community interventions are as yet minimal. Perhaps due to the perceived rarity of these disorders, wide-scale community interventions are not practiced. Another possibility for the lack of community-level intervention is the inherent challenge of the societal standard of beauty and appearance should such interventions be proposed. Changes at the community level require a concerted effort toward abolishing the value placed on thinness. Currently, the fervor does not appear to exist to orchestrate such a rebellion.

ADAPTATIONS FOR DIVERSITY

Ethnicity

The cultural norms of the United States have historically been dominated by the values of the White middle class. Although the stereotypical picture of the eating disordered client is a young White American adolescent female, the recent increase of anorexia and bulimia among non-White women must be explored (Root, 1990). In addition, binge eating disorder and obesity have been commonly identified among people of color (Klesges et al., 1996). An important consideration, given the impact of the media on eating disorders, is that few non-White women are featured in the media, and those that do appear tend to have physical characteristics that are similar to the White standard of beauty (Osvold & Sodowsky, 1993). It is as yet unclear what impact these images have on women of color.

A further consideration is that because eating disorders have been related to socioeconomic status, the increasing status of non-White populations in the United States may serve to increase their vulnerability to eating disorders (Anderson & Hay, 1985). Additionally, Hsu (1987) has noted that as African Americans become more upwardly mobile they may be more likely to adopt traditional While middle-class values and the related disorders as well. As African Americans more commonly live biculturally, an internalized devaluing of their own race can occur. This can result in greater acceptance of White standards, especially given the lack of African American role models. The typical help-seeking patterns and underutilization of mental health services by people of color may, however, continue to obscure the prevalence of the disorders among these groups (Root, 1990; Striegel-Moore & Smolak, 1996). Although Dolan

(1991) warned against using broad statements about racial groups, the discussions of cultural considerations that follow attempt to highlight the similarities and differences among cultures with respect to eating disorders.

African American Women. Historically, African American women have not been at risk for developing anorexia or bulimia due to several protective factors. They have typically not identified with the standards of the White culture (including the standards for thinness), and they have displayed greater acceptance of their body sizes, despite being heavier than their White peers (Altabe, 1998; Gray, Ford, & Kelly, 1987). Even among the high-risk group of ballet dancers, black females have reported lower rates of disturbed eating (Hamilton, Books-Gunn, & Warren, 1985). Most eating disorders develop during adolescence, and among African American women this period has been brief by White standards. Eating disorders among this population tend to develop at a later age (Anderson & Hay, 1985). The socialization of many African American women also may differ from that of women in the White culture. African American women are expected to be independent and successful, in contrast to the White values for women to be attractive and feminine (Osvold & Sodowsky, 1993). African American women may be raised with a more pragmatic attitude with an emphasis on self- and community pride rather than on appearance.

A survey of 507 male and female undergraduate students at a Black university revealed that 3% of the sample fit the *DSM-IV* criteria for bulimia. When compared to a similar White sample, however, the African American students reported less emphasis on food and weight (Gray et al., 1987). A more recent study of 123 African American college women found rates of bulimia symptoms comparable to those found in similar White samples (Lester & Petrie (1998). Among this sample, identification with White culture was not related to bulimic symptomology. Having internalized societal standards of attractiveness was, however, found to be predictive of bulimic symptoms, suggesting a less direct path of influence.

Silber (1986) has suggested that the rarely seen case of anorexia among African Americans and Hispanics may be due more to misdiagnosis than from scarcity of the disorder. Although it has been concluded that the symptoms present themselves similarly in Caucasian and African American women (Anderson & Hay, 1985), Osvold and Sodowsky (1993) highlighted the importance of culture in the etiology of anorexia nervosa.

One study compared eating and psychological pathology between White and minority women and found that there were no differences in eating disorder symptomology between the two groups (le Grange, Telch, & Agras, 1997). Unfortunately, little can be gleaned from these findings given the considerable within-group differences among the minority group (Striegel-Moore & Smolak, 1996). Findings from one ethnic sample can not necessarily be generalized to another, and non-Whites can not be adequately investigated as if they were a single group.

A recent literature review revealed that African American adolescent girls typically identify a larger size as more ideal than their Caucasian peers and are more likely to perceive that friends and family want them to be larger. African American adult women report some weight consciousness, but little social pressure to be thin and a more positive body image than White women (Crago, Shisslak, & Estes, 1996; Klesges et al., 1996).

African American women are more likely to have binge eating disorder and the resulting consequence of obesity (Klesges et al., 1996). In a study of 351 White, Hispanic, and Black women (Fitzgibbon et al., 1998), depression was found to be predictive of binge eating among Whites, and depression and higher weight predictive among Hispanic women. Depression, higher weight, and body image were not found to predict binge eating in Black women, indicating that other variables need to be investigated.

Counselors and researchers are urged to be conscious of the later aged occurrence of anorexia and bulimia among African American women. Additionally, as acculturation to the dominant White culture increases, a higher incidence of eating disorder symptoms among African American women is likely.

A greater understanding of the factors believed to be protective against anorexia and bulimia might lend needed information to the prevention efforts for all groups. If messages sent to children in the Black community help these children guard against unrealistic appearance goals, these messages should be incorporated into the rearing of all children. These may be messages that place African American women at greater risk for binge eating disorder, however.

Hispanic Women. Studies of eating disorders among Latina women are quite limited. One study compared the treatment outcomes of 10 Hispanic women (6 Mexican Americans, 2 Colombians, and 2 Mexicans) and 20 White women with diagnoses of anorexia nervosa in San Diego (Heibert, Felice, Wingard, Munoz, & Ferguson, 1988). No differences between the two groups were reported with regard to clinical characteristics or treatment outcome. Another study (Smith & Krejci, 1991) with a large male and female high school sample (327 Hispanics, 129 Native Americans, and 89 Whites) found considerable eating pathology among the Hispanic group. On most measures of disturbed eating (fasting, induced vomiting, bingeing) the Hispanic group scored comparably to the White group, but not as high as the Native American group. A recent review of the literature has echoed this conclusion (Crago et al., 1996).

Risk factors among minority populations have also begun to be investigated. One comparison of body dissatisfaction among White, Hispanic, and Asian American sixth- and seventh-grade girls (mean age 12.4 years) found that the Hispanic girls had the highest level of body dissatisfaction, followed by Asian American and White girls respectively (Robinson et al., 1996). If body dissatisfaction is indeed a precursor to eating disorder pathology, this finding suggested that these two groups are at greater risk than has previously been assumed. This was found to be the case in an investigation of 120 Mexican American, lower socioeconomic status, adolescent women (Joiner & Kashubeck, 1996). Among this sample, body dissatisfaction was significantly related to anorexic and bulimic symptomology. Reported eating disorder symptoms were not, however, related to acculturation level among this sample.

The prevalence of eating pathology among Latina women has likely been underestimated. It appears that Hispanic girls and women are engaging in disturbed eating behaviors at a rate that is similar to that among Whites. This disturbing trend suggests that the interaction between ethnicity, social environment, self-perception, and level of acculturation remains a rich direction for future clinical investigation.

Native American Women. Few data are available on the prevalence of eating disorders among Native American women, who are the least researched ethnic group in the eating disorders literature. One study found that among 85 Chippewa girls and women living on a reservation in Michigan, 74% reported dieting in order to lose weight, and of those, the majority had purged, used diet pills, and fasted (Rosen et al., 1988). Although generalizations cannot be made from this sample, the prevalence of eating disorders among Native American women may have been previously underestimated.

A similar conclusion has been drawn by Smith & Krejci (1991). In a comparison of disturbed eating patterns among Native American, Hispanic, and White high school students, the Native American group scored higher than the comparison groups on all measures of disturbed eating. The Native American group were heavier than the comparison group, and students who were heavier reported more body dissatisfaction, greater fear of weight gain, more frequent extreme dieting, and more frequent vomiting as a weight control technique. Crago et al. (1996) have concluded that Native Americans have more eating disturbances than any other ethnic group or their White counterparts. The few studies to include Native Americans have had small samples, however, which limits generalizability. Further exploration is needed before any reasonable conclusions can be drawn about eating disorders among Native Americans.

Asian American Women. Although anorexia is well known in Japan (including a specially named binge episode related to anorexia), studies of eating disorders among Asian American women have rarely been reported in the literature. Studies of other Asian populations are also rare. High rates of body image distortions and body dissatisfaction has been observed among school children and adolescents in Japan (Ohtahara, Ohzeki, Hanaki, Motozumi, & Shiraki, 1993). Individual case studies have also been reported involving two women of Chinese descent who were raised in England (Schmidt, 1993). The bicultural existence and family histories of obesity are cited as onset and maintenance factors.

A recent investigation of White, Hispanic, and Asian sixth- and seventh-grade schoolgirls identified rates of body dissatisfaction among the Asian group that were higher than those of the White group, but not as high as those of the Hispanic group (Robinson et al., 1996). The investigators contended that body dissatisfaction may be more common among the Asian population than has been recognized. Similar results were obtained by Sanders & Heiss (1998), who found that female Asian immigrant college students reported similar eating attitudes and body dissatisfaction but a greater fear of fat than their Caucasian counterparts. It is not clear whether this translates to a higher prevalence of eating disorders as well because others have found less body image dissatisfaction among Asian American men and women than among Whites or Hispanics in a sample of 315 college students (Altabe, 1998). Contradictory evidence may be related to sampling differences. It can not be assumed that acculturated Asian Americans are similar to recent Asian immigrants with respect to eating disorder behaviors, and this distinction tends to be overlooked. Asian American populations have been among the least-researched ethnic group in the United States. Without adequate data, speculation about the prevalence or course of eating disorders within this population is unwise.

International Women. The literature has begun to accumulate evidence suggesting that the risk for eating disorders among international women increases with the level of acculturation of White standards. Assuming a continuum of eating disorder symptomology, Hooper and Garner (1986) compared Black, White, and mixed-race schoolgirls in Zimbabwe on eating disorder symptomology. The White group showed the greatest symptomology, the Black group showed the lowest, and the mixed-race group had scores that fell between the comparison groups. The researchers concluded that the acculturation and adoption of Western ideals influence the development of eating disorders.

Even Caucasians from different cultures have been susceptible to the influences of American White, middle-class standards. Van den Broucke and Vandereycken (1986) studied 14 European exchange students in the

United States who had been diagnosed with an eating disorder during their year-long stay. Although most evidenced at least minor eating disorder symptomology prior to departing from home, the challenges of adolescence combined with the culture shock, separation from family, and the stress of academic and social adjustment served to exacerbate the disorders.

It has been suggested that eating disorders may present similarly in countries outside the United States, but that cultural issues may also affect the presentation. A cross-cultural study of 132 American and Austrian college females found that the American group had higher rates of depression and alcohol and drug abuse (Mangweth, Pope, Hudson, & Biebl, 1996). This was true for both the bulimic group and the control group. This finding suggests that the depression and substance abuse associated with bulimia in the United States may be more a function of the culture than the eating disorder.

Non-Western cultures do not seem to manifest eating disorders with the diagnostic criteria used in Western cultures. India, for example, tends to exhibit milder forms of eating disturbances and identifies a minor disorder known as eating distress syndrome (Srinivasan, Suresh, & Jayaram, 1998). It has been noted that greater eating disturbances are seen in the young female college students in India, indicating that as Western norms infiltrate the culture, greater severity of eating problems may be anticipated.

Some recent research with ethnically diverse samples has provided inconsistent evidence. For example, a large survey of female subscribers (9,971 women) to *Consumer Reports* found that there were no differences between the White, African American, Hispanic, Native American, and Asian American women with respect to reported binge eating behavior (le Grange, Stone, & Brownell, 1998). Black women were found to purge more than the other groups, and Asian American women more frequently endorsed exercise as weight control. This sample was identified as being above the median income level of the United States, which was likely to skew the results but may suggest that socioeconomic status level remains an important variable.

Another study of 36,320 7th- to 12th-grade boys and girls found results inconsistent with other literature (Story, French, Resnick, & Blum, 1995). For both boys and girls, higher socioeconomic status was related to greater weight satisfaction and fewer unhealthy weight control practices. Self-report indicated that compared to White females, African American girls vomited more often, Hispanic girls used diuretics more frequently, and Asian American girls reported more binge eating. Among this sample, Black and Native American girls had greater body satisfaction.

Another study with a large ethnically diverse sample (17,159 White, Black, Asian American, Native American, and Hispanic adolescent females) found that among all ethnic groups body dissatisfaction and perceptions of being overweight were correlated with restricting, purging, and binge eating (French et al., 1997). The researchers concluded that, overall, the non-White groups have lower prevalence of dieting and weight concerns, but that the "ethnic subculture does not appear to protect against the broader sociocultural factors that foster body dissatisfaction among adolescent females" (p. 315). It may be, as these authors have suggested, that the discrepancies between studies are due to the within-group cultural differences of the ethnic groups. Such inconsistencies make it difficult to draw conclusions about eating disorders within non-White groups. Pumariega (1997) has warned that the protective factors of the native culture of people of color are eroding as adolescents, hungry for acceptance by the mainstream culture, abandon native values. He has recommended continued investigations to address the cultural values, beliefs, and level of acculturation.

Recommendations for counseling women of color and of nondominant cultures include an awareness of the cultural aspect of the disorders. It may be necessary to assess the extent of identification a woman has with her own ethnic culture and that of the dominant White society in addition to the eating disorder diagnostic criteria (Osvold & Sodowsky, 1993), criteria that Root (1990) has reminded us were developed from observations of White clients. It should be noted that others have found level of acculturation to be unrelated to eating disorder symptomology (Joiner & Kashubeck, 1996). The relationship between body dissatisfaction, eating disorder symptomology, and cultural background requires further research. Greater attention to the effects of racism is also warranted (Crago et al., 1996). Feelings of low self-esteem, social isolation, and attempting to be accepted by the dominant culture may make one vulnerable to developing eating disorder symptoms. In the meantime, mental health professionals should be cognizant of the socially sanctioned stereotypes of women of color and avoid such stereotypes from influencing the assessment process (Root, 1990).

Prevention efforts among ethnically diverse groups should address the previous lack of prevention involvement in communities of color. Outreach programs can be established with these communities only after allowing for time to build relationships with key leaders and showing genuine interest in the group (Root, 1990). Outreach and prevention programs need to take into account the norms of the community with regard to help-seeking patterns, beliefs about causation and healing, and meaning of the disorder. This strategy might allow for greater inclusion of people of color into research protocols and prevention/treatment programs.

(For recommendations regarding inclusion of people of color in empirical studies, see Root, 1990.)

Gender

Females have been the most affected by eating disorders, but the prevalence among males may be underestimated (Lachenmeyer & Muni-Brander, 1988). Steiger & Houle (1991) have suggested that similar factors that make women vulnerable operate to make men vulnerable as well. One risk factor is that of athletic involvement, especially in sports that have a weight or physical appearance orientation, such as wrestling or body building (Anderson, 1999; Franco et al., 1988). A second risk factor for men is a history of obesity (Anderson, 1999; Franco et al., 1988). Males with bulimia were found to have relatively higher current weights and histories of higher past adolescent and prepubescent weights. A third risk factor for men is homosexuality. It appears that the heterosexual male population is more protected from standards emphasizing physical appearance, but that gay men feel more pressure to be thin or attractive (Anderson, 1999; Schneider & Agras, 1987).

Although men tend to score lower on the Eating Disorders Inventory (EDI) drive-for-thinness scale and report less body dissatisfaction (Grogan, Williams, & Conner, 1996; Schneider & Agras, 1987), a correlate of the drive for thinness among women may be the drive for fitness among men (Ussery & Prentice-Dunn, 1992).

The strongest predictors of bulimia among men were found by Ussery and Prentice-Dunn (1992) to be similar to the predictors of bulimia among women, that is, the restrained eating, lack of interoceptive awareness, and lack of confidence in identifying one's emotions that lead to underdeveloped coping skills. However, in a comparison of men and women with comparable bulimic histories, Schneider and Agras (1987) found some gender differences. Men with bulimia were noted to differ from women with bulimia in that they are less likely to identify the intake of large amounts of food as a binge, less likely to report laxative, diuretic, or diet pill use, and less likely to exercise excessively. Men also report greater success with diet plans than do women. Further, women tend to binge in private, but male binges tend to occur during mealtime with larger quantities of food, and men are less likely to report feeling guilty about eating in public. Among the eating disorders, men are most likely to develop binge eating disorder (American Psychiatric Association, 1994).

An exception to the previous discussions of ethnicity is the report of an investigation of bulimia among African American college students, in which Black males were more likely than their Caucasian counterparts to report significantly more frequent bingeing, dieting, and fasting (Gray et al., 1987).

It has been suggested that men and women are differentially affected by the cultural pressure for weight and body shape. Social cues that determine appropriate or desired weight hold women to a more stringent standard (Schneider & Agras, 1987). Recent evidence has suggested that men may be also influenced by media images (Grogan et al., 1996). Both men and women in this study experienced a drop in body esteem after viewing same-gender models' photographs. A similar investigation, however, found that only women were negatively affected by viewing slim, physically fit, same-gender models in the media (Kalodner, 1997).

In addition, males with bulimia may go undiagnosed. Men may experience greater embarrassment at acknowledging symptoms that have been characterized as a disorder of adolescent females (Schneider & Agras, 1987). Although eating disorders occur more rarely in men, and even more rarely in men of color, the disorders do exist in these populations (Anderson, 1999; Gray et al., 1987; Lawlor, Burket, & Hodgin, 1987), and risk factors alone may not alert the clinician. For example, eating disorders have been present in male clients who come from lower socioeconomic groups and do not fit the typical clinical picture. Clinicians should be cautious of dismissing this diagnosis among atypical populations.

Affectional Orientation

Homosexuality has been reported to be a risk factor for developing eating disorders among men, but not women. Most samples of eating disordered females report very small percentages of identified lesbians (Herzog, Newman, Yeh, & Warshaw, 1992). For women, homosexuality may offer protection from a vulnerability to eating disorder symptomology. Several factors have been cited as potential explanations for this phenomenon. Unlike heterosexual women, lesbian women are reported to be more satisfied with their bodies (Bergeron & Senn, 1998; Herzog et al., 1992).

In a study of 64 heterosexual and 45 homosexual unmarried women, Herzog et al. (1992) found that significantly more heterosexual women wanted to lose weight, despite the fact that the lesbian women among the sample were heavier than the heterosexual women. Although both groups chose ideal weights below the appropriate life weight tables (Metropolitan Life Insurance, 1983), lesbian women were more likely to choose higher weights, closer to the norm. The heterosexual women were more likely to diet and were more susceptible to the image society portrays as the female ideal. Similar conclusions were drawn by Bergeron & Senn (1998), who found that heterosexual women reported more negative attitudes toward their bodies than did lesbian women, even though there were no significant differences in their weights. Heterosexual women in this predominantly White sample also identified an ideal weight that was lower than that chosen by the lesbian women. It may be, as Brown (1987) has noted, that feminist ideology rejects the cultural standards of beauty as well as reduces the guilt associated with eating that is found in the majority of traditional female culture.

Herzog et al. (1992) have concluded that the dissatisfaction with one's body that increases the risk of eating disorders among the heterosexual female population is less prominent among the lesbian population and may explain the lower incidence of eating disorders among lesbian women. Others have contended that young lesbians may also value society's ideal of thinness, but that sexual relationships with women promote greater acceptance of the female form (Beren, Hayden, Wilfley, & Striegel-Moore, 1997). Interviews with 26 lesbian college students yielded evidence of considerable internal conflict between feminist values and the social pressure toward female thinness. Caution is warranted, however, in discarding the potential eating disorder diagnosis among lesbians. The incidence of anorexia and bulimia among lesbian women is low, but not absent; and the prevalence of binge eating disorder has been virtually ignored in the literature.

Gay men have been reported to have eating disorder symptomology (primarily anorexia and bulimia) at higher rates than are found among heterosexual men (Anderson, 1999; Yager, Kurtzman, Landsverk, & Wiesmeier, 1988). Compared to heterosexual men, gay men have been more likely to be underweight, to chose an ideal weight that is lower, and to believe that a thinner body type is more attractive to potential partners (Herzog, Newman, & Warshaw, 1991). These researchers also reported that heterosexual men were less likely to be influenced by their perceptions of women's preferences for male physique, and that their desired weight was less than these men believed women preferred.

When 48 nonclinical homosexual men were compared to 300 nonclinical heterosexual men, the gay male sample was reported to present past problems with binge eating, use of diuretics, feeling fat despite others' perceptions of them, and feeling terrified of becoming fat. Additionally, gay men scored higher than their heterosexual peers on the EDI scales of drive for thinness, interoceptive awareness, bulimia, body dissatisfaction, ineffectiveness, and maturity fears, and the total overall score.

There has been speculation that findings of higher than expected rates of disordered eating among the gay male population may be related to a tendency toward the effeminate for at least some gay men (Yager et al., 1988). A more reasonable explanation might be that some gay men feel the same pressure that heterosexual women feel to be attractive to other males and might be more conscious of the competition for partners. This explanation is further supported by the long tradition among men in general to seek attractive partners. Herzog et al. (1991) have noted that gay males may fear weight gain more that heterosexual males because weight gain would surpass their ideal body weight and the weight they believe would be most attractive to a male partner.

The rise of AIDS among the gay male population may ameliorate the emphasis on thinness within this group. Some authors have noted that the physical deterioration associated with AIDS has fostered a slang for the disease (slims) in some countries (Mickalide, 1990). This association may help to diminish the thin ideal.

Investigations of eating pathology among the gay and lesbian culture is in preliminary stages, and explanations of the increased prevalence in the gay male population can only be speculative. In addition, binge eating disorder has not been adequately studied among gay and lesbian groups.

Athletes

Despite anecdotal data, evidence has suggested that athletes are not, as a group, at greater risk for developing eating disorders, particularly anorexia and bulimia. Certain sport groups do, however, increase the vulnerability for developing eating disorder symptoms (Stoutjesdyk & Jevne, 1993). Among a sample of 191 Canadian athletes, eating disorder prevalence was not higher for females than is found in the general and college populations. The prevalence of disturbed eating patterns for men was, however, higher than has been reported in college and general populations. For women, the risk factors included being involved in a sport that emphasized leanness or physical appearance (such as diving or gymnastics) or that had weight restrictions (such as judo or lightweight rowing). For both men and women, eating disorder symptomology was related to the level of competition. Only those athletes who regularly competed on the national or international level showed elevated scores on a measure of disturbed eating behaviors and attitudes. A conclusion was that the combination of high-level competition and weight or aesthetic considerations within the sport makes for a vulnerability to disturbed eating.

Similarly, Depalma et al. (1993) studied 131 lightweight college football players and found that 9.9% fit the criteria for an eating disorder and that 42% evidenced disturbed eating patterns. Wrestlers and body builders are also at high risk for eating disorder pathology. Steen and Brownell (1990) found that 30% to 40% of high school and college wrestlers reported pathological eating, including food restriction, fasting, vomiting, using laxatives and diuretics, and bingeing after matches. Preoccupation with weight and food was common among this sample of 431 male wrestlers. Goldfield, Harper, and Blouin (1998) reviewed the literature on eating disturbances in body builders and concluded that severe dieting, preoccupation with weight and shape, body image distortions, and diagnosable eating disorders are relatively common among serious recreational and competitive body builders. The eating disturbances combined with lower body fat than is considered healthy make this a particularly high-risk sport.

Among the female athletic community, two risk factors have been identified (Powers & Johnson, 1996). *Appearance thinness* refers to the belief that judges reward thinner competitors in sports like gymnastics and figure skating. *Performance thinness* refers to the belief that lower body fat enhances performance, particularly in sports like track and swimming where endurance is required. Despite the lack of convincing evidence, this belief is so strongly held among coaches, trainers, and athletes that it has become an assumption of the culture of competition.

Dancers have long been considered to be at high risk for the development of eating disorders; however, this generalization has been challenged. Hamilton, Brooks-Gunn, Warren, and Hamilton (1988) have contended that those ballet dancers who are most successful show rates of eating disorder pathology similar to those found in the general population. Dancers struggling to gain recognition in a major dance company, however, are more likely to report eating pathology. This pattern is reported to hold true for dancers in both American and Chinese ballet companies.

Johnson et al. (1989) have noted a steady increase in the use of exercise as a purging strategy, especially in recent years as the standard of thinness for women is being replaced with the standard of physical fitness or strength. Given this trend, they warned those involved in the supervision of athletics, such as athletic trainers, to be observant of suspicious behavior. Trainers may be the initial contact for someone struggling with an eating disorder, and they need to be informed and capable of providing a safe environment for the potential disclosure of psychological problems.

Proposed prevention efforts are aimed at educating athletes and sports management personnel (coaches and trainers) in the dangers of disturbed eating (Grandjean, 1991; Thompson & Sherman, 1993). The female athlete triad (disturbed eating, amenorrhea, and osteoporosis) carries considerable health risks, has become more common, and is now attracting the attention of eating disorder prevention experts in athletics. Recent efforts of the USA Gymnastics governing board have included increasing the age limit to 16 for gymnastics in the 2000 Olympics and providing sport psychology and nutrition consultants for the national teams. The National Collegiate Athletic Association (NCAA) has also undertaken a research and prevention program for eating disorders within college athletics (Powers & Johnson, 1996). In addition to increasing the awareness of eating disorder warning signs, it is recommended that weight be de-emphasized and that group weigh-ins be eliminated. In sports where weight is a determinant for competition, such as wrestling, unhealthy weight management strategies should not be condoned, even passively (Thompson, 1998).

SUMMARY

A clear conclusion is that eating disorders reflect an interaction of social, interpersonal, intrapersonal, and physical variables. The societal ideal for people, especially women, to be thin and attractive promotes greater pressure for women with regard to appearance and places them at greater risk for developing anorexia and bulimia. It is during adolescence or young adulthood that these disorders manifest, usually as a means of coping with problems or life transitions. Other risk factors include higher socioeconomic status, participation in some types of athletics, disturbed family dynamics, and low self-esteem. Binge eating disorder is a more recently acknowledged syndrome that threatens to afflict more individuals and often results in obesity and its associated health and social risks. Although a small proportion of the population may develop a clinical eating disorder, great numbers of individuals suffer with subclinical symptoms of disturbed eating and dieting patterns.

Treatment may include individual, group, and/or family counseling. A medical evaluation and nutritional counseling are also recommended. In severe cases, inpatient or pharmacological treatment may be warranted. Treating the eating disordered client requires patience and an understanding of the psychological depth of the disorder. Recovery from an eating disorder is often a slow process, and the relapse rate is high.

Prevention efforts at the individual, family, school, and community levels should be considered by those involved with adolescents or young adults, especially those youths in high-risk groups. Special attention should be paid to atypical groups such as people of color and men. These groups are least likely to be identified as at risk for an eating disorder and may be neglected in treatment and research of eating disorders.

The power of society and the media should not be overlooked. It is the responsibility of each individual to challenge the damaging and demeaning messages of our culture. It is equally important to teach our youth to challenge those same messages, whether the messages stem from the media, their peers, their families, or their own internalized belief systems.

REFERENCES

Agras, W. S. (1996). Short-term psychological treatments for binge eating. In C. G. Fairburn & G. T. Wilson (Eds.), *Binge eating* (pp. 270-286). New York: Guilford Press.

Altabe, M. (1998). Ethnicity and body image: Quantitative and qualitative analysis. *International Journal of Eating Disorders, 23,* 153–159.

Anderson, A. E. (1999). Eating disorders in males: Critical questions. In R. Lemberg (Ed.), *Eating disorders: A reference sourcebook* (pp. 73–78), Phoenix, AZ: Oryx Press.

Anderson, A. E., & DiDomenico, L. (1992). Diet vs. shape content of popular male and female magazines: A dose-response relationship to the incidence of eating disorders? *International Journal of Eating Disorders, 11,* 283–287.

Anderson, A. E., & Hay, A. (1985). Racial and socioeconomic influences in anorexia nervosa and bulimia. *International Journal of Eating Disorders, 4,* 479–487.

American Psychiatric Association. (1994). *Diagnostic and statistical manual of the mental disorders* (4th. ed.). Washington, DC: Author.

Armstrong, J. G., & Roth, D. M. (1989). Attachment and separation difficulties in eating disorders: A preliminary investigation. *International Journal of Eating Disorders, 8*, 141–155.

Beattie, H. J. (1988). Eating disorders and the mother-daughter relationship. *International Journal of Eating Disorders, 7*, 453–460.

Berel, S., & Irving, L. M. (1998). Media and disturbed eating: An analysis of media influence and implications for prevention. *Journal of Primary Prevention, 18*, 415–430.

Beren, S. E., Hayden, H. A., Wilfley, D. E., & Striegel-Moore, R. H. (1997). Body dissatisfaction among lesbian college students. *Psychology of Women Quarterly, 21*, 431–445.

Bergeron, S. M., & Senn, C. Y. (1998). Body image and sociocultural norms. *Psychology of Women Quarterly, 22*, 385–401.

Betz, N. E., & Fitzgerald, L. F. (1993). Individuality and diversity: Theory and research in counseling psychology. *Annual Review of Psychology, 44*, 343–381.

Brown, L. (1987). Lesbians, weight, and eating: New analyses and perspectives. In Boston Lesbian Psychologies Collective (Eds.), *Lesbian psychologies* (pp. 294–310). Chicago: University of Illinois Press.

Bruce, B., & Agras, W. S. (1992). Binge eating in females: A population-based investigation. *International Journal of Eating Disorders, 12*, 365–374.

Bruch, H. (1973). *Eating disorders*. New York: Basic Books.

Carter, J. C., Stewart, A., Dunn, V. J., & Fairburn, C. G. (1997). Primary prevention of eating disorders: Might it do more harm than good? *International Journal of Eating Disorders, 22*, 167–172.

Cohn, L., & Maine, M. (1998). More harm than good. *Eating Disorders, 6*, 93–95.

Connor-Greene, P. A. (1988). Gender differences in body weight perception and weight-loss strategies of college students. *Women and Health, 14*, 27–42.

Coric, C., & Murstein, B. I. (1993). Bulimia nervosa: Prevalence and psychological correlates in a college community. *Eating Disorders, 1*, 39–51.

Crago, M., Shisslak, C. M., & Estes, L. S. (1996). Eating disturbances among American minority groups: A review. *International Journal of Eating Disorders, 19*, 239–248.

Depalma, M. T., Koszewski, W. M., Case, J. G., Barile, R. J., Depalma, B. F., & Oliaro, S. M. (1993). Weight control practices of lightweight football players. *Medicine and Science in Sports and Exercise, 25*, 694–701.

Dolan, B. (1991). Cross-cultural aspects of anorexia nervosa and bulimia: A review. *International Journal of Eating Disorders, 10*, 67–78.

Fairburn, C. G., & Carter, J. C. (1997). Self-help and guided self-help for binge-eating problems. In D. M. Garner & P. E. Garfinkel (Eds.), *Handbook of treatment for eating disorders* (2nd ed., pp. 494–499). New York: Guilford Press.

Fitzgibbon, M. L., Spring, B., Avellone, M. E., Blackman, L. R., Pingitore, R., & Stolley, M. R. (1998). Correlates of binge eating in Hispanic, Black, and White women. *International Journal of Eating Disorders, 24*, 43–52.

Franco, K. S. N., Tamburrino, M. B., Carroll, B. T., & Bernal, G.A.A. (1988). Eating attitudes in college males. *International Journal of Eating Disorders, 7*, 285–288.

Franko, D. L. (1998). Secondary prevention of eating disorders in college women at risk. *Eating Disorders, 6*, 29–40.

French, S. A., Story, M., Neumark-Sztainer, D., Downes, B., Resnick, M., & Blum, R. (1997). Ethnic differences in psychosocial and health behavior correlates of dieting, purging, and binge eating in a population-based sample of adolescent females. *International Journal of Eating Disorders, 22*, 315–322.

Friedman, S. S. (1998). Girls in the 90s: A gender-based model for eating disorder prevention. *Patient Education and Counseling, 33*, 217–224.

Garfinkel, P. E., & Walsh, B. T. (1997). Drug therapies. In D. M. Garner & P. E. Garfinkel (Eds.), *Handbook of treatment for eating disorders* (2nd ed., pp. 372–380). New York: Guilford Press

Garner, D. M., Garfinkel, P. E., Schwartz, D., & Thompson, M. (1980). Cultural expectations of thinness in women. *Psychological Reports, 47*, 483–491.

Garner, D. M., Vitousek, K. M., & Pike, K. M. (1997). Cognitive-behavioral therapy for anorexia nervosa. In D. M. Garner & P. E. Garfinkel (Eds.), *Handbook of treatment for eating disorders* (2nd ed., pp. 94–144). New York: Guilford Press.

Goldfield, G. S., Harper, D. W., & Blouin, A. G. (1998). Are bodybuilders at risk for an eating disorder? *Eating Disorders, 6*, 133–157.

Graber, J. A., & Brooks-Gunn, J. (1996). Prevention of eating problems and disorders: Including parents. *Eating Disorders, 4*, 348–363.

Grandjean, A. C. (1991). Eating disorders: The role of the athletic trainer. *Athletic Training, 26*, 105–112.

Gray, J. J., & Ford, K. (1985). The incidence of bulimia in a college sample. *International Journal of Eating Disorders, 4*, 201–211.

Gray, J. J., Ford, K., & Kelly, L. M. (1987). The prevalence of bulimia in a Black college population. *International Journal of Eating Disorders, 6*, 733–740.

Grogan, S., Williams, Z., & Conner, M. (1996). The effects of viewing same-gender photographic models on body-esteem. *Psychology of Women Quarterly, 20*, 569–575.

Hall, A. (1985). Group psychotherapy for anorexia nervosa. In D. M. Garner & P. E. Garfinkel (Eds.), *Handbook of psychotherapy for anorexia nervosa and bulimia* (pp. 462–475). New York: Guilford Press.

Hamilton, L. H., Brooks-Gunn, J., & Warren, M. P. (1985). Sociocultural influences on eating disorders in professional ballet dancers. *International Journal of Eating Disorders, 4*, 465–477.

Hamilton, L. H., Brooks-Gunn, J., Warren, M. P., & Hamilton, W. G. (1988). The role of selectivity in the pathogenesis of eating disorders in ballet dancers. *Medicine and Science in Sports and Exercise, 20*, 560–565.

Heibert, K. A., Felice, M. A., Wingard, D. L., Munoz, R., & Ferguson, J. A. (1988). Comparison of outcome in Hispanic and Caucasian patients with anorexia nervosa. *International Journal of Eating Disorders, 7*, 693–696.

Herzog, D. G., Newman, K. L., & Warshaw, M. (1991). Body dissatisfaction in homosexual and heterosexual males. *Journal of Nervous and Mental Disease, 179*, 356–359.

Herzog, D. G., Newman, K. L., Yeh, C. J., & Warshaw, M. (1992). Body image satisfaction in homosexual and heterosexual women. *International Journal of Eating Disorders, 11*, 391–396.

Herzog, D. B., Sacks, N. R., Keller, M. B., Lavori, P. W., von Ranson, K. B., & Gray, H. M. (1993). Patterns and predictors of recovery in anorexia nervosa and bulimia nervosa. *Journal of the American Academy of Child and Adolescent Psychiatry, 32*, 835–842.

Hooper, M. S., & Garner, D. M. (1986). Application of the eating disorders inventory to a sample of Black, White, and mixed-race schoolgirls in Zimbabwe. *International Journal of Eating Disorders, 5*, 161–168.

Huon, G. F. (1996). Health promotion and the prevention of dieting-induced disorders. *Eating Disorders, 4*, 27–32.

Hsu, L. K. G. (1987). Are eating disorders becoming more common in Blacks? *International Journal of Eating Disorders, 6*, 113–125.

Jasper, K. (1993). Monitoring and responding to media messages. *Eating Disorders, 1*, 109–114.

Johnson, C. L., Tobin, D. L., & Steinberg, S. L. (1989). Etiological, developmental, and treatment considerations for bulimia. In L. C. Whitaker & W. N. Davis (Eds.), *The bulimic college student* (pp. 57–73). New York: Haworth Press.

Joiner, G. W., & Kashubeck, S. (1996). Acculturation, body image, self-esteem, and eating-disorder symptomology in adolescent Mexican American women. *Psychology of Women Quarterly, 20*, 419–435.

Kalodner, C. R. (1997). Media influences on male and female non-eating-disordered college students: A significant issue. *Eating Disorders, 5*, 47–57.

Keel, P. K., Heatherton, T. F., Harnden, J. L., & Hornig, C. D. (1997). Mothers, fathers, and daughters: Dieting and disordered eating. *Eating Disorders, 5*, 216–228.

Killen, J. D. (1996). The development and evaluation of a school-based eating disorder symptoms prevention program. In L. Smolak, M. Levine, & R. Striegel-Moore (Eds.), *The developmental psychopathology of eating disorders* (pp. 313–339). Mahwah, NJ: Erlbaum.

Killen, J. D., Taylor, C. B., Hayward, C., Haydel, K. F., Wilson, D. M., Hammer, L., Kraemer, H., Blair-Greiner, A., & Strachowski, D. (1996). Weight concerns influence the development of eating disorders: A 4-year prospective study. *Journal of Consulting and Clinical Psychology, 64*, 936-940.

Killen, J. D., Taylor, C. B., Hammer, L. D., Litt, I., Wilson, D. M., Rich, T., Hayward, C., Simminds, B., Kraemer, B., & Varady, A. (1993). An attempt to modify unhealthful eating attitudes and weight regulation practices of young adolescent girls. *International Journal of Eating Disorders, 13*, 369–384.

Klesges, R. C., DeBon, M., Meyers, A. (1996). Obesity in African American women: Epidemiology, determinants, and treatment issues. In J. K. Thompson (Ed.), *Body image, eating disorders, and obesity* (pp. 461–478). Washington, DC: American Psychological Association.

Kog, E., & Vandereycken, W. (1985). Family characteristics of anorexia nervosa and bulimia: A review of the research literature. *Clinical Psychology Review, 5*, 159–180.

Lacey, J. H., Coker, S., & Birtchnell, S. A. (1986). Bulimia: Factors associated with its etiology and maintenance. *International Journal of Eating Disorders, 5*, 475–487.

Lachenmeyer, J. R., & Muni-Brander, P. (1988). Eating disorders in a nonclinical adolescent population: Implications for treatment. *Adolescence, 90*, 303–312.

Lawlor, B. A., Burket, R. C., & Hodgin, J. A. (1987). Eating disorders in American Black men. *Journal of the National Medical Association, 79,* 984–986.

Lee, N. F., & Rush, A. J. (1986). Cognitive-behavioral group therapy for bulimia. *International Journal of Eating Disorders, 5,* 599–615.

le Grange, D., Stone, A. A., & Brownell, K. D. (1998). Eating disturbances in White and minority female dieters. *International Journal of Eating Disorders, 24,* 395–403.

le Grange, D., Telch, C. F., & Agras, W.S. (1997). Eating and general psychopathology in a sample of Caucasian and ethnic minority subjects. *International Journal of Eating Disorders, 21,* 285–293.

Lester, R., & Petrie, T. A. (1998). Physical, psychological, and societal correlates of bulimic symptomology among African American college women. *Journal of Counseling Psychology, 45,* 315–321.

Levine, M., Smolak, L., & Schermer, F. (1996). Media analysis and resistance in elementary school children in the primary prevention of eating problems. *Eating Disorders, 4,* 310–322.

Levine, M., Smolak, L., & Striegel-Moore, R. (1996). Conclusion, implications, and future directions. In L. Smolak, M. Levine, & R. Striegel-Moore (Eds.) *The developmental psychopathology of eating disorders* (pp. 399–416). Mahwah, NJ: Erlbaum.

Lundholm, J. K., & Waters, J. E. (1991). Dysfunctional family systems: Relationship to disordered eating behaviors among university women. *Journal of Substance Abuse, 3,* 97–106.

Mangweth, B., Pope, H. G., Jr., Hudson, J. I., & Biebl, W. (1996). Bulimia nervosa in Austria and the United States: A controlled cross-cultural study. *International Journal of Eating Disorders, 20,* 263–270.

Mann, T., Nolen-Hoeksema, S., Huang, K., Burgard, D., Wright, A., & Hanson, K. (1997). Are two interventions worse than none? Joint primary and secondary prevention of eating disorders in college females. *Health Psychology, 16,* 215–225.

Marcus, M. D. (1997). Adapting treatment for patients with binge eating disorder. In D. M. Garner & P. E. Garfinkel (Eds.), *Handbook of treatment for eating disorders* (2nd ed., pp. 484–493). New York: Guilford Press

Metropolitan Life Insurance Company. (1983). Metropolitan height and weight tables. *Statistical Bulletin of the Metropolitan Life Foundation, 64,* 2–9.

Mickalide, A. D. (1990). Sociocultural factors influencing weight among males. In A. M. Anderson (Ed.), *Males with eating disorders* (pp. 30–39). New York: Brunner/Mazel.

Mintz, L. B., & Betz, N. E. (1988). Prevalence and correlates of eating disordered behavior among college women. *Journal of Counseling Psychology, 35,* 463–471.

Mitchell, P. B. (1988). The pharmacological management of bulimia nervosa: A critical review. *International Journal of Eating Disorders, 7,* 29–41.

Moriarty, D., Shore, R., & Maxim, N. (1990). Evaluation of an eating disorder curriculum. *Evaluation and Program Planning, 13,* 407–413.

Murray, S. A., Touyz, S. W., & Beumont, P. J. (1996). Awareness and perceived influence of body ideals in the media: A comparison of eating disorder patients and the general community. *Eating Disorders, 4,* 33–46.

Ohtahara, H., Ohzeki, T., Hanaki, K., Motozumi, H., & Shiraki, K. (1993). Abnormal perception of body weight is not solely observed in pubertal girls: Incorrect body image in children and its relationship to body weight. *Acta Psychiatrica Scandinavica, 87*, 218–222.

Omizo, S. A., & Omizo, M. M. (1992). Eating disorders: The school counselor's role. *The School Counselor, 39*, 217–224.

Osvold, L. L., & Sodowsky, G. R. (1993). Eating disorders of White American, racial and ethnic minority American, and international women. *Journal of Multicultural Counseling and Development, 21*, 143–154.

Pelch, B. L. (1999). Eating-disordered families: Issues between generations. In R. Lemberg (Ed.), *Eating disorders: A reference sourcebook* (pp. 121–123). Phoenix, AZ: Oryx Press.

Pike, K. M., & Wilfley, D. E. (1996). The changing context of treatment. In L. Smolak, M. Levine, & R. Striegel-Moore (Eds.), *The developmental psychopathology of eating disorders* (pp. 365–397). Mahwah, NJ: Erlbaum.

Piran, N. (1996). The reduction of preoccupation body weight and shape in schools: A feminist approach. *Eating Disorders, 4*, 323–333

Polivy, J., & Federoff, I. (1997). Group psychotherapy. In D. M. Garner & P. E. Garfinkel (Eds.), *Handbook of treatment for eating disorders* (2nd ed., pp. 462–475). New York: Guilford Press

Polivy, J., & Herman, C.P. (1987). Diagnosis and treatment of normal eating. *Journal of Consulting and Clinical Psychology, 55*, 635–644.

Polivy, J., & Herman, C. P. (1996). Etiology of binge eating: Psychological mechanisms. In C. G. Fairburn & G. T. Wilson (Eds.), *Binge eating: Nature, assessment, and treatment* (pp. 173–205). New York: Guilford Press.

Powers, P. S., & Johnson, C. (1996). Small victories: Prevention of eating disorders among athletes. *Eating Disorders, 4*, 364–377.

Pumariega, A. J. (1997). Body dissatisfaction among Hispanic and Asian American girls. *Journal of Adolescent Health, 21*, 1.

Robinson, T. N., Killen, J. D., Litt, I. F., Hammer, L. D., Wilson, D. M., Haydel, K. F., Hayward, C., & Taylor, C. B. (1996). Ethnicity and body dissatisfaction: Are Hispanic and Asian girls at increased risk for eating disorders? *Journal of Adolescent Health, 19*, 384–393.

Root, M. P. P. (1990). Disordered eating in women of color. *Sex Roles, 22*, 525–536.

Rosen, L. W., Shafer, C. L., Dummer, G. M., Cross, L. K., Deuman, G. W., & Malmberg, S. R. (1988). Prevalence of pathogenic weight-control behaviors among Native American women and girls. *International Journal of Eating Disorders, 7*, 807–811.

Sanders, N. M., & Heiss, C. J. (1998). Eating attitudes and body image of Asian and Caucasian college women. *Eating Disorders, 6*, 15–28.

Sargent, J., Liebman, R., & Silver, M. (1985). Family therapy for anorexia nervosa. In D. M. Garner & P. E. Garfinkel (Eds.), *Handbook of psychotherapy for anorexia nervosa and bulimia*. New York: Guilford Press.

Schmidt, U. (1993). Bulimia nervosa in the Chinese. *International Journal of Eating Disorders, 14*, 505–509.

Schneider, J. A., & Agras, W. S. (1987). Bulimia in males: A matched comparison with females. *International Journal of Eating Disorders, 6*, 235–242.

Schwartz, R. C., Barrett, M. J., & Saba, G. (1985). Family therapy for bulimia. In D. M. Garner & P. E. Garfinkel (Eds.), *Handbook of psychotherapy for anorexia nervosa and bulimia*. New York: Guilford Press.

Silber, T. J. (1986). Anorexia nervosa in Blacks and Hispanics. *International Journal of Eating Disorders, 5,* 121–128.

Silverstein, B., Perdue, L., Peterson, B., & Kelly, E. (1986). The role of the mass media in promoting a thin standard of bodily attractiveness for women. *Sex Roles, 14,* 519–532.

Smith, J. E., & Krejci, J. (1991). Minorities join the majority: Eating disturbances among Hispanic and Native American youth. *International Journal of Eating Disorders, 10,* 179–186.

Smolak, L., & Levine, M. P. (1996). Adolescent transitions and the development of eating disorders. In L. Smolak, M. P. Levine, & R. Striegel-Moore (Eds.), *The developmental psychopathology of eating disorders* (pp. 207–234). Mahwah, NJ: Erlbaum.

Srinivasan, T. N., Suresch, T. R., & Jayaram, V. (1998). Emergence of eating disorders in India: Study of eating distress syndrome and development of a screening questionnaire. *International Journal of Social Psychiatry, 44,* 189–198.

Steen, S. N., & Brownell, K. D. (1990). Patterns of weight loss and regain in wrestlers: Has the tradition changed? *Medicine and Science in Sports and Exercise, 22,* 762–768.

Steiger, H., & Houle, L. (1991). Defense styles and object-relations disturbances among university women displaying varying degrees of "symptomatic" eating. *International Journal of Eating Disorders, 10,* 145–153.

Story, M. (1986). Nutrition management and dietary treatment of bulimia. *Journal of the American Dietetic Association, 86,* 517–519.

Story, M., French, S. A., Resnick, M. D., & Blum, R. W. (1995). Ethnic/racial and socioeconomic differences in dieting behaviors and body image perceptions in adolescents. *International Journal of Eating Disorders, 18,* 173–179.

Stoutjesdyk, D., & Jevne, R. (1993). Eating disorders among high performance athletes. *Journal of Youth and Adolescence, 22,* 271–282.

Striegel-Moore, R. (1993). Etiology of binge eating: A developmental perspective. In C. G. Fairburn & G. T. Wilson (Eds.), *Binge eating: Nature, assessment, and treatment* (pp. 144–172). New York: Guilford Press.

Striegel-Moore, R., & Smolak, L. (1996). The role of race in the development of eating disorders. In L. Smolak, M. P. Levine, & R. Striegel-Moore (Eds.), *The developmental psychopathology of eating disorders* (pp. 259–284). Mahwah, NJ: Erlbaum.

Stunkard, A. J. (1993). A history of binge eating. In C. G. Fairburn & G. T. Wilson (Eds.), *Binge eating: Nature, assessment, and treatment* (pp. 15–34). New York: Guilford Press.

Thompson, R. A. (1998). Wrestling with death. *Eating Disorders, 6,* 207–210.

Thompson, R. A., & Sherman, R. T. (1993). Reducing the risk of eating disorders in athletics. *Eating Disorders, 1,* 62–78.

Troop, N. A., & Treasure, J. L. (1997). Psychosocial factors in the onset of eating disorders: Responses to life events and difficulties. *British Journal of Medical Psychology, 70,* 373–385.

Ussery, L. W., & Prentice-Dunn, S. (1992). Personality predictors of bulimic behavior and attitudes in males. *Journal of Clinical Psychology, 48,* 722–729.

Van den Broucke, S., & Vandereycken, W. (1986). Risk factors for the development of eating disorders in adolescent exchange students: An exploratory survey. *Journal of Adolescence, 9*, 145–150.

Vandereycken, W. (1993). The sociocultural roots of the fight against fatness: Implications for eating disorders and obesity. *Eating Disorders, 1*, 7–16.

Westphal, V. K., & Smith, J. E. (1996). Overeaters Anonymous: Who goes and who succeeds? *Eating Disorders, 4*, 160–170.

Wilson, G. T., Fairburn, C. G., & Agras, W. S. (1997). Cognitive-behavioral therapy for bulimia nervosa. In D. M. Garner & P. E. Garfinkel (Eds.), *Handbook of treatment for eating disorders* (2nd ed., pp. 67–93). New York: Guilford Press.

Wilson, G. T., Nonas, C. A., & Rosenblum, G. D. (1993). Assessment of binge eating in obese patients. *International Journal of Eating Disorders, 13*, 25–34.

Wiseman, C. V., Gunning, F. M., & Gray, J. J. (1993). Increasing pressure to be thin: 19 years of diet products in television commercials. *Eating Disorders, 1*, 52–64.

Yager, J., Kurtzman, F., Landsverk, J., & Wiesmeier, E. (1988). Behaviors and attitudes related to eating disorders in homosexual male college students. *American Journal of Psychiatry, 145*, 495–497.

Yanovski, S. Z., Nelson, J. E., Dubbert, B. K., & Spitzer, R. L. (1993). Association of binge eating disorder and psychiatric comorbidity in obese subjects. *American Journal of Psychiatry, 150*, 1472–1479.

9 | Children Having Children: Teenage Pregnancy and Parenthood

Ardis Sherwood-Hawes

The incidence of adolescent pregnancy and parenthood in the United States has remained at an alarmingly high level for the past 30 years. During the 1970s, numerous studies indicated that one of the most profound trends among American adolescents was a significant increase in both pregnancy (Dryfoos & Heisler, 1978) and the subsequent rearing of offspring by single, school-age mothers (Ogg, 1976). A study by Ogg (1976) indicated that the number of one-parent families had increased seven times as rapidly as the number of two-parent families, and according to Nye (1976), school-aged children between 14 and 16 years of age represented the most rapidly increasing group of single parents.

Although the size of the adolescent population in the United States has decreased considerably over the past 30 years (Voydanoff & Donnelly, 1990), birth rates of United States adolescents increased substantially during the 1980s, and rates accelerated sharply from 1986 to 1991, increasing 24% during this time period ("State Specific," 1997). Recent reports have indicated an encouraging reversal in these dire statistics. Between 1991 and 1996, adolescent birth rates declined by 12%. These decreases are nationwide and encompass all ages and racial and ethnic groups. The percentages are greater for younger adolescents, ages 10 to 14 (14%), and African American adolescents (23%), and the largest drop in pregnancy and childbearing rates occurred among married adolescents (Wingert, 1998). Hispanic American youth, ages 15 to 19, who have the highest rate of pregnancy and childbearing among American adolescents, sustained the lowest birthrate decline, 5% between the years of 1995 and 1996. Abortion rates have also decreased for all racial and ethnic groups, and this descent denotes a reduction in rates of adolescent pregnancy (Dionne, 1998; Smith & Ramirez, 1997; "State Specific," 1997; Wingert, 1998).

Despite the reduction in adolescent pregnancy and childbearing rates, the overall birthrate for United States adolescents is still as high or higher than rates 20 years ago (Smith & Ramirez, 1997). It is estimated that almost 1 million adolescent women (Kiselica, Stroud, Stroud, & Rotzien, 1992; Wingert, 1998) or 8% of children age 14, 18% of children ages 15 to 17, and 22% of adolescents ages 19 to 20 become pregnant each year (Bell, 1997). The vast majority of these pregnancies are unintended (Bell, 1997; Mapanga, 1997; White & White, 1991), yet over 50% of these pregnancies result in live births ("State Specific," 1997). Thus each year a greater percentage of our nation's youth are bearing children before they complete their education or secure their economic future (Patterson, 1990). Over 9,000 of these infants are reared by children under the age of 14, and almost 5,000 of these infants are the second child born to 16-year-old mothers (McCullough & Scherman, 1991). Only 5% of the more than 500,000 infants born each year to American adolescents are placed for adoption (Cervera, 1993a; Voydanoff & Donnelly, 1990). In addition, 80% of adolescent parents do not marry, and the preponderance of these infants are reared by single mothers with meager assistance from fathers of the children (Bell, 1997; Mapanga, 1997; Wingert, 1998).

Although the rates of adolescent pregnancy and childbearing in the United States are decreasing, the percentages of adolescent pregnancy, abortion, and childbirth in the United States are significantly higher than in other industrialized nations (Allen-Meares, 1989; Bell, 1997; Christopher & Roosa, 1990; Meyer, 1991; "State Specific," 1997). American adolescents under the age of 15 are five times more likely to give birth than same-age adolescents in comparable countries (Allen-Meares, 1991). Conversely, the rate of sexual activity among United States adolescents is predominately the same or lower than other analogous nations (Allen-Meares, 1989; Freeman, 1989). (Sexual activity denotes initiation of intercourse. Note that studies have rarely investigated alternate expressions of sexual behaviors among adolescents—Furstenberg, Brooks-Gunn, & Chase-Lansdale, 1989).

Although adolescents in Sweden become sexually active at earlier ages than United States adolescents, the United States pregnancy rate is three times higher than that of Sweden (Alan Guttmacher Institute, 1994; Foster, Green, & Smith, 1990) and two times higher than rates in Canada or England (Bell, 1997). (Noteworthy is that Sweden has the highest, and Canada the lowest, percentage of sexually active adolescents—Foster et al., 1990). In addition, the United States has the same percentage of sexually active adolescents as the Netherlands (Voydanoff & Donnelly, 1990) but a pregnancy rate nine times higher than the Netherlands (Bell, 1997). Most researchers attribute these disturbing statistics to higher levels of consistent and effective use of contraceptives among adolescents in other countries (Christopher & Roosa, 1990).

Sexual activity among adolescents has steadily increased over the past 30 years, and present day adolescents are engaging in sexual intercourse at much younger ages. One national school-based survey revealed that 53% of all high school students have experienced sexual intercourse, and only 52.3% of those sexually active students reported using a condom during last coitus (Azzarto, 1997). The results from another school-based survey of over 8,000 high school students documented that 59% of students experienced coitus, and 40% of the sexually active students reported sexual intercourse with four or more partners (Koniak-Griffin & Brecht, 1997).

There are many interrelated social, economic, family, and biological factors that contribute to the current trend in adolescent sexuality patterns (Brewster, Billy, & Grady, 1993; Hofferth, 1991; White & White, 1991). For example, over the past century, young women in industrialized nations have been reaching menarche at younger ages. Menarche, or biological maturity, is caused by the increased production of sex hormones, and this increase is positively correlated with sexual activity (Allen-Meares, 1991; Voydanoff & Donnelly, 1990). Although the average age of menarche is currently slightly over 12 years, the number of children who reach biological maturity at age 9 or younger is rising. These young adolescents may be biologically equipped to produce children, but they rarely have the developmental maturity to cope with their emerging and often bewildering sexual urges, or to understand and prevent pregnancy (Patterson, 1990).

Concurrently, societal changes have overtly and covertly impacted the sexual behavior of young people. Contemporary adolescents experience much more social freedom than did adolescents in the first half of the 20th century. Television, automobiles, telephones, computers, and changes in family structure all contribute to the increased autonomy of today's young people. Families are typically smaller and no longer include extended family members, such as grandparents or other relatives. Children often live in single-parent families, and opportunity for adult supervision is reduced. Even in two-parent households, both parents typically work outside the home, and children have greater spans of time for unsupervised activity with their own peers. When adolescents have expanded periods of unsupervised free time, they become more susceptible to peer pressure and have increased opportunities to experiment with drugs, alcohol, and sexual activity. Research suggests that sexual intercourse among adolescents is more likely to occur in homes with little or no adult supervision (McCullough & Scherman, 1991).

In addition, contemporary children have more exposure to external influences that shape the formation of their value systems. Mass media messages have a powerful impact on the belief systems of young people, and in recent years, media messages have consistently indicated that social attitudes are more permissive toward the expression of sexuality through premarital sexual activity. Our culture condones explicit sexual themes in advertising, the entertainment industry, and all forms of mass media, and these sexual messages convey information to our nation's young about societal expectations toward the development of gender roles, sexuality, and male and female relationships. Conversely, as we bombard our children with confusing sexual images and messages, our culture often denies realistic and complete sexuality information to our young people. Unfortunately, these skewed messages may be the primary source of sexual education for our children. Thus adolescents may be engaging in sexual activity at younger ages not only because of earlier physical maturation and the accompanying sexual feelings, but also because of permissive societal attitudes regarding premarital or extra-marital sexual intercourse, media messages that promote and glamorize sexuality, unsupervisored free time, and inadequate training on issues related to sexuality (Croft & Asmussen, 1992; Furstenberg et al., 1989; Plotnick, 1993).

Although young people are becoming physically mature and progeni-tive at younger ages, they may lack the capacity or maturity to prevent pregnancy or protect themselves from sexually transmitted diseases (STDs) and human immunodeficiency virus (HIV), the precursor of acquired immune deficiency syndrome (AIDS) (Patterson, 1990). At pre-sent, adolescents are the population considered to be most vulnerable to HIV, and everyday, due to spontaneous unprotected sexual activity, many of our nation's young people are being exposed to, and possibly contract-ing HIV (Allen-Meares, 1991; Barth, Fetro, Leland, & Volkan, 1992; Cervera, 1993b). One in four new HIV infections occurs among people who are younger than age 20 (Azzarto, 1997), and adolescent parents are considered to be at even greater risk of contracting HIV than nonparent-ing adolescents (Koniak-Griffin & Brecht, 1997).

Many professionals attribute the failure of the United States culture to address adequately issues of adolescent pregnancy and effectively pre-vent childbearing during adolescence to a lack of specific definition of the problem. Should the primary focus of programs be on abstinence, or should pregnancy be prevented through the promotion of effective and regular use of contraception? Or would a multidimensional approach be more effective in preventing adolescent pregnancy and childbearing? The outcome of the solutions designed to reduce the rate of adolescent preg-nancy depends on how our society defines the problem of adolescent childbearing (Croft & Asmussen, 1992).

The focus of this chapter is on prevention and based on the assumption that universal remedies are necessary for the successful reduction of ado-lescent pregnancy and childbearing. Therefore, this chapter concentrates on a community-oriented approach to the prevention of adolescent preg-nancy and childbearing. The chapter first defines the problem and con-siders antecedents for at-risk adolescent sexual behavior and the consequences of that behavior. The chapter then provides a case study; discusses individual, family, school, and community approaches to prevention; and examines community, individual, and school intervention strategies. The chapter concludes with an exploration of adaptations for diversity and a case study aftermath.

PROBLEM DEFINITION

An enormous amount of research has been conducted to identify factors associated with rates of adolescent sexual activity, pregnancy, and childbirth. The majority of this research has investigated the characteristics of adolescent mothers to determine what type of female child is most likely to become pregnant and the childbearing consequences for these young mothers (Brooks-Gunn & Furstenberg, 1989; Christmon, 1990; Dearden, Hale, & Alvarez, 1992; Freeman, 1989; Meyer, 1991; Watson & Kelly, 1988). This research, which predominately focuses on unmarried adolescents, seems to infer that adolescent pregnancy is acceptable if the female is married.

The cultural bias that places the responsibility of fertility control on the female has led to a dearth of investigative reports on adolescent fatherhood, and even less research on the immediate and long-term consequences for infants born to adolescent parents (Brooks-Gunn & Furstenberg, 1989; Meyer, 1991). Recent studies on adolescent fathers revealed that male and female adolescents who are at risk for early parenthood share many of the same characteristics. Therefore, this chapter predominately uses a gender-neutral approach for the discussion of variables related to adolescent pregnancy and childbearing.

Research has connected adolescent pregnancy and parenthood to a complex and interrelated combination of factors based on culture, economy, family, education, environment, and human development and behavior (Azzarto, 1997; Brewster et al., 1993; Hofferth, 1991; Kiselica et al., 1992). For example, a well-developed body of literature has demonstrated that use of chemical substances and early school withdrawal are substantially conjoined with premature initiation of unprotected sexual behavior (Allen-Meares, 1991; Brooks-Gunn & Furstenberg, 1989). This empirical research suggested that use of drugs and alcohol is strongly indicative of future detrimental behavior. However, these studies do not clearly demonstrate whether chemical usage is a cause of deleterious conduct, or an identifier of underlying issues that predispose at-risk behaviors in adolescence (Bayatpour, Wells, & Holford, 1992). Many professionals maintain that chemical substance use is a response to a combination of factors, none of which is causative. Perhaps adolescents, in part, use substances to cope with debilitating emotions (e.g., rage, depression) that emanate due to life stressors or previous traumatic occurrences (Adger, 1991).

When considering the link between noncompletion of education and alcohol abuse, professionals might ask, Does alcohol abuse cause declines in academic performance or do students begin to use alcohol as a method to cope with academic difficulties, and their subsequent feelings of discouragement and failure? These theories are further illustrated by studies indicating that the use of chemical substances is positively correlated to a history of physical and /or sexual abuse (Bayatpour et al., 1992; Berenson, San Miguel, & Wilkinson, 1992; Schamess, 1993). Survivors of abuse, especially sexual abuse, often manifest feelings of low-self esteem, unresolved anger, helplessness, and hopelessness, and experience a sense of powerlessness in their relationships. These children may use alcohol and drugs to mask their painful emotions, or the chemical usage may be an unconscious attempt to gain assistance from outside authorities. Research has also suggested that childhood abuse is strongly linked to calamitous decisions about sexuality and sexual behavior. Recent studies revealed that children who have survived or are being traumatized by sexual abuse are more likely to become sexually active at younger ages and are at heightened risk for adolescent pregnancy and parenthood (Bayatpour et al., 1992; McCullough & Scherman, 1991; Plotnick, 1993; Rhodes, Fischer, Ebert, & Meyers, 1993; Schamess, 1993). In addition, research has demonstrated a positive correlation between childhood emotional problems and high risk for contracting HIV and STDs (Azzarto, 1997; Koniak-Griffin & Brecht, 1997).

ANTECEDENTS FOR AT-RISK ADOLESCENT SEXUAL BEHAVIOR

Adolescent sexual activity, use of contraception, and responses to unplanned parenthood are dependent on many variables. Most adolescents do not intend to become pregnant. The initiation of sexual intercourse is often perceived as an unexpected and spontaneous event, as something that just "happened" (Brooks-Gunn & Furstenberg, 1989, p. 251). Generally, sexual intercourse is precipitated by a serious relationship, although younger adolescents are less likely to be engaged or involved in a steady relationship when they become sexually active. The risk of pregnancy and childbirth is linked to individual beliefs about contraception, decisions about usage, knowledge about effective methods of birth control, and attitudes toward adolescent parenthood (Voydanoff & Donnelly, 1990).

Many younger adolescents are sexually active for approximately 1 year prior to using contraception (Allen-Meares, 1989). The major reasons for this delay include procrastination, fear of parental reprisal, belief that pregnancy is impossible, and fear about the safety of methods of birth control (Zabin, Stark, & Emerson, 1991). Adolescents who clearly understand that pregnancy can result from even one unprotected sexual encounter are somewhat more inclined to use effective contraception than those who do not understand the risks of unprotected sex (Voydanoff & Donnelly, 1990). Moreover, complete and comprehensive information regarding the risks for AIDS has increased adolescent abstinence and use of protection during intercourse (Wingert, 1998).

Many of the antecedents associated with adolescent pregnancy and childbearing echo conditions linked to disadvantaged socioeconomic status, so it is not surprising that researchers have found that adolescents from impoverished backgrounds tend to become sexually active at younger ages, are less inclined to use effective contraception, and are, therefore, more likely to become adolescent parents (Voydanoff & Donnelly, 1990). The Alan Guttmacher Institute (1994) reported that although only one third of the United States adolescent population lives in substandard socioeconomic conditions, 83% of adolescent parents derive from poor and low-income families. Studies have consistently recapitulated that, regardless of racial or cultural background, all adolescents who experience socioeconomic advantage, family stability, and higher levels of religiosity are more likely to delay onset of sexual intercourse or use contraception at initial intercourse than adolescents from disadvantaged socioeconomic backgrounds and/or unstable family environments. Some studies have indicated that White adolescents are more likely to use contraception than Black adolescents, but when socioeconomic status, family stability, and community milieu are considered, these differences dramatically decrease (Voydanoff & Donnelly, 1990). Likewise, adolescents who chose abortions over childbearing are more likely to live in higher socioeconomic environments, be successful in school, have parents and friends who have positive attitudes toward abortion, reside in communities that provide accessible public-funded abortions, and tend to have fewer friends or relations who are adolescent parents (Furstenberg et al., 1989). Less than 5% of all pregnant adolescents release their infants for formal adoption, and the vast majority of these adoptees are children born to White adolescents from advantaged socioeconomic backgrounds (Cervera, 1993a; Resnick, Blum, Bose, Smith, & Toogood, 1990). Formal adoption is rarely an accepted practice among families of African heritage, although frequently young children are informally adopted by relatives. These adoption customs may have evolved due to the generations of racial discrimination experienced by Black people in America (Brooks-Gunn & Furstenberg, 1989) and related fears of Black genocide.

Developmental Influences

Childhood development is a gradual, steady process that ranges from the dependency of infancy to the self-sufficiency of adulthood (Allen-Meares, 1991). The outcome of this maturation interval is dependent on an interaction between children's unique characteristics, capabilities, and their environment. Throughout this period, children need consistent attachments to adults who protect them and provide the nurture and structure necessary for healthy development. Under satisfactory conditions, as their cognitive processes mature, children are gradually encouraged and allowed to become more autonomous and responsible for their behaviors. When children experience adverse childhood conditions, such as neglect, emotional or physical abandonment, poverty, instability, and emotional, mental, or physical abuse, they may experience delays in their developmental growth and fail to form the skills necessary to cope with the challenges and stressors of adolescence and adulthood.

> Youth who live in deprived surroundings, lacking food, clothing, and appropriate housing may not receive what they need from their environment to grow and develop into healthy functioning individuals, and thus could be at risk for a variety of behavioral problems. (Allen-Meares, 1991, p. 332)

Interpersonal Influences

Sexual activity and responses to pregnancy among adolescents are highly connected to their observations and discernment about normative behavior in their families of origin and peer groups (Brooks-Gunn & Furstenberg, 1989; Voydanoff & Donnelly, 1990). There is a significant probability that adolescents who anticipate a positive response to early parenthood from family or friends will become adolescent parents. This risk is increased when their families or peer group members have a history of adolescent pregnancy and childbearing (Resnick et al., 1990). Conversely, adolescents who expect negative reactions from significant others are more likely to delay or avoid pregnancy through use of reliable contraception (Freeman, 1989). Furthermore, there may be many other underlying multidimensional factors that influence adolescent sexual behavior. For example, pregnancy may be perceived as a method to identify with the value systems of families or peers, as a way to maintain relationships with the family or with sexual partners, or as a means to declare independence from the family. Childbearing may be perceived as an avenue to freedom and autonomy, or as a way to escape from unsatisfactory or intolerable family conditions (Bell, 1997; Cervera, 1993b; Freeman, 1989; White & White, 1991).

Adolescents who are reared in families that have experienced separation or divorce and families headed by single parents are at elevated risk for early pregnancy. When parents divorce, the lines of communication between parents and children can become distorted and disrupted. Family income may become drastically reduced, and this economic hardship can create stress within the family and adversely affect the parent's ability to nurture and structure their children effectively. Children may be required to cope with reductions in emotional support and simultaneously deal with overwhelming changes, such as a different school, community, or residence. During these difficult times, adolescents may rely more on peers for emotional support and, subsequently, become more susceptible to at-risk behaviors (McCullough & Scherman, 1991; Voydanoff & Donnelly, 1990).

Environmental Influences

Communities can impact the sexual behavior of young people through educational standards, labor markets conditions, attitudes about sexual education, and policies regarding abortion. Children growing up in economically depressed environments have reduced rates of high school completion and lowered expectations toward their future socioeconomic status. Academic performance is significantly connected to adolescent sexual behavior. Students who are academically successful and internalize aspirations for higher education are more likely to delay initiation of sexual intercourse or use effective measures to prevent pregnancy than students who experience difficulty in school, do not visualize themselves as successful students, and have diminished educational and vocational goals (Bloch, 1991; Brewster et al., 1993; Kiselica et al., 1992; Plotnick, 1993; Whitbeck, Hoyt, Miller, & Kao, 1992).

Career and educational aspirations may be tied to adolescents' perceptions of the opportunity structure of their communities. A high school diploma probably means less to adolescents who lack the resources to pay for college, or to those who live in communities with high rates of unemployment. These adolescents may have learned through observation that higher education and career achievement are unattainable goals, and may perceive parenthood as the only route to independence and adulthood. These helpless, hopeless beliefs about future possibilities are exacerbated when parents have not completed high school or are unemployed. (Note that numerous studies have indicated that daughters are significantly influenced by their mother's educational achievement—Voydanoff & Donnelly, 1990). Furthermore, unlike other adolescent at-risk behaviors, such as suicide, substance abuse, and violence, pregnancy and parenthood are customarily positive and valued occurrences.

In disadvantaged communities, vocational resources and job opportunities may be limited, and when the probability for adequate employment is low, the costs of early childbearing are also low (Patterson, 1990). Young women are particularly impacted by community employment practices. Community values on women in the work force affect opportunities, pay scales, and career advancement for women, and contribute to decisions young women make about their pursuit of and attainability of career goals (Brewster et al., 1993). Adolescent women tend to prevent pregnancy through abstinence or birth control when they expect to achieve higher wages through career development (Plotnick, 1993)

Federal, state, and local policies that regulate family planning education as well as accessibility and financial costs of abortion also affect rates of adolescent pregnancy and childbearing (Plotnick, 1993). Research has consistently revealed that availability of abortion does not influence adolescent decisions on the initiation of sexual activity, or their decisions regarding the use of contraception. However, abortion availability increases the probability that pregnant adolescents will terminate unintended pregnancies through abortion and, therefore, decreases the percentage of adolescent childbearing. Data have disclosed that communities with restricted availability to abortion have higher rates of adolescence childbirth, and that birthrates are dramatically reduced when states adopt liberalized laws on abortion (Hofferth, 1991; Plotnick, 1993). In addition, adolescents who live in communities that tend to deny or hide factual sexual information from children may find it difficult to acknowledge, understand, and cope with their maturing sexuality, and may become at greater risk for unplanned pregnancies (Brewster et al., 1993). For example, a community that prohibits the discussion of contraception in the public schools influences the availability of birth control information for adolescents who live in the community and reduces the likelihood adolescents will effectively contracept if they chose to become sexually active.

In socioeconomically disadvantaged communities, adolescents, regardless of gender, race, or ethnicity, realistically may not be sacrificing much in income potential or future financial stability by not postponing parenthood. Furthermore, childbearing may allow them to become accepted as adult members of the community (Plotnick, 1993). The literature invariably shows that when young people believe they have the opportunity to achieve educational and career goals, they are less apt to become pregnant and jeopardize the achievement of these goals (Brewster et al., 1993).

CONSEQUENCES

The human and economic consequences of adolescent childbirth are enormous. Whether married or unmarried, adolescent mothers are susceptible to numerous pregnancy-related complications, such as toxemia of pregnancy (eclampsia) and maternal mortality. The high percentage of negative outcomes of adolescent pregnancy is often associated with inadequate prenatal care, poor nutrition, and physical immaturity (White & White, 1991). Current data have suggested that reproductive immaturity, pregnancy hormonal deficiencies, distress, and underdeveloped body size significantly contribute to the incidence of premature parturition among adolescents (Stevens-Simon, Kaplan, & McAnarney, 1993). Babies born to adolescent mothers are vulnerable to the adverse effects of premature birth, such as low birth weight, infant mortality, neurological disorders, intellectual impairment, and developmental delays (Allen-Meares, 1989). The risks are even greater among socioeconomically disadvantaged Black adolescents who face the additional distress of discrimination. Studies have indicated the mortality rate of infants born to young Black mothers is almost twice that of infants born to young White mothers (Rhodes et al., 1993).

Infants born to adolescents may be further jeopardized due to the socioeconomic circumstances of their parents. Adolescent parents are less likely to complete high school, less likely to find stable employment, and more likely to live in poverty and become dependent on some form of public assistance. The majority of these young families live in substandard, unsafe, or crowded housing, are nutritionally deprived, and have restricted access to adequate cultural and social advantages. Children of economically disadvantaged families are less healthy and have higher mortality rates than children of economically advantaged families. These children are vulnerable to the adverse conditions associated with poverty, and their quality of life is reduced at the onset of conception (Bloch, 1991; Cervera, 1993a; Combs-Orme, 1993; Foster et al., 1990; Mapanga, 1997).

The development of effective pregnancy prevention programs is essential to the welfare and prosperity of our society. Economically, it is far less costly to prevent adolescent pregnancies than it is to direct interventions toward the financial, emotional, and educational assistance of adolescent parents (Hofferth, 1991).

CASE STUDY: THE STORY OF MARY

Several years ago, Mary was referred to the women's program at a community college by the local Job Opportunities and Basic Skills (JOBS) training program. At that time, she was 32 and the single parent of three children, ages 15, 14, and 8. Her downcast demeanor conveyed a sense of desperation, and her facial expression reflected her feelings of distress and apprehension toward this initial contact. She wore no makeup, yet it was apparent she had made an effort to dress appropriately for this appointment. Despite her intense fear of speaking with a college counselor, Mary courageously began to communicate her feelings of despair, helplessness, and hopelessness about her life situation. Her disclosure revealed that she felt depressed and a sense of shame about her circumstances, and that she possessed a drastically limited reservoir of effective life and social skills. Despite her dangerously low sense of self-esteem, Mary demonstrated high intelligence, a yearning for change, the ability to perceive, accept, and internalize encouragement, and a tremendous source of intrinsic strength. It was apparent that buried beneath the layers of abuse, neglect, and trauma was the spirit of a remarkable and talented young woman.

Mary was born when her mother, Sue, was 17, and her father, Jim, 19. She was the oldest of three children. Mary's childhood was chaotic and consisted of extended periods of abandonment and terror. Jim fluctuated between bouts of severe depression and violent rages. Sue was withdrawn and chronically depressed. During her early childhood, Mary's father periodically abused alcohol and began to batter her mother. Her earliest memories of police intervention began when Mary was about 5 years old, and she remembers a woman came to talk with her. She was told to "keep her mouth shut," and she obediently refused to answer the woman's questions. The authorities did not pursue any further action. Mary's mother attempted to modify Jim's behavior by maintaining a perfect home environment (e.g., clean house, prompt meals, invisible children). Mary's job was to keep the younger children quiet and out of the way; thus she and her mother "became responsible" for the control of Jim's behavior.

When Mary was 8, Jim lost his job and Sue began work as a swing shift waitress. Mary was given the adult responsibilities of child care, meal preparation, and other household chores. Her father's drinking escalated, and he either forced the children to spend the evening in their bedroom or went to the local bar. At this time, he began to physically abuse Mary. The children were often awakened in the middle of the night by violent arguments that culminated in the physical abuse of Sue. Neighbors periodically requested the police to intervene with this pattern of domestic violence, and the police would come, tell Jim to stop beating Sue, and Sue to stop provoking Jim's anger.

During her first 2 years of school, Mary was the ideal student. She loved being at school, was bright, eager to learn, and a "model female" student (quiet, nondisruptive, compliant). During her third and fourth year of elementary school, Mary's academic performance began to decline dramatically. She was frequently absent. By middle school, Mary was seriously struggling with her school work. She had difficulty concentrating, neglected her homework assignments, and was not involved in any extracurricular activities. She had few friends, rarely smiled, and quietly occupied a desk in the back of the classroom. By the time Mary entered high school, she believed she hated school.

Mary ran away from home when she was 13. The authorities brought her back to her parents. She ran away again at 14, was placed in juvenile detention for 3 days, and returned to her parents. At 15, she made friends with a group of young people who manifested serious at-risk behaviors and began regularly skipping school, using drugs and alcohol, and having unprotected sexual intercourse with her boyfriend, Allen. Mary was apprehensive about becoming sexually active but complied due to peer pressure and her desire to please Allen. The lack of adequate nurture and positive structure in Mary's childhood was directly correlated to the formation of her sense of low self-esteem and her inability to care for herself effectively and assertively.

Mary does not remember learning about birth control at home or at school. She did know what condoms were, but Allen refused to use them. Mary was 16 and Allen 17 when their first child was conceived.

Mary lived in an academically disadvantaged community that had a high rate of unemployment. Jobs were particularly scarce for women. Mary can remember her parents telling her that college was impossible for "people like them." When she learned she was pregnant and would not be able to complete high school, Mary did not believe these events would make a big difference in the quality of her future life. The parents of both children considered marriage to be the only alternative. Mary and Allen quit school, and Allen got a job at a gas station.

Mary and Allen's marriage was quite similar to the marriage of Mary's parents. Allen continued to abuse drugs and alcohol, and after a few years, domestic violence became a regular part of their relationship. They divorced when Mary was 29. Since then, she and her children have relied on public assistance programs for survival.

APPROACHES TO PREVENTION

Individual

The normal course of adolescent development is filled with upheaval and overwhelming physical, emotional, mental, and social changes. During this passage from childhood to adulthood, adolescents experience myriad transformations, including an accelerated growth in cognitive abilities. This gradual transition from concrete operational responses to more formal operational thinking generally begins during late childhood and early adolescence. The development of flexible and abstract thinking patterns enables most older adolescents to consider logically the possibilities and subsequent ramifications of certain behaviors, such as unprotected sexual activity or use of alcohol (Allen-Meares, 1991; Brooks-Gunn & Furstenberg, 1989). However, because of the heightened egocentrism and narcissism typical of adolescence, this exploration has a tendency to be self-directed, and adolescents may alternate between concrete and abstract modes of thinking. Consequently, adolescents often become fixated on the here and now, have difficulty determining long-term consequences of intentions, and make decisions solely based on immediate self-gratification (Blinn & Stenberg, 1993).

In addition to the cognitive, physical, emotional, and relational changes of adolescence, young people are faced with the simultaneous emergence of intensified feelings of sexuality and the need to develop a mature value system and formulate guidelines for social and intimate relationships. Social and romantic relationships are critical to the developmental process of adolescence. This process enables children to learn and practice the skills that are necessary for the formation of more permanent relations, such as marriage and parenthood.

While young people attempt to cope with the multitude of psychosocial stressors associated with adolescent development, they also strive to establish a unique sense of identity. Identity formation and emotional emancipation from parents are crucial tasks for adolescents (Allen-Meares, 1991; Croft & Asmussen, 1992). During this progressive and difficult process, adolescents struggle toward the achievement of emotional, financial, and functional independence. When differentiation of self from parents is not encouraged or permitted, the adolescent potential to become maturely responsible for self and others may become thwarted (Freeman, 1989).

Adolescents often need practical assistance in building self-esteem and developing life management skills (McCullough & Scherman, 1991). Advocates of the cognitive-behavioral approach to prevention of at-risk behaviors propose that adolescents engage in certain behaviors because they lack relevant information and the skills necessary to utilize that information effectively in life situations. Many proponents of this approach advocate a four-step model to facilitate responsible sexual behavior in adolescents. The first two steps involve comprehending and storing information on sexuality and reproduction as well as on the consequences of sexual experimentation and use of chemical substances. This knowledge is generally transmitted, integrated, and practiced in a small-group format. The second two steps are decision making and decision implementation. Adolescents learn to transform abstract information into everyday reality and how to investigate potential consequences of behaviors. Simulated role-plays and feedback help group members personalize knowledge about sexuality and drugs, practice newly acquired skills, and learn assertive behaviors (Allen-Meares, 1991).

How might Mary's life have been different if she had received training in assertiveness, self-esteem, and other life management skills? The coping and problem-solving skills Mary received from her parents were minimal and often dysfunctional. Her father repeatedly coped through alcoholism and abusive behavior, and her mother usually coped through depression and submissive behavior. She learned helpless and hopeless behaviors from both parents. The nonintervention of authorities (police, children's services , school professionals) reinforced her sense of powerlessness. Children have an intrinsic need for positive life-sustaining messages, and such interventions might have significantly altered the course of Mary's life.

Family

The quality of the relationship between parents and adolescents contributes to childhood manifestation of at-risk behaviors. Parental rejection or a lack of warmth and affection is related to emotional problems and developmental delays in moral reasoning, and adolescents who experience deficient communication with parents may become susceptible toward unsafe activities such as drug abuse or unprotected sexual experimentation (Brooks-Gunn & Furstenberg, 1989). Parental neglect, rejection, or abuse is much more predictive of at-risk behaviors in children than is family conflict (McCullough & Scherman, 1991). Studies have suggested that female adolescents from emotionally inadequate environments often become depressed and seek to compensate for this lack of love and support by establishing intimate relationships with nonfamily members. Young males are likely to counterbalance lack of nurture by abusing drugs and alcohol (Whitbeck et al., 1992). Additionally, research has indicated that adolescent sexual activity is highly associated with parental responses to structure. When parents provide structure with abuse, or fail to provide structure (e.g., rules, guidelines, instruction, discipline) and convey a sense of apathy or powerlessness toward parental responsibilities, their offspring have a propensity toward early initiation of sexual activity (Brooks-Gunn & Furstenberg, 1989; Voydanoff & Donnelly, 1990).

Many children are not nurtured by a stable and functional family atmosphere that promotes support and encouragement, and teaches effective problem-solving and coping skills. When parents do not demonstrate or model adequate life skills, children may perceive their own situation as hopeless and fail to develop the necessary skills for survival and growth. In addition, adolescents and children who have not been exposed to self-sustaining skills may become overwhelmed by the natural, yet stressful, circumstances of maturation and development (e.g., academic achievement, formation and maintenance of relationships, peer pressure, sexual growth) and may perceive themselves as powerless. This sense of powerlessness is positively associated with early sexual activity (White & White, 1991).

The family milieu has a most powerful impact on the successful development of our society's children. Young people learn how to function as adults and how to parent their future children in their families of origin. Parents can optimally influence their children's sexual behaviors by (a) providing consistent nurture and structure, (b) limiting opportunities for sexual experimentation, (c) imparting concrete information about sexual intercourse and reproduction, and (d) sharing personal beliefs and values about sexuality (Voydanoff & Donnelly, 1990). Research has revealed that children who are encouraged to discuss sexuality, pregnancy, and contraception openly with their parents generally use protection if they become sexually active (Barth et al., 1992). Communities can promote favorable family interactions by offering parenting programs for adults who were not taught adequate life management skills in their own families of origin. In addition, parental involvement is vital to the efficacy of school or community-based pregnancy prevention programs. Program facilitators can offer workshops on issues related to adolescent sexuality, provide parents with outlines of course curriculum, and encourage family discussions so parents can integrate their value system into education material (Croft & Asmussen, 1992).

How might Mary's life have been different if the authorities had mandated various interventions for this young family when the unstable conditions first became apparent? Might her life story have changed if her father had receive early alcohol abuse and anger management counseling? Perhaps he had a condition that could have been ameliorated by medical treatment and mental health services. Could her parents have benefited from receiving parenting and life management training? Could mental health counseling have assisted her mother in her ability to more effectively care for herself and her children?

School

The three basic strategies for school-based pregnancy prevention programs can be organized according to the principal objectives of each approach: abstention from or delay or reduction of sexual activity, provision of information and methods to prevent pregnancy and childbearing, and enhancement of self-esteem and instruction on meaningful alternatives to childbearing (Foster et al., 1990; Hofferth, 1991, Plotnick, 1993).

Two major types of educational programs emphasize abstinence or delay of sexual activity. The first includes traditional sex education courses that provide information on sexuality, reproduction, and life management skills (e.g., decision making, problem solving, goal setting). The second teaches assertiveness skills to facilitate a healthy response to sexual proclivity (Hofferth, 1991). The goal of 94% of these programs is to provide education so adolescents can make informed decisions about sexuality. Around 80% of these programs concentrate on education about reproduction, and 40% attempt to reduce adolescent childbearing through promotion of abstinence (Barth et al., 1992).

Traditional Sex Education.   Traditional sex education courses attempt to delay or reduce sexual activity by providing formal instruction about sexuality and reproduction. These programs may also offer training on life management skills and social action skills (e.g., sexual and social responsibility, conflict resolution, interpersonal relationships and communication skills) to encourage informed and healthy choices about potential sexual behaviors (Plotnick, 1993).

Close to 90% of all large school districts offer some form of sexual education (Barth et al., 1992), but there are serious limitations connected with most school programs. School-based sexuality education is often noncomprehensive and restricted to topics of biology and reproduction. Educators often avoid the discussion of controversial or sensitive subjects, such as birth control or homosexuality, because of perceptions that this information is unacceptable to parents and other community members (Croft & Asmussen, 1992; Franklin, Grant, Corcoran, Miller, & Bultman, 1997). (Community members may be more receptive to school-based sexuality education if educators changed the title from sex education to sexuality education—Croft & Asmussen, 1992). Consequently, less than half of school programs provide complete information on sexuality or how to use and where to obtain birth control (Barth et al., 1992). In addition, adults, not adolescents, determine the informational content of the courses.

Surveys have revealed that young people are less interested in learning the biological facts of reproduction than in receiving education on contraception and on social issues surrounding sexuality. Most adolescents want factual and complete information about sexuality, STDs, and HIV/AIDS, and they assert that concealing information interferes with their ability to make responsible decisions about future sexual intentions. They regard the tendency of adults to withhold information and decide what children should and should not know about sexuality as an irresponsible action (Croft & Asmussen, 1992). Many professionals agree and maintain that children must be give detailed information on all the methods that will provide protection from disease and prevention of pregnancy (abstinence through birth control) before they can make healthy choices about sexual activity (Allen-Meares, 1989; Barth et al., 1992).

Prevention of at-risk behaviors is a process that begins in early childhood and continues through the latter stages of life. Unfortunately, the majority of traditional sexuality programs are severely time limited (Croft & Asmussen, 1992) and do not accommodate the developmental learning processes of children. Studies have indicated that this hasty, sporadic approach to sexuality education is not effective in reducing the rate of adolescent pregnancy. Moreover, prevention programs often target at-risk groups too late in the developmental cycle (Allen-Meares, 1991).

Many professionals maintain that an effective prevention program for at-risk behaviors of children and adolescents needs to encompass grades K–12 and include comprehensive, developmentally appropriate information that incorporates all aspects of human sexuality and sexual behavior. These programs are not designed to teach young people how to have sex but to help them better understand their emerging sexuality as well as to learn ways to cope with this mysterious yet natural part of maturation. This learning process begins in early childhood and includes components other than sexual behaviors, such as self-esteem, respect for self and others, sexual responsibility, interpersonal relationship skills, and life management skills (Croft & Asmussen, 1992). The results from school programs that have integrated comprehensive sexuality education in class curriculum for grades K–12 have been highly favorable. Although abstinence is encouraged throughout the educational process, the programs also promote consistent use of effective contraception for young people who chose to become sexually active. Evaluations of these programs reveal this approach dramatically reduces the rate of premature sexual experimentation and pregnancy (Christopher & Roosa, 1990).

Research has consistently revealed that sex education and family life courses significantly increase student knowledge about reproduction and the biological aspects of sexuality but have little influence on adolescent sexual behavior or rates of pregnancy (Barth et al., 1992; Hofferth, 1991; Voydanoff & Donnelly, 1990). The results of a meta-analysis of adolescent pregnancy by Franklin et al. (1997) indicated that pregnancy prevention programs had no effect on adolescent sexual activity across age, gender, and ethnicity, and that programs emphasizing contraception, knowledge building, and distribution of birth control were successful in reducing rates of pregnancy and childbearing. Research has also demonstrated that sexuality education that includes a contraception component does not increase sexual activity among adolescents, even when participants are 14 years and younger (Franklin et al., 1997; Sellers, McGraw, & McKinlay, 1994).

How might Mary's life have been different if her elementary school had included a prevention program for at-risk students? Could the existence of such a program have encouraged teachers to become more aware of her emotional difficulties? What if teachers had received training to help them detect early signals of potential school withdrawal? What if they had been given a convenient source for referral? Might early intervention have empowered Mary to complete her education and realize her full human potential?

Life Management Skills Training. Life skills educators maintain that analytical reasoning processes are necessary to make rational decisions about future sexual behavior. During life management skills training, adolescents are presented with factual information about reproduction and taught problem-solving, decision-making, and interpersonal communication skills. Research has suggested that interactions that provide nonjudgmental instruction and encourage self-determination have a more enduring impact on human growth and development. Consequently, many family life educators recommend that educators provide complete information and withhold value judgments on sexual or contraceptive behavior, and that adolescents ultimately be allowed to determine their own sexual goals and objectives. This approach provides concrete birth control instruction but also encourages abstinence or delays in sexual activity. Adolescents learn how to anticipate and recognize at-risk situations, problem-solve ways to avoid engaging in unprotected intercourse, and simultaneously form and maintain relationships with their peers (Hofferth, 1991). During this didactic process, it is important for educators to use language that facilitates adolescents' comprehension and internalization of proffered messages (Freeman, 1989). Studies have shown that students who participate in life skills programs have better problem-solving, negotiation, and communication skills; greater comprehension of reproduction and contraception; and more favorable attitudes toward regular and effective family planning than do nonparticipating students (Hofferth, 1991).

Adolescents learn best through action, and it is important to get them involved in their own learning processes. Role-plays provide a safe medium in which adolescents can experiment, practice, and become comfortable with healthy decisions regarding their sexuality. Drama and exercises are also excellent interventions for adolescents. For example, all middle school students in one innovative program are given the assignment of caring for an "infant" for 7 days. These infants are actually 10-pound sacks of kitty litter wrapped in pink or blue bags. Students must have these infants with them at all times and tote their children around school in infant carriers. After school or during the weekend, these students must arrange and pay (either through barter or money) for child care. This exercise is an excellent learning tool to help adolescents learn about how it feels to be responsible for a helpless infant. Most begin the week in high excitement, choosing names and dressing their babies in purloined baby clothes. Toward the end of the week, they are scrounging for babysitters, hoping to survive the weekend, and anticipating their impending freedom from parenthood. Other pregnancy prevention programs offer a more technologically advanced method to teach adolescents about the responsibilities of parenthood. Students receive computerized life-sized dolls that are programed to mimic the behaviors of a newly born infant. These dolls awaken and cry at random hours over a 24-hour period, demand to be fed every few hours, have crying cycles, and manifest typical behaviors of normal infants.

The decision tree is another exercise that assists adolescents in the realization that behaviors have consequences. This task helps adolescents carefully scrutinize a proposed action and the outgrowth of that contemplated behavior. The tree's branches sprout with decisions, possible consequences, and potential outcomes of each decision. For example, a heterosexual adolescent considering sexual intercourse looks beyond the decision of initiating sexual activity to the next option, the decision whether to contracept. If the adolescent elects to contracept, he or she next determines whether to obtain information about the effectiveness of various types of birth control and evaluate those potential methods. The decision tree now expands to include choices on whether to learn how to contracept effectively and where to obtain birth control. If the adolescent decides not to contracept, he or she plans for the possibility of a pregnancy or a sexually transmitted disease. If pregnancy occurs, further decisions include choices of abortion, marriage, child support, adoption, or single parenthood (Kriepe, 1983).

How might Mary's life have been different if she had been encouraged in self-determination and taught she had the right to make healthy decisions about her body, her emotions, and her future goals? Might she have avoided seeking affirmation through the relationship with Allen?

Adolescent Family Life Act. In response to the escalating rates of adolescent pregnancy and childbearing, and the adverse outcomes associated with adolescent parenthood, Congress passed the Adolescent Family Act (AFLA) of 1981. This is the first federal program devoted exclusively to addressing concerns about adolescent pregnancy. Proponents of the AFLA assert that premature sexual activity is the main problem, and pregnancy, STDs, HIV/AIDS, and childbirth can all be avoided if sexual intercourse is postponed. AFLA programs promote abstinence as a primary prevention for all adolescents and secondary intervention strategies to ameliorate the negative outcomes of childbearing for adolescent parents and their infants. Programs for the AFLA are designed by the Office of Adolescent Pregnancy Programs, and planners assume that the development of internal controls (e.g., self-responsibility, self-determination) will enable adolescents assertively to resist social and personal influences, such as peer pressure, media messages, and natural sexual urges (Christopher & Roosa, 1990; White &

White, 1991). These programs promote abstinence through developmentally appropriate skill-building exercises and activities, and rely on the use of peer counselors as well as parental involvement and support (Hofferth, 1991).

The AFLA reports of positive results in interpersonal growth and decreases in sexual activity should be cautiously considered because detailed evaluations of AFLA programs are rare, unscientific, nontechnical, brief in content, and methodologically unsound (White & White, 1991). The few scientific studies have indicated that abstinence programs do not influence sexual decisions of adolescents who are not yet sexually active and suggested that this strategy has little effect on the behavior of sexually active adolescents (Plotnick, 1993). Research by Christopher and Roosa (1990) disclosed that programs that rely exclusively on a premarital abstinence approach are not effective in reducing adolescent sexual activity or pregnancy rates. In fact, a study of Success Express, an AFLA program that targets midlevel school children, revealed an increase of sexual activity among participants, particularly male adolescents. In addition, the dropout rate for this program was very high, indicating that students at risk were not motivated to complete the program. Programs that focus on abstinence as the only alternative to pregnancy ignore young people who have already experienced coitus. This exclusion includes the many adolescents who have been forced to endure sexual intercourse through rape or sexual abuse. Moreover, sexually active adolescents may resist courses that strictly promote abstinence because they may hear the message that they have done something bad or wrong, and may feel defensive, ashamed, and immobilized (Christopher & Roosa, 1990). In addition, adolescents may discredit messages that emphasize the importance of preventing unwanted pregnancies through abstinence when they perceive having a child as a positive life experience (Ravert & Martin, 1997). Thus Koniak-Griffin and Brecht (1997) have maintained the promotion of abstinence for every adolescent may create a situation that places adolescents who have experienced sexual exposure at increased risk for contracting STDs and HIV. Programs need to focus on reduction of risk-taking behaviors, emphasize the use of condoms as a protection from AIDS (not strictly pregnancy), and promote effective contraception and condom usage with every sexual encounter.

School-Based Clinics (SBCs). Modern children are faced with learning how to handle multiple adverse environmental conditions, and when they have not been taught effective coping skills, they may respond to environmental deficiencies with behaviors such as suicide attempts, drug or alcohol abuse, and unprotected sexual experimentation. Comprehensive mental health services are vital to this population, and it is imperative that these services are accessible to targeted populations.

School-based clinics can fulfill this need (Harold, 1988). SBCs are administered by the school system, located on site at the school or near school grounds, and are a convenient method to serve the mental and physical health needs of students comprehensively. However, although SBCs improve the health care received by students, they show little impact on sexual behavior, use of contraception, and adolescent rates of pregnancy and childbirth.

Research has indicated that community-based clinics located near, but not on, school grounds and not administered by the school system are more effective in reducing adolescent pregnancy rates (Franklin et al., 1997; Hofferth, 1991; Plotnick, 1993). These statistics may be due to several factors. Although SBCs can serve a vast number of students, clinic schedules revolve around school hours and the school year, and the population served is restricted to registered students. In addition, family planning is generally not a major focus at these clinics. Even when family planning is stressed, students may feel apprehensive about obtaining contraception at the clinic because of problems with confidentiality. Unfortunately, information from student files may be accessible to teachers, or clinic staff may divulge personal information to other school employees. Personnel may not be cognizant of the ethical, moral, and legal aspects or, more importantly, the realistic repercussions of these breaches of confidentiality. Fear of discovery is one of the major reasons adolescents practice unprotected sexual intercourse, and when they believe their privacy may be violated, they avoid using the SBCs' contraceptive services (Zabin et al., 1991).

Community

Community members, parents, and educators are searching for strategies to reduce the escalating rates of adolescent pregnancies and the growing exposure of our nation's youth to STDs, HIV, and AIDS (Barth et al., 1992). Allen-Meares (1991) proposed that to be effective, prevention programs for at-risk behaviors must (a) target multiple systems (e.g., family, school, community) and use diverse strategies to transmit information, (b) direct intervention efforts toward the entire community, (c) encompass all adolescents and reject assumptions that subgroups are the only students at risk, and (d) focus efforts on encouragement, success, and advantage rather than on deviance or etiology of the problem. Brewster et al. (1993) maintained that the community context is a major influence on the sexual behavior of community youth and suggested that three interwoven factors are crucial to the prevention of pregnancy among adolescents:

1. *community and family attitude.* Adolescents need structured information about appropriate modes of behavior. It is the responsibility of adults to model and define social norms that proscribe,

constrain, and delineate acceptable, healthy, and successful behaviors, and clearly communicate the realistic consequences of at-risk behaviors.

2. *provision of hope and possibilities.* Children who reside in communities that empower and encourage goal achievement as well as provide career-related opportunities have positive expectations toward successful accomplishment of educational and vocational goals.

3. *access to contraception.* There needs to be a concerted community and parental effort toward the exposure of youth to knowledge of the reproductive system, complete and factual information about contraception, and accessible family planning clinics.

Family Planning Services. Contraceptive use among adolescents in recent decades has increased. This trend may be due to an elevated societal concern over the possibility of exposure to AIDS and an impetus toward providing information on protection against this syndrome. However, the majority of sexually active adolescents either randomly use ineffective methods of birth control or completely avoid contraceptive use (Zabin et al., 1991). Studies have indicated that adolescents who experience sexual intercourse at younger ages are more likely to contracept inconsistently, choose ineffective methods of contraception, or engage in unprotected sexual intercourse. Thus adolescents with meager understanding about their sexuality and how to protect themselves sexually are least likely to use contraception.

Simple awareness about sexuality and contraception rarely changes contraception behaviors. Concrete, practical instruction about birth control is positively correlated to contraception use at first intercourse, regular contraception use, and choice of more effective methods of sexual protection. Research has consistently shown that comprehensive knowledge of contraception, more than knowledge of reproduction, significantly lowers practices of unprotected sexual activity among sexually active adolescents. Unfortunately, information about contraception is usually gained from peers, and misinformation about availability, cost, effectiveness, safety, and proper utilization is prevalent (Barth et al., 1992).

Statistics have indicated that adolescents who do use some form of protection often choose methods that are inexpensive and easy to obtain. These methods are generally the least effective forms of birth control. The most effective modes of contraception (e.g., birth control pill, injections,[1]

---

[1]Many professionals maintain that the recent decline in rates of adolescent pregnancy and childbearing is positively correlated with the increased use of an injectable form of birth control called Depo-Provera. Depo-Provera is simple to use and requires one visit every 3 months to a clinic for an injection (Kluger, 1998; Wingert, 1998).

diaphragm, cervical cap) require contact with medical personnel and instruction on usage. Nonprescription methods of protection (e.g., foam, gel, condoms) are not as effective in preventing pregnancy, but condoms are imperative for protection against AIDS. Adolescents who use condoms rarely receive instruction on correct condom application and removal, and improper use of condoms further increases adolescent risk for pregnancy and AIDS (Voydanoff & Donnelly, 1990).

Family planning services promote sexually responsible behavior by concentrating on increasing regular and effective use of contraception among sexually active youth. It is well documented that family planning programs that distribute contraception and offer information and guidance on abortion and adoption are the most effective method for reducing adolescent birth rates. However, studies have not clearly shown whether these services decrease rates of adolescent pregnancy. Studies have also demonstrated that family planning service effectiveness is enhanced when combined with sexuality education, and sexuality education is more effective when combined with direct access to contraception. Note that research has not indicated that these services encourage or increase sexual activity among adolescents (Franklin et al., 1997; Hofferth, 1991; Sellers et al., 1994). After reviewing the literature that examines the impact of social policies on adolescent pregnancy and childbearing, and the effectiveness of various programs, Plotnick (1993) concluded that "policies that offer tangible family-planning services and that improve access to and affordability of abortion are more likely to succeed than those that focus on changing personal attitudes and values" (p. 327). He further stated that policies that improve educational and economic opportunities for adolescents are likely to have an indirect, yet important, long-term impact on reducing future adolescent pregnancy and childbearing rates.

How might Mary's life have been different if she had received information that helped her understand her sexuality, her need for intimate relationships, and her emerging sexual desires? What if she (and Allen) had received concrete complete information on human sexuality and use of contraception? Might they have avoided pregnancy?

Residential Programs. Prevention works best when it targets communities instead of families and individuals within society (Freeman, 1989) and is directed toward reshaping community climates. Comprehensive residential programs that provide multidimensional services for adolescents can help communities reach goals of reducing at-risk behaviors among children (Hofferth, 1991). These community-based centers can foster propitious changes in community characteristics that can positively impact community youth. Residential programs have several major advantages. The centers are open during periods of idle time, such as weekends, after school, and during vacations, and are available to all adolescents, including those who are withdrawn, suspended, or expelled from school. More importantly, when programs are situated in close proximity to families and the residential environment, family and community members become more involved, and programs are able to tailor strategies that accurately reflect and address conditions within the community (Freeman, 1989; Foster et al., 1990).

Needs Assessment. The development and strategic planning stages of a comprehensive community-based prevention center for adolescents require extensive cooperative efforts among educators, parents, and community members (Croft & Asmussen, 1992). Community involvement in the goal-development stages of prevention programs is vital to the future success of proposed projects. Involvement not only cultivates the commitment necessary to project sustentation but also critically promotes the identification and resolution of potential areas of disagreement among community members (Foster et al., 1990).

During the planning stages, it is important to administer a systematic and accurate assessment of the specific needs of targeted communities. Communities are unique and have precise needs, and generalized programs may fail in certain communities because the needs of the community are not addressed. The needs assessment should focus on (a) identification of existing community resources, (b) limitations in necessary resources, (c) how available resources can be used advantageously, and (d) strategies to make resources available and accessible to community youth (Freeman, 1989). The needs assessment can be accomplished through written questionnaires, semistructured interviews, and the use of focus groups (Croft & Asmussen, 1992; Nix, Pasteur, & Servance, 1988). Surveys should include a reliable sample of all community residents (e.g., all ages, economic and educational levels, racial and ethnic groups). After the initial contact that identifies the needs of the community, it may be necessary to gather additional information to further define requirements and specify priorities. In addition, although different groups may agree on certain needs, they may perceive these needs as requiring disparate solutions. For example, adults may devise solutions that do not accommodate the requisites of community youth, and thus jeopardize the successfulness of programs (Freeman, 1989).

Spaha is a successful community program for adolescents that operates on a limited budget, with one paid director and adult volunteers. Adolescents are active in the needs assessment process, and their opinions are crucial in determining the services offered by Spaha (Azzarto, 1997). One service requested by adolescents was a female support group, and Azzarto (1997) recommended this intervention as a strategy to prevent at-risk behaviors for young women. Research has indicated that low self-esteem, isolation, and lack of positive interactions with adults are related to at-risk behaviors (e.g., unprotected sexual inter-course and increased exposure to HIV/AIDS and STDs). Support groups can provide an unconditionally accepting environment in which young women can improve self-esteem through (a) cultivation of healthy relationships with peers and nondidactic, nonjudgmental adults, and (b) development of self-identity by sharing and exploring personal beliefs, behaviors, and feelings.

Life Options Programs. Evidence has strongly indicated that student employment opportunities are positively associated with delays in childbearing, and multidimensional programs that combine employment, sexuality and contraception instruction, and life options training significantly decrease rates of adolescent pregnancy and childbearing (Christopher & Roosa, 1990; Hofferth, 1991; Plotnick, 1993). The goals of life options programs are to help adolescents understand the consequences of early parenthood, motivate them to defer childbearing, teach life management and interpersonal skills, and provide social and economic alternatives to parenthood. Program strategies include personal counseling, career and vocational training, human development courses, and work opportunities.

High unemployment rates for adolescents within their immediate community can decrease opportunities for work experiences and prevent the acquisition of career-related knowledge. In economically depressed communities, it is difficult for adolescents to internalize an image of themselves as responsible, working adults. This frustration of the ability to visualize and develop career goals can negatively impact the self-worth of male and female adolescents. Furthermore, adults in economically disadvantaged communities are also impacted by high rates of unemployment and may be less capable of modeling positive career-related behaviors and providing adequate guidance about career preparation (Freeman, 1989).

Hofferth's (1991) review of the effectiveness of programs for high-risk adolescents revealed some promising results for community-based prevention programs. Research data from Youth Incentive Entitlement Plot Projects (Olsen & Farkas, 1987) indicated that when adolescents are guaranteed a job (part-time during the school year and full-time during summer vacation), they are more likely to delay childbearing. The program evaluations demonstrated that after 2 years, program participants, when compared to the control group, had substantially higher levels of knowledge about sexual reproduction and contraception, had a greater tendency to delay initiation of sexual activity, and were more likely to use contraception when sexually active. There was a 30% decrease in pregnancy rates for older adolescents compared to a 58% increase in nonparticipants.

A more comprehensive approach was developed in 1985 by Public/Private Ventures. This experimental project, Summer Training and Education Program (STEP), was designed to reduce rates of early school withdrawal, school suspension, course failure, and pregnancy rates among adolescents from disadvantaged socioeconomic backgrounds. The randomly selected STEP participants were provided with remedial education (90 hours of reading and math tutoring), sexuality education and life skills training (18 hours of learning how to make responsible decisions about social and sexual behaviors), work experience (80 hours of part-time work provided by the local youth jobs program), and a comprehensive support system throughout the entire year. The control group received full-time summer employment and no other special treatment. Program evaluations revealed that the experimental group showed increases in effective use of contraception when sexually active and were more likely than the control group to delay initiation of sexual intercourse.

How might Mary's life have been different if, since childhood, she had carried an image of herself as a productive, worthy, self-empowered, and satisfied working adult? What if she had been encouraged to set goals and to visualize herself as capable of achieving these goals, and could depend on obtaining the resources necessary for attaining these goals?

INTERVENTION STRATEGIES

There are critical implications for intervention that must be integrated into adolescent pregnancy and parenting program development. Successful intervention strategies enable teens, both male and female, to avoid additional pregnancies and provide compelling reasons for them to do so. Intervention programs for pregnant or parenting adolescents predominately focus on adolescent females[2] and are directed toward the facilitation of healthy pregnancies for mother and infant, completion of education, resolution of immediate and long-term social and emotional difficulties, deferral of subsequent pregnancies, and acquirement of self-sufficiency skills, economic independence (Hofferth, 1991), and parenting skills. Pregnant and parenting adolescents frequently need preliminary subsistence assistance, and this support is typically acquired from parents, public assistance, nutritional programs such as food stamps or the Special Supplemental Food Program for Women, Infants, and Children (WIC), that provides nourishment for eligible pregnant and lactating women and children up to 5 years of age. Evaluations of WIC show this

---

[2]It is important to note that intervention programs often neglect the needs of adolescent fathers, despite data that indicate fathers who participate in such programs are more involved with prenatal care, and offspring of participating fathers have higher birth weights than do infants of nonparticipating fathers (Softas-Nall, Baldo, & Williams, 1997).

program is successful in improving the outcome of pregnancy for mother and infant and can have the strongest impact on at-risk adolescent mothers (Allen-Meares, 1989). The two major public sources for assistance are Aid to Families With Dependent Children (AFDC) and Medicaid. Medicaid has eliminated a previous connection with AFDC and is now expanded to provide health care assistance to multifarious groups of women (Combs-Orme, 1993).

An important function of intervention programs is to provide information and referrals to accessible resources. Thus professionals who work with adolescent parents should be familiar with and understand the eligibility requirements and application procedures of all federal, state, and local services available to adolescent parents. In addition to financial, medical, and nutritional assistance, referrals can include mental health and other support services, adoption/abortion clinics, child care, programs that provide clothing and other basic needs, housing, educational options (e.g., alternative schools, high school equivalency program, community colleges, vocational training—Combs-Orme, 1993), and parent education classes. Mapanga (1997) has promoted the services of midwives and community health nurses, either at health centers or with community outreach programs, as a resource for adolescent parents and pregnancy prevention programs. Midwives and nurses can provide information about sexuality, contraception, and the prevention of HIV/AIDS, and offer comprehensive services with prenatal and postnatal care.

Adolescent mothers list transportation, child care, support groups, and counseling services as top priorities for assistance programs. Support groups are an important intervention for pregnant and parenting adolescents. Approval and support from peer groups is an imperative need for most adolescents. Unfortunately, pregnant female adolescents are often rejected by their friends and classmates (Blinn & Stenberg, 1993). These young mothers feel comfortable with other young women who are experiencing similar situations and value the acceptance, nurture, encouragement, and constructive feedback that peer groups can provide. In addition, young mothers report that lack of transportation is a serious obstacle to completing education and obtaining medical assistance. Even when financial assistance is provided for child care, the use of public transportation to get their child to day care, go to school, and pick up the child after school is often perceived as an overwhelming barrier (McCullough & Scherman, 1991).

Community

Although early and regular prenatal and postnatal care significantly reduces the health risk to infants and their mothers, utilization of available services by low-income pregnant and parenting women is extremely low. Research has indicated several factors that may contribute to the underutilization of prenatal and postnatal services for pregnant and parenting mothers who are economically disadvantaged. These include (a) reduction of services due to governmental cutbacks, (b) difficulties with child care and transportation, (c) programmatic barriers (e.g., inefficiencies, confusion about eligibility, application procedures, long lines, extensive waiting periods), (d) inappropriate behavior of staff (e.g., judgmental attitude, intrusiveness, discrimination), and (e) treatment and assessment strategies that are biased toward the dominant segment of the population. Women who experience discrimination, depression, or other psychological difficulties, or who feel disempowered are the population that will benefit most from these services, yet they typically do not initiate and sustain program assistance (Rhodes et al., 1993).

The tendency to defer prenatal care is further increased among disadvantaged adolescents, and the youngest adolescent group, whose babies are at the greatest risk, are the least likely to seek medical assistance (Combs-Orme, 1993). It is important that professionals consider the unique adolescent characteristics that can underlie adolescent disuse of medical care. Adolescents may fail to seek prenatal care due to immature cognitive processes and lack of knowledge. Their thinking processes are often concrete and existential, and the concept of a child developing within the body of a young female may be too abstract for them to understand (Christopher & Roosa, 1990). Younger adolescents may not be knowledgeable about the symptoms of pregnancy and may not initially realize they are pregnant. Sometimes adolescents delay the commencement of prenatal care during the critical first trimester because they are undecided on how to resolve the pregnancy or want to deny the fact they are pregnant. Denial can emanate from magical thinking processes (ignore it and it will go away) or as a way to cope with the perceived consequences of discovery. For example, adolescents may avoid acknowledging the pregnancy because they fear parental reactions or are anxious about medical tests and pelvic examinations (Combs-Orme, 1993).

Public nutritional resources are available to pregnant and lactating adolescents, yet many young women do not take advantage of these services (Combs-Orme, 1993). Typically, adolescents gain less weight during pregnancy, and their nutritional intake is often poor. Consequently, they are at heightened risk for being malnourished during gestation. Inadequate maternal weight gain in adolescents is positively correlated to the maternal and neonatal risks linked to adolescent childbearing (Stevens-Simon et al., 1993).

Many factors are associated with poor nutrition and insufficient weight gain among pregnant adolescent females. Adolescents frequently experience feelings of negativity about their body image. These feelings are especially intense during periods of rapid growth and extensive physical changes. Studies have indicated that when adolescent women are pregnant, their perceptions of self-image, self-esteem, and self-identity are further diminished. This may lead to an increased need to conform to the current societal message that only extremely thin women are attractive and thus create a conflict between complying with the societal mores of thinness and the need to gain weight during pregnancy (Blinn & Stenberg, 1993). Malnourishment is exacerbated by the combination of reduced nutritional consumption and an immature reproductive system that requires additional sustenance. Reduced nutritional intake could be due to typical teenage eating habits (e.g., skipping meals, eating junk food) or may derive from conditions in which adolescents are unable to afford sufficient amounts of healthy food or from supplemental food programs that do not meet the special nutritional needs of pregnant adolescent females. Further, adolescent mothers are vulnerable to depression, and this affective disorder can precipitate a failure to thrive in children. Adolescents who fail to gain weight during gestation should be evaluated for depression (Combs-Orme, 1993).

Pregnancy prevention and intervention programs for adolescents need to include information on nutritional requirements during pregnancy and stress how weight gain is necessary for the health of the mother and unborn child (Blinn & Stenberg, 1993).

Individual

It is imperative that professionals consistently consider the individual developmental stages of the pregnant adolescent. "It is easy to forget that pregnant adolescents are still children, subject to the same cognitive and emotional limitations as any child" (Combs-Orme, 1993, p. 353). Ideally, adolescence is a time for children to define and establish self-identity, and to learn and practice the skills of adulthood. Conversely, pregnancy is a time for adults to prepare for childbirth and learn to meet the impending needs of their unborn child. The conflict between these natural processes can manifest in intensified feelings of distress and instability in adolescents as they struggle to fulfill both developmental tasks (Christopher & Roosa, 1990). Professionals can facilitate healthy resolution of this dichotomy by focusing interventional efforts toward the needs of both parents (male and female) and their infant. When adolescents are assisted in fulfilling developmental goals, and resolving their feelings about the pregnancy, they become more capable of nurturing and caring for their unborn or newborn infant (Combs-Orme, 1993).

The combination of the immature cognitive processes of adolescence and the trauma of pregnancy may distort young people's ability to make rational decisions on how to resolve the pregnancy. Thus many adolescent parents may need crisis intervention counseling when they first admit they are pregnant. They may feel overwhelmed and immobilized, and need strategies that can assist them in becoming calmer, less emotional, and more capable of solving problems and making crucial, life-consequential decisions (e.g., adoption, abortion, marriage, employment, education). It is important that health care workers assist adolescents in planning for their future and urge them not to lose sight of their long-term dreams. This encouragement needs to be directed toward both male and female adolescents. A study by Softas-Nall, Baldo, and Williams (1997) demonstrated that intern counselors may be more likely to influence adolescents fathers to drop out of school and seek employment to provide financial support for their child. This study indicated that male adolescents who were of Hispanic descent were the population least encouraged to pursue high school completion and higher education. In addition, adolescents often experience instant gratification when they earn a minimum wage, and they may tend to discard long-term plans for education and career. Professionals can help adolescents problem solve, make long-range plans, and realize their former goals are not only accessible and attainable but also vital to their future quality of life (Combs-Orme, 1993; Kiselica et al., 1992).

Programs and policies need to encourage single fathers to establish paternity legally for their children. Fathers who do so have a basis for asserting their rights with regard to regular visitation (if the father is the noncustodial parent), adoption, parenting practices, and custody decisions (e.g., paternal, maternal, shared). Legal paternity permits children to have knowledge of the identity of their fathers, allows them access to Social Security or military benefits, provides them with the opportunity to seek important medical information about their fathers, and, when followed by adequate child support, enhances their economic well-being. Paternity should be legally established as soon after the birth of the child as possible at a stage when the father is most motivated to become involved with prenatal and postnatal care as well as with decisions regarding the future well-being of the child. It has also been suggested that minors be approached differently than single fathers who are legal adults. For example, with cases involving noncustodial unmarried fathers under 18, financial obligations might be postponed until adulthood, with provisions for token financial support, and guidelines that specifically outline other paternal responsibilities toward care of the child (e.g., regular visitation, transportation to day care and medical services) might be developed.

School

Many studies have indicated that postnatal services are effective in reducing subsequent pregnancies for adolescent mothers. A longitudinal study conducted by Seitz and Apfel (1993) examined the effects of female adolescents' postnatal attendance at a public alternative school for pregnant adolescents.

This school adheres to the regular school calendar, schedule, and curriculum, and provides students with medical services, prenatal and parenting classes, life management skills training, and mental health counseling. The goal of school personnel is to promote and encourage development of self-sufficiency skills. Usually pregnant adolescents remain at the alternative school until their infant is born, and return to regular school the first quarter following the birth. However, students who deliver during the third quarter are allowed to complete the fourth quarter at the alternative school. Consequently, students who experience parturition January through April are permitted to remain at the school longer than students who deliver May through August.

Information gathered by Seitz and Apfel (1993) on 102 alternative school female students revealed that students who were allowed to remain at the alternative school for 7.1 weeks or longer were almost three times less likely to have a second child within a 2-year period than were students who returned to regular school in less than 7.1 weeks. After 5 years, over half of the single child group had not delivered a second child. Adolescents who did not give birth to a second child within 2 years had significantly better educational outcomes (e.g., passing grades, high school diploma) than did students who delivered a second child. In addition, adolescent mothers who deliver a second child within 2 years are inclined to have larger families, abandon hope for educational and vocational achievement, and rely on public assistance to support their families.

Seitz and Apfel (1993) proposed that there is a critical interval during the second postnatal month in which adolescents make pivotal decisions about future sexual responsibilities and the consequences of their sexual behaviors. The availability of an effective support system during this time period promotes the probability that young mothers will make decisions that lead to more positive life outcomes. It appears "that intervention with economically disadvantaged women is especially effective when it begins during the pregnancy with the first-born child and continues postnatally" (p. 580).

ADAPTATIONS FOR DIVERSITY

Our society is failing to educate approximately one third of our population (Bloch, 1991). The risk for noncompletion of education is dramatically increased for adolescent parents, young people who live in urban areas, and members of certain ethnic and racial groups (Barber & McClellan, 1987). For example, high school noncompletion rates are dangerously high for students of Native American and Puerto Rican descent (Barber & McClellan, 1987). Research that investigated conditions leading to high rates of high school noncompletion has predominantly focused on the individual, family, and socioeconomic status as possible contributing factors. Despite the vast amount of research directed toward identifying students who are at high risk for early school withdrawal, not one component or a combination of circumstances has emerged that clearly predicts adolescent at-risk behavior (Bloch, 1991).

Some studies have seemed to indicate that lower economic status, limited educational background of parents, and being born to a certain ethnic or racial group are highly predictive of at-risk behaviors such as drug abuse, adolescent pregnancy, or high school noncompletion. Meyer (1991) found a cultural bias in the majority of medical and social research:

> The terms *inner city, urban,* and *lower socioeconomic status* were frequently conflated with Blacks and other minorities. This conflation makes Blacks and/or other minorities of higher socioeconomic status (in addition to Whites of lower socioeconomic status) virtually invisible. It also does not differentiate among factors associated with economic status, minority status, and/or cultural factors. Conflating race and ethnic group with socioeconomic status may also serve to perpetuate discrimination by normalizing the privileged status of the majority group in our society. (p. 221)

For example, many people believe that adolescent pregnancy and childbirth are primarily African American problems. The facts are that although the rate of Black adolescent childbirth is higher than the rate for European American adolescents, the incidence of White adolescent childbirth is much greater than that of Black adolescents. Furthermore, racial differences in rates of sexual activity, pregnancy, and childbirth have declined in recent years. During the past 40 years, the rate of pregnancy has increased by more than 300% for White adolescents and by 12% for Black adolescents (Meyer, 1991), and in the 1990s, the pregnancy rate for Black adolescents has reduced more significantly than the rate for White adolescents.

Few studies have researched the impact of teachers and the educational system on high school noncompletion rates and the instructional institution's role in determining educational outcome (Dearden et al., 1992). The research focus on factors that are beyond the scope of influence of public agencies may significantly contribute to the paucity of studies that investigate the school system as a possible contributing variable of high school noncompletion rates. If educators believe that certain at-risk behaviors and subsequent school withdrawal are racially or ethnically related, and maintain there is little they can do to change the circumstances, they may make few attempts to reduce the dropout rates among these populations (Bloch, 1991).

If as profiles of dropouts seem to indicate, schools are not successful with identifiable groups of students, it is not enough to know it is so, one must ask *why* it is so. Have schools acted in ways that may be interpreted as alienating to students with cultural backgrounds different from the dominant culture? In general, what interactions between schools and students are counterproductive to learning, indeed to staying? How can schools change these interactions? (p. 44)

Ultimately, the standard public education system is not sufficiently responsive to the needs of culturally diverse groups, and many students are underserved because of the tenacious disposition to advance and preserve educational procedures that predominately comply with requirements of the dominant culture. Research needs to address the interaction between school systems and populations that are at higher risk for high school noncompletion because they do not conform to the profile of an average student, and to investigate educational procedures that are successful in reducing their withdrawal from school (Bloch, 1991).

Studies also need to be directed toward examining the behaviors students exhibit prior to withdrawal so educators can plan more effective strategies for prevention. Students may delay physical withdrawal from school until they are in junior high or high school, but they may begin to leave emotionally and mentally in much earlier grades. In addition, students who behave in ways that increase the possibility of suspension or expulsion from school may be surreptitiously withdrawing from school. When a student who has negative experiences in school is suspended, the suspension may be reinforcing for that student. Is it possible that our educational system discourages the participation of students who do not fit the norm of the average student and covertly or overtly attempts to remove these students from the system? The consequences to breaking rules in school seem to be irrevocably connected to subsequent denial of education. Does it make sense to suspend or expel a student for truancy?

The tendency of research to focus on factors unrelated to school responsibility for dropout behaviors may emanate from ideology that promotes the belief that it is easier to fix certain students so they can better function in the traditional educational setting than it is to change the education system to accommodate the diverse needs of students. When students feel culturally or racially isolated, and when their style of learning does not conform to the traditional modes of education, they may feel discouraged, disempowered, and alienated, and thus cease to pursue their education. All students have the right to feel involved and accepted in the classroom, and educators must examine their roles in the estrangement of certain students (Wehlage & Rutter, 1986). The focus of prevention must shift from attempting to mold students to adapt to standard educational criteria to determining how the school system can be restructured to recognize and respond to the diverse requirements of all students.

CASE STUDY AFTERMATH

Mary enrolled in the community college and used various free services (e.g., personal counseling, group counseling, and human resource classes) to learn more effective life management skills and to improve her emotional well-being. She received her associate degree in 1993, and her bachelor of arts in psychology in 1995. She completed her master's degree in 1998 and is currently fulfilling her vocational dream of counseling children from disadvantaged environments.

SUMMARY

The continued increase of pregnancy rates among adolescents in the United States implies that the strategies established by current programs to prevent adolescent pregnancy are not working. Many variables contribute to the effectiveness of intervention programs. For example, problem definition, setting, project design, curriculum, and execution of services are important determinants of program performance. However, even excellently designed pregnancy prevention programs may be unsuccessful when the target group is already engaging in risk-taking activity. Studies have suggested that pregnancy prevention programs may be more successful when they incorporate multiple systems (e.g., community, family, school) and when participants have not yet experienced sexual intercourse. Consequently, professionals recommend starting comprehensive sexuality education in elementary school because programs that target preadolescents have a greater likelihood of reaching young people before they become sexually active. However, many adults believe sexuality education promotes sexual activity and resist comprehensive sexuality programs, especially those that provide information about birth control or that encompass preadolescents. Although studies reveal sexuality education does not encourage or increase sexual experimentation, program developers often comply with societal preferences, modify middle school and high school curriculum, and avoid offering sexuality education to elementary school students. Regardless of this attempt to deny sexuality education to our nation's children, more preadolescents are initiating sexual activity each year. Unfortunately, because of their lack of knowledge and immature thinking processes, American children are becoming increasingly vulnerable to the negative consequences of unprotected sexual activity (e.g., HIV/AIDS, STDs, pregnancy). Moreover, when children rear children, the repercussions for the young parents, their offspring, and our society are enormous. Thus the development of responsible and effective pregnancy prevention programs is essential for the protection and preservation of our nation's future generations.

REFERENCES

Adger, H. (1991). Problems of alcohol and other drug use and abuse in adolescents. *Journal of Adolescent Health, 12,* 606–613.

Alan Guttmacher Institute. (1994). *Sex and America's teenagers.* New York: Author.

Allen-Meares, P. (1989). Adolescent sexuality and premature parenthood: Role of the Black church in prevention. *Journal of Social Work and Human Sexuality, 8*(1), 133–142.

Allen-Meares, P. (1991). Educating adolescents on the dangers of premature childbearing and drug use: A focus on prevention. *Child and Adolescent Social Work, 8* (4), 327–338.

Azzarto, J. (1997). A young women's support group: Prevention of a different kind. *Health and Social Work, 22*(4), 299–305.

Barber, L., & McCellan, M. (1987). Looking for America's dropouts: Who are they? *Kappan, 69,* 256–263.

Barth, R., Fetro, J., Leland, N., & Volkan, K. (1992). Preventing adolescent pregnancy with social and cognitive skills. *Journal of Adolescent Research, 7*(2), 208–232.

Bayatpour, M., Wells, R., & Holford, S. (1992). Physical and sexual abuse as predictors of substance use and suicide among pregnant teenagers. *Journal of Adolescent Health, 13*(2), 128–132.

Bell, A. (1997). Pregnant on purpose. *Teen Magazine, 41*(8), 106.

Berenson, A., San Miguel, V., & Wilkinson, G. (1992). Violence and its relationship to substance abuse in adolescent pregnancy. *Journal of Adolescent Health, 13*(6), 470–474.

Blinn, L., & Stenberg, L. (1993). Feelings about self and body during adolescent pregnancy. *Families in Society: The Journal of Contemporary Human Services, 74*(5), 292–290.

Bloch, D. (1991). Missing measures of the who and why of school dropouts: Implications for policy and research. *Career Quarterly, 40,* 36–47

Brewster, K., Billy, J., & Grady, W. (1993). Social context and adolescent behavior. The impact of community on the transition to sexual activity. *Social Forces, 71*(3), 713–740.

Brooks-Gunn, J., & Furstenberg, F., Jr. (1989). Adolescent sexual behavior. *American Psychologist, 44*(2), 249–257.

Cervera, N. (1993a). Decision making for pregnant adolescents: Applying reasoned action theory to research and treatment. *Families in Society: The Journal of Contemporary Human Services, 74*(6), 355–365.

Cervera, N. (1993b). Serving pregnant and parenting teens. *Families in Society: The Journal of Contemporary Human Services, 74*(6), 323.

Christmon, K. (1990). Parental responsibility and self-image of African American fathers. *Families in Society: The Journal of Contemporary Human Services, 71*(9), 563–567.

Christopher, F., & Roosa, M. (1990). An evaluation of an adolescent pregnancy prevention program: Is "Just say no" enough? *Family Relations, 39,* 68–72.

Combs-Orme, T. (1993). Health effects of adolescent pregnancy: Implications for social workers. *Families in Society: The Journal of Contemporary Human Services, 74*(6), 344–354.

Croft, C., & Asmussen, L. (1992). Perceptions of mothers, youth, and educators. A path toward detente regarding sexuality education. *Family Relations, 41*, 452–459.

Dearden, K., Hale, C., & Alvarez, J. (1992). The education antecedents of teen fatherhood. *British Journal of Educational Psychology, 62*(1), 139–147.

Dionne, E., Jr. (1998, May 11). Some good news about teen pregnancy. *Nation's Cities Weekly, 21*(19), 10.

Dryfoos, J., & Heisler, T. (1978). Contraceptive services for adolescents: An overview. *Family Planning Perspectives, 10*, 229–233.

Foster, H., Green, L., & Smith, M. (1990). A model for increasing access: Teenage pregnancy prevention. *Journal of Health Care for the Poor and Underserved, 1*(1), 136–146.

Franklin, C., Grant., Corcoran, J., Miller, P., & Bultman, L. (1997). Effectiveness of prevention programs for adolescent pregnancy: A meta-analysis. *Journal of Marriage and the Family, 59*(3), 551–567.

Freeman, E. (1989). Adolescent fathers in urban communities: Exploring their needs and role in preventing pregnancy. *Journal of Social Work and Human Sexuality, 8*(1), 113–131.

Furstenberg, F., Jr., Brooks-Gunn, J., & Chase-Lansdale, L. (1989). Teenaged pregnancy and childbearing. *American Psychologist, 44*(2), 313–320.

Harold, N. (1988). School-based clinics. *Health and Social Work, 13*(4), 303–305.

Hofferth, S. (1991). Programs for high-risk adolescents: What works? *Evaluation and Program Planning, 14*, 3–16.

Kiselica, M., Stroud, J., Stroud, J., & Rotzien, A. (1992). Counseling the forgotten client: The teen father. *Journal of Mental Health Counseling, 14*(4), 338–351.

Kluger, J. (1998, October 26). The hot shot. *Time*, p. 69.

Koniak-Griffin, D., & Brecht, M. (1997). AIDS risk behaviors, knowledge, and attitudes among pregnant adolescents and young mothers. *Health Education and Behavior, 24*(5), 613–623.

Kriepe, R. (1983). Prevention of adolescent pregnancy: A developmental approach. In E. R. McAnarney (Ed.), *Premature adolescent parenthood and pregnancy* (pp. 37–59). New York: Grune & Stratton.

Mapanga, K. (1997). The perils of adolescent pregnancy. *World Health, 50*(2), 16–18.

McCullough, M., & Scherman, A. (1991). Adolescent pregnancy: Contributing factors and strategies for prevention. *Adolescence, 26*(104), 809–816.

Meyer, V. (1991). A critique of adolescent prevention research: The invisible White male. *Adolescence, 26*(191), 217–222.

Nix, L., Pasteur, A., & Servance, M. (1988). A focus group study of sexually active Black male teenagers. *Adolescence, 23*(91), 741–751.

Nye, F. (1976). *School-age parenthood: Consequences for babies, mothers, fathers, grandparents, and others*. Pullman: Washington State University, Cooperative Extension Service.

Ogg, E. (1976). *Unmarried teenagers and their children* (Public Affairs Pamphlet No. 537). New York: Public Affairs Press.

Olsen, R., & Farkas, G. (1987). *The effect of economic opportunity and family background on adolescent fertility among low-income Blacks* (Final report to NICHD, Grant No. R01- HD-19153). Columbus: Ohio State University.

Patterson, D. (1990). Gaining access to community resources: Breaking the cycle of adolescent pregnancy. *Journal of Health Care for the Poor and Underserved, 1*(1), 147–149.

Plotnick, R. (1993). The effect of social policies on teenage pregnancy and child-bearing. *Families in Society: The Journal of Contemporary Human Services, 74*(6), 324–328.

Ravert, A., & Martin, J. (1997). Family stress, perception of pregnancy, and age of first menarche among pregnant adolescents. *Adolescence, 32*(126), 261–269.

Resnick, M., Blum, R., Bose, J., Smith, M., & Toogood, R. (1990). Characteristics of unmarried adolescent mothers: Determinants of child rearing versus adoption. *American Journal of Orthopsychiatry, 60*(4), 577–584.

Rhodes, J., Fischer, K., Ebert, L., & Meyers, A. (1993). Patterns of service utilization among pregnant and parenting African American adolescents. *Psychology of Women Quarterly, 17,* 257–274.

Schamess, S. (1993). The search for love: Unmarried adolescent mothers' views of, and relationships with, men. *Adolescence, 28*(110), 425–438.

Seitz, V., & Apfel, N. (1993). Adolescent mothers and repeated childbearing: Effects of a school-based intervention program. *American Journal of Orthopsychiatry, 63*(4), 572–581.

Sellers, D., McGraw, S., & McKinlay, J. (1994). Does the promotion and distribution of condoms increase teen sexual activity? *American Journal of Public Health, 84,* 1952–1959.

Smith, S., & Ramirez, S. (1997). Teenage birthrates—variations by state. *Public Health Reports, 112*(2), 173.

Softas-Nall, B., Baldo, T., & Williams, S. (1997). Counselor trainee perception of Hispanic, Black, and White teenage expectant mothers and fathers. *Journal of Multicultural Counseling and Development, 25*(4), 234–243.

State specific birth rates for teenagers—United States, 1990–96. (1997). *Journal of the American Medical Association, 278*(14), 1143–1147.

Stevens-Simon, C., Kaplan, D., & McAnarney, E. (1993). Factors associated with preterm delivery among pregnant adolescents. *Society for Adolescent Medicine, 14*(4), 340–342.

Voydanoff, P., & Donnelly, B. (1990). *Adolescent sexuality and pregnancy.* Newbury Park, CA: Sage.

Watson, F., & Kelly, M. (1988). Targeting the at-risk male: A strategy for adolescent pregnancy prevention. *Journal of the National Medical Association, 81*(4), 453–456.

Wehlage, G., & Rutter, R. (1986). Dropping out: How much do schools contribute to the problem? *Teachers College Record, 87,* 374–392.

Whitbeck, L., Hoyt, D., Miller, M., & Kao, M. (1992). Parental support, depressed affect, and sexual experience among adolescents. *Youth and Society, 24*(2), 166–177.

White, C., & White, M. (1991). The Adolescent Family Life Act: Content, findings, and policy recommendations for pregnancy prevention programs. *Journal of Clinical Child Psychology, 20*(1), 58–70.

Wingert, P. (1998). The battle over falling birthrates. *Newsweek, 131*(19), 40.

Zabin, L., Stark, H., & Emerson, M. (1991). Reasons for delay in contraceptive clinic utilization. *Journal of Adolescent Health, 12,* 225–232.

10 | A Future in Jeopardy: Adolescents and AIDS

Lizbeth A. Gray, Reese M. House, and
Donna A. Champeau

Education, Compassion, and Reason

Amy is an 18-year-old American adolescent. She has just tested HIV positive. She is fairly certain she contracted the virus through sexual contact, although she is not sure when or with whom. She frequented many parties in which alcohol was abundant, and she, along with many of her friends, drank to the point of passing out. A few times while she was drinking at these parties, she had sexual intercourse. She found it hard to say no to sexual advances when she was under the influence of alcohol. Because of her current HIV status, many of her friends have rejected her, and even members of her immediate family are afraid at times to be around her.

Talking about high-risk groups for HIV/AIDS, projected numbers, causal agents, transmission processes, and prevention strategies in an intellectual and objective manner is relatively easy. Speaking of the possibility of Amy's death and dying process is harder. To embrace the pain that her family experiences is difficult, and to deal with institutions and communities that contribute to a family's pain through roadblocks erected from ignorance is frustrating. This chapter focuses on HIV/AIDS information that we need to know as counselors and other professionals working with adolescents. What we are asking readers to do is learn about HIV/AIDS, integrate the information, and open their hearts to the anguish that HIV/AIDS is causing in our society. We must learn to understand this disease with our minds and our hearts.

There is mounting evidence that the human immunodeficiency virus (HIV), which causes AIDS (acquired immunodeficiency syndrome), is spreading rapidly among adolescents in the United States. As of June 1998, 3,302 adolescents between the ages of 13 and 19 had been diagnosed with AIDS (Centers for Disease Control and Prevention [CDC], 1998). This small number is misleading because HIV has an average latency of 10 years. The CDC reported in June 1998 that 23,729 Americans between the ages of 20 to 24 years had been diagnosed with AIDS. Due to the long

281

latency period, virtually all of these young adults are believed to have contracted the virus while in their teens. Ramifications of this crisis are far reaching, and there is no doubt that the health and welfare of today's adolescents are in jeopardy. The HIV/AIDS pandemic is having a tremendous social and psychological impact on individuals, families, schools, and communities.

There is no cure for HIV disease and no vaccine; thus adolescents will continue to be vulnerable to HIV infection and AIDS for the foreseeable future. Adolescents are at risk for HIV because they are sexually active, often do not use condoms, may have multiple sexual partners, and do not use precautions if they believe that their partner is safe. A small percentage of adolescents are also injection drug users (IDUs). The antecedents for these behaviors are many. As adolescents continue to engage in unprotected sex and to use drugs intravenously, the risk escalates.

Adolescents have a hard time believing that contracting HIV is a possibility for them. Only a small number of the thousands of adolescents infected with HIV are aware of their seropositive status, and those who know they are positive often keep it secret to avoid rejection by friends or family. Because their peers do not manifest symptoms of the syndrome, it is easy to understand why adolescents in general do not see themselves at risk for HIV/AIDS. The image of AIDS as a disease of gay men and IDUs has also allowed youth to feel invulnerable to HIV. Even adolescent boys who experiment with unprotected sex with other males may not see themselves at risk if they do not self-identify as gay. Others believe that they cannot get HIV/AIDS from someone with whom they are in love or with whom they engage in serial monogamy. It is difficult to counter these myths when messages from some parents, churches, and government agencies continue to put forth the idea that monogamy, marriage, and love are equated with health while promiscuity and drug addiction are the sole source of HIV/AIDS.

Adolescents take risks on a daily basis. No magic instruments have been found to prevent adolescents from becoming pregnant, to help them refrain from drunk or dangerous driving or stop drug abuse. Indeed, the only possible effective tools in the fight against the spread of HIV are education, compassion, and reason. Prevention and intervention programs must be offered that are sensitive and take into consideration the multicultural needs of adolescents, families, schools, and communities. Contemporary and accessible services that address developmental needs must be designed for all adolescents. The role of the family must be targeted in all HIV/AIDS education efforts. States must include HIV/AIDS prevention programs as an integral part of comprehensive school health education for all public school students. There is a need to develop special educational outreach programs for hard-to-reach groups of adolescents engaging in behaviors that put them at risk of becoming HIV infected.

This chapter first focuses on the specifics of the HIV/AIDS problem and presents a case study that helps to illustrate individual, family, school, and community approaches to prevention as well as strategies for working with HIV-diagnosed youth and related ethical issues. The chapter concludes with a discussion of adaptations for diversity. An appendix provides a listing of national AIDS resources to help counselors as they strive for education, reason, and compassion in working with adolescents with AIDS.

PROBLEM IDENTIFICATION

Factual Information About HIV/AIDS

The cause of AIDS is believed to be a retrovirus that targets and destroys certain white blood cells essential to the functioning of the body's immune system (Levy et al., 1984). Once the immune system is severely depressed, opportunistic infections develop that typically cause death. When an individual contracts the AIDS virus, he or she is infected for life. To date, there is no cure for HIV, but because treatment in recent years has been promising and mortality rates have dropped, there seems to be a false sense of security among the younger population. It is still important to remember that although vaccines to prevent HIV infection are being developed, none are predicted to be effective in the near future (Rosenberg & Biggar, 1998).

HIV is not as contagious as other well-known viruses such as the common cold and is not transmissible through casual social contact such as coughing, sneezing, shaking hands, sharing eating utensils, or using the same telephone. The virus is actually quite fragile and is quickly killed on environmental surfaces when treated with disinfectants. Medical authorities repeatedly state that transmission only occurs through three modes: unprotected high-risk sexual contact, exposure to infected blood or blood products (e.g., sharing needles, blood transfusions), and passage of the virus from a woman to her fetus or newborn infant. In addition to blood and semen, vaginal and cervical secretions are known to contain the virus and may account for female-to-male transmission. It is thought that the vast majority of HIV-infected persons are carriers who are unaware that they have been exposed to the virus but are nevertheless capable of infecting others. Saliva, tears, urine, cerebrospinal fluid, and feces may also contain traces of the virus in infected persons, but not in amounts sufficient to transmit the virus to another person (Fan, Conner, & Villarreal, 1996)

Since HIV/AIDS was first reported in the United States, the predominant number of persons diagnosed have been homosexual or bisexual males. In other areas of the world, however, heterosexual transmission of HIV accounts for the clear majority of cases. In the United States the percentage of heterosexual AIDS cases increases each year. Of the total AIDS cases reported among adults and adolescents as of June 1998, 9% contracted the virus through unprotected heterosexual activity (CDC, 1998). HIV/AIDS is a problem among all races, but a disproportionate number of African Americans and Hispanics are infected with the virus in the United States. Approximately 36% of AIDS cases in the United States are among African Americans, who comprise 12% of the American population, and 18% are among Hispanics, who comprise 6% (CDC, 1998).

The average time between HIV infection and the onset of symptoms is approximately 10 years (CDC, 1998; Levy et al., 1995; Smith, McGraw, Crawford, Costa, & McKinlay, 1993). Symptoms include tiredness, fever, loss of appetite and weight, diarrhea, night sweats, and swollen lymph glands, all of which are similar to the symptoms of the common cold and flu. Unlike the common cold, symptoms of the person with AIDS are ongoing and persistent. Further, the virus frequently affects the brain and central nervous system causing confusion or dementia. People living with AIDS (PLWAs) frequently contract life-threatening infections such as Pneumocystis carinii pneumonia, or a type of cancer known as Kaposi's sarcoma. With the advent of improved medical practices, experimental drug treatment, and new FDA approved drugs, people are living longer with AIDS. Age-adjusted death rates from HIV infection in the United States declined 47% from 1996 to 1997, and HIV infection fell from 8th to 14th among leading causes of death in the nation (CDC, 1998). These figures mean that new treatments have been very effective in extending lives, but they do not mean that there has been a reduction in HIV transmission. Other available data suggest that the annual number of new HIV infections in the United States has not declined in recent years, and the total number of people living with AIDS is still increasing (CDC, 1998).

Adolescents Are At Risk

In 1996, AIDS had become the number 6 killer of youth 15 to 24 years of age (CDC, 1996). HIV is primarily spread among adolescents through unprotected sexual contact with an infected person or by sharing a needle with an infected person in the course of intravenous drug use. A survey conducted by the Division of Adolescent and School Health of the National Center for Chronic Disease Prevention and Health Promotion at the Centers for Disease Control and Prevention stated that 86% of all college students reported having engaged in sexual intercourse. And of the 62.4% who were sexually active within the 30 days preceding the survey, only 27.9% said they used a condom most of the time or always (CDC, 1996). These statistics, along with the fact that adolescents are initiating sexual intercourse at younger ages, indicate that many of the nation's younger people continue to be at considerable risk for HIV infection. An examination of sexual risk-taking behavior of high school students from 1991 to 1997 concluded that students are more aware of their risks and are using condoms more often when engaging in sexual intercourse (DiClemente, 1998). However, risk reduction behaviors among our nation's youth still need improvement. The reality is that young people are more aware of their risks for HIV infection but continue to view themselves as not vulnerable (Henderson, 1998). There is still a gap between awareness and subsequent risk reduction behaviors. It is important that counselors, and other professionals who deal with youth, not take a back seat on these issues.

Increasing the adolescent's risk for HIV/AIDS is the high percentage of teens who have tried drugs or who use drugs and alcohol on a regular basis. Use of alcohol or drugs such as amphetamines (speed), amyl nitrite (poppers), cocaine, and marijuana impair judgment and increase the chances of risky sexual behaviors or the sharing of needles (Smith & Katner, 1995).

For a variety of reasons from sexual attraction and curiosity to a means of financial support, some adolescents experiment sexually with homosexual/bisexual men and/or intravenous drug users; thus a bridge or chaining effect is established for transmission of the virus to the larger adolescent population. As a result, they typically contract HIV/AIDS from such chained contact rather than from direct homosexual contact or intravenous drug use.

With these disconcerting facts, there is some encouraging news. Accurate AIDS knowledge gained by adolescent boys leads to more tolerant attitudes (Steitz & Munn, 1993). Eighty-five percent of college students surveyed said PLWAs should be allowed to attend public schools (up from 63% in 1988); and only 33% said they would be worried for their personal health if a co-worker had AIDS (down from 50% in 1988) (Gray, 1994). In this same college student study, undergraduates also showed a greater willingness to talk with potential partners about protection against HIV, and four times as many students in 1993 expressed willingness to test for HIV than 5 years earlier.

Overall, due to the high frequency of sexual activity, failure to use condoms and spermicides, lack of access to good preventative health care, drug involvement, and the chain effect resulting from experimentation with homosexual contact and injection drug use, adolescents are particularly vulnerable to contracting HIV/AIDS. The fact that they are not changing risky behavior supports the premise that it is very difficult to convince adolescents to believe in the dangers of HIV/AIDS. This is due to several factors including their susceptibility to peer pressure; propensity to take risks, including sexual and drug experimentation; sense of invulnerability and immortality; and difficulty grasping the long-term adverse consequences of current behavior (Bowler, Sheon, D'Angelo, & Vermund, 1992). In addition, there is some concern that the new drug therapies may give the false impression that the pandemic is nearing its end (DiClemente, 1998).

Response of Adolescents

Panic, hysteria, and denial are common responses to HIV/AIDS among adolescents. When examining these psychological reactions, it is critical to understand the way in which parental and community attitudes affect adolescents' thinking. Often public attitudes about HIV/AIDS, based in part on misinformation and fear of sexuality and AIDS, manifest themselves through adolescents.

Adolescents' anxiety of contracting a deadly disease through sexual activity is heightened by the embarrassment about sexual intimacy that is common to the normal developmental processes of adolescents. Many adolescents seem to have factual information about reproduction, birth control, and safer sex practices but lack the skills and maturity necessary to talk effectively about these issues with a partner.

Similarly, some adolescents exhibit a lack of concern or denial with respect to the AIDS epidemic, believing that they are invulnerable. This belief in personal invulnerability, particularly in relationship to health issues, is also an intrinsic developmental feature of adolescents and points to maturity as one key factor in developing a healthy sexuality. Most adolescents judge their risk level by imagining a stereotype of who will be involved in a negative event such as contracting HIV/AIDS (Weinstein, 1984). People tend to associate AIDS with gay men or injection drug users and distance themselves from the possibility of contracting AIDS (Henderson, 1998). Weinstein (1984) has labeled this process as *unrealistic optimism*.

CASE STUDY: AMY

Amy is one of thousands of American adolescents who is HIV positive. Although there will be similarities between her experiences and those of others, it is important to realize that her situation is unique only to her. Each adolescent is an intricate map of emotions, cognitions, personal experiences, physical needs, relationships, and genetic composition, and consequently, counselors and other professionals must expect that there will be no two cases exactly alike. We can learn from Amy. We must remember that the following situation does not offer a prescription for responses to all youth who are struggling with HIV/AIDS.

Identifying Characteristics. Amy is an 18-year-old White female who tested HIV positive 6 months ago. She currently lives with her family.

Presenting Problem. Amy's presenting problem was "Please help me. I am afraid I may get sick and die."

Family History. Amy is the oldest of five children. She has three brothers ages 15, 14, and 11 and one sister age 9. The family had been active in the Catholic Church, and the two younger children attend Catholic schools. Her father is 45 years old and works in middle management in a high-tech corporation. Her mother is 43 years old and works part-time as a librarian at the city library.

Amy describes a history of "happy family vacations" and frequent outings until her preteen years. In the last year, the family has experienced financial stress and subsequent withdrawal of the father due to a "need to make more money." The mother expresses that at the same time she has felt "helpless about the entire situation," and she sees herself providing continuity to the family. In the absence of her father, Amy describes taking over the role of second parent to the two younger children.

Educational History. Amy's grades in high school have ranged between C+ and A−. She is particularly gifted at computer science. Amy has always been a vocal student in the classroom, and she describes her senior year of high school as "pretty good."

Social History. Amy has always been a well-liked student and a "party girl." Since her diagnosis, some of her friends have acted cool and aloof toward her. She cannot help thinking their distance is because of her HIV-positive status. She no longer attends parties because she is not very often asked to go to them.

Employment History. Amy works in the public library and also has a part-time job at the local bakery. She is afraid to tell her employers of her HIV-positive status for fear that they may treat her differently.

Medical History. Amy had no significant medical history other than normal childhood illnesses prior to her HIV-positive diagnosis. Amy has had sex with approximately five young men. She remembers two experiences of sexual intercourse in which a condom was not used. Currently she shows no sign of a compromised immune system.

Mental Status. Amy appeared agitated and restless, and was able to make eye contact only for short periods of time. During the initial contact she was teary eyed, admitted great fear, and expressed confusion and helplessness.

She struggled to maintain her composure throughout the session. She was reluctant to talk about her sexual history, although she seemed quite willing to relate other information about her past. She expressed bitterness toward her family and friends for "avoiding me like the plague." There was no evidence of tangential thinking or suicidal ideation.

APPROACHES TO PREVENTION

Counselors as Educators

In the absence of treatments or vaccines that are effective and available for everyone, we must still rely on risk and harm reduction prevention/education programs to reduce the incidence rate of HIV/AIDS in adolescents such as Amy. The goal of such programs is prevention of the spread of the virus through behavioral change. It is critical for counselors and other professionals to expand the definition of helping by accepting the responsibility to provide prevention education about HIV/AIDS. Education may be done with individuals, with families, in the schools, in community programs, or in whatever milieu adolescents are found.

In order to present effective prevention programming, counselors and other professionals need to be both knowledgeable about AIDS-related issues and comfortable talking about sexuality. In a national survey of counselor education programs, 243 programs identified AIDS as high priority for inclusion in curricula. Yet nearly 40% of the responding programs did not include any AIDS training in their curricula (Gray & House, 1996; House, Eicken, & Gray, 1995). This lack of training suggests that many counselors entering the profession may not be prepared to assist clients with AIDS-related issues. It is essential that these counselors learn about HIV/AIDS through attending appropriate continuing education seminars and workshops.

Sexual comfort is the most important qualification of professionals who work with HIV/AIDS and adolescents. No matter how carefully organized HIV/AIDS curricula and outreach strategies are, embarrassed or fearful professionals can inadvertently sabotage HIV/AIDS prevention efforts. Counselors and other professionals are part of a larger American society that typically receives inaccurate information and powerful negative messages about sexuality, both of which can impede talking comfortably about this topic. Communication about sexual issues is frequently made difficult by the profound emotional impact that sexual vocabulary carries. Confusion also arises because sexual terms lack precision. Consequently, not only is effective communication with adolescents diminished, but also HIV/AIDS professionals may transfer negative emotional feelings to the youth with whom they work.

It is erroneous to assume that counselors have developed sexual comfort as part of their training. One survey of counselor education programs indicated that only 42% offered discrete sexual counseling courses (Gray & House, 1996). The majority of programs did not require sexuality courses for master's programs in counseling. No counselor education program surveyed indicated that sexual training for counselors was overemphasized.

Becoming sexually comfortable is an ongoing process that is circular and interactive in nature. The sexually uncomfortable person sets an awkward professional atmosphere that invites inhibition. Conversely, success as an HIV/AIDS educator may contribute to the development of a positive self-concept in youth. In order to work with adolescents at risk for HIV/AIDS, counselors and other professionals must consciously begin the process of increasing their own sexual comfort. This journey begins by actively addressing the factors that are likely to contribute to physical, mental, or emotional constraint in the role of HIV/AIDS educator and prevention specialist. These factors are:

- inaccurate sexual knowledge;
- inaccurate knowledge about HIV/AIDS;
- lack of an explicit sexual vocabulary;
- limited practice in talking about sexuality and HIV/AIDS;
- lack of identification and resolution of personal sexual issues; and
- sexual values and biases (e.g., homophobia) that interfere with openness to alternative lifestyles for others.

Prevention via Counseling Individuals

As counselors and other professionals work with adolescents in an HIV/AIDS prevention mode, they find at least two groups of adolescents: adolescents whose behavior is currently high risk, and those who may be concerned and anxious but whose behavior is not high risk. This second population has been referred to as the worried well. Working with adolescents can take many forms. One is an individual counseling model with nine guidelines. The key to the effectiveness of applying the model's concepts is the personal approach of the counselor. Creating a comfortable environment, as suggested earlier, is paramount. Both an understanding of the developmental issues that adolescents face and respect for adolescent culture are necessary.

The individual counseling model's guidelines are to

1. provide information about HIV/AIDS;
2. address the difficulties of implementing safer sex plans;
3. introduce assertiveness techniques and methods for resisting peer pressure;

4. respond to the emotional and psychological confusion surrounding sexual behaviors and relationship dynamics;
5. work to build self-esteem;
6. incorporate exploration about sexual decision making;
7. utilize active counseling techniques, such as role-plays, so that adolescent clients can rehearse discussing safer sexual behavior and asserting boundaries with prospective partners;
8. assist the adolescent client in exploring personal values in order to come to terms with similarities and differences between values of self and family of origin; and
9. refer the adolescent client to community resources for assistance with medical, legal, and social service issues related to HIV/AIDS.

These guidelines are incorporated into the following simulations of school counselor responses to adolescents in Amy's high school.

1. *Information*
   Adolescent: I heard that Amy has HIV. I thought only gay men got HIV.
   Counselor: I'm glad that you are concerned about Amy and about HIV/AIDS. However, HIV is not just a disease of the gay population. Anyone can get HIV if they put themselves at risk. For example, if a person is sexually active, he or she needs to protect himself or herself by using condoms. (The counselor could provide a pamphlet with more information about HIV/AIDS and teens or refer to an appropriate community agency if providing direct information is not an option.)
2. *Safer sex plan*
   Adolescent: I heard that Amy did not use condoms with those guys. But, forget it, I'm not using condoms . . . they are too stupid.
   Counselor: At first it is hard to use condoms. What is stupid about them for you? (The counselor and adolescent could discuss safer sex practices—or where to get safer sex information—keeping in mind that the less behavior the counselor asks someone to change the more likely the behavior change will occur. The key concept is, "What is the least amount of change that will protect you from being at risk for HIV/AIDS?")
3. *Assertiveness*
   Adolescent: Since hearing about Amy, I think I want Steven to use a condom. But he says, "No f . . . ing way will I wear that raincoat on my dick."
   Counselor: It is sometimes hard to stand up for what you believe, when people you care about think differently. How about practicing some ways to tell Steven you really mean it about wearing a condom? (Skills, such as using "I" language, making eye con-

tact, voice and tone level, and outcome clarification can be utilized when helping adolescents assert themselves.)

4. *Confusion*

   Adolescent: Pam doesn't want to sleep with me anymore. She's afraid she will get AIDS. But it feels so good to be with her.

   Counselor: If sexual intercourse is the source of Pam's concern, what other ways can you be close to her? (A discussion might follow regarding relationships, especially the confusion that often exists between emotional closeness and sexuality.)

5. *Self-esteem*

   Adolescent: I think maybe I deserve to get HIV like Amy. I've never been popular enough to have one real boyfriend so I take who I can. Mary called me a royal sluthead the other day.

   Counselor: Sounds like you don't like yourself very much. We all do things we don't feel good about and things we do feel good about. Let's talk about when you feel good about yourself and when you don't.

6. *Decision making*

   Adolescent: Some of the guys only go out with girls who—you know—do it. I don't know what to do anymore because of this HIV thing that Amy has.

   Counselor: Making these decisions is not easy. It would be great if there was a right answer that I could give you. What is most important is to help you decide which sexual activities feel right for you and how to be responsible with your choices. (The counselor might want to use the decision-making model [Table 10–4] or the listing of sexual activities model [Table 10–2] included in this chapter. These models speak to safer sex activities and emphasize that sexuality includes a broad range of activities, including abstinence, and is not limited to penile-vaginal intercourse.)

7. *Communication about safer sex and relationship boundaries*

   Adolescent: The speaker at the AIDS assembly said we're supposed to talk to our sexual partners about safer sex and other stuff. But what do you say? And what's this "other stuff"?

   Counselor: It is hard to talk about sex. This county health brochure is a place to start. Let's go over it together. Then we can talk—or you can talk to the health clinic staff—about the other stuff like your values, birth control, your feelings about the relationship, and your and your partner's sexual needs.

8. *Values*

   Adolescent: My mom thinks that I shouldn't be Amy's friend because she's HIV positive. But I like her better than any of the other girls in the neighborhood.

   Counselor: It sounds like you and your mom have a difference in values. Sometimes people that we care about believe differently than we do. How can I help you talk to your mom about these differences? (This might lead into a discussion of personal and parental values and how we decide what is right for each of us.)

9. *Referral*

Adolescent: I don't know quite how to tell you this, but I am worried that I might be HIV positive like Amy. Last week I slept over at a friend's house, and we messed around. That friend was with Amy one time.

Counselor: I appreciate your honesty. I have the name of a confidential community clinic that you can go to for information about HIV/AIDS and testing. Tell me more about your concerns.

Working Directly With Families as a Preventative Measure

Although the majority of parents agree it is their responsibility to provide sexuality education to their children, they frequently feel ill prepared to do so. Similarly, parents often struggle with the complexities and specifics regarding HIV/AIDS education even though they might want to be directly involved with their adolescents. It is important to recognize that working with parents, in order to help them effectively educate their own children, is an important role of the counselor and other professionals.

Parent/adolescent education courses about HIV/AIDS are an appropriate and useful prevention measure. For example, classes where mothers and adolescent daughters participate are currently a popular and effective way to enhance communication about sensitive issues like sexuality within families. This model has been extremely effective with younger children in that they need to have messages reinforced by their family members. Seemingly, the same holds true for HIV/AIDS education.

All formal AIDS education programs for adolescents, whether in the school, church, or community setting, should solicit parental input. Parents must be involved in not only the development of curricula but also the implementation. It is exciting to see school- and community-based AIDS educational programs in which parents observe and participate with the educational process. AIDS prevention measures that include homework assignments that encourage family communication are more likely to achieve the final goal: safer behavior that reduces HIV risk for adolescents.

Prevention in the Schools

Most schools have been directly impacted by HIV/AIDS. Some, as in the case of Amy, have a student who has been diagnosed HIV positive; others have students whose family members or friends have HIV or AIDS. Counselors and other professionals need to take the lead in making sure that appropriate HIV/AIDS education is implemented in the schools. In addition to HIV/AIDS curricula, counselors and other professionals can help organize activities such as HIV/AIDS awareness programs, school fund-raisers for local prevention programs, and a school health resource center. One specific strategy that many organizations have found effective is to have HIV-positive persons tell their personal stories (Stewart & Beazley, 1993). Another is large city schools that have incorporated school health clinics on their campuses. Models for such endeavors can be found through contacting Advocates for Youth, which is included in the appendix at the end of this chapter.

Over 10 years ago, the former U.S. Surgeon General C. Everett Koop (1988) specifically called for schools to start frank discussions about sexuality and teach children about HIV/AIDS and its dangers at the lowest grade possible. Most state health departments have developed AIDS curricula for youth unique to the values and concerns of each geographical area. To achieve optimum effectiveness, HIV/AIDS curricula must include information that is age specific and must be viewed in terms of a larger health context. For example, in a school setting such information could be included in a communicable disease or health education unit that can be taught as part of a comprehensive K-12 health education curriculum. Such programs must be geared toward adolescents' own needs, perceptions, fears, and concerns and be sensitive to the contemporary youth culture. HIV/AIDS curricula may be viewed as five separate, yet interfacing, content areas that include medical information, risky and safer sexual behaviors, common myths and misinformation, effective sexual decision-making skills, and effective sexual communication skills. Tables 10–1 through 10–5 present examples of the content that can be included in these topical areas. Other curricula examples can be found by contacting the Sexuality Information and Education Council of the United States (SIECUS) that is included in the appendix to this chapter.

Table 10–1 | HIV/AIDS Curricula: Medical Information

The most recent medical information about HIV/AIDS includes four areas: cause, acquisition, treatment, and prevention. The questions that follow are typical questions about the four areas that could be utilized when educating adolescents about HIV/AIDS.

- **What is HIV/AIDS?** HIV/AIDS is a disorder of the immune system in which the system is weakened and is unable to prevent life-threatening infections.

- **How is HIV/AIDS transmitted?** The AIDS virus is spread by unprotected high-risk sexual contact, needle sharing, exposure to infected blood products, and, less commonly, through tainted transfused blood or its components. The virus may also be transmitted from infected mother to fetus or infant during pregnancy, birth, or shortly after birth through breast feeding.

continues

Table 10–1 | continued

- **How is HIV/AIDS not transmitted?** The AIDS virus is not spread by casual contact such as hugging, kissing, holding hands, touching objects handled by an infected person, toilet seats, dishes, or telephones.

- **Who can get HIV/AIDS?** Anyone who has unprotected high-risk sexual contact with an infected person or who shares needles is at risk for HIV. This risk is increased by having multiple sexual partners.

- **Is there a test for HIV?** A blood test can usually identify the presence of antibodies to the AIDS virus. Consult your local AIDS project or state/county health division for the latest information.

- **Is there treatment for AIDS?** There is no cure for HIV/AIDS. However, treatments for AIDS-associated infections are improving, and thus people are living longer with HIV/AIDS.

Table 10–2 | HIV/AIDS Curricula: Risky and Safer Sexual Behavior

It is important to include the latest available information about risky and safer sexual behavior in HIV/AIDS curricula for adolescents. Please consult your local or state health agency for the latest updates. When educating adolescents about the risky to safe behaviors identified here, the use of straightforward language is necessary.

- **Risky behaviors** include vaginal and anal intercourse without a condom, oral-anal contact (rimming), putting a hand or fist into vagina or anus (fisting), fingers, tongue, or penis touching the vagina during menstruation, sharing sex toys (e.g., vibrators), piercing the skin, oral sex without a condom, masturbation on open/broken skin.

- **Safer behaviors** include vaginal intercourse with a condom,* anal intercourse with a condom, oral sex on a man with a condom, oral sex on a woman with use of a dental dam.

- **Safe behaviors** include kissing if neither person has open cuts or sores, masturbation on healthy skin, touching, massage, fantasy, parallel masturbation, solitary masturbation, clothed body to body rubbing, consensual voyeurism, exhibitionism.

- **The safest behavior** is abstinence from sexual contact.

---

*Use of the condom: It is only with the proper use of a condom that HIV transmission can be prevented. Condoms can break or slip off during sexual intercourse. There is a correct procedure for applying a condom. It is important to put the condom on the penis prior to any sexual contact. Applying the condom includes squeezing and holding the end of the condom while unrolling it over the entire erect penis. The man must withdraw the penis while still erect to prevent the condom from slipping off and leaking. Condoms must not be reused. Latex condoms are effective barriers against the virus; natural animal skin condoms are not effective. Extra protection is provided by latex condoms that have spermicidal jelly containing nonoxynol-9. If additional lubrication is used, it is important to avoid oil-based lubricants such as Vaseline, mineral oil, or cold cream. Oil-based lubricants can erode and create holes in the condom. A recommended option is the water-based lubricating jelly K-Y.

Table 10–3 | HIV/AIDS Curricula: Common Myths and Misinformation

It is critical for the educator to dispel common myths and misinformation about HIV/AIDS. The following six myths typically are found in the adolescent population.

1. Only gay men and lesbians get HIV/AIDS.
2. Only the sexually promiscuous get HIV/AIDS.
3. Donating and receiving blood in the United States is unsafe.
4. Casual contact such as touching, sneezing, having a meal with/sharing eating utensils with someone who has HIV/AIDS, or sharing a bathroom or going to the same school with a person with HIV/AIDS, can transmit the virus.
5. HIV/AIDS can be transmitted through saliva, sweat, and tears.
6. Alcohol and drugs do not increase the risk of contracting HIV/AIDS.

Table 10–4 | HIV/AIDS Curricula: Sexual Decision-Making Model

Effective sexual decision-making skills need to be taught in terms of a larger frame of personal values. This exercise is one example of a sexual decision-making model for adolescents

Check any of the reasons listed below that you used in deciding to become involved in the following sexual behavior:_____
                                                                    (behavior)

_____ I wanted to find out what it felt like.
_____ I was sexually excited.
_____ I wanted to be as experienced as my friends are.
_____ I was talked into it.
_____ I didn't really decide—it just sort of happened.
_____ I felt it would make me feel more mature or adult.
_____ My partner and I decided we were ready for it.
_____ I felt it was about time I tried it.
_____ My parents said it would be okay.
_____ Other: _____

Check any of the reasons listed below that you used in deciding not to participate in the following sexual behavior:_____
                                                                    (behavior)

_____ I was scared.
_____ I didn't really like the person.
_____ My parents would disapprove.
_____ I wasn't sure how to do it.
_____ I don't believe people my age should be doing that.
_____ I wanted to wait until I was in love.
_____ I was afraid of getting caught.
_____ My partner wouldn't agree to it.
_____ I was afraid of getting a sexually transmitted disease.
_____ I was afraid of getting HIV/AIDS.
_____ I was afraid it would result in pregnancy.
_____ Other: _____

continues

Table 10–4 | continued

Possible Sexual Behaviors
- abstinence from all sexual activity
- holding hands
- hugging
- kissing
- french kissing
- cuddling and caressing
- breast fondling
- rubbing bodies to orgasm
- mutual masturbation
- parallel masturbation
- cunnilingus
- fellatio
- intercourse between the thighs
- intercourse between the breasts
- vaginal intercourse
- anal intercourse
- analingus (rimming)
- brachioproctic sex (fingers/fist in anus)
- sex toys
- sexual reading material
- pornography
- heterosexual involvement
- homosexual involvement
- bisexual involvement
- sex with strangers
- sex with more than one person at a time
- precommitment to partner sexual involvement
- monogamy
- serial monogamy
- use of condoms during oral sex
- use of condoms during vaginal sex
- use of condoms during anal sex
- birth control

Note: From *About Your Sexuality,* by D. Calderwood, 1983, Boston, Beacon Press. Adapted with permission.

Table 10–5 | HIV/AIDS Curricula: Sexual Communication Skills

Effective sexual communication skills are critical for developing a healthy sexuality. Listed here are several areas that need to be talked about with a prospective partner prior to a sexual relationship. Counselors and other professionals can use many creative methods to operationalize communication about these issues. Possibilities include role-plays, fishbowls, mock advertisements, and use of art, dance, music, and film.

1. Feelings
2. Significance of the sexual encounter
3. Sexual preferences and needs
4. Birth control methods
5. Safer sex plans including abstinence

Prevention in the Community

Building prevention programs in the community takes place through utilizing networker and advocacy processes. The role of networker and advocate requires being knowledgeable about the particular political issues the HIV/AIDS crisis poses. Typical political problems include lack of funding for research and social services, community values that prevent or thwart education about sexual issues, and religious and moral views that might reject some sexual behavior.

Some people believe that promotion of safer sexual behaviors encourages sexual activity among adolescents. Others say that sexuality education belongs in the home, school, *and* community. It is safe to say that opinions are polarized regarding HIV/AIDS prevention for adolescents. All too evident is that some individuals have an intense emotional investment in their value position about HIV/AIDS and sex education. When working in the community setting, it is realistic to expect opposition and to be prepared to counter it (Collison et al., 1998).

Advocates, for example, must take into consideration the basic fundamentals of community change. The counselor and other professionals must become familiar with the power structure of the community as well as lines of decision making within specific agencies or programs. Effective community involvement can make a difference between success and failure in addressing HIV/AIDS issues. All points of view must be represented before and during the development of a prevention program. This can be done, in part, by seeking participation from select members of the community who represent diverse populations. These members may disagree about the need for HIV/AIDS education, but at the same time may be willing to work toward common community goals. Including adolescents and parents is critical. Additionally, networking with other educators, regionally and nationally, who have successfully addressed controversy in their own communities provides a reference for strategic planning.

When talking with community members about building or expanding an HIV/AIDS prevention program, it is important to correct misunderstandings by providing the most current and accurate factual information about HIV/AIDS. Professionals can use statistics that speak specifically to their community. For example, in Amy's community many of the citizens appear to believe that HIV/AIDS is predominantly a disease afflicting gay men. However Amy, like many other individuals, was infected via heterosexual contact. There are ample data indicating that heterosexual transmission, worldwide, is becoming the most common form of infection. Women, in particular, are becoming infected with HIV at an alarmingly rapid rate (Harvey & Spigner, 1995). These data are important so parents with heterosexual children recognize the need to educate their children that HIV/AIDS does concern them.

Some community education experts (Cohen & Wiseberg, 1990; House & Walker, 1993) specifically mention that cooperation from churches is essential for effective community educational programs. Although some religious organizations have taken positions opposing HIV/AIDS education on moral grounds, others are willing and eager to participate in educational efforts. For example, the American Friends Service Committee, a Quaker organization, purports that withholding information about safer sexual behavior is immoral because of health implications.

Community members who are angry, confused, or anxious about HIV/AIDS, deserve the help of professionals who are sensitive to local community concerns. Yet the public must recognize that the goal of HIV/AIDS prevention programs is to focus on health issues, not to get roadblocked by differing views of morality. Calamidas (1991) stressed that:

> . . . educators should not be intimidated into offering educational programs that are weakened in order to avoid controversy. . . . educators must emphasize that they are compelled to discuss all aspects of controversial and ethical issues and it is imperative that they be allowed to freely answer all questions . . . if educators acknowledge that values and value positions are inherent to the educational program and that the primary value of concern is *health*, controversy can be reduced. (pp. 56–57)

INTERVENTION STRATEGIES

Working With HIV-Diagnosed Youth From a Family, School, and Community Model

Counselors and other professionals need to undertake multifaceted roles when working with an HIV-diagnosed youth. No singular intervention is effective. Different roles include, but are not limited to, intervening with HIV-positive adolescents and also their families, schools, and communities. A systems approach to intervention is critical. However, it is important for the counselor or other professional to be aware of conflicting responsibilities inherent in these roles.

Counseling the HIV/AIDS-diagnosed youth takes sensitivity and skill. The adolescent who has HIV/AIDS is facing a life-threatening illness, probable death, and stigmatization by some individuals in society. The adolescent is likely to be confused about the medical aspects of the disease. He or she may feel extremely guilt ridden and regretful about past sexual experiences or drug use. Other emotional responses of HIV-positive adolescents include fear, anger, denial, and pain.

The family of the HIV-positive adolescent is also struggling with its own set of issues. For example, Amy's family consists of three brothers, ages 15, 14, and 11, and one sister, age 9. Amy's siblings have all felt stigmatization and ostracism since their sister's diagnosis became public. They are aware that Amy may die at a young age. This possibility overwhelms both parents, and they have responded through withdrawal and verbal helplessness. Each of the siblings has responded differently with his or her own unique issues.

Further, an adolescent's school community is affected by an HIV-positive diagnosis. From the case study of Amy, it is possible that several other adolescents may be directly linked to the original HIV carrier. These adolescents, like Amy, may have since had unprotected sexual experiences. Many of Amy's classmates and their parents are reacting to the information that Amy is HIV positive with hostility. Teachers and administrators from Amy's school are immobilized. There has been no organized response by the school to the panic exhibited by students and parents. The teachers struggle, from lack of experience and education, with how best to address their own feelings and those of the student body.

The community at large in which the HIV-positive youth lives needs attention. Counselors and other professionals need to be proactive with local community agencies to insure that Amy receives the care and treatment to which she is entitled. As in the landmark case of one teenager, Ryan White, Amy may need social, political, and legal advocacy to help her fight social injustices that impact adolescents with HIV/AIDS. (Ryan White contracted AIDS as a child from blood transfusions. He lived in Kokomo, Indiana, and was not allowed to continue enrollment in his local school.)

Table 10–6 presents one model of how to work with the adolescent with HIV/AIDS utilizing a multidimensional approach integrating for all components of the system. It is important to remember that the suggested steps are not linear, and emphasis is dependent upon the relationship with a particular adolescent and his or her family, school, and community. Therapeutic issues usually center around helping people find the personal strength and resources to cope with a positive diagnosis. The two most important aspects of counseling with a person who is HIV positive and others affected by the illness are a willingness to be there as a compassionate listener and a commitment to advocate assertively for the rights of the individual with HIV/AIDS.

An example of how the counselor or other professional might begin to respond to Amy, the 18-year-old who is HIV positive, by using the guidelines from Table 10–6 as the framework for counselor or other professional intervention is as follows.

Assessing. Amy currently feels well physically. Her psychological stress, however, is high; her core issues seem to be fear of death and abandonment as well as guilt about her sexual contact with several partners. Currently, her emotional support system is not strong, but the possibility of building

Table 10–6 | Guidelines for Counseling the HIV/AIDS-Diagnosed Youth: Utilizing a Multidimensional Model for all Components of the System

- **Assessing**
  1. Degree of medical illness
  2. Degree of psychological stress
  3. Degree of social isolation-support systems
  4. Significant others and family responses
  5. Management of daily living
  6. Financial need

- **Educating**
  1. Effects of the virus
  2. Health care, insurance, and social security issues
  3. Transmission of the virus
  4. Sexual activity options

- **Assisting**
  1. Networking with social agencies
  2. Responding to employment, housing, and discrimination needs
  3. Developing support systems

- **Counseling**
  1. Providing an emotionally caring atmosphere
  2. Confronting denial about the HIV/AIDS diagnosis
  3. Confronting rejection and stigma issues
  4. Addressing loss and grieving issues
  5. Teaching stress identification and reduction techniques
  6. Bridging communication with friends and family

- **Advocating**
  1. Social
  2. Political
  3. Legal

support exists with parents, siblings, former friends, and teachers. Some of Amy's daily needs are being met. For example, her parents provide basic food and shelter. She is currently receiving consistent health care from a family physician and infectious disease specialist. However, the family's financial situation prior to the illness was tenuous and is further stretched by the high medical costs associated with HIV/AIDS.

Educating. It is important that Amy, her family, and other individuals understand the life cycle of HIV/AIDS and its related infections. With accurate information about HIV, educated choices can be made. One reason for some of the emotional and relational rejection may be due to misinformation. In addition, Amy and her family need accurate information about the effects of medications Amy is taking so that they can distinguish between side effects and the symptoms of the infections associated with HIV/AIDS. If there is understanding about the course of the virus, family and friends will be able to make the most of the times when she is feeling well. Because there is a connection between physiological responses of the body and health habits, it is imperative that Amy eat and sleep well.

Assisting.   It is essential to work with community agencies that can provide outside assistance for Amy. These include, but are not limited to, local HIV/AIDS projects and county and state health departments. Frequently, services are duplicated and/or ignored due to lack of coordination. It is especially critical to help facilitate the effective use of multiple helping systems. For example, support groups usually exist for persons with HIV/AIDS, and volunteers may be available to help with transportation and other practical needs. This kind of intervention gives an HIV-positive person opportunities to leave the house occasionally and relieves stress on the family as primary caregivers. The issues of medical expenses for the family and future hospitalization also need to be addressed through linking with appropriate agencies, such as social security, home health care, and legal aid. The student body at large and the staff of the school may also have special needs due to public awareness of Amy's diagnosis. For example, an aggressive HIV/AIDS education program should be implemented in the school to reduce unnecessary fear.

If Amy is interested, efforts might be made to help her continue part-time employment at the library and bakery. If Amy's health deteriorates, the school needs to be contacted and a plan initiated so Amy can continue her high school education. Special services of the high school should be identified.

Although it is not fully functioning, Amy's primary support system is her family. Family meetings should be held to work with the withdrawal patterns of her brothers and sister, the distancing of her father, and the helplessness of her mother. It might be important for the family to understand the caretaker role Amy plays as oldest sibling in the family, and the possible fears that family members associate with the prospect of losing that caretaker. The family needs to come to terms with the stigma that they associate with having a child/sibling who has HIV/AIDS. Family members must be assisted to recognize the critical part they play in supporting Amy, and that their support is intrinsically connected to her well-being.

Another potential support system for Amy is the many female friendships at school. These girls, and their parents, need special outreach efforts to reestablish positive relationships. Amy's teachers, especially those (such as the computer specialist) that she felt close to, also need to be utilized as potential support people.

Counseling.   When establishing a counseling relationship with Amy, the counselor must be particularly emotionally supportive. It is important for the counselor to commit to a long-term counseling relationship with Amy.

The first step in the process is to assist Amy in expressing her emotions in a safe and nonjudgmental setting. Amy, seemingly, is experiencing many emotions, including regret and anger. In order to work with Amy about these issues, it is essential to create a trusting bond. The pain associated with her sense of emotional abandonment by her family and rejection by her friends must also be addressed. The counselor can help Amy begin to face her diagnosis by encouraging her to grieve and deal with her many losses. Because research has suggested that increases in stress levels exacerbate the rate of HIV-related infections, the counselor is obligated to teach stress identification and stress reduction techniques or refer to appropriate professionals (e.g., licensed masseuse, biofeedback technician, nutritionist) (Moffatt, Spiegel, Parrish, & Helquist, 1989).

Family members may benefit from counseling as well. As parents or siblings, family members may experience feelings of shock, embarrassment, hurt, and anger. Seemingly simplistic questions may be present: What to say to other family members, friends, and neighbors? More complicated situations such as understanding medication regimens and interactive effects also are common for the family. The strain of a life-threatening illness is intense for everyone involved, and the strain frequently effects the family's other relationships.

Ethical Issues in Counseling With the HIV/AIDS Adolescent

The development of HIV/AIDS and resulting deaths raise endless ethical questions for the counselor. According to Manuel et al. (1990), the literature surrounding HIV/AIDS and ethics can be divided into the following eight categories: (1) quarantine and isolation of HIV patients; (2) discriminatory measures concerning specific population groups; (3) nonrespect of the confidential nature of medical information; (4) application of the penal code; (5) screening, compulsory notification, and registration; (6) protection of blood given for transfusion; (7) research on drugs and vaccines; and (8) fundamental rights of the person with HIV/AIDS.

One primary ethical concern is confidentiality limits with the HIV/AIDS client who continues to be sexually active without informing his or her partner. The question that continues to be debated asks, At what point, if any, do counselors breach a confidential relationship with a client who has the AIDS virus to preserve society's goals of health and safety (Gray & Harding, 1988; Harding, Gray, & Neal, 1993)? This ethical dilemma highlights the fine line between individual freedom and the health and welfare of society at large. As there is no dominant legal precedent to look to for guidance on this issue, it is likely that statutes will vary from state to state (Harding et al., 1993).

Limits of confidentiality in the counseling relationship have previously been defined in terms of "clear and imminent danger" (ACA, 1995) to self or others, ordinarily seen in the context of client suicide and homicide. However, ethical standards do not precisely define how clear and imminent danger relates to the sexually active and noninforming individual with HIV. Some professional associations, however, have delineated policy regarding this issue. The American Counseling Association has not (Harding et al., 1993). ACA ethical standards do obligate the counselor to consult with other professionals whenever possible. Counselors who find themselves struggling with the conflict that exists between confidentiality issues and clear and imminent danger guidelines should, at the least, consult with other professionals as a part of their decision-making process.

Counselors as Referral Agent

Referral can be utilized in a variety of circumstances surrounding HIV/AIDS and adolescents. The first may be when counselors recognize that their own biases and values are interfering with delivering appropriate services, whether working at the individual, family, school, or community level. At this time it is critical for counselors to refer in a manner that does not negatively impact adolescents or their families. A second reason for referral may arise when a problem is so specialized that it requires unique assistance that counselors cannot provide. A third reason is that working as personal counselor with HIV-positive adolescents, their families, and significant others presents potential role conflicts.

It is important for counselors to be familiar with existing resources or how to find them. State, county, and community health departments have current information and services about HIV/AIDS and are considered a major information source. In addition, HIV/AIDS organizations that specifically focus on providing services, such as volunteer transportation and meals, are available in most large communities. Many national helping professional organizations, such as ACA, can provide guidance for locating appropriate resources. Advocates for Youth is one of the primary HIV/AIDS and adolescent resource centers that counselors should identify. The center provides bibliographies, curricular information, pamphlets, materials for parents, videos, and leader resources. The CDC provides updated statistics and medical information about HIV. The nonprofit organization Sexuality Information and Education Council of the United States (SIECUS) has the largest sexuality library in the United States and is rich with examples of HIV/AIDS curricula. These three organizations, and other resources, are included in the appendix at the end of this chapter.

ADAPTATIONS FOR DIVERSITY

Curricula and counseling services must be accessible to people from a wide variety of cultural and ethnic backgrounds. HIV/AIDS does not exclude any culture, and neither should HIV/AIDS prevention curricula and intervention programs. In many cases, however, HIV/AIDS programs are developed for European American middle-class adolescents and their families. This section discusses some specific considerations for working with youth of color and the harder-to-reach youth.

Working With Youth of Color

Youth of color are at higher risk for contracting HIV/AIDS, as indicated by the disproportionate percentage of African American and Hispanic people affected by HIV infection and AIDS since the beginning of the epidemic. Injection drug use and other risk-taking behaviors among low-income African American and Hispanic populations are most often attributed to the low incomes and resulting poverty of these groups (De Le Cancela, 1989; Mays & Cochran, 1988). Further, minority adolescents have cultural or linguistic barriers that make it likely that standard educational programs will not work. Sensitivity to cultural values, religious beliefs, and social customs increases the likelihood that adolescents will understand, and incorporate the information being conveyed to them. Social networks are powerful forces in both the African American and Hispanic cultures. Counselors should utilize these networks in preventive education and intervention programs. Showing family, relatives, and peers specific ways they can help reduce risk-taking behaviors in adolescents is an important strategy. Atwood (1993) proposed a systemic approach to behavior change with African American and Hispanic youth. Her approach, like that of the authors of this chapter, views the adolescent as a member of a family, a school, a community, and also of the larger social system. Thus messages that focus on the adolescent as a responsible member of a family and a social network are more helpful than the individualistic message of "protect yourself."

Cross-age helping, in which adolescents play an important role in the educational and social service enterprise as volunteer educators, is another important strategy when working with high-risk adolescents from underrepresented populations. Older adolescents can teach younger ones in any prevention program. Peer counseling groups can be established to discuss reasons for having sexual relationships (see Table 10–4). Reasons might include wanting to be loved, wanting to be accepted, needing closeness and nurturance, proving masculinity or femininity, participating in the rites of passage into maturity, wishing to conform to peer group expectations, rebelling against parents, curiosity, and needing to know whether they are sexually attractive and acceptable to members of the opposite sex (Atwood, 1993; Calderwood, 1983).

Working With the Special Needs of Harder-to-Reach Youth

Adolescents within the mainstream of the school system can benefit from traditional school based HIV/AIDS education, but adolescents outside the school system need to be reached through specially designed programs. The harder-to-reach adolescent often is the poor student, the dropout, the homeless, the incarcerated, the runaway, the drug abuser, and the gay and bisexual youth. Many members of these adolescent groups are frequently kicked out of their homes because their families are unable to accept their behavior, do not have money to support them, or believe they cannot handle them. More than 1 million adolescents run away each year (Advocates for Youth, personal communication, August 1994). "Various community surveys and youth shelter data suggest that somewhere between 1 and 1.3 million adolescents are in emergency shelters or on the streets in any given year" (Athey, 1991, p. 518). These runaways are escaping stressful environments and most often are victims of extremely dysfunctional families.

Street kids have been labeled *throwaways*. These adolescents frequently engage in survival sex to meet financial needs. It is estimated that there are nearly 1 million adolescent prostitutes in the United States (Athey, 1991). It is clear from studies of homeless youth and their risk behaviors that many of these adolescents are already HIV positive.

Gay and bisexual males are currently and have always been the number 1 high-risk group for HIV/AIDS in the United States. It is generally thought that 10% of the adult population is gay; that means 1 out of every 10 children in a classroom will eventually identify themselves as gay. Gay youth are constantly pressured into a male-female lifestyle by a society that assumes everyone is heterosexual. It is not surprising that gay youth have become one of the biggest subgroups that make up the street kid phenomenon. The pain and fear of struggling with sexual identity creates a lonely world not often shared with anyone. If the adolescents' gay orientation is known, they often lose their family and peer group support system.

Almost two decades into the epidemic, it is clear that preventive strategies among gay youth are failing, and that a second wave of HIV-positive youth is emerging. A 1993 report from the San Francisco Health Commission found that almost 12% of 20- to 22-year-old gay men surveyed were HIV positive, as were 4% of the 17- to 19-year-olds. If those figures are not quickly reversed, health officials say, the current generation of young urban gay men will have as high an infection rate by the time they reach their mid-30s as middle-aged gay men are thought to have today—close to 50% (Bull & Gallagher, 1994, p. 38).

Unfortunately, educators still argue about what constitutes safer sexual behavior and tend to promote dialogue only about abstinence (Collins & Stryker, 1997). This educational approach leaves all adolescents, but gay youth in particular, unsure of exactly how to protect themselves. What further complicates this situation is that educators disagree about whether AIDS prevention for gay youth should focus narrowly on safer sex practices or more broadly on issues of personal responsibility and relational dynamics. When sexual arousal and/or love comes into the picture, it is easy to forget what is intellectually known about safer sex. "Contrary to what some conservative critics believe, research indicates that lust is not the only factor that incites unsafe sex among gay men" (Bull & Gallagher, 1994, p. 38).

Counselors and other professionals must challenge their own heterosexual and/or homosexual assumptions. They must make a conscious effort to look for youth in classrooms and in community programs who are grappling with sexual identity issues. It is important to listen in a nonjudgmental fashion and help them find support in their struggle. Counselors and other professionals must help gay youth face at least two major issues: isolation and possible rejection by family, and life-threatening illness as a result of unprotected high-risk sexual experiences. Through proactive and supportive interventions it is possible to meet their needs. Consequently, this may prevent some of them from becoming runaways engaging in survival sex—and almost certainly contributing to the HIV/AIDS pandemic.

Abstaining from sexual experiences is not a realistic vision for many of the adolescents who are functioning in a survival mode. Emphasis needs to be placed upon outreach programs that move outside of the classroom and into the streets. Counselors and other professionals must be creative and develop prevention programs using whatever methods work to meet the special needs of the harder-to-reach youth. If adolescents cannot come to counselors and other professionals, then they must go to the adolescents with information about HIV, counseling, and testing (Clark, Brasseux, Richmond, Getson, & D'Angelo, 1998). Workers from programs for runaway children in New York City cruise the streets until 5:00 a.m. each morning offering hot chocolate, sandwiches, and condoms. The language counselors and other professionals use may need to be changed. Terms such as *intercourse* and *oral sex* may need to be thrown out the window for *fucking* and *sucking*. Along with professionalism, counselors must bring their own street smarts when talking to adolescents if high-risk behavior for HIV/AIDS is going to be changed.

Other youth groups that are difficult to reach include the physically disabled, developmentally delayed, or mentally ill. It is erroneous to assume that these adolescents are refraining from sexual activity or drug use. These groups are frequently neglected in HIV/AIDS education efforts.

Recently, sexuality education organizations have designed programs that include these populations. More efforts are needed in these areas.

SUMMARY

This chapter emphasizes the importance of counselors and other professionals working as prevention and intervention specialists with individuals, families, schools, and communities. Educational processes have been stressed. It is a grave mistake, however, to assume that education equals factual information and that this, by itself, translates into behavioral change. Counselors and other professionals must be progressive, compassionate, and creative. They must also apply reason to their work. They need to break through resistance to behavioral change because of strong, misguided, mind sets. Adolescents believe "this won't happen to me." Uninformed parents believe "only gay males and injection drug users contract HIV/AIDS." Bigots purport "people with AIDS are our modern day lepers." These irrational beliefs can no longer be tolerated.

Researchers are currently struggling to acquire the information and medical technology needed to develop a cure for HIV/AIDS. The outlook for a cure in the near future is not optimistic; some say we must learn to live with some form of HIV as long as there are human beings on this planet. Others say that even with a cure, elements such as poverty, racism, sexism, and homophobia will continue to contribute to the far-reaching consequences of HIV/AIDS. But as deep-seated and seemingly intractable as these problems are, they are not excuses to remain stagnant in our efforts. We must go forward to the best of our abilities. And we must continue our involvement in the social, psychological, political, legal, and ethical ramifications of HIV/AIDS. We are not powerless. We certainly have the skills and knowledge to impact the course of negative societal reactions. Most assuredly, we have the ability to help many adolescents change their behavior. Most of all we can provide and foster compassion for those youth diagnosed with HIV/AIDS. Assuming the responsibility of addressing HIV/AIDS is a legacy of counselors and other professionals worth remembering.

REFERENCES

American Counseling Association. (1995). *Code of ethics and standards of practice.* Alexandria, VA: Author.

Athey, J. L. (1991). HIV infection and homeless adolescents. *Child Welfare, 52,* 517–528.

Atwood, J. D. (1993). AIDS in African American and Hispanic adolescents: A multisystemic approach. *American Journal of Family Therapy, 21*, 333–351.

Bowler, S., Sheon, A. R., D'Angelo, L. J., & Vermund, S. H. (1992). HIV and AIDS among adolescents in the United States: Increasing risk in the 1990s. *Journal of Adolescence, 15*, 345–371.

Bull, C., & Gallagher, J. (1994, June 17). The lost generation: A second wave of HIV infections among young gay men leaves educators worried about the future of the epidemic. *The Advocate*, pp. 36–44.

Calderwood, D. (1983). *About your sexuality*. Boston: Beacon Press.

Calamidas, E. G. (1991). Reaching youth about AIDS: Challenges confronting health educators. *Health Values, 15*, 55–61.

Centers for Disease Control and Prevention. (1996). Youth risk behavior surveillance—United States, 1995. *Morbidity and Mortality Weekly Report, 45*, 8–19.

Centers for Disease Control and Prevention. (1998). *HIV/AIDS Surveillance Report, 10*, 1–40.

Cohen, R., & Wiseberg, L. S. (1990). *Double jeopardy—threat to life and human rights: Discrimination against persons with AIDS*. Cambridge, MA: Human Rights Internet.

Clark, L. R., Brasseux, C., Richmond, D., Getson, P., D'Angelo, L. J. (1998). Effect of HIV counseling and testing on sexually transmitted diseases and condom use in an urban adolescent population. *Archives of Pediatrics and Adolescent Medicine, 152*, 26.

Collins, C., & Stryker, J. (1997). *Should we teach only abstinence in sexuality education?* San Francisco: Center for AIDS Prevention Studies.

Collison, B. B., Osborne, J. L., Gray, L. A., House, R. M., Firth, J., & Lou, M. (1998). Preparing counselors for social action. In C. C. Lee & G. R. Walz (Eds.), *Social action: A mandate for counselors* (pp. 263–177). Alexandria, VA: American Counseling Association.

De La Cancela, V. (1989). Minority AIDS prevention: Moving beyond cultural perspectives toward sociopolitical empowerment. *AIDS Education and Prevention, 1*, 949–957.

DiClemente, R. J. (1998). Preventing sexually transmitted infections among adolescents: A clash of ideology and science. *Journal of the American Medical Association, 279*, 1574–1575.

Fan, H., Conner, R. F., & Villarreal, L. P. (1996). *AIDS: Science and society*. Sudbury, MA: Jones & Bartlett.

Gray, L. A. (1994). *Five years later: Students know more about AIDS, still have unprotected sex* [Press release]. Corvallis: Oregon State University Information Services.

Gray, L. A., & Harding, A. K. (1988). Confidentiality limits with clients who have the AIDS virus. *Journal of Counseling and Development, 66*, 219–223.

Gray, L. A., Eicken, S., & House, R. M. (1996). Human sexuality instruction in counselor education curricula: Changes over a 5-year period. *Family Journal, 4*(3), 208–216.

Harding, A. K., Gray, L. A., & Neal, M. (1993). Confidentiality limits with clients who have HIV: A review of ethical and legal guidelines and professional policies. *Journal of Counseling and Development, 71*, 297–305.

Harvey, M. S., & Spigner, C. (1995). Factors associated with sexual behavior among adolescents: A multivariate analysis. *Adolescence, 30*, 253–264.

Henderson, C. W. (1998, January 15). Study reveals views of young people toward sex, health, AIDS. *AIDS Weekly Plus*, pp. 18–19.

House, R. M., Eicken, S., & Gray, L. A. (1995). A national survey of counselor education programs regarding HIV/AIDS. *Journal of Counseling and Development, 74*, 5–11.

House, R. M., & Walker, C. M. (1993). Preventing AIDS via education. *Journal of Counseling and Development, 71*, 282–289.

Koop, C. E. (1988). In *AIDS and the education of our children* (pp. 5–35). Washington, DC: U.S. Department of Education.

Levy, J., Hoffman, A., Kramer, S., Landis, J., Shimabukaro, J., & Oshiro, L. (1984). Isolation of lymphocytopathic retroviruses from San Francisco patients with AIDS. *Science, 225*, 840–842.

Levy, S. R., Perhats, C., Weeks, K., Handler, A. S., Zhy, C., & Flay, B. R. (1995). Impact of a school-based AIDS prevention program on risk and protective behavior for newly sexually active students. *Journal of School Health, 65*, 145–151.

Manuel, C., Enel, P., Charrel, J., Reviron, D., Larher, M. P., Thirion, X., & Sanmarco, J. L. (1990). The ethical approach to AIDS: A bibliographical review. *Journal of Medical Ethics, 16*, 14–27.

Mays, V. M., & Cochran, S. D. (1988). Issues in the perception of AIDS risk and risk reduction activities by African American and Hispanic/Latina women. *American Psychologist, 43*, 949–957.

Moffatt, B., Spiegel, J., Parrish, S., & Helquist, M. (1989). *AIDS: A self-care manual.* Santa Monica, CA: IBS Press.

Rosenberg, P. S., & Biggar, R. J. (1998). Trends in HIV incidence among young adults in the United States. *Journal of the American Medical Association, 229*, 1894–1899.

Smith, K. W., McGraw, S., Crawford, S. L., Costa, L. A., & McKinlay, J. B. (1993). HIV risk among Latino adolescents in two New England cities. *American Journal of Public Health, 83*, 1395–1399.

Smith, M. U., & Katner, H. P. (1995). Quasi-experimental evaluation of three AIDS prevention activities for maintaining knowledge, improving attitudes, and changing risk behaviors of high school seniors. *AIDS Education and Prevention, 7*, 391–402.

Steitz J. A., & Munn, J. A. (1993). Adolescents and AIDS: Knowledge and attitude. *Adolescence, 28*, 609–619.

Stewart, S. A., & Beazley, R. P. (1993). Meeting a person with AIDS in the classroom: An evaluation. *Canadian Journal of Public Health, 84*, 265–267.

Weinstein, N. D. (1984). Why it won't happen to me: Perceptions of risk factors and susceptibility. *Health Psychology, 3*, 431–457.

APPENDIX 10–1

NATIONAL AIDS RESOURCES

Advocates for Youth
1025 Vermont Avenue, NW, Suite 200
Washington, DC 20005
Phone: (202) 347-5700
E-mail: www.advocatesforyouth.org

Advocates for Youth (formerly the Center for Population Options), a national education and advocacy organization, is dedicated to improving the quality of life of adolescents by preventing risk-taking behaviors and too early childbearing. Advocates for Youth offers a variety of services, including training for youth services professionals, materials development and distribution, peer education, and technical assistance. The Advocates for Youth Resource Center maintains an extensive collection of materials, the focus of which is major journals, including back issues on adolescent sexuality issues. The center also houses books and newspaper articles as well as a large video collection on topics such as HIV/AIDS, adolescents, pregnancy, and general family planning issues.

AIDS Information Network
1211 Chestnut Street
Philadelphia, PA 19107
Phone: (215) 575-1125
E-mail: aidsinfo@cr.tpath.org

The AIDS Information Network (AIN), formerly the AIDS Library of Philadelphia, provides comprehensive, current information on all aspects of HIV/AIDS to anyone who wants it. The AIDS Information Network is the largest AIDS-related lending library designed for public use in the United States and one of the few AIDS organizations with a trained librarian on staff. The library provides referrals, a newsletter, general and specific information on HIV/AIDS, research assistance, displays, speakers, and bibliographies and resource listings.

American Civil Liberties Union Foundation, AIDS Project
125 Broad Street, 18th Floor
New York, NY 10004-2400
Phone: (212) 576-2627
E-mail: aclu@aclu.org; www.aclu.org/

The AIDS Project of the American Civil Liberties Union (ACLU) Foundation undertakes litigation, public policy advocacy, and public education on civil liberties issues raised by the AIDS crisis. The project is headquartered in New York, staffed by four attorneys and two support personnel, and supplemented by a legislative expert in Washington, D.C., and five ACLU affiliate attorneys whose efforts focus on HIV/AIDS-related issues.

American Foundation for AIDS Research
120 Wall Street, 13th Floor
New York, NY 10005-3902
Phone: (212) 806-1600; (800) 392 6327
E-mail: www.amfar.org/content.html

The American Foundation for AIDS Research (AmFAR) is the nation's leading nonprofit organization dedicated to the support of HIV/AIDS research, education, prevention, and sound public policy. AmFAR identifies unmet needs in HIV/AIDS biomedical research (including clinical research), the social sciences, education for prevention, and public policy development. The foundation has provided nearly $58 million to innovative projects in these vital areas. In support of scientific research, AmFAR selects innovative proposals and approaches, and awards grants in basic science, social research, clinical research, public policy, and education.

CDC National AIDS Clearinghouse
P.O. Box 6003
Rockville, MD 20849-6003
Phone: (800) 458-5231
E-mail: www.cdcnpin.org/

The Centers for Disease Control and Prevention (CDC) National AIDS Clearinghouse (NAC) is a national reference, referral, and publication distribution service for AIDS and HIV information. CDC NAC is a comprehensive information service for public health professionals, educators, social service workers, attorneys, human resource managers, and employers. Information services are provided by telephone or mail. The clearinghouse maintains several computerized databases, which reference specialists with a broad knowledge of AIDS organizations and materials access to answer inquiries, make referrals, and help locate publications about HIV infection and AIDS.

CDC National AIDS Hotline

P.O. Box 13827
Research Triangle Park, NC 27709
Phone: (800) 342-AIDS
E-mail: nahl@asha.emcdc.gov

The Centers for Disease Control and Prevention (CDC) National AIDS Hotline provides current and accurate information about HIV infection and AIDS to the general public. Callers access the hotline any time, day or night, to receive information. The hotline provides callers with descriptive information about HIV and AIDS; confidential information about preventing and reducing the risk of transmitting HIV infections; information about counseling, testing, and support services; referrals for local legal, financial, and treatment resources; and HIV/AIDS publications.

Center for Women Policy Studies, National Resource Center on Women and AIDS

1211 Connecticut Avenue, Suite 312
Washington, DC 20036
Phone: (202) 872-1770

The Center for Women Policy Studies established the National Resource Center on Women and AIDS to fill the vacuum in public policy discussion of HIV/AIDS and to address, from women's perspectives, critical policy issues for women of color and low-income women related to the AIDS crisis. A centralized information resource for researchers, policy makers, advocates, and caregivers, the resource center annually publishes the *Guide to Resources on Women and AIDS,* with a state-by-state directory of programs serving women and case studies of exemplary programs. The center develops policy options to ensure that women's needs are met in biomedical and behavioral research, clinical trials of AIDS treatments, development of HIV prevention strategies and risk reduction education, and delivery of health care and social services.

Gay Men's Health Crisis

119 West 24th Street
New York, NY 10011-0022
Phone: (212) 807–6664
E-mail: www.gmhc.org/index.html

The Gay Men's Health Crisis (GMHC) is a community-based, volunteer AIDS service organization that pursues a threefold mission: services, education, and advocacy for people whose lives are affected by HIV. GMHC provides individual and group support, financial advocacy, recreational opportunities, and crisis intervention services. Legal services are provided to ensure that people with HIV infection can live full, productive lives in the face of possible legal difficulties. GMHC uses many avenues in addition to a hotline to reach its audiences: publications, videos, safer sex workshops, outreach into communities of color, information tables on city streets, distribution of condoms and safer sex guidelines to bars and clubs, and educational programs for mental health professionals and employers.

Hemophilia and AIDS/HIV Network for the Dissemination of Information, National Hemophilia Foundation
116 West 32nd Street, 11th Floor
New York, NY 10001
Phone: (212) 328-3777; (800) 42-Handi
E-mail: handi@hemophilia.org; www.hemophilia.org

As the HIV/AIDS information center of the National Hemophilia Foundation (NHF), the Hemophilia and AIDS/HIV Network for the Dissemination of Information (HANDI) is the hemophilia community's link to available resources dealing with hemophilia and HIV. HANDI provides information, resources, and referrals on hemophilia and HIV/AIDS to people with hemophilia, their families, and the professionals who care for them, as well as to NHF chapters, other hemophilia organizations, and the general public.

Multicultural Training Resource Center, Multicultural AIDS Resource Center
1540 Market Street, Suite 320
San Francisco, CA 94102
Phone: (415) 777-3229; (800) 871-6688
E-mail: marcc@polarisinc.com

The Multicultural Training Resource Center (MTRC) of San Francisco was established in 1984 as the first national center to provide multicultural and culturally specific HIV/AIDS and substance abuse prevention services. MTRC views multiculturalism as a concept that celebrates culture and cultural differences without limiting its definition to race, ethnicity, and color, thereby including women, the elderly, lesbians, homosexuals, and the homeless.

National Association of People With AIDS
1413 K Street, NW, 7th Floor
Washington, DC 20005
Phone: (202) 898-0414
E-mail: www.napwa.org

The National Association of People With AIDS (NAPWA) serves as a national voice for all those infected and affected by HIV/AIDS. Funded by the Centers for Disease Control and Prevention, private corporations, other donors, and membership fees, NAPWA achieves its mission through three mechanisms: (1) information dissemination, (2) public policy advocacy, and (3) technical assistance to organizations. NAPWA's primary requesters are people with HIV/AIDS and related AIDS service organizations, including NAPWA's affiliate people with AIDS coalitions.

National Coalition of Hispanic Health and Human Services Organizations
1501 16th Street, NW
Washington, DC 20036
Phone: (202) 387-5000
E-mail: info@cossmho.org; www.cossmho.org

The mission of the National Coalition of Hispanic Health and Human Services Organizations (COSSMHO) is to improve the health and well-being of all Hispanic communities in the United States by conducting national demonstration programs, coordinating research, and serving as a source of information, technical assistance, and policy analysis. COSSMHO addresses HIV/AIDS in the Hispanic community through the Community HIV and AIDS Technical Assistance Network (CHATAN), which provides technical assistance on the local, state, regional, and national levels by identifying, implementing, and assessing culturally appropriate intervention strategies.

National Minority AIDS Council
1931 13th Street, NW
Washington, DC, 20009
Phone: (202) 483-6622
E-mail: www.nmac.org

The National Minority AIDS Council (NMAC) is dedicated to developing leadership within communities of color to address the challenges of HIV/AIDS. NMAC provides technical assistance, public policy advocacy, conferences, research and treatment advocacy, and three newsletters: *CONNECTIONS* (technical assistance), *Update* (public policy), and *Treatment Alert* (research and treatment advocacy).

National Native American AIDS Prevention Center
3515 Grand Avenue, Suite 1200
Oakland, CA 94610
Phone: (510) 444-2051
E-mail: nnapc@aol.com; www.nnaapc.org

The National Native American AIDS Prevention Center (NNAAPC) is directed and managed by and for American Indians, Alaskan natives, and Hawaiian natives. NNAAPC operates a national, toll-free, Indian-specific, AIDS hotline and a clearinghouse for native-specific HIV/AIDS and sexually transmitted disease information. The center also publishes a yearly newsletter, *Seasons.*

National Pediatric and Family HIV Resource Center
University of Medicine and Dentistry of New Jersey
Francis-Xavier Bagnood Center
30 Bergen Street, ADM C #4
Newark, NJ 07103
Phone: (973) 972-0410
E-mail: ortegaes@umdnj.edu

The National Pediatric HIV Resource Center (NPHRC) serves professionals who care for children and families with HIV infection and AIDS. The center, funded in part by the Maternal and Child Health Bureau of the Health Resources and Services Administration, offers consultation, technical assistance, and training for medical, social service, and planning personnel. The center, which is staffed by professionals including a physician, nurse, psychologist, and social worker, receives numerous requests for assistance from providers working with HIV-infected children as well as from the general public. Consultation is provided to organizations designing new programs and modifying existing ones to serve children, youth, and families with HIV. Technical assistance is provided in areas such as developing family education materials, conducting needs assessments, evaluating programs, and designing systems of care that are family centered, community based, and culturally competent. Training and clinical fellowships are available to physicians, nurses, social workers, mental health professionals, and other providers.

National School Boards Association, HIV/AIDS Education Project
1680 Duke Street
Alexandria, VA 22314
Phone: (703) 838-6722
E-mail: www.nsba.org/schoolhealth/

Funded by the Centers for Disease Control and Prevention, the HIV/AIDS Education Project of the National School Boards Association (NSBA) helps school board members, superintendents, and other school-affiliated personnel to deal effectively with the issues of HIV and AIDS in schools.

Planned Parenthood Federation of America
810 Seventh Avenue
New York, NY 10019
Phone: (212) 541-7800
E-mail: www.plannedparenthood.org

The Planned Parenthood Federation of America (PPFA) is a federation of 132 nonprofit affiliates operating 900 clinics in 49 states and the District of Columbia. The affiliates provide reproductive health care and sexuality education to nearly 5 million men and women each year. Services include contraception, abortion, sterilization, and infertility services. PPFA also sponsors and advocates biomedical, socioeconomic, and demographic research regarding reproductive health issues. PPFA produces educational materials, acts as a clearinghouse, and provides community education through the affiliates. Most PPFA affiliates offer anonymous or confidential HIV testing and counseling to clients. All affiliates provide HIV educational materials, safer sex counseling, and referral services.

Project Inform
205 13th Street, Suite 2001
San Francisco, CA 94103
Phone: (415) 558-8669; (800) 822-7422 (hotline)

The three main goals of Project Inform (PI) are (1) to inform those infected by HIV (or at risk of infection) of lifesaving strategies such as early diagnosis and early intervention, (2) to give people and their health care providers the means to make informed choices about the most promising treatment options, and (3) to change research and regulatory polices that delay or prevent access to treatment. Anyone can call the toll-free treatment hotline for up-to-date HIV treatment information.

Sex Information and Education Council of the United States
130 West 42nd Street, Suite 3500
New York, NY 10036
Phone: (212) 819-9770

The Sex information and Education Council of the United States (SIECUS) was founded to provide health care professionals, educators, policy makers, students, and ethnic minorities with information and education on family life and related issues. SIECUS provides information to more than 12,000 people a year, serving all populations and racial and ethnic minorities. SIECUS' Mary S. Calderone Library provides library and information services by telephone or mail and in person at SIECUS headquarters in New York City. The library contains a unique collection of 5,000 sexuality-related resources, of which about 10% are related to HIV and AIDS. The AIDS collection comprises books, current journal articles, HIV/AIDS-related newsletters, and vertical files. The library is open by appointment for SIECUS members; information requests are accepted by telephone and mail.

11 | I Don't Want to Live: The Adolescent at Risk for Suicidal Behavior

David Capuzzi and Douglas R. Gross

The adolescent at risk for suicidal preoccupation and behavior has become an increasing concern for schools and communities throughout the United States. Between 1960 and 1988 the suicide rate among adolescents increased much more dramatically than it has in the general population. The adolescent suicide rate rose by 200% compared to an increase in the general population of approximately 17% (Garland & Zigler, 1993). Much of the current literature (Coy, 1995: Zenere & Lazarus, 1997) ranks suicide, following accidents, as the second leading cause of death for our nation's youth.

The topic of adolescent suicide has been a major focus for newspaper features, television specials, and legislative initiatives as the problem of adolescent suicide has reached epidemic proportions (Hafen & Frandsen, 1986). Estimates such as "7,000 teenagers each year commit suicide, while an additional 400,000 try unsuccessfully to end their own lives" (Hafen & Frandsen, 1986) are based on incomplete data (Curran, 1987) yet provide the basis for ranking suicide as the second leading cause of death among the 11- to 24-year-old age group. According to some experts (Hafen & Frandsen, 1986), one teenager attempts suicide every 90 seconds, and one completes the act of suicide every 90 minutes.

This chapter first defines the problem by looking at ethnic differences, methods, risk factors, precipitants, myths, and profiles, and then presents a case study and explores individual, family, and school and community approaches to prevention. The chapter continues with thorough examination of intervention strategies, including guidelines for identifying, counseling, and managing youth at risk for suicide as well as guidelines for actions to take in the case of attempted or completed suicide. A brief look at adaptations for diversity concludes the chapter.

PROBLEM DEFINITION

Ethnic and Gender Differences

The suicide rate is higher among adolescent males than among females (although adolescent women attempt three to four times as often as adolescent men). Caucasian, adolescent males complete suicide more often than any other ethnic group (Canetto & Sakinofsky, 1998; Metha, Weber, & Webb, 1998). A number of explanations to account for the differences in rates between genders and races have been proposed, but no clear answers have been found. As early as 1954 (Henry & Short) an explanation based on a reciprocal model of suicide and homicide was suggested in which some groups were seen as more likely to express frustration and aggression inwardly and others were more likely to express it outwardly. Empirical data, however, do not support this reciprocal relationship. Some models used to explain racial differences in suicide have suggested that the extreme stress and discrimination that African Americans in this country confront helps to create protective factors, such as extended networks of social support, that lower the risk and keep the suicide rates for African American adolescents lower than those of Caucasian adolescents (Bush, 1976; Gibbs, 1988). Noteworthy, however, is that despite the overall pattern suggested by the data, during the period between 1980 and 1994, the suicide rates for African American adolescent males showed a 320% increase in the 10 to 14 age group and a 196% increase in the 15 to 19 age group (Metha et al., 1998).

Native Americans have the highest adolescent suicide rates of any ethnic group in the United States. There is considerable variability across tribes. The Navajos, for example, have suicide rates close to the national average of 11 to 13 per 100,000 of the population; some Apache groups have rates as high as 43 per 100,000 (Berlin, 1987). The high suicide rates in the Native American population have been associated with factors such as alcoholism and substance abuse, unemployment, availability of firearms, and child abuse and neglect (Berman & Jobes, 1991). In general, less traditional tribes have higher rates of suicide than do more traditional tribes (Wyche, Obolensky, & Glood, 1990). Suicide rates for both Asian American and Hispanic American adolescents continue to be lower than those for African American and Native American youth even though the 1980–94 time period bore witness to much higer rates than previously recorded (Metha et al., 1998).

Methods

The use of firearms outranks all other methods of completed suicides; firearms are now being used by both genders. Studies in the United States have shown that availability of guns increases the risk of adolescent suicide (Brent et al., 1993). The second most common method is hanging, and the third most common is gassing. Males use firearms and hanging more often than do females, but females use gassing and ingestion more often than do males for completed suicides (Berman & Jobes, 1991). The most common method used by suicide attempters is ingestion or overdose.

Risk Factors

As noted by Garland and Zigler (1993) and Shaffer and Craft (1999), the search for the etiology of suicide spans many areas of study. Risk factors that have been studied include neurotransmitter imbalances and genetic predictors, psychiatric disorders, poor self-efficacy and problem-solving skills, sexual or physical abuse, concerns over sexual identity or orientation, availability of firearms, substance abuse, violent rock music, divorce in families, unemployment and labor strikes, loss, disability, giftedness, and phases of the moon. It is important to note that almost all adolescent suicide victims have experienced some form of psychiatric illness. The most prevalent psychiatric disorders among completed adolescent suicides appear to be affective disorders, conduct disorder or antisocial personality disorder, and substance abuse (Shaffer, 1988; Shaffer & Craft, 1999). Among affective disorders, particular attention should be paid to bipolar illness and depressive disorder with a comorbidity such as attention deficit disorder, conduct disorder, or substance abuse (Rohde, Lewinsohn, & Seeley, 1991).

The suicide of a family member or a close friend of the family can be a risk factor for adolescent suicide; prior attempts also escalate risk. Further, an adolescent experiencing a physical illness that is chronic or terminal can be at higher risk (Capuzzi, 1994). Many researchers have studied cognitive and coping style factors, such as generalized feelings of hopelessness and poor interpersonal problem-solving skills, as risk factors for adolescent suicide (Garland & Zigler, 1993). High neuroticism and low extraversion, high impulsiveness, low self-esteem, and an external locus of control have also been studied and can be used to predict risk (Beautrais, Joyce, & Mulder, 1999). The best single predictor of death by suicide seems to be a previous suicide attempt (Shaffer, Garland, Gould, Fisher, & Trautman, 1988). Some studies have indicated that as many as 40% of attempters will make additional suicide attempts and that as many as 10% to 14% of these individuals will complete suicide (Diekstra, 1989).

Precipitants

Completed suicide is often precipitated by what, to the adolescent, is interpreted as a shameful or humiliating experience (e.g., failure at school or work, interpersonal conflict with a romantic partner or parent). There is mounting evidence indicating that adolescents who do not cope well with major and minor life events and who do not have family and peer support are more likely to have suicidal ideation (Mazza & Reynolds, 1998). The humiliation and frustration experienced by some adolescents struggling with conflicts connected with their sexual orientation may precipitate suicidal behavior (Harry, 1989), although being gay or lesbian, in and of itself, may not be a risk factor for suicide (Blumenthal, 1991). Hoberman and Garfinkel (1988) found the most common precipitant of suicide in a sample of 229 youth suicides to be an argument with a boyfriend, a girlfriend, or a parent (19%) followed by school problems (14%). Other humiliating experiences, such as corporal punishment and abuse, also serve as precipitants; the experience of sexual or physical assault seems to be a particularly significant risk factor for adolescent women (Hoberman & Garfinkel, 1988).

Understanding the Myths

The biggest problem connected with the topic of adolescents at-risk for suicide is the fact that parents, teachers, mental health professionals, and the adolescent population itself are not made aware of a variety of myths and misconceptions as well as the signs and symptoms associated with adolescent suicide. Because subsequent case study, prevention, and intervention information in this chapter is based on prior awareness of these two areas, the information that follows about myths and then the suicidal profile is pertinent.

Disqualifying the myths and misconceptions surrounding the topic of adolescent suicide at the beginning of any initiative to provide prevention, crisis management, and postvention services is important. Some of the most commonly cited misconceptions include the following (Capuzzi, 1988, 1994; Capuzzi & Gross, 1996):

- *Adolescents who talk about suicide never attempt suicide.* This is probably one of the most widely believed myths. All suicidal adolescents make attempts (either verbally or nonverbally) to let a friend, parent, or teacher know that life seems to be too difficult to bear. Because a suicide attempt is a cry for help to identify options, other than death, to decrease the pain of living, always take verbal or nonverbal threats seriously. Never assume such threats are only for the purpose of attracting attention or manipulating others. It is better to respond and enlist the aid of a professional than it is to risk the loss of a life.
- *Suicide happens with no warning.* Suicidal adolescents leave numerous hints and warnings about their suicidal ideations and intentions. Clues can be verbal or in the form of suicidal gestures such as taking

a few sleeping pills, becoming accident prone, and reading stories focused on death and violence. Quite often, the social support network of the suicidal adolescent is small. As stress escalates and options, other than suicide, seem few, suicidal adolescents may withdraw from an already small circle of friends, making it more difficult for others to notice warning signs.

- *Adolescents from affluent families attempt or complete suicide more often than adolescents from poor families.* This, too, is a myth. Suicide is evenly divided among socioeconomic groups.

- *Once an adolescent is suicidal, he or she is suicidal forever.* Most adolescents are suicidal for a limited period of time. In the experience of the authors, the 24- to 72-hour period around the peak of the crisis is the most dangerous. If counselors and other mental health professionals can monitor such a crisis period and transition the adolescent into long-term counseling/therapy, there is a strong possibility there will never be another suicidal crisis. The more effort that is made to help an adolescent identify stressors and develop problem-solving skills during this postsuicidal crisis period and the more time that passes, the better the prognosis.

- *If an adolescent attempts suicide and survives, he or she will never make an additional attempt.* There is a difference between an adolescent who experiences a suicidal crisis but does not attempt suicide, as in the example just given, and the adolescent who actually makes an attempt. An adolescent who carries through with an attempt has identified a plan, had access to the means, and maintained a high enough energy level to follow through. He or she may believe that a second or third attempt may be possible. If counseling/therapy has not taken place or has not been successful during the period following an attempt, additional attempts may be made. Most likely, each follow-up attempt will become more lethal.

- *Adolescents who attempt or complete suicide always leave notes.* Only a small percentage of suicidal adolescents leave notes. This is a common myth and one of the reasons why many deaths are classified and reported as accidents by friends, family members, physicians, and investigating officers when suicide has actually taken place.

- *Most adolescent suicides happen late at night or during the predawn hours.* This myth is not true for the simple reason that most suicidal adolescents actually want help. Mid to late morning and mid to late afternoon are the time periods when most attempts are made because a family member or friend is more likely to be around to intervene than would be the case late at night or very early in the morning.

- *Never use the word* suicide *when talking to adolescents because using the word gives some adolescents the idea.* This is simply not true; you cannot put the idea of suicide into the mind of an adolescent who is not suicidal. If an adolescent is suicidal and you use the word, it can help an adolescent verbalize feelings of despair and assist with establishing rapport and trust. If a suicidal adolescent thinks you know he or she is suicidal and realizes you are afraid to approach the subject, it can bring the adolescent closer to the point of making an attempt by contributing to feelings of despair and helplessness.

- *Every adolescent who attempts suicide is depressed.* Depression is a common component of the profile of a suicidal adolescent, but depression is not always a component. Many adolescents simply want to escape their present set of circumstances and do not have the problem-solving skills to cope more effectively, lower stress, and work toward a more promising future.

- *Suicide is hereditary.* Suicide tends to run in families, just as physical and sexual abuse does, and has led to the development of this myth. Suicide is not genetically inherited. Members of families do, however, share the same emotional climate because parents model coping and stress management skills as well as high or low levels of self-esteem. The suicide of one family member tends to increase the risk among other family members that suicide will be viewed as an appropriate way to solve a problem or set of problems.

    In conjunction with this myth, it should be noted that some adolescents are predisposed, because of genetic factors, to depression as a response to life circumstances. Because of the connection between depression and suicide, many have mistakenly come to the belief that suicide can be genetically inherited.

Recognizing the Profile

A number of experts (Beautrais et al., 1999; Capuzzi, 1994; Capuzzi & Golden, 1988; Curran, 1987; Davis, 1983; Hafen & Frandsen, 1986; Hussain & Vandiver, 1984; Johnson & Maile, 1987; Mazza & Reynolds, 1998) believe that about 90% of the adolescents who complete suicide (and lethal first attempts can result in completions) give cues to those around them in advance. Whether these cues or hints are limited or numerous depends on the adolescent because each adolescent has a unique familial and social history. It is important for adults (and young people as well) to recognize the signs and symptoms to facilitate intervention. A comment such as "I talked with her a few days ago and she was fine—I am so shocked to learn of her death" may mean that no one was aware of the warning signs. One of the essential components of any staff development effort is teaching the profile of the suicidal or potentially suicidal adolescent so that referral and intervention can take place. Behavioral, verbal, and cognitive cues (thinking patterns and motivations) and personality traits are the four areas described here.

Behaviors.

- *Lack of concern about personal welfare.* Some adolescents who are suicidal may not be able to talk about their problems or give verbal hints that they are at risk for attempting suicide. Sometimes such adolescents become unconcerned with their personal safety in the hopes that someone will take notice. Experimenting with medication, accepting dares from friends, reckless driving, and carving initials into the skin of forearms are all ways of gesturing or letting others know "I am in pain and don't know how to continue through life if nothing changes."
- *Changes in social patterns.* Relatively unusual or sudden changes in an adolescent's social behavior can provide strong cues that such a young person is feeling desperate. A cooperative teenager may suddenly start breaking the house rules that parents have never had to worry about enforcing. An involved adolescent may begin to withdraw from activities at school or end long-term friendships with school- and community-related peers. A stable, easygoing teenager may start arguing with teachers, employers, or other significant adults with whom prior conflict was never experienced. Such pattern changes should be noted and talked about with an adolescent who does not seem to be behaving as he or she usually has in the past.
- *A decline in school achievement.* Many times, adolescents who are becoming more and more depressed and preoccupied with suicidal thoughts are unable to devote the time required to complete homework assignments and maintain grades. If such an adolescent has a history of interest in the school experience and has maintained a certain grade point average, loss of interest in academic pursuits can be a strong indication that something is wrong. The key to assessing such a situation is the length of time the decline lasts.
- *Concentration and clear thinking difficulties.* Suicidal adolescents usually experience marked changes in thinking and logic. As stress and discomfort escalate, logical problem solving and option generation become more difficult. It becomes easier and easier to stay focused on suicide as the only solution as reasoning and thinking become more confused and convoluted. "It may become more and more obvious that the adolescent's attention span is shorter and that verbal comments bear little relationship to the topic of a conversation" (Capuzzi, 1988, p. 6).
- *Altered patterns of eating and sleeping.* Sudden increases or decreases in appetite and weight, difficulty with sleeping, or wanting to sleep

all the time or all day can all be indicative of increasing preoccupation with suicidal thoughts. These altered patterns can offer strong evidence that something is wrong and that assistance is required.

- *Attempts to put personal affairs in order or to make amends.* Once a suicide plan and decision have been reached, adolescents will often make last minute efforts to put their personal affairs in order. These efforts may take a variety of directions: attempts to make amends in relation to a troubled relationship, final touches on a project, reinstatement of an old or neglected friendship, the giving away of prized possessions (skis, jewelry, compact discs, collections).

- *Use or abuse of alcohol or drugs.* Sometimes troubled adolescents use or abuse alcohol or other drugs to lessen their feelings of despair or discontent. Initially, they may feel that the drug enhances their ability to cope and increases feelings of self-esteem. Unfortunately, the abuse of drugs decreases ability to communicate accurately and problem solve rationally. Thinking patterns become more skewed, impulse control lessens, and option identification decreases. Rapid onset of involvement with illicit or over-the-counter drugs is indicative of difficulty with relationships, problem solving, and ability to share feelings and communicate them to others.

- *Unusual interest in how others are feeling.* Suicidal adolescents often express considerable interest in how others are feeling. Because they are in pain, but may be unable to express their feelings and ask for help, they may reach out to peers (or adults) who seem to need help with the stresses of daily living. Such responsiveness may become a full-time pastime and serve to lessen preoccupation with self and to serve as a vehicle for communicating, "I wish you would ask me about my pain," or "Can't you see that I need help too?"

- *Preoccupation with death and violence themes.* Reading books or poetry in which death, violence, or suicide is the predominating theme can become the major interest of an adolescent who is becoming increasingly preoccupied with the possibility of suicide. Such adolescents may be undecided about the possibility of choosing death over life and may be working through aspects of such a decision with such reading. Other examples of such preoccupation can include listening to music that is violent; playing violent video games; writing short stories focused on death, dying, and loss; drawing or sketching that emphasizes destruction; or watching movies or videos that emphasize destruction to self and others.

- *Sudden improvement after a period of depression.* Suicidal adolescents often fool parents, teachers, and friends by appearing to be dramatically improved, after a period of prolonged depression, in a very short period of time. This improvement, which can sometimes take place overnight or during a 24-hour period, encourages friends and family to interpret such a change as a positive sign. It is not unusual for such a change to be the result of a suicide decision and the formulation of a concrete suicide plan on the part of the adolescent at risk. It may mean that the suicide attempt (and the potential of completion) is imminent and that the danger and crisis are peaking. The important point for family and friends to remember is that it is not really logical for a depression to lessen that rapidly. It takes time, effort, and, at times, medical assistance, to improve coping skills and lessen feelings of depression just as it took time (months or years) to develop nonadaptive responses to people and circumstances and feelings of hopelessness.

- *Sudden or increased promiscuity.* It is not unusual for an adolescent to experiment with sex during periods of suicidal preoccupation in an attempt to refocus attention or lessen feelings of isolation. Unfortunately, doing so sometimes complicates circumstances because of an unplanned pregnancy or an escalation of feelings of guilt.

Verbal Cues.   As noted by Schneidman, Farbverow, and Litman (1976), verbal statements can provide cues to self-destructive intentions. Such statements should be assessed and considered in relation to behavioral signs, changes in thinking patterns, motivations, and personality traits. There is no universal language or style for communicating suicidal intention. Some adolescents will openly and directly say something like "I am going to commit suicide" or "I am thinking of taking my life." Others will be far less direct and make statements such as "I'm going home," "I wonder what death is like," "I'm tired," "She'll be sorry for how she has treated me," or "Someday I'll show everyone just how serious I am about some of the things I've said."

The important thing for counselors, parents, teachers, and friends to remember is that when someone says something that could be interpreted in a number of ways, it is always best to ask for clarification. It is not a good idea to make assumptions about what a statement means or to minimize the importance of what is being communicated. Suicidal adolescents often have a long-term history of difficulty with communicating feelings and asking for support. Indirect statements may be made in the hopes that someone will respond with support and interest and provide or facilitate a referral for professional assistance (Capuzzi & Gross, 1996).

Thinking Patterns and Motivations.   In addition to the areas previously described, thinking patterns and motivations of suicidal adolescents can also be assessed and evaluated. For such an assessment to occur, it is necessary to encourage self-disclosure to learn about changes in an adolescent's cognitive set and distortions of logic and problem-solving ability. As noted by Velkoff and Huberty (1988), the motivations of suicidal adolescents can be understood more readily when suicide is viewed as fulfilling one of three primary functions: (1) an avoidance function, which protects the individual from the pain perceived to be associated with a relationship or set of circumstances; (2) a control function, which enables an adolescent to believe he or she has gained control of someone or something thought to be out of control, hopeless, or disastrous; and (3) a communication function, which lets others know that something is wrong or that too much pain or too many injuries have been accumulated.

Suicidal adolescents often distort their thinking patterns in conjunction with the three functions of avoidance, control, and communication so that suicide becomes the best or only problem-solving option. Such distortions can take a number of directions. All-or-nothing thinking, for example, can enable an adolescent to view a situation in such a polarized way that the only two options seem to be continuing to be miserable and depressed or carrying out a suicide plan; no problem-solving options to cope with or overcome problems may seem possible (Capuzzi, 1988; Capuzzi & Gross, 1996). Identification of a single event that is then applied to all events is another cognitive distortion, that of overgeneralization. Being left out of a party or trip to the mountains with friends may be used as evidence for being someone no one likes, a loser, or someone who will always be forgotten or left out. "I can't seem to learn the material for this class very easily" becomes "I'm never going to make it through school" or "I'll probably have the same difficulties when I start working full time." Adolescents who are experiencing stress and pain and who are becoming preoccupied with suicidal thoughts often experience more and more cognitive distortions. Such distortions result in self-talk that becomes more and more negative and more and more supportive of one of the following motivations for carrying through with a suicide plan:

- wanting to escape from a situation that seems (or is) intolerable (e.g., sexual abuse, conflict with peers or teachers, pregnancy);
- wanting to join someone who has died;
- wanting to attract the attention of family or friends;
- wanting to manipulate someone else;
- wanting to avoid punishment;
- wanting to be punished;
- wanting to control when or how death will occur (an adolescent with a chronic or terminal illness may be motivated in this way);
- wanting to end a conflict that seems unresolvable;
- wanting to punish the survivors; and
- wanting revenge.

Personality Traits. As noted by Capuzzi (1988), it would be ideal if the research on the profile of the suicidal adolescent provided practitioners with such a succinct profile of personality traits that teenagers at risk for suicide could be identified far in advance of any suicidal risk. Adolescents who fit the profile could then be assisted through individual and group counseling and other means. Although no consensus has yet been reached on the usual, typical, or average constellation of personality traits of the suicidal adolescent, researchers have agreed on a number of characteristics that seem to be common to many suicidal adolescents:

- *Low self-esteem.* A number of studies (Beautrais et al., 1999; Cull & Gill, 1982; Faigel, 1966; Stein & Davis, 1982; Stillion, McDowell, & Shamblin, 1984) have connected low self-esteem with suicide probability. The counseling experience of the authors as well as the experience of other practitioners seems to substantiate the relationship between low self-esteem and suicide probability. Almost all such clients have issues focused on feelings of low self-worth, and almost all such adolescents have experienced these self-doubts for an extended time period.
- *Hopelessness/helplessness.* Most suicidal adolescents report feeling hopeless and helpless in relation to their circumstances as well as their ability to cope with these circumstances. The research support (Beautrais et al., 1999; Cull & Gill, 1982; Jacobs, 1971; Kovacs, Beck, & Weissman, 1975; Peck, 1983) for verification of what clinicians report is growing. Most practitioners can expect to address this issue with suicidal clients and to identify a long-term history of feeling hopeless and helpless on the part of most clients.
- *Isolation.* Many, if not most, suicidal adolescents tend to develop a small network of social support. They may find it uncomfortable to make new friends and rely on a small number of friends for support and companionship. (This may be the reason why so often those around a suicide victim state they did not notice anything unusual. The suicidal adolescent may not be in the habit of getting close enough to others so that changes in behavior or outlook can be noted.) A number of authorities (Hafen, 1972; Kiev, 1977; Peck, 1983; Sommes, 1984; Stein & Davis, 1982) seem to support this observation.
- *High stress.* High stress coupled with poor stress management skills seem to be characteristic of the suicidal adolescent. A number of studies have addressed this trait in terms of low frustration tolerance (Cantor, 1976; Kiev, 1977).
- *Need to act out.* Behaviors such as truancy, running away, refusal to cooperate at home or at school, use or abuse of alcohol or other drugs, and experimentation with sex are frequently part of the pattern present in the life of a suicidal adolescent. Such behaviors may be manifestations of depression. Adults often remain so focused on the troublesome behavior connected with an adolescent's need to act out that underlying depressive episodes may be overlooked.

- *Need to achieve.* Sometimes adolescents who are suicidal exhibit a pattern of high achievement. This achievement may be focused on getting high grades, being the class clown, accepting the most dares, wearing the best clothes, or any one of numerous other possibilities. In the counseling experience of the authors, this emphasis on achievement often is a compensation for feelings of low self-esteem. Readers should be cautioned, however, about jumping to the conclusion that every adolescent who achieves at a high level is suicidal. This trait, along with all of the other traits and characteristics connected with the profile of the suicidal adolescent, must be assessed in the context of other observations.

- *Poor communication skills.* Suicidal adolescents often have a history of experiencing difficulty with expression of thoughts and feelings. Such adolescents may have trouble with identifying and labeling what they are feeling; self-expression seems awkward if not stressful. It is not unusual to discover that adolescents who have become preoccupied with suicidal thoughts have experienced a series of losses or disappointments that they have never been able to discuss and, understandably, integrate or resolve.

- *Other directedness.* Most suicidal adolescents are *other* rather than *inner* directed. They are what others have told them they are instead of what they want to be; they value what others have said they should value instead of what they deem to be of personal value and worth. This trait may also be linked to low self-esteem and may lead to feelings of helplessness or inability to control interactions or circumstances around them.

- *Guilt.* Usually connected with feelings of low self-esteem and a need to be other directed, the guilt experienced by many suicidal adolescents is bothersome and sometimes linked to a wanting-to-be-punished motivation for suicide. "Nothing I do seems to be good enough" or "I feel so bad because I disappointed them" or "I should not have made that decision and should have known better" are statements common to the guilt-ridden suicidal adolescent.

- *Depression.* Depression is a major element (Mazza & Reynolds, 1998) in the total profile of the suicidal adolescent. Hafen and Frandsen (1986) pointed out that there are sometimes differences between depression in an adult and depression in an adolescent. Adults are often despondent, tearful, sad, or incapable of functioning as usual. Although adolescents sometimes exhibit these characteristics, they may also respond with anger, rebelliousness, truancy, running away, and using and abusing drugs. Those adults and peers who associate depression only with feelings of sadness and despondency may not recognize depression in adolescents who mask the depression with behavior that creates discomfort in family and school environments.

As noted by Capuzzi (1988),

> Given the complexity of being an adolescent in the late 1980s, coupled
> with the normal ups and downs of the developmental stage of adoles-
> cence, it is normal for every adolescent to experience short periods of
> depression. But when depressive periods become more and more fre-
> quent, longer and longer, and of such intensity that the adolescent has
> difficulty functioning at school and at home, they could be a strong
> warning sign of suicide potential, especially if other aspects of behavior,
> verbalization, motivations, and cognitive distortions have been
> observed. (p. 10)

It is extremely important for counselors and other professionals who
may be working with suicidal adolescents to complete additional
coursework or training experiences to learn about the different types
of depression. Although familiarity with resources and guidelines
such as those provided by McWhirter & Kigin (1988) and the *DSM-
IV* (American Psychiatric Association, 1994) are readily available to
mental health practitioners, case supervision and consultation may
be needed to determine accurately the nature of a depressive
episode. Well-meaning practitioners frequently fail to discriminate
between depression created by a constellation of factors (negative
self-talk, poor problem-solving skills, high stress) and depression
that is a result of the body chemistry an adolescent inherited at birth.
Treatment or counseling plans are different based on the kind of
depression being experienced. Counselors, therapists, and core or
crisis team members need to liaison with nurse practitioners and
psychiatrists when medical assessment and subsequent medication
are appropriate for depression.

- *Poor problem-solving skills.* Most parents notice differences in the
  problem-solving ability of their children. Some children are more
  resourceful than others in identification of problem resolution
  options. Suicidal adolescents seem, in the experience of the authors,
  to have less ability to develop solutions to troublesome situations or
  uncomfortable relationships. This may be a reason why suicidal preoccupation can progress from a cognitive focus to an applied plan
  with little dissonance created by the formulation and consideration
  of other problem-solving options and decisions.

CASE STUDY

Jim was a 17-year-old high school junior and the son of affluent, well-edu-
cated parents. Jim's dad was a successful attorney, and his mom was an
assistant superintendent for the local school district. Jim's sister, Janell,

was 15, well liked, a cheerleader, and involved in a variety of school and community-related activities. Janell had a beautiful singing voice and frequently accepted prominent roles in school, church, and community musical productions.

Although Jim had a few close friends, he preferred to spend most of his time reading and studying and was a straight "A" student. He accepted an opportunity to spend most of his junior year traveling and studying in Europe and thought such an experience would provide an excellent educational option as well as time away from his parents. Jim resented the high expectations his parents placed on both him and Janell and felt that his father did not approve of an earlier decision not to participate in varsity sports. Both parents, Jim felt, pressured him to be involved in school and community civic and social organizations; Jim preferred more solitary and intellectual pursuits. Jim felt somewhat self-conscious and awkward in social situations and never felt that he could present himself as well as his sister or in a way acceptable to his parents. He felt directed and criticized by both parents and resented the fact that his parents always seemed too busy to listen to him talk about things of importance to him. He really resented his father's lack of approval and felt that no one in his family seemed to really understand his point of view.

Jim had experienced periodic episodes of depression, and because he had decided that it was best not to talk with family members about his feelings, he usually tried to keep his sister and his parents from knowing that he felt really down. Jim noticed that his depression was worst when he was under a lot of stress with respect to completing class assignments and during times that his parents pressured him into social situations. Bob, Jim's best friend, got so concerned about Jim toward the end of the exam period in the spring of their sophomore year that he told Jim's parents. Jim's parents took him to a psychiatrist who prescribed an antidepressant and recommended weekly therapy. Jim's parents were angry with their son, resented the additional expense, and demanded that Jim get better as soon as possible. Janell hoped her friends would not find out because she was in the midst of being nominated for Queen of the Rose Festival and had already been selected as a Rose Festival Princess. Jim did not like the psychiatrist and felt as criticized by him as he did by his parents. He disliked the side effects of the medication, often skipped his weekly therapy session, and could hardly wait to leave home in late August to attend the orientation session at Cambridge prior to initiation of his travel/study itinerary.

Shortly after Thanksgiving Jim's parents received a call from Switzerland; Jim had nearly died after an overdose of his medication and was recovering in a hospital in Zurich. Jim was sent home during the first part of December.

APPROACHES TO PREVENTION

Individual

Individually focused preventive counseling with Jim could have been focused in several ways. Jim could have benefitted from a therapeutic relationship that included self-esteem enhancement as part of the treatment plan. If counseling/therapy had been initiated during elementary school years, Jim might not have responded with depression and, to a great extent, isolation and withdrawal from all but a few friends who provided a limited network of social support. Jim might also have been encouraged to share feelings and communicate with his parents. He also could have benefitted from assertiveness training to assist him with sending needed messages to his parents at times when his parents were more preoccupied with career-related responsibilities and interests. Jim's counselor/therapist could probably have worked with him to become more aware of stressors, and more adept at managing stress and/or removing stressors from his environment. Possibly, the combination of efforts made by his parents in couples counseling and by Jim in the context of his individual work could have resulted in outcomes very different than those described in the case study.

Family

Most suicidal adolescents have developed their at-risk profiles over time beginning during early childhood. In families in which there is more than one child, it is often easy for parents to identify differences in self-esteem, communication skills, stress management, and problem solving. By the time a child is in elementary school, there may be visible indicators or traits that, if no intervention takes place, result in the child's involvement in one or several at-risk behaviors. In the opinion of the authors, such a child, by the time the middle school or junior high transition occurs, is vulnerable to becoming pregnant, contracting AIDS, abusing drugs, developing an eating disorder, dropping out of school, or attempting or completing suicide.

Jim's family could have noted Jim's low self-esteem, discomfort with respect to sharing feelings, depression, response to stress, poor stress-management skills, and his resentment toward them. They might have been able to detect changes in his thinking patterns or fluctuations in day-to-day behaviors had they developed a relationship with him that included more open lines of communication. Jim's parents didn't realize that their son experienced even higher levels of stress in conjunction with the European study program and felt compelled to succeed at all costs. Jim also did not anticipate the amount of interchange and collaboration required by the group-living situations he found himself in as he and his peers and teachers traveled from one community to another and had begun to feel less self-assured than ever. Ideally, Jim's parents should have sought counseling assistance for themselves and their son when Jim was in elementary school.

School and Community

There are a number of steps that can be taken to involve both the school and the community in prevention efforts. In general, it is easier to initiate efforts in the school setting than it is in the context of a mental health center because schools can easily access young people, reach and prepare school faculty and staff, involve parents, and collaborate with mental health professionals from the surrounding community.

A number of steps must be taken to facilitate a successful school-community prevention effort. These include negotiation with administrators, faculty/staff in-service, preparation of crisis teams, providing for individual and group counseling options, parent education, and classroom presentations.

Negotiation With Administrators. There is a compelling need for prevention, crisis management, and postvention programs for the adolescent suicide problem to be put in place in elementary, middle, and high schools throughout the country (Metha et al., 1998; Zenere & Lazarus, 1997) . Based on the experience of these authors in the process of working with school districts all over the country, one of the biggest mistakes made by counselors, educators, and coordinators of counseling/student services is to initiate programs and services in this area without first obtaining commitment and support of administrators and others in supervisory positions. Too often efforts are initiated and then canceled because little or no negotiation with those in decision-making positions has taken place. Building principals and superintendents must be supportive; otherwise all efforts are destined for failure. Developing understanding of the parameters connected with suicide prevention and intervention must start with the building principal and extend to all faculty and staff in a given building so that advance understanding of why quick action must take place is developed. During a crisis schedules must be rearranged, and faculty and staff may be called upon to teach an extra class or assist with an initial assessment. Everyone connected with a given building must have advance preparation.

In addition to the groundwork that must be done on the building level, it is also important to effect advance communication and planning on the district level. The superintendent, assistant superintendent, curriculum director, staff development director, student services coordinator, and research and program evaluation specialist must all commit their support to intervention efforts. When administrators have the opportunity to listen to an overview of proposed efforts and ask questions, a higher level of commitment can be established, and efforts can be more easily expedited. The probability of extending proposed programming to all schools in a given district is also increased.

Faculty/Staff In-Service.   Because teachers and other faculty and staff usually learn of a student's suicidal preoccupation prior to the situation being brought to the attention of the school counselor or another member of the core or crisis team (assuming such a team exists), *all* faculty and staff must be included in building and/or district level in-service on the topic of adolescent suicide. Teachers, aides, secretaries, administrators, custodians, bus drivers, food service personnel, librarians, and school social workers all come in contact with adolescents at risk for suicide. It is imperative that all such adults be educated about both adolescent suicide and building and district policies and programs for prevention, crisis management, and postvention. There are a growing number of publications that provide excellent guidelines for elements of prevention programming focused on school faculty and staff (Davidson & Range, 1999; Metha et al., 1998; Zenere & Lazarus, 1997). When a young person reaches out to a trusted adult, that adult must have a clear understanding and a considerable amount of self-confidence so that he or she knows exactly what to say and do as well as what not to say and do.

Many schools and school districts have actually precipitated suicide attempts by not providing for faculty/staff in-service on the topic prior to introducing discussion among student groups. When middle and high school students participate in educational programs on the topic of adolescent suicide, they begin to realize that they, as well as some of their friends, are at risk, and they approach admired adults for assistance. Adults in the school who have no knowledge of what to do and who have not had the opportunity to have their questions answered and their apprehension lowered may be threatened by what a student is sharing and fail to make appropriate comments and decisions. Highly stressed, depressed, suicidal adolescents do not have the perspective to realize that such responses are connected with discomfort on the part of the adult and have little to do with what could be interpreted as disapproval and lack of acceptance. Awkward and minimal responses to suicidal self-disclosure on the part of a trusted adult can be interpreted as the loss of the last link to society and provide additional reinforcement for finalizing a suicide plan.

It is unethical not to prepare school faculty and staff in advance of the presentation of information on suicide to the students in a school. To do so could also become the basis for legal action by parents and family members. Much of the content in this chapter can become the basis for necessary in-service efforts.

Preparation of Crisis Teams. Many schools have crisis or core teams composed of faculty, staff, and parents connected with a particular building. These teams often exist in conjunction with a program for the prevention and intervention efforts necessary to cope with the drug problem among the young people in today's schools. Such teams usually consist of some combination of teachers, counselors, parents, social workers, school psychologists, school nurses, and school administrators. Usually these teams have been educated about traits that place adolescents at risk for substance use and abuse and have had supervision and instruction on the use of appropriate communication, diagnostic, and intervention skills necessary to begin the long-term process of recovery from alcoholism and other addictions.

With education beyond that which is provided during the faculty/staff in-service discussed previously as well as additional supervision and evaluation of clinical skills, a core or crisis team can be taught how to facilitate prevention efforts in a school as well as how to respond to a student already experiencing a suicidal crisis or in need of postvention efforts. In addition, such a team can be expected to write a policy statement that covers all parameters connected with prevention, crisis management, and postvention efforts. Such a policy could be adopted in other schools; in reality, except for specifics connected with a given building, the same policy statement should be adopted and followed throughout a school district. It is important to realize that everyone who is called upon to assist a suicidal adolescent must know what to do. Confusion or lack of certainty about a chain of command or notification of parents procedures can result in delays and interfere with efforts to save a young person's life!

Individual and Group Counseling Options. Prior to providing students with any information about suicide and suicide prevention efforts in a school, arrangements must be made for the individual and group counseling services that will be needed by those who seek assistance for themselves or their friends. Unless such counseling options are available, any effort at prevention, crisis management, or postvention will be doomed to failure. This may present a problem to school personnel, particularly on the secondary level, unless there is a commitment on the part of administrators to free counselors from scheduling, hall monitoring, and other duties not related to the emerging role of the counselor of the 21st century. Working with suicidal adolescents requires a long-term commitment on the part of those interested in intervening. No counselor, psychologist, or social worker can undo the life experiences and self-perceptions of a lifetime without providing consistent, intensive opportunities for counseling.

If the school district cannot make a commitment to providing counseling, then arrangements for referral to community agencies and private practitioners must be made. It is important to provide adolescents and their families with a variety of referral possibilities along with information on fee schedules. There may be some question about whether the school district will be liable for the cost of such counseling if the referral is made by the school. (This issue should be explored by whatever legal counsel is retained by the district.) The dilemma, of course, is that unless counseling takes place when a suicidal adolescent has been identified, the probability is high that an attempt or a completion will take place. If the school is aware of a teenager's suicidal preoccupation and does not act in the best interests of such a teenager, families may later bring suit against the district. Counselors in the school and members of the mental health network in the community must preplan to work in concert for the benefit and safety of adolescents at risk for suicide.

Parent Education. Parents of students in a school in which a suicide prevention program is to be initiated should be involved in the school's efforts to educate, identify, and assist young people in this respect. Parents have a right to understand why the school is taking such steps and what the components of a school-wide effort will be. Evening or late afternoon parent education efforts can be constructive and engender additional support for a school or school district. Parents have the same information needs as faculty and staff with respect to the topic of adolescent suicide. They will be more likely to refer themselves and their children to the school for assistance if they know of the school's interest in adolescent suicide prevention, have had an opportunity to ask questions about their adolescent sons' and daughters' behavior, and have been reassured about the quality and safety of the school's efforts.

Classroom Presentations. Debate surrounding the safety of adolescent suicide prevention programs that contain an educational component that is presented to adolescents continues. This debate is similar to the one that emerged years ago when schools initiated staff development and classroom presentations on the topic of physical and sexual abuse. There are a number of advocates of education and discussion efforts that are focused on students in conjunction with a school-wide suicide prevention effort (Capuzzi, 1988, 1994; Capuzzi & Golden, 1988; Curran, 1987; Ross, 1980; Sudak, Ford, & Rushforth, 1984; Zenere & Lazarus, 1997). Providing adolescents with an appropriate forum in which they can receive accurate information, ask questions, and learn about how to obtain help for themselves and their friends does not precipitate suicidal preoccupation or attempts (Capuzzi, 1988, 1994; Capuzzi & Gross, 1996). Because newspaper and television reports of individual and cluster suicides do not usually include adequate education on the topic, and because many films have unrealistically presented or romanticized the act of suicide, it is important for schools to address the problem in a way that provides information and encourages young people to reach out for help prior to reaching the point of despair.

A carefully prepared and well-presented classroom presentation made by a member of the school's core team (or another presenter who has expertise on the topic) is essential. Such a presentation should include both information on causes, myths, and symptoms as well as information about how to obtain help through the school. **Under no circumstances should media be used in which adolescents are shown a suicide plan.** In addition, on the elementary level, school faculty should not present programs on the topic of suicide prevention; their efforts are better focused on developmental counseling and classroom presentations directed at helping children overcome traits (such as low self-esteem or poor communication skills) that may put them at risk for suicidal behavior at a later time. Although these efforts should be continued through secondary education, middle and high school students are better served through presentations that address adolescent suicide directly. (Middle and high school students almost always have direct or indirect experience with suicide and appreciate the opportunity to obtain information and ask questions.)

INTERVENTION STRATEGIES

Individual and Family

There are times that adolescents at risk for suicide are not identified until a crisis state has been reached. In such circumstances, it is important for all concerned to initiate action for the purpose of assessing lethality and determining appropriate follow-up. Because many professionals who are not counselors lack experience with adolescents who are in the midst of a personal crisis, the guidelines that are included here may prove helpful. Please note that these guidelines can be read in the context of working with Jim. The assumption that one would have to make, however, is that all the adults traveling with Jim and his peers had participated in staff development efforts and included a counselor or other professional who could assess suicidal risk. An additional assumption is that families would be supportive of the use of these guidelines, either because they realized that the situation had escalated beyond their capacity to handle the situation, or because they had participated in a school-sponsored presentation to the community on the topic of adolescent suicide prevention and intervention.

1. *Remember the meaning of the term* **crisis management.** When thinking of crisis management, it is important to understand the

meaning of the word *crisis* as well as the word *management*. The word *crisis* means that the situation is not usual, normal, or average; circumstances are such that a suicidal adolescent is highly stressed and in considerable emotional discomfort. Adolescents in crisis usually feel vulnerable, hopeless, angry, low in self-esteem, and at a loss for how to cope. The word *management* means that the professional involved must be prepared to apply skills that are different from those required for preventive or postvention counseling. An adolescent in crisis must be assessed, directed, monitored, and guided for the purpose of preventing an act of self-destruction. Because adolescents who are experiencing a suicidal crisis may be quite volatile and impulsive, the need for decisive, rapid decision making on the part of the intervener is extremely important.

2. *Be calm and supportive.* A calm, supportive manner on the part of the intervener conveys respect for the perceptions and internal pain of an adolescent preoccupied with suicidal thoughts. Remember that such an adolescent usually feels hopeless and highly stressed. The demeanor and attitude of the helping person are pivotal in the process of offering assistance.

3. *Be nonjudgmental.* Statements such as "you can't be thinking of suicide; it is against the teachings of your church" or "I had a similar problem when I was your age, and I didn't consider suicide" are totally inappropriate during a crisis situation. An adolescent's perception of a situation is, at least temporarily, reality, and that reality must be respected. The same caution can be applied to the necessity of respecting a suicidal adolescent's expression of feelings whether these feelings are those of depression, frustration, fear, or helplessness. Judgmental, unaccepting responses and comments only serve to further damage an already impaired sense of self-esteem and decrease willingness to communicate. Adolescents could sink further into depression or increase their resolve to carry through with a suicide plan if others are critical and unwilling to acknowledge what appear, to the adolescent, to be unsurmountable obstacles.

4. *Encourage self-disclosure.* The very act of talking about painful emotions and difficult circumstances is the first step in what can become a long-term healing process. A professional helper may be the first person with whom such a suicidal adolescent has shared and trusted in months or even years, and it may be difficult to do simply because of lack of experience with communicating thoughts and feelings. It is important to support and encourage self-disclosure so that an assessment of lethality can be made early in the intervention process.

5. *Acknowledge the reality of suicide as a choice, but do not normalize suicide as a choice.* Practitioners need to let adolescents know

that they are not alone and isolated with respect to suicidal preoccupation. Practitioners also need to communicate the idea that suicide is a choice, a problem-solving option, and that there are other choices and options. This may be difficult to do in a way that does not make such an adolescent feel judged or put down. An example of what could be said to an adolescent in crisis is "It is not unusual for adolescents to be so upset with relationships or circumstances that thoughts of suicide occur more and more frequently; this does not mean that you are weird or a freak. I am really glad you have chosen to talk to me about how you're feeling and what you are thinking. You have made a good choice since, now, you can begin exploring other ways to solve the problems you described."

6. *Actively listen and positively reinforce.* It is important, during the initial stages of the crisis management process, to let the adolescent at risk for suicide know you are listening carefully and really understanding how difficult life has been. Not only will such careful listening and communicating, on the part of the professional, make it easier for the adolescent to share, but it also will provide the basis for a growing sense of self-respect. Being listened to, heard, and respected are powerful and empowering experiences for anyone who is feeling at a loss for how to cope.

7. *Do not attempt in-depth counseling.* Although it is very important for a suicidal adolescent to begin to overcome feelings of despair and to develop a sense of control as soon as possible, the emotional turmoil and stress experienced during a crisis usually makes in-depth counseling impossible. Developing a plan to begin lessening the sense of crisis an adolescent may be experiencing is extremely important, however, and should be accomplished as soon as possible. Crisis management necessitates the development of a plan to lessen the crisis; this plan should be shared with the adolescent so that it is clear that circumstances will improve. Counseling/therapy cannot really take place during the height of a suicidal crisis.

8. *Contact another professional.* It is a good idea to enlist the assistance of another professional, trained in crisis management, when an adolescent thought to be at risk for suicide is brought to your attention. School and mental health counselors should ask a colleague to come into the office and assist with assessment. It is always a good idea to have the support of a colleague who understands the dynamics of a suicidal crisis; in addition, the observations made by two professionals are more likely to be more comprehensive. Because suicidal adolescents may present a situation that, if misjudged or mismanaged, could result in a subsequent attempt or completion, it is in the best interests of both

the professional and the client for professionals to work collaboratively whenever possible. It should also be noted that liability questions are less likely to become issues, and professional judgment is less likely to be questioned, if assessment of the severity of a suicidal crisis and associated recommendations for crisis management have been made on a collaborative basis.

9. *Ask questions to assess lethality.* A number of dimensions must be explored to assess lethality. This assessment can be accomplished through an interview format (a crisis situation is not conducive to the administration of a written appraisal instrument). The following questions help determine the degree of risk in a suicidal crisis; all of them do not need to be asked if the interview results in the spontaneous disclosure of the information:

- *"What has happened to make life so difficult?"* The more an adolescent describes the circumstances that have contributed to feelings of despair and hopelessness, the better the opportunity for effective crisis management. The process of describing stress-producing interpersonal situations and circumstances may begin to lower feelings of stress and reduce risk. It is not unusual for an adolescent in the midst of a suicidal crisis to describe a multifaceted set of problems with family, peers, school, and drugs. The more problems an adolescent describes as stress producing and the more complicated the scenario, the higher the lethality or risk.

- *"Are you thinking of suicide?"* Adolescents who have been preoccupied with suicidal thoughts may experience a sense of relief to know there is someone who is able to discuss suicide in a straightforward manner. Using the word *suicide* will convey that the helping professional is listening and is willing to be involved; using the word *suicide* will not put the idea of suicide in the mind of a nonsuicidal adolescent. This particular question need not be asked until such time the assessor has developed the rapport and trust of the adolescent; timing is important in this regard so that it is relief rather than resistance that is experienced on the part of the adolescent.

- *"How long have you been thinking about suicide?"* Adolescents who have been preoccupied with suicide for a period of several weeks are more lethal than those who have only fleeting thoughts. One way to explore several components of this question is to remember the acronym *FID*. When asking about suicidal thoughts, ask about *frequency* or how often they occur, *intensity* or how dysfunctional the preoccupation is making the adolescent ("Can you go on with your daily routine as usual?"), and *duration* or how long the periods of preoccupation last. Obviously, an adolescent who reports frequent periods of preoccupation so intense that it is difficult or impossible to go to school, to work, or to see friends, and for increasingly longer periods of time so that periods of preoccupation and dysfunction are merging, is more lethal than an adolescent who describes a different set of circumstances.

- *"Do you have a suicide plan?"* When an adolescent is able to be specific about the method, the time, the place, and who will or will not be nearby, the risk is higher. (If the use of a gun, knife, medication, or other means is described, ask if that item is in a pocket or purse and request that the item be left with you. Never, however, enter into a struggle with an adolescent to remove a firearm. Call the police or local suicide or crisis center.) Most adolescents will cooperate with you by telling you about the plan and allowing you to separate them from the means. Remember, most suicidal adolescents are other-directed; such a trait should be taken advantage of during a crisis management situation. Later, when the crisis has subsided and counseling is initiated, the adolescent's internal locus of control can be strengthened.

- *"Do you know someone who has committed suicide?"* If the answer is "yes," the adolescent may be of higher risk, especially if this incident occurred within the family or a close network of friends. Such an adolescent may have come to believe that suicide is a legitimate problem-solving option.

- *"How much do you want to live?"* An adolescent who can provide only a few reasons for wishing to continue with life is of higher risk than an adolescent who can enumerate a number of reasons for continuing to live.

- *"How much do you want to die?"* The response to this question provides the opposite view of the preceding question. An adolescent who gives a variety of reasons for wishing to die is more lethal than an adolescent who cannot provide justification for ending life. It may be unnecessary to ask this question if the previous question provided adequate data.

- *"What do you think death is like?"* This question can be an excellent tool for assessment purposes. Adolescents who do not seem to realize that death is permanent, that there is no reversal possible, and that they cannot physically return are at higher risk for an actual attempt. Also, adolescents who have the idea that death will be romantic, nurturing, or the solution to current problems are at high risk.

- *"Have you attempted suicide in the past?"* If the answer to this question is "yes," then the adolescent is more lethal. Another attempt may occur that could be successful because a previous attempter has the memory of prior efforts and the fact that he or she conceptualized and carried through with a suicide plan. An additional attempt may correct deficits in the original plan and result in death.

- *"How long ago was this previous attempt?"* This question should be asked of any adolescent who answers "yes" to the previous question. The more recent the previous attempt, the more lethal the adolescent and the more critical the crisis management process.
- *"Have you been feeling depressed?"* Because a high percentage of adolescents who attempt or complete suicide are depressed, this is an important question. Using the acronym FID to remember to ask about frequency, intensity, and duration is also helpful in the context of exploring an adolescent's response to this question. As previously discussed, a determination needs to be made relative to the existence of clinical depression if such a condition is suspected. Adolescents who report frequent, intense, and lengthy periods of depression resulting in dysfunctional episodes that are becoming closer and closer together, or are continuously experienced, are at high risk.
- *"Is there anyone to stop you?"* This is an extremely important question. If an adolescent has a difficult time identifying a friend, family member, or significant adult who is worth living for, the probability of a suicide attempt is high. Whoever the adolescent can identify should be specifically named; addresses, phone numbers, and the relationship to the adolescent should also be obtained. (If the adolescent cannot remember phone numbers and addresses, look up the information, together, in a phone book.) In the event it is decided that a suicide watch should be initiated, the people in the network of the adolescent can be contacted and asked to participate.
- *"On a scale of 1 to 10, with 1 being low and 10 being high, what is the number that depicts the probability that you will attempt suicide?"* The higher the number, the higher the lethality.
- *"Do you use alcohol or other drugs?"* If the answer to this question is "yes," the lethality is higher because use of a substance further distorts cognition and weakens impulse control. An affirmative response should also be followed by an exploration of the degree of drug involvement and identification of specific drugs.
- *"Have you experienced significant losses during the past year or earlier losses you've never discussed?"* Adolescents who have lost friends because of moving, vitality because of illness, or their family of origin because of a divorce are vulnerable to stress and confusion and are usually at higher risk for attempting or completing suicide if they have been preoccupied with such thoughts.

- *"Have you been concerned, in any way, with your sexuality?"* This may be a difficult question to explore, even briefly, during a peaking suicidal crisis. Generally, adolescents who are, or think they may be, gay or lesbian are at higher risk for suicide. It is quite difficult for adolescents to deal with the issue of sexual orientation because of fear about being ridiculed or rejected. They may have experienced related guilt and stress for a number of years never daring to discuss their feelings with anyone.
- *"When you think about yourself and the future, what do you visualize?"* A high-risk adolescent will probably have difficulty visualizing a future scenario and will describe feeling too hopeless and depressed to even imagine a future life.

As noted at the beginning of this discussion, it is not necessary to ask all of these questions if the answers to them are shared during the course of the discussion. Also, it is appropriate to ask additional questions after a response to any of the questions when it seems to be constructive to do so. It should be noted that the interviewing team must make judgments about the truthfulness of a specific response by considering the response in the total context of the interview.

10. **Make crisis management decisions.** If, as a result of an assessment made by at least two professionals, the adolescent is at risk for suicide, a number of crisis management interventions can be considered. They may be used singly or in combination; the actual combination will depend upon the lethality determination, resources and people available, and professional judgment. It is the responsibility of the professionals involved, however, to develop a crisis management plan to be followed until the crisis subsides and long-term counseling or therapy can be initiated.

- *Notification of parents.* Parents of minors must be notified and asked for assistance when an adolescent is determined to be at risk for a suicide attempt. Often, adolescents may attempt to elicit a promise of confidentiality from a school or mental health counselor who learns about suicidal intent. Such confidentiality is not possible; the welfare of the adolescent is the most important consideration, and parents should be contacted as soon as possible.

  Sometimes parents do not believe that their child is suicidal and refuse to leave home or work and meet with their son or daughter and members of the assessment team. At times parents may be adamant in their demands that the school or mental health professional withdraw their involvement. Although such attitudes are not conducive to the management of a suicidal crisis, they are understandable because parents may respond to such information with denial or anger to mask true emotions and cope with apprehensions that perhaps their child's situation reflects their personal inadequacies as people and parents. Because an adolescent at risk for a suicide attempt cannot be left unmonitored, this provides a dilemma for a school or a mental health agency. Because conforming to the wishes of noncooperative parents places the adolescent at even greater risk, steps must be taken despite parental protests. Although some professionals worry about liability issues in such circumstances, liability is higher if such an adolescent is allowed to leave unmonitored and with no provision for follow-up assistance. Schools and mental health centers should confer with legal counsel to understand liability issues and to make sure that the best practices are followed in such circumstances.

- *Considering hospitalization.* Hospitalization can be the option of choice during a suicidal crisis (even if the parents are cooperating) when the risk is high. An adolescent who has not been sleeping or eating, for example, may be totally exhausted or highly agitated. The care and safety that can be offered in a psychiatric unit of a hospital is often needed until the adolescent can experience a lowered level of stress, obtain food and rest, and realize that others consider the circumstances painful and worthy of attention. In many hospital settings, multidisciplinary teams (physicians, psychiatrists, counselors, social workers, nurses, nurse practitioners, teachers) work to individualize a treatment plan and provide for outpatient help as soon as the need for assistance on an inpatient basis subsides.

- *Writing contracts.* At times, professionals may decide that developing a contract with the adolescent may be enough to support the adolescent through a period of crisis and into a more positive frame of mind, after which the adolescent will be more receptive to long-term counseling or therapy. Such a contract should be written out and signed and dated by the adolescent and the counselor. The contract can also be witnessed and signed by other professionals, friends, or family members.

    Contracts should require the adolescent to

    —agree to stay safe;
    —obtain enough food and sleep;
    —discard items that could be used in a suicide attempt (guns, weapons, medications);
    —specify the time span of the contract;
    —call a counselor or crisis center if there is a temptation to break the contract or attempt suicide;
    —write down the phone numbers of people to contact if the feeling of crisis escalates; and
    —specify ways time will be structured (walks, talks, movies).

- *Organizing suicide watches.* If hospital psychiatric services on an in-patient basis are not available in a given community and those doing the assessment believe the suicide risk is high, a suicide watch should be organized by contacting the individuals that the adolescent has identified in response to the question, "Is there anyone to stop you?" After receiving instruction and orientation from the professional, family members and friends should take turns staying with the adolescent until the crisis has subsided and long-term counseling or therapy has begun. In the opinion of the authors, it is never a good idea to depend on a family member alone to carry out a suicide watch; it is usually too difficult for family members to retain perspective. Friends should be contacted and included in a suicide watch even though confidentiality, as discussed earlier, cannot be maintained.

School and Community

When an adolescent has attempted or completed a suicide, it is imperative, particularly in a school setting, to be aware of the impact of such an event on the "system." Usually, within just a few hours, the fact that an adolescent has attempted or completed suicide has been chronicled through the peer group. This could present a problem to the faculty and staff in a given school building because not answering questions raised by students can engender the sharing of misinformation or rumors and encouraging open discussion could embarrass an attempter upon his or her return.

The following guidelines should prove helpful. Had Jim been in the regular school program when he made his attempt, these guidelines would have been put into effect immediately.

1. The principal of the building in which a student has attempted or completed suicide (even though such an incident most likely occurred off the school campus) should organize a telephone network to notify all faculty and staff that a mandatory meeting will take place prior to school the next morning. (Prior to the meeting, the principal should confirm the death through the coroner's office or through the student's family.) The principal should share information and answer questions about what happened during such a meeting. *In the case of a suicide completion, it is recommended that the principal provide all faculty and staff with an announcement that can be read—in each class rather than over a public address system—so that everyone in the school receives the same information. The announcement should confirm the loss and emphasize the services the school and community will be providing during the day and subsequent days. Details*

about the circumstances or the family of the deceased should not be given so that confidentiality is maintained in that regard.

2. Faculty and staff should be instructed to answer student questions that spontaneously arise but should be told not to initiate a discussion of suicide in general.

3. Faculty and staff should be told to excuse students from class if they are upset and need to spend time in the office of the building counselor or of another member of a core or crisis team.

4. Parents who are upset by the suicidal incident should be directed to a designated individual to have questions answered. Parents should also be provided with options for counseling, whether this counseling is provided by school personnel or referred to members of the mental health community.

5. At times, newspaper and television journalists contact the school for information about both the attempt or the completion and the school's response to the aftermath. Again, it is important to direct all such inquiries to a designated individual to avoid the problems created by inconsistency or sharing inaccurate information.

6. If a suicidal attempt occurs prior to the initiation of prevention and crisis management efforts in a given building, it is not a good idea to initiate classroom mental health education immediately even if faculty, staff, and core teams have been prepared and a written policy has been developed. Allow sufficient time to pass to prevent embarrassment to the returning student and his or her family.

7. Be alert to delayed or enhanced grief responses on the part of students prior to the anniversary of a suicide completion. Often students will need opportunity to participate in a support group with peers or individual counseling prior to and, perhaps, beyond the anniversary date.

8. Do not conduct a memorial service on the school campus after a suicide because doing so may provide reinforcement to other students preoccupied with suicidal ideation. This means that it is unwise to conduct an on-campus memorial service after a death for any reason; it is difficult to explain why a student who has suicided is not being remembered when another student, faculty, or staff has been memorialized previously. *Excuse students to attend the off-campus memorial or funeral. Do the same thing after deaths for other reasons.*

9. Early in the sequence of events, as listed in these guidelines, one or two individuals from the school should contact the family and ask if there is any support it might need that the school can provide. It is a good idea to offer such assistance periodically, as time passes, because so many families are left alone with their grief once the memorial or funeral has taken place.

ADAPTATIONS FOR DIVERSITY

Information contained in the Problem Definition section of this chapter suggests a number of adaptations for diversity, particularly with respect to prevention efforts. Because data suggest that Caucasian adolescent males are the highest risk group for suicide, extra efforts should be make to involve those young men, who may be vulnerable, in early prevention efforts. Individual and group counseling, focused on some of the personality traits described earlier, could and should be initiated in the elementary school years. Such early prevention efforts are preferable to waiting until suicidal preoccupation develops and behavior can be observed. Because Native Americans have the highest adolescent suicide rates of any ethnic group in the United States, teachers, counselors, and parents should be alerted to early signs so that efforts can be made to avert the development of at-risk behaviors.

The etiology of suicide is something that all adults should be made aware of so that young people experiencing psychiatric illness, abuse, confusion about sexual identity, and chronic or terminal physical illness can be monitored, supported, and referred for counseling/therapy when needed. Staffing sessions should be routinely conducted in elementary, middle, and high school settings so that young people who may be at risk for suicide attempts or completions could be routinely monitored and assisted. Because we know that adolescents who experience what they interpret as shameful or humiliating experiences with peers and with family members may, at times, be at high risk, these young people should also be the focus of observation and action should the need for prevention or intervention efforts be identified. In general, the more adults can be made aware of both risk factors and the suicidal profile, the earlier and more effective the prevention or intervention efforts.

SUMMARY

The authors believe that individuals who are interested in working with suicidal youth must obtain more extensive information than that provided in this chapter. In addition, such individuals should obtain supervision from professionals qualified to provide such supervision after observing actual assessment interview and counseling/therapy sessions. Generally, neither assessment, preventive, or postvention sessions should be attempted by anyone who has graduated from a graduate program with *less than* a 2-year coursework and practicum/internship requirement. (In the case of counselors, such a graduate program should follow the standard set by the Council for the Accreditation of Counseling and Related Educational Programs.) In addition, membership in the American Association of Suicidology, participation in workshops and conferences focused on the topic of adolescent suicide, and consistent reading of the *Journal of Suicide and Life-Threatening Behavior* and other books and journals are imperative.

Readers should also be cautioned not to use the material in this chapter as the sole basis for mental health education on the topic of adolescent suicide prevention or faculty/staff development in schools. This chapter provides an overview and an excellent starting point for professionals. Those without expertise on the topic or graduate preparation as a counselor, social worker, psychologist, or psychiatric nurse will not be able to answer questions of clients, families, and other professionals on the basis of reading a single chapter on this topic. Finally, anyone reading this chapter should be cautioned against initiating an adolescent suicide prevention, crisis management, and postvention program without writing a description of the various components so it can be checked by other professionals (including attorneys) and followed by all those involved in such an initiative.

An adolescent who becomes suicidal is communicating the fact that he or she is experiencing difficulty with problem solving, managing stress, expressing feelings. It is important for us to respond in constructive, safe, informed ways because the future of our communities (whether local, national, or international) is dependent upon individuals who are positive, functional, and able to cope with the complex demands of life. As research and clinical experience provide additional and more sophisticated information about adolescent suicide, it will be necessary to incorporate this information into prevention, crisis management, and postvention efforts. To abdicate our responsibility to do so would communicate a lack of interest in the youth of today and a lack of concern about the future of society.

REFERENCES

American Psychiatric Association. (1994). *Diagnostic and statistical manual of mental disorders* (4th ed.). Washington, DC: Author.

Beautrais, A. L., Joyce, P. R., & Mulder, R. T. (1999). Personality traits and cognitive styles as risk factors for serious suicide attempts among young people. *Journal of Suicide and Life-Threatening Behavior, 29*, 37–47.

Berlin, I. N. (1987). Suicide among American Indian adolescents: An overview. *Journal of Suicide and Life-Threatening Behavior, 17*, 218–232.

Berman, A. L., & Jobes, D. A. (1991). *Adolescent suicide: Assessment and intervention.* Washington DC: American Psychological Association.

Blumenthal, S. J. (1991). Letter to the editor. *Journal of the American Medical Association, 265,* 2806–2807.

Brent, D. A., Perper, J. A., Moritz, G., Baugher, M., Schweers, J., & Roth, C. (1993). Firearms and adolescent suicide: A community case-control study. *American Journal of Diseases in Children, 147,* 1066–1071.

Bush, J. A. (1976). Suicide and Blacks. *Journal of Suicide and Life-Threatening Behavior, 6,* 216–222.

Canetto, S. S., & Sakinofsky, I. (1998). The gender paradox in suicide. *Journal of Suicide and Life-Threatening Behavior, 28,* 1–23.

Cantor, P. (1976). Personality characteristics found among youthful female suicide attempters. *Journal of Abnormal Psychology, 85,* 324–329.

Capuzzi, D. (1988). *Counseling and intervention strategies for adolescent suicide prevention.* (Contract No. 400–86-0014). Ann Arbor, MI: ERIC Counseling and Personnel Services Clearinghouse.

Capuzzi, D. (1994). *Suicide prevention in the schools: Guidelines for middle and high school settings.* Alexandria, VA: American Counseling Association.

Capuzzi, D., & Golden, L. (Eds.) (1988). *Preventing adolescent suicide.* Muncie, IN: Accelerated Development.

Capuzzi, D., & Gross, D. (1996). "I don't want to live": The adolescent at risk for suicidal behavior. In D. Capuzzi & D. Gross (Eds.), *Youth at risk: A prevention resource for counselors, teachers, and parents* (2nd ed., pp. 353–282). Alexandria, VA: American Counseling Association.

Coy, D. R. (1995). The need for a school suicide prevention policy. *National Association of Student Services Professionals Bulletin, 79,* 1–9.

Cull, J., & Gill, W. (1982). *Suicide probability scale manual.* Los Angeles: Western Psychological Services.

Curran, D.F. (1987). *Adolescent suicidal behavior.* Washington, DC: Hemisphere.

Davidson, M. W., & Range, L. M. (1999). Are teachers of children and young adolescents responsive to suicide prevention training modules? Yes. *Death Studies, 23,* 61–71.

Davis, P.A. (1983). *Suicidal adolescents.* Springfield, IL: Charles C Thomas.

Diekstra, R. F. (1989). Suicidal behavior in adolescents and young adults: The international picture. *Crisis, 10,* 16–35.

Faigel, H. (1966). Suicide among young persons: A review of its incidence and causes, and methods for its prevention. *Clinical Pediatrics, 5,* 187–190.

Garland, A. F., & Zigler, E. (1993). Adolescent suicide prevention: Current research and social policy implications. *American Psychologist, 43*(2), 169–182.

Gibbs, J. T. (1988). Conceptual, methodological, and sociocultural issues in Black youth suicide: Implications for assessment and early intervention. *Journal of Suicide and Life-Threatening Behavior, 18,* 73–79.

Hafen, B. Q. (Ed.). (1972). *Self-destructive behavior.* Minneapolis, MN: Burgess.

Hafen, B. Q., & Frandsen, K. J. (1986). *Youth suicide: Depression and loneliness.* Provo, UT: Behavioral Health Associates.

Harry, J. (1989). *Sexual identity issues. Report of the Secretary's Task force on Youth Suicide: Vol. 2. Risk factors for youth suicide* (DHHS Publication No. ADM 89–1622). Washington, DC: Government Printing Office.

Henry, A. F., & Short, J. F. (1954). *Suicide and homicide.* Glencoe, IL: Free Press.

Hoberman, H. M., & Garfinkel, B. D. (1988). Completed suicide in children and adolescents. *Journal of the American Academy of Child and Adolescent Psychiatry, 27*, 688–695.

Hussain, S. A., & Vandiver, K. T. (1984). *Suicide in children and adolescents.* New York: SP Medical and Scientific Books.

Jacobs, J. (1971). *Adolescent suicide.* New York: Wiley-Interscience.

Johnson, S. W., & Maile, L. J. (1987). *Suicide and the schools: A handbook for prevention, intervention, and rehabilitation.* Springfield, IL: Charles C Thomas.

Kiev, A. (1977). *The suicidal patient.* Chicago: Nelson-Hall.

Kovacs, M., Beck, A., & Weissman, A. (1975). The use of suicidal motives in the psychotherapy of attempted suicides. *American Journal of Psychotherapy, 29,* 363–368.

Mazza, J. J., & Reynolds, W. M. (1998). A longitudinal investigation of depression, hopelessness, social support, and major and minor life events and their relation to suicidal ideation in adolescents. *Journal of Suicide and Life-Threatening Behavior, 28,* 358–374.

McWhirter, J. J., & Kigin, T. J. (1988). Depression. In D. Capuzzi & L. Golden (Eds.), *Preventing adolescent suicide* (pp. 149–186). Muncie, IN: Accelerated Development.

Metha, A., Weber, B., & Webb, L. D. (1998). Youth suicide prevention: A survey and analysis of policies and efforts in the 50 states. *Journal of Suicide and Life-Threatening Behavior, 28*(2), 150–164.

Peck, D. (1983). The last moments of life: Learning to cope. *Deviant Behavior, 4,* 313–342.

Rohde, P., Lewinsohn, P., & Seeley, J. R. (1991). Comorbidity of unipolar depression: Comorbidity with other mental disorders in adolescents and adults. *Journal of Abnormal Psychology, 100,* 214–222.

Ross, C. (1980). Mobilizing schools for suicide prevention. *Journal of Suicide and Life-Threatening Behavior, 10,* 239–243.

Schneidman, E., Farberow, N., & Litman, R. (1976). *The psychology of suicide.* New York: Jason Aronson.

Shaffer, D. (1988). The epidemiology of teen suicide: An examination of risk factors. *Journal of Clinical Psychiatry, 49,* 36–41.

Shaffer, D., & Craft, L. (1999). Methods of adolescent suicide prevention. *Journal of Clinical Psychiatry, 60,* 70–74.

Shaffer, D., Garland, A., Gould, M., Fisher, P., & Trautman, P. (1988). Preventing teenage suicide: A critical review. *Journal of the American Academy of Child and Adolescent Psychiatry, 27,* 675–687.

Sommes, B. (1984). The troubled teen: Suicide, drug use, and running away. *Women and Health, 9,* 117–141.

Stein, M., & Davis, J. (1982). *Therapies for adolescents.* San Francisco: Jossey-Bass.

Stillion, J., McDowell, E., & Shamblin, J. (1984). The suicide attitude vignette experience: A method for measuring adolescent attitudes toward suicide. *Death Education, 8,* 65–81.

Sudak, H., Ford, A., & Rushforth, N. (1984). Adolescent suicide: An overview. *American Journal of Psychotherapy, 38*(3), 350–369.

Velkoff, P., & Huberty, T. J. (1988). Thinking patterns and motivation. In D. Capuzzi & L. Golden (Eds.), *Preventing adolescent suicide* (pp. 111–147). Muncie, IN: Accelerated Development.

Wyche, K., Obolensky, N., & Glood, E. (1990). American Indian, Black American, and Hispanic American youth. In M. J. Rotheram-Borus, J. Bradley, & N. Obolensky (Eds.), *Planning to live: Evaluating and treating suicidal teens in community settings* (pp. 355–389). Tulsa: University of Oklahoma Press.

Zenere, F. J., II, & Lazarus, P. J. (1997). The decline of youth suicidal behavior in an urban, multicultural public school system following the introduction of a suicide prevention and intervention program. *Journal of Suicide and Life-Threatening Behavior, 27*(4), 387–403.

12 | I Am Somebody: Gang Membership

Sonja Burnham and Mit Arnold

Gangs have been present in history for centuries. Literature and music reveal the existence of groups that meet the criteria established by Jackson and McBride (1987): "A gang is a group of people that form an allegiance for the common purpose, and engage in unlawful or criminal activity" (p. 20). Spergel (1990) added to a clear definition of gang activity by stating that "the principal criterion currently used to define a *gang* may be the group's participation in illegal activity" (p. 179). Robin Hood and his Merry Men are most recognizable as a group that fits these definitions. Robin Hood's gang was using force and weapons to prey on the rich to provide for the poor. Literature and popular movies have romanticized their behavior, but they were still operating outside the law.

Gangs have existed in the United States since the Revolutionary War. One notable example was Jean Laffite who led his buccaneers against the British in Louisiana in support of General Andrew Jackson. The days of the Wild West were notorious for gangs. The most notable of these may have been Jesse James and his brother Frank who were legendary for their activities. In response to the early gangs, government officials offered rewards for the capture of these individuals (Jankowski, 1991).

Gangs are having an enormous impact on all of society, in all parts of the country. No geographical area, racial or cultural group, or school district is immune to problems that may be traced to some aspect of gang activity. Because the gang problem has become so extensive, approaches to prevention of increased gang activity and intervention of existing gang activity needs to be undertaken simultaneously. Approaches to prevention of gang involvement concern not just gang members, but families, schools, communities, and others who are involved with these groups.

This chapter first defines the problem by looking at gangs in the past, factors for gang involvement in the present, including characteristics of gangs and male and female gang members, and ethnic gangs. A case study profiles a young man involved in gangs as a way of understanding the reality of those factors. The chapter then considers approaches to prevention and intervention strategies at individual, family, school, and community levels and concludes with a discussion of adaptations for diversity. The appendix to the chapter contains a multiple-choice quiz (with answers) that can help to focus attention on important points concerning gangs.

PROBLEM DEFINITION: PAST AND PRESENT

Youth gangs began emerging in America during the shift from an agrarian society to an industrialized one. During the 1920s cities that were becoming industrialized grew rapidly. Cities such as New York, Boston, and Chicago were becoming urbanized. Large numbers of immigrants from varying cultures flocked to these cities seeking a better life for themselves and their children. They were not accepted into the mainstream culture, which was White, Anglo-Saxon, and Protestant. The parents worked at low-paying menial jobs that barely allowed them to earn a living while trying to assimilate into the culture; the youth banded together for socialization and protection as they experienced adolescence in an unfamiliar country that was frustrating and alien to them. Dozens of gangs made up of members from similar racial, ethnic, and cultural backgrounds emerged. These gangs began to become destructive and often to be well known by their gang names and unique clothing (Sachs, 1997). The youth tended to continue in these gangs throughout their adult live.

Thrasher (1926), an early investigator of gang activity during the late 1920s, viewed youth gangs as means to socialize young delinquents to organized crime, to turn the youth into gangsters, as the adult men were known. The large urban areas were the birthplace of many of the notorious Mafia gangs, and gang wars ensued over territory and other activities such as bookmaking, extortion, gun running, and liquor sales. Because southern cities experienced less rapid growth, and immigrants did not migrate to the South in as large numbers, economic growth as well as gang growth moved in that region at a slower pace.

During the 1930s and 1940s a change occurred within the overall racial and cultural makeup of gangs. African American, Puerto Rican, and Mexican American gangs began to outnumber the previously predominant White gangs. Gang wars escalated with the use of handguns, knives, chains, and other self-made implements. Drug use among gang members increased as well as drug trafficking. Gang conflicts continued through the 1950s and saw a slight decrease during the 1960s, perhaps because of the Vietnam War.

Estimates of gang activity today vary. The U.S. Department of Justice has estimated that more than 16,000 different gangs, with more than

500,000 gang members, are active (Huff, 1998); estimates in the *American Bar Association Journal* have put the figures nearer to 23,338 different gangs and a membership of 665,000 (Gibeaut, 1998). Figure 12–1 shows the major gangs found in the United States and their major locations (Los Angeles and Chicago) as well as the various types of gangs throughout the country. As the figure indicates, the Crips and the Bloods, which were the two most powerful Black gangs during the first half of the 20th century, continue in a dominant position in Los Angeles.

Factors for Gang Involvement

From the early 1900s researchers have continued to look at gang involvement, attempting to uncover the factors that underlie gang activity and explain the continued growth and spread of gangs in the United States. Miller (1958), for example, looked at gang members and how they had been reared and found that it was not unusual for gang members to come

Figure 12–1 | U.S. Gangs

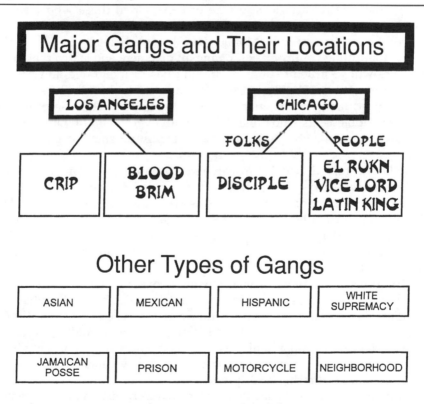

Various gangs and/or sects may join forces or war with other factions.

from a matriarchal environment. Gang members from these homes, he held, were often models for younger members who learned their sex-role behavior from the more experienced gang members who were similar to them in ethnic and cultural background. For another example, some theorists viewed gangs as a subculture that is the result of lower class male youth being unable to attain wealth and success through traditional and acceptable means (Cloward & Ohlin, 1960; Cohen, 1955). Because working class youth often are not adequately trained to meet the requirements of middle-class society, gangs are the means of reacting to and making adjustments in their lives in order to find their own social status and acceptance. Further, gangs have an organizational structure that spells out rules concerning expected levels of aggressive behavior as well as the status and prestige earned as a result of adhering to these rules (Bernard, 1990). Matza (1964) disagreed with the subculture theory, instead viewing adolescents as being suspended between childhood and adulthood and seeing this time as a period of risk for males who are discovering their identities and trying to become aligned with a peer group. Because these youth fear losing status by not being accepted, they are easy targets for gangs that specify a rigid structure of behavior in those who want to become members.

For yet another example, Morales (1992) viewed the family as a crucial factor for putting youth at risk for gang involvement and stated that those families whose structure and functioning has disintegrated and broken down through poverty, alcoholism, drug addiction, chronic illnesses, and incarcerated family members put youth at great risk. Thus, according to Morales, adolescents who are involved with overwhelming family problems seek gang membership as a way to belong and gain recognition and protection.

Other factors linked by researchers to gang involvement include delinquency (Curry & Spergel, 1992), lower socioeconomic status (Hirschi, 1969), ethnic minority status and identity (Gray-Ray & Ray, 1990; Hagadorn, 1991; Vigil, 1988), and lack of influence by parents (Fagan, 1989; Fagan, Piper, & Moore, 1986). However, there is little empirical evidence to show how gang members differ from non-gang-member youth.

The psychosocial control theory, which concerns the factor of delinquency and its relation to gang involvement, has been both influential and supported by research. Internal control was emphasized by Hirschi (1969), for example, as the mechanism for explaining conformity and delinquency, with such factors as poor family relations and failure in school being indicators of increased potential for delinquency. A new version of the theory (Gottfredson & Hirschi, 1990) presented six factors of adolescents who have high self-control that are thus factors inversely related to delinquency and, consequently, gang membership. These are the

1. ability to defer gratification;
2. stamina to persist in a course of action;
3. ability to be cognitive and verbal;
4. ability to engage in long-term pursuits;
5. ability to perceive the value of cognitive and academic skills; and
6. possession of sensitivity and feelings of altruism toward others.

Many factors for gang involvement already described were supported in a study by Dukes and Martinez (1994) that examined the precursors and consequences associated with gang membership in the United States. These researchers found that nearly 1 of every 20 youths in the study were active gang members, and that those who were active gang members came from poor backgrounds and were living away from their parents. Findings also revealed that those youth who were gang members or wannabes had the lowest self-esteem and poorest psychosocial health, and, in addition, were members of minority ethnic groups. Thus they also had less resistance to peer pressures.

Gang Characteristics.   In the last decade, as researchers have worked with specific gangs in specific areas of the country in order to identify factors that can be ameliorated, gang structures and characteristics have been described. Spergel (1995), for example, defined three major types of delinquent youth culture or gang activity that can be characterized by (a) racket activities, (b) violent conflict, and (c) theft. He further stated that without appropriate analysis of the particular community's gang activity, the intervention into and prevention of these activities will be extremely difficult. Klein, Maxon, and Miller (1995), for another example, studied Chicanos and Black gangs in Los Angeles for several decades and concluded that the leadership of these gangs is of paramount importance. However, this leadership is not a position, but more a collection of functions with the gang leader's duties varying with each function, such as fighting, athletics, or girls. Skolnick (1995), for yet another example, concluded that there are two types of gangs: entrepreneurial and cultural. He proposed that the more a gang is involved in the drug trade, the less it becomes a cultural phenomenon and the more it becomes a business enterprise—which presents great difficulty when intervention strategies are sought to decrease gang activity. A related finding, by Knox, Laske, and Tromanhauser (1992), who researched gangs over the last decade, is that there is a direct correlation between the presence of gangs in and around schools and increases in school violence.

Yablonsky (1997), after a review of the research available on gangs, reached the following conclusion about gang characteristics:

1. Gangs are fiercely involved with their territory, their hood, or barrio and will fight ferociously to protect their turf.

2. There are different levels of participation in gangs, in part due to age, and these can be characterized by core or marginal participants.
3. Diverse patterns of leadership exist in gangs.
4. Many gangs are totally and intensely involved in the commerce of drugs.
5. Gangs, in part, are generated by their cultural milieu in response to a society that blocks opportunity to achieve the success goals of the larger society. (p. 184)

Gang Member Characteristics.   A typical gang member is usually male, a poor student, or a school dropout. He is unemployed and often unemployable and has a police record. Because the gang provides identity, status, and a surrogate family, members develop complete loyalty. Some family members support their children's involvement in gangs in order to support their own drug habits. In general, gang members are from a lower economic background and are very prevalent in African American and Hispanic populations. However, Caucasians join gangs such as skinheads, hell's angels, and satanic groups. The gang members tend to stay on their turf and commit crimes against those who are unable to defend themselves. Their violent work has the advantage of being done during the nighttime hours, from speeding cars, through overpowering victims by their numbers, and shooting from roofs and other familiar vantage points (McCarthy, 1998).

To charactize gang members fully, however, *gang member* needs to be defined. According to Yablonsky (1997), the word *member* as defined in the dictionary—"one of the individuals composing a group; a constituent part of a whole" (*Merriam-Webster's*, 1995, p. 724)—does not necessarily fit most gang members because gangs are neither distinct nor clearly delineated groups. In his research he has instead observed three general but distinct statuses of gang membership:

1. *wannabes (Wbs):* These are youth from about age 9 to age 13 who aggresively seek roles and status in a gang.
2. *gangbangers (Gs):* These youth are ages 13 to 25 and already accepted as gang members. This group is considered the core—or soldiers—of a gang and comprises about 80% of members in the contemporary multipurpose violent gang.
3. *older (or original) gangsters (OGs):* These youth are usually founders of the gang and have achieved permanent status in their gang. Many OGs are retired or semiretired but continue to maintain the permanent status of OG. Note that *gangster* is a term often used in place of *gang member*.

Wannabes in general seldom attend school and come from dysfunctional families in which their parents are often into drugs and alcohol, and often abuse them sexually, physically, and emotionally. Wannabes work for older gangsters, often as mules for drugs, and their ultimate goal is to become a gangbanger. As wannabes work for gangbangers and older gangsters, and commit violent acts to prove their worthiness to be a gangbanger, they are often promoted into the full status of a gangbanger. Generally, wannabes continue a life of crime and violence and serve time in prison.

The general public carries a misconception that all individuals involved with gangs participate to a similar degree. As just noted, some gang members are only involved in gang activities in a limited way while others—primarily gangbangers and old gangsters—have daily involvement in gangs. The gangbangers and old gangsters are not only fully committed to their gang but also often live near each other. Generally the gang serves all their social needs. Marginal gang members are often designated as more active participants if they are seen with other core gang members, dress in a similar manner to those gang members, and are caught in activities associated with certain gangs. Police and other authorities will label such individuals as gang members, sometimes even after the gang affiliation has terminated (Yablonsky, 1997). For these individuals, shedding the gangster label is almost impossible because law enforcement agencies are slow to believe that a gang member at any level has disaffiliated with the gang. (About half of all active gang members in the United States today have tried to quit gang life—National Gang Crime Research Center, 1998.) Core gang members are totally involved with the activities of the gang and become vehemently encouraging and supportive of violent behavior. Many gangbangers are swept into a delusionary state of being persecuted by police, other gangs, or anyone who gets in their way. These gang members believe that self-esteem, status in the world, and pleasurable activities are all tied to the gang. They may be easier to recognize because they have 24-hour participation and involvement and live out the paranoid gangster code of ethics and lifestyle. No matter what the level of involvement may be, gang members share the beliefs and values that allow them to behave in ways that will gain them prestige, acceptance, and status in the gang world. Gang members often use graffiti to advertise what gangs control certain regions. These are often elaborate and symbolize various gang codes, slogans, or affiliations, as shown in Figure 12–2.

Gang members, because of their dysfunctional backgrounds, are almost always in some way emotionally on the edge. The sociopathic personality that some gang members exhibit contributes to the total involvement and commitment that they have to their gang. The attitudes these gang members have set them up for violence in all their interactions.

Figure 12–2 | Examples of Gang Graffiti in Memphis: Colors, and Speech and Dress Codes

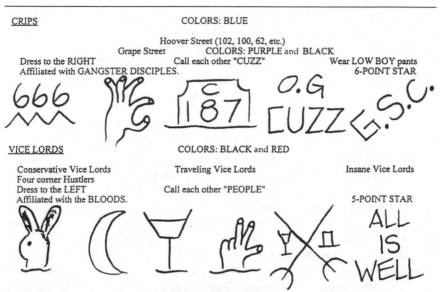

CRIPS COLORS: BLUE

Hoover Street (102, 100, 62, etc.)
Grape Street COLORS: PURPLE and BLACK
Dress to the RIGHT Call each other "CUZZ" Wear LOW BOY pants
Affiliated with GANGSTER DISCIPLES. 6-POINT STAR

VICE LORDS COLORS: BLACK and RED

Conservative Vice Lords Traveling Vice Lords Insane Vice Lords
Four corner Hustlers
Dress to the LEFT Call each other "PEOPLE"
Affiliated with the BLOODS. 5-POINT STAR

Gang members look at females as sex objects to be treated in any way they chose for their own pleasure. These attitudes can be clearly heard in much "gangsta" rap. Their attitude toward females in general is one of disdain, with gang members delineating their women as either whores or saints. The whores are only there to be used in any manner gang members choose while the saints are there to mother their children and be idolized. Often gang members are overtly homophobic and will present themselves with a macho image in order to dismiss the insecurities they may have about their own masculinity (Yablonsky, 1997). In prisons, aggressions toward homosexuals, or perceived homosexuals, can be brutal beatings, often leading to death.

While acting out irrational violent behavior, core sociopathic gang members tend to show little social conscience or real concern for others. Empathy for others is not a primary concern for gangsters. Their only concern is for their own emotional and material comfort. In short, these individuals exhibit the following characteristics: "(a) limited feelings of guilt, (b) few feelings of compassion or empathy for others, (c) behavior which is dominated by egocentrism and satisfying their own goals, and (d) manipulation of others for immediate self-gratification" (Yablonsky, 1997, p. 113).

It is the norm for gang members to have low self-esteem. Their violent behavior serves to allow them some means to stroke their egos. Violence often allows them to become enmeshed in a state of euphoria. They get their highs from the violent, brutal acts that they perpetrate in order to gain these feelings. Their ability to rationalize away this behavior is a function of gang involvement.

It is no wonder that gangs offer a seductive alternative to impoverished, unadventurous, or humdrum lives. Youth who see gang members wearing cool clothes and jewelry and buying sought-after material goods of the moment are lured into aspiring to be one of them. Joining a gang also gives members protection from other gangs, because protecting their own home boys is paramount for gang members.

Females in Gangs.   Most research on gangs and gang membership has focused on males and their drug use, family dysfunction, peer pressure, and self-esteem. Even though females have committed crimes side by side with male gang members, females have been most often briefly discussed and perceived as playing secondary roles in most gangs. Their main role has been usually defined as one of providing sexual services to male gang members (Yablonsky, 1997).

Female gang members have become more independent and liberated through the 1980s and 1990s, however, and have taken on roles more comparable to those of male gang members. Serious crime by females has steadily increased over the past two decades (Campbell, 1987, 1992; Spergel, 1992; Taylor, 1993). Further, "since the 1980s females in gangs have become more violent and more and more oriented to male crime" (Fishman, 1992); "female gang members are hard core and deadly" (Taylor, 1993, p. 45); and females in gangs have committed serious crimes such as drive-by shootings, armed robberies, muggings, and automobile thefts as well as drug dealing (Covey, Menard, & Franzese, 1992; Molidor, 1995). The increased level of violence is often attributed to the availability of guns and other sophisticated weapons.

Despite substantiation of increased violent behaviors and criminal activities, female gang members are nevertheless usually not studied separately. This may be because most gang researchers have been male and most perceptions of females have come from male gang members (Korowitz, 1986). Research is particularly needed into the girl-only gangs that have gained some national attention, even though information on these gangs is not easily located (LeBinh, 1997).

In one of the few studies of female gang members, Molidor (1996) conducted interviews to learn about criminal behavior as well as the physical, sexual, and psychological abuses the females experienced as gang members. Factors for female gang involvement were found to be similar to those of male gang members (Molidor, 1996), with lack of education and severely dysfunctional family life as major factors (Covey et al., 1992). Many young females came from homes and neighborhoods in which alcohol and drug use and distribution were prevalent. Female initiations into gangs were also often severely painful and humiliating. However, once the females were part of a gang, they too felt they belonged to a family and acquired a sense of power.

In a comparative study of females involved in gangs and other adolescent females, Shulmire (1996) collected data focused on family demographics and family relationships, school functioning, psychosocial functioning, and level of contacts with gangs. Among findings were that

- mothers of gang-involved females had lower educational levels than mothers of the other females;
- gang-involved females reported feeling mistreated at home more often than other females;
- gang-involved females revealed problematic relationships with their fathers; and
- the friendship patterns and social-structural considerations of gang-involved females were connected to gang membership.

Gang membership for females appears to be tied to personal self-esteem, relationships to members of their families of origin, and their environment, school, and neighborhood. These females will need to have their needs met in these areas if they are to choose an alternative lifestyle. In addition, even though current research into female gang members has revealed that their factors for gang involvement are similar to many of those observed for male gang members, prevention and intervention for females in gangs may need to be developed separately from those for males involved in gangs.

Ethnic Gangs

Because gangs fulfill needs that are traditionally fulfilled by an individual's home and school, it is logical to expect that disenfranchised youth of all races will participate in gang activities. Gang membership tends to reflect the local ethnic population and varies geographically. For example, Asian gangs are found in the Northwest and other locations with significant Asian populations. In Los Angeles, where Hispanics make up the largest minority group, Hispanic gang membership is significant. Any organized response to gang activity must include knowledge of the culture and its influence on members of the gang. The brief descriptions of Asian, African American, Hispanic, and White supremacist gangs that follow illustrate the commonalities and ethnic influences (Palmer, 1992).

Asian Gangs. Most Asian gang members arrived in the United States as minors or young adults. These adolescents and young adults, with no support system and often without knowledge of the majority language, are at high risk to associate with gang members who are of their race and speak the same language. This bond increases their alienation from the mainstream culture. Due to experiences in their homelands, many Asians do not trust the police and rely on gangs for protection and problem solving. Unemployment and lack of marketable skills make Asian gang members look to extortion, physical assaults, residential robbery, and burglary as means to get money.

Palmer (1992) described three levels of the Asian gangs. A *casual gang* is a group of friends who operate together in committing crime by consensus with no leadership. These members participate in the most violent of crimes. The *informal gang* is headed by a charismatic leader, but gang membership fluctuates and is transient in nature. The *formal gang* has an even more defined administrative structure with a defined chain of command.

Extortion is acknowledged to be the most prevalent form of crime committed by Chinese gang members, and their primary source of income. Through extortion, the gangs exert their control on the Chinese community. Police estimate that more than 90% of Chinese business owners regularly pay one or more gangs. When retail businesses refuse to pay, their shops may be vandalized, burglarized, or set on fire. Asian gangs were once thought of as being exclusively ethnic Chinese. However, with the migration of Southeast Asians into the United States, gang membership presently includes Cambodian and Vietnamese youth. Organized crime is the thrust of much of the literature on Asian gangs (Palmer, 1992).

African American Gangs. African American gangs often exist in neighborhoods where household heads are single females and gang affiliations regularly occur. Gangs tend to form in sets based on a locality. Gang names include surnames, such as Crips or Bloods, with the full name being, for example, the Rolling 70s Crips or the Insane Gangsta Bloods. Black gangs exist in the same territory as other ethnic gangs, but typically do not fight across ethnic boundaries. Little formal administrative structure exists (unlike the Asian gangs). Gang members frequently sell crack cocaine and heroin, but it is unusual for gang members to use these drugs. Most Black gang members drink beer and smoke marijuana. Gang members are totally opposed to authority. Teenage parents teach their children gang signs and dress them in gang colors. Gang members frequently recruit their siblings. Dress and color are important symbols of some types of African American gangs, and gang members may adopt certain items of clothing that are worn in designated colors or in specific ways. For example, members of the LA-based African American gang, the Crips, wear blue clothing to display their loyalty (as they do in Memphis—see Figure 12–2). Their rival gang, the Bloods, wear red clothing. Although the colors differ, the articles of clothing that identify an individual as a gang member are often the same.

Examples include bandannas, colored shoelaces, or a particular style of trousers. These gangs have their own brand of violence and revenge. Drive-by shootings can result from disagreement over turf. Other activities include robberies and assaults, prostitution, and sale of sophisticated weapons (Jackson & McBride, 1987).

Hispanic Gangs.   Hispanic gangs were recorded in Southern California in the early 1900s. Hispanic immigrants from various sections of Mexico formed gangs to defend their newly acquired territory. Then, as now, Hispanic gangs form alliances for purposes of strength. Their belief that the gang is more important than the individual reflects a value in their culture (Morales, 1982).

Hispanic gangs are generational and primarily male. Young males are known as PeeWees or lil Winos. An individual gang member who lives to age 22 becomes a *veterano*. Veteranos act as advisers to younger gang members, and they also hide members, dispose of weapons, and arrange meeting places. Gangs are usually named after the street, housing project, or barrio from which the gang originates. Members identify closely with their neighborhood (or hood), and it is this name they tattoo on themselves and write on walls throughout the city. Gangs are composed of divisions roughly based on age cohort. In a sense, the gang is similar to an army, with the divisions operating with some autonomy while still loyal to the hood. These gangs ostensibly operate to protect the hood but actually are operating to promote prized violent behaviors. The size of the gang roughly correlates to the size of the barrio in which the gang lives. Gangs range in size from 30 members to 300 members. Gang boundaries are dynamic, changing as members move in and out, often in response to a specific situation. For core members, the gang becomes a total institution, much like a commune or a military unit, completely absorbing the individual into the subculture. Core members of the gang interact with one another according to established patterns that are binding to them as gang members, and that are clearly identifiable, both by other gang members and by others not involved in the gang. Interaction within the gang is specific and ritualistic in form, with sanctions applied whenever someone does not adapt to the patterned form of behavior. Members from rival gangs challenge each other to test group fidelity and to establish membership. The challenge is one of the rituals that clearly identifies gang membership and intensifies the sense of belongingness to the group (Morales, 1992).

White Supremacist Groups.   White supremacists are often referred to as skinheads because of their closely cropped hair or shaved heads. The movement began in England in 1968 and moved formally into the United States in 1984. In 1986, the Skinheads of America formed an alliance with the Aryan Nation, an existing White supremacist organization. This group believes that the White race is superior to all others. They do not believe in mixing the races. Skinheads promote racial hatred and violence by distributing literature targeting people of color, gays, lesbians, and Jews. They seek to intimidate and harass individuals through physical attacks and through racial slurs. Disenfranchised adolescents who are experiencing academic problems, or drug and alcohol abuse, or who have been physically or sexually abused are especially at risk. At-risk youth are recruited through school activities, literature, and on the Internet. The goal of the gang is to gain superiority and power through intimidation. Gang members dress in military-style clothes, steel-toed boots, and T-shirts with White Pride logos. Symbols used by skinheads include the circled swastika, an upside-down two-sided ax, a circled A, and a rifle sight (Palmer, 1992). A 1988 nationwide survey of neo-Nazi skinheads indicated continued membership growth and a persistent propensity for engaging in violence—mainly against racial and religious minorities. The gangs are composed overwhelmingly of teenagers, many as young as 13 and 14 years of age. It is alarming to note that the skinheads provide a recruitment pool for other White supremacy groups, such as the Order, the Nationalist Socialist Vanguard, and the White Aryan Resistance. White supremacy groups draw from skinhead gangs in the effort to recruit "soldiers dedicated to the cause" (Palmer, 1992).

CASE STUDY: ANTHONY

Anthony, a 13-year-old New York youth, lives in Brooklyn's dangerous, gang-infested Bedford Stuyvesant section. It is one of the oldest Black ghettos in the United States. He lives on the fourth floor of a crumbling tenement with his aunt and sleeps on a mattress in a room he shares with cousins. His mother is a 31-year-old crack addict who is in and out of jail. His father, with whom he has had little contact except when he was being beaten by him, is also an addict and is in prison doing time for dealing drugs. This boy carries a .25 automatic for protection like most of his home boys. He seldom attends school, so is therefore unable to read or write well. He smokes marijuana and drinks heavily. He wears designer jeans, a T-shirt, and a $45 pair of Pumas with starched shoelaces.

By the time Anthony was around 9 or 10 years old, he was exhibiting pregang behaviors in elementary school. In fact, he was usually found during recess playing "gangs" with others who were from similar backgrounds. As Anthony became old enough to move closer to gang members, he did so at first by volunteering to do simple errands, such as running money or drugs between members. This was almost inevitable because both his parents modeled violent behavior and were heavy drug users.

Anthony continued his move toward gangs by being willing to do any errand or activity that brought him closer to an actual gang member. He isolated himself from any friends who were not interested in gangs, and soon he was a loner on the streets. He quit attending school regularly. In effect, he had no parents to monitor his activities, or other relatives to model more acceptable behaviors and to encourage him to stay in school.

As he grew older, Anthony began to wear the colors of his chosen gang and became involved in wannabe gang behaviors that broke the law and involved violence. The police labeled him as a gang member even though he was still only an apprentice. Anthony was on his way to becoming fully involved in gang activities.

APPROACHES TO PREVENTION

The emergence and spread of gang activity has no geographical boundaries. Gangs in the United States, which started in largely urban areas, have now spread to small town U.S.A. Even rural areas are feeling the impact of some gang activity. Often gang-like activities are perpetrated by gang wannabes instead of hard-core gangsters. The presence of individuals willing to strive for the gang lifestyle in any location sends a message to all. Those who are concerned with trying to reclaim these individuals from gangs and redirect them into socially acceptable lifestyles know that a variety of interventions must be used. It is also clear that even with some successful interventions, the social system that promotes and tolerates injustice and encourages gang activity must be changed. Disintegrating families, drugs, lack of economic opportunities, unacceptable ways to gain social status, and poor social support structures such as schools and community agencies are all areas that need to be addressed. Because the problem is large and spreading, it requires strategies that are undertaken concurrently in order to make any successful impact. Programs that offer the best hope for success are those that lead these youth back from lives of crime and violence to a society that can offer them an attainable social status, and social programs that help them to realize the need for change while offering a clear path to follow.

Individual

The initial approach to lessening the number of youth joining and remaining in gangs has to be one-to-one approach. To prevent young boys and girls from meeting their needs by affiliating with gangs, as Anthony did, the individual within the family is the first line of attack. Youth need to know and value themselves so that they are able to value others. There must be a new route available to these at-risk youth that invites them to value themselves.

The following list of critical ages and activities describes life-span development of gang members and illustrates how early these young gang wannabes begin to develop, how young boys and girls may begin their journey to violence and often death.

Average Age	Activity
8.9 years	First heard anything about gangs
9.2 years	First bullied by someone in a gang
9.2 years	First met someone in a gang
10.4 years	First bullied someone else in school
11.3 years	First fired a pistol or revolver
11.3 years	First saw trauma (killing or injury) from gang violence
12.0 years	First joined the gang
12.0 years	First arrested for a criminal offense
12.3 years	First got his or her own gun
13.0 years	First got a permanent tattoo
16.5 years	Age of typical current gang member
24.1 years	Age they expect to get married
26.1 years	Age they expect to quit the gang.
59.5 years	Age they expect to die.

Note that even though gang members think they will leave their gang and live until at least 60, the grim reality is that many die very young (Knox, 1998).

To combat this scenario of events, young people must desire to resist gangs. Adults who work with youth, like Anthony in the case study, must find ways to help them meet their needs through ways that are both non-violent and acceptable. If family is not available, other youth often are ready to assist at-risk youth.

Peer helping programs have been developed across the country, and because it is peer groups interacting in these programs, they often have more chance of being successful. Peer pressure, which can negatively affect the choices youth make, can also be a powerful positive prevention tool.

One-to-one mentoring programs have also been developed based on positive role modeling. Youth who are at risk for gang involvement are particularly receptive to the positive effects of being mentored by a successful role model, and research has demonstrated that at-risk minority youth paired with successful role model minorities are greatly benefited (Landre, Miller, & Porter, 1997). One such program is Big Brother/Big Sister, a well-recognized, long-established program that pairs a child with an adult for the purpose of guidance and friendship. Other programs, sponsored by local agencies, community groups, and business and industry, are additionally available in most communities. When at-risk youth experience one-to-one mentoring and interact with a positive mentor similar to themselves, they often become able to look toward a gang-free future.

Family

According to many surveys and task forces, the number 1 tool for fighting gang involvement is parent involvement. Strong families are a major asset. Some states have enacted strong laws that hold parents accountable for the actions of their children, especially in school. Even single-parent families can begin very early to instill in their children a sense of worth and respect for themselves and others.

Many anti-gang programs are in operation across the nation. Those that are successful (a) provide more leisure-time activities with youngsters; (b) support a tougher law enforcement against gang activities in the community; (c) increase efforts to dry up sources of gang revenue, such as drugs and narcotics; and (d) increase parental supervision of children, including their activities and their friends (Moore, 1998).

Parents can also fight gangs by becoming better parents, that is, by improving their skills and taking more serious responsibility for their children. Parents who become effective gang fighters

- monitor the company their children keep;
- monitor their children's whereabouts;
- keep their children busy with positive activities at school, at church, or in organized recreational activities;
- model good behavior for their children and let them know how they are valued as individuals;
- spend time with their children and include them in family activities often; and
- watch for signs of pregang behavior, and at the first sign, intervene quickly and seek help from school, community groups, and law enforcement. Police officials are willing to help deter youth from gang involvement (McCarthy, 1998).

School

In recent years, youth have become anxious about their safety because of increased violence in the schools; and research has clearly illustrated that increased violence in communities and school come with gang involvement. Although not all school violence is gang related, there is enough gang-related violence to cause many schools to adopt a dress code with zero tolerance for gang paraphernalia, such as gold chains, baggy pants, and bandanas (see Figure 12–2). Special drug and gang prevention officers often are seen patrolling the halls of many urban schools. Metal detectors are commonplace, and a sense of being under siege often pervades the school setting. Strong schools, however, are a major asset in blocking gang activity. School is a perfect place to identify and work closely with troubled students such as gang wannabes. Schools can also help make sure that parents are involved with their children at school every step of the way, even if it means trying unconventional things such as having parents' night on a Saturday morning when parents can attend, and providing day care for younger children in the family. School counselors, teachers, and administrators must all take an active role in finding more appropriate ways of dealing with all the issues underlying drug activity. They must work closely with law enforcement and with social service agencies that can provide services that may shore up a disintegrating family (Lieutenant W. Hissong, Southaven, MS, police force gang specialist, personal communication, March 22, 1999). For example, creative scheduling of school instruction and atypical school hours might serve to meet the needs of students who come from homes where the eldest become parents to younger siblings.

Gang members are often bright and resourceful. They belong to organizations that have elaborate social and organizational structures that must be known and remembered. The systems of codes and symbols of typical gangs attest to the fact that many gang members possess exceptional cognitive abilities. For example, gangs use alphabets that are individualized for their own gang (see Figure 12–3 for partial alphabets), and they communicate using these alphabets so other gangs or law enforcement will not detect their plans. Gangs are dynamic groups that change over time and are influenced by their environment. For example, some gangs that previously used symbols such as bandanas, hats, or baggy clothes to identify themselves have now gone to more public symbols, such as apparel from the NFL and NBA.

Schools are recognizing and changing their approach to academic accountability. With academic competence also comes a measure of social prestige. This can go a long way in keeping marginal gang wannabes in the mainstream of the school culture (Dunston, 1993; Meeks, Heit, & Page, 1995).

Gang prevention programs must emphasize increasing the self-esteem of at-risk youth. Interventions to build self-esteem rest on the assumption that if a person likes himself or herself, he or she will be less likely to engage in activities that are harmful to self or others (Wilson-Brewer & Jacklin, 1990). Self-esteem enhancement is a long-term process. It must begin with healthy parenting practices, be nourished by the community, and be consistently enhanced by schools through activities that give adolescents a feeling of belonging and accomplishment. Juarez (1992) has suggested that self-esteem activities target male youth due to their dominant role in gang activities. Alternative community support systems that

Figure 12–3 | Alphabets

enhance self-esteem development should focus on manhood development with emphasis on rites-of-passage programs to assist male teens in the move from adolescence into adulthood.

Among effective approaches to prevention that can be employed in school settings are two techniques that have been demonstrated to be successful: conflict resolution education and dispute mediation training. One of the first conflict resolution curricula for adolescents was developed by Prothrow-Smith (1987). Participants learn how to communicate in such a way as to not escalate the conflict, to utilize problem-solving skills, and to maintain self-control through anger management. Conflict resolution education focuses on the use of peers as dispute mediators. Selected students are trained in communication, leadership, problem solving, and assertiveness. In middle schools, peer mediators resolve playground conflicts. In high schools, they may resolve disputes in interpersonal relationships. Teachers, security personnel, and others may receive dispute mediation training so they can help to resolve problems that are inherent in their work.

The ultimate goal of gang awareness and prevention activities is to provide safe and secure school campuses where students can learn and teachers can teach effectively (Elder, Fisher, & Forthman, 1994). If successful prevention of gang involvement is the goal, students must be involved in school-based programs from an early age (Landre et al., 1997). One definitive way to accomplish this is to invest as much money in hiring elementary school counselors as school systems do in hiring high school counselors (Peep, 1996). Additionally, all school staff, including auxiliary personnel, need to be educated in gang awareness and prevention (Trump, 1993b).

Children who are economically deprived need to be provided with choices at school that will make dropping out less likely. Teaching methods and materials need to be evaluated for appropriateness to real life situations. Youth grow up today in an MTV fast-paced world. Much of what happens at school is not relevant or presented in a palatable way. Instructional methods such as cooperative learning, cross-age tutoring, and team building can all help increase students' involvement and interaction with teachers (Bodinger-deUriate, 1993). Changes in the power structure in school also help drive children away. Children need to be respected no matter what their socioeconomic status is or from what cultural background they have come (Lal, Lal, & Achilles, 1993). School needs to be a caring and nurturing environment that encourages students to be involved and connected with their peers and teachers.

School programs with the best chance for preventing gang involvement offer gang prevention topics such as (a) consequences of gang membership, (b) gang resistance skills and assertiveness training skills (Elder et al., 1994; Meeks et al., 1995), (c) coping and stress management skills, (d) decision-making skills, (e) conflict prevention/peer mediation, (f) character development and responsibility, and (g) drug and substance abuse prevention (Meeks et al., 1995; Miars, 1996; Trump, 1993b). One program that presents a number of these gang prevention skills is Gang Resistance and Education Training (GREAT), which has been presented to eighth graders. Preliminary results have suggested that students who complete this program report more prosocial behavior than their peers who do not complete the program or who do not participate in the program (Esbersen & Osgood, 1997).

Another program that offers students training in coping skills is the Improving Social Awareness—Social Problem-Solving (ISA) Project. This program includes instruction in critical thinking skills and problem solving at the elementary level, and targets topics such as substance abuse or gang resistance at the secondary level.

Drug abuse training and abuse prevention are essential components of school-based gang prevention programs (Trump, 1993a) because drug abuse is closely related to gang activity. One program containing these components is the Drug Abuse Resistance Education (DARE) program, which is widely used in school settings and is highly supported by law enforcement.

Other school (and community) programs that provide students with alternatives in learning and playing that have great promise include using sports and field trips, which provide students opportunities they might never have otherwise because of their financial and family circumstances, and incorporating opportunities for vocational training and job placement into the curriculum (Bodinger-deUriet, 1993). Research has suggested that youth who are in gangs will select reputable employment over crime if given that option. Job placement and job tryouts need to be funded for at-risk youth so that they will aspire toward long-term employment once they finish school (Taylor, 1990). The School-to-Work Opportunities Act, signed into law in 1994, provides for funding to support a comprehensive high-quality, school-to-careers transition system to enable all students to successfully enter the workplace. A major component of this initiative is to ensure that all students, even those with academic deficiencies or disabilities, are provided adequate training that will lead to jobs offering livable wages and advancement (Moore, 1998).

Community

Taylor (1990) suggested that what is necessary for the control or reduction of gangs is the availability of jobs and the larger world of business and industry. Gang members often get involved in gangs via involvement in the drug traffic. All youth want to have a certain level of material goods. We see this in advertisements that play to the wants and peer pressures of our youth. When youth get involved in gangs, even in a minor way, they make a lot more money than can be made at a fast food restaurant or car wash. Many more jobs must be developed for youth that pay more than minimum wage. Communities must make a concerted effort to contribute to this concept through local business and industry.

Many communities have struggled with youth violence and gang development. A number of programs have been developed and implemented at local levels, and some have produced positive results. No one program, no set of strategies, can be considered the answer to the multifaceted and complex problem of gang involvement, however. As the 21st century arrives, Americans need to be ready to take back the youth of our society from gangs. In order to do this, there must be dramatic changes in families, schools, communities, and in this nation. No one group is able to do the work alone. Individual groups and programs need to form coalitions and collaborative groups that tie programs together and make them successful as well as cost- and time-effective. An example is the 100-man march several years ago that began an active involvement of minority men with each other, their children, and youth in their communities. It is grassroots efforts like this that help to reduce gang violence.

INTERVENTION STRATEGIES

Individual

Two strategies for dealing with individual gang members, especially those still on the fringes, are counseling and the use of psychodrama. Both of these intervention strategies have an effective therapeutic component and can be easily incorporated with other programs in schools, through community agencies, or in prisons. Counseling is most effective with marginal gang members or wannabes because it teaches new behavioral alternatives that allow these youth to become involved in constructive activities. Group counseling can provide opportunities for members to help each other gain insights and see their faulty thinking and behavior patterns. Group counseling is like a gang interaction. Members are more comfortable and able to participate fully in the activity. Positive changes often occur through working in this type of group because all the members are working from a similar family and community background (Yablonsky, 1997).

Psychodrama differs from counseling because the primary activity is for the individual to work through his or her personal, home, and community problems by acting them out using an alter ego. The success of this intervention is rooted in the fact that if gang members are able to take a minute and work through some of their reactionary behavior in a role-play setting before they actually carry out their behavior in reality, chances are greater that the negative behavior can be thwarted. If, for example, a male gang member has reacted to a minor threat from one of his own gang by vowing to kill him, he can instead role-play through the drama in his head, work through some of the anger, and particularly work on what consequences await him if he goes through with this threat. Often, after psychodrama occurs, underlying causes may surface that have triggered an inappropriate reaction to a relatively minor problem. Counseling and psychodrama have great value when working with gangsters. They provide direct training to those involved, allow opportunities for individuals to vent their anger and rage in a controlled environment, and slow down events so that gangsters can take time to see and understand what is actually taking place.

Gangsters live in the moment and react to whatever stimuli are affecting them. They need a mechanism by which they are given a chance to think through their behavior or make changes in their initial behavioral reaction to the stimuli. Psychodrama and group counseling allow gangsters to learn from each other in an open environment that what causes their violent impulses is often based on the emotional, physical, or sexual abuse they may have received as young children in a dysfunctional family system (Yablonsky, 1997).

Family

Today, many families are headed by a single parent, usually the mother, who is the only wage earner and, therefore, is unable to monitor the children. For these families, after-school and weekend programs often provide a safe haven for latchkey youngsters as well as give parents peace of mind while they are at work. For example, the Family Network Partnership is a program jointly sponsored by a university and community agency to help support families by providing recreation, tutoring, and peer helping (Moore, 1998). Most low-income families are unable to afford recreational activities or pay for tutoring.

Schools

Schools are also beginning to be more of a clearinghouse for family resources by sending home information to parents via school newsletters and other community publications. The intervention most needed in schools usually is during the hours of 3:00 p.m. until 7:00 p.m., which is often referred to by law enforcement as the prime time for crime. With good after-school programs, youth can be kept busy and will not have to spend time engaged in unproductive or unlawful activities (Moore, 1998). Many parent-teacher groups are beginning to see this need, and parent volunteers are investing their time with groups of youth after school by providing them with interesting and enjoyable activities.

Many schools are also used in the summer for remedial and recreational activities. Youth whose parents are unable to afford camps and sports activities need alternatives that provide safe and constructive programming for their children.

Community

One of the earliest interventions was begun by the New York City Youth Board in 1946. It was known as the detached worker project. This project had the following goals: (a) reduced antisocial behavior, particularly street fighting; (b) friendly interactions with other street gangs; (c) increased democratic participation within the gangs; (d) broadened social horizons; (e) responsibility for self-direction; (f) improved personal and

social adjustment of the individual; and (g) improved community relations. In this model a professional, such as a social worker or police officer, works directly with a gang on its own turf. Each professional is
assigned to a particular gang. Even though this approach has some success, the project worker often can not provide the proper interventions
commensurate with the level of gang involvement. Marginal gang members can often be helped by getting them to counseling groups, providing
recreation to fill some of their time and connect them with more whole-
some male role models, and providing job opportunities for them. Core
gang members require a more intense level of intervention. Problems
occur when project workers make incorrect diagnoses of gang structure
and makeup. These programs also require that an effective police presence is available in the community (Yablonsky, 1997).

The detached worker project model takes apart a gang's structure. It
deals first with the marginal gang members or wannabes to help redirect
their energies by providing constructive activities that will utilize their
time as well as supply acceptable social interaction, thereby drawing
them more into the mainstream of society.

Another early program that emerged in cities like New York, Chicago,
and Boston during the 1930s was known as the Adult Youth Association
(AYA) approach. Settlement houses or community recreation centers were
developed to deal with youth in these areas, where boredom, low economic status, and cultural differences were all contributing to the alienation of young men.

The AYA approach is primarily based on the premise that male youth,
in particular, need good role models to learn basic acceptable socialization
skills, and that the role models can be provided by community volunteers
working with at-risk youth in recreational endeavors and other social
activities. It is also based on the knowledge that even in ghetto areas it is
not unusual to see known gang members involved in a pickup game of
basketball. The success of this approach is based on the fact that community volunteers can better know and serve the needs of the community's
youth because they are members of the same community (Yablonsky,
1997). This type of program often draws on its own success stories for
future volunteers. Those at-risk individuals who were able to turn their
lives around often return to their own neighborhoods to become the
youth leaders and role models for the next generation.

Because the AYA is well integrated into each community, and the
workers are members or returning members of that community, the
chance of successful outcomes is raised. The fact that AYAs use recreation as a focus often leads to teams and leagues developing in one or
more sports. Those at-risk youth who belong to these leagues often
replace the idea of being in a gang with the idea of joining an athletic
league and derive the positive aspects of this organization. Marginal

gang members, who may disengage more easily because of their low level of gang involvement, may replace the benefits of gangs with those of a sports league. The most important aspect of any AYA is to allow the recreational and social activities to evolve naturally through the interaction of the local community volunteers and the youth. If communities bring already developed programs to neighborhoods without allowing for local youth to participate in the planning, the chance for success is diminished.

Throughout the 1990s gangs have continued to grow in numbers and strength, and have become more violent. Many communities have attempted to fight back against gang proliferation and expansion. According to Miller (1990), success requires a nationwide program that can give communities a framework and process by which local organizations could be informed of current methods and tools and supported financially.

A Presidential Committee on Juvenile Delinquency and Youth Crime developed such a program during the administration of President John Kennedy. To deter gang violence, federal offices were to be established to oversee the national anti-gang effort, to provide remedial programs to needy areas of the country, and to follow the effects through research and evaluation. When President Kennedy was assassinated, program funding ceased.

Many major cities have responded to the increased proliferation and intensity of violence, choosing methods that fit their city's needs. Austin, Texas, long plagued with gangs, experienced several acutely violent and savage murders in 1990 that alerted the entire city to the need for action. All elected officials made controlling gang activity their number 1 priority. A task force of elected officials, schools, social services, and citizens worked from a multidisciplinary approach to find ways to control gang activity. City officials felt the Austin police force should have a special unit devoted to gangs. The criminal intelligence unit started publishing bulletins about gang activities. Police were given special training on how to recognize and report gang activity, and local prosecutors were committed to making gang-related crime the top prosecution priority. In addition, a public service media campaign was developed, and gang unit efforts were complemented by beefed up budgets to social service, health, and child care agencies. As a result, Austin now has several programs that work toward controlling and eliminating the level of gang crime that was apparent in 1990.

A study completed in 1996 by the Police Executive Research Forum (PERF) examined the history and nature of gangs as well as the responses of public agencies to gangs from 1991–96 in five major citiies: Austin, Chicago, Kansas City (KS), Metro-Dade (FL), and San Francisco (Painter & Weisel, 1997). The study also reviewed how individual police responded to particular local gang problems. Each city worked to find solutions that fit its particular needs because no one anti-gang program works for all cities, given the diversity of region, race, and culture. This study, for example, suggested that all gang activity is not necessarily tied to heavy drug activity, that the city's geographical location may influence the amount of drug activity, and that this, in turn, may have an influence on gang activity. From the PERF study's highlights of what each of the five cities has done to respond to gangs and their affiliated activities, it seems clear that each community will have to find its own most appropriate ways to respond to local gang activity. This will require a collaborative community approach, carried out by a well-informed, trained police force and supported by governmental leadership.

Taylor (1990) suggested strategies that should be incorporated in any community team effort. One is that the community needs to put up a strong fight against the negative effects of drugs, and this fight needs to start at home at an early age. Another is to get parents talking with their children. Being a good role model is paramount, but parents must be explicit in their zero tolerance for any drug activity. Yet another is to encourage strong homes. Whether they are in a Chicago ghetto or in a more rural area of Colorado, such homes form the foundation for anti-drug, gang-free communities. Even poor families' or single parents' homes can be strong against the issues that support gang activity.

To be successful in preventing gang activity in communities, programs need a strong theoretical framework. However, this is an area that is extremely complex and not easily researched (Miller, 1990). The lack of systematic evaluation plans to determine long-term effectiveness of prevention and intervention strategies is one major cause of promising programs being scrapped before they are fully implemented. The only data collected and used to judge success or failure are often increases or decreases in crime statistics during new-program implementation. Community programs also need a two-pronged program so as to include prevention as well as intervention (Regini, 1998).

The American gang policy, developed by the National Gang Crime Research Center in Chicago, adopted a zero tolerance to gangs and gang activity in the 1980s. Its slogan was "Say no to gangs." There was funding to fight the drug aspect of gangs, but not enough. For the 21st century, the center's gang policy is adopting a negative tolerance toward gangs. This policy's slogan is "Say goodbye to gangs." This policy states that the cost is high for doing gang business. Money will be available to use civil, administrative, and criminal sanctions to prevent new recruits and target hardcore gang members for stiff sentences. All economic incentives must be removed from gang involvement. New and smarter laws will need to be passed to deal with gangs. The message must be sent to gangs in a strong and consistent way that gang terror is over (National Gang Crime Research Center, 1998).

ADAPTATIONS FOR DIVERSITY

Prevention and intervention strategies will be of little value to those who work to block gang involvement if there is not a basic understanding of the ethnic and cultural factors that influence individuals. People have always clustered together in groups for social interaction, protection, self-development, and simply because of their proximity to each other. Basic social expressions such as language, norms, sanctions, and values reveal valuable information (Axelson, 1999). This information is critical when developing the best approaches to diverse gangs.

All individuals come from their own particular ethnic and cultural group. Ethnic characteristics can be traced back to national origins or geographic regions. Culture is learned from experiences in the environment. Because the United States is a pluralistic society in terms of culture, there are a variety of ethnic groups to address. There are also subcultures that are racial, ethnic, regional, economic, or social communities that are distinctly different from other dominant groups in society. Gangs can be considered a subculture (Baruth & Manning, 1991).

Knowing that gangs represent diverse ethnic and cultural groups is of great importance when choosing approaches to block their influence and spread, as the earlier discussion of ethnic gangs has suggested. In the case of Anthony, whose ethnic roots are African American, his cultural roots or learned experiences are steeped in the drug-infested and extreme poverty of his ghetto, and place him at extremely high risk of joining a gang. It is easy to recognize that Anthony views the gang as a way of meeting his need to be part of a culture that offers him friends for social interaction, a unique language, a set of values, and codes to live and work by, even though the work is crime related.

For those who work with gangs, it is imperative that the ethnic and cultural backgrounds of specific gangs are reviewed as prevention programs are planned or interventions are undertaken. Uninformed assumptions about how gangs view the world or what norms or values they adhere to will not lead to successful outcomes. Providing opportunities that offer gang members a chance to reclaim ethnic pride or learn to function in an acceptable cultural milieu will enhance the likelihood of a successful outcome.

SUMMARY

Gangs have been around for decades. Their influence on society is felt by all Americans. The financial and individual losses to communities and families can be seen in towns, large and small. Gang members are a diverse group, but they all seek to have their individual social and emotional needs met through gang involvement. Being part of a gang organization allows them to feel protected and affirmed by those who matter to them, and to have a sense of belonging in an environment that alienates them from mainstream culture. Many factors in families, schools, and communities influence gang wannabes to become gang members. Thus it is important to intervene very early with potential gang members with interventions developed to combat the causes that are individual to each community while providing ongoing prevention activities. Effective laws and law enforcement are also needed. Diversity issues in gangs need to be addressed in order to find ways to solve the problems specific to a geographical region, large city, or small town in America. It is only when communities work collaboratively with all the resources they have toward strong prevention programs and effective intervention activities that progress will be achieved.

REFERENCES

Axelson, J. (1999). *Counseling and development in a multicultural society* (3rd ed.). New York: Brooks/Cole.

Baruth, L. G., & Manning, M. L. (1991). *Multicultural counseling and psychotherapy: A life-span perspective*. New York: Macmillan.

Bernard, T. J. (1990). Angry aggression among the truly disadvantaged. *Criminology, 28*, 73–75.

Bodinger-deUriate, C. (1993). *Membership in violent gangs fed by suspicions*. Los Alamitos, CA: Southwest Regional Laboratory. (ERIC Document Reproduction Service No. ED358 399)

Campbell, A. (1987). Self-definition by rejection. The case of gang girls. *Social Problems, 34*, 451–456.

Campbell, A. (1992). *The girls in the gang*. Malden, MA: Blackwell.

Cloward, R. A., & Ohlin, L. E. (1960). *Delinquency and opportunity: A theory of delinquent gangs*. New York: Free Press.

Cohen, A. K. (1955). *Delinquent boys: The culture of the gang*. New York: Free Press.

Covey, H. C., Menard, S., & Franzese, R. J. (1992). *Juvenile gangs*. Springfield, IL: Charles C Thomas.

Curry, G. D., & Spergel, I. A. (1992). Gang involvement and delinquency among Hispanic and African American adolescent males. *Journal of Research in Crime and Delinquency, 29*, 273–291.

Dukes, R. I., & Martinez, R. (1994). The impact of ethgender on self-esteem among adolescents. *Adolescence, 29*, 105–115.

Dunston, M. S. (1993, March/April). Signs of the times: Gangs and their symbols. *Police Marksman*, pp. 16–38.

Elder, R., Fisher, C., & Forthman, J. A. (1994). *On alert! Gang prevention school in-service guidelines*. Sacramento, CA: California Department of Education. (ERIC Document Reproduction Service No. ED 370 170)

Esbersen, F. A., & Osgood, D. W. (1997, November). National evaluation of G.R.E.A.T. *National Institute of Justice Research in Brief*. Washington, DC: Author.

Fagan, J. A. (1989). The social organization of drug use and drug dealing among urban gangs. *Criminology, 27,* 633–669.

Fagan, J. A., Piper, E. S., & Moore, M. (1986). Violent delinquents and urban youth. *Criminology, 23,* 439–466.

Fishman, L. T. (1992, March). *The Vice Queens: An ethnographic study of Black female gang behavior.* Paper presented at the annual meeting of the American Society of Criminology, Chicago.

Gibeaut, J. (1998). Gang busters. *American Bar Association Journal, 84,* 64–69.

Gottfredson, M., & Hirschi, T. (1990). *A general theory of crime.* Stanford, CA: Stanford University Press.

Gray-Ray, P., & Ray, M. C. (1990). Juvenile delinquency in the Black community. *Youth and Society, 22,* 67–84.

Hagadorn, J. M. (1991). Gangs, neighborhoods, and public policy. *Social Problems, 38,* 529–541.

Hirschi, T. (1969). *Causes of delinquency.* Berkeley: University of California Press.

Horowitz, R. (1986). Remaining an outsider: Membership as a threat to research rapport. *Urban Life, 1,* 409–430.

Huff, C. R. (1998, March). Criminal behavior of gang members and at-risk youths. *National Institute of Justice Research Review.*

Jackson, R., & McBride, D. (1987). *Understanding street gangs.* Sacramento, CA: Custom.

Jankowski, M. S. (1991). *Islands in the street: Gangs and American urban society.* Berkeley: University of California Press.

Juarez, P. D. (1992). The public health model and violence prevention. In R. C. Cervantes (Ed.), *Substance abuse and gang violence* (pp. 43–59). Newbury Park, CA: Sage.

Klein, M., Maxson, C., & Miller, J. (Eds.). (1995). *The modern gang reader.* Los Angeles, CA: Roxbury.

Knox, G. (1998). What do we know about the gang problem in American today? *Official Proceedings of the 1998 Second International Gang Specialist Training Conference, 1,* 419.

Knox, G., Laske, D., & Tromanhauser, E. (1992). *Schools under siege.* Dubuque, IA: Kendal/Hunt.

Lal, S. R., Lal, D., & Achilles, C. M. (1993). *Handbook on gangs in schools: Strategies to reduce gang-related activities.* Newbury Park, CA: Corwin Press.

Landre, R., Miller, M., & Porter, D. (1997). *Gangs: A handbook for community awareness.* New York: Facts on File.

LeBinh, P. (1997). *Girl-only gangs: A bibliography.* (ERIC Document Reproduction Service No. ED 413 275)

Matza, D. (1964). *Delinquency and drift.* New York: Wiley.

McCarthy, C. (1998). What are gang characteristics? *Official Proceedings of the 1998 Second International Gang Specialist Training Conference, 1,* 443.

Meeks, L., Heit, P., & Page, R. (1995). *Violence prevention: Totally awesome teaching strategies for safe and drug free schools.* Blacklick, OH: Meeks Heit.

Merriam Webster's collegiate dictionary (10th ed.). (1995). Springfield, MA: Merriam-Webster.

Miars, R. D. (1996). Stress and coping in today's society. In D. Capuzzi & D. Gross (Eds.), *Youth at risk: A prevention resource for counselors, teachers, and parents* (2nd ed., pp. 129–147). Alexandria, VA: American Counseling Association.

Miller, W. (1958). Lower class culture as a generating milieu of gang delinquency. *Journal of Social Issues, 14,* 5–19.

Miller, W. B. (1990). Why the United States has failed to solve its youth gang problem. In C. R. Huff (Ed.), *Gangs in America.* Newbury Park, CA: Sage.

Molidor, C. E. (1996). *Female gang members: A profile of aggression and victimization.* (ERIC Document Reproduction Service No. EJ 530 433)

Moore, M. (1998). Investing in our children: Report on youth violence and school safety. *Official Proceedings of the 1998 Second International Gang Specialist Training Conference, 1.*

Morales, A. (1992). A clinical model for the prevention of gang violence and homicide. In R. C. Cervantes (Ed.), *Substance abuse and gang violence* (pp. 105–120). Newbury Park, CA: Sage.

Morales, A. (1982). The Mexican American gang member: Evaluation and treatment. In R. M. Becerra, M. Karno, & J. Escobar (Eds.), *Mental health and Hispanic Americans: Clinical perspectives.* New York: Grune & Stratton.

National Gang Crime Research Center. (1998). A message from the National Gang Crime Research Center: Understanding the "negative tolerance" policy on and about gangs. *Journal of Gang Research, 5*(3), 76.

Painter, E., & Weisel, D. (1997). Crafting local responses to gang problems: Case studies from five cities. *Public Management, 79*(7), 75.

Palmer, M. (1992). *Gang profiles.* Portland, OR: Northeast Coalition of Neighborhoods.

Peep, B. B. (1996). Lessons from the gang: What gang members think about their schools suggests new direction for classroom reform. *The School Administrator, 53,* 26–31.

Prothrow-Smith, D. (1987). *Violence prevention curriculum for adolescents.* Newton, MA: Education Development Center.

Regini, L. A. (1998). Combating gangs. *F.B.I. Law Enforcement Bulletin, 67,* 1–5.

Sachs, S. L. (1997). *Street gangs awareness: A resource guide for parents and professionals.* Minneapolis, MN: Fairview Press.

Shulmire, S. R. (1996). *A comparative study of gang-involved and other adolescent women.* (ERIC Document Reproduction Service No. ED 412 477)

Skolnick, J. (1995). Gangs and crime old as time: But drugs change gang culture. In M. Klein, C. Maxon, & J. Miller (Eds.), *The modern gang reader.* Los Angeles, CA: Roxbury.

Spergel, I. A. (1990). Youth gangs: Continuity and change. In M. Tonry & N. Morros (Eds.), *Crime and justice: A review of research* (pp. 171–275). Chicago: University of Chicago Press.

Spergel, I. A. (1992). Youth gangs: An essay review. *Social Service Review, 6,* 121–140.

Spergel, I. A. (1995). *The youth problem.* New York: Oxford University Press.

Taylor, C. (1990). *Dangerous society.* East Lansing: Michigan State University Press.

Tayor, C. S. (1993). Female gangs: A historical perspective. In C. S. Taylor (Ed.), *Girls, gangs, women, and drugs* (pp. 13–47). East Lansing: Michigan State University Press.

Thrasher, T. (1926). *The gang: Study of 1,313 gangs.* Chicago: University of Chicago Press.

Trump, K. S. (1993a). *Youth gangs and schools: The need for intervention and prevention strategies.* Cleveland, OH: Cleveland State University. (ERIC Document Reproduction Service No. ED 361 457)

Trump, K. S. (1993b). Tell teen gangs: School's out. *American School Board Journal,* pp. 39–42.

Vigil, D. (1988). *Barrio gangs: Street life and identity in southern California.* Austin: University of Texas Press.

Wilson-Brewer, R., & Jacklin, B. (1990). *Violence prevention strategies targeted at the general population of minority youth.* Paper presented at the Forum on Youth Violence in Minority Communities: Setting the Agenda for Prevention, Atlanta, GA.

Yablonsky, L. (1997). *Gangsters: Fifty years of madness, drugs, and death on the streets of America.* New York: New York University Press.

APPENDIX 12–1

Questions

Multiple Choice (Place answer in the blank):

__c__ 1. Which ethnic gangs exhibit a structural hierarchy?
    a. Asian
    b. African American
    c. Hispanic
    d. White supremacist

__a__ 2. Which ethnic gang type practices extortion?
    a. Asian
    b. African American
    c. Hispanic
    d. White supremacist

__b__ 3. Heroin is the primary drug sold by which ethnic group?
    a. Asian
    b. African American
    c. Hispanic
    d. White supremacist

__d__ 4. Which ethnic group recruits for neo-Nazi type activities?
    a. Asian
    b. African American
    c. Hispanic
    d. White supremacist

__c__ 5. Which ethnic group is generational?
    a. Asian
    b. African American
    c. Hispanic
    d. White supremacist

Please answer *True* or *False* to the following questions:

__F__ 6. Gangs are a recent phenomena in our society.
__T__ 7. Those individuals involved in gangs do so because they want to be with their own racial/cultural group.
__F__ 8. Gangs are generally found only in urban areas.
__T__ 9. Those who aspire to gang affiliation are known as *wannabes*.
__F__ 10. The impact of gangs on society is minimal to the average citizen.
__T__ 11. Some research has found that gang involvement is more likely for those with poor family ties.
__T__ 12. Gang members often continue their involvement as adults.

_T_ 13. Gang members seek to gain recognition, protection, and a sense of belonging.

_T_ 14. Leadership in gangs is not well structured and organized.

_T_ 15. Research has been done to show that adolescents who have high self-control are less likely to be involved in gangs.

Matching (put correct letter on the line):

_c_	16. Wannabe	a. serve as advisers to young gang members
_d_	17. Gangster	b. signs and symbols representing gangs
_b_	18. Graffiti	c. youth seeking status in a gang
		d. term used in place of gang member
_a_	19. Veteranos	e. Term for White supremacist in America
_e_	20. Skinhead	

13 | Death in the Classroom: Violence in Schools

Michael T. Barta

Our schools are in difficulty. High dropout rates, bulging special education programs, and the increase in violence in our schools corroborate this statement. Behavior appears to be the external manifestation of an internal state of being. If this is the case, then these behaviors speak volumes to the state and quality of the delivery of education in the United States. Violence, taken as a single entity, demonstrates that our children are not getting their needs met in appropriate ways. A great number of our children feel as if they don't belong. These children also feel unheard, incompetent, unchallenged, and powerless. Is there any wonder why youth choose to act out in violent or aggressive ways when they constantly carry such unmet needs? Aggressive youth view violence as a legitimate means of solving interpersonal problems (Dodge, 1986; Slaby & Guerra, 1988). Currently, schools are under attack by critics for seeming to care more about performance on standardized tests than meeting the student's needs for comfort and safety. Many schools across the nation give annual tests to demonstrate the achievement of higher standards. As of yet, there is no proof that meeting these standards will meet our youth's needs.

The model presented in this chapter is based on meeting youth's needs within the classroom through the use of a need-based preventative program. However, to do this it is necessary to focus on the needs of the family, school, and community. For general purposes, at times, the term *community* is used simultaneously with *school board*. The school board, in essence, acts as the voice of the community, reflecting the community's needs, values, and recommendations. The prevention team consists of students, parents, teachers, administrators, and school board members (community). The school-wide prevention team assesses, delivers, and evaluates the performance of this program. The main argument for this purposed program is that youth who do not get their needs satisfied in appropriate ways will find other, more destructive ways to get their needs met. Schools need to focus as much energy on youth as they do on the content. Educators must take the responsibility to reform the schools before any more children have to die in the classroom.

This chapter outlines a model that uses, but is not entirely based on, William Glasser's list of universal needs. Glasser (1998) stated that people have five needs that must be met consistently throughout life. These needs have no hierarchical structure, which means that the meeting of one need is not contingent upon the meeting of other needs. Glasser's need list includes love or belonging, freedom (personal choice), power (accomplishment or achievement), fun (a sense of learning and exploration), and survival (our most basic physical and emotional needs). Through better meeting the needs of youth, schools can take preventive steps in bringing an end to destructive behavior.

Before focusing on the needs model, the chapter considers recent violence in the schools, briefly explores the problem, discusses family, school, and community influences, and presents reflections on Littleton. Using the needs-based model in a team approach to violence prevention is then broadly explored, and the chapter concludes with discussions of need-based intervention and diversity teams. Hopefully the strategies presented in the chapter will offer fresh hope to all involved in the process of education.

VIOLENCE IN OUR SCHOOLS

Violence has become a part of the daily lives of students, families, schools, and communities. On June 16, 1998, Kip Kipland, a 15-year-old boy, was formally charged with aggravated murder and aggravated attempted murder. He was charged after killing his parents, driving to school and opening fire in a crowded school cafeteria. When the shooting was over, two classmates were dead and several others were wounded. At no time in history has there been the number of violent crimes and reports of aggression in our schools as there is today. Juvenile arrests for murder between 1985 and 1994 increased 150% (Traub, 1996). The problem of violence in the classroom is not confined to inner-city schools. Arrests in rural communities showed that violent crimes increased 15.2% from 1992 to 1993 (Federal Bureau of Investigation [FBI], 1994).

The literature concerning violence continues to paint a bleak picture. In 1997, the U.S. Department of Education conducted a study with a sample of 1,234 schools. The results of this study found that during the 1996–97 school year there were 4,170 cases of rape and sexual battery, 7,150 cases of robbery, and 10,950 physical attacks or fights with weapons reported in the schools. The study also showed that there were 98,490 reported cases of vandalism, 115, 500 reports of larceny, and 187, 890 reports of physical attack or fights without a weapon (Mansfield, Alexander, & Farris, 1991).

The frequency of violence in our schools points to the need for reform. Everyday in our schools our youth face traumatic situations: 3 under 25 die from HIV infection, 6 under 20 commit suicide, 13 are homicide victims, 16 are killed by firearms, 316 children under 18 are arrested for violent crimes, 1,420 babies are born to teen mothers, 3, 356 students drop out of school, 5,702 children under 18 are arrested, and 13,076 public school students are suspended (Campbell & Dahir, 1997). Without question, schools must develop new creative ways to meet and satisfy the needs of students.

When thinking of violence in schools, most tend to visualize guns and gang members. Yet there are subtler forms of violence that occur daily. Bullying is a specific form of violence that afflicts physical and/or psychological harm on individuals. It is estimated to affect 15% to 20% of the U.S. population (Batsche & Knoff, 1994). Bullying victims are likely to be seen as powerless, as having poor social contacts and support systems at school. They have other traits that single them out from the rest of the school population (Furlong, Chung, Bates, & Morrison, 1995). Students who do not feel a sense of belonging are often targeted for violence. Those who stand out in a crowd, such as special education students, are more likely to be victimized than students in regular education (Morrison, Furlong, & Morrison, 1994).

PROBLEM EXPLORATION

Violence touches the student's life in many ways. Studies have shown that youth exposed to violence suffer decreases in academic achievement, less supportive interpersonal relationships, withdrawn and negative social behavior, and an increased risk of becoming violent themselves (Bell & Jenkins, 1993). Schools, in order to increase the student's success, must find ways to enhance the sense of security needed by all students. Even when schools have protective measures in place (e.g., security personnel and metal detectors), students remain frightened. How can we expect our youth to learn in environments that resemble prisons more than safe places of academic enrichment? What has been tried?

Many approaches have tried to identify and deal effectively with aggressive and violent students. Suspension and expulsion put youth back into the community where they can freely practice negative behaviors. Strumphauser (1986) described the futility of these methods to deal with violence. In his opinion a more ineffective social program could not be designed. To remove the youth from the very society to which they must learn to adapt is using punishment as the only learning principle to change behavior. This removal not only includes suspension and expulsion but also the removal of the youth from regular education into self-contained special education classrooms. Obviously, the continued rise in violence and aggression in our schools proves these attempts ineffective for preventing or reducing violence. It appears that many interventions used by schools tend to be based on removing the youth from the school. Currently the mode of dealing with violence shows an overwhelming tendency to be reactive and punitive. Teachers and administrators use coercion, suspension, and expulsion as a means to curb violent behavior. These practices add to the problem by being mild forms of violence in themselves. The question is not what to do with violent students; the question is how to prevent the need for violence and aggressive behavior in students.

The use of behavior modification also appears to be ineffective in stopping aggression and violence. Applied behavioral analysis often uses the psychology of operant conditioning, which is mostly reactive and coercive. Teachers randomly reinforce positive behavior in the hope of having other youth follow in kind. For youth who have emotional need deficits, behaviorism only increases the problem. Behavior modification is an educated guess as to what youth need. Molding their behavior removes the choices, freedoms, and feelings of belonging that are essential for personal growth. Behavioral approaches focus on the external rather than internal reasons for behavior. Attempting to control the external environment of students strips them of their individuality. They are made to perform for rewards that often have no relation to what they want or need. Instead of using external forms of control, educators will do well to focus on students' perception of their needs.

Zero tolerance is another popular method of dealing with the growing problem of aggression and violence. Zero tolerance translates into suspension and expulsion for students. The strategy removes students from environments in which they can learn appropriate social skills, learn prosocial behavior, and be exposed to caring adults. Zero tolerance removes students from productive environments and places them in the community where they have access to drugs, negative role models, and uncaring adult support systems (Nelson, 1997). With violence escalating, the causes and conditions that surround the violent youth must be explored. The examples just noted bring clarity to some of the current ineffective methods of prevention used in our schools to detour violence.

FAMILY, SCHOOL, AND COMMUNITY INFLUENCE

Explorations of family, school, and community areas—and of the need for change—provide assistance in efforts to understand the violent student's worldview.

Family

Youth today face many problems concerning family issues. Single-parent households, divorce, dual-income families, and youth abuse within the family leave youth with no significant support systems or role models. Abused and neglected youth have been shown to manifest more aggressive behaviors than nonabused (Egeland, Sroufe, & Erickson, 1983). It appears that families are not providing a consistent foundation of support for youth. Interactions between children and troubled families tend to teach and maintain deviant patterns of behavior (Patterson, 1982). Youth are currently identified as the problem rather than being seen as a symptom of a larger family problem. Interventions after the child displays violent tendencies denies the intuitive understanding that these behaviors do not develop overnight (Nelson, 1997).

Schools

Another significant predictor of aggressive behavior is exposure to violence. A study of middle and high school students in an inner-city area revealed that 35% of students had witnessed a stabbing, 39% had witnessed a shooting, and 24% stated that they had witnessed a killing (Shakoor & Chalmers, 1991). It appears that youth learn to be violent by modeling aggression that is acted out at home, in schools, or in the community.

The choice of content-based instruction plays a significant role in the youth's feelings of frustration and failure. Schools, due to the public demand for excellence, often place more emphasis on content than the social and emotional needs of youth. In turn, problems arise from these needs going unmet. Once a youth has expressed an aggressive or violent attitude, his or her chances of positive interactions with teachers are severely limited. Soriano, Soriano, and Jimenez (1994) found that teachers tend to make fewer academic interactions with students who display aggressive behaviors. By overlooking this population, educators overlook those who need the help most.

Community

Communities can contribute to creating violence in our youth. When communities lack adequate recreational and adult-sponsored activities, youth are allowed to meet their own needs, often in unproductive ways. The community's general functioning will be better off if aggressive and violent behaviors are dealt with in appropriate ways. The use of suspension and expulsion with problem youth increases the burden on the community. Youth taken out of a structured environment and placed on the streets are able to act out their aggressive behaviors more freely. The absence of meaningful recreational and vocational opportunities supports delinquent behavior (Strumphauser, Aiken, & Veloz, 1977). A program of prevention that deals with the unmet needs of youth can effectively reduce the number of youth removed from the schools. Communities want safe and productive youth yet often do nothing to create these conditions. The community's environment, attitudes, values, and behavior play a crucial role in the development of youth. Communities fail when they do not recognize the importance of providing safe, caring environments for this population. High proportions of youth are living in environments in which they have witnessed or experienced violence either in their families, schools, or communities. This exposure to violence has tremendous detrimental emotional and behavioral health effects on our youth (O'Keefe, 1997). The existing problems in families, educational systems, and communities need to be seen realistically and dealt with effectively.

Need for Change

From the perspective of the educational system, educators can not continue to use coercion as a means to control youth. Youth today have more struggles than they did even a generation ago. Society has moved from meeting basic needs in the home or in the community to transferring responsibility onto an ill-prepared school system. When school programs are based on content and not the needs of the youth, youth are not getting needs met anywhere. Aggression and violence have no place in schools, yet by ignoring the youth's needs, our schools are contributing to creating violent and aggressive behavior. Nelson (1997) has shown that the implementation of a universally based, school- or district-wide intervention program greatly reduces the frequency of expulsions, suspensions, and emergency removals based on violent and aggressive behavior.

Using William Glasser's list of universal needs can be a collaborative, integrative, and supportive way to focus on the needs of youth, families, schools, and our communities. This approach promises to treat the youth across his or her entire social milieu. The youth, the family, the school, and the community will all benefit from need gratification. Acting as a whole, the levels within this system can meet and sustain all needs from an internal perspective. The methods used here are based on reciprocity within the system, which means that when one group's needs are met, that group has more energy, time, and resources to help meet the needs of the other groups. The sense of belonging created by this method allows everyone say in how the program is run. Contributions made by the school and the community ultimately reinforce the health and satisfaction of the community.

A need-based model is built around the needs of youth. The entire focus asks the family, the school, and the community to place the youth at the center of need gratification. Through their efforts, the families, the school, and the community can expect capable, fully functioning youth who no longer use violence and aggression to meet needs.

The school board is the voice of the community, communicating its needs, and recommendations. Currently, the school board directs what will be taught in schools and how this information will be delivered. The administration then tells the teachers what content is acceptable for use in the classroom. In most schools, the administration also dictates how this information is delivered. Teachers focus on the distribution of information to the students. New and young teachers, educated with fresh, creative strategies, are forced to comply with the existing educational system.

It is understood that youth need to learn how to read, write, and calculate. However, it is equally important that youth learn to understand and deal with their needs effectively. A need-based system allows the youth, the school, the family, and the school board to have their needs met on a consistent basis. Meeting the youth's needs allows him or her freely to create, belong, explore, accomplish, and flourish. Meeting youth's needs in healthy ways takes away their maladaptive responses to life. Violence occurs when there is a threat to one's well-being. When one of the five universal needs goes unmet on a consistent basis, the first response is fear and aggression. If these needs are not met in appropriate ways, youth find destructive ways to meet them. Gangs serve as a good example of this premise. A gang can be viewed as a maladaptive attempt to gratify needs. A youth who joins a gang is given a strong sense of belonging. He or she also gets a sense of power (usually through numbers and weapons), fun (through vandalism, drinking, drugs, and unloving sex), survival (a false sense of being cared for of taking care of each other), and freedom (making choices that are not congruent with societies' values). Although the need gratification produced by belonging to a gang can be viewed as pathological, it does provide the individual with the opportunity to have his or her needs met on a consistent basis.

Youth are encouraged to join gangs because schools are not meeting their needs. Teachers, administrators, and service personnel have access to the nation's youth an average of 180 days per year. Teachers see youth 8 hours a day, 5 days a week, and spend 7,200 hours per year with them. With single-parent families, double-income families, and troubled families, school personnel possibly have more access to youth than any other institution or person. Schools have a valuable opportunity to reach the youth's five basic needs and encourage positive growth. Unfortunately, schools have assumed that the youth are getting these needs met elsewhere even when statistics and common sense tell them otherwise. Kazdin (1991) pointed out that if youth who exhibit signs of aggressive behavior are not provided with effective interventions to these behaviors by the age of 8, the chances are that these youth will need lifelong support and be consistent problems to society.

Families, schools, and the community must focus on what our youth need to be emotionally and mentally healthy. Youth should not be expected to disregard their emotional needs in the process of mastering instructional content. How can youth be expected to learn when they are hungry? When they feel no sense of belonging? When they have no opportunities to explore, have fun, or find their own interests? How can youth possibly be interested in the content taught when there is absolutely no sense of accomplishment in the task for him or her?

Families face the same dilemma. How can parents be involved when they do not have enough time to raise their own youth? When the sense of family and belonging is laid by the wayside in pursuit of money and material goods? Families have difficulty in attaining feelings of stability when their youth's needs for safety and security in the educational system are not being met. Education must begin to satisfy these needs before violence can be eradicated from the schools.

The same questions can be asked regarding teachers and administrators. How can teachers expect to have a sense of belonging in the schools when they have to follow strict standards of achievement that inhibit all sense of creativity? How can teachers and administrators be expected to teach youth with limited funds and materials? How can teachers not suffer burnout while trying to find the correct balance between the content-oriented curriculum and the obvious needs of the students they teach? How can society expect teachers to focus on effective teaching when they are frustrated by extremely low pay, and hold feelings of being unvalued? Administrators need the freedom to lead effectively. How can an administrator lead when the teacher meets his or her action with resistance? When teachers' only sense of accomplishment rests on the scores of the youth within their school?

Communities have needs, too. They need to feel a sense of belonging to the rest of society. Communities need recreational facilities and areas of open space. Communities need to feel that their youth are becoming sturdy citizens. When this model is employed, the youth, the family, the school, and the community can all have their needs met while at the same time eradicating violence and aggression.

REFLECTIONS ON LITTLETON

The Event

Cassie Bernall, Matt Kechter, Corey DePooter, Rachel Scott, John Tomlin, Laura Townsend, Danny Rohrbough, Kelly Flemming, Steven Curnow,

Isaiah Shoels, Daniel Mauser, Dave Sanders, Kyle Velasquez, Eric Harris, and Dylan Klebold are the 15 most recent victims of our educational system. On Tuesday, April 20, 1999, at 11:30 a.m., two youths walked into a Littleton, Colorado, high school with two shotguns, a semiautomatic pistol, a 9-mm semiautomatic rifle, and over 20 self-made bombs to kill their peers and teachers. These two students obviously did not feel a part of their school. Instead, they turned to other students with the same sense of despair. In this despair, the two gunmen found companionship that set them on a deadly course. The Trench Coat Mafia seems like a name that a youth would make up during make-believe play. For these students it meant belonging.

We can expect more incidents like this as long as we continue to neglect our youth's basic needs. The needs of survival, belonging, adventure, exploration, accomplishment, and freedom of choice obviously were not met in the two gunmen in appropriate ways. When our students do not have their needs met in appropriate ways, they will find a way to meet them in destructive ways. These two high school students were very successful in meeting their own needs. They killed for power and for the sense of accomplishment they sorely craved. They joined together and became a killing team to feel a sense of belonging. They made a free choice, a choice that would leave others dead and wounded. Their laughter could be heard in the halls of the school in the adventure of execution-style killings. They obviously believed that their actions would live on in the minds and hearts of millions, that they would survive.

Each one of the needs talked about in this chapter was met when the two high school students in Littleton, Colorado, decided to meet their own needs.

The rage shown in this incident is unfathomable. Colorado sits in shock and disbelief just 24 hours after the shooting stopped. Columbine High School in Littleton, Colorado, was described as a place that was proud of their S.A.T. scores and sports teams. Fifty youths in the school of 1,800 have straight As and over 200 have a 3.8 grade point average. Columbine is also typical of every other high school in America, stratified by cliques.

Eric Harris, 18, and Dylan Klebold, 17, belonged to a group that called themselves the Trench Coat Mafia. They were outsiders, a group that did not fit in with the youth who were popular. The stratification at this particular high school turned deadly. Eric and Dylan found belonging in other damaged and shunned individuals. They found power in relating to this century's greatest madman, Adolph Hitler. They found a perverted sense of fun from torturing animals, setting fires, building bombs, and destroying lives. They believed they would survive this ordeal, and in a way they have succeeded. The memory of this event will last forever. Eric and Dylan wrote poems about death, listened to German bands, talked about their admiration for Adolph Hitler, and wore swastikas. Their friends describe them as normal. They liked to play violent video games, watch TV, and play role-playing games. A year ago they were both convicted of felony theft, one count of felony trespass, and a misdemeanor for breaking into a car and stealing radio equipment. Instead of reform, they were sent to a diversion program for first-time juvenile offenders (Erin, Lipsher, & Young, 1999). No one had taken the gunmen seriously. People in the school saw them as rebels or villains, but most described them as losers (Johnson & Brook, 1999).

People inside the school described the horror. They said that the gun shots and explosions seemed to go off for hours. Students sprinted through hallways or ran outside and climbed over cars for safety. There was smoke, blood, dead bodies, and a torrential rain streaming from the sprinkler system. Students in the science wing witnessed a teacher stumble into their classroom after being shot two times in the back. They described seeing his teeth break out when his face hit the floor. The students in the science room took off their shirts to mop up the blood (Wilgonen, 1999). In the cafeteria a teacher screamed, "Get down!" Chaos overwhelmed the cafeteria as hundreds of students scrambled to get under tables. Eric and Dylan just kept firing. In the library students heard explosions as pieces of the ceiling fell around them. The students in the library heard the gunmen say, "This is for making fun of us, this is revenge." The assailants walked up to a student and said, "Look at this nerd," and killed him. Then they said, "Look at this nigger," and they killed him, too (Callahan, 1999). How tragic that in the aftermath the cliques broke down and could be seen on national TV hugging and grieving together (Rimen, 1999).

The Reactions

Here are two personal reactions to the Littleton, Colorado, tragedy. One is that of this chapter's author, Michael Barta, and the other is that of a graduate student in school counseling and special education at the University of Northern Colorado, Suzy Trukenbrod.

- *Michael:* How ironic that as this chapter was being created, 14 students and one teacher were killed in the nation's worst school shooting spree, just 50 miles from our home town. No longer is the violence out there; the violence has affected our own community. I was in a gymnasium locker room when I first heard a young woman sobbing on the radio. The girl described how the gunmen shot people at random. The mind is an incredible instrument: when I first heard the woman sobbing, I thought I was listening to a local radio station that plays comedy. I felt sick when reality hit, and my mind said, "This is not funny." I was stunned with a deep sense of sadness. I felt depression, hopelessness, and panic. It is one thing when there is a school shooting 2,000 miles away; it's another thing when it happens in your community. Another young woman came on the radio, and through her sobs I heard her say, "How can this be happening? Schools are supposed to be safe."

- *Suzy:* I spent the day crying, partly for myself and partly for the family and friends of the students. A feeling of helplessness comes over a person in times of tragedy. Disbelief that such a thing could happen in a state that is so beautiful. Feelings that no matter what you do it's not enough. Is this really the case? Is there nothing we can do? Or is it in times like these that we have to take a step forward and do more than just talk? It is times like these, desperate times, when we need to take the risks that can make the difference. Watching the students and the families recount their stories of the last 36 hours shocked me. It opened my eyes to the world we are living in and has affected my thinking.

- *Michael:* This tragedy brings back many of my high school experiences. I was a scrawny, pimple-faced kid who was afraid of girls. I can identify with the feelings of isolation and inferiority still present in our young people today. My solution didn't involve guns; instead I turned to drinking a half-dozen beers with friends on Friday nights. I can identify with our youth's feeling of unworthiness.

- *Suzy:* I sent out an e-mail after this event to let the people I love know that I cared for them. The responses I got from these people were amazing. They reflected on their own school experiences and how this incident would have been unfathomable when they were in school. This was unfathomable to the students at Littleton High School. What is so devastating about school violence is that it catches you where you least expect it.

- *Michael:* What I've seen in the aftermath of this tragedy is the overwhelming sense of how people identify with both the victims and the perpetrators. This type of event brings to the surface our own experiences and emotions, our own difficulties and struggles. We don't condone the shooting, but we seem to all identify with the feelings of rejection, isolation, and loneliness. We identify with being social outcasts in our own schools, homes, or communities. This incident brings to light just how many people in our society feel like they don't belong. It frightens us to have these feelings brought into our awareness. It is horribly frightening to identify with the rage that was present in these two young men. We identify with the rage of being put down and the rage of not belonging. We make the assumption that violence only happens in inner-city schools, but the perpetrators of this crime drove to school in a BMW.

- *Suzy:* We seem to be a nation of hypocrites. Constantly telling our students to respect the people in their lives as we drive down the road screaming at the person in the car next to us. What message are we truly sending? It is said that actions speak louder than words. Maybe we need to start teaching our youth through our actions. Our youth are screaming, and only through incidents when others are killed do we hear them. We have heard their screams seven times in the last 2 years. When do we start listening and stop just hearing? What does it take until we make the necessary changes? When will there be enough dead youth? The initial signs may be small, but we need to take notice. It is our responsibility as educators to make our schools safe, not the responsibility of the police officer who gets placed in the school.

- *Michael:* Radio talk shows have tried desperately, 24 hours a day, to make sense of the shooting. Shock has turned to anger. Everyone affected by this event is trying to find someone to blame. The teachers, the police, the counselors, the Internet, and the boys' families have all been the targets of blame. We are all to blame for ignoring our youth's needs. It appears that our nation is set on proving worth externally, and we have forgotten our inner natures. Our quiet desperation is no longer quiet.

- *Suzy:* We are in the age of bigger is better: SUVs, big screen TV, and more powerful computers. If you don't have the biggest and the best you might as well have nothing at all. WRONG! We have lost the values that started our great nation. We have lost the mentality that hard work and dedication will help us succeed. If we put forth an effort to change, and help one student, we are successful. If we keep one student from picking up a gun to hurt himself or herself or another student, we are making progress.

- *Michael:* Just last year our government spoke of reducing violence by getting families more involved with schools and raising standards of achievement. It appears that high academic standards may be part of the problem. They create competition and alienation. Focusing on high academic standards distracts teachers and parents away from the warning signs of aggression. This incident has shocked me. A mass murder happened not far from my desk, as I sat working on a chapter concerning school violence. I felt a sense of powerlessness in the midst of violence. I am but one voice; who will listen? We all must listen to the cries of our youth.

- *Suzy:* We must create the environment that makes students feel that they belong. We must create the environment in which students have power and input. We must create an environment that is so sacred that the thought of destroying it is unthinkable. We are the people that make school safe. We are the people that make school fun. We are the people that make school a place that is respected. We do not work in a dictatorship. Take the time to listen to your students. Take 10 minutes a day to talk to a student and be sure it is a different student every day. Reach out and become a part of their lives. Take interest in their interests. Help them actually learn respect and concern. Fill their minds with knowledge and their hearts with enough care to lead us into the next millennium. Our nation's future depends on what we are doing in our classrooms, and the skills we are teaching our students.

- *Michael:* No one took the two gunmen seriously. For over a year the two had dressed in dark trench coats, worn make-up, and painted their fingernails black. The two had been producing pipe bombs in their basements. They felt isolated and alone. Other students told teachers and parents of their concern, but the pleas fell on deaf ears. Concerned parents had even gone to the police with threatening e-mail from the two suspects, only to be turned away. Teachers, administrators, and counselors all missed seeing the signs of trouble. In spite of metal detectors and guards within our schools, our system still can not identify youth that are at risk for violent actions. Once again, we heard the cry for help after 15 people lay dead.

APPROACHES TO PREVENTION: A NEED-BASED PREVENTION PROGRAM

Is it a fantasy, or can our schools possibly become community-based centers that provide a safe, nurturing environment in which youth can learn and grow? Many protagonists of this type of system could say that "Education is for teaching youth how to read, write, and calculate!" Other opponents to a need-based system may argue that by controlling the youth's environment, they will finally work harder. However, the advocates of a need-based system see that through basic need gratification youth will learn. Youth who have unfulfilled needs cannot respond to the content-based instruction of our schools. When a person's needs are unfulfilled, his or her energy is spent trying to fill the need. How can schools better provide an environment that both addresses these needs and at the same time meet the demands of a content-based curriculum?

Using the work of William Glasser (1998), the focus becomes the five universal needs innate to all humans. These needs are not hierarchical; therefore, one need is not more important than another, although it is important that all needs are met.

- *Survival* includes our basic needs for water, food, and shelter. In the United States today, the need for survival has gone beyond the basic requirements for life and is more associated with security and longevity. Through exercising, eating healthy food, and being active, life becomes more meaningful.

- *Power* can be defined as the need for achievement, self-worth, and recognition.
- *Freedom* is the basic need to move from place to place, feel internally free, and be able to make choices.
- *Fun* is associated with the need to laugh, play, and recreate. In essence, fun is the need for renewal.
- *Belonging* is the need that drives people to care for others and to seek relationships.

Schools did not become violent overnight. Any new program is going to take time and dedication by many people; however, the time and dedication required for a need-based prevention program far outweighs the cost of youth's lives.

Setting Up the Program

The school psychologist or a school counselor acts as the leader or director of the school-wide prevention program. Setting up the program can be done in four steps:

1. *Hold a general meeting to form specific need-based prevention teams.* The teams—student, school, family, and school board prevention teams—should consist of students, parents, teachers, administrators, and school board members and represent the entire population within their particular sector. For example, the student prevention team members are the voice of all students within this school, depending of the scope of the model. Likewise the parents on the family prevention team speak for all parents, and the teachers on the school prevention team speak for all teachers. The number of volunteers for each team is not important, although the teams should remain fairly small in order to maintain focus and direction. The teams should also represent all levels of the student and community population.
2. *Break out the prevention teams individually so they can organize, exchange information, and clarify roles and responsibilities.* The school counselor or school psychologist acting as leader should hand out role definitions to each team. Each team is responsible for specific tasks that affect its specific population. A special team to deal with diversity (discussed later in the chapter) should also meet at this time. Each prevention team should focus on its particular responsibility—which is to do a needs analysis of its specific population to determine what that population's specific needs are.
3. *Reconvene the specific prevention teams to determine when the next general program meeting will be held.* At this next general meeting the

prevention teams can consolidate their individual needs assessments and develop a prevention plan that can be utilized throughout the school system or district.

4. *Adjourn to administer the needs assessments.*

Team Role.   The roles of each specific team are as follows:

- **Student prevention team:** Is the responsible voice of the students. Through a needs assessment, this team determines what is required in order to get the needs of belonging, power, freedom, fun, and survival met. This team should be supervised during the initial stages to provide reality to the requests. It is important, however, to allow students to be in charge of ideas and suggestions. The students will then relay their findings to the other school-wide prevention program teams.

- **School prevention team:** Consists of several teachers within the school and at least one administrator. If possible, the teachers should be representative of different grade levels within the school. This team's responsibility is first to assess what materials, programs, and facilities are currently in place to meet the youth's needs. Assessing what currently exists for need gratification saves time and money in later steps. Next, the school prevention team determines what needs to be done (needs assessment) within the classroom and the school to meet the youth's needs of belonging, freedom, power, fun, and survival. Finally, this team determines what teachers and administrators require in order to get their own needs met within the school environment. The school prevention team is responsible for the implementation of programs to meet the youth's needs.

- **Family prevention team:** Consists of members of the community who have youth or recently had youth in the schools. The family prevention team focuses on the needs of parents and families within the community. Their first task is to determine what is currently in place within the community to meet the needs of families. Next, this team analyzes what is required in order for families to better meet the needs of their youth. Finally, the family prevention team creates programs or raises resources to help families meet the needs of the youth. This step may, for example, include forming parent support groups, holding informal discussions concerning parenting skills, or creating a day care exchange program.

- **School board prevention team:** Made up of several members from the current school board. The school board prevention team acts as the voice of the community. This team has the primary responsibility to solicit opinions from members of the community via phone interviews or mailed surveys. After the initial assessment, the school board prevention team determines what is currently in place within the community that can be utilized to meet the youth's five needs. Next, the team determines what specifically is required at the community level to meet the needs of youth. For instance, is there a need for more programs to promote belonging (e.g., boys clubs, girls clubs)? Does the community need to provide more open space or recreational activities? Finally, the school board prevention team determines what the community as a whole needs to provide its citizens with feelings of belonging, power, freedom, fun, and survival.

Team Responsibilities. As the individual prevention teams discuss their roles and responsibilities, the following lists can help each focus more directly on its tasks.

- **Student prevention team responsibilities:** With the help of a teacher, parent, or other adult volunteer, the student team
  —solicits information from other students;
  —determines what programs, activities, or people are in place within their school or community to help them feel a sense of comfort, belonging, excitement, exploration, and achievement;
  —analyzes what will be required in their school or community to help students meet these needs; and
  —determines what their peers need in the school and the community to feel a sense of belonging, power, freedom, fun, and survival.
- **Family prevention team responsibilities:** The family team
  —solicits information from families in the community;
  —determines what is currently in place within the school or community to help families meet the needs of their youth;
  —analyzes what is required at the family level to help families better meet the needs of their youth; and
  —determines what families need in order to feel a sense of belonging, power, freedom, fun, and survival within the school community.
- **School prevention team responsibilities:** The school prevention team
  —solicits information from teachers and administrators within the school district;
  —determines what is currently in place in the school and community to help meet youth's needs;
  —analyzes what is required to help meet the needs of the youth in the school; and
  —determines what teachers and administrators need in order to gain a sense of belonging, power, freedom, fun, and survival within the school community.

- **School board prevention team responsibilities:** The school board team
  —solicits information from members of the community;
  —determines what is currently in place in the community to help meet the needs of youth;
  —analyzes what is required to meet the needs of the youth at the community level; and
  —determines what the school board needs in order to feel a sense of belonging, power, freedom, fun, and survival within the school board and the broader community.

After the individual prevention teams review their responsibilities, they can begin to focus on the need assessment component of this program. Each team will administer and evaluate its specific need assessments. The need assessments of all teams will be consolidated at the next general meeting to form a plan.

Conducting Need Assessments

The need assessments are conducted in each specific population by the need-based prevention team that represents that population. The assessments can be made formally, as in the classroom, or informally, through interviews over the telephone or mail. (How the diversity team can conduct a need-based assessment for diverse and multicultural populations is discussed later in the chapter.)

Each prevention team is responsible for assessing and implementing the materials and programs that best help meet the five needs. Examples of need assessments for each of the five prevention teams, which can be informal yet focus on each of the five need areas, and which can be expanded to fit each group's specific needs, are as follows:

- **Student need assessment:** This assessment, which should be given at the beginning of the school year, or any time a new student comes into the school or district, asks students to
  —describe what activities make you feel like a part of this school. What could be added, or what would interest you? (*belonging*);
  —describe how you like to be recognized for your work or achievements (*power*);
  —describe activities that make learning fun and exciting (*fun*);
  —describe what interests you have and how you would like to learn more about these interests (i.e., more field trips, reading, writing, visuals) (*freedom*); and
  —describe what you need to be prepared for school and ready to work (*survival*).

- **Family need assessment:** This assessment asks parents to
  —describe what your family needs to feel connected to each other, the school, and the community (i.e., someone to talk with, more family programs, more time) (*belonging*);
  —describe what your family needs to get and maintain a sense of worth (*power*);
  —describe what your family needs in order to have the ability to make choices (i.e., time, money, day care) (*freedom*);
  —describe what your family finds exciting and fun. Do you have the means to do these activities? (*fun*); and
  —describe what your family needs to feel more safe and secure (*survival*).
- **School need assessment:** This assessment asks teachers and administrators to
  —describe what you need to feel that you are a valuable part of this school (*belonging*);
  —describe what you need to feel recognized for your work (*power*);
  —describe the areas of the school in which you need more choices (*freedom*);
  —describe what you need to feel that your job is fun and fulfilling (*fun*); and
  —describe what you need to run your classroom or your school effectively (*survival*).
- **School board need assessment:** This assessment asks school board members to
  —describe what the school board needs to feel connected with the schools and the community (*belonging*);
  —describe what the school board needs from the youth and the schools in order to feel recognized (*power*);
  —describe what the school board needs in order to make choices concerning the progress of the students and the schools (*freedom*);
  —describe what the school board needs in order to feel enjoyment and gratification in its endeavors (*fun*); and
  —describe what the school board needs to provide support to the schools and the community effectively (*survival*).

It is important to keep the needs assessments short and simple in order to facilitate later phases.

Developing and Implementing the Plan

The need-based program is developed and implemented with the following steps:

1. Determine what is already in place to meet the need of youth
2. Analyze the needs assessments
3. Determine the specific needs of students, parents/families, schools, and school boards/communities
4. Consolidate needs
5. Plan for implementation
6. Implement the program
7. Evaluate the program

After the individual prevention teams have conducted needs assessments for their specific populations, the school- or district-wide prevention program team discusses, analyzes, and consolidates the needs assessments of each individual team. Each individual prevention team then develops a plan for its specific population; the school- or district-wide prevention program team evaluates these plans. Implementation of the plans is discussed at this point. All individual prevention teams should remain in constant contact to ensure that all are working toward the same goal. The school- or district-wide prevention program team meets monthly to discuss positive or negative findings within the program based on reports from the individual prevention teams. Ultimately, each individual team is responsible for creating and implementing the specific plans that were developed based on its needs analysis. The community determines and implements resources, time, and personnel in order to better meet youth, family, and school needs. The school is in turn responsible for determining, creating, and implementing a program that best meets the needs of youths and their families. Families are responsible for meeting the needs of their youths in appropriate ways at home, and for helping the school to meet their youths' needs. The students are responsible for helping each other feel a sense of belonging, personal choice, responsibility, accomplishment, and learning.

Evaluating the Plan

Once the plan has been initiated, the school- or district-wide prevention program team needs to take the seventh step, that is, to evaluate the original plan, to assess if the original plan is working or if the plan needs revision. At its monthly meetings, the school- or district-wide prevention program team should continue to discuss how the program is operating and should focus on any problems, concerns, or unmet needs. The school- or district-wide prevention program team should also continue to discuss the successes it finds within the new program. The meetings should be positive and productive, and each individual prevention team should feel safe to voice concerns or ask for help with further facilitation of needs.

INTERVENTIONS

Interventions in schools usually come after an incident or a crisis has occurred. In some cases, the intervention comes too late and youth are killed or seriously wounded. Interventions up to this point have had the tendency to be punitive and coercive. When an intervention takes place the youth is usually removed from the school, the home, or the community. Current responses to violence are unsystematic and applied only when youth act out (Nelson, 1997). In the need-based model, the intervention is a continued part of the prevention plan. The intervention teams are comprised of the same members that make up the prevention teams. The goal of these teams is to utilize the monthly evaluation meetings to uncover any possible problem areas. If each team takes a responsible approach, each youth should be known on an individual basis by that team. If behavior becomes destructive, the specific intervention team can immediately meet to discuss and rectify the situation. Should an incident occur, the team can analyze, create, and implement a strategy to meet the needs of the youth across all levels—home, school, or community. The best way to intervene in a situation is to make sure it does not need to happen in the first place.

ADAPTATIONS FOR DIVERSITY

Available data show that youth of color are the most affected by violence (Ammerman & Hersen, 1992). Schools are becoming more diverse, and we must find ways to deal effectively with the diverse needs of these new populations. Racism, classism, and racial privilege all show a positive relation to school violence (Soriano et al., 1994). As diversity increases so does the chance of violent interactions. Different values, needs, and cultural expectations cause friction when met with old or established ways of behavior. The present educational system needs to continue to improve methods for dealing with both multiculturalism and diversity. Many of the traditional approaches to teaching were developed for a monocultural population. A need-based program, based on individual needs, can meet these needs from the individuals' cultural, racial, or ethnic point of view. In Los Angeles alone, over 120 different languages are spoken within the schools (Youth's Planning Council Strategic Plan Development Committee, 1992). Schools often lack the necessary training to deal with diverse populations. Educators must understand the social, cultural, and ethnic differences of people before they can be effective.

The need-based model meets the needs of youths, families, and communities from their own points of view. This is important when dealing with cultural and diverse populations. Therefore, in addition to the student, family, school, and community prevention teams, this model includes a diversity prevention team. The diversity team consists of individuals from any number of groups. When speaking of diversity in this model, we mean a group of people who make up nontraditional populations (e.g., non-White, disabled, gay or lesbian, lower income). The purpose of this diversity prevention team is to make sure that the normally underrepresented populations in the school and community have a voice. The team's main goal is to find and relate the diverse needs of the individuals who are from these nontraditional populations. Not only will the diversity prevention team help traditional members of society understand the needs of this diverse population, but it will also act as a sounding board for all issues of diversity in the schools. Our educational system often disregards the tremendous richness people of diversity have to offer. We can eliminate the friction caused by a growing diverse population in our schools by providing guidance to traditional students, teachers, and families.

The diversity prevention team is part of the larger school- or district-wide prevention program eam. This team also uses the five needs developed by William Glasser to meet youths' needs. Following are the suggested responsibilities of the diversity prevention team and examples of diversity need assessments.

- **Diversity prevention team responsibilities:** The diversity prevention team
  —solicits information from nontraditional members of the school and the community;
  —determines how the diverse population's needs differ from those of the traditional population in the schools and the community;
  —determines what is in place within the schools and the community to meet the diverse needs of the youth;
  —determines what the youth need (within their own cultural context) to feel a sense of belonging, power, freedom, fun, and survival;
  —determines what is required to get their own needs met as a team; and
  —develops and brings a diversity awareness program to community leaders, schools, families, and youth.

The added step in this process will ensure that the diversity team is understood within the context of the entire group.

- **Diversity need assessment:** Again, needs assessments are given to the specific populations through the need-based prevention team

that represents that population. This assessment asks nontraditional members of the school and community to
—describe what people of diversity need to feel connected to each other, the school, and the community (*belonging*);
—describe what people of diversity need in order to get and maintain a sense of worth (*power*);
—describe what people of diversity need in order to have the ability to make choices (*freedom*);
—describe what people of diversity need to feel a sense of excitement and adventure (*fun*); and
—describe what people of diversity need in order to feel more safe and secure (*survival*).

SUMMARY

This need-based prevention program is designed to find and meet youths' needs based on the five universal needs created by William Glasser. The premise of the program relies on the assumption that if youth get their needs met in appropriate ways they will not have to resort to violence and aggressive behavior. The need-based prevention program is not designed to take the focus off learning. Rather, the program is an additional tool in the learning process. As a result of focusing on meeting the youth's needs, students, families, schools, and the community can expect to see the need for violence and aggressive behaviors eradicated. A need-based prevention program does not tax our school's time, money, or faculty. With the dedicated efforts of a handful of individuals, schools can again be safe, comfortable places of learning. Once a need-based prevention program is in place, it seems likely that our educational system will be better able to meet both the emotional needs of the individual and the content and instructional needs of the school. With the removal of suspension and expulsion, educators can focus more on helping the youth learn not only content but also valuable life skills. Schools can once again have a sense of community, exploration, excitement, and fun.

REFERENCES

Ammerman, R. T., & Hersen, M. (Eds.). (1992). *Assessment of family violence: A clinical and legal source book*. New York: Wiley.
Batsche, G., & Knoff, H. (1994). Bullying and victims: Understanding a pervasive problem in schools. *School Psychology Review, 3*, 165–174.
Bell, C. C., & Jenkins, E. J. (1993). Community violence and youth on Chicago's south side. *Psychiatry, 56*, 46–53.

Callahan, P. (1999, April 21). A day of devastation. *The Denver Post*, p. A8.

Campbell, C. A., & Dahir, C. A. (1997). *Sharing the vision: The national standards for school counseling programs*. Alexandria, VA: American School Counseling Association.

Dodge, K. A. (1986). A social information-processing model of social competence in youth. In M. Perlmutter (Ed.), *Minnesota symposium on child psychology* (pp. 77–125). Hillsdale, NJ: Erlbaum.

Egan, T. (1999, April 21). Violence by youth looking for answers. *The New York Times*, p. A21.

Egeland, B., Sroufe, L. A., & Erickson, M. (1983). The developmental consequences of different patterns of maltreatment. *Child Abuse and Neglect, 7*, 459–469.

Erin, E., Lipsher, S., & Young, R. (1999, April 21). Videos, poems foreshadowed day of disaster. *The New York Times*, p. A21.

Federal Bureau of Investigation. (1994). Uniform crime report for the United States 1993. Washington DC: U.S. Government Printing Office.

Furlong, M. J., Chung, A., Bates, M., & Morrison, R. L. (1995). Who are the victims of school violence? A comparison of student nonvictims and multivictims. *Education and the Treatment of Youth, 18*, 282–298.

Glasser, W. (1998). *Choice theory: A new psychology of personal freedom*. New York: HarperCollins.

Johnson, D., & Brook, J. (1999, April 21). Two suspects hadn't been taken seriously. *The New York Times*, p. A1.

Kazdin, A. E. (1991). Aggressive behavior and conduct disorder. In T. R. Kratoch & R. J. Morris (Eds.), *The practice of child therapy* (2nd ed., pp. 174–221). New York: Pergamon Press.

Mansfield, W., Alexander, D., & Farris, E. (1991). Teacher survey on safe, disciplined, and drug-free schools. Washington, DC: National Center for Education Statistics.

Morrison, G. M., Furlong, M., & Morrison, R.L. (1994). School violence to school safety: Reframing the issues for school psychologists. *School Psychology Review, 23*, 236–256.

Nelson, C. M. (1997). Aggression and violent behavior: A personal perspective. *Education and the Treatment of Youth, 20*, 250–262.

O'Keefe, M. (1997). Adolescents' exposure to community and school violence: Prevalence and behavioral correlates. *Journal of Adolescent Health, 20*, 368–376.

Patterson, G. R. (1982). *Coercive family process*. Eugene, OR: Castilia.

Rimen, S. (1999, April 21). Good grades, good teams, some bad feelings. *The New York Times*, p. A12.

Shakoor, B. H., & Chalmers, D. (1991). Co-victimization of African American youth who witness violence: Effects on cognitive, emotional, and behavioral development. *Journal of the National Medical Association, 83*, 233–238.

Slaby, R. G., & Guerra, N. G. (1988). Cognitive mediators of aggression in adolescent offenders: I. Assessment. *Developmental Psychology, 24*, 580–588.

Soriano, M., Soriano, F. I., & Jimenez, E. (1994). School violence among culturally diverse populations: Sociocultural and institutional considerations. *School Psychology Review, 23*, 216–235.

Strumphauser, J. S. (1986). *Helping delinquents change: A treatment of social learning approaches*. New York: Haworth Press.

Strumphauser, J. S., Aiken, T. W., & Veloz, E. V. (1977). Eastside story: A behavioral analysis of a high juvenile crime community. *Behavioral Disorders, 2,* 76–84.

Traub, J. (1996, November). The criminals of tomorrow. *The New Yorker,* pp. 56–65.

Wilgonen, J. (1999, April 21). Behind every door: Different tales of terror. *The New York Times,* p. A1.

Youth's Planning Council Strategic Plan Development Committee. (1992, July 1). Who are the youth of Los Angeles? *Interim Report.*

My deepest gratitude goes to Suzy J. Trukenbrod for her help with editing and for sharing her personal reactions to the incident at Littleton.

14 | I Can't Live Without It: Adolescent Substance Abuse From a Cultural and Contextual Framework

Alberta M. Gloria and Sharon E. Robinson Kurpius

In 1997 high rates of drug use continued at all grade levels, but survey data indicated a slowdown of use and the beginning of a positive turnaround of attitudes, particularly among eighth graders. Twelfth graders continued to show increases in the use of drugs such as marijuana, cocaine, LSD, and cigarettes. Tenth graders also showed increases such as in lifetime use of marijuana, past month use of tranquilizers, and in being drunk daily. (National Institute on Drug Abuse [NIDA], 1998a)

This brief overview of recent research (NIDA, 1997b), heard on the NIDA's information phone line, indicates that the United States continues to fight drug and alcohol abuse. The fight against drugs is imperative as the United States has the highest rate of illicit drug use among the world's industrialized nations (Oyemade & Washington, 1990). Of particular concern is the use of drugs by our most precious resource: adolescents and youth.

Adolescent substance abuse often results in harm not only to youth but also to families, communities, and society as a whole. Alcohol use is associated with 60% of all murders, 40% of all assaults, and 33% of all rapes and child molestation (U.S. Department of Health and Human Services, 1984). Not only are criminal justice systems experiencing the exploding impact of substance abuse, so are health care systems. An estimated $114 billion has been spent on social and economic costs related to alcohol and drug issues. Although the yearly estimated costs spent on health care, lost productivity, and legal and social support systems are extreme, monetary amounts do not describe the emotional, social, and psychological costs to families and communities (Funkhouser & Denniston, 1992).

Several questions exist regarding adolescent substance use prevention and intervention. What drugs are being used and abused? Which adolescents are most at risk for substance abuse? What psychosociocultural factors influence adolescent substance use and abuse? What can be done? Unfortunately, these questions are not easily answered. As an initial step in understanding substance use and abuse issues, it is imperative to contextualize the discussion of these concerns. In addition, several assumptions about drugs and drug use need to be addressed. It is important to emphasize that drugs are not inherently good or bad and that drug use is not necessarily the same as drug abuse. Instead, what influences value judgments regarding certain chemical substances is who takes them, for what purposes they are taken, when and where they are taken, and how much and how frequently they are taken (Robinson, 1989). For instance, the scenario in which an adult has a beer after work may be viewed very differently than one in which an adolescent has a beer after school. Although the first scenario may be perceived by some as relatively benign, the second may be viewed as bad and the user as at-risk for abuse.

Examining historical and legal events, physiological perspectives, psychosocial factors, and cultural and contextual differences may be helpful to understanding adolescent drug use and abuse. Thus this chapter first provides a historical and legal perspective of drug use and a description of physiological mechanisms of drug use. The chapter continues with a summary of current drugs commonly used by adolescents and a discussion of the psychosociocultural influences of drug use. The case of Deanna, a Native American adolescent struggling with alcohol and drug use, is presented. Prevention and intervention strategies for educators, counselors, parents, and families are then highlighted within the systemic contexts of schools, families, and communities. The chapter concludes with an exploration of available resources and information.

CHRONOLOGY OF HISTORICAL AND LEGAL EVENTS

The United States has an extensive history of establishing laws in an attempt to regulate substances. In order to understand the historical context of drug use, a chronological timeline is presented.

1791	Whiskey was first taxed.
1842	Opium was taxed.
1914	An estimated 1 in every 400 Americans were addicted to opium or its derivative.

1919–29	Physicians and druggists were arrested for prescribing drugs to addicts. The illegal drug trade flourished as they protected themselves by refusing to treat addicts.
1920	Prohibition laws regarding alcohol were instituted, but many continued to use alcohol illegally.
1932	Marijuana was considered the assassin of youth by the Federal Bureau of Narcotics (Mandel & Feldman, 1986).
1933	The Eighteenth Amendment (i.e., Prohibition Amendment) was repealed.
1937	The Marijuana Tax Act legally controlled marijuana.
1956	The Narcotics Drug Control Act mandated tough penalties for heroin-related offenses, including sanctioning the death penalty for anyone caught selling heroin to a minor.
1962	The White House Conference on Drugs, convened by President John F. Kennedy, advocated medical treatment for drug abuse.
1964–70	This was a time of drug consciousness with pro-drug advocacy.
1967	*In re Gault* established rights for minors, including the right to receive a notice of charges, to obtain legal counsel, to confront and cross-examine witnesses, to avoid self-incrimination, to receive a transcript of legal proceedings, and to have an appellate review. These rights do *not* include a right to bail or a trial by jury.
1970	The Controlled Substances Act expanded the role of community mental health centers and hospitals in drug abuse treatment; established maximum penalties for manufacturing, distributing, and possessing drugs; and supported drug education.
1973	President Richard Nixon proclaimed a War on Drugs, increasing the federal anti-drug budget from $40 million in 1969 to $750 million in 1973 (Mandel & Feldman, 1986).
1980s	Use of marijuana, sedatives, tranquilizers, and hallucinogens declined. Cocaine and stimulant use steadily increased.
1982	In *Hutto v. Davis*, Davis was sentenced to 40 years for possession of 9 ounces of marijuana with the intent to sell. The U.S. Supreme Court ruled against Davis' appeal of cruel and unusual punishment (Inciardi, 1986).
1986	The Anti-Drug Abuse Act was developed to curb drug trafficking. The United States worked with international governments to monitor international borders (Public Law 99-570). The Drug-Free Schools and Communities Act passed, providing the Department of Education with $200 million for drug abuse education in the schools (Business Research Publications, 1987).
1988	The Anti-Drug Abuse Act appointed a drug policy director and established a zero tolerance policy for those who manufacture, import, distribute, or use illicit drugs (Public Law 100-690).

1990s Youth continue to believe in their invincibility, assuming that they will not become addicted to chemical substances. Drugs of the 90s include heroin, metamphetamines, marijuana, alcohol, and cigarettes.

PSYCHOPHYSIOLOGY OF DRUGS

Phases

Although the psychophysiology of different drugs may vary, all drugs go through a series of phases. For some drugs these phases are predictable and occur in short time periods, whereas the process for others is erratic and of greater duration (Julien, 1978). First, a drug is absorbed. Although there are several ways for drugs to be introduced into the body, oral ingestion is the most common mode of entry. When drugs such as alcohol, tranquilizers, and stimulants are swallowed, they are absorbed through the intestinal walls into the blood stream. Smoked/inhaled drugs (e.g., marijuana, nicotine, and inhalants) enter the bloodstream through the lungs. Drugs (e.g., heroin) that are injected directly into a vein (i.e., mainlining) or under the skin (i.e., skin-popping) are directly absorbed into the blood stream. Snorted drugs (e.g., cocaine, crank) are absorbed through the mucous membranes.

After being introduced into the body, a drug is transported to the part of the body where it will exert its action. A drug's effect, however, depends on the type, potency, and purity of the drug; the contaminant used to cut the drug; the personality and physiology of the user; and the social environment in which the drug is taken. Finally, the drug's action is stopped as the body metabolizes the drug, and the drug is finally excreted.

The Nervous System

The nervous system is made up of the central nervous system (CNS) and the peripheral nervous system (PNS). Comprised of the brain and the spinal cord, the CNS is responsible for interpreting and acting on body sensations. The PNS is comprised of various nerve processes that connect the CNS with receptors, muscles, and glands. The PNS can be subdivided into the somatic nervous system and the autonomic nervous system. The somatic nervous system interfaces with the CNS to control voluntary muscular actions such as arm and leg movements. In contrast, the autonomic nervous system controls involuntary body actions such as heart rate, digestion, and breathing. The autonomic nervous system is comprised of the sympathetic and parasympathetic nervous systems that stimulate or inhibit an organ's activities.

Drugs influence specific structures of the brain that are responsible for particular thoughts and behaviors. For instance, the cerebral cortex controls reasoning, language, and sensory discrimination, and the basal ganglia maintain good muscle tone. The hypothalamus is involved in eating, drinking, temperature, and sex drive, whereas the limbic system is involved in emotions, physical activity, and memory. Further, the medial forebrain bundle is known as the pleasure center, the brainstem controls respiration and vomiting, and the medulla oblongata is involved in aggression (Goldberg, 1982).

Chemical messengers that carry information throughout the nervous system can be classified as either hormones or neurotransmitters. Although drugs can influence the release of hormones by a gland into the blood, their major impact is on neurotransmitters, chemicals released by nerve cells throughout the CNS. Neurotransmitters influence the transmission of nerve impulses from one nerve cell to another. The major neurotransmitters that interact with psychoactive substances are acetylcholine, dopamine, norepinephrine, serotonin, GABA, and endorphins. The influence of different drugs on neurotransmitters varies, and the exact process of influence continues to be explored (Lewis, Dana, & Blevins, 1988).

Behaviors are influenced when drugs excite, inhibit, or block the actions of neurotransmitters. For instance, cocaine is believed to block a nerve cell's reuptake of norepinephrine and dopamine in areas such as the medial forebrain bundle, resulting in a feeling of euphoria for an extended time. In contrast, tranquilizers block the reuptake of dopamine in the basal ganglia, resulting in muscle relaxation. Tranquilizer abuse, however, can result in muscle rigidity. Influencing the neurotransmitters in the medulla oblongata, PCP or angel dust can result in violent and bizarre aggressive behaviors.

Although research on the interaction of neurotransmitters, drugs, and behavior is just beginning to uncover these complex relationships, it is clear that psychoactive drugs affect the chemical pathways of the body. When drugs are abused, overused, or combined, the effects can be dangerous or even deadly. For instance, the result of combining alcohol with sedatives, barbiturates, or tranquilizers may be respiratory failure. Because drugs interfere with the normal functioning of the nervous system and other organs in the body, the decision to use drugs should be exercised with caution and information. Further, adolescent drug users must be aware that research has not yet fully discovered the many physiological or psychological influences caused by drug side effects.

UNDERSTANDING DRUGS AND THEIR EFFECTS

Although adolescents report use of illicit drugs such as methamphetamines (speed, chalk, ice, crystal, glass), heroin (smack, skag, junk), and phencyclidine (PCP, ozone, wack, rocket fuel), the reported use of these and other drugs has remained relatively stable (NIDA, 1997a, 1997b). Although not illegal, adolescents can also easily access chemicals such as diet pills, over-the-counter stimulants, (e.g., NoDoz), coffee, or buzz beans (chocolate-covered coffee beans). For purposes of this review, however, only alcohol, nicotine, marijuana, and inhalants are reviewed.

Alcohol

An estimated 24 gallons of beer, 2 gallons of distilled spirits, and over 2 gallons of wine are sold each year for every man, woman, and child in the United States. The two alcoholic beverages most consumed are beer and wine. In particular, wine coolers have become popular among youth (Avis, 1990). The sweet, fruity taste of wine coolers often prevents adolescents from considering that wine coolers have a higher alcohol content than a can of beer. Interestingly, it is estimated that children and adolescents view 25 to 50 alcohol commercials for every anti-drug message (e.g., Partnership for a Drug-Free America) (Strasburger, 1989).

Found in all alcoholic beverages, ethanol acts as a depressant on the CNS (Raskin & Daley, 1991). When an individual's blood alcohol level (BAL) is .04% (usually after one or two alcoholic beverages), the cerebral cortex becomes less efficient such that an individual has decreased alertness, relaxed inhibition, impaired judgment, increased heart rate, and a general sense of feeling good (Avis, 1990). As a person's BAL increases, judgment ability declines, reaction time is slowed, and both sensory and motor capabilities are impaired. Most states define drunkenness at a BAL of .10%. Intoxication is officially reached at .20% BAL, stupor at .30% BAL. A BAL of .35% and over can result in respiratory failure and death. The vomiting reflex (controlled by the brainstem) can be activated at .12% BAL. Alcohol also causes a lower level of blood flow to the brain, decreasing oxygen levels as well as nutrient and waste removal. In addition, alcohol-related changes in cortical functions can also result in behavioral changes. The more rapid the intake of alcohol, the greater the behavioral changes as the individual becomes less inhibited. Because alcohol is metabolized at a slow rate of oxidation, it has a long duration of action (Ray & Ksir, 1987).

Physical damage due to alcohol use is rare in adolescents as they have probably not been abusing for a long enough period of time for damage to occur. Withdrawal symptoms for adolescents who have been heavy alcohol users include tremors, perspiring, agitation, disorientation, and brief seizures. With prolonged abuse, however, gastritis with hemorrhaging and inflammation of the pancreas can result. Bleeding, severe vomiting, and changes in the blood necessitate hospitalization. Chronic alcoholism in adults can result in chronic liver disease, inflammation of various nerves, and impaired memory (Schonberg & Schnoll, 1986).

The single best predictor of drug abuse is early age of onset of use (Ungerleider & Seigel, 1990). Interestingly, research has indicated that almost 24% of all college students report that they first drank alcohol in middle or junior high school. Research has also showed that the earlier adolescents begin to drink, the heavier the alcohol use by their college years (Robinson, Gloria, Roth, & Schuetter, 1993). Other research found that the lifetime prevalence of alcohol use was 81.7% for high school seniors, 72% for 10th graders, and 53.8% for 8th graders. When binge drinking was examined, 31.3% of high school seniors, 25.1% of 10th graders, and 25.1% of 8th graders reported that they had consumed five or more drinks in a row (NIDA, 1997b).

Nicotine

Nicotine, the primary active ingredient in tobacco, is ingested through cigarettes, cigars, pipes, and smokeless tobacco (chew). The most popular method of ingesting nicotine is by smoking. Although cigarette smoking has decreased over the last 40 years, 35% of all adolescents still report tobacco use (Robinson et al., 1993). Specific to cigarettes, an estimated 4.1 million adolescents between the ages of 12 and 17 are smokers (NIDA, 1997a). Adolescent girls are more frequent users of cigarettes, whereas adolescent boys are more likely to use smokeless tobacco than their female counterparts.

The pharmacological and behavioral processes that determine physiological tobacco addiction are complex as nicotine acts as both a stimulant and sedative to the CNS. Specifically, nicotine results in a rapid and evenly absorbed distribution or kick because of the sudden release of epinephrine. The epinephrine stimulates the CNS to release glucose for energy. After the glucose is used by the body, a period of low energy leads the user to seek or use more nicotine (NIDA, 1998b). When nicotine is absorbed, it is carried on droplets of tar (Avis, 1990). The amount of tar in a cigarette varies from 7mg for a low-tar cigarette to 15mg for a regular cigarette. The half-life of nicotine is 2 hours; however, regular smoking results in an accumulation of nicotine in the body. Thus daily smokers are exposed to the effects of nicotine 24 hours a day (NIDA, 1998b).

Smokers have increased heart rates because the carbon monoxide in cigarette smoke causes them to lose 15% of the oxygen-carrying capacity of their blood. Further, decreased blood flow (and oxygen) to the skin results in smokers appearing older than nonsmokers. Smoking also makes artery walls less flexible, increasing the risk and severity of hardening of the arteries. In addition, smokers have a higher expectancy rate of lung cancer, emphysema, and bronchial disorders (NIDA, 1998b). The negative health effects of secondhand or sidestream smoke are also a concern, particularly for nonsmokers. Research has shown that nonsmoking spouses of smokers have a higher rate of lung cancer than do spouses of nonsmokers. Further, young children and infants exposed to secondhand smoke also have more respiratory and asthma problems (Avis, 1990).

Despite warning labels placed on cigarette packages and advertisements regarding the dangers of smoking, the prevalence rate of adolescents who smoke remains high. Further, research indicated that current smokers have substantially higher rates of alcohol use (12.8%) and other drug use (14.7%) than do nonsmokers (2.5% and 2.6%, respectively). Similarly, almost three quarters of those adolescents who had previously smoked cigarettes indicated that they also smoked marijuana (NIDA, 1997a).

Marijuana

Currently, there are over 200 slang terms for marijuana, including *herb*, *boom*, *Jane*, and *gangster*. Marijuana is generally smoked as a cigarette (a joint or nail) or in a pipe or bong. More recently, blunts—cigars that have been emptied of tobacco and filled with marijuana—are being used. Marijuana is the most widely used illegal drug in the United States and is generally the first illegal drug that adolescents use. Marijuana consists of the dried, shredded flowers and leaves of the hemp plant, and its psychoactive effect is achieved through the chemical delta-9-tetrahydrocannabinol (THC). There are various grades or types of marijuana, including sensinilla, containing as much as 8% THC, and hashish, containing up to 50% THC. Marijuana sold on the street is estimated to contain between 2 and 5% THC. Although the general use of marijuana is below that of the late 1970s and early 1980s, adolescent use increased in the early 1990s, and recent research has indicated that there has been an increase in the number of 10th and 12th graders who have used marijuana at least once in their lives (NIDA, 1998d).

When marijuana is smoked, THC is rapidly absorbed into the blood. Although marijuana creates a sedative, dreamy high, it alters the metabolization of serotonin and dopamine. Further, the long half-life of marijuana means that daily smokers may be continually high as the marijuana is never out of body's system. Schonberg and Schnoll (1986) cited considerable research on the negative effects of marijuana on brain, cardiovascular, pulmonary, endocrine, and psychological functioning. For instance, marijuana affects the transfer of information from short- to long-term memory, decreasing an individual's ability to learn (Kingery-McCabe & Campbell, 1991). Heavy marijuana smoking has also been linked to the amotivational syndrome of lethargy and decreased motivation in adolescents. In particular, youth who use marijuana before or during the school day impair their desire and ability to learn. Many of the effects of smoking marijuana are similar to those of drinking alcohol, including lowered secretions of sex hormones; impaired motor coordination, reaction time, and sensory perception; and decreased ability to follow moving objects. With poorer motor coordination and distorted time and distance perceptions, those who drive under the influence of marijuana have the same safety risks as those who drive under the influence of alcohol.

Although current research has not indicated whether or not physiological addiction to marijuana occurs, research on the effects of marijuana is still in its infancy. There is an increasing belief that marijuana smoke affects the lungs in a manner similar to tobacco smoke. Chronic smoking of marijuana impairs airflow in the lungs and is more likely to produce daily coughs, symptoms of bronchitis, and more frequent chest colds (NIDA, 1998d). As users inhale more deeply to hold marijuana smoke in their lungs, the amounts of tar and carbon monoxide absorbed by marijuana smokers are three to five times greater than for tobacco smokers (NIDA, 1998d). Only long-term research will be able to verify the relationship between marijuana smoking and cancer.

Inhalants

Inhalants include solvents, gases, and nitrites. Solvents are household substances such as paint thinner, degreasers, gasoline, glue, and office supply substances such as correction fluids or felt-tip markers. Gases include butane lighters, whipping cream dispensers (i.e., whippets), spray paint, hair spray, and medical anesthetic gases such as ether, chloroform, and nitrous oxide. Adolescents between the ages of 11 and 15 are the primary users of inhalants, as inhalants are inexpensive, readily available, and perceived as a substitute for alcohol.

Inhalants contain volatile hydrocarbons that cause a strong short-lived, euphoric high. Inhaled through the nose or mouth (huffing), inhalants can cause intoxicating effects that last only a few minutes or several hours if repeatedly ingested (NIDA, 1998c). Symptoms of inhalant use are similar to those of alcohol use, including "lack of coordination, restlessness, excitement, confusion, disorientation, difficulty in walking (ataxia), delirium, and coma" (Schonberg & Schnoll, 1986, p. 54). One-time use of inhalants can cause death by acute intoxication as oxygen is displaced in the lungs (NIDA, 1998c). Further, sudden sniffing death can occur when excessive exercise and stress immediately follow inhalant abuse. Although adolescents may enjoy the giddy high associated with sniffing, chronic use of inhalants can result in hearing loss (from paint sprays and glues), limb spasms (from glues, gasoline, and whipping cream dispensers), brain damage (from paint sprays and glues), and bone marrow damage (from gasoline) (NIDA, 1998c).

According to data from the National Household Survey on Drug Abuse (NIDA, 1997a), 1.3 million (5.9%) adolescents reported the use of inhalants at least once during their lifetime, and 900,000 (4%) reported using inhalants in the past year. Data from NIDA's (1997b) Monitoring the Future Study indicated that the annual rate of inhalant use among high school seniors rose from 3.0% in 1976 to an all-time high of 8% in 1995. This research also indicated that one in five eighth grade students had used inhalants at least once in their lives.

PSYCHOSOCIOCULTURAL INFLUENCES OF SUBSTANCE USE

In addition to the physiological influences of drug use, scholars and researchers have identified psychological and sociocultural influences of adolescent substance use and abuse. In synthesizing the literature, a continuum that is a current model of substance use as well as brief reviews of contextual and cultural concerns that relate to adolescent substance use are provided. The significance of cultural contexts and racial/ethnic differences in understanding adolescent substance use is also discussed.

Continuum of Drug Use: A Psychosocial Perspective

Muisener (1994) created a drug use and experience continuum for adolescents that is known as the adolescent chemical use experience (ACUE) continuum. Like other psychosocial frameworks of drug use (e.g., Avis, 1990), the ACUE continuum considers social and environmental factors that influence drug use. Although the stages of Muisener's model overlap and cut-off points are arbitrary, it provides a framework within which to distinguish the different substance use experiences of adolescents.

Experimental use is the first stage of the ACUE continuum. Looking to "learn the mood swing" (Macdonald & Newton, 1981), experimenters try drugs feeling bored or curious, hoping to have fun, or responding to peer pressure (Jalali, Jalali, Crocette, & Turner, 1981). The number of trials that constitute experimental use varies. For instance, Avis (1990) defined *experimental use* as 10 or fewer experiences with a given drug, whereas Miller (1989) defined *experimentation* as using any given drug four or five times. Experimental users are aware of the differences between having fun and getting into danger, typically only use alcohol or marijuana, and are not likely to develop serious drug problems.

Social use with peers is the second stage of drug use. Muisener (1994) indicated that "the social stage is fairly adaptive and normative for many adolescents" (p. 6). It is the context within which the adolescent "seeks the mood swing" (Macdonald & Newton, 1981) that defines social use. Circumstantial or situational use of drugs (e.g., drinking at a weekend party with friends) has been considered "quasi-normal" (Avis, 1990; Ungerleider & Seigel, 1990). Adolescents who misuse or overindulge in use of substances at this stage, however, are at risk for continued drug use (Muisener, 1994).

Operational use, considered entry into substance abuse, is the third stage of the ACUE continuum. In this stage, adolescents actively engage in and are fascinated by the drug effects, and have a "preoccupation with the mood swing" (Macdonald & Newton, 1981). There are two types of operational users. Muisener (1994) described the first type as "pleasure pursuant" users who seek the effects of the drug to feel good. The second type consists of "pain-avoidant" or "compensatory" users (Nowinski, 1990) who use drugs to avoid dealing with painful feelings or to cope with life events and concerns. Pain avoidant and compensatory users are of particular concern: those who often establish potentially dysfunctional coping styles instead of learning more effective coping strategies are at higher risk for drug abuse.

Dependent use is the last stage of the ACUE continuum. Adolescents use chemicals in order to feel normal and are described as "compulsively consumed with urges to experience the mood swing from drugs" (Muisener, 1994, p. 8). These adolescents devote a great deal of time and energy to getting high and becoming connoisseurs of street drugs. For these users, also known as compulsive users, drugs are an escape or a means to avoid discomfort rather than experience pleasure (Avis, 1990). As a result, an adolescent's sense of self and identity is often interwoven with drug use, and he or she is at a higher risk for health concerns.

All adolescents differ in their experiences across the ACUE continuum (Muisener, 1994). Of those adolescents who are experimental or social drug users, only a fraction will progress to the extreme stage of dependency. When considered at a national level, however, this represents approximately 1 million teenagers—a staggering number. Similarly, approximately 4% to 5% of teens between the ages of 15 and 19 use illicit drugs regularly. However, as Muisener pointed out, those adolescents who abuse substances can regress to less problematic stages of use at a later time.

Cultural and Contextual Considerations of Drug Use

What is known currently about adolescent substance use is primarily based on data from White adolescents (Rebach, 1992; Wang, Bahr, & Marcos, 1995). Although this research provides a starting point from which to address preliminary concerns and issues, contextual and cultural considerations need to be integrated in order to be relevant and appropriate for other populations. Environmental contexts and constructs of race and ethnicity are generally not examined relative to adolescent substance use (Jillson-Broostrom, 1993; Wang et al., 1995). Because each individual has cultural values and a cultural understanding of the world (i.e., a world-view), it is necessary to delineate some of the different cultural and contextual issues that need to be considered relative to adolescent substance use. Further, the large differences between and within ethnic groups also need to be considered such that aggregation of individuals or groups does not continue.

Differences in family size often reflect the extended family in the home and thus need to be considered as potential influences. In examining family structure, the average Black household contains 2.9 persons as compared to 2.5 for Whites, 3.6 for Hispanics, 3.4 for Asian Americans, and 3.1 for American Indians (O'Hare, 1992). By age, American Indians are the youngest ethnic group with 37.4% being 18 years of age or younger, followed by Hispanics (36.7%), African Americans (33.8%), Asian Americans (30.4%), and Whites (25.1%) (U.S. Bureau of Census, 1992).

The Asian American population is estimated to be growing at the fastest rate of any U.S. ethnic group (U.S. Bureau of Census, 1992). Asian Americans are the most diverse group within the United States and are 22% Chinese, 21% Filipino, 19% Japanese, 10% Korean, and 10% Asian Indian (U.S. Bureau of the Census, 1990). Given the changing demography, programs that address acculturative stress (Smart & Smart, 1994) and language barriers are needed. These considerations are also relevant for the Hispanic/Latino populations. The Mexican-origin population (60%) constitutes the largest group of Hispanics/Latinos, followed by South and Central American Latinos (22%), Puerto Ricans (12%), and Cubans (5%) (Chapa & Valencia, 1993). The American Indian population is also highly diverse, with more than 500 federally recognized tribal entities and 300 federal reservations (Klein, 1993). However, American Indians share the loss of tribal and individual decisions as a result of federal and governmental control (Thurman, Swaim, & Plested, 1995).

Another consideration is that the birth rate of biethnic or biracial children is higher than any other group. Increased attention to identity concerns for these adolescents is warranted (Herring, 1997).

Racial/Ethnic Differences in Substance Use

In a review of the substance use research published in *Sociological Abstracts, Psychological Abstracts,* and *Social Science Index,* Rebach (1992) found that White youth tend to use alcohol and most other drugs at higher rates than do Asian, Black, or Hispanic youth. American Indian students had the highest alcohol use rate, whereas Blacks had the highest abstention rate from alcohol. Black and Hispanic youth began marijuana use at a later age and were less likely to become heavy users than were their White counterparts. Lex (1987) also found similar heterogeneous drinking patterns and specific psychological, medical, and social consequences among racial/ethnic minority groups.

Rebach (1992) noted that health problems are a major consequence of racial/ethnic minority substance use. For example, esophageal cancer and cirrhosis of the liver are the most frequent health problems associated with alcohol use among racial/ethnic minorities (Herd, 1988). Alcohol-related health problems among American Indians occur two to five times more often than in the general population (Rebach, 1992). Another consequence of substance use among racial/ethnic minorities is a disproportionately high number of violent crimes and arrests (Rebach, 1992). Because racial/ethnic minority adolescents are highly influenced by their families and extended families (Ho, 1992; Marín, 1991), effecting change utilizing the support of families is essential (Goddard, 1993). For this reason, prevention and intervention programs need to utilize the family systems to change drug use patterns.

Ultimately, there is no typical profile of an adolescent drug abuser. The factors that influence adolescent substance use vary and require comprehensive and multidimensional prevention and intervention approaches. These approaches must be culturally congruent at the individual, familial, and community levels through the integration of psychological, social, and cultural contexts.

CASE STUDY: DEANNA

Deanna is a 16-year-old high school sophomore who lives in a medium sized town in the southwestern United States and who self-identifies as Navajo. Although her grandparents still live on a Navajo reservation, her family moved to town where job opportunities were better for her parents. In addition, many members of her extended family live in the same community. Deanna is the oldest of five children and is often the primary caretaker for her younger brothers and sisters who range in age from 2 to 12. Because of her many responsibilities at home, she has not been able to become actively involved in school activities such as sports, even though she is one of the best sprinters in her gym class.

In Deanna's family, her mother is the primary bread winner, whereas her father changes jobs frequently due to his drinking. Deanna's mother has training as a legal secretary and is employed by a small law firm. Her father does not have any specialized training and works as a manual laborer. When her father is out of work, family arguments escalate and his drinking increases. When this occurs, the children have learned to stay out of the way and not to provoke him.

Deanna has a tendency to be self-effacing, has difficulty with ambiguity, and yearns for social recognition and attention. At school, she seems to lack self-confidence and goes along with others in order to be accepted. Although intelligent, Deanna's grades are mediocre. Noting that she has become even less motivated to do classwork and often seems unable to pay attention in class, her teachers have referred her to the school counselor.

In her discussions with the counselor, Deanna finally admits that she has been getting drunk at least once a month since she was 13 years old and that she occasionally smokes marijuana. When things are bad at home, alcohol and marijuana help her to escape and forget her family's problems. She also claims that she "needs to drink and do pot" in order to be accepted and that "all of my friends do it."

DRUG PREVENTION AND INTERVENTION

The primary question that frequently arises when dealing with adolescent drug use is, What can parents, educators, and counselors do to prevent or deter adolescents from using drugs? Traditionally, prevention and education regarding substance abuse among children and adolescents have been targeted toward families and schools (Robinson, 1989). If intervention rather than prevention is warranted for adolescent substance abuse, it often occurs in more structured settings such as treatment programs targeted for individuals. Treatment programs vary by type, services, and setting. For instance, settings include short-term inpatient crisis care, inpatient programs, day care programs, residential treatment, halfway houses, and outpatient treatment programs. Although all programs make extensive use of group and individual therapy, they also "require some parental and/or familial involvement in the program and attempt to provide family counseling" in an effort to focus on the "underlying problems" in the family milieu (Kusnetz, 1986, p. 151). The more actively involved and supportive the family, the greater the chance of recovery for the substance abuser. Programs offered at the community level can be designed to provide either prevention or intervention.

Individual-Based Interventions

When an adolescent is using alcohol and other chemical substances, individual counseling is often warranted. Individual counseling can be obtained from community mental health agencies, hospitals, managed health care organizations (HMOs), and private practice therapists. Some HMOs provide both in- and outpatient drug and alcohol counseling, although the number of sessions is often limited. An experienced counselor who is nonjudgmental can provide a safe and trusting environment that will most likely elicit the adolescent's willingness to participate.

Motivation is also critical for stopping alcohol and drug abuse. More successful adolescents recognize that they have a problem and want to change (Kusnetz, 1986). Those adolescents who are less likely to be successful are referred by the criminal justice system, have used drugs for a longer time, are more immersed in the drug culture, come from families in which the adults are substance abusers, and have histories of violence and gang involvement (Kusnetz, 1986). Regardless of the history of the abuser, self-motivation and family involvement are paramount for change to occur.

Exploring the adolescent's perceptions of home, school, and peers can help the counselor to identify the motives, beliefs, and behaviors that contribute to his or her substance use. Counseling should also address self-esteem, self-efficacy, anger, hopelessness (e.g., "nothing is going to get better"), and the need to belong. Issues of identity (cultural, racial, or sexual) also need to be considered because identity development is central to psychological adjustment (Phinney, Lochner, & Murphy, 1990). For some adolescents, level of acculturation also needs to be assessed. For instance, counselors must understand the environmental and internal stresses experienced by adolescents as they balance their native and host culture values (Gloria & Peregoy, 1996). This concern is particularly relevant for biracial adolescents (Herring, 1997). Similarly, addressing environmental concerns of racism and discrimination is needed, particularly as many racial and ethnic minority or gay/lesbian/bisexual adolescents often feel hopeless, isolated, or alienated. For instance, in an exploratory study of 83 youth between the ages of 14 and 18, Freeman (1990) found ethnic differences in adolescent experiences. Many White students (85%) indicated that conflicts arising from parental, peer, or role model expectations were major contributors to their substance abuse. In contrast, almost all Hispanic youth (98%) discussed cultural identity concerns and reported that using drugs helped minimize environmental stresses such as racism.

Individual interventions for Deanna. Because Deanna has been using alcohol for over 3 years and has been experimenting with marijuana, she could benefit from interventions designed to decrease these at-risk behaviors. If individual interventions are conceptualized as changing an individual's behaviors, then both group and one-on-one approaches can be utilized. Therapeutic interventions with Deanna could foster discussion of what is happening at home and at school, and how this relates to her substance use. The counselor can discuss with Deanna how her self-perceptions (e.g., low self-esteem and low self-efficacy) and her desire for peer recognition could be related to her at-risk behaviors. Involving Deanna in group counseling with similar at-risk youth could foster her life coping skills and her sense of self-worth while providing her with accurate information about potential consequences of her drug use behaviors. Deanna could probably benefit from being in a group that included other Navajo adolescents, thus reinforcing her cultural identity and increasing her overall sense of self-worth.

Family-Based Interventions

As families are the most essential socialization system for children (Oyemade & Washington, 1990), they must be an integral component of broad-based prevention and intervention programs. The literature indicates inconsistencies regarding the influence of family on adolescent drug use. Abusive, alcoholic, single-parent, and blended families, families with latchkey children, families with inconsistent limit setting and rules for behavior, and families with low bonding have been related to adolescent drug use. Regardless of the extent of family difficulties, the role of the family in preventing adolescent substance use can be significant (Wang et al., 1995).

Although parents may be knowledgeable about alcohol and drug use, they may be unaware or deny that their children have been exposed to or have used alcohol/drugs. Furthermore, it is often difficult for parents and families to acknowledge that substance abuse is occurring in a child or family member, and their attitudes often deter them from acting against drug use (e.g., talking with their children about the dangers of drug use) (Burns & Margarella, 1990). Recognizing and requesting help with the problem may trigger intense feelings of anger, hurt, betrayal, or failure for parents. Additional barriers to parents addressing substance use with their children include a lack of time, a misperception of their child's world, difficulty in communicating with their children regarding sensitive issues, not wanting to appear as if they mistrust their children, and lacking current information (Burns & Margarella, 1990).

If parents suspect that their child is using drugs, they are encouraged to talk with their child about their concern and why the drug is harmful (NIDA, 1984). Parents need to communicate that they are opposed to any drug use and that they intend to enforce that position. Parents are encouraged to be "understanding (I realize you're under a lot of pressure from friends to use drugs); firm (As your parent I cannot allow you to engage in harmful activities); and self-examining (Are my own alcohol and drug consumption habits exerting a bad influence on my child?)" (NIDA, 1984, pp. 4-5). Sarcasm, accusations, and sympathy-seeking or self-blaming behaviors will only make a child defensive and inattentive to parents. Acknowledging that one's child is using drugs and the need for assistance does not imply parental failure but instead reflects caring and parental support.

A confrontation with a child regarding drugs can be charged with many emotions; however, parents are encouraged to remain calm, open, loving, and firm. Parents need to listen to their children and not just give advice. Teaching children how to make responsible decisions, to accept the consequences of their decisions, and to love themselves is essential. Parents also need to know the differences between firmness and punishment. Children respect fair limits that take into consideration their age and maturity level. Consistency in setting limits helps a child understand acceptable parameters for behavior. Although adolescence is a time for individuals to seek independence, autonomy, and self-identity (Miller, 1989), most adolescents need and want some parental direction. A balance between adolescent autonomy and family is needed, particularly as low family attachment and involvement has been associated with increased risk of adolescent substance abuse (Hawkins, Catalano, & Miller, 1992; Wang et al., 1995). This balance is particularly relevant for adolescents and families who value familialism and interdependence (Gloria & Peregoy, 1996; Ho, 1992).

Parents and family play a critical role in adolescent substance abuse interventions as they are the single most important contributors to an adolescent's environment. Specifically, parents transmit cultural values and beliefs and have the ability to provide support, encouragement, and acceptance within the family. As the adolescent's substance use and the family environment reciprocally affect one another, parents are instrumental in bringing the family to counseling or applying other intervention strategies.

Parents can look for changes in mood, attitude, grades, peer group, extracurricular activities, and interpersonal interactions as indicators of possible adolescent substance use. When parental discipline designed to change an adolescent's substance use behaviors is not effective, a family systems approach in counseling is warranted. Within a family systems framework, counselors focus on both the adaptive and maladaptive exchanges among family members and between the adolescent and his or her environment (Ho, 1987). Emphasis is on improving the transactions that occur within the family, using the family as a natural support system, and applying the life events and experiences of the family system (Ho, 1987).

A second recommended intervention focuses on communication dynamics within the parent-adolescent relationship. Adolescents often feel that parents criticize, make demands, control, and rarely listen. Further, many believe that their parents do not understand their pressures, concerns, or feelings. The need for effective communication is important in light of research findings that weak family relations, low bonding, perceived lack of support, and high number of family conflicts are related to a higher frequency and severity of substance use (Rhodes & Jason, 1988). Although the content of what is being said is important, parents also need to listen for the feelings that accompany the message (Daroff, Marks, & Friedman, 1986, 1990). Hearing the underlying emotional message may be difficult or painful, and thus parents may find a third party, such as a counselor, helpful in facilitating, teaching, and modeling communication with their adolescents.

Rutter (1987) has indicated that a good parent-child relationship serves as a buffer between the environment and the child and subsequently increases the child's self-esteem. Additional family factors that promote a positive outcome for adolescents include rewarding them for independence with moderate risk taking, encouraging them to assume responsibility, and modeling examples of helpfulness and caring (Werner, 1984). Parents often have to be taught these behaviors in a way that helps adolescents develop maturity and good decision-making skills. Further, as some cultures value interdependence of family members, counselors can create a balance of adolescent-parent involvement. Such a balance would provide for culturally relevant and meaningful intervention (Thurman et al., 1995).

A third family-based intervention is based on a behavioral framework. The goal is to replace maladaptive substance use behaviors with healthy adaptive behaviors (McWhirter, McWhirter, McWhirter, & McWhirter, 1993). For instance, behaviors that adolescents are more likely to engage in (e.g., participating in after-school activities, going out with friends, talking on the phone) can reinforce those behaviors that they are less likely to engage in (e.g., cleaning their room, making curfew, completing chores). The first step of a behavioral intervention is to determine what the adolescent considers to be positive reinforcements. Each positive reinforcement needs to be salient, available, and able to be allotted in graduated portions by parents.

Another behavioral intervention is applying logical consequences for adolescent behaviors. This approach challenges adolescents to take responsibility for their behaviors. As logical consequences are applied firmly and consistently, these behaviors must be accompanied by discussion and respect (Daroff et al., 1990). As with positive reinforcements, logical consequences differ for each adolescent. Being grounded for a weekend may seem drastic and earth shattering for one adolescent, but endurable or irrelevant for another. To prevent the challenging of parental authority, inappropriate and unacceptable behaviors must be clearly defined and specific at the start of the behavioral intervention.

Behavioral contracting between parents and adolescents allows for the specific determination of rules and consequences while providing a catalyst for clear communication. Defining acceptable and unacceptable behaviors and identifying logical and feasible consequences (e.g., grounded for the weekend versus forever) can help to ensure success of such interventions. A possible contract might include no drinking at parties, no ditching classes, and no mouthing off to teachers. Privileges such as telephone use, peer interactions, and dating need to be linked to specific acceptable behaviors such as consistent school attendance and honoring curfews. As adolescents fulfill requirements, terms of the contract can be renegotiated, thereby increasing their self-efficacy and sense of responsibility.

>*Family interventions for Deanna.* Deanna could benefit from her family being more aware of the impact family dynamics can have on adolescents' self-worth and behaviors. Unfortunately, Deanna's father is modeling maladaptive coping with life's problems by his drinking. Family counseling could not only address Deanna's behaviors but also could help her father develop more effective strategies for dealing with his problems. In addition, more open and effective communication between Deanna and her parents could be facilitated. Because the extended family is considered part of the primary family for American Indians (LaFromboise, Berman, & Sohi, 1994), perhaps the counselor can explore how members of the extended family could help relieve some of the stresses resulting in Deanna's drinking and smoking marijuana. Further, Deanna seems to have limited time available because she is needed at home, and perhaps a contract can be developed between Deanna and her parents that could allow her to join the school track team or do some other valued school activity if she meets specific goals with respect to her school work and her alcohol and marijuana use behaviors.

School-Based Interventions

The primary arena for substance abuse recognition, prevention/education, and intervention is the school system. Teachers and school counselors are often the first to recognize substance use behaviors. As early detection is central to decreasing adolescent drug use, they play critical roles in intervention efforts. Teachers and school counselors who provide nurturing and understanding learning environments at school often create a refuge from the home environment (Werner, 1984). A respected school counselor or teacher who is perceived as open and receptive is most likely to have success as adolescents struggle with developmental concerns of boundary, trust, and identity (Fields, 1992; McKim, 1991). These trusted relationships allow for disclosure of family, peer, or school difficulties as well as drug use.

During the 1960s and 1970s, educators fought drug abuse by focusing on knowledge and attitudes, with the assumption that changes in substance use behaviors would follow (Schinke, Botvin, & Orlandi, 1991). Single dimension, information only, and one-shot presentations (with no follow-up programming), however, have minimal impact on substance use (Gonet, 1998). Examining 143 adolescent drug prevention studies, Tobler (1986) identified five major prevention strategies: knowledge-oriented strategies only, affective strategies only, social influence and life skills approaches, knowledge plus affective strategies, and alternative strategies.

Prevention and intervention strategies can be both informal and formal. For instance, the "Just Say No" approach of telling adolescents to refuse drugs is an example of an informal, unidimensional, simplistic approach to a multidimensional, complex problem. Students are told to respond behaviorally without addressing the cognitions or feelings that are often involved in making such a decision. More importantly, such programming is based only on the premise that the inability to "say no" is due to one's deviance, with no social and cultural considerations or factors integrated into the program's premise. However, substance use is often specifically a coping response to social and environmental factors beyond an individual's control, such as "ignorance, poverty, racism, prejudice, substance use, sexual/physical abuse as a child, dysfunctional family life, and/or mental incompetence" (Warheit & Gil, 1998, p. 39).

Other informal approaches involve developing a working partnership with the parents to prevent further drug use. Depending on parental cooperation and school counselor availability, workshops can be conducted after normal school hours for students and their parents. Information and skill-based training, such as assertiveness training and decision-making skills, can help students make informed decisions about substance use (McWhirter et al., 1993). Although these workshops are not intended to serve as individual or group counseling, they can help students identify situations and circumstances that promote and maintain their substance use (McWhirter et al., 1993). School counselors can apply innovative strategies in their workshops such as talks by recovered abusers, movies, group outings, and drug-free parties. In addition to workshops, school counselors can serve as liaisons to parents regarding adolescents' behavior and academic performance. For changes to occur, students must perceive the counselor's role as an advocate and support, not as a "narc" or another adult who does not understand.

School counselors can also coordinate academic and vocational opportunities for students in the school system and the community. Alternative school programs such as early release for work-study programs, vocational school training, and individually paced programs, may provide students with an avenue to continue their education in an environment more receptive to their interests and needs.

Another informal school-based intervention targets naturally occurring peer groups. Because most students trust and relate to their peers, peer support and education groups are effective ways of relaying information to adolescents (Robinson Kurpius, in press). Peer discussion groups allow students to discuss their experiences and difficulties with peer pressure and peer acceptance. Students can find validation in knowing they are not alone in their experiences and feelings. Similarly, finding out that not everyone is using drugs can help to dispel adolescent drug myths. Most importantly, the group can help foster healthy peer relationships that promote self-growth. Programs such as Students Against Drunk Driving (S.A.D.D.) are an example of this type of intervention. Involvement in extracurricular activities such as sports, clubs, or music programs can also serve as an informal source of adolescent support.

There are a multitude of formal, structured programs for prevention and intervention of adolescent substance use. Multicomponent programs are more effective than unidimensional approaches (Gonet, 1998). For instance, in Botvin's (1986) Life Skills Training Program, trained teachers and older peers from the 11th and 12th grades structured a prevention program targeted for junior high students. Utilizing components of short- and long-term consequences of drug use (e.g., biofeedback after smoking cigarettes), critical thinking and decision-making skills, anxiety management skills, social skills to resist peer pressure, and self-image development, Botvin accessed the affective, cognitive, and behavioral components of adolescents. Similarly, prevention and intervention programs need to help adolescents to increase their sense of self-efficacy about making decisions through addressing the four senses of (1) belonging, (2) usefulness in life, (3) competency and being valued by others, and (4) self-empowerment (Kassebaum, 1990).

Another widely used structured program that utilizes multiple components is the Growing Healthy Program, which has been shown to reduce alcohol, drug, and cigarette use among adolescents (Dryfoos, 1990). Promoted by the National Center for Health Education (National Diffusion Network, 1986), this health education program for kindergarteners through seventh graders combines general health issues with reading, arts, sciences, and physical education to address issues of body systems, safety, nutrition, hygiene, fitness, mental health, and healthy lifestyles. Using audiovisuals, models, workshops, and students' parents, this program integrates school, family, and community in prevention efforts. Girl Power! is a more recent campaign that started in 1996. Sponsored by the Department of Health and Human Services, this program is designed to serve girls between the ages of 9 and 14. Strong no-use messages are integrated into self-defined groups that address self-esteem, self-identity, and empowerment issues.

Other school-based, noncurricular programs include in-house psychoeducational programs and support services. Dryfoos (1990) reviewed the popular Student Assistance Program (SAP) that utilizes full-time professional counselors to provide alcohol and drug abuse prevention and intervention services to 11th and 12th graders. Services include (1) group, individual, and family counseling; (2) resources for students who are struggling academically; and (3) consultations with parents and community leaders. Because SAP counselors are typically employed by external organizations, they are not under the same confidentiality and time constraints as school guidance counselors. Evaluation research of SAP approaches has indicated significant reductions in alcohol and marijuana use along with significant increases in academic performance.

Another school-based program is the Talented At-Risk Girls: Encouragement and Training for Sophomores (TARGETS) project that has been offered through Arizona State University since 1992. This project, sponsored by the National Science Foundation, focuses on the career aspirations and at-risk behaviors of teenage girls. Through activities such as future day fantasies, individual career counseling sessions, and group discussions of at-risk behaviors such as alcohol and drug use, sexuality, and suicide, adolescent girls are provided with self-care knowledge and encouragement to pursue their career dreams. Long-term follow-up with over 300 girls has revealed that this program enhances career aspirations, job and future self-efficacy, and self-esteem while decreasing substance use behaviors (Kerr & Robinson Kurpius, 1999).

Unfortunately, most commercial curriculum packages are not supported by empirical research and have not been systematically evaluated (Bangert-Drowns, 1988; Dryfoos, 1990). Some of these programs include Children Are People, All Stars, 8:30 Monday Morning, DARE, Lions/Quest Program—Skills for Adolescents, Project Pride, and Get High on Yourself. Although these programs address drug problems from multiple perspectives, objective and valid evaluation continues to be problematic.

Regardless of whether the school-based programs are formal or informal, they should address the primary factors involved in the etiology of substance abuse. These factors include peer use of illicit substances (Kandel & Yamaguchi, 1985), peer pressure (Brook, Whiteman, & Gordon, 1983; Brook, Whiteman, Gordon, Nomura, & Brook, 1986), early antisocial behavior (Hawkins, Lishner & Catalano, 1985), familial relations (Hawkins et al., 1983; Wang et al., 1995), cultural influences (Gloria & Peregoy, 1996; Thurman et al., 1995; Trimble, Bolek, & Niemcryk, 1992), and media influences (Vega & Gil, 1998b). Also, as pointed out by Dryfoos (1990), incorporating behavioral, cognitive, and affective strategies is important in all prevention efforts. Wallack and Corbett (1990) called for a "broader, more comprehensive, and multifaceted approach to prevention [intervention] that takes a variety of societal and cultural factors into account while also focusing on environmental factors" (p. 5).

School-based interventions for Deanna. Perhaps the most appropriate school-based intervention for Deanna is the TARGETS program. By participating in this research-based program, Deanna could be exposed to both group and individual counseling that could support increased efforts at school and decreased substance use. The program also addresses self-esteem and self-efficacy issues. These are particularly relevant for Deanna given her need to fit in, to use substances to escape, and to allow her peers to influence her behaviors. In addition to TARGETS, it could be helpful if Deanna were involved in an ongoing school-based support group of peers who are struggling with similar problems. Given Deanna's high need for approval and peer acceptance, she might do well in a peer-led group.

Community-Based Interventions

Community interventions can be provided in a wide variety of ways. Popular media prevention strategies (e.g., comparing a brain on drugs to an egg sizzling in a frying pan) have questionable effects on drug use behaviors. In particular, information contained in these strategies does not effectively communicate the reality of drug use or abuse that is relevant and applicable to students. That is, if adolescents experiment with drugs and do not experience adverse effects, the parallel of a fried brain may not seem applicable to them. This type of commercial fosters an information gap between the reality of drugs and the intended message. Less credence is also given to public service announcements made by movie stars and athletes when some of these same individuals are later found to be using substances.

McWhirter et al. (1993) identified five community-based programs presently available for adolescents: drug-free programs, residential treatment facilities, therapeutic communities, day care programs, and aftercare programs. Drug-free programs are usually outpatient programs within a residential treatment program. Activities range from individual and group counseling to challenging experiential programs. Residential treatment facilities are inpatient and focus on long-term recovery. Requiring the adolescent to live on-site, these programs focus on resocializing youth by teaching new life skills. For adolescents from racial/ethnic minority backgrounds in particular, learning and applying bicultural skills in order to manage different cultures is necessary.

A similar residential type of treatment program is therapeutic communities, designed for adolescents who are recovering substance use offenders and who are referred from the juvenile court system. Focusing on extinguishing substance use, therapeutic communities rely on peer influence and group action to change attitudes and destructive behavior. Day care programs, however, typically are less structured than residential programs. Their services usually include academic learning and counseling as well as supervised social activities. Aftercare programs target the adolescent who has been discharged from treatment. The premise of these programs is that treatment is a lifelong process.

Other community-based interventions often involve law enforcement systems that collaborate with the community. Police often talk with the parents of the adolescent arrested for a substance use offense. Police, parents, schools, and community task forces can work together effectively to design community-wide prevention and intervention programs to combat adolescent substance use. For instance, boys and girls clubs and community YMCAs provide alternative activities. Adult volunteers and recovered users often staff these programs, providing healthy, productive, and positive role models. Such organizations bring individuals, schools, and communities together to share responsibility for preventing and intervening in adolescent substance use and abuse.

> *Community-based interventions for Deanna.* Getting Deanna involved in the local YMCA or community sports team could be beneficial. In addition, she could benefit from being active in tribal-based activities. These interventions could foster a sense of belonging as well as pride in who she is—both as a Native American and as an athlete. She could benefit from more positive individual, social, and environmental experiences, and these community interventions have the probability of providing her with the positive individual and group-member recognition she needs and wants.

Considerations for Substance Abuse Prevention and Intervention: Adaptations for Diversity

In that many adolescent prevention and intervention programs do not include cultural or contextual issues, Wallack and Corbett (1990) called for "a combination of approaches affecting different aspects of the political, social, and cultural environment, in addition to the individual" (p. 17). Specifically, attention to the environmental issues of discrimination and racism are of particular concern for all adolescents. Labouvie (1986) found that a sense of powerlessness or helplessness was related to heavy substance abuse. Substance use "helped" adolescents achieve a sense of emotional self-regulation. Given that approximately 10% of adolescents are lesbian, gay, or bisexual (Berk, 1993), same-sex interests often result in familial and internal conflict (Herring, 1997). Accordingly, these youth are vulnerable to alcohol and drug use as they often feel rejected by the self and the heterocentric values of the United States.

Underscoring the importance of integrating contextual and cultural considerations into prevention and intervention programming, Oetting, Beauvais, and Edwards (1988) identified ineffective strategies for working with American Indian adolescents. For example, programs that were identified as ineffective for American Indians were those that focused on improving self-esteem; viewed alcohol as a substitute for social acceptance; perceived alcohol use as by depressed, anxious, or emotionally disturbed youth; and did not actively or completely exclude alcohol use. However, although some preventive activities may be ineffective for one specific cultural group, the same activities may be effective with adolescents from other cultural backgrounds. Adolescent substance abuse is a serious issue; therefore, researchers, parents, school systems, and counselors cannot afford to administer one-size-fits-all prevention or intervention programming.

ACCESSING RESOURCES AND INFORMATION

In accessing information about substance use prevention and intervention, there are several alternatives from which to choose. First, the public library is an excellent source for information about state laws related to drugs. Learning about state laws and the legal rights of minors can be helpful in providing straight talk and accurate information about drugs. Second, if parents or adolescents are concerned about openly seeking information, a variety of free publications, pamphlets, posters, and other drug education information can be ordered by phone. For instance, the first research-based drug prevention guide for children and adolescents (*Preventing Drug Use Among Children and Adolescents*) is available through the National Clearinghouse for Alcohol and Drug Information (NCADI) at 1-800-729-6686. The publication *Keeping Youth Drug Free* is also available from NCADI. It is estimated that NCADI receives over 250,000 inquiries and distributes over 20 million information products each year.

The Internet is another rich source of information regarding substance use and abuse prevention. A variety of government and private agency web sites are available and user friendly. For families interested in surfing the web to gain information about drugs, Internet addresses to visit include

- *www.health.org* to access the Substance Abuse and Mental Health Services Administration;
- *www.nida.nih.gov* to access the National Institute on Drug Abuse;
- *www.niaa.nih.gov* to access the National Institute on Alcohol Abuse and Alcoholism; and
- *www.whitehousedrugpolicy.gov* to access the Office of National Drug Control Policy.

Within most sites, links and programs specifically target adolescents and different racial and ethnic minority groups. Most information is easy to read and presented in a fun and attention-getting fashion. Most sites also provide additional links (i.e., other sites of potential interest) and referral information. Addresses and phone numbers for different prevention and treatment organizations are also generally provided. The majority of information on web sites can be downloaded for parents or adolescents to use in later discussions. Further, the NIDA Infofax provides a 24-hour toll-free phone line from which drug information can be ordered via fax or mail. Audio information on topics such as the health effects of drugs, drug use and AIDS, and drug treatment and prevention can also be listened to in English or Spanish. The phone numbers are 1-888-644-6432 and 1-888-889-6432 (hearing-impaired).

SUMMARY

Simply stated, "no single strategy has demonstrated long-term impact" (Wallack & Corbett, 1990, p. 15) on adolescent drug abuse. Prevention of substance abuse is a shared responsibility among adolescents, families, schools, and communities. Both prevention and intervention programs need to focus on adolescents' behaviors, feelings, and thoughts (Dryfoos, 1990) within a culturally and socially congruent environment (Gloria & Peregoy, 1996; Trimble et al., 1992). The focus and manner in which programs focus on adolescents, however, must be informed by cultural values and beliefs specific to group and subgroup norms (Gloria & Peregoy, 1996; Thurman et al., 1995; Trimble et al., 1992; Vega & Gil, 1998a). That is, prevention and intervention programs must be designed to be congruent with the values and worldview of the culture within which they are implemented. Although we may never totally stop substance use or abuse, one of our most important tasks is to prepare our youth to be wise decision makers and to draw upon their cultural, social, and familial strengths and supports.

REFERENCES

Avis, H. (1990). *Drugs and life*. Dubuque, IA: William C. Brown.

Bangert-Drowns, R. L. (1988). The effects of school-based substance abuse education—a meta-analysis. *Journal of Drug Education, 18,* 243–265.

Berk, L. E. (1993). *Infants, children, and adolescents*. Boston: Allyn & Bacon.

Beschner, G. (1986). Understanding teenage drug use. In. G. Beschner & S. Friedman (Eds.), *Teen drug use* (pp. 1–18). Lexington, MA: D.C. Heath.

Botvin, G. (1986). Substance abuse prevention efforts: Recent developments and future directions. *Journal of School Health, 56,* 369–374.

Brook, J. S., Whiteman, M., & Gordon, A. S. (1983). Stages of drug use in adolescence: Personality, peer, and family correlates. *Developmental Psychology, 19,* 269–277.

Brook, J. S., Whiteman, M., Gordon, A. S., Nomura, C., & Brook, D. W. (1986). Onset of adolescent drinking: A longitudinal study of intrapersonal and interpersonal antecedents. *Advances in Alcohol and Substance Abuse, 5,* 91–110.

Burns, C., & Margarella, M. (1990). Reaching parents. In *Communicating about alcohol and other drugs: Strategies for reaching populations at risk* (pp. 211–247, Office for Substance Abuse Prevention Monograph B5, DHHS Publication No. ADM 90-1665). Washington, DC: U.S. Government Printing Office.

Business Research Publications. (1987, September). Education department starts school year with "Challenge" public service campaign. *Substance Abuse Reports, 18,* 3–4.

Chapa, J., & Valencia, R. R. (1993). Latino population growth, demographic characteristics, and educational stagnation: An examination of recent trends. *Hispanic Journal of Behavioral Sciences, 15,* 165–187.

Daroff, L. H., Marks, S. J., & Friedman, A. S. (1986). Adolescent drug abuse: The parents' predicament. In G. Beschner & A. S. Friedman (Eds.), *Teen drug use* (pp. 185–209). Lexington, MA: D.C. Heath.

Daroff, L. H., Marks, S. F., & Friedman, A. S. (1990). The parents' predicament. In A. S. Friedman & S. Granick (Eds.), *Family therapy for adolescent drug abuse* (pp. 85–108). Lexington, MA: Lexington Books.

Dryfoos, J. G. (1990). *Adolescents at risk: Prevalence and prevention.* New York: Oxford University Press.

Fields, R. (1992). *Drugs and alcohol in perspective.* Dubuque, IA: Brown.

Freeman, E. M. (1990). Social competence as a framework for addressing ethnicity and teenage alcohol problems. In A. R. Stiffman & L. E. Davis (Eds.), *Ethnic issues in adolescent mental health* (pp. 247–266). Newbury Park, CA: Sage.

Funkhouser, J. E., & Denniston, R. W. (1992). Historical perspective. In *A promising future: Alcohol and other drug problem prevention services improvement* (pp. 5–15, Office for Substance Abuse Prevention Monograph B10, OHHS Publication No. ADM 92-1807). Washington, DC: U.S. Government Printing Office.

Gloria, A. M., & Peregoy, J. J. (1996). Counseling Latino alcoholics and other substance users/abusers: Cultural considerations for counselors. *Journal of Substance Abuse Treatment, 13,* 119–126.

Goddard, L. L. (1993). The role of the family in alcohol and other drug use prevention. In *The second national conference on preventing and treating alcohol and other drug abuse, HIV infection, and AIDs in Black communities: From advocacy to action* (pp. 161–173, Center for Substance Abuse Prevention Monograph 13). Washington DC: U.S. Department of Health and Human Services, Public Health Service.

Goldberg, S. (1982). *Clinical neuroanatomy made ridiculously simple.* Miami, FL: MedMaster.

Gonet, A. M. (1998). Groups for drug and alcohol abuse. In K. C. Stoiber & T. R. Kratochwill (Eds.), *Handbook of group intervention for children and families* (pp. 172–192). Needham Heights, MA: Allyn & Bacon.

Hawkins, J. D., Catalano, R. F., & Miller, J. Y. (1992). Risks and protective factors for alcohol and other drug problems in adolescence and early adulthood: Implications for substance abuse prevention. *Psychological Bulletin, 112,* 64–105.

Hawkins, J. D., Lishner, D. M., & Catalano, R. F. (1985). Childhood predictors and the prevention of adolescent substance abuse. In C. L. Jones & R. J. Battejes (Eds.), *Etiology of drug abuse: Implications for prevention* (pp. 75–126, Research Monograph 56). Rockville, MD: National Institute on Drug Abuse.

Herd, D. (1988). Drinking by Black and White women: Results from a national survey. *Social Problems, 35,* 493–505.

Herring, R. D. (1997). *Counseling diverse ethnic youth: Synergetic strategies and interventions for school counselors.* Fort Worth, TX: Harcourt Brace College.

Ho, M. K. (1987). *Family therapy with ethnic minorities.* Newbury Park, CA: Sage.

Ho, M. K. (1992). *Minority children and adolescents in therapy.* Newbury Park, CA: Sage.

Hutto v. Davis, 454 U.S. 370 (1982).

Inciardi, J. A. (1986). Getting busted for drugs. In G. Beschner & A. S. Friedman (Eds.), *Teen drug use* (pp. 63–83). Lexington, MA: D.C. Heath.

In re Gault, 387 U.S. 1 (1967).

Jalali, B., Jalali, M., Crocette, G., & Turner, F. (1981). Adolescents and drug use: Toward a more comprehensive approach. *American Journal of Orthopsychiatry, 51*, 1.

Jillson-Broostrom, I. (1993). Health and related data for racial/ethnic populations in the United States: Realities and need. In *The second national conference on preventing and treating alcohol and other drug abuse, HIV infection, and AIDs in Black communities: From advocacy to action* (pp. 247-264, Center for Substance Abuse Prevention Monograph 13). Washington DC: U.S. Department of Health and Human Services, Public Health Service.

Julien, R. M. (1978). *A primer of drug action* (2nd ed.). San Francisco: Freeman.

Kandel, D. B., & Yamaguchi, K. (1985). Developmental patterns of the use of legal, illegal, and medically prescribed psychotropic drugs from adolescence to young adulthood. In C. L. Jones & R. J. Battejes (Eds.), *Etiology of drug abuse: Implications for prevention* (pp. 193–235, Research Monograph 56). Rockville, MD: National Institute on Drug Abuse.

Kassebaum, P. (1990). Reaching families and youth from high-risk environments. In *Communicating about alcohol and other drugs: Strategies for reaching populations at risk* (pp. 11–119, Office for Substance Abuse Prevention Monograph B5, DHHS Publication No. ADM 90-1665). Washington, DC: U.S. Government Printing Office.

Kerr, B., & Robinson Kurpius, S. E. (1999). *Guiding girls in engineering, math, and sciences: A year-end report.* Arlington, VA: National Science Foundation.

Kingery-McCabe, L. G., & Campbell, F. A. (1991). Effects of addiction on the addict. In D. C. Daley & M. S. Raskin (Eds.), *Treating the chemically dependent and their families* (pp. 57–78). Newbury Park, CA: Sage.

Klein, B. T. (Ed.). (1993). *Reference encyclopedia of the American Indian* (6th ed., pp. 35–39). West Nyack, NY: Todd.

Robinson Kurpius, S. E. (in press). Peer counseling. In A. E. Kazdin (Ed.), *Encyclopedia of psychology.* Washington, DC: American Psychological Association and Oxford Press.

Kusnetz, S. (1986). Services for adolescent substance abusers. In G. Beschner & A. S. Friedman (Eds.), *Teen drug use* (pp. 123–153). Lexington, MA: D.C. Heath.

Labouvie, E. W. (1986). Alcohol and marijuana use in relation to adolescent stress. *International Journal of Addictions, 21*, 333–345.

LaFromboise, T. D., Berman, J. S., & Sohi, B. K. (1994). American Indian women. In L. Comas-Díaz & B. Greene (Eds.), *Women of color: Integrating ethnic and gender identities in psychotherapy* (pp. 30–71). New York: Guilford Press.

Lewis, J. A., Dana, R. O., & Blevins, G. A. (1988). *Substance abuse counseling: An individualized approach.* Pacific Grove, CA: Brooks/Cole.

Lex, B. W. (1987). Review of alcohol problems in ethnic minority groups. *Journal of Consulting and Clinical Psychology, 55*, 293–300.

Macdonald, D. I., & Newton, M. (1981). The clinical syndrome of adolescent drug abuse. *Advances in Pediatrics, 28,* 1–15.

Mandel, J., & Feldman, H. W. (1986). The social history of teenage drug use. In G. Beschner & A. S. Friedman (Eds.), *Teen drug use* (pp. 19–42). Lexington, MA: D.C. Heath.

Marín, G. (1991). Influence of acculturation on familialism and self-identification among Hispanics. In M. E. Bernal & G. P. Knight (Eds.), *Ethnic identity: Formation and transmission among Hispanics and other minorities* (pp. 181–196). Albany: State University of New York Press.

McKim, W. A. (1991). *Drugs and behavior: An introduction to behavioral pharmacology* (2nd ed.). Englewood Cliffs, NJ: Prentice Hall.

McWhirter, J. J., McWhirter, B. T., McWhirter, A. M., & McWhirter, E. H. (1993). *At-risk youth: A comprehensive response.* Pacific Grove, CA: Brooks/Cole.

Miller, P. H. (1989). *Theories of developmental psychology* (2nd ed.). New York: Freeman.

Muisener, P. P. (1994). *Understanding and treating adolescent substance abuse.* Thousand Oaks, CA: Sage.

National Diffusion Network. (1986). *Education programs that work* (12th ed.). Longmont, CO: Sophris.

National Institute on Drug Abuse. (1984). *Parents: What you can do about drug abuse.* (DHHS Publication No. ADM 1267). Washington, DC: U.S. Government Printing Office.

National Institute on Drug Abuse. (1997a). *1996 National Household Survey on Drug Abuse.* Rockville, MD: U.S. Department of Health and Human Services.

National Institute on Drug Abuse. (1997b). *Monitoring the Future Study* [On-line]. Available: http://www.nida.nih.gov/infofax/HSYouthtrends.html

National Institute on Drug Abuse. (1998a). *Infofax phoneline* (1.888.644.6432). Rockville, MD: U.S. Department of Health and Human Services.

National Institute on Drug Abuse. (1998b). *Cigarettes and other nicotine products* [On-line]. Available: Http://www.nida.nih.gov/Infofax/tobacco.html

National Institute on Drug Abuse. (1998c). *Inhalants* [On-line]. Available: Http://www.nida.nih.gov/Infofax/inhalants.html

National Institute on Drug Abuse. (1998d). *Marijuana* [On-line]. Available: Http://www.nida.nih.gov/Infofax/marijuana.html

Nowinski, J. (1990). *Substance abuse in adolescent and young adults: A guide to treatment.* New York: Norton.

Oetting, E. R., Beauvais, R., & Edwards, R. (1988). Alcohol and Indian youth. Social and psychological correlates and prevention. *Journal of Drug Issues, 18,* 87–102.

Oyemade, U. J., & Washington, V. (1990). The roles of family factors in the primary prevention of substance abuse among high-risk Black youth. In A. R. Stiffman & L. E. Davis (Eds.), *Ethnic issues in adolescent mental health* (pp. 267–284). Newbury Park, CA: Sage.

O'Hare, W. P. (1992). America's minorities—the demographics of diversity. *Population Bulletin, 47,* 1–47.

Phinney, J. S., Lochner, B. T., & Murphy, R. (1990). Ethnic identity development and psychological adjustment in adolescence. In A. R. Stiffman & L. E. Davis

(Eds.), *Ethnic issues in adolescent mental health* (pp. 53–72). Newbury Park, CA: Sage.

Raskin, M. S., & Daley, D. C. (1991). Introduction and overview of addiction. In D. C. Daley & M. S. Raskin (Eds.), *Treating the chemically dependent and their families* (pp. 1–21). Newbury Park, CA: Sage.

Ray, O., & Ksir, C. (1987). *Drugs, society, and human behavior*. St. Louis, MO: Times Mirror/Mosby College.

Rebach, H. (1992). Alcohol and drug use among American minorities. In J. E. Trimble, C. S. Bolek, & S. J. Niemcryk (Eds.), *Ethnic and multicultural drug abuse: Perspectives on current research* (pp. 23–57). Binghamton, NY: Harrington Park Press.

Rhodes, J. E., & Jason, L. A. (1988). *Preventing substance abuse among children and adolescents*. New York: Pergamon Press.

Robinson, S. E. (1989). Preventing substance abuse among teenagers: A school and family responsibility. *Counseling and Human Development, 21*, 1–8.

Robinson, S. E., Gloria, A. M., Roth, S. L., & Schuetter, R. M. (1993). Patterns of drug use among male and female undergraduates. *Journal of College Student Development, 34*, 130–137.

Rutter, M. (1987). Psychosocial resilience and protective mechanisms. *American Journal of Orthopsychiatry, 57*, 316–331.

Schinke, S. P., Botvin, G. J., & Orlandi, M. A. (1991). *Substance abuse in children and adolescents: Evaluation and intervention*. Newbury Park, CA: Sage.

Schonberg, S. K., & Schnoll, S. H. (1986). Drugs and their effects on adolescent users. In G. Beschner & A. S. Friedman (Eds.), *Teen drug use* (pp. 43–62). Lexington, MA: D.C. Heath.

Smart, J. S., & Smart, D. W. (1994). The rehabilitation of Hispanics experiencing acculturative stress: Implications for practice. *Journal of Rehabilitation, 60*, 8–12.

Strasburger, V. C. (1989). Why just say no won't work. *Journal of Pediatrics, 114*, 676–681.

Thurman, P. J., Swaim, R., & Plested, B. (1995). Intervention and treatment of ethnic minority substance abusers. In J. F. Aponte, R. Y. Rivers, & J. Wohl (Eds.), *Psychological interventions and cultural diversity* (pp. 215–233). Boston, MA: Allyn & Bacon.

Tobler, N. (1986). Meta-analysis of 143 adolescent drug prevention programs: Quantitative outcome results of program participants compared to a control or comparison group. *Journal of Drug Issues, 16*, 537–567.

Trimble, J. E., Bolek, C. S., & Niemcryk, S. J. (Eds.). (1992). *Ethnic and multicultural drug abuse: Perspectives on current research*. Binghamton, NY: Harrington Park Press.

Ungerleider, J. T., & Seigel, N. J. (1990). The drug abusing adolescent: Clinical issues. *Adolescence: Psychopathology, Normality, and Creativity, 13*, 435–442.

U.S. Bureau of the Census. (1990). *1990 Census of population and housing B summary tape file 1: Summary population and housing characteristics*. Washington, DC: U.S. Government Printing Office.

U.S. Bureau of the Census. (1992). *1990 Census of population, 1990 CP-1-4, general population characteristics*. Washington, DC: U.S. Government Printing Office.

U.S. Department of Health and Human Services. (1984). *Alcohol and health: Fifth special report to the U.S. Congress* (Publication No. ADM 84-1291). Washington, DC: U.S. Government Printing Office.

Vega, W. A., & Gil, A. G. (Eds.). (1998a). *Drug use and ethnicity in early adolescence.* New York: Plenum Press.

Vega, W. A., & Gil, A. G. (1998b). Prevention implications and conclusions. In W. A. Vega & A. G. Gil (Eds.), *Drug use and ethnicity in early adolescence* (pp. 177–196). New York: Plenum Press.

Wallack, L., & Corbett, K. (1990). *Illicit drug, tobacco, and alcohol use among youth: Trends and promising approaches in prevention* (Office for Substance Abuse Prevention Monograph 6). Washington, DC: U.S. Government Printing Office.

Wang, G. T., Bahr, S. J., & Marcos, A. C. (1995). Family bonds and adolescent substance use: An ethnic group comparison. In C. K. Jacobson (Ed.), *American families: Issues in race and ethnicity* (pp. 463–492). New York: Garland.

Warheit, G. J., & Gil, A. G. (1998). Substance use and other social deviance. In W. A. Vega & A. G. Gil (Eds.), *Drug use and ethnicity in early adolescence* (pp. 37–70). New York: Plenum Press.

Werner, E. E. (1984). Resilient children. *Young Children, 40,* 68–72.

15 Nowhere to Turn: Homeless Youth

Melissa Stormont

The face of the homeless person has changed over the past several decades. Often now the face is that of a child: a child without a home. Families with small children now represent up to 43% of the homeless population (Dail, 1993). Conservative estimates indicate that at least 500,000 youth are homeless in the United States (National Coalition for the Homeless, 1994b; Shane, 1996). Schools and communities need to extend outreach efforts to identify children who are homeless as they are entitled to the same free and appropriate education as their peers who have homes (Shane, 1996). To ensure their appropriate education, professionals who work with children need to be educated on homelessness in general and on the unique needs and characteristics of children who are homeless.

Children who are homeless are at great risk for academic and behavioral problems in school (Butler, 1989; Danseco & Holden, 1998; Lewis & Doorlag, 1987; Reeves, 1988). These children may look and act different than their same age peers, and these differences demand sensitivity and understanding from teachers and other professionals who work with these youth. It is evident that the educational needs of homeless children warrant collaborative outreach efforts and interventions from teachers, counselors, administrators, and communities. Every professional involved needs to be aware of the resources available to assist homeless children. Schools must better prepare themselves to reach and to teach children who are homeless as, sadly, such children are consistently ignored by both schools and society.

This chapter first describes homelessness, both demographically and more descriptively using a case study. Next, the chapter delineates preventative measures for ending homelessness by presenting the causes of homelessness for individuals and families and then the ways that the community, the government, and other profit or not-for-profit agencies can provide outreach efforts. The chapter then describes interventions that can be driven by the schools for individual students who are homeless and their families and presents possible links from the school to the community to help meet the educational needs of these students. Adaptations for diversity and other considerations for working with homeless children are detailed next. The chapter concludes with an exploration of ways to end the cycle of homelessness by conducting outreach efforts and supporting the development of life and job skills for street youth.

HOMELESSNESS DEFINED

Homelessness means having a primary residence that is a public or private shelter, emergency housing, hotel or motel, or any other public space including public parks, cars, abandoned buildings, or aqueducts (National Coalition for the Homeless, 1990). Other definitions of homelessness include having to double up in housing with friends and family members (National Coalition for the Homeless, 1998c). Regardless of how homelessness is defined, being homeless means more than not having a fixed place to sleep. Homeless people have nowhere to put the things they cherish, things that connect them to their past. They have often lost contact with their family and friends and may have to uproot their children from school. Homelessness means suffering the frustration and degradation of living hand to mouth, and depending on the generosity of strangers or the efficiency of a government agency for survival.

At least 1 million families in the United States are homeless, with incidence rates increasing at a rate of 25% a year (National Coalition for the Homeless, 1990). From the most recent statistics available, it is clear that the faces of the homeless have changed drastically since the days of the White, male, alcoholic, skid row bum. According to the National Coalition for the Homeless (1998b), 40% of the homeless in the United States are families and 25% are children. Within these families half of the children are under the age of 6. They may never go to school, or they may enter school for the first time at a late age.

Conservative estimates indicate that one in five homeless children are not currently in school (Cherey, 1995; National Coalition for the Homeless, 1994a). Further, research has found that homeless children who are attending school are significantly more likely than children who are poor but housed to have missed more than 3 weeks of school in the last 3 months (Wood, Valdez, Hayashi, & Shen, 1990). One reason given for missing school is that families are in transition. Homeless children may also miss school due to frequent sick days. Unfortunately, the problem of homelessness in children is not decreasing. In fact, children are the fastest growing group of the homeless population (National Coalition for the

Homeless, 1994a; Shane, 1996). Worestendiek's research in Philadelphia found a 25% increase of children in homeless shelters between 1988 and 1993 (as cited in Shane, 1996).

Homeless children come from all geographical areas. Many state-level studies continue to support that homelessness is a problem present in nonmetropolitan areas (National Coalition for the Homeless, 1993). Children who are homeless also represent different ethnicities. However, a disproportionate number of minorities, especially African Americans, are represented in the homeless population (Shane, 1996). According to one report that delineated the percentage of the homeless by ethnicity, 58% of the population of homeless were African American, 29% were Caucasian, 10% were Hispanic, 2% were Native American, and 1% were Asian American (National Coalition for the Homeless, 1998c). Children may have different needs according to their different cultural backgrounds that will need to be addressed in a culturally sensitive way. (These adaptations for diversity are presented later in the chapter.) Overall, most homeless children have different needs from children who are not homeless, and they may have extensive problems in school. The following case of a homeless family illustrates the problems that the children might face in school.

Case Study: Homeless Family

It was 3:00 a.m. At a local gas station, a man was trying to bum $5 worth of gas off the attendant as his family waited, shivering, in their junky car. The attendant obliged the family and called a local homeless shelter asking if they would let the family stay even though its doors were closed for the night. The children arrived at the shelter, hungry and cold. Their parents tucked them in and stayed up for a while chatting with the volunteers. They were homeless because of one bill they could not pay, their electric bill. They tried to survive in their trailer without heat, lights, or hot water, but it was too hard on their children.

The children woke up and ate breakfast. Their clothes were wrinkled. They were dirty and extremely tired. They went to school after less than 3 hours of sleep. What will their teachers think when they fall asleep in class? How will they get food for lunch? What will their peers think? They came to school dirty, wearing the same clothes as the day before looking different from their peers. What can these children talk about with their peers? They have had to grow up too fast. Their worries are not the same as other children's. They are worried about their next meal and where they will seek shelter. However, their needs are the same as other children's: They need a home and all of the securities that come with it. They also need an education.

Consequences for Children

The case example suggests what the consequences of homelessness may be for youth in the classroom. In addition to not having a neat appearance or clean clothes, homeless youth who attend school typically do not have school records, immunization records, a permanent address, transportation, school supplies, gym shoes, appropriate clothing, or a full stomach (Gonzalez, 1990). For example, one study found that 15% of homeless children had incomplete immunizations (Bass, Brennan, Mehta, & Kodzis, 1990). Other studies have found that homeless children also tend to have chronic health problems and typically do not get medical care (Bass et al., 1990; Burg, 1994; Shane, 1996), and that health care problems appear to be more prevalent in homeless children than in children who are poor but have housing (Wood et al., 1990). In addition, research has found that homeless children have both more health problems and more barriers to obtaining adequate health care than children who are poor but live in low-income housing (Burg, 1994).

These physical insufficiencies only begin to describe these children's lives. Children who are homeless may go home to a shelter where there is often noise, inconsistency in adult supervision (e.g., shelter rules vs. parents' rules), no place to do homework, no privacy, and no resources. Additionally, homeless children are at risk for having been exposed to domestic violence (Eddowes & Hranitz, 1989; Shane, 1996). According to Maslow's hierarchy of needs, shelter, security, and food must be obtained before reaching higher order needs such as psychological and self-actualization needs (Maslow, 1968). Thus the additional problems associated with homelessness are profound for children. Not only are homeless children not getting the most basic needs fulfilled, but also their psychological health is at stake (Harrington-Lueker, 1989). These children may experience numerous emotions related to their homelessness including embarrassment, anxiousness, fear, low self-esteem, depression, suspiciousness, and feelings of helplessness (Bassuk & Rosenberg, 1988; Harrington-Lueker, 1989). These childrens' adult worries make it understandable that they might not care about completing their homework.

PREVENTION: CAUSES OF HOMELESSNESS

The best way to prevent the problems of homeless youth is to prevent homelessness. Homelessness, however, is a complicated social issue that requires a multilevel approach. Providing permanent affordable housing is only part of the solution. Ending homelessness is a matter of providing people with opportunities for housing, decent wages, health insurance, treatment for health problems, and an education. It is also a matter of understanding the issues surrounding families who become homeless and respecting their needs. The solution for ending homelessness needs to be addressed at individual, family, school, and societal levels.

Individual

Poverty, Unemployment, Low Wages. Since 1970 there has been a substantial increase in the number of persons living in poverty; and by 1996 the number of poor Americans exceeded 36.5 million (National Coalition for the Homeless, 1998b). There has also been an increase in the number of Americans living in extreme poverty, with 40% of people who are poor living on incomes that are well below the poverty level. Factors that contribute to poverty include falling wages and unemployment. The basis of employment in the United States has changed dramatically over the past 20 years from a highly paid manufacturing-based economy to a low-paid service-based structure. The result of this shift is reflected in the growing number of people who are made homeless due to under-employment. Nationally, the United States lost 882,000 manufacturing jobs between 1980 and 1988. Although new jobs were created during this time period, 88% were in retail and restaurant work (HomeBase, 1993).

Unemployment is also considered a leading cause of increased home-lessness (National Coalition for the Homeless, 1998a). In June 1993, a 7% unemployment rate translated to 8.9 million workers out of work (National Coalition for the Homeless, 1993), and 1.7 million people were considered as long-term unemployed. Once people become homeless, it is increasingly difficult to find a job because, without a home, they do not have a permanent address or telephone number to include on job applications. Further, work alone does not mean that a family will be able to rise out of poverty. Jobs need to provide enough compensation for a family to survive. Overall, 60% of new jobs created since 1979 pay less than $7,000 a year (HomeBase, 1993). By the end of the 1980s, 49% of employed taxpayers (47.2 million people) had annual incomes below $20,000 (Bartlett & Steele, 1992). Under these low-wage conditions, after paying rent, a family is hard pressed to stretch the remaining dollars to pay for food, let alone insurance, telephone, medical expenses, clothing, and school. If there are pre-school-aged children in the home, it is often not economical for both parents to work because their wages are likely to be devoted entirely to child care expenses. For a single parent, holding a job may not be an option unless the child attends school or free child care is available. In addition, most low-paying jobs do not include health care benefits. Accordingly, the serious illness of one family member can lead to tremendous financial hardship or homelessness.

Increased Costs of Housing/Lack of Low-Income Housing. Federal standards specify that housing should not exceed 30% of a household's income. However, almost two thirds of renters who are poor pay 50% or more of their income for housing (Dolbeare, 1991). In fact, rent for a one-bedroom apartment is unaffordable for at least one third of renters in all 50 states. More recent reports continue to stress that the lack of affordable housing is a major problem leading to homelessness (National Coalition for the Homeless, 1998a). Although federal, state, and local housing assistance programs are available to the low-income community, only one third of low-income renter households receive such assistance (Dolbeare, 1991). When the task of trying to obtain affordable housing interacts with the low wages that people who are impoverished receive, finding housing becomes almost impossible. The National Coalition for the Homeless (1998a) reported that "in the median state a minimum-wage worker would have to work 83 hours each week to afford a two-bedroom apartment at 30% of his or her income, which is the federal definition of affordable housing" (p. 2).

In 1968, housing legislation was passed to create 6 million units of federally subsidized low-income housing. By the late 1970s, only 2.7 million had been built (National Coalition for the Homeless, 1990). The prospects of additional low-income housing in the future are dubious. It was estimated that a loss of 1 million units will occur over a 20-year period due to subsidy expirations, opt-out provisions in Section 8 contracts, and losses due to physical or financial collapses (HomeBase, 1993). Recent reports have documented that between 1993 and 1995 alone, 900,000 housing units were lost (National Coalition for the Homeless, 1998a).

Reductions in Federal and State Entitlement Programs. National and state policy changes since the Reagan era of the 1980s have greatly impacted people with low incomes. Federal housing programs designed to create or subsidize low-cost housing were cut as much as 75% under President Reagan's administration (National Coalition for the Homeless, 1990). As many states have faced severe fiscal distress, they also have made drastic cuts in programs that assist the poor. State programs such as Aid to Families With Dependent Children (AFDC), general assistance benefits, and Supplemental Security Income for the elderly poor and the differently abled were cut more sharply in 1990 and 1991 than in any year since the early 1980s (Center on Budget and Policy Priorities, 1992). In 1992, 44 states cut or froze their AFDC benefits. Similar reductions occurred in 40 states in 1991. These reductions were more than any decreases since 1981. Overall, over a 24-year period (1970–94), AFDC benefits for families of three fell 47% (National Coalition for the Homeless, 1998a). A new program entitled Temporary Assistance to Needy Families (TANF) was designed to replace AFDC; however, TANF typically only provides assistance to people who are 75% below the level of poverty. General assistance benefits were also reduced or eliminated in 22 states from 1991 to 1992. Twenty-six of 27 states either froze or cut Social Security benefits for poor elderly and disabled recipients during 1992 (Center on Budget and Policy Priorities, 1992). These cutbacks have left holes in the safety net. Without these benefits to fall back on, many people were and are destined for economic hardship and homelessness.

Failure of the Health Care System. The health care system in the United States is severely lacking. Over 40 million Americans have no health care insurance, and there is a shortage of substance abuse treatment programs and community facilities for people who are chronically mentally ill (National Coalition for the Homeless, 1993). For homeless people with addictions, the traditional substance abuse treatment methods are inadequate. Issues of poverty, physical and mental illness, and remediating skill deficits are rarely included as a part of treatment but are blatant barriers to a homeless person's potential life of stability and self sufficiency. The programs that do exist are unable to meet the service demands. In one 1991 study of local treatment programs for the homeless, results indicated that 80% of the local programs were forced to turn away homeless clients seeking help. In addition, there is a lack of supportive, alcohol- and drug-free housing. In the state of Massachusetts, only 185 openings were available in drug-free housing for the 25,000 homeless people who received treatment annually.

People with chronic mental illness also face a shortage in appropriate housing, which relegates many to the streets. During the 1960s, deinstitutionalization became the treatment policy for serving the mentally ill. As a part of that policy, 2,000 federally supported community mental health centers were planned, but less than 800 were actually established (National Coalition for the Homeless, 1993). Although the increase of homeless people is often attributed to the deinstitutionalization of persons with mental illness during the 1970s, the federal government has established that this movement was not the primary cause of increased homelessness. In fact, the dramatic increases in the homeless population occurred much later than the 1970s. It was the decade of the 1980s, characterized by poverty and a lack of affordable housing, that resulted in growing numbers of people finding themselves on the street.

Families

To prevent homelessness for families it is important to understand the unique needs of families who are homeless. Such families typically become homeless for the same reasons as other individuals with the exception of mothers who become homeless due to fleeing domestic violence. (The needs of single mothers are distinct and addressed in the Adaptations for Diversity section.) The best way to prevent homelessness for families is to identify families at risk for homelessness and provide support services. It is more cost-effective to spend money preventing homelessness by preventing evictions (e.g., providing vouchers to landlords for past payments, legal assistance, cash assistance programs), keeping families in shared housing situations, and assisting families who are living in condemned buildings by providing them with transition help than it is to support families in shelters once they become homeless (Lindblom, 1996). More important than cost-effectiveness is the fact that once families are homeless, the road to reestablishing self-sufficiency is much more difficult, and the effects of homelessness on children may be traumatizing not solely because of the lack of permanent housing but also because of the other risks that may accompany homelessness (Bassuk & Weinreb, 1994).

Families may experience great hardship when they become homeless. If there is a father present, he is often separated from the rest of the family. It is also not uncommon for children to be divided and placed in different shelters due to space requirements or possibly placed in foster care due to a family's homelessness (Bassuk & Weinreb, 1994; Shinn & Weitzman, 1996). For many families the way to end homelessness and secure a stable residence includes many important factors. Research on service providers' opinions toward what was important for homeless families to possess, secure, and keep affordable housing included mothers' motivation, financial and food assistance, employment opportunities, housing, coping skills, education, and training (Buckner, Bassuk, & Zima, 1993). Even though service providers in this study recognized that most of the mothers are working, and that many suffer from depression, they nevertheless cited mothers' motivation and attitude (not the provision of support services) as the most important factor for obtaining and sustaining housing.

A better approach for service agencies working with homeless families is not to assume that mothers can "motivate themselves" or that families are not already motivated. In actuality, homeless families spend an inordinate amount of time, energy, and persistence trying to meet the basic needs of their family. On the average, a homeless family spends 37 hours a week trying to obtain food, clothing, shelter, child care, public assistance, and job training (HomeBase, 1993). Therefore, it is important for shelters and programs to support families in obtaining their basic needs. This family focus is supported in a review of the literature which stipulated that "Residential programs meant for women with young children ought to consider all aspects of families and children" (Buckner et al., 1993, p. 395).

Schools

It is very important that children who are homeless attend school and are provided the same quality education as their peers who are not homeless (Bassuk & Weinreb, 1994). According to the Stewart B. McKinney Homeless Assistance Act of 1986, parents can keep their children in the same school or reenroll them in the school district where they are living temporarily. It is important that children who are homeless and attend school have teachers, principals, counselors, and communities willing to do their part to ensure that the children are educationally successful. (The role of the school in supporting children and their families is addressed in detail in the Interventions section.)

Community Programs

It is obvious that the prevention of homelessness has to include a multi-faceted effort that considers both the needs of the family (housing) and the needs of individuals within a family (mental health treatment). Many researchers group the causes of homelessness at the individual level (e.g., mental health problems, substance abuse) and the external/systemic level (e.g., lack of affordable housing, falling wages, cutbacks in federal programs) (Buckner et al., 1993; Herron & Zabel, 1995; Tracey & Stoeker, 1993). Because there are so many causes of homelessness, it is critical that mental health and other supports are provided on an individual basis for families in addition to temporary or permanent housing (Buckner et al., 1993). It is also critical that community workers help remove barriers to ensure that children who are homeless receive adequate health care including immunizations and wellness checkups. One study removed some of the barriers to adequate health care for families by providing transportation, including taxi vouchers or bus tokens, to health care facilities (Danseco & Holden, 1998). Communities can also help remove barriers by keeping children who are homeless in school and by helping to ensure that children are receiving an appropriate education in a comfortable environment once in school. (Community involvement in the education of homeless children is covered in the Interventions section.)

Even with the complexity of ending homelessness, the most frequently cited cause of and solution for ending homelessness is, not surprisingly, providing safe and affordable low-income housing (Tracy & Stoeker, 1993). Indeed, researchers have concluded that "Until this country establishes a comprehensive housing policy, there is little hope that our other efforts on behalf of children can be sustaining" (Bassuk & Weinreb, 1994, p. 56).

INTERVENTIONS

Hoping that the government will recognize these tragic problems and change inadequate policies is unrealistic. The sad truth is that thousands of families are destined for homelessness. Thus individual parents and professionals need to work with families and communities to design and implement effective interventions that will ensure that homeless youth are receiving the education that they need and deserve.

Individuals: Parents

To ensure that their children are receiving an appropriate education, parents need to know their rights within the educational system, including their childrens' right to receive an appropriate education as stated in the Stewart B. McKinney Homeless Assistance Act of 1986 and its recent amendments (Foscarinis, 1996). Parents can contact a local shelter, social service agency, or church for assistance in obtaining the information related to their rights. Parents can also work as an advocate for other homeless families and inform them of their educational rights.

These suggestions may be idealistic considering the magnitude of the problems that parents who are homeless are typically experiencing. Therefore, schools must take a leadership role in bridging the gap between homeless shelters and the schools. Schools are an important socializing agent, second only to the family (Kauffman, 1993). As such, school personnel need to consider what effect they will or can have on every individual student's future success in life. Counselors, teachers, and administrators may not be able to influence the quality of a student's life outside of school. However, they can influence a student's life once that child is seated in a classroom. As Kauffman wrote, "In our culture, success or failure at school is tantamount to success or failure as a person . . ." (p. 225).

Individuals: School Counselors

School counselors' knowledge and sensitivity to serving homeless children in the schools makes them the best coordinators of resources for these individuals. The complex emotional and educational needs of homeless children match the training and work of school counselors. In addition, it is mandated by the 1994 amendments to the Stewart B. McKinney Act that local and state educational agencies communicate and coordinate services with local and state housing authorities (Foscarinis, 1996). School counselors could coordinate efforts to educate teachers and administrators on the characteristics and educational needs of children who are homeless. One guide for the selection of interventions is to conduct research on child characteristics that may help buffer homeless children under extreme stress from experiencing major trauma from their experience. Counselors can coordinate school and community efforts to address some of these protective factors, including developing strong physical health, high self-esteem, positive social skills, planning abilities, success in school, strong support systems, family closeness, and positive school experiences (Garmezy & Rutter as cited in Wagner, Schmitz, & Menke, 1996).

To help children who are homeless succeed in school, counselors also need to help teachers modify their classroom to accommodate homeless children's behavioral and social difficulties by being aware of models that have been effective for children (Gonzalez, 1990). It is important to note that each child is different, and some children who are homeless may not need any additional interventions. However, teachers should be prepared to use modifications and interventions if and when they are needed. Counselors should also be knowledgeable about the services (state and local) available for homeless children and help coordinate community efforts to advocate for the educational needs of these children. Counselors could also work with administrators to develop or institute programs such as programs to increase retention of students (HomeBase, 1993). Further, counselors could help arrange for independent study options and other special adaptations for students who are homeless, which may possibly increase their opportunities for success in school.

Individuals: Teachers

Teachers should have in-service training, which could be organized by school counselors and administrators, on general information related to homelessness, children's characteristics, suggested classroom modifications, and ways to facilitate positive self-esteem and success in school (Eddowes & Hranitz, 1989; Wagner et al., 1996). Children who are homeless are more likely than their peers to be doing poorly or failing in school (Bassuk & Rosenberg, 1988) and to have repeated a grade in school (Wood et al., 1990). It is, therefore, particularly important that teachers are aware of the diverse needs of these children and can create individualized interventions for them. This individualization requires that teachers be cognizant of what constitutes success in school. For example, two studies have documented what elementary (Hersh & Walker, 1983) and secondary (Kerr & Zigmond, 1986) teachers believe are important student characteristics or skills for school success. These critical skills are that a student

- follows established classroom rules;
- listens to teacher instructions;

- complies with teacher commands;
- does in-class assignments as directed;
- produces work of acceptable quality given his or her skill level;
- has good work habits (e.g., makes efficient use of class time, is organized, stays on task);
- makes her or his needs known in an appropriate manner;
- expresses anger appropriately; and
- behaves appropriately in nonclassroom settings and respects property and the rights of others.

If we consider the children in the case study, it is easy to discern that achieving these competencies may be problematic. Thus the following suggestions for teacher interventions are focused on academic adaptations for achieving success, behavioral management, emotional well-being, and self-esteem, and on educating other students about the characteristics and problems faced by children who are homeless. Some of the interventions are relatively easy and require only a small time commitment from teachers. Others, however, may be too demanding for some teachers. Counselors should help teachers decide which of these suggestions are feasible for them. Counselors could then employ some of the modifications themselves (e.g., teaching social skills 1 day a week).

Academic Adaptations. Teachers should administer quick, informal assessments to students who are homeless. Teachers also need to develop an assessment and work folder for the student that can be easily transferred to another school. In order to do adaptations, a teacher needs to analyze informal assessment data and begin instruction in various areas accordingly. Teachers should begin instruction in content areas at a place where the child can succeed. Teachers should also be very systematic and not assume that children have gone through the curriculum with the same consistency as their peers. That is, children who have been chronically homeless may have moved schools or been absent from school during times that certain basic prerequisite skills were taught. It is, therefore, important that teachers never assume that because a student is at a certain grade level that he or she has all of the foundation skills. Criterion-based assessments can help teachers determine skills that have been mastered and where there are deficits in knowledge that need to be remediated.

In addition, there are many small changes a teacher can make in terms of homework assignments. If students have difficulty completing written work, a teacher can adjust the amount of work required by students or change the output requirements (e.g., a child could recite a story into a tape recorder instead of writing it out). Teachers should modify homework assignments for a child who has no place to work after school (Eddowes & Hranitz, 1989). A teacher can also help promote organizational abilities for students who are homeless by having a private area in the classroom that is the students' place to keep their work. Students should be allowed to post their work in a special place to help them take pride in what they have done.

Behavioral Management. Children who are homeless often live in a hectic environment outside of school. Therefore, these children should be provided with a positive supportive classroom in school. Teachers should always set up conditions in which children can succeed academically and socially and then praise them accordingly. In addition, teachers should give clear, concise rules and be consistent when enforcing them (Eddowes & Hranitz, 1989). Teachers should also take the time to explain to the children why the rules are necessary. Teachers then need to inform shelter officials and parents of all rules and assignments. Special rewards and contingency plans can be arranged for children who need encouragement to complete their homework.

Emotional Well-Being. Counselors should make sure that teachers are sensitive to homeless children's well-being at all times. Teachers should be aware of the physical as well as emotional risk factors associated with homelessness. They should make accommodations such as the following simple modifications within the classroom that can promote social and emotional well-being. For example, to eliminate embarrassing situations, teachers should make other arrangements if children celebrate their birthdays by bringing treats (Indiana Department of Education, 1988). For another example, social growth could be facilitated by establishing a buddy system for homeless children; the teacher could state that the child is new in the school and then praise peers for making the child feel comfortable (Gonzalez, 1990). Other examples of interventions teachers can implement that may help include

- emphasizing classroom survival skills such as listening, asking for help, and following classroom rules (Indiana Department of Education, 1988; Wagner et al., 1996);
- employing social skills training with the entire class from simple skills (saying please and thank you) to more complex skills (inappropriate comments) (Indiana Department of Education, 1988; Wagner et al., 1996); and
- relieving anxiety through having a supportive, noncompetitive classroom (Wagner et al., 1996).

Above all, teachers with students who are homeless should make school a safe place where the children can learn and see hope for their futures.

Educating Other Students. Unfortunately many adults still have some misconceptions regarding the homeless population. A large sample of the general population reported that they thought more than half of the homeless population were drug addicts, and 37% reported that they thought that being homeless was freeing in that people would not have the same worries that other adults have (Link et al., 1996). Clearly, all students should be educated on factors related to homelessness. When they learn about the factors of homelessness, other students may become more compassionate to children who are in this situation. Hopefully, this process will aid in the successful social integration of students who are homeless into our schools.

HomeBase, a project in San Francisco, has developed a packet that includes classroom activities a teacher can use to introduce homelessness, to look at its causes and effects, and to explore taking action on homelessness. The lesson plans are detailed and varied for age appropriateness (grades K–3, 4–8, and 9–12). In the K–3 lesson on introducing students to homelessness, for example, students are asked to discuss the importance of homes (see Figure 15–1). As illustrated in Figure 15–2, students then use a picture of a house to answer open-ended questions on, for example, what they like to do in their home, why their home is important to them, and what people do in their homes (HomeBase, 1993). Figure 15–3 outlines classroom activities for each level and gives topical, material, and planning information. This packet could be an excellent resource for any school. Teachers could use this packet as a base from which to make their own unique lesson plans in similar formats.

Individual: Principals

Principals also need to get involved with homeless children's education when the children initially arrive at school, while they are enrolled, and when they leave. Upon arrival to a new school, children should be met and closely monitored by the principal (Gonzalez, 1990). This may help a child feel welcome and important. Once children are attending school, counselors and principals should establish immediate academic assessments of them, particularly if they have been out of school for a long period of time (Indiana Department of Education, 1988). Medical, counseling, and nutritional consultations for these children should be arranged through the school system. Schools could also be opened earlier and closed later to serve children food and give them adequate shelter (most shelters make families leave before school begins and do not open until late evening) (Eddowes & Hranitz, 1989).

When homeless children are leaving school, the principal should give them a transfer card and possibly contact the next school the child will be attending (Indiana Department of Education, 1988). It is important to

Figure 15–1 | Sample Lesson Plan for Elementary Students on Homelessness

---

Introduction to Homelessness

Level: K-3

Topic: The Importance of a Home

Materials: Drawing/painting materials, magazines/newspapers, "My Home" drawing

Time: 2 periods

Suggested Activity:

   Part 1: Have students draw/paint a picture of, make a collage of, or "build" a house.

   Part 2: Have students complete the "My Home" drawing individually or as a group.

Discussion:

   ✔ What is in a home?

   ✔ Who lives in a home?

   ✔ How many people live in a home?

   ✔ What types of homes are there besides a house?

   ✔ Where do you find a home?

   ✔ What do you do in a home?

   ✔ How do you get a home?

Note: From *Reaching and Teaching Children Without Housing: Improving Educational Opportunities for Homeless Children and Youth,* by HomeBase (p. 27), 1993, San Francisco: Author. Copyright 1993 by the Center for Common Concerns. Reprinted with permission.

minimize the stress of moving from school to school (Bassuk & Weinreb, 1994). Making the transition to a new school smooth for children helps to ensure that they feel welcome and that parents do not have to worry about obtaining appropriate documentation.

Empowering Families

There are many kinds of support that families need from community agencies and schools. Researchers have suggested that the needs of families and their children be addressed through an interdisciplinary team headed by a case manager (Wagner et al., 1996). As already indicated, the

Figure 15–2 I Sample Activity for Elementary Students on Homelessness

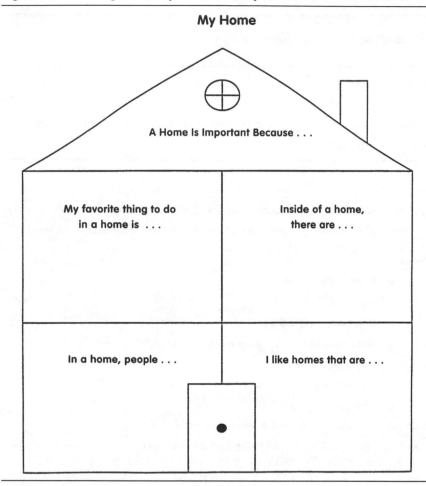

Note: From *Reaching and Teaching Children Without Housing: Improving Educational Opportunities for Homeless Children and Youth*, (p. 28), by HomeBase, 1993, San Francisco: Author. Copyright 1993 by the Center for Common Concerns. Reprinted with permission.

coordination of the community agencies is mandated by law, and the school counselor or a social worker can coordinate this team.

In coordinating services for families, it is important that the teams make sure that families and children are provided a safe and secure shelter facility that has a consistent routine and structure (Bassuk & Weinreb, 1994). The shelters can also make programmatic changes to help encourage the restabilization of families. For example, shelters can allow families

Figure 15–3 | Classroom Activities Outline

Classroom Activities Outline

ELEMENTARY SCHOOL	Level	Topic	Materials	Time
Introduction to Homelessness	K-3	The Importance of a Home	Drawing/painting materials, magazines/newspapers, "My Home" drawing	2 periods
Causes of Homelessness	K-3	Losing a Home	"Oakland" story	1 period
Effects of Homelessness	K-3	What Happens to Someone When They Don't Have a Home	"If I Didn't Have a Home . . ." exercise	1 period
Taking Action on Homelessness	K-3	Doing Something to Help	Paper, pens, envelopes or drawing materials	1 period

MIDDLE SCHOOL	Level	Topic	Materials	Time
Introduction to Homelessness	4-8	Stereotypes About Homelessness	Drawing materials, "People Without Homes"	1 period
Causes of Homelessness	4-8	Living in San Francisco	Budgeting worksheet, classified ads	2 periods
Effects of Homelessness	4-8	Life Without a Home	San Francisco Examiner article	1 period
Taking Action on Homelessness	4-8	Making a Difference	Varying	1 period

HIGH SCHOOL	Level	Topic	Materials	Time
Introduction to Homelessness	9-12	Stereotypes About People Without Homes	"How Homelessness Happens," "Homelessness Outline"	1 period
Causes of Homelessness	9-12	Living in the Bay Area	Budgeting worksheets, classified ads	2 periods
Effects of Homelessness	9-12	How Homelessness Changes Your Life	"Daily Log," "Shelter Rules and Regulations"	1 period
Taking Action on Homelessness	9-12	Thinking About Change	Varying	1 period

Note: From *Reaching and Teaching Children Without Housing: Improving Educational Opportunities for Homeless Children and Youth* (p. 26), by HomeBase, 1993, San Francisco: Author. Copyright 1993 by the Center for Common Concerns. Reprinted with permission.

to stay for 24 hours (Bassuk & Weinreb, 1994). This will enable one family member to work while the other family members stay in a safe environment. Research has shown that most parents who are homeless have full- or part-time jobs, and eliminating the stress of worrying about their families' safety may help more parents maintain their jobs (Danseco & Holden, 1998).

Research has also shown that preventative solutions for homelessness, according to service providers, include affordable housing, job training, education in daily living skills, rebuilding self-esteem, substance dependency treatment, and providing mental health services (Tracy & Stoeker, 1993). Research has further shown that other critical aspects of any program designed to help establish and sustain families in affordable housing include parent education, job training, encouraging problem-solving skills, and building support networks (Bassuk & Weinreb, 1994; Wagner et al., 1996).

In addition to providing these important prevention interventions to empower families, an interdisciplinary team could support families in meeting the physical needs of their children and in removing barriers to receiving adequate health care. The team should also assist parents and children in managing the emotional distress associated with being homeless and help families achieve renewed hope and build on existing social support systems or create new ones (Wagner et al., 1996).

These activities and goals are very similar to those included in a framework for empowering families of children with special needs (Turnbull & Turnbull, 1997). This framework emphasizes the importance of treating each family individually, understanding family factors that will affect empowerment (family members' knowledge, skills, motivation), and the importance of using certain guidelines for collaborating with families. The guidelines, referred to as the eight necessary obligations for professionals to recognize, work on, and attend to in order to achieve reliable alliances with families, include "knowing yourself, knowing families, honoring cultural diversity, affirming family strengths, promoting family choices, envisioning great expectations, communicating positively, and warranting trust and respect" (Turnbull & Turnbull, 1997, p. 47).

Community Outreach

Teachers and principals are busy with the demands of school that already extend their work beyond an 8-hour school day, and asking them to become advocates for homeless children may appear beyond their call of duty. However, there are successful outreach strategies to help fulfill these responsibilities that, again, can be coordinated by the counselor. Counselors could begin by setting up networks with local shelters and emergency housing facilities. This could allow counselors and/or teachers to visit shelters on a monthly basis to meet with homeless families and keep them informed about their children's progress. Counselors and administrators could appoint a person to be the educational coordinator between the schools and shelters. This person might be a volunteer from the community because it is important that the community also take responsibility for this serious societal problem.

Communities need to be aware of the prevalence of homelessness and the need for volunteers to help homeless families. The identification of homeless students who need help getting to school is a first step in terms of outreach. Community advocates are needed to help identify students who are not currently receiving an education. This could be done through posting flyers in hotels/motels and in other places people without homes may be living (e.g., bus depots, drop-in centers, bridges) (HomeBase, 1993). Outreach to those students who have not accessed educational services is critical. It is also important to have continuous lines of communication open with local shelters and churches who house students currently in school. Volunteers should be recruited to get homeless parents involved and interested in their children's education. Community help is critical for ensuring that the lines of communication remain open among schools, parents, and shelters (Eddowes & Hranitz, 1989).

Counselors can be key agents in initiating community assistance, which may be provided in various forms. For example, communities could help make sure that children without homes have transportation to and from school (Gonzalez, 1990). Schools could collaborate with day care centers to establish free care before and after school and transportation (Gonzalez, 1990). Another transportation option is for parents who live near a homeless shelter to volunteer to pick up children from the shelter and take them to school. This could also provide good opportunities for social interactions with other children if they were transported in a group.

Parents in the community could be assigned a child who is homeless for whom they could provide, for example, birthday treats, school supplies, or clothing (Gonzalez, 1990). If the child moves but is in the same area, the family that originally sponsored the homeless child should remain the same, thus providing valuable continuity. People in the community could also be encouraged to interact with homeless youth prior to or following school or to volunteer time to tutor or assist them once or twice a week (Gonzalez, 1990).

State residency laws cannot be used to ban homeless children from schools. The Stewart B. Mckinney Homeless Assistance Act of 1986 has stated that homeless children are entitled to free, appropriate education (National Coalition for the Homeless, 1990). However, there are no laws requiring in-depth identification of such children so that they can be educated in the schools based on their unique needs. Thus it is up to communities and, more specifically, to shelters and social services to work together as a coalition to protect the rights of these children to a free and appropriate education.

ADAPTATION FOR DIVERSITY

Within homeless families there are many additional factors for professionals to consider, including the children's risk for academic and emotional problems, single mothers, and cultural diversity. Understanding the characteristics of these diversities will help further outreach efforts as well as efforts to design more appropriate interventions.

Risk for Academic and Emotional Problems

Given that impoverished children are at increased risk for academic and emotional problems (Lewis & Doorlag, 1987), it is not surprising that children who are poor and without homes are also at risk. Homeless children experience academic and behavioral and emotional problems, and these problems manifest themselves at all ages (Bassuk & Rubin, 1987; Whitman, Accardo, Boyert, & Kendagor, 1990; Wood et al., 1990). Specifically, homeless children have significantly more behavior problems than children who are poor but housed (Wood et al., 1990). A particular characteristic that is important to consider for homeless school-aged children is their increased risk for depression. Research has found that the vast majority of these children have depressive symptomatology, with up to 66% showing symptoms at a level severe enough to warrant a clinical evaluation (Bassuk & Rubin, 1987; Wagner et al., 1996).

Depression in children has been linked to decreased academic performance (Schmitz, 1993, as cited in Wagner et al., 1996). A study reporting that 30% of homeless children had repeated a grade in school (Danseco & Holden, 1998) has provided some support for this depression-academic performance link within the population of homeless children. However, whether this is because of depression, academic skill deficiencies, or failure due to not completing assignments needs to be addressed so teachers and other professionals can better tailor interventions to students.

Children living in extremely stressful conditions may suffer emotionally. Being aware of the high risk for depression in this population can help direct the screening of homeless children at an early age for both behavioral and academic problems and individualized interventions. Recognizing that homeless children may manifest temporary behavior problems related to the anxiety that they are experiencing because of their situation is important. For example, a homeless child may display classic symptoms of hyperactivity (e.g., difficulty attending to tasks), but it may be because this student is preoccupied with his or her family's difficulties and more pressing problems and is not focused on the teacher's lecture or a class activity. Thus problems that will be ameliorated by providing permanent shelter to a child and assisting his or her family should be differentiated from more permanent problems that are related to extreme levels of depression, anxiety, and learning difficulties.

Assessing students and determining what is the main cause of school difficulties is also important because children who are homeless are at risk for academic problems and developmental delays that may be due to learning disabilities or mild mental retardation (Bassuk & Rubin, 1987;

Whitman et al., 1990; Wood et al., 1990). Research has found that 9% of homeless preschoolers failed two sections of the Denver Developmental Screening Test and 15% failed one (Wood et al., 1990). Other research has found that 35% of school-age homeless youth scored one standard deviation below the mean on an intelligence test (Whitman et al., 1990). One explanation for high rates of mild disabilities among homeless children is their high risk for lead exposure (Burg, 1994), which has been linked to higher incidence of learning disabilities (Lerner, Lowenthal, & Lerner, 1995). Additionally, mothers' inadequate prenatal care and/or drug use as well as children's lack of postnatal health care also place such children at risk for mild disabilities.

Single Mothers

A large percentage of homeless families are headed by a single female. An extensive review of the literature in this area makes it clear that these single mothers with children are a distinct subgroup within the population of the homeless and have different psychological and demographic characteristics. The needs of homeless mothers with small children are also very different from the needs of other homeless people (Buckner et al., 1993). According to Burt and Cohen (as cited in Buckner et al., 1993), homeless mothers caring for children are younger, less educated, and have been homeless for shorter periods of time than single women who are homeless but not caring for children. Mothers who are homeless are less likely than unaccompanied single females to be alcoholics and less likely to suffer from mental illnesses or substance dependency that requires hospitalization. However, mothers are more likely to report greater degrees of psychological distress than single women.

The psychological distress for homeless mothers appears to be much greater than the distress of poverty alone. Thus even though mothers caring for dependent children appear to have less major substance abuse and fewer mental health problems than other homeless people, mothers living in shelters have more substance abuse problems than mothers who live in low-income housing (Wood et al, 1990), which may be related to the psychological distress homeless mothers report. The psychological distress related to being a homeless mother may, in addition, be due to the events that precipitated homelessness and/or the lack of outside support available once homeless. That is, many women with children are homeless because they are fleeing domestic violence (Dail, 1993). According to the National Coalition for the Homeless (1998a), 44% to 50% of women are homeless due to the fact that they are fleeing domestic abuse. Sadly, the stress related to being homeless with children and the lack of support from immediate family and friends may ultimately drive many mothers back to their abusers.

This lack of support that homeless mothers report is a major consideration for working with this diverse population. Research has found that 26% of homeless women report no consistent support (Dail, 1993). Related research has documented that 43% of mothers who are homeless report minimal or limited support from other people (Bassuk & Rubin, 1987). The lack of support is much more profound for mothers who are homeless when compared to mothers who are poor but living in low-income housing. One study that predominantly included African American mothers (Letiecq, Anderson, & Koblinsky, 1998) found that mothers in low-income housing see and/or talk to more friends and relatives on a weekly basis than mothers who are homeless. Furthermore, mothers who are homeless report fewer people that they can count on in times of need and less family support in the last 6 months than mothers in low-income housing. Another study (Bassuk & Rosenberg, 1988) found that 22% of homeless mothers cannot name one person who is a support to them, whereas the majority of housed mothers can name three or more sources of support. In addition, the mothers who are homeless report twice the rate of domestic abuse as the mothers who are housed, and almost one third cite their child as a main source of support. A further study (Bassuk & Rubin, 1987) similarly found that 24% of mothers who are homeless report that their child is their major source of support.

The mothers who are not receiving much support from relatives and friends may face a major child care dilemma. They cannot leave their children in shelters or in temporary housing situations where they are often not separated from other homeless populations that possibly include substance abusers as well as those who are mentally ill or violent (Dail, 1993). The following eloquently describes the plight of single mothers with children:

> It is obvious that these mothers are extraordinarily stressed and are facing almost insurmountable problems of single parenting under the difficult circumstances of poverty, lack of extended family support, lack of affordable child care available to them if they could work, and being without a home. In reality, any smaller combination of these circumstances could render almost anyone immobilized, and it is highly unlikely that any improvement can occur without ongoing social assistance and interpersonal support. (Dail, 1993, p. 59)

Cultural Diversity

In addition to cultural differences related to marital status and gender, ethnicity and geographical location need to be considered when working with homeless children. There is extreme disparity between the percentage of minorities in the general population and the percentage of minorities who are homeless. In fact, researchers have documented percentages of homeless minorities as high as 85% in certain areas (Danseco & Holden,

1998). More conservative estimates indicate that at least half of mothers who are the heads of homeless families are ethnic minorities (Dail, 1993). Thus when implementing preventative and secondary interventions, it is important to recognize that the homeless population is different from the general population. With this knowledge, preventative outreach approaches should target community and state-run services that serve minority groups, particularly African Americans, and support families who are teetering on the brink of homelessness. Once African American mothers become homeless, it is very important to provide linkages with social service organizations and other sources of support because this group may be particularly subject to alienation or a lack of support from family and friends (Letiecq et al., 1998).

There is also a misconception in the general public that homelessness is an urban problem. Indeed, rural homelessness may be increasing at a faster rate than urban homelessness, and the demographic characteristics of the rural homeless are different from the urban homeless (Herron & Zabel, 1995). Specifically, rural people who are homeless are more likely to be Caucasian than their urban counterparts (Herron & Zabel, 1995; National Coalition for the Homeless, 1998c). Other reports have documented that homeless people in rural areas may be more likely to be homeless due to domestic violence (Aron & Fitchen, 1996). Another important consideration for working with homeless populations in rural areas is that it may be more difficult to identify rural families who are homeless because they may have a stronger support network and may be living in temporary residences with family and friends, or because they may be living in wooded camp areas or other remote areas (Aron & Fitchen, 1996).

Honoring cultural diversity when working with all families is important, and being culturally sensitive without being stereotypic is equally important (Turnbull & Turnbull, 1997). Professionals need to understand the impact that culture has on how individuals perceive the world (Watson, 1996). Examples of arrangements that professionals providing services to families who are homeless could make to be culturally sensitive include ensuring that the provider and the family have a language and/or cultural match, having flexible hours and accepting walk-ins, and using clergy and/or respected members of cultures (e.g., healers) in interventions (Watson, 1996).

BREAKING THE CYCLE OF HOMELESSNESS FOR STREET YOUTH

Homeless youth living on the streets without parents are beginning to be the subject of much-needed research. This is important because these homeless adolescents are at risk for many negative outcomes, and if left without resources and assistance, they are likely to re-create the cycle of homelessness for their children.

The number of adolescents (under 18 years of age) who are considered homeless street youth ranges from 250,000 to 1,000,000 (Robertson as cited in Unger et al., 1998). Homeless adolescents are a difficult population to identify because as many as 85% may not use homeless shelters (Greenblatt & Robertson, 1993). Once adolescents do arrive at shelters, however, the shelters need not only to have places for them to stay but also to provide an array of services. A study that documented the efforts of one city to establish more shelters for homeless adolescents also stressed the importance of coordinating services for these adolescents once they are in emergency housing facilities (Yates, Pennbridge, Swofford, & Mackenzie, 1991). These services include providing transportation to health care services or providing access for mobile teams to provide services within shelters, and supporting youth in acquiring independent living skills.

The need for interventions and outreach programs for this population is clear. Many street youth report psychological problems including depression, low self-esteem, and suicidality (Greenblatt & Robertson, 1993; Kennedy, 1991; Unger, Kipke, Simon, Montgomery, & Johnson, 1997). The prevalence of psychological disorders in homeless adolescents is reported to be three times higher than in adolescents who were not homeless, and the rates of drug and alcohol abuse are five to eight times higher (Greenblatt & Robertson, 1993). Note that adolescents who are homeless may have had major family crises leading to their situation that may make them even more vulnerable to having psychological problems once living on the streets or in temporary housing situations (Greenblatt & Robertson, 1993; Kennedy, 1991).

In addition, homeless youth engage in high-risk behavior, possibly to physically and/or psychologically survive on the street, such as drug use, unprotected sex, and unprotected sex with intravenous drug users (Greenblatt & Robertson, 1993; Kipke, O'Connor, Palmer, & Mackenzie, 1995; Rotheram-Borus, Parra, Cantwell, Gwadz, & Murphy, 1996). The repercussions for such high-risk behaviors include contracting sexually transmitted diseases including HIV/AIDS. According to one study, (Sweeney, Lindegen, Buchler, Onorato, & Janssen, 1995), 4% of teenagers who are homeless test positive for HIV, with rates as high as 17% for teenage boys who engage in sex with men.

To work effectively with homeless adolescents, educators and service providers must understand the needs of this population as well as the barriers to providing services to this population. The immediate needs include the physical needs for shelter, clothing, and food, and the medical need for education on behaviors that place them at risk for HIV infection (Greenblatt & Robertson, 1993; Shane, 1996). One barrier to providing services may be a lack of understanding of the day-to-day lifestyle of adolescents living on the streets (Lloyd & Kuszelewicz, 1995). Another barrier may be that many adolescents distrust adults and will not access services themselves. So the question is, How can professionals best work with this population of homeless youth?

Successful programs documented in the literature include storefront services for youth to drop in and pick up information about AIDS (Lloyd & Kuszelewicz, 1995) and focus groups led by adults who have similar demographic characteristics, and who have possibly been homeless themselves. A comprehensive intervention program employed in one study included small group sessions facilitated by a trained leader with a similar demographic background as well as individual counseling when needed. The interventions included information on (a) general knowledge of HIV and AIDS, (b) the importance of using coping skills effectively, and (c) resources available to adolescents. The study found that the number of sessions that adolescents participated in correlated with a reduction in high-risk behavior and an increase in consistent condom use.

A consistent and sensitive outreach approach that provides ongoing information in many different formats on the risks of certain behaviors may thus be the best intervention option. Fear tactics should not be employed because they may alienate the youth that need the information the most (Lloyd & Kuszelewics, 1995). Educators and professionals should remember, however, that this group of youth may be very challenging to reach. Youth who are homeless take risks every day just to survive.

In developing outreach efforts for adolescents, consider that not all street youth or potential street youth are so hard to find. Because research has documented that younger adolescents (12 to 15 years old) have different characteristics when compared with older adolescents (16 to 23 years old), and that two thirds of younger adolescents have attended school in the past month compared to only 27% of older adolescents (Unger et al., 1998), school-based services can provide early assistance to the younger population of homeless adolescents and attempt to get them off the streets as quickly as possible

Preventative measures to target youth who are having problems in school and provide appropriate services should also be considered. Many adolescents who are runaway youth report recent school stressors, including failing a grade, being expelled, and/or having particular problems with teachers (Rotheram-Borus, Rosario, & Koopman, 1991).

Other documented characteristics of younger adolescents are that they are more likely to be female, more likely to have been homeless for shorter periods of time, and more likely to have stayed in a residence in the past year when compared with older adolescents. Younger adolescents are also more likely to rely on other people for shelter and money and to cite gang affiliations as their peer group, possibly because they have difficulty making it alone on the streets (Unger et al., 1998). (Both younger and older adolescents reported that they engage in illegal activities at rates of

40% to 45% to get money.) Overall, then, professionals may be better able to assist younger adolescents and help them get off the streets. Further, early intervention is very important with young adolescents who are living on the streets because the risks of drug and alcohol abuse and depression are higher for adolescents who have been on the street for more than 1 year (Unger et al., 1997).

In addition to younger adolescents, another group of homeless adolescents who are easy to find are those in foster care. Between 20% and 25% of youth who are released from foster care when they are 18 go directly to homeless shelters (Azar, 1995; Nazario, 1993). Not only are these youth not linked with a place to stay, but they are also not transitioned into the workforce. Although it is important that adolescents are provided with life skills such as knowing how to select and prepare for future employment, and although emancipation plans are required for foster youth over 16 years of age, many teens in foster care do not receive life skills and many do not have a high school diploma (Nazario, 1993). This makes their job prospects even worse. Educators and community organizations need to work with social services to support the provision of life and job skills to adolescents in foster care.

The need to support life and job skills is especially important for adolescent females who are on the street or in foster care. According to a report for the Children's Defense Fund by Mihaly (as cited in Shane, 1996), many young mothers who become homeless were in foster care or on the street as teenagers. Other research has also found that many homeless adolescents grew up in homeless families (Campbell & Peck, 1995). Therefore, homeless adolescent females are particularly in need of social services to develop life and job skills so as to achieve self-sufficiency and to prevent more lives from being subjected to the hard life on the streets.

SUMMARY

Children who are homeless may suffer physically, psychologically, socially, and academically. It is unconscionable that many of these children are not being served when a portion of this population could be readily identified through homeless shelters and other social agencies. Given a problem of this magnitude, who will advocate appropriate education for homeless children? Homeless families may not be aware of the educational rights of their children or may feel powerless to change the status quo. Thus not only must there be provisions for homeless children in the classroom, but their parents must also be informed and involved. Counselors, teachers, administrators, and communities need to take the initiative for both passing laws and educating parents about their rights.

Research on homeless children is growing but still scarce despite the large numbers of homeless children in the United States. More information regarding homeless children and the barriers they face within and outside of the school system is needed. Similarly, future research should reveal successful classroom models that meet the needs of homeless children. Additionally, the prevalence of homelessness and the needs of homeless children must be recognized by state departments of education. Once educational departments have a clear picture of homelessness in their state, they should apply for federal grants to fund their interventions.

The implications of not identifying and intervening with children who are homeless include thousands of children growing up uneducated and bitter. How can children be involved in a society they do not understand or respect? How can they find empowerment and break the cycle of homelessness if no program has identified them and provided opportunities? It is devastating and unconscionable that homeless children even exist in this country. Our society is destined for even greater tragedy if the educational rights and opportunities for homeless children are not mandated and vigorously upheld. The suggestions presented in this chapter combined with a collaborative effort among counselors, teachers, administrators, and communities is one part of a strategy for ensuring an educational home in all children's futures.

REFERENCES

Aron, L. Y., & Fitchen, J. M. (1996). Rural homelessness: A synopsis. In J. Baumchi (Ed.), *Homelessness in America* (pp. 81–85). Phoenix, AZ: Oryx Press.

Azar, B. (1995, November). Foster care has bleak history. *APA Monitor, 26*(11), 8.

Bartlett, D. L., & Steele, J. B. (1992). *America: What went wrong.* Kansas City, KS: Andrews & Micheal.

Bass, J. L., Brennan, P., Mehta, K. A., & Kodzis, S. (1990). Pediatric problems in a suburban shelter for homeless families. *Pediatrics, 85*(1), 33–38.

Bassuk, E., & Rubin, L. (1987). Homeless children: A neglected population. *American Journal of Orthopsychiatry, 57,* 279–286.

Bassuk, E., & Rosenberg, L. (1988). Why does family homelessness occur? A case-control study. *American Journal of Public Health, 78,* 783-788.

Bassuk, E. L., & Weinreb, L. (1994). The plight of homeless children. In J. Blacher (Ed.), *When there's no place like home: Options for children living apart from their natural families* (pp. 37–62). Baltimore, MD: Paul H. Brookes.

Buckner, J. C., Bassuk, E. L., & Zima, B. T. (1993). Mental health issues affecting homeless women: Implications for intervention. *American Journal of Orthopsychiatry, 63,* 385–399.

Burg, M. A. (1994). Health problems of sheltered homeless women and their dependent children. *Health and Social Work, 19,* 125–131.

Butler, O.B. (1989). Early help for kids at risk: Our nation's best investment. *NEA Today*, 7(6), 50–53.

Campbell, C. A., & Peck, M. D. (1995). Issues in HIV/AIDS service delivery to high-risk youth. In G. A. Lloyd & M. A. Kuszelewicz (Eds.), *HIV disease: Lesbians, gays, and the social services* (pp. 159–178). New York: Haworth Press.

Center on Budget and Policy Priorities. (1992). *The states and the poor.* Washington, DC: Author.

Cherey, D. (1995). The homeless. In N. L. Herron & D. Zabel (Eds.), *Bridging the gap: Examining polarity in America* (pp. 167–195). Englewood, CO: Libraries Unlimited.

Danseco, E. R., & Holden, E. W. (1998). Are there different types of homeless families? A typology of homeless families based on cluster analysis. *Family Relations, 47,* 159–165.

Dail, P. W. (1993). Homelessness in America: Involuntary family migration. *Marriage and Family Review, 19*(1–2), 55–75.

Dolbeare, C. (1991). *Out of reach: Why every day people can't find affordable housing.* Washington, DC: Low-Income Housing Information Service.

Eddowes, E. A., & Hranitz, J. R. (1989). Educating children of the homeless. *The Educational Digest, 55,* 15–17.

Foscarinis, M. (1996). The federal response: The Steward B. McKinney Homeless Assistance Act. In J. Baumohl (Ed.), *Homelessness in America* (pp. 160–171). Phoenix, AZ: Oryx Press.

Gonzales, M. L. (1990, June). School + home = a program of reducating homeless students. *Phi Delta Kappan*, pp. 785–787.

Greenblatt, M., & Robertson, M. J. (1993). Lifestyles, adaptive strategies, and sexual behaviors of homeless adolescents. *Hospital and Community Psychiatry, 44,* 1177–1183.

Harrington-Lueker, D. (1989, July). What kind of school board member would help homeless children? *American School Board Journal*, pp. 12–19.

Hersh, R. H., & Walker, H.M. (1983). Great expectations: Making schools effective for all students. *Policy Studies Review, 2,* 147–188.

Herron, N. L., & Zabel, D. (1995). *Bridging the gap: Examining polarity in America.* Englewood, CO: Libraries Unlimited.

HomeBase. (1993). *Reaching and teaching children without housing: Improving educational opportunities for homeless children and youth.* San Francisco: Author.

Indiana Department of Education. (1988). *Education of homeless youth.* Indianapolis, IN: Author.

Kauffman, J. M. (1993). *Characteristics of emotional and behavioral disorders of children and youth* (5th ed.). New York: Merrill.

Kennedy, M. R. (1991). Homeless and runaway youth mental health issues: No access to the system. *Journal of Adolescent Health, 12,* 576–579.

Kerr, M. M., & Zigmond, N. (1986). What do high school teachers want? A study of expectations and standards. *Education and Treatment of Children, 9,* 239–249.

Kipke, M. D., O'Connor, S., Palmer, R., & Mackenzie, R. G. (1995). Street youth in Los Angeles: Profile of a group at high risk for human immunodeficiency virus infection. *Archives in Pediatric Adolescent Medicine, 149,* 513–519.

Lerner, J.W., Lowenthal, B., & Lerner, S.R. (1995). *Attention deficit disorders: Assessment and teaching.* Pacific Grove, CA: Brooks/Cole.

Letiecq, B. L., Anderson, E. A., & Koblinsky, S. A. (1998). Social support of homeless and housed mothers: A comparison of temporary and permanent housing arrangements. *Family Relations, 47,* 415–421.

Lewis, R. B., & Doorlag, D. H. (1987). *Teaching special students in the mainstream.* New York: Merrill.

Lindblom, E. N. (1996). Preventing homelessness. In J. Baumohl (Ed.), *Homelessness in America* (pp. 187–200). Phoenix, AZ: Oryx Press.

Link, B. G., Phelan, J. C., Stueve, A., Moore, R.E., Bresnahan, M., & Struening, E. L. (1996). Public attitudes and beliefs about homeless people. In J. Baumohl (Ed.), *Homelessness in America* (pp. 143–148). Phoenix, AZ: Oryx Press.

Lloyd, G. A., & Kuszelewics, M. A. (Eds.). (1995). *HIV disease: Lesbians, gays, and the social services.* New York: Haworth Press.

Maslow, A. H. (1968). *Toward a psychology of being* (2nd ed.). New York: Van Nostrand.

National Coalition for the Homeless. (1990). *Homelessness in America: A summary.* Washington, DC: Author.

National Coalition for the Homeless. (1993). *The problems of homelessness: Causes and trends.* Washington, DC: Author.

National Coalition for the Homeless. (1994). *Education of homeless children and youth.* Washington, DC: Author

National Coalition for the Homeless. (May, 1998a). *Why are people homeless?* NCH Fact Sheet # 1 [On-line]. Available: http://nch.ari.net/causes.html

National Coalition for the Homeless. (1998b). *How many people experience homelessness?* NCH Fact Sheet # 2 [On-line]. Available: http://nch.ari.net/numbers.html

National Coalition for the Homeless. (1998c). *Who is homeless?* NCH Fact Sheet # 3 [On-line]. Available: http://nch.ari.net/who.html

Nazario, S. (1993, December 12). Sex, drugs, and no place to go. *Los Angeles Times,* p. A1.

Reeves, M. S. (1988, April). Self-interest and the common weal: Focusing on the bottom half. *Education Week,* pp. 14–21.

Rotheram-Borus, M. J., Parra, M., Cantwell, C., Gwadz, M., & Murphy, D. A. (1996). Runaway and homeless youths. In R. J. DiClemente, W. B. Hansen, & L. E. Ponton (Eds.), *Handbook of adolescent health risk behavior* (pp. 369–391). New York: Plenum Press.

Shane, P. G. (1996). *What about America's homeless children?* Thousand Oaks, CA: Sage.

Shinn, M., & Weitzman, B. C. (1996). Homeless families are different. In J. Baumohl (Ed.), *Homeless in America* (pp. 109–122). Phoenix, AZ: Oryx Press.

Stewart B. McKinney Homeless Assistance Act of 1986, P.L. No. 100-77 & 11301 et seq., 101 Stat. 482 (1987).

Sweeney, P., Lindegren, M. L., Buehler, J. W., Onorato, I. M., & Janssen, R. S. (1995). Teenagers at risk of human immunodeficiency virus type 1 infection. *Archives in Pediatric Adolescent Medicine, 149,* 521–528.

Tracy, E., & Stoecker, R. (1993). Homelessness: The service providers' perspective on blaming the victim. *Journal of Sociology and Social Welfare, 20*(3), 43–59.

Turnbull, A. P., & Turnbull, H. R. (1997). *Families; professionals and exceptionality: A special partnership* (3rd ed.). Upper Saddle River, NJ: Merrill.

Unger, J. B., Simon, T. R., Newman, T. L., Montgomery, S. B., Kipke, M. D., & Albornoz, M. (1998). Early adolescent street youth: An overlooked population with unique problems and service needs. *Journal of Early Adolescence, 18,* 325–348.

Unger, J. B., Kipke, M. D., Simon, T. R., Montgomery, S. B., & Johnson, C. J. (1997). Homeless youths and young adults in Los Angeles: Prevalence of mental health problems and the relationship between mental health problems and substance abuse disorders. *American Journal of Community Psychology, 25,* 371–394.

Wagner, J., Schmitz, C.L., & Menke, E. (1996). Homelessness and depression in children: Implications for intervention. In *The Hatherleigh guide to child and adolescent therapy* (pp. 79–102). New York: Hatherleigh Press.

Watson, V. (1996). Responses by the states to homelessness. In J. Baumohl (Ed.), *Homelessness in America* (pp. 172–178). Phoenix, AZ: Oryx Press.

Whitman, B. Y., Accardo, P., Boyert, M., & Kendagor, R. (1990). Homelessness and cognitive performance in children: A possible link. *Social Work, 35,* 516–519.

Wood, D. L., Valdez, R. B., Hayashi, T., & Shen, A. (1990). Health of homeless children and housed, poor children. *Pediatrics, 86,* 858–866.

Yates, G. L., Pennbridge, J., Swofford, A., & Mackenzie, R. G. (1991). The Los Angeles system of care for runaway/homeless youth. *Journal of Adolescent Health, 12,* 555–560.

16 This Isn't the Place for Me: School Dropout

James W. Kushman, Conrad Sieber, and
Paula Heariold-Kinney

School dropout is a highly visible sign of a society that has failed to prepare its youth for successful transition into adulthood. It is an issue that should be of great concern to school and community counselors working with young people and their families. School dropout is a problem that has gained much public attention. Census data reported by the National Center for Education Statistics (NCES) (McMillen, Kaufman, Hausken, & Bradby, 1993) indicate that high school noncompletion rates among 16- to 24-year-olds generally declined from the early 1970s through the 1980s. In 1992 there was an 11% dropout rate as defined by NCES. This translated into about 3.4 million youth who risked unproductive lives because they had not completed high school and were, therefore, unprepared for 21st century jobs. More recently, Mortenson (1997) reviewed census data on high school dropouts and also concluded that in the 1980s there was a trend toward declining dropout rates. However, that trend reversed as the 1990s progressed, and an October 1995 Census Bureau report indicated that dropout rates had increased 56.8% between 1990 and 1995. In addition, as defined in the Census Bureau's *Current Population Survey on School Enrollment*, the 1995 dropout rate for the nation was 5.4%, up from 4.0% in 1990 and 1991 (Mortenson, 1997). Thus high school dropout continues to be of great concern because of its negative impact on the social and economic health of the country (Asche, 1993).

Note that estimates of the dropout rate can vary to a surprising degree, as just illustrated, depending on how *dropout* is defined and measured. Sources of dropout statistics include special U.S. census surveys, large national samples of youth who are tracked over time such as the High School and Beyond data, and data compiled by state departments of education and local school districts. Caution needs to be exercised in comparing dropout rates from different data sources. In the past there was no consistent agreed-upon method for measuring school dropout. In fact, NCES has been working since the early 1990s to resolve this problem (Hoffman, 1995) and has collaborated with states and school officials to develop a uniform definition of *dropout*. The Common Core of Data (CCD) Agency Universe Survey, first used for reporting purposes during the 1991–92 academic year, has standardized the way dropouts are defined and counted. School districts in most every state across the country have agreed to report rates of dropouts in the 7th through 12th grade by gender across five racial/ethnic categories. *Dropout* is defined as a student who has been enrolled at any time during the previous school year and is not enrolled on October 1 of the current school year. Furthermore, a student can only be categorized as having dropped out if he or she has *not* completed a high school diploma or another state- or district-approved educational program; or is *not* temporarily absent due to suspension or school-approved illness (Hoffman, 1995). Thus in tracking changes in dropout rates, it may be most helpful to look at differences year to year within the same data set, at least until this more uniform method of reporting data is not only in common use but also readily accessible in the educational research literature.

It is clear that the dropout problem does not affect all groups equally. Poor and minority students tend to experience the highest dropout rates, and males show higher rates than females. Since 1990 the dropout rate for males increased 2% while that for females moved up by .5%. During the same period, the dropout rate for Hispanics increased more than that of Anglo and African American students (Mortenson, 1997). Rumberger (1993) completed an extensive review of the research literature on dropouts. With regard to the possible interaction between race/ethnicity and socioeconomic status, he concluded that there is empirical support from studies of nationwide data that indicate that much, if not all, of the differences in dropout rates among various racial groups can be explained by socioeconomic status. That is, when socioeconomic status is held constant, much of the difference in dropout rates among various racial/ethnic groups disappears or is greatly diminished. Because ethnic minorities tend to be highly represented among the poor, it is not surprising that the dropout problem is often most concentrated in large urban areas where poor and minority students tend to live. It is not uncommon for 25% to 50% of the students in some inner-city high schools to drop out. However, it is an error to conclude that the dropout problem is simply an inner-city minority problem because substantial numbers of suburban and Anglo students also drop out.

There are both moral and economic implications of students dropping out. A society based on democratic ideals cannot simply sacrifice or write off large numbers of youth who, because of their failure in school, gravely limit their potential and future well-being. In fact, public education was founded on the belief that citizens need to be educated to be capable of participating in a democratic society (Peck, 1993). In addition, there are also serious economic consequences created by an undereducated population. Large numbers of dropouts weaken the economy because they place a burden on unemployment and welfare services, not to mention the criminal justice system. Dropouts run the risk of becoming costly to society rather than productive and contributing members. The problem is exacerbated by the postindustrial economy, in which important jobs require more education and problem-solving and thinking skills. Coupled with the changing nature of work is the fact that ethnic groups with high dropout rates, such as Hispanics, will continue to compose a greater share of the work force. Mortenson (1997) put it this way:

> Since about 1973 the labor market has been brutally redistributing income among workers according to their educational attainment. Those who have the most formal education have the highest incomes, have experienced real gains during the last two decades. Those with the least formal educations have the lowest incomes, have experienced substantial real declines in their incomes and living standards. (p. 94)

He concluded that

> this redistribution . . . clearly signals the end of the high-wage—low-skill labor economy. The bottom line is simple: neither individuals, nor families, nor communities, nor states, or the country can afford to passively watch increases in high school attrition. By every measure we know of, individuals who choose this course are also choosing more poverty with neither hope for improvement nor an expectation of a social safety net to save them from their chosen adversity. In their downward spiral they will effect their families, their communities, their states, and the country as a whole. (pp. 94–95)

In addition to economic problems, high school dropouts are also more likely to engage in high-risk behaviors, such as premature sexual activity, early pregnancy, crime and delinquency, alcohol and drug abuse, and suicide attempts (Asche, 1993).

That young people do not complete school is a moral, social, and economic tragedy. In a general sense, counselors can play an important role by helping at-risk youth recognize the risks associated with dropping out of school. Counselors must help at-risk youth see the connection between present choices to stay in or leave school, and the future personal consequences of not completing their education.

Although the label *dropout* is conveniently applied to large numbers of students who do not finish school, such a label belies the fact that they are a diverse group who leave school for many different reasons. The implication is that there is no single cure-all that can be uniformly applied by counselors and educators. Helping potential dropouts requires a clear understanding that the problem is complex and multifaceted. Bickel, Bond, and LeMahieu (1988) pointed out that the term *dropout* itself is potentially misleading because it implies an event instead of a process, that is, a single decision point to leave school, with the student as the sole decision maker. Such is far from reality. Some students merely fade out after a period of feeling alienated from school. Others can be subtly or not so subtly pushed out by a school culture or school personnel that do not want to deal with them any longer. Still others are pulled out, either by more important demands on their time such as parenting or having to work, or by negative community influences. It is also important to remember that some students leave school but do return, perhaps to attend alternative education programs.

As yet, a precise typology of early school dropouts has not been developed. However, Orr (1987) developed a four-part typology that distinguishes between qualitatively different types of students whose risk of dropping out varies:

1. students experiencing some problems in school with a marginal risk of dropping out;
2. those interested in staying in school but who cannot because of personal circumstances such as parenthood or the need to work;
3. students at high risk of dropping out as indicated by poor attendance, lack of interest, and low grades; and
4. those who have left school and are in need of special services to complete their education and become better prepared for the transition to work.

This typology illuminates the complexity of the problem and the diversity of students whom we conveniently call dropouts. It is clear that different students leave school under different circumstances and for various reasons, even students within the same school.

In this chapter, some of the complexity of the dropout problem is examined by focusing on four points of intervention: the student, the family, the school, and the community. Two broad strategies of intervention are explored: the clinical approach, which focuses on the individual, and the systemic approach, which emphasizes the larger system in which the individual functions.

PROBLEM DEFINITION

A useful distinction for designing counseling interventions is to think of variables as falling into two broad categories: demographic correlates, which represent the students' more stable background, and early warning signs, which are more immediate and alterable student characteristics.

Demographic Correlates

It has been well documented that some racial minorities—Native Americans, Hispanics, and African Americans—are more likely to drop out than Whites, and that males are more likely to drop out than females. Race seems to be important, but what factors underlie racial differences? Data from NCES indicate fewer racial differences when family income levels are accounted for. African American and White dropout rates are virtually the same when income level is held constant. However, Hispanic dropout rates are higher than those of African Americans and Whites at the low- and middle-income levels. Thus, although dropout rates are higher among students of color, these differences seem more likely to be a result of poverty and social class than race. Language is also a factor for Hispanic and other immigrant students who may have limited English-speaking capabilities. Among Hispanics who speak English well, the dropout rate is 17% compared to a dropout rate of 83% for Hispanics who speak no English at all (McMillen et al., 1993). Rumberger (1993) noted this result may be due to the understandably high correlation between language proficiency and both academic achievement and grade retention, each of which is directly correlated with higher dropout rates.

A cultural difference argument has also been made to explain why certain minority groups fail more often in school. Ogbu (1995) summarized six types of cultural and language barriers faced by minorities:

- cross-cultural misunderstanding;
- language and communication barriers;
- differences in conceptual knowledge;
- differences in teaching and learning styles;
- cultural hegemony (i.e., in the United States dominant Whites have been the majority culture that defines what is mainstream and controls many of the resources); and
- differences in cultural frames of reference.

Ogbu (1995) proposed that it is the cultural frames of reference barrier that helps explain why some minority groups, such as African Americans, seem to have a harder time achieving in school than other minority groups. He defines *cultural frames of reference* as "the correct or ideal way to behave within the group (i.e., acceptable attitudes, beliefs, preferences, and practices)" (p. 272). The ways in which cultural frames of reference affect minorities' interpretation of cultural boundaries (i.e., the boundaries that demarcate one culture from another) is viewed as different for voluntary versus involuntary minorities. Voluntary minorities are characterized by having acted on the choice to immigrate to the United States and are often more successful in schools because they view cultural boundaries as challenges to overcome. Therefore, they are more successful at crossing over these boundaries to learn school culture and language. Involuntary minorities, such as African Americans, whose ancestors were brought to the United States against their will as slaves, are in Ogbu's analysis more likely to experience an oppositional cultural frame of reference in relation to the dominant culture. This produces ambivalence about crossing cultural boundaries, an ambivalence that is based on an interpretation of cultural differences as barriers and markers of cultural group identity. Involuntary minorities' ambivalence and attention to defining their cultural group identity, at least in part, through cultural boundaries produces hesitancy about crossing over them. Thus these minorities have mixed feelings about learning and fully entering the school culture. This process creates more academic difficulties for them and less academic success. In this analysis, the school culture, often a reflection of this society's dominant Anglo culture, presents true barriers that create dissonance and possibly an approach-avoidance problem for involuntary minorities.

Thus social, ethnic, class, and cultural background are the major demographic correlates of school dropout. Some evidence suggests that racial/ethnic differences in dropout rates are greatly mediated by socioeconomic status. Students who traditionally have not been part of the American mainstream, such as the poor and people of color, may experience greater difficulty in school. Schools are not always responsive to the needs of different ethnic, class, and cultural groups. Although why some groups drop out more than others is not fully understood, it seems clear that such differences are best understood in terms of underlying factors, such as poverty, family circumstances, language skills, cultural differences, and how these are interpreted by minorities and the dominant cultural group. Unfortunately, schools have often been slow to respond to cultural diversity and thus have failed to capitalize on the dynamic resources and opportunities for learning created by pluralism. Yet we do live in an increasingly pluralistic society. Counselors working with at-risk youth need to be sensitive to the diversity of backgrounds and cultures from which today's students come, and educators in general must work harder to create school environments of inclusion for all cultural groups. This includes confronting the difficult problem of underachievement among lower socioeconomic status students. Clearly, counselors can play a role in raising the consciousness of teachers and administrators to these cultural dynamics, and can be proactive in working as change agents in helping schools use practices, procedures, and organizational structures that promote inclusion.

Early Warning Signs

The factors just described represent relatively stable and unchangeable characteristics of the individual. Another set of variables include characteristics and circumstances that are more immediate and alterable through educational and counseling interventions. Studies of early warning signs have identified a variety of school and personal factors that help predict dropping out. These variables fall into four categories:

- *poor academic performance:* This area is usually evidenced by low grades, low test scores, and being held back one or more grades before high school (i.e., retention). School counselors do need to communicate with teachers so that patterns of low performance or academic failure can be identified early. Academic performance is intertwined with behavior and affective problems with which counselors deal directly.
- *behavior problems:* This area is usually evidenced by disruptive classroom behavior, cutting classes, truancy, and suspension.
- *affective characteristics:* These include poor or unrealistic self-concepts and feelings of alienation—that is, students feeling that they do not fit into the school or classroom.
- *personal circumstances:* Many student circumstances, such as teen pregnancy, teen parenting, having to work, and having to care for sick or elderly family members, can conflict with school demands. Counselors can play a critical role in helping students find ways to balance school and outside demands, and in advocating for students who require school or community services such as teen parent programs.

Obviously, some of these variables can occur early in a student's academic career, and the question of how early potential dropouts can be identified is crucial. As in other areas of counseling, early identification is a delicate matter. Although from a prevention standpoint it is desirable to identify potential dropouts as early as possible, caution must be exercised. It is imperative to avoid harsh labels that lead to stereotyping by teachers and students, and to a negative self-concept and lowered aspirations among those so labeled.

How early can potential dropouts be identified? Certainly earlier than high school and even as early as the primary grades. An exemplary, although by no means recent, study was completed by Lloyd (1978). Lloyd's analysis of a group of 1,500 students successfully discriminated school dropouts from school graduates based on third- and sixth-grade student characteristics. For the third grade, a combination of four factors was found to discriminate dropouts from graduates with 75% accuracy: (1) achievement scores (especially in reading), (2) global ability (IQ test), (3) socioeconomic status and family background characteristics, and (4) retention (nonpromotion). The same characteristics were found to hold for the sixth grade, with the addition of school attendance. Although such variables are predictive of dropping out, it is important to keep in mind that they are not foolproof. For example, in Lloyd's discriminant analysis, one quarter of the students were misclassified based on third-grade characteristics, which means that some students do succeed despite early warning signs to the contrary. However, success is much more likely when prevention and early intervention measures are taken by counselors and other school staff.

Keith and Schartzer (1995) examined family-school involvement factors of Mexican American students in the 8th grade for their predictive value in predicting dropouts at the 10th-grade level. As others have, they found that children who are currently doing well in school are most likely to stay in school. Students getting poor grades and low achievement test scores in the 8th grade were at risk for dropping out by the 10th grade. In terms of family involvement, those Mexican American students with parents who engaged them in discussing school activities, who had high educational aspirations for their children, and who were proficient in the English language, were less likely to drop out of school by the 10th grade. Again, it should be noted that language proficiency correlates well with academic achievement and that it is academic achievement that predicts dropout rates (Rumberger, 1993).

Underlying Causes

Up to now we have described the important correlates of dropping out, but this is far from a deep understanding of the complex underlying causes of dropout behavior. Researchers who have studied these underlying causes include Rumberger (1993), who classified the variables correlated with dropout rates into four categories: family background, school, community, and student. These categories are highly intercorrelated. For example, family background characteristics, which are an important influence on dropout behavior, include socioeconomic status, which is typically a composite of family income and level of parent education and by itself one of the most powerful dropout predictors. For another example, student and school characteristics play an important role in dropouts' descriptions of the evolving process of alienation and disengagement from academics and school. These students self-report making less effort, being less engaged in academic subjects, spending less time on homework, paying less attention in class, and cutting classes more often (Rumberger, Ghatak, Poulos, & Ritter (1990).

Other research into underlying causes has focused on family processes associated with dropping out. For example, parenting styles were found to be influential in an evaluation of family processes of a matched group of students who remained in or dropped out of high school (Rumberger et al., 1990). One finding was that parenting that is too permissive seems to lead to excessive adolescent autonomy and increased peer group influence. Because these overly permissive parents are not involved in their children's education, and do not provide guidance and support for their adolescent students' decision making, the students not only are left to develop on their own but are also more likely to drop out. Another finding was that parenting that provides "proper academic encouragement" is most likely to result in students' completing high school. As previously noted, Keith and Schartzer (1995) found that Mexican American parents who discuss school activities with their children and have high educational aspirations for their students are less likely to see their teenagers become dropouts. In addition, a parenting style that is engaged, authoritative, and participatory seems to help students develop an internal locus of control, the sense that their own actions and efforts influence desired outcomes such as high school graduation. This is important because dropouts are often found to have an external locus of control (i.e., a belief that desired outcomes are caused by external factors beyond the individual's control such as chance or luck) (Rumberger et al., 1990).

Research on dropouts is limited by the same kinds of difficulties found in research on student achievement (Rumberger, 1993). Because there are a large variety of factors that influence dropouts (student, family background, school, and community characteristics), and because these factors are highly intercorrelated, examining and isolating the influence of any one factor is difficult. Furthermore, these studies are correlational, and no matter how many factors are accounted for, causation cannot, with total confidence, be presumed from correlation. For that matter, even when two factors are correlated and causation can be reasonably presumed (such as with depression and poor grades), it is hard to tell which is the cause and which the consequence. Further, dropping out is a long-term process of disengagement and/or exclusion that requires longitudinal research to understand fully the process and those influences that shape it. However, longitudinal research is more difficult and costly to conduct. Dropping out is clearly a complex process most likely caused by a combination of factors. The presumed causes of school dropout thus involve a set of related variables that cut across the student's experiences and behaviors, the school environment, and support systems outside of the school including parents, peers, and the community (Rumberger, 1993). Although these influences may be difficult to disentangle, they do suggest multiple points at which counselors and educators can intervene. These include the following:

1. *Student behaviors within the school*
   - poor academic performance;
   - cutting classes; and
   - noninvolvement in school life outside the classroom.

2. *Student behavior outside of school*
   - excessive absenteeism;
   - increased hours spent working or in illegal activities; and
   - drug and alcohol use.
3. *Student affect*
   - feelings of hopelessness;
   - feeling helpless and not in control of events that affect one's life; and
   - lowered self-esteem.
4. *Student life circumstances*
   - teen pregnancy or parenting; and
   - social and economic hardships that place adult demands on young people.
5. *School climate*
   - quality of teacher-student interactions and relationships;
   - degree to which school creates an environment of inclusion for all students;
   - effective but fair school discipline procedures;
   - activities that create social connections bonding the student to the school;
   - teaching practices that create meaningful learning opportunities that can be applied outside the school setting; and
   - flexibility to create accommodations for students who must combine school with family responsibilities or work.
6. *Home and family*
   - parental interest and involvement in the student's school experiences and progress;
   - parental expectations of good academic performance and accomplishment;
   - parenting styles that support students taking responsibility for their behavior and include parental guidance in decision making; and
   - identification and intervention with abusive parents.
7. *Community*
   - negative peer influences that can accelerate student disengagement; and
   - availability of community support programs (e.g., teen mother services) through counseling agencies, churches, and volunteer groups.

Several larger themes underlie these variables and potential interventions. The first is the *opportunity to learn*. At-risk students may require more opportunity to learn (i.e., more time allowed for learning tasks), given their poor academic performance. Unfortunately, time is a limited resource for some at-risk youth who have legitimate adult responsibilities outside of school such as teen parenting or work.

A second theme is *motivation*. Simply having students spend more time in learning tasks will not suffice if they are not motivated to learn. If they are to become motivated, at-risk youth must believe that they can succeed in school and must perceive some present and future value for their hard work. They must come to believe in a positive future and job opportunities beyond high school.

A third theme, related to motivation, is *commitment*. Commitment can be viewed as the opposite of alienation, a condition that characterizes many dropouts and their teachers. In order for students to feel committed to school, they need teachers and counselors who are themselves committed to their students and school, and students need to feel involved in school life outside the classroom.

The last theme is *empowerment*. Empowering students with some legitimate responsibilities (e.g., a say in discipline policies, curriculum choices) should lead to increased identification and affiliation with school. Empowering teachers and counselors with the responsibility and decision-making power they need to help students is likewise important.

CASE STUDIES

The research findings are perhaps best illustrated through case studies, which can provide a richer, up-close look at school dropout and its causes. Two case studies are presented here, one on an individual student, the other on a school. This illustrates a dual focus on both the individual dynamics of dropout and understanding how the system contributes to this process.

The Story of a Disaffected Student in Portland

Shamica is a 15-year-old freshman attending a comprehensive high school in Portland, Oregon. She entered high school with reading and math achievement scores below the ninth-grade level. Shamica has no stable or supportive family structure, and she has not had one for much of her life. Her mother deserted her when she was in sixth grade, and she lived in several foster homes. At the time of this case study, she lived with her sister's 24-year-old friend and her live-in boyfriend. Shamica is a heavy-set girl who looks older than her 15 years. She is very loud and boisterous in classes, and was suspended from school the second week into the semester as well as several times since for attendance, tardiness, and behavior problems. She is awaiting an alternative placement because she is not earning enough credits to complete her ninth-grade year.

When talking about school, her teachers, and her living situation, Shamica expresses a sense of helplessness, bewilderment, and rejection. Here is one of her typical statements:

> My teachers don't care about me anyway! Whenever I try to do right, they are still in my face. Even when I put my hand up, they don't call on me. So when I yell out the answer, they tell me to put my hand up first. I don't even care.

When referring to her living situation, she responds with some sadness. Her body language becomes that of a much younger girl, and her voice grows quiet. She describes her living situation in the following way:

> I have lived all over the place. Every time I move, I lose more clothes because my foster parents take them. Even though I don't like where I live, at least I have my own bedroom. But every time they get mad at me, they tell me that they are going to throw me out. I try to stay out of their way or stay in my room when I am home. When I get married, I'm not ever going to let anything happen to my kids.

Shamica is a living example of the evidence showing the importance of family support in keeping young people in school (Horn, 1992; Keith & Schartzer, 1995; Rumberger, 1993; Rumberger et al., 1990). She illustrates how parents and home life can influence dropout behavior. Shamica's low self-esteem, acting out, and low grades can bep seen as attempts to get attention, although in a negative way. Her lack of a stable family structure, which if present could have eased her feelings of isolation and hopelessness, seems to play a significant role in Shamica's inability to succeed in school. She also demonstrates in her comments a sense that the school and her teachers have given up on her, and she seems to have no place to turn in order to solve her problems.

The Story of a School in Harlem

Using ethnography and the methods of qualitative social science research, Michelle Fine (1986) provided an excellent illustration of how a variety of school factors can contribute to school dropout through an in-depth case study of a comprehensive high school in upper Manhattan. Although this study occurred over a decade ago, it remains instructive. Some of the themes it raises resonate with many school reform practices that involve creating school environments that are more engaging and successful in educating members of diverse cultural groups who come from lower socioeconomic backgrounds. The school being evaluated was in a poor area of the city, had low-income students who were primarily African American and Hispanic, and was characterized as having a good reputation for safety and stability. To identify some of the structural characteristics of the school that lead to dropout, Fine conducted observations in classrooms and other school settings, looked at student autobiographies, conducted in-home interviews with 30 recent dropouts and 15 who had dropped out 4 years earlier, and administered surveys to 350 ninth graders, some of whom were interviewed later. Her results revealed that different students express different reasons for dropping out. Some of the students were very critical of schooling and its worth in obtaining a job or a good income. Others had to attend to family health or economic needs that interfered with school. Still others simply felt a sense of helplessness and hopelessness in the midst of poverty and their own school failure. Another group felt pushed or thrown out by school personnel who did not want to deal with them any more. There was no single self-reported reason, even within the same school and urban environment.

Fine (1986) described the subject of her case study as a school that had a disproportionate share of low-achieving students, insufficient resources, and overcrowded classrooms. Teachers and administrators in this school were predominantly White, and students were predominantly African American and Hispanic, which contributed to poor communication and a lack of understanding between teachers and students. Classrooms were organized more around control than conversation, more around the authority of the teacher than autonomy of students, and focused more on competition than collaboration. Fine noted that often when students talked to each other to cooperate it provoked accusations of cheating from their teachers.

Fine (1986) used the term *disempowerment* to explain the process of dropping out. Many teachers reported a sense of disempowerment, felt that no one listened to them, believed that school policy did not reflect what was really important for students and that students could not be helped. Teacher feelings of disempowerment or helplessness carried over to students, many of whom in turn developed feelings of powerlessness and alienation, and eventually dropped out.

The disempowerment hypothesis is consistent with research findings on the psychological state of dropouts. Two important variables here are locus of control and learned helplessness (e.g., Seligman, 1991). As previously mentioned, dropouts are often found to have a more external locus of control for desired outcomes as compared to graduates, who tend to have an internal locus of control and believe their efforts and actions can lead to achieving their goals. Thus dropouts more often have feelings of little personal control over what happens to them and often feel helpless to improve their circumstances.

The study of this Harlem school illustrates at least two ways high schools contribute to school dropout. Because students experience high school in many different ways, some students may see no value in completion and little connection between what goes on in school and their present experiences. Others have personal circumstances that prevent them from fully participating, and still others are pushed out because of behavior problems or because they do not fit into the dominant school culture. Concerning the latter point, some students experience cultural alienation because their language and culture are not reflected in the adults who run the school. Until schools are able to address the diversity of student experiences and needs, they will continue to lose too many students.

A second way that large high schools help create dropouts is that they are often bureaucratic places for both students and staff. This often leads to a sense of powerlessness, helplessness, and futility in a school environment that promotes a feeling of anonymity and actually interferes with the development of caring relationships between teachers, counselors, administrators, parents, and students. Because of organizational structures, policies, and procedures designed to process large groups of students through the educational system, teachers and counselors feel that they can do little to help students, and students sense that the staff is uncaring. An unproductive cycle of helplessness and blame can result, and students drop out. However, this cycle can be broken, and schools can create more meaningful learning experiences for students by empowering both students and staff to share responsibility for creating quality learning environments in which students achieve their academic goals. Decentralizing power by sharing responsibility for decision making about issues such as fair discipline policies, making curriculum and instruction more engaging and connected to the real world, improving school climate, and changing school scheduling are examples of ways to change schools in order to give greater ownership to teachers, students, and parents.

APPROACHES TO PREVENTION

Much research has been done to identify the characteristics of students who are at risk of dropping out. The question now becomes what to do about students once they are identified as possessing these characteristics. Counselors and school administrators are continually searching for new approaches that will help them implement effective strategies that prevent students from leaving school. Generally, there are two types of approaches: the clinical approach and the systemic approach. The clinical approach focuses on direct student and family interventions; the systemic approach is concerned with the structure of schools and communities and how their interrelationships affect the dropout process.

Clinical Approach: Treating the Student and Family

The clinical approach is probably the more common and familiar to counselors because it deals directly with the student and his or her family. This approach asks the question, "What's wrong with the student?" It looks at predictors intrinsic to the student who is at risk of dropping out. In most cases, this approach addresses questions in three areas:

1. *The home*
   - Does the student come from a low-income family, a family with limited formal education, or a family with serious financial problems?
   - Does the student come from a poorly functioning, high-stress, or chaotic family in which parents are overly permissive and lack involvement with their children, or in which there is substance abuse?
   - Were the parents or siblings dropouts?
   - Is the student psychologically, sexually, or physically abused in the home?
2. *Personal traits or circumstances*
   - Does the student have a predominantly external locus of control?
   - Is the student's estimation of his or her self-worth poor or overly focused in unhealthy ways on factors such as physical appearance or materialism?
   - Does the student exhibit a lack of motivation characterized by a sense of discouragement, boredom, or disengagement from school?
   - Is the student pregnant?
   - Does the student have substance abuse problems and/or an eating disorder?
   - Has the student repeated grades (i.e., retention)?
   - Is the student clinically depressed or does he or she have an anxiety disorder and/or another mental health problem?
3. *School behaviors*
   - Is the student frequently absent?
   - Does the student often cut classes?
   - Is there a lack of interest and follow through in school work?
   - Does the student exhibit hostility, unruliness, passivity, or apathy?
   - Does the student have difficulty with reading?
   - Does the student have problems in establishing and maintaining social relationships or with communication skills?

The astute counselor must zero in on these factors and begin to develop a planned, coordinated response of prevention and treatment. Educational and counseling strategies to address the dropout problem include special education, remediation, and alternative education.

Special education has been an approach for the student whose behavior and poor academic performance indicate that he or she needs something educationally different than the traditional school program. Special education may have prevented some students from dropping out of school because of individualized instruction and small class size. However, for other special education students who truly did not have a handicapping learning condition but were culturally different and had language barriers that interfered with their learning, special education may have led to feelings of alienation and unworthiness, and thus intensified their feelings of failure. Counselors should be aware that with special education students, or other special populations, attention may need to be paid to building self-worth.

Remediation has been another method for addressing the academic problems students experience in school. One remedial approach is retention, and many students who are at risk of dropping out have been retained in at least one grade. Another remedial approach is ability grouping, which places underachievers in slower classrooms so that they can catch up. In general, schools have responded to the problems of under-achieving and at-risk students by sorting and selecting these students into homogeneous groups (Lesters & McDill, 1995). The problem with ability grouping is that students in slow classrooms may experience shame and lowered self-esteem, and as a result, more behavioral problems can occur. Further, placing students of lower academic achievement together in the same classroom neither improves student achievement nor seems to change self-concept (Kulik, 1993; Lesters & McDill, 1995). In fact, ability grouping may adversely affect the potential dropout because a social hierarchy is inadvertently set up that negatively stigmatizes lower achieving students. The experience of social hierarchy and issues of inclusion can be heard in the words of one high school student who participated in a study of an urban school's dropout prevention program: "It was the cream-of-the-crop students who got all the attention from teachers when I was in high school. Those were the kids who got college prep classes and extra time from teachers" (Sims, 1997, p. 11). However, when lower achieving students are mixed with average and high-ability students, negative stereotypes are avoided, and the slow students may become more challenged and improve. It is important to point out that remedial strategies can be effective if potential negative consequences are foreseen and addressed. This can be accomplished, for example, by grouping students for only part of the day in so-called pull-out programs and providing individualized instruction in the classroom so that these students can succeed. Students tutoring other students and cooperative learning are other effective strategies for students who need remediation.

One of the most successful approaches for addressing the needs of at-risk students is to place them in an alternative program. *Alternative education* is a label for a variety of nontraditional school programs that are usually housed in separate buildings away from the traditional school.

There is no single alternative education model, nor do these programs always serve the same populations. One type of alternative education program is the special school for high-risk students who have been repeatedly suspended, have significant behavior problems that disrupt classes, or otherwise do not seem to fit in at conventional schools. Alternative schools of this type employ individualized academic instruction along with counseling services that are designed to better meet the needs of at-risk youth. Although alternative schools aim to change the student and therefore come under the clinical approach, these schools also represent systemic interventions because the school and its program are structured around the needs of students. The alternative school is a good example of combining the clinical and systemic approaches.

An effective alternative program better meets the needs of at-risk youth because of smaller class and school size, and more personal attention. Characteristics of a successful alternative program also include autonomy from the regular school, highly committed staff, many curricular options, experiential education involving work in community settings, and a supportive atmosphere resembling a family setting. In this system, the need for counseling and psychological assistance can be addressed within the school or through off-campus referral (Wehlage, 1991). Alternative programs can provide a safe, caring environment that for many students is the one place where they receive positive attention. For some students, the alternative school may be the only stable home or family they have. Thus at-risk students tend to prefer alternative to traditional schools and feel better about themselves in this learning environment that provides personalized student-teacher relationships and in which the school develops a community of support (Wehlage, 1991).

In discussing clinical approaches, the importance of collaborative relationships between schools and social service agencies must be stressed. As the research reviewed earlier clearly indicated, at-risk students in many cases have problems other than experiencing failure and frustration in school. Behavioral or psychological difficulties that students exhibit in school may alert counselors to other problems in the student's life. It is important that the whole student be addressed, not his or her behavior alone. In some school districts, student service centers have been developed in order to personalize counseling, career, health, and other support services that are essential to address fully the needs of at-risk youth. If student services are not available via the school district, counselors and administrators should take steps to bring these services to the school or provide transportation for students to community agencies. Support and counseling services are also important for parents of at-risk youth who may be contributing to the students' failure in school. Wehlage and Stone (1996) analyzed data from the Center on Organization and Restructuring of Schools (CORS) for 24 restructured schools to assess the impact of school organization on the development of social, health, and career-related services. A middle and high school were then chosen for more extensive case study. The study found that adding health and social services to bureaucratically organized schools was unlikely to prove effective. Instead, to make these services work well, they should be integrated into the school so that they become part of a school community with a common vision and a shared sense of responsibility for student learning. Additional student services do little good if they are not viewed as central to the shared educational mission of the school. The case study of the successful middle school program concluded by stating, "Let there be no doubt that building community [within the school] was and still remains hard work. It is a job that is never finished. . . . From the earliest days, faculty took very explicit steps to insure that their community included the students. . . . In the end the school represented a collective vision of how to best address the academic and nonacademic needs of their pupils" (Wehlage & Stone, 1996, pp. 31–32). In creating a program of successful social and health services, the school worked closely with many agencies and utilized the skills of many different professionals, but the school staff insisted that collaboration with service providers support the school vision, and it was the faculty that determined how the service center and school would mesh to create an integrated program.

All the strategies described here can have positive effects on students who are experiencing failure, frustration, and unhappiness in school. However, the clinical approach in and of itself may not solve the problems of potential school dropouts, especially when many of the causes lie in our schools, families, and communities rather than residing solely within the student dropouts themselves. The intention of clinical interventions is to help students, but some carry a negative stigma that result in doing as much harm as good. For example, students who are placed in slow classrooms for several consecutive years are in danger of being negatively labeled throughout the rest of their school careers. Although school systems have begun looking more closely at mainstreaming special education students, the numbers of students who are moved into regular programs may still be too few, especially for certain groups such as African American adolescents. Another concern is equity. In many instances, students who are placed in special programs, including alternative schools, can receive a watered-down version of the curriculum with lower academic performance expectations, leaving these students unprepared for postsecondary education or the working world. When expectations are lowered for students who are enrolled in special programs, their failure can become a self-fulfilling prophecy.

Although dealing with the individual and his or her family represents an important prevention strategy, there are several other limitations to the clinical approach. One is that the goal of some counseling programs is simply to help at-risk students feel good about themselves rather than to improve academic performance. It is important to remember that students generally feel good about themselves when they are successful in their endeavors, including academics, and are making a contribution to their families and communities. A more basic limitation of the clinical approach is that too often it assumes the problem lies solely within the student. Efforts are geared toward fixing the student so that he or she will function better in the traditional school. For instance, counselors can become unwitting accomplices in reproducing a social system within the school that seeks to "help" students adjust to a school environment that, however unconsciously, may actually exclude these students because they come from a group that does not fit into the school's dominant culture (Fine, 1990). Furthermore, by "treating" the disaffected student, the meta-message sent by the counselor can be that there is something inherently wrong with the student that limits his or her ability to adjust, when in reality the student may be having a normal response to a school environment that is based on exclusion. Another down side to the clinical approach is that it often has little if any impact on difficult-to-change factors outside the school, such as the effects of poverty and poorly functioning families. Furthermore, schools with large numbers of at-risk students can begin to become social service agencies rather than educational organizations. These inherent limitations have led some to consider the systemic approach, a more powerful method of serving the whole student in context.

Systemic Approach: Changing the School and Community

The systemic approach focuses on changing the educational system to meet the needs of at-risk students. The educational system includes both the school and its interactions with the surrounding community. Systemic interventions are more difficult to implement than clinical ones, and therefore, in the past many school districts have shied away from them. High levels of commitment from the community, school board, superintendent, principals, staff, parents, and students are required for the systemic approach to work. However, pressures for school reform, improved academic achievement for all students including those who are underachieving, and accountability at the school level have been changing this calculus throughout the 1990s.

The systemic approach recognizes the strong influence on students of social environments created within families, communities, and the school itself. Factors such as poverty and low parent educational attainment as well as school factors such as hierarchies and bureaucracies that make schools unresponsive to changes in the families, cultural groups, and communities they serve are not accepted as excuses or insurmountable barriers to successfully educating all students. Systemic/environmental factors are taken into consideration in designing schools that are responsive to the whole student and to all students. For many at-risk youth, school is a place where they feel isolated and discouraged. Because of their circumstances and backgrounds (e.g., having to work to support self or family, feeling culturally or racially isolated, being poor, possessing a learning style that does not mesh with traditional ways of teaching), school can become a place of frustration, further reinforcing a sense of exclusion. In the case of female students who become pregnant or are already teen mothers, dropping out may be the only solution if accommodations cannot be made for their educational and personal needs (e.g., class scheduling, day care, prenatal care), or in cases in which the school climate treats teen pregnancy as shameful leading to these young women's exclusion from the school community at a time of heightened vulnerability. For most young people, the way to handle an extremely frustrating situation is to rebel and act out, or simply to leave the situation—as many students do when they drop out of school.

A progressive school district that supports the systemic approach recognizes the fact that with the diverse demographic makeup of today's student population it is necessary to design a flexible system around the needs of students and their families. This helps schools become more student-centered so that curriculum, instructional methods, and academic achievement goals are informed by knowledge of the students and their needs. Here the community and families are viewed as being in partnership with the school rather than as part of the problem. Factors within the school that can impede student success and serve as obstructions for at-risk students as well as students in general include

1. *organizational structure:* The organizational structure of the school can be a major barrier to student success. To begin with, many urban schools, and a rapidly increasing number of suburban schools, are too large. Students who attend a large school with large class sizes tend to feel overwhelmed and defeated, especially in transition years such as the sixth and ninth grades. The at-risk student may already be skeptical as she or he enters middle or high school. These students need to feel accepted and involved, which is almost impossible to accomplish in a large school. For a synthesis of relevant research on this subject, see Dryfoos (1990), who has focused on the debilitating effects that large high schools have on students.

   School hours are another part of the organizational structure that can make it difficult for at-risk students who have to work while attending school. School hours are usually scheduled from 8 a.m. to 3 p.m., leaving little flexibility for working students.

Class scheduling can also be unrealistic. High school classes are often set up for 50-minute periods, during which time students are expected to digest all of one subject such as math. The bell rings, indicating it is time to move on to the next class and subject. By the time the student returns to math, perhaps after missing class the next day because of an assembly, the concept of the math problem is lost and so is the student. Far better would be completing the math problem without regard for ringing bells. The point is that in most traditional schools teaching of subjects is not integrated. The organizational structure that impacts instructional methods is not organized to encourage transfer of subject matter from one class to another, and teachers usually have little time to cross subject lines by meeting and planning with other teachers in order to integrate information.

2. *procedural practices:* Procedural practices are those practices and policies set up to ensure that the school runs smoothly and to protect the safety of students and staff. Rules and discipline fall under procedural practices. When the emphasis is on rules that are not meaningfully connected to the learning and community development goals of the school, the rules can actually serve as barriers to learning opportunities and relationships. Rules of this sort can be experienced as arbitrary and lacking in meaning and common sense. The problem with the thoughtless application of uniform rules is that they sometimes become more important than educating the student. It makes little sense to suspend a student who is skipping school or to give a failing grade to a student who, for some understandable reason, is having difficulty with a subject. The disciplinary action does little to solve the problem. Such rules do not help the at-risk student and may convey the message that no one really cares if he or she succeeds. Although there should be clear limits and consequences for not following school rules, rules should not be designed to impinge on educating the student. At-risk students are the ones who suffer most from inflexible, unrealistic discipline policies regarding attendance, tardiness, and dress codes. Educators need to review school rules to examine the tension between the letter of the law and the spirit of the law. Unless school rules are founded on a spirit of creating learning opportunities, meaningful relationships, and inclusion, they will hinder—not help—the educational process. Thoughtful development and application of rules in which educators use good judgment and see discipline as creating learning opportunities takes more time and energy but is also more likely to create a caring, sane, and respectful learning environment for students from diverse backgrounds and experiences.

3. *instructional strategies:* Limited or inflexible instructional strategies and poor pedagogy harm even the most gifted students. Students have different learning styles. Teaching styles that fit a single rather than a variety of learning styles can be detrimental, especially for at-risk students. A curriculum based on seat time rather than competence can also be a barrier for students who work at a slower pace and need more time. Further, a curriculum that is meaningless and disconnected from the student's out-of-school life can result in boredom and disengagement. Some of the brightest students have dropped out of school due to boredom and not being challenged.

Fine (1990) spoke convincingly of schools that create environments through organizational structure, policies, and teaching strategies in which whole groups of students are exposed to systematic exclusion processes that are rationalized by the ideologies of "merit-choice-and-tradition." Her analysis is that public schools serve as "moral communities" (i.e., they function through collective consideration of fairness, reallocation of resources, and personal sacrifice for others' benefit). Public education at its most basic level assures legal access to every child, access that is deemed essential for social and economic participation in a democratic society. Now that legal access has been granted, according to Fine, the focus should shift to social justice considerations and the differential experiences and outcomes that occur for students of diverse backgrounds. She exhorted us to recognize that political negotiations, although often unacknowledged, determine who enters, remains in, and becomes excluded from these communities. School policies and practices regularly monitor who gets what, how much they get, in what contexts, for how long, and toward what ends. Other decisions that are negotiated include who is entitled to special resources and how school populations should be distributed by race, gender, and class to assure diversity, equity, and excellence. Through extensive case studies involving public and private high schools, she used qualitative research methods to conclude that a systematic pattern of exclusion exists in schools for certain groups, a pattern rationalized by the notion of common good.

Fine (1990) also critiqued the ideology of school exclusion. She found evidence of school exclusion practices in the language of school officials who commonly used terms like *academic inability, parental choice,* and *tradition.* Such language provides coherence and meaning to those individuals and institutions that help create school environments that have the underlying dynamics of exclusion. She observed that "the image of a single common good unravels once the diverse needs and entitlements of those placed outside the 'deserving' community are revealed" (p. 24). In fact, schools may often maintain a sense of meaning and identity by creating images of *discarded others.* In her study, those groups of others that threaten the traditional school community were dropouts, low-income students, students of color, and young women (i.e., whose potential impact, should they be admitted to an all male school, was being studied). "Stripped to its barest core," Fine noted, "those who belonged, including faculty and parents, seemed to believe they were simply smarter, classier, or more masculine" (p. 24). Through research and (in one case) litigation, schools based on exclusion in which insiders were held together by commonly defined groups of outsiders were exposed. The consequences of this exclusion were high dropout rates, the sense of many students being "pushed out," socially deficient education, and students trained to think they were deserving based on their race and class. This, said Fine, leads to publicly sanctioned communities of exclusion lacking in diversity and critique and in which students are sheltered from a rich education. Worse, Fine observed, were the young men and women who learned to view public exclusion as natural, justifiable, and even necessary for the common good. Although sobering in its implications, Fine's analysis, given poor educational outcomes for disadvantaged and minority students, should be considered.

To address the issue of inclusion and extend the analysis beyond the school itself, the systemic approach challenges schools to consider the community as an asset instead of a problem, and to reach out to parents, businesses, and other community stakeholders. The goal is to forge partnerships with parents and the larger community because all have a vested interest in seeing that students are successful. These partnerships often take the form of parent involvement programs, school-business compacts, and restructured schools that give parents more voice in everyday school decisions about discipline, scheduling, curriculum and instruction, and other areas that directly affect students.

It is important to change the paradigm for understanding the families of at-risk students from a deficit to an asset model that sees parents and the community as having strengths that the school can build on. In distressed neighborhoods, communities are usually seen as possessing deficits rather than strengths. Parents of at-risk students are more often seen as part of the problem rather than part of the solution. Yet even in neighborhoods and families with serious problems, there are strengths. These assets include parents who want their children to succeed; businesses that are willing to help by providing tutors, mentors, and real-world learning opportunities; and other agencies that are concerned about student welfare but who have limited access to the schools. Note that connecting the community to their schools is of particular importance to counselors. It is school counselors who are often in a position to make the connections to community, social, and health services because counselors understand child and adolescent development and know the non-instructional services students need.

Some schools have experimented with becoming integrated service centers in which the school becomes the place where all services are under one roof and thus easily accessible (Wehlage & Stone, 1996). In these centers, students not only receive their education but also have direct access to counseling, psychological, health, and social services. The centers try to cut through the turf issues and red tape that often result when schools work with outside service agencies. This approach has received substantial support through funding offered by the U.S. Department of Education's 21st Century Community Learning Centers Program. Schools in urban and rural areas can apply for funds to support expanded after-school (i.e., extended day) programs focused on academic assistance, social service, and cultural, recreational, and arts programs through partnerships with community agencies and groups, such as health and human services, and businesses. One significant part of this program is offering family and adult services to meet the needs of parents of disadvantaged students.

In Rumberger's (1993) critical analysis of the research on dropouts, especially as it applied to Hispanic children, he concluded that dropping out is more a social than an educational process. That is, research has identified three major sources of influence on dropping out and other behaviors of young people. These are families, schools, and communities. Each plays a significant and often additive role in influencing attitudes, behaviors, and academic performance. Thus each needs to be addressed in resolving the dropout problem. Rumsberger concluded that solutions probably require fundamental systemic changes throughout the school system rather than individual programmatic interventions solely focused on intervening with potential dropouts. He acknowledged the real challenges in pursuing these systemic changes and envisioned two possible paths for school involvement in reorganizing how they accomplish their learning objectives. On the one hand, he noted, some believe the educational system can be a catalyst for social change; but on the other hand, critics point out that too often the schools reinforce and perpetuate social class and ethnic differences.

Several prominent school restructuring models for at-risk students stress the idea of greater partnership between the school and the community it serves. One is James Comer's School Development Program (Comer, 1988). The model focuses on responding to the child development and relationship needs of poor and minority students that are usually not well addressed by schools, but when left unaddressed, impede academic progress. The model stresses applying child development principles to school decisions, which are made collaboratively by staff and parents working together under a site-based participatory management structure. The school is governed by a school planning and management team consisting of staff and parents. A unique feature of this model is that the school management works closely with a mental health team consisting of the social worker, counselor, special education teacher, and psychologist. In this structure, the mental health and child development experts are involved in important school matters rather than being isolated from the decision-making process. Decisions are based not only on students' academic needs but also on their child development needs. Another important part of the model is that it creates less dissonance between the school and the home because it increases parent involvement in the school. Parents become partners with the school staff to ensure that child development and learning goals are achieved. This is a promising model for at-risk students because it illustrates how teachers, administrators, mental health staff, and parents can work together in partnership. Instead of one group blaming the other, everyone becomes responsible for seeing that students succeed. Comer (1998) has elaborated on his ideas for serving disadvantaged youth and their families by emphasizing the importance of local community involvement in creating solutions instead of a sole reliance on the schools for problem solving.

Another model for at-risk students is Henry Levin's Accelerated Schools (Levin, 1987; Levin & Chasin, 1994). At the heart of Levin's model is a belief in building on strengths. Students at risk are seen as having strengths, including their own experience, culture, language, and learning style, that a school can build on in designing curriculum and instructional programs. The model stresses greater parent involvement, empowering school staff and parents in school decision making, and the school's responsibility for accelerating, instead of slowing, the learning of all students. The idea is to think of the school community in broader terms than just staff, and to involve parents and other community members in meaningful ways.

The main advantage of the systemic approach is that the school, families, and community assume shared responsibility for the educational and developmental needs of students. The school seeks to create an environment of inclusion for all students and establishes high but attainable academic goals and expectations. The school works cooperatively with social service agencies while maintaining a focus on creating learning opportunities and academic success. The school also works with other community groups and organizations to bring available resources to bear in order to create an effective learning community. By using an asset-versus-deficit model of families, parents, and the community, each becomes part of the solution rather than the problem. Resources are redefined as being much broader than just financial and as including parent skills that can be utilized within the school. Schools create environments and learning programs adapted to the needs of students rather than to the needs and convenience of the school bureaucracy. Our society has thrust upon schools the difficult but not impossible challenge of becoming more flexible for a diverse population while raising educational standards. The challenge is to apply the research on at-risk students toward restructuring the system to better meet their needs. What is not often recognized is that this approach not only works to the advantage of the potential dropout but also to the assurance of good education for all students.

INTERVENTION STRATEGIES

The approaches discussed in the preceding section tend to be broad strategies for the prevention of school dropout. Because school dropout is a process and not a single event, and because it relates to many risk factors throughout a student's life and school career, it is difficult to distinguish between prevention and intervention strategies. Intervention strategies may be viewed as more closely targeted—although still related to the broad prevention strategies discussed earlier. Together they define a comprehensive approach to the wide array of school dropout issues. Interventions, like prevention, can be divided into clinical approaches (student and family issues) and systemic approaches (school and community issues).

Clinical Approach: Treating the Student and Family

A lack of family involvement can play a significant role in dropout behavior. As in the case study of Shamica, if the family structure is not stable, the school and social agencies must intervene by providing students with the support they need to succeed in school. It cannot be assumed that each student comes to school with a strong family support system. At Garfield High School in Los Angeles, Jaime Escalante (i.e., the math teacher who became famous for raising math scores at a primarily low-income Hispanic high school as depicted in the film, *Stand and Deliver*) reached out to parents to form parent support groups after finding out that many students did not have the resources in their own homes to study. Parents volunteered their homes for students to form study groups. In addition, many parents encouraged other parents to attend parent conferences at the school.

Even with supportive families, the school system needs to reach out to parents to establish rapport. Parents should be made to feel that the school is a partner in education, rather than an authority figure. Parents should be encouraged to talk about their children with teachers, administrators, and other school personnel, and educators should remember to listen. This is important because the school staff cannot understand the child's behavior until they know more about the family's dynamics. Most families want their children to succeed. However, in many instances, families are intimidated by school personnel and feel that their opinions, even about their own children, are not valued by the school professionals. Students who see that their parents are valued and accepted feel valued themselves. Whatever the situation, the school's greeting should be friendly and relaxed. It is difficult for a family to discuss a problem with those who look or act as if the parent is a bother or wish they were not there. If families are in need of social services, they should be advised of these services, but in a way that avoids embarrassment. Training staff to listen to, and work with parents, is important in helping students stay in school.

If at-risk students are to succeed, they need supportive family structures. Families can help their children by reading and talking to them from a young age, by taking an interest in their school work and homework, and by asking questions and encouraging their children to make decisions. Families should try hard to provide a stimulating learning environment for their children by playing games, engaging in family activities, having positive discussions about school and their child's social life during meals, and encouraging responsible movie and television viewing. Families need to provide an environment in which their child feels safe, loved, and nurtured. As Rumberger (1993) concluded, parenting styles can and do make a difference for the social and academic success of children. Although rigid authoritarianism that does not flex with the growing capabilities of adolescence is problematic, so is overly permissive parenting in which parents abdicate and transfer their responsibilities for guidance and support to their child's peer group. For some parents, counselors may be able to assist by finding parenting workshops and other community resources.

The case study of Shamica showed a student with a tendency for being boisterous and acting out in school, which caused her to be suspended on several occasions. In addition, she was a young woman who was overweight and recognized that she was not making good choices in selecting healthy foods. Intervention strategies that might work for Shamica come in many different forms. The first and most important intervention is recognizing the underlying causes of difficult or problematic student behaviors. School staff need to connect with students who do not have strong family structures as soon as possible and help them develop some type of support system. The support system should include at least one caring adult such as a counselor, teacher, or other staff member who takes special interest in that student. Counselors and other staff should do everything possible to show positive feelings toward students experiencing difficulties. They should make praise and compliments both specific and sincere, such as, "You look proud of the way you finished that project. I know that you must feel good about it!" Students should be made to know that their behavior has a positive effect on others. Students should be listened to as much as possible without judging. Their feelings should be acknowledged without always offering advice. School counselors should do something special for the discouraged student by taking time to talk to them one on one.

An important point about intervening with the individual student is that students should be empowered not enabled. The worst possible insult to an at-risk student is to enable them. Empowerment teaches students responsibility and makes them feel that they are in control of their lives rather than having others control them. Regardless of the students' gender, race, or culture, high and attainable expectations should be maintained at all times. Students realize immediately if expectations are low but will rise to the level of their teachers' expectations. In evaluating K–12 instructional programs, there is a paradox in how expectations operate within many classrooms. That is, we often assume teachers' expectations shape student self-expectations and thus performance. But instead, underachieving students often demonstrate their lower self-expectations, which in turn seems to lower teacher expectations, so that the teachers begin to reflect back to students their own lower self-estimates. This dynamic could be another reason that grouping students by level of current academic achievement may lead to self-fulfilling prophecies of poor academic achievement, especially for lower achieving students.

On the social side, students who are exhibiting at-risk behaviors should be encouraged to participate in extracurricular activities. Students who participate in these activities respond more positively to school and may be more motivated to achieve academically, possibly because their participation bonds these students to other members of the school community such as friends and adults.

The school counselor has a role in helping at-risk students. The counselor is someone that a student should be able to count on. Counselors should, as much as possible, get to know the students on a personal level and to reward them for even small successes. Counselors can help organize meaningful school activities, such as wellness weeks, diversity seminars, and leadership training. Student groups can also be organized using peer facilitators to assist students in discussing current youth issues and ways of promoting better study skills. The school counselor should be a resourceful person with whom an at-risk student can connect.

Systemic Approach: Changing the School and Community

In terms of specific systemic interventions at the school level, schools should create a student-centered environment where the curriculum is made relevant and stimulating. Schools should stress relationships through the restructuring process by developing opportunities for greater racial/cultural interaction, understanding, trust, and caring between teachers and students. As in the case study of the inner-city school, when both students and staff feel alienated from each other and from school life, feelings of disengagement and helplessness result for everyone. Most teachers feel that their best experiences in school are when they connect with students personally and are able to help them in some way. However, most traditional schools as currently structured allow teachers little time to do this. John Maguire (Center for Arts in the Basic Curriculum, 1993) of the Claremont Graduate School has stated that "When relationships are wrong between teachers and students, for whatever reason, we can restructure until the cows come home but transformation won't take place." When one high school student was asked what the problem of his schooling was, he replied, "This place hurts my spirit." A process that can help bring a school-wide focus to constructive and healthy relationships is that of community building (e.g., Peck, 1987). An African proverb states that "It takes a whole village to raise a child." A supportive and involved community is essential, especially in areas where many community risk factors can work against school success. In addition to community building and relationship issues, the curriculum and its delivery are also important foundations for student success.

A central thesis of this chapter is that educational practices that prevent school dropouts are most often the very same practices and organizational structures that improve learning for all students, not simply at-risk or vulnerable students. Many times the most powerful and also the most challenging interventions are systemic in nature and address all components of the systems that influence student attitudes, behaviors, and values (e.g., Rumberger, 1993). Fortunately, the school reform movement and increasing public and political pressure to raise academic achievement for all students has led many school districts to use systemic interventions involving school reorganization to address and improve the problem of underachievement and unacceptably high dropout rates. For instance, in a comprehensive review of 5 years of research on school restructuring by the Center on Organization and Restructuring of Schools (CORS), Newman and Wehlage (1995) evaluated organizational structures that led to the quality education of diverse groups of students. They analyzed data from four sources: the School Restructuring Study (SRS); the National Educational Longitudinal Study of 1988 (NELS: 1988); the study of Chicago School Reform, which included survey data from 8,000 teachers and principals of 400 elementary and 40 high schools; and a longitudinal case study of school restructuring in eight schools. The researchers examined the process of reorganizing school structures, policies, and practices and focused on the interrelationships among administrators, teachers, students, families, and the community. They concluded that it was imperative that these groups join together with a clear and sustained focus on improving the quality of learning in their schools. When schools strayed from this focus, systemic changes to improve learning and academic performance were undermined. Similarly, Shouse (1995) used NELS: 1988 data to evaluate the effects of academic press (i.e., school focus on high academic standards) and of developing a sense of community within the schools. He concluded that community development within the schools when academic press is weak may actually diminish student achievement, especially among lower socioeconomic schools. In fact, for low- and middle-income schools, the combination of strong academic press and communal organization constituted the strongest influence on achievement. Thus equity within schools was furthered by this approach.

Newman and Wehlage (1995) have made recommendations in three primary areas for systems-level interventions in school organization to foster quality learning: teacher pedagogy, the professional community of educators, and external agencies and parents. First, authentic teacher pedagogy (i.e., the methods of instruction and assessment of student learning outcomes) communicates to students the significance of what they are learning. Authentic instruction is focused on teaching for conceptual understanding, which requires greater depth of student cognitive processing and more connection to the world beyond the classroom. This emphasizes teaching methods that help students apply their academic learning in contexts beyond the school. Second, schools focused on quality learning should promote professional community among their educators through organizational practices of shared school governance, small school size, parent involvement, and other structural conditions that support the experience of professional community. Third, supportive external agencies and parents are needed to help create the organizational capacity to promote quality student learning. The most influential groups in this regard are often districts, states, parents, and private nonprofits that support school reform.

The Detroit schools provide an example of an urban district struggling to make systems-level changes at the high school level to decrease dropout rates and increase student achievement (Syropoulos, 1997). The focus of this systemic intervention was to restructure the ninth grade with the goals of improving academic performance, helping students develop positive attitudes toward learning, improving the school climate, and decreasing unacceptably high double-digit dropout rates. At the end of the second year of reorganization, a program evaluation was completed that included surveys of administrator, principal, teacher, and student attitudes and examination of objective data such as dropout rates, grades, and achievement test scores. Syropoulos (1997) concluded that students, teachers, and principals viewed the organizational changes positively. More specifically, the district restructuring of the high school ninth-grade program was encouraged to continue to decrease student alienation by breaking the large schools into small stable units to increase personal attention from staff. Such changes took the form of creating schools within schools, expanding the role of the homeroom teacher to include mentoring and personal guidance, expanding class time through use of block scheduling to decrease the amount of student movement from class to class, creating student clusters to increase peer support so students remain with the same group as they move through classes, and developing alternative and mini schools that reach out to disaffected students through compensatory education and more personalized attention. This reorganization also offered instructional and direct noninstructional services, including on-campus assistance for counseling and psychological needs as well as tutorials with student assistants under teacher supervision. Family involvement initiatives to encourage parent participation with their children in instructional and noninstructional activities also occurred.

By the end of the second year, those high schools participating in the evaluation had lowered dropout rates among 9th-grade students, although the dropout rates of 10th-grade students actually increased. This led the evaluator to conclude that the reorganization program needed to be expanded to include the 10th grade. In the area of ongoing improvement and organizational change, principals expressed the need for teachers to realize that to be effective with broad groups of students they must vary their instructional methods. Among teacher concerns were students who lacked reading skills, student attendance, and class size—which led to recommendations for decreasing class size, increasing parental involvement, and having common teacher preparation periods. Results of the systemic changes most appreciated by students were opportunities for "learning new things," being helped to get along with other people, and working cooperatively with other students. Students were concerned about not having enough activities in their schools and experiencing a lack of cooperation in the ninth-grade restructuring efforts among some teachers and counselors.

School reform, reorganization, and restructuring initiatives focused on improving the learning experiences and academic performance of students from diverse ethnic, class, and cultural backgrounds have demonstrated success. Two key components of these systemic changes are a focus on academic press/quality learning and community development within schools. Especially for lower and middle-income students these processes seem powerful and effective (Shouse, 1995). Reorganization and school restructuring focus on organizational structures, policies, procedures, instructional methods, social service delivery, and the relationships among students, parents, teachers, counselors, administrators, and community agencies. The emphasis is on creating learning environments that are inclusive, hold high and attainable expectations for students, and see parents and the community as partners with resources instead of as adversaries solely defined by their problems. Systems-level change means we must all change together and reexamine our relationships with one another, or learn to accept high dropout rates and poor student achievement.

ADAPTATIONS FOR DIVERSITY

Throughout this chapter, we have emphasized that school dropouts come from many diverse backgrounds and circumstances, and that it is the school's responsibility to respond to student diversity so that all students have an opportunity to succeed. Two specific diversity issues are important to understanding and preventing school dropout.

The first issue is family diversity. The demographics of the current American family play a large part in prevention and intervention strategies for at-risk students. Hodgkinson and Hamilton-Outtz (1992), and Hamilton-Outtz (1993), in their demographic profiles of American families, stated that most Americans still live in some type of family arrangement, but the traditional definition no longer applies to the majority. There are more married couple families without children than married couple families with children, more families with stepchildren, many more single-parent families, more fathers raising their children alone, and many more mothers in the labor force. What this indicates is that there are many families who are struggling and facing more challenging lifestyles. Therefore, schools have a greater responsibility to provide for the diversity of families they serve. School counselors and other school staff should be prepared to deal with students who may have only one parent living with them, who have less adult supervision before and after school, and whose family situations are less stable than in the past. In fact, less adult time for children and adolescents outside of the school day may be one of the biggest contributors to child/adolescent alienation and problem behavior.

The second diversity issue is the ethnic and cultural mix of today's students and how schools respond to these changing demographics. It is one that we have touched upon throughout this chapter. School systems, particularly those in urban areas and certain states, are dealing with increasingly diverse student bodies. The demographic trends indicate that the bulk of the population growth in the United States in the last decade was primarily due to the increased number of minorities, many of whom are immigrants from poor, third-world countries. In states like Texas and California, minorities are becoming the majority. These minority groups include Hispanics, African Americans, Asians, Pacific Islanders, Native Americans, and Alaska natives. Hodgkinson and Hamilton-Outtz (1992) pointed out that one fallacy of the current debate on educational standards is the belief that all states begin at the same starting line in the race for educational excellence. The demographic trends suggest instead that some states more than others are dealing with poor, minority immigrant families who have greater basic needs.

As discussed earlier, minority status is correlated with poverty, and the data show quite clearly that poverty status is linked to many risk factors that predict school dropout. We cannot talk about ethnic diversity without recognizing that many minorities are from poor families who have not been included in or had full access to the so-called American mainstream. Thus ethnic diversity raises two challenges for schools: dealing with students from different social as well as cultural and language backgrounds. This diversity means that students not only come to school with different languages, cultural values, and learning styles, but also with vastly different life experiences and economic opportunities.

Poverty and its constellation of risk factors are major issues in many states and communities. Among the more prominent poverty-related risk factors are increased teen pregnancy, less access to health care, and increased violence and criminal behavior. In high-poverty areas, schools that empower students and their families, provide more access to health care and social services, and deliver programs to prevent school and community violence will be a necessary part of a comprehensive dropout prevention strategy.

Educational equity is an important issue that relates to the cultural and social diversity of today's students. Educational inequity often comes in the form of lowered expectations that emanate from deeply held beliefs about the ability of different groups to succeed and can result in the creation of schools that exclude whole groups of students. Expectations that are lowered because a student is from a particular ethnic background or because the student is poor can be not only devastating and humiliating but also waste human resources. Some teachers treat poor students differently from middle-class students, believing that poor students are not as capable as those from more affluent families. The same holds true for African American, Hispanic, and Native American students. Students who are made to feel that they are not valued are more likely to drop out. Ironically, these students may not have suffered from low self-esteem until they were put into a situation where little was expected of them. It is only when a student begins to question his or her self-worth that insecurities and low self-esteem are created. When students' social class and ethnicity are accepted by other students, teachers, and school counseling staff, they are much more likely to feel good about themselves and succeed. In the case of minority groups, this is more likely to happen if teachers and counselors are representative of the cultural groups making up the student body.

Aside from underlying staff attitudes and expectations, a more obvious type of educational inequity is placing at-risk students in programs that fail to equip them with a quality education. Some alternative programs do an excellent job of building a comfortable shelter for the damaged student but may put the student in jeopardy if academic goals and expectations are drastically lower than those for students in the traditional school. At-risk students may later feel they have been cheated because they are still not equipped to work and survive in our society.

The school system that is committed to helping at-risk students and educating its entire population will attempt to restructure itself in order to meet the needs of all students. The role that counselors play in this reformation stage is crucial because counselors may know the multiple needs of students better than anyone else in the building. Counselors need to act as guides who instill in students hope for the future, and as student advocates within the school system.

SUMMARY

The school dropout problem involves many of the personal, family, and social issues discussed throughout this book. The problem is serious and eventually harms young people and their families and communities as well as our society. Counselors must help students realize that the easy choice to leave school is not necessarily the best for them in the long run. Young people who do not complete their high school education often feel deep regret later in life. As our society and economy continue to change, dropouts will find it increasingly difficult to lead productive and satisfying lives. There is neither a single type of dropout nor a single magic intervention that will help all of those who are at risk of leaving school. In addressing this multifaceted problem, counselors must assess many aspects of student functioning, including student experiences outside of school, to develop effective interventions that address the whole student.

School counselors are an important link to families and community agencies whose help may be needed by students. Likewise, community counselors need to coordinate their services with schools. Furthermore, schools must be more sensitive to the needs of students and their families through more responsive structuring, scheduling, programs, and policies. Counselors can be effective advocates for at-risk youth in school committees and other forums to ensure that schools recognize and respond to the needs of a diverse student population.

The role of the counselor in helping potential dropouts should be, first, to give sound guidance to those who are already experiencing problems and to establish primary prevention programs. Second, counselors should serve to facilitate communication between students and school staff, parents, and community agencies so that all work together to build a climate of learning, caring, and respect. For students who are disengaged from school or feel that they are being treated unfairly, caring and respect are needed before any counseling intervention can be effective. Principles of community building can serve as a framework for these efforts. Third, the counselor should be an advocate for and friend to students who may feel lost or shuffled from teacher to teacher in large schools. Teachers often only feel responsible for part of the student's school experience—that is, for student learning in a specific subject area. Counselors may be in a better position to deal with the whole student and provide continuity throughout the student's school career, especially in large schools that can be chaotic places at times. Districts should also pay attention to early intervention during elementary grades so that problems can be identified and dealt with quickly and more effectively.

Most high school counselors agree that supportive guidance and counseling can help at-risk students have a more positive and productive school experience, especially those students who lack support at home. Counselors are often responsible for helping students make decisions about the direction of their education. Unfortunately in most cases, a counselor's daily routine involves scheduling and dealing with behavior problems more than with working as a team with teachers and other staff to develop systemic solutions. Counselors need to take the lead in redefining their roles to be more congruent with the development of systems-level changes and improvement. Student problems are too often addressed piecemeal in schools instead of through integrated academic, career, and social services.

Districts truly interested in dropout prevention and improving student achievement use systems-level analysis and intervention. They realize that counseling should be integrated into the total educational program. In addition to providing guidance and day-to-day assistance with discipline, counselors should be full partners in developing and implementing programs designed to foster child development and increase student academic success. Counselors and administrators alike must define a larger role for counselors. To take on this larger role, counselors must receive adequate training in advocacy, program development, systems theory, and organizational change skills. Counselors and their districts need to develop a broader view of the counseling role, to expand that role beyond the practice of individual counseling, to make counselors more involved in organizational change and systems-level interventions. This role requires skill in working with organizational dynamics and leadership development. In the movement to reshape education, much research has been done to describe and understand the dropout problem, but little has been said about the importance of school guidance and counseling. School and community counselors are too often underutilized resources in helping at-risk youth. Counselors can be major contributors to the success of students who experience problems in school. As the movement to improve schools continues, an expanded and more proactive role for school and community counselors needs to be developed.

REFERENCES

Asche, J. A. (1993). *Finish for the future: America's communities respond.* Alexandria, VA: National Association of Partners in Education.

Bickel, W. E., Bond, L., & LeMahieu, P. G. (1988). *Students at risk of not completing high school.* Unpublished manuscript, University of Pittsburgh.

Center for Arts in the Basic Curriculum (CABC) Staff. (1993, February 4). What do we want our schools to do? *CABC Newsletter*, p. 4.

Comer, J. P. (1988). Educating poor and minority children. *Scientific American, 259*(5), 28–34.

Comer, J. P. (1998). *Waiting for a miracle : Why schools can't solve our problems—and how we can.* New York: Dutton.

Dryfoos, J. G. (1990). *Adolescents at risk: Prevalence and prevention.* New York: Oxford University Press.

Fine, M. (1986). Why urban adolescents drop into and out of public high school. *Teachers College Record, 87*, 393–409.

Fine, M. (1990). "The public" in public schools: The social construction/constriction of moral communities. *Journal of Social Issues, 46*, 107–119. (ERIC Document Reproduction Service No. ED316601)

Hamilton-Outtz, J. (1993). *The demographics of American families: Review.* Washington, DC: Institute for Educational Leadership.

Hodgkinson, H. L., & Hamilton-Outtz, J. (1992). *The nation and the states: A profile and data book of American diversity.* Washington, DC: Institute for Educational Leadership.

Hoffman, L. M. (1995). *State dropout data collection practices: 1991–92 school year.* Washington, DC: National Center for Education Statistics. (ERIC Document Production Service No. ED383735)

Horn, L. (1992). *A profile of parents of eighth graders: National Education Longitudinal Study of 1988.* Washington DC: National Center for Educational Statistics.

Keith, P. B., & Schartzer, C. L. (1995, August). *What is the influence of Mexican American parental involvement on school attendance patterns?* Paper presented at the annual meeting of the American Psychological Association, New York. (ERIC Document Production Service No. ED415450)

Kulik, J. A. (1993, Spring). An analysis of the research on ability grouping. *National Research Center on the Gifted and Talented Newsletter*, pp. 8–9. (ERIC Document Production Service No. ED367095)

Lesters, N., & McDill, E. L. (1995). *Rising to the challenge: Emerging strategies for educating youth at risk* (Urban Monograph Series). Oak Brook, IL: North Central Regional Education Lab. (ERIC Document Production Service No. ED397202)

Levin, H. M. (1987). Accelerated schools for disadvantaged students. *Educational Leadership, 44*(6), 19–21.

Levin, H. M., & Chasin, G. (1994). Thomas Edison accelerated elementary school. In *Yearbook of the National Society for the Study of Education: Creating new educational communities, schools, and classrooms where all children can be smart* (p. 94). Chicago: University of Chicago Press. (ERIC Document Production Service No. ED375502)

Lloyd, D. N. (1978). Prediction of school failure from third-grade data. *Educational and Psychological Measurement, 38*, 1193–1200.

McMillen, M. M., Kaufman, P., Hausken, E. G., & Bradby, D. (1993). *Dropout rates in the United States: 1992.* Washington, DC: National Center for Education Statistics.

Mortenson, T. G. (1997). Postsecondary education opportunity: The Mortenson research seminar on public policy analysis of opportunity for postsecondary education, 1997. *Postsecondary Education Opportunity*, 55–66. (ERIC Document Production Service No. ED416754)

Newman, F. M., & Wehlage, G. G. (1995). *Successful school restructuring: A report to the public and educators*. Washington, DC: American Federation of Teachers. (ERIC Document Production Service No. ED387925)

Ogbu, J. U. (1995). Cultural problems in minority education: Their interpretations and consequences. Part two: Case studies. *Urban Review, 27*, 271–297.

Ogbu, J. U. (1992). Understanding cultural differences and school learning. *Education Libraries, 16*, 7–11.

Orr, M. T. (1987). *What to do about dropouts: A summary of solutions*. New York: Structural Employment/Economic Development Commission.

Peck, M. S. (1993). *A world waiting to be born: Civility rediscovered*. New York: Bantam Books.

Peck, M.S. (1987). *A different drum*. New York: Simon & Schuster.

Rumberger, R. W. (1993). Chicano dropouts: A review of research and policy issues. In R. R. Volencio (Ed.), *Chicano school failure and success: Research and policy agendas for the 1990s*. Bristol, PA: Folmer Press.

Rumberger, R. W., Ghatak, R., Poulos, G., & Ritter, P. L. (1990). Family influences on dropout behavior in one California high school. *Sociology of Education, 63*, 283–299.

Seligman, M.E.P. (1991). *Learned optimism*. New York: Knopf.

Shouse, R. C. (1995). *Academic press and school sense of community: Sources of friction, prospects for synthesis*. Arlington, VA: National Science Foundation. (ERIC Document Production Service No. ED387868)

Sims, A. (1997). Project choice: Lessons learned in dropout prevention. Kansas City, MO: Ewing Marion Kauffman Foundation. (ERIC Document Production Service No. ED416283)

Syropoulos, M. (1997). *Evaluation of the 1996–97 ninth-grade restructuring program: Area E*. Detroit, MI: Research and Evaluation Specialists. (ERIC Document Production Service No. ED418188)

Wehlage, G. (1991). School reform for at-risk students. *Equity and Excellence, 25*, 15–24.

Wehlage, G. G., & Stone, C. (1996). School–based student and family services: Community and bureaucracy. *Journal of Education for Students Placed At Risk, 1*, 299–317. (ERIC Document Production Service No. ED383497)

Index